UNIX® System Administration Handbook

Evi Nemeth
Garth Snyder
Scott Seebass

Computer Science Department
University of Colorado

Prentice Hall
Englewood Cliffs, New Jersey 07632

Library of Congress Cataloging-in-Publication Data

Nemeth, Evi. (date)
Unix system administration handbook / Evi Nemeth, Garth Snyder, Scott Seebass.
p. cm.
Includes index.
ISBN 0-13-933441-6
1. UNIX (Computer operating system) I. Snyder, Garth.
II. Seebass, Scott. III. Title.
QA76.76.063N45 1989
005.4'3--dc20 89-32379
CIP

Editorial/production supervision: bookworks
Cartoons by: Tyler Stevens
Manufacturing buyer: Robert Anderson
UNIX® is a registered trademark of AT&T.
Prentice Hall Software Series, Brian W. Kernighan, *Advisor*

The publisher offers discounts on this book when ordered in bulk quantities. For more information, write or call:

Special Sales
Prentice-Hall, Inc.
College Technical and Reference Division
Englewood Cliffs, NJ 07632
(201) 592-2498

Printed in the United States of America
10 9 8

ISBN 0-13-933441-6

Prentice-Hall International (UK) Limited, London
Prentice-Hall of Australia Pty. Limited, Sydney
Prentice-Hall Canada Inc., Toronto
Prentice-Hall Hispanoamericana, S.A., Mexico
Prentice-Hall of India Private Limited, New Delhi
Prentice-Hall of Japan, Inc., Tokyo
Simon & Schuster Asia Pte. Ltd., Singapore
Editora Prentice-Hall do Brasil, Ltda., Rio de Janeiro

Contents

Foreword

The administration of UNIX systems has always been a somewhat neglected subject. I think this happened for several reasons, all connected to various aspects of its unusual history.

First, the creation and early spread of the system took place among devotees, people who soon became knowledgeable of its nooks and crannies. These groups were often irritated by the formalities and procedures common in the big computer centers that were the chief computational resources during the 1970s, and they were ingenious in developing their own wizardly administrative recipes, instead of relying on cookbooks.

Second, a typical UNIX system inhabits a computing niche unusual until recently. Most commonly, such systems are either medium-size machines serving a single department in a company or university, or workstations used by a single person, but connected by a network to many other systems. For the most part—though there are now exceptions—UNIX systems are not big machines with professional, on-site staff from the manufacturer or a big computer center, nor personal computers owned by isolated individuals. For a large machine, it is expected that professionals will provide the support. For the personal computer, the manufacturer is expected to write the administrative cookbook for the limited range of uses to which the machine will be put. The purchasers of a mid-range machine may find themselves suddenly nominated to be the staff; this can make them feel nearly as much on their own as if they had bought a personal computer, but they must face the complexities of keeping an eye on multiple users, dealing with one or more networks, and handling the other daunting conundrums that turn up.

Finally, UNIX systems come from a variety of sources. Although there is a common core of useful administrative tools and procedures, not all suppliers provide a useful degree of support. Also, many sites import substantial amounts of software from university distributions, Usenet, or other places that provide the programs, but little else.

Despite the problems, many of the purveyors of UNIX systems do a good job of telling their customers how to run them. Nevertheless, a comprehensive book discussing administration is clearly needed. The manufacturer's theory of what you want to do is not necessarily your own, and the documentation may be scattered; your supplier may be more talented at building hardware than at generating useful manuals; or you may be using popular software that didn't come in the box.

Therefore, this book is most welcome.

Dennis Ritchie

Preface

Introduction

This book is about how to "do" UNIX system administration the right way. The techniques we will teach you are simple, efficient, and effective.

There are now over a million UNIX sites, and the pace at which new installations are added is steadily increasing. Computer vendors like UNIX because it is accessible and relatively easy to adapt to a new machine; the cost of porting UNIX is insignificant compared to the cost of writing a proprietary operating system. Computer buyers like UNIX because it's easy to find people who already know how to use it and because it allows them to create an expandable system without being tied to one particular vendor. Everybody wins.

UNIX is also a very elegant operating system. It is flexible, so that you never have the sense that you are fighting the system to force it into a mold it was never meant to fit. It is consistent, so that only one set of paradigms need be learned. It is powerful, so that the faculties of the system can be brought to bear against practically any problem.

Unfortunately, UNIX is also cryptic, idiosyncratic, and unstandardized. Learning to use or administer UNIX requires a significant time investment. Once the initial period of frustration is over, however, you have a very powerful tool at your disposal.

Running a UNIX system is fun because you get to use the system for what it does best: writing, installing, and maintaining software. Since a high degree of automation can be grafted into UNIX administration, you will rarely find yourself repeating tiresome chores by hand. Just as in user-level UNIX, the standard paradigms, once learned, are clear and consistent.

UNIX System Administration Handbook is intended primarily for people with little or no background in system administration, but it is more than just a tutorial. Chapters are organized as much for reference as for straight-through reading. We hope that you'll be able to find what you need just by scanning the table of contents, but we've also taken pains to make the index accurate and thorough. We want this book to be indispensable.

We assume throughout that you are already familiar with the basics of UNIX and know how to use the shell and commands such as **mkdir**, **vi**, and **sh**. If you don't, you *must* supplement this book with some additional reading. Consult the UNIX bibliography at the end of this book for some specific recommendations.

How this book differs from the UNIX manuals

Most UNIX systems come with enough documentation to kill a cow; you may wonder why a book about system administration is even necessary. The problem, as we see it, is that the standard documents describe various commands and subsystems *in isolation*, without providing a framework to tie them together. Manuals always tell you *how* to do things without ever telling you *why* you want to do them. And *why*, after all, is what system administration is all about.

UNIX machines used to be big and expensive, and the support personnel used to be specialists. Now you can buy a desktop UNIX system for $2000. The big-system paradigm has been shattered. We believe that as time goes on, UNIX administration will become less of an atomic specialty and more a component of many people's jobs.

Without guidance, it's easy for a new administrator to lose sight of ultimate goals in a sea of documentation or to inadvertently skip over one or more critical areas through failure to realize that they are important. That is where this book fits in. While we can't claim that *everything* you need to know is included, we can guarantee that after reading it you will know pretty much what UNIX administration involves and how to go about it.

Hardware and software discussed

There are two main flavors of UNIX: AT&T's System V and the University of California at Berkeley's 4.*X* BSD (Berkeley Software Distribution). System V is oriented towards business, and so stability, simplicity, and maintainability are among its strengths. BSD embodies a number of advanced concepts not present in System V but is not as well supported. In past years BSD UNIX has maintained a technological lead over System V, but current trends in the System V world appear to be closing this gap.

Most of the computers at our site run some form of BSD, but some run System V variants and some run both at the same time. *The emphasis of this book is on BSD*. However, the two versions are often close enough so that by noting differences between the two we have produced a book that should be useful for either flavor.

Paradoxically, the differences among the various ports and versions of AT&T UNIX are sometimes much greater than the differences between BSD and "standard" System V. The information in this book regarding AT&T must therefore be taken with a grain of salt; when we say that something functions in a certain way under AT&T UNIX we mean that it is true for at least one major version and is usually true for several. Our closest reference machines are an AT&T 3B15 running System V.2.1.1 and an AT&T 3B2 running System V.3, but we've used a variety of other sources in trying to present a fair and balanced image of the AT&T world.

In this book, the letters "BSD" mean Berkeley UNIX 4.2, the version of BSD that most commercial ports are based on. We also cover Berkeley release 4.3, but everything specific to this revision is identified as such. Similarly, the letters "ATT" represent our homogenized view of AT&T UNIX.

Some machine-specific material has been introduced into this book in an effort to illustrate the variations among different flavors of UNIX. The four systems we've used as examples are:

- DEC Vaxen running pure BSD
- Sun Microsystems Sun3's running Sun UNIX
- Pyramid 90x's running dualPort OSx
- ATT 3B15 running System V.2

These are all nice systems; however, the fact that they appear in this book should not be construed as an endorsement. We've selected these four because they show some degree of variation from one another without being so widely separated that all comparisons are moot. Machine-specific examples are clearly marked.

Revisions 4.0 and higher of Sun's UNIX show significant deviations from BSD, especially with respect to the placement and format of system files. This book is still valid as a general reference for such systems; however, when we mention material specific to Suns in this book we are speaking mostly of revisions 3.2 and 3.4.

Organization

It would be nice if operating systems were designed so that they could be explained in a linear way, without having to unravel a complex web of interrelations in order to create a coherent presentation. Alas, an operating system designed in this way would be easy to understand but probably not very useful. UNIX is especially horrible to explain because so little is built into the operating system itself; instead, much of the action shamelessly takes place in the context of user space—right in your living room, as it were.

Consequently, we've chosen an organization for this book that is chronological rather than conceptual. Rather than starting with the most basic facts and gradually building up to more complex abstractions, topics are introduced in the order that you would probably want to activate them in a new system. We like this organization because it tells you what you need to know *when you need to know it* and because we feel that it increases the value of each chapter as reference material. Except for two or three chapters that are fairly light, you will find the level of presentation fairly even.

The first six chapters of this book are presented in a sequence you should find useful if you are bringing up a system straight from the packing crate. In this section are contained the bare essentials, things you need to know just to get the system up and running. Chapters 7-14 introduce the various kinds of hardware that are typically used with UNIX and discuss how to install, configure, and operate this equipment. Chapters 15-19 discuss five important UNIX software subsystems: electronic mail, telephone communication, network news, backups, and accounting. The rest of the chapters represent a grab-bag of UNIX topics, some of which may not concern you.

Attitude preadjustment

As a new UNIX system administrator, you are about to begin a long and complex project. As you work, keep in mind the five following rules. If you adhere to their spirit your success will be practically automatic.

Be consistent

As long as you know exactly what you have done and how to undo it, you won't lose comprehension of the system you have created. The best way to maintain comprehension is to keep good documentation, but this is hard to do consistently. The next best thing is to pick standard ways of performing system tasks, standard places to put various types of files, standard coding practices, etc., and stick to them.

Learn more than you think you need to know

The more complete your comprehension of how your system works, the easier your life becomes. Time invested in learning about the system is paid back later many times over. In the long run, it will not save you time to learn the absolute minimum necessary for the completion of a particular job.

Read the manuals

The manuals are the final authority on your system, and you should know their contents. This is not to say that you should read them from cover to cover — far from it! There is a sizable portion of the UNIX manuals that you may never have occasion to use. But when you learn a new command, you *should* skim its manual page. You will often find hidden features that are just right for your particular application.

Do things right the first time

Don't patch something sloppily intending to come back later to fix it up. You won't. Make allowances for changes that might occur to your system; don't "hard-wire" system-dependent information into your programs and scripts. Make everything as bulletproof as possible. Assume Murphy's Law.

Have fun

There is pleasure in doing things well, and this applies no less to computer administration than to any other activity. If you get frustrated or overstressed, work on something else for a while (if you can). The more good associations you develop with your administration duties, the better off you and your system will be.

Send us bug reports

Please feel free to send suggestions, comments, and bug reports to us via electronic mail at sa-book@boulder.Colorado.EDU.

Good luck!

Evi Nemeth
Garth Snyder
Scott Seebass

Acknowledgments

First and foremost we would like to thank Tyler Stevens, a graduate student in English with a degree in computer science, who "tylerized" our grammar, punctuation, and an occasional incredibly awkward sentence. Tyler also did all the interesting illustrations in the book.

Next we would like to thank Trent Hein, who took time out of his busy schedule to read the entire manuscript and provided lots of technical detail nit-picking.

There were a host of folks who we did not lean on as much as Tyler and Trent, but who read parts of the book and provided valuable comments:

Eric Allman
Jeremy Brest
Brent Browning
Jeff Forys
Andrew Gollan
Bob Gray
Jeff Haemer
Paul Kooros

Alan Krantz
Kirk McKusick
Phil Rice
Nancy Seebass

We would like to thank the following people for letting us include their code in our appendices:

Bob Coggeshall
Jeff Forys
Andrew Gollan
Andy Rudoff
Sylvan Ruud
Cliff Spencer

We would also like to acknowledge some UNIX old-timers who provided historical information:

Eric Allman
Stu Feldman
Brian Kernighan
Kirk McKusick
Dennis Ritchie
Jerry Saltzer
Heidi Stetner
and, of course, Biff.

Many thanks to our technical reviewers, Brian Kernighan and Sheila Katzen, and the editorial staff at Prentice Hall, especially Karen Fortgang and John Wait.

A grant from AT&T provided support for a System Administration Workshop where we tried out some of the material before committing it to print.

Finally, the Computer Science Department at the University of Colorado, where we wrote and rewrote the book, deserve many thanks for providing computing resources and putting up with us.

1

Where to Start

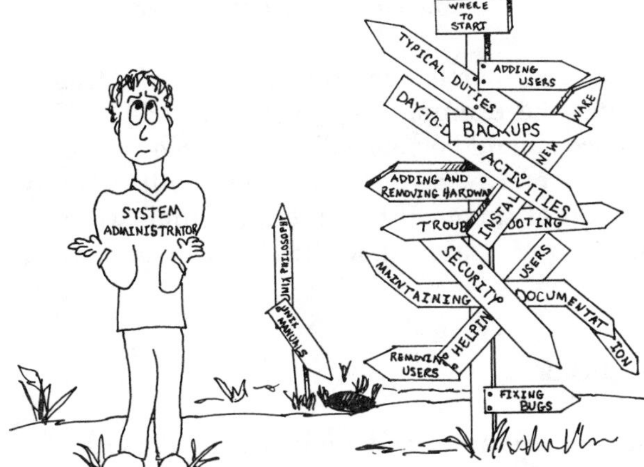

If you are reading this book, you are probably already a system administrator, or you are thinking of becoming one. This chapter is designed to give a general overview of the tasks involved in being a system administrator and to give a few simple hints on how to make the job easier.

1.1 Notation and conventions used in this book

Throughout **UNIX System Administration Handbook**, command names and their literal arguments are **boldfaced**. Wild cards, such as command arguments that should not be taken literally, are *italicized*. For example:

> **ls -l** *dir1 dir2*

In general, we use the same command syntax as the UNIX manual pages: Anything within square brackets ("[" and "]") is optional, and anything followed by an ellipsis ("...") may be repeated more than one time.

Simple command sequences are placed directly in the body text (e.g., "the **ls -l** command"); longer commands and interactive examples are indented and separated from the rest of the text by blank lines. Output produced by a specific command is always set in a constant-width font (`like this`); this convention also identifies code fragments and example text from various UNIX files. For example, use of the **echo** command might be illustrated with

```
% echo "UNIX is yummy"
UNIX is yummy
```

The percent symbol is the default C-shell prompt.

Filenames, pathnames, user names, and group names are not specially marked unless their function is not clear; in this case they are quoted.

If a command sequence is unique to a particular version of UNIX, this is mentioned in the text surrounding the example. If no version of UNIX is specified, it means that the sequence should be generally applicable. Because there are so many different flavors of UNIX, few commands will actually work in exactly the same way on all of them. If in doubt, the final word on command usage is your system documentation, not this book or any other source.

1.2 Typical duties of the system administrator

The duties of a system administrator are numerous and varied. This section gives an overview of some tasks that the typical system administrator is expected to perform. These duties do not necessarily have to be done all by one person, and at many sites the work is distributed among several people. However, there needs to be at least one person who understands all of the duties that must be performed and makes sure that someone is doing them.

1.2.1 Adding and removing users

It is the system administrator's responsibility to add accounts for new users and to remove the accounts of users who are no longer active. The process of adding and removing users can be somewhat automated, but there are still decisions, such as choosing the user name and locating the home directory, that must be made before a new user can be added.

When a user should no longer have access to the system, his login must be disabled for security and administrative reasons, and all his files must be disposed of so that they do not use up valuable system resources.

1.2.2 Adding and removing hardware

When new hardware is purchased, or when hardware is moved from one machine to another, the system must be configured to recognize and use that hardware. This may range from the simple task of adding a terminal to the complex job of adding a disk drive.

Hardware is of no use if the system is not properly configured to use it. There are many systems that have complex and expensive pieces of hardware such as floating point boards that are never accessed because no one took the time to make sure the system was set up right. Always configure your hardware properly.

When hardware is removed, the system must be reconfigured to avoid any problems that may occur. These problems range from the system not being able to boot to wasting memory by including unneeded device drivers.

1.2.3 Performing backups

Performing backups is one of the most important jobs of the system administrator, and also the job that is most often ignored or sloppily done. Backups are time-consuming and boring, but they are absolutely necessary. Backups can be automated and delegated to an underling, but it is still the system administrator's job to make sure that backups are executed correctly and on schedule.

1.2.4 Installing new software

When new software is acquired, it must be installed and tested. When the new software is working correctly, the users must be informed of its availability and location. Local software should be installed in a place that makes it easy to differentiate it from the software included with the UNIX release. This makes the task of installing a new release of UNIX much simpler, because the local software can be easily saved and reinstalled on the new system.

1.2.5 Day-to-day activities

There are numerous daily activities that must be performed. These include making sure that mail and news are working correctly, insuring that uucp connections to other sites are completing, and keeping an eye on the availability of system resources such as disk space.

1.2.6 Troubleshooting

Like all things, UNIX systems and the hardware they run on occasionally break down. It is the system administrator's job to play mechanic by diagnosing the problem and calling in experts if necessary. Finding the problem is often harder than fixing it. Many system administrators also consider keeping up with new developments and changes in UNIX as part of their job.

1.2.7 Maintaining local documentation

As your system is changed to suit your needs, it begins to differ from the plain-vanilla system that your documentation describes. It is the system administrator's duty to document all aspects of the system that are specific to the local environment. This includes documenting any software that is installed but did not come with the operating system, documenting where cables are run and how they are constructed, maintaining maintenance records for all hardware, and recording the status of backups.

1.2.8 Fixing bugs

Bugs in UNIX distributions occur more often than one might expect. Bug reports and fixes may be sent by the software distributor or found on network news. The system administrator must install and test bug fixes as they arrive. Most known bugs are fixed in the next release of the software — but new releases usually introduce new bugs of their own.

1.2.9 Security

The system administrator must implement a security policy and periodically check to see that the security of the system has not been violated. On low-security systems, this may only involve checking to make sure no one is playing games during the day. On a high-security system it may involve periodically checking for various types of unauthorized access.

1.2.10 Helping users

Although helping users with their various problems is rarely included in a system administrator's job description, it claims a significant portion of most administrators' workdays. System administrators are bombarded with problems ranging from "My SNOBOL program worked yesterday and now it doesn't! What did you change?" to "I spilled coffee on my keyboard! Should I pour water on it to wash it out?" — usually uttered in tones of utmost anguish and urgency.

1.2.11 System accounting

UNIX allows usage records to be kept for various resources such as CPU time and printer usage. Most sites do not keep accounting information, but it is not difficult to do and can be quite informative. In some situations, the administrator may be expected to summarize accounting records and send out invoices at the end of the month.

1.3 The UNIX manuals

The UNIX manuals contain all the information needed to keep the system running, yet that information is sometimes hard to find and often cryptic. The system administrator **must** have a complete set of manuals for the particular version of UNIX that is being used. Additional copies of the manuals may be obtained from the software vendor, from the Usenix Association (for BSD), and sometimes from private publishing houses. Buying printed versions of the manual is usually cheaper than making photocopies.

In early versions of the manuals, all of the short reference manual pages were organized in sections and placed in Volume 1. Longer tutorials and installation guides were placed in Volume 2. ATT manuals had Volumes 2A and 2B, and BSD added Volume 2C. On systems with sufficient disk space, the Volume 1 manuals should be kept on-line, allowing quick and easy access. On many BSD systems, the Volume 2 manuals are also kept on-line in the directory /usr/doc.

The organization of sections in Volume 1 varies from system to system. On BSD systems there are nine sections broken down as follows:

- Section 1 - User commands
- Section 2 - System calls
- Section 3 - Library routines
- Section 4 - Device drivers
- Section 5 - File formats
- Section 6 - Games
- Section 7 - Miscellaneous: ASCII, macro packages, etc.
- Section 8 - Commands for system administration
- Local - Locally installed manual pages

The notation **tty**(1) refers to the user-level **tty** command described in Section 1, and the notation **tty**(4) refers to the terminal device driver described in Section 4. Many ATT systems are similarly organized, except that maintenance commands are kept as a subsection of user commands rather than having their own manual section.

troff input for the on-line manuals is kept in the directories /usr/man/man*X*, where *X* is a digit 1 through 8 or "l" for the local section. Preformatted versions of the manuals are kept in /usr/man/cat*X*; all manual pages may be preformatted with the **catman** (BSD) or **makecats** (ATT) command if space permits.

In some modern releases, the longer manuals are divided according to functions such as text formatting, C programming, etc. In these releases the system administrator's information is often separated into a distinct volume. The best way to determine the organization of your particular set of manuals is to simply peruse them.

1.4 The UNIX philosophy

The UNIX philosophy is to keep things small and modular. Although some recent versions of UNIX violate this philosophy, these rules are still good to keep in mind when writing programs and scripts. It is much easier to find a bug in a process that is divided into several distinct parts than a bug in one huge program. Another benefit is that some modules may be reused in other programs that require the same sort of functionality, saving time and effort. UNIX provides excellent utilities for connecting several modules together, so there is very little overhead involved in modularization.

2

Booting and Shutting Down

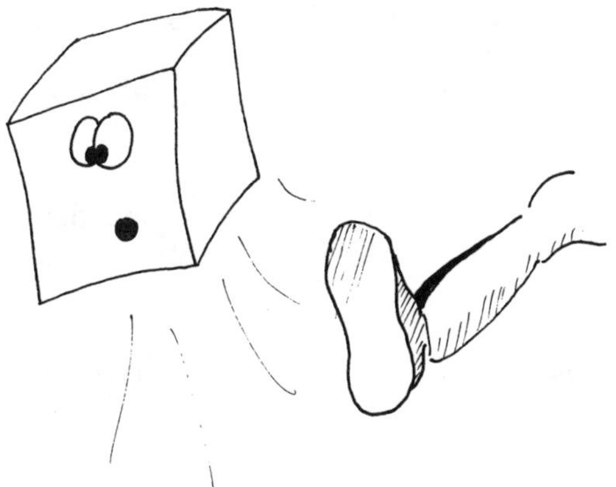

UNIX is a complex operating system, and turning UNIX systems on and off is more complicated than just flipping a power switch. Both operations must be performed correctly in order for the system to stay healthy.

2.1 Bootstrapping

Bootstrapping is the process of starting up a computer from a halted or powered-down condition. During bootstrapping, the operating system is loaded into memory and its execution is begun. A variety of initialization tasks are performed, and the system is then opened up to users. Because none of the normal functionality of the operating system is available while the computer is being initialized, the computer must "pull itself up by its bootstraps," so to speak; hence the name. *Bootstrapping* is often abbreviated to *booting*.

It is important that the system administrator understand what is happening as the system comes up, as boot time is a period of special vulnerability.

Errors in configuration information, missing or unreliable equipment, and inconsistent or damaged filesystems can all prevent a computer from coming up, and bad initialization instructions can cripple it by neglecting or misapplying important operations.

Boot configuration is often one of the very first tasks an administrator must perform on a new system. Unfortunately, it is also one of the most difficult, and it requires some familiarity with other aspects of the UNIX operating system. Even though this chapter appears early in the book, it references material that is not introduced until much later. In particular, familiarity with the material in Chapter 4: *The Filesystem*, Chapter 8: *Configuring the Kernel*, and Chapter 20: *Daemons* will prove very helpful. If your system already boots without any problem, *skip this chapter and come back to it later*.

An additional caveat: The booting process is very hardware dependent. What follows is generically true but may differ slightly from reality for your particular system.

In this section, we will first present an overview of the bootstrapping procedure, and then we'll examine two sample initialization scripts in more detail. At the end of this section are some troubleshooting hints for extreme situations.

2.1.1 The bootstrapping process

There are two routes by which most UNIX hardware can boot: automatic and manual. In automatic booting, the system performs the complete boot procedure on its own, without any external assistance. In manual booting, the system follows the automatic procedure up to a point, but turns control over to the operator before any initialization scripts are read. The computer is in single-user mode at this time, so no other users can log in. The operator can resume the automatic boot procedure after setting the date, checking the disks, and performing whatever other operations are necessary.

In day-to-day operation, automatic booting is used almost exclusively. A typical boot procedure for a modern machine is to turn on the power and wait for the system to come on-line! Nevertheless, it is important to understand your automatic boot procedure and know how to perform a manual boot.

Except for operator intervention and the necessity of manually checking the filesystems, the two boot procedures are identical. Manual booting is normally used only when the system is partially broken or has just crashed, or when the system administrator wants to make some repairs.

2.1.1.1 Steps in the boot process

A typical bootstrapping procedure can be divided into seven distinct phases:

- Loading UNIX into memory
- Initialization of the kernel
- Hardware probing and configuration
- Creation of spontaneous system processes
- Operator intervention (single-user boot only)
- Execution of initialization scripts
- Multi-user operation

2.1.1.2 Loading UNIX

UNIX is itself a program, and the first of the bootstrapping tasks is to load this program into memory so that it can be executed. The program that implements UNIX is called the kernel, and its pathname is vendor dependent but usually /unix or /vmunix.

Most UNIX systems implement a two-stage loading process. During the first stage, a small boot program is read into memory from disk or tape and executed. This program arranges for the second stage to occur, the loading of the kernel itself.

This phase of the bootstrapping process occurs completely outside the domain of UNIX, so there is no standardization whatsoever.

2.1.1.3 Initialization of the kernel

In this phase of bootstrapping, the kernel is executed and begins to initialize itself. One of the first things the kernel does is perform tests to find out how much memory is available. Since the kernel runs in constant memory, it knows right from the start how much memory to reserve for itself, its internal data storage areas, and its I/O buffers. On most systems, you will see a message on the console reporting the total amount of machine memory and the amount remaining after the kernel has extracted its share.

2.1.1.4 Hardware probing and configuration

After the kernel has its own act together, it checks out the machine's environment to see what hardware is present. When you construct a kernel for your system, you tell it what hardware devices it should expect to have to deal with; when the kernel begins to execute, it tries to find and initialize each device that you have told it about. Most kernels will print out a line of cryptic information about each device they find.[1]

The device information provided at kernel configuration time is often underspecified. In these cases, the kernel tries to determine the other information that it needs by probing the bus for devices and asking the appropriate device drivers for information. Any device that is missing or does not respond for some other reason may be marked as nonexistent and have its driver disabled, so that even if the device is later reconnected it will not be usable until the machine is rebooted.

2.1.1.5 Creation of spontaneous system processes

Once basic initialization is complete, the kernel creates some processes in user space. The number and nature of these processes varies from system to system. On BSD systems, there are three:

- **swapper** - process 0
- **init** - process 1
- **pagedaemon** - process 2

Of these three, only **init** is a "real" process; **swapper** and **pagedaemon** are actually parts of the kernel that have been faked up to look like processes for scheduling reasons. These processes are described in Chapter 20: *Daemons.*

At this point, the kernel's role in bootstrapping is complete. However, none of the processes that handle basic operations, such as accepting logins on terminals, have been created, nor have most of the all-important daemons been started up. All of these things are started (indirectly in some cases) by **init**.

2.1.1.6 Operator intervention (single-user boot only)

If the system is to be brought up in single-user mode, **init** is notified of this as it starts up. **init** simply creates a shell on the system console and waits for it to terminate (via <Control-D> or **exit**) before continuing with the rest of its startup regimen. The single-user shell is always the Bourne shell **sh** (not the C-shell **csh**) and runs as "root", UNIX's privileged user.

[1]This information is similar in form and content to the device information you supply when configuring the kernel.

From this shell, the operator can execute commands in much the same way as when logged in on a multi-user system. However, only the root partition is mounted at this time, so the operator must mount other filesystems by hand in order to use programs that do not live in /bin or /etc. Mounting of filesystems is covered in Chapter 4: *The Filesystem*. No daemons are running at this point, so commands such as **mail** that depend upon server processes will not function correctly.

The **fsck** command, which examines disks to insure the consistency of the information they contain, is automatically run when no single-user phase is involved in the bootstrapping. When the system is brought up single-user, however, this command must be run by hand. The use of **fsck** is discussed in Chapter 4: *The Filesystem*.

Another operation that is frequently performed in single-user mode is setting the system's clock with the **date** command. Many newer computers have internal clocks that maintain the correct time even when power to the computer is turned off, so setting the date on these systems is not necessary. Some systems can find out the time from other computers on their network.

2.1.1.7 Execution of initialization scripts

The next step in the bootstrapping procedure is the execution of the command scripts /etc/rc*. These are just ordinary shell scripts, so **init** spawns a copy of **sh** to interpret them. The exact names, contents, and organization of these files vary from version to version. Sun, for example, has the files /etc/rc, /etc/rc.local, and /etc/rc.boot. In some cases (such as 4.3BSD), **init** executes only one script, and this master script is responsible for starting up each of the others. On other systems, **init** may run each script separately. Look in your system's manuals under **rc** for the complete scoop.

Some tasks that are often performed in the /etc/rc scripts are:

- Setting the name of the computer (BSD and some ATT)
- Setting the time zone (ATT only)
- Checking the disks with **fsck** (only if not a single-user boot)
- Mounting the system's disk partitions (see Chapter 4)
- Removing files from the /tmp directory
- Notifying the kernel of additional swap partitions (see Chapter 4)
- Starting up daemons and network services (see Chapter 20)
- Turning on accounting and quotas (see Chapters 19 and 22)
- Configuring network interfaces (see Chapter 14)

Most /etc/rc scripts are quite verbose and print out a description of everything they do as it is done. This is a tremendous help if the system hangs up midway through booting or if you are trying to locate an error in one of the startup scripts.

2.1.1.8 Multi-user operation

After all the initialization scripts have been run, the system is fully operational except for the fact that no one can log in. In order for logins to be accepted on a particular terminal, there must be a **getty** process listening on the terminal's hardware port — thus far, no **getty**'s have been created.

After the /etc/rc* scripts have completed, **init** goes to work spawning these listening processes, completing the boot process. On BSD systems, **init** has only two states: single-user and multi-user. On modern ATT systems, **init** has one single-user and a number of multi-user *run levels* which determine which resources are enabled. Section 9.4.2 describes the **init** run levels. UNIX's handling of terminals is a separate subject which is addressed in Chapter 9, so we will not go into more detail at this point. Just keep in mind that **init** continues to perform an important role in terminal handling even after bootstrapping is complete.

2.1.2 A closer look at the /etc/rc* scripts

In this section, we will pick through a sample /etc/rc and /etc/rc.local file from a Vax running 4.3BSD. While we've taken out some lines that were unduly site-specific, we will go through the files in essentially their native state. Since the scripts vary so much from one system to another, we want to stress that there is not necessarily anything wrong with your system's rc files if they don't look anything like ours.

2.1.2.1 A sample /etc/rc script

```
HOME=/; export HOME
PATH=/bin:/usr/bin
```

These first two lines set the HOME and PATH environment variables to their appropriate values. The commands executed during boot are for the most part basic system commands, hence the straightforward search path. Note that there are no spaces around the equal signs or the colon in the second line.

```
if [ -r /fastboot ]; then
    rm -f /fastboot
    echo "Fast boot, skipping fsck" > /dev/console
```

Here the script tests for the existence of a file called /fastboot. If it exists, the script deletes the file and prints a message on the console stating that **fsck**, the filesystem consistency check program, will not be run. The reason for this is that **fsck** may take a long time to run, and if all you want is a quick and dirty reboot, it is convenient to have a way of bypassing the **fsck** sequence without booting into single-user mode. The BSD commands **fastboot** and **fasthalt** create the /fastboot file automatically.

```
elif [ $1x = autobootx ]; then
    echo "Auto reboot in progress..." > /dev/console
    date > /dev/console
    /etc/fsck -p > /dev/console
    case $? in
    0)
        date > /dev/console ;;
    2)
        exit 1 ;;
    4)
        /etc/reboot -n ;;
    8)
        echo "Auto reboot failed - help!" > /dev/console
        exit 1 ;;
    12)
        echo "Reboot interrupted" > /dev/console
        exit 1 ;;
    *)
        echo "Unknown error in reboot" > /dev/console
        exit 1 ;;
    esac
else
    date > /dev/console
fi
```

This fragment of the /etc/rc file describes what happens if the /fastboot file does not exist (notice the `elif`) and the script was invoked with the argument "autoboot" to indicate that there should be no single-user phase in the boot procedure. The date and a message stating that an automatic reboot is in progress are printed on the system console. The **fsck -p** command is then run to automatically check all the filesystems listed in /etc/fstab, and the exit code it returns is examined to determine whether or not the disk check was successful.

If the exit code is zero, then the **fsck** was successful and the date of completion is echoed to the console. With the exception of exit code four, each of the other codes causes the script to terminate. When **init** sees that the script has failed, it does not continue to multi-user mode but backsteps instead to the single-user shell, allowing the operator to take remedial action.

An exit code of four indicates that the root partition was repaired and that the bootstrapping process must be restarted from the beginning in order for the repairs to take effect, hence the execution of the **reboot** command. Note the **-n** option to reboot, which prevents the kernel from flushing its internal disk cache and wiping out the repairs that **fsck** just made.

Note that if the "autoboot" argument is *not* passed into the script, the date is simply printed on the console and no disk checks are done. This is why **fsck** must be run manually when the system is booted single-user. Some versions of the /etc/rc file operate backwards with respect to the "autoboot" argument – the script assumes that an automatic boot is in progress unless a "single-user" argument is passed in.

The following lines help to deal with the case in which a machine crashes while its /etc/passwd file is being edited. The password file is critical to the operation of the system because it contains the information necessary to allow users to log in. Because /etc/passwd is so important, it is best not to edit it directly. Some BSD systems provide the **vipw** program to edit /etc/passwd. **vipw** makes a copy of /etc/passwd in /etc/ptmp and invokes your editor (as specified by the EDITOR environment variable, or **vi** if unspecified) on the copy. This insures that /etc/passwd is never left in a strange or inconsistent state while being edited, and prevents more than one person from editing the passwd file at a time. On some systems, **vipw** is also responsible for creating a hashed version of the passwd file via **mkpasswd**.

```
if [ -s /etc/ptmp ]; then
    if [ -s /etc/passwd ]; then
        ls -l /etc/passwd /etc/ptmp > /dev/console
        rm -f /etc/ptmp
    else
        echo "Passwd recovered from ptmp" > /dev/console
        mv /etc/ptmp /etc/passwd
    fi
elif [ -r /etc/ptmp ]; then
    echo 'removing passwd lock file' > /dev/console
    rm -f /etc/ptmp
fi
```

The first line of this section of code thus checks to see if the /etc/ptmp file exists and is not empty. If that's true, then someone must have been editing the passwd file when the system went down. A check is then made to see if the /etc/passwd file is missing or zero length; if it is, then "Passwd recovered from ptmp" is printed on the console and /etc/ptmp becomes the actual /etc/passwd file. Otherwise, both files are simply **ls**'ed and the /etc/ptmp file is removed. If the /etc/ptmp file exists, but is empty, it is simply removed and a message is printed on the console.

The next two lines clear out /etc/mtab, where information about the mounted filesystems is stored. First, all active filesystems are unmounted, and then the file /etc/mtab is truncated to zero length. (It isn't actually possible to unmount the root partition, so **umount -a** doesn't really do quite what the **-a** "for all" flag suggests.) Mounting of filesystems is discussed in Chapter 4.

```
/etc/umount -a
cat /dev/null > /etc/mtab
```

Next, all standard filesystems are mounted with the **mount** command, and paging and swapping are enabled on disk partitions designated for this purpose in /etc/fstab. The "2>&1" construct insures that both regular and diagnostic output will be sent to the system console.

```
/etc/mount -a > /dev/console 2>&1
/etc/swapon -a > /dev/console 2>&1
```

The script next addresses the handling of disk quotas.

```
echo -n 'checking quotas:' > /dev/console
/etc/quotacheck -a -p > /dev/console 2>&1
echo ' done.' > /dev/console

/etc/quotaon  -a
```

The first three lines validate and update disk quota information for each partition. The last line then enables quotas on all partitions on which they are appropriate, as specified in /etc/fstab. Quotas are discussed in Chapter 22.

```
rm -f /etc/nologin
```

The /etc/nologin file is removed if it exists. On some systems, the **login** program looks for this file when a user attempts to log in. If it exists, its contents are printed on the user's terminal and the user is not allowed to log in. Programs such as **shutdown** create this file to keep users from logging into a system that will soon be brought down. /etc/nologin may also be created by hand if it is ever necessary to keep users off the system. The **-f** option to **rm** is used to prevent an error message from appearing if /etc/nologin does not exist.

```
rm -f /usr/spool/uucp/LCK.*
```

This line removes any spurious uucp lock files, so that uucp will assume that the system's modems are initially available. Uucp is discussed in Chapter 16.

```
chmod 666 /dev/tty[pqrs]*
```

Access permissions on the system's pseudo-terminals are set to allow anyone to read and write from them.

```
sh /etc/rc.local
```

At this point in the /etc/rc file, the /etc/rc.local script is executed. Note that /etc/rc.local is executed in its own shell, not by the same shell that executes /etc/rc. The rc.local script contains similar commands to the /etc/rc script; we will examine a sample /etc/rc.local in a moment.

The next task on /etc/rc's list of things to do is clear out the /tmp directory, where programs usually put their temporary files. Since the **vi** and **ex** editors also put their temporary files here, /etc/rc attempts to salvage any files that users were editing when the system went down by running the program **ex3.7preserve** inside the /tmp directory. This program finds all the editor files and squirrels them away in the /usr/preserve directory, where they can be recovered by use of the **vi -r** or **ex -r** commands. It also sends mail to the owners of the files telling them that this has happened.

```
echo "Preserving editor files" > /dev/console
(cd /tmp; /usr/lib/ex3.7preserve -a)
```

Note that **cd /tmp ; /usr/lib/ex3.7preserve -a** is enclosed in parentheses. This causes the two commands to be executed in a subshell, preventing the working directory of the main script from becoming /tmp.

```
echo "Clearing /tmp" > /dev/console
(cd /tmp; find . ! -name . -exec rm -r {} \; )
```

These lines print a descriptive message on the console and delete the remaining files in /tmp. This approach assumes that /tmp is not a separate disk partition; if this isn't true, then care must be taken not to remove /tmp's "quotas" file and lost+found directory. On some systems, subdirectories of /tmp are not removed.

```
echo -n "Standard daemons:" > /dev/console
/etc/update; echo -n ' update' > /dev/console
/etc/cron; echo -n ' cron' > /dev/console
echo '.' > /dev/console
```

The **update** and **cron** daemons are started here. A classification heading is first printed, and the name of each daemon is printed as it is started up. This code is typical of all daemon-starting runs in the /etc/rc* files, so the code for starting the remaining daemons (of which there are many) is not shown.

```
/etc/accton /usr/adm/acct;
```

This line turns on the system's cpu accounting procedures and directs that per-process accounting information be saved in the file /usr/adm/acct.

```
date > /dev/console
exit 0
```

At the very end of the script, the date is printed on the console, and the script exits with a successful return code (zero). It is important that the script specify a successful exit code so that **init** will know that execution of the entire script was successful and allow the machine to continue to the multi-user state.

2.1.2.2 A sample /etc/rc.local script

While all of the commands executed in /etc/rc are important to insure correct functioning of the system, nothing in /etc/rc was specific to any particular machine: The hostname was not set, no particular hardware was referenced or configured, and no local daemons were started. All of these things happen in /etc/rc.local.

```
PATH=/etc:/bin:/usr/ucb:/usr/bin
```

Just as in /etc/rc, the first thing that happens is an adjustment to the script's search path. Note that this assumes the /usr filesystem is already mounted.

```
hostname boulder
hostid `hostname`
```

The first line sets the name of the machine to "boulder". The second line initializes the machine's host identification number to its Internet address; the **hostname** command returns the name of the machine, and the **hostid** command looks this name up in the /etc/hosts file.

```
/etc/ifconfig lo0 localhost up arp >/dev/console
/etc/ifconfig de0 128.138.240.4 up subarp netmask \
    0xffffff00 arp broadcast 128.138.240.255 >/dev/console
/etc/ifconfig de1 128.138.238.18 up subarp netmask \
    0xffffff00 arp broadcast 128.138.238.0 >/dev/console
```

These lines configure the machine's Ethernet interfaces using the **ifconfig** command. The "lo0" interface is a local software loopback without any actual hardware. "de0" and "de1" are actual connections to local Ethernets. **ifconfig** is discussed in Chapter 14.

```
strings /vmunix | grep UNIX > /tmp/t1
tail +2 /etc/motd >> /tmp/t1
mv /tmp/t1 /etc/motd
```

These three lines adjust the /etc/motd file, which is displayed when a user logs in, to contain the correct kernel identification string. Recall that /vmunix is the UNIX kernel – among the printable strings in this file will be one that identifies the kernel and its compilation date like this:

4.3 BSD UNIX #30: Sat Jan 9 18:52:07 MST 1989

The first of the command lines grabs this string out of /vmunix and puts it into a temporary file. The second line grabs everything from the old /etc/motd file from the second line on, and appends it to the temporary file. Finally, the temporary file is moved to become the actual /etc/motd. If the first line of the /etc/motd file is always the kernel identification string, then this has the effect of automatically updating the first line of the /etc/motd file every time the machine is bootstrapped.

```
echo 'Checking for core dump...' > /dev/console
savecore /users/crash > /dev/console 2>&1
```

In case the system is being bootstrapped after a crash, these lines invoke the **savecore** command to preserve an image of the kernel right after it encountered the fatal error in the /users/crash directory. A **savecore** operation assumes that the kernel was able to dump its address space onto a swap partition before exiting; the choice of partition is specified at kernel configuration time. Since crash dumps can be large, it is a good idea to clean out /users/crash on a regular basis, or to have this function performed by **cron**. Crash dumps are discussed in Chapter 4: *The Filesystem*.

2.1.3 What to do if the system won't boot

Some things that can keep a UNIX system from successfully booting are:

- Hardware problems
- Defective boot floppies or tapes
- Damaged filesystems
- Improperly configured kernels
- Errors in the /etc/rc* scripts

2.1.3.1 Hardware problems

There is not much you can do about these problems but have them repaired by a technician. Before you call out for maintenance, though, be sure that the problem is really with the hardware. If when booting you consistently receive a message informing you of a memory defect or other similar ailment, it is a good bet that the problem is with the hardware.

If, on the other hand, the machine simply does nothing or hangs up midway through the boot sequence, there are a couple of things you should try before calling the hardware people.

First, check the power supply to each piece of equipment. This may seem almost too obvious to mention, but it is surprising how often this step is overlooked, even by people who should know better. Some power problems are not obvious; for example, DEC's Unibus has its own power supply that must be turned off when swapping Unibus boards around. It is easy to forget to power the bus back up.

Second, check for any kind of problem that could impair communication between components of the computer system. Check all cables to be sure they are firmly connected, and be sure that all disk drives are on-line. Don't forget the Ethernet connections, especially on machines that bootstrap off of the net rather than a disk drive.

Third, check the fault lights on each piece of equipment that has them. Hard disks almost always have them, and many printers and computers do as well. Some computers (Pyramids and Suns, for example) have several fault lights that can identify problems with some degree of specificity.

Fourth, try power-cycling the equipment. Turn the power to the computer and all peripherals completely off. On Vaxen, be sure to turn off the LSI 11 support processor. Wait ten seconds or so before restoring power to allow any internal capacitors to discharge.

Fifth, try cooling down the machine room a few degrees. Computer equipment is somewhat temperature-sensitive. If the temperature of your machine room is too warm, it is likely to cause malfunctions.

Sixth, if the boot procedure *does* get as far as the kernel's initial probing of devices before encountering problems, try to verify the presence of each of your devices in the kernel's diagnostic printouts. If the kernel doesn't see a device that it should be seeing, the device is broken or it's not connected properly.

Seventh, most systems come with a set of stand-alone diagnostic programs that can help track down infirmities in the system's hardware. The diagnostics are usually run on the bare hardware, so they can be used even if UNIX can't be booted. The depth of coverage of these tests and their method of operation vary from machine to machine, but most will include at least memory, CPU, and bus tests. Consult your manuals.

If these procedures fail to identify the problem, call your service person.

Naturally, the best defense against hardware problems is to take good care of your hardware in the first place. Chapter 13: *Hardware Maintenance Tips* lists a number of simple maintenance procedures you can use to reduce your risk of problems. It is important to be constantly on the lookout for potential trouble spots. Your system's console message log (usually /usr/adm/messages) will contain a copy of any hardware error messages that are printed to the system's console. It is normal for certain devices to experience a few errors every so often, but if you see a sudden increase in errors this may indicate that a device is about to fail.

2.1.3.2 Defective boot floppies or tapes

If your system uses a bootstrap floppy disk or tape, it is important that you keep a backup copy of it. Most manufacturers will provide a backup floppy with the system, but it is still better to make your own if software for doing this is provided, so that both original copies are preserved in a virgin state. This is especially true if your hardware configuration is recorded on the floppy, as this may change and need updating.

Failures of this type have different symptoms from system to system, but it is easy to determine whether or not the boot floppy is the problem by simply trying to boot off a different copy.

2.1.3.3 Damaged filesystems

This is perhaps the scariest type of failure, since it is possible that the system's files or even in rare cases a disk drive itself may be damaged beyond recovery. The symptoms vary depending upon whether the damage is soft (scrambled information on the disk) or hard (a disk head crash), and upon which disk partitions are affected. If you believe that your disks have problems, you should understand the material in Chapter 4 before trying to fix them.

If the root partition cannot be read, it will not be possible to load the kernel, and the system may behave as if a hardware problem were at fault. Unless you have had the foresight to prepare an alternative root partition (preferably on a different disk drive), this kind of situation can be almost hopeless. In the worst-case scenario, you will have to go back to the original UNIX tapes and reinitialize the entire system to its distributed state. If you have recent backups, the loss of data from this operation will be minimized.

If you do opt to configure your system with a backup root partition, it is important that you duplicate the contents of the master root onto the slave root every so often with the **dd** command to keep the two in sync. This can be done most easily by running a script out of **cron**. Be cautious, though, since on some systems it is possible to copy partitioning information and boot blocks when **dd**ing the root partition, thus accidentally relabeling the destination disk.

You must also make whatever other preparations are necessary to allow you to boot off the alternative partition. For systems with boot tapes or boot floppies, this may mean configuring a special tape or disk that will try to load the kernel from the alternative partition rather than the standard one. Your manuals should have information on how to do this.

In less severe instances of root partition damage, the boot procedure may proceed part way, but crash before the **fsck** checks are reached. Pay close attention to the message printed by the kernel as the system crashes, as it will tell you if the crash is really filesystem-related. *Any* kind of message about inodes, superblocks, maps, or filesystems probably indicates one of these problems. Here are a few representative BSD filesystem crash messages:

```
ialloc: dup alloc      namei: null cache ino           free: bad size
bread: size 0          namei: duplicating cache        free inode isn't
getfs: bad magic       free: freeing free block        clrblock
mkdir: dquot           ifree: freeing free inode
```

In this situation, the first thing to do is try to boot single-user. If the machine cannot even be booted single-user, the system has real problems and you should try to get help.

Once in single-user mode, you'll have access to only the most basic and important UNIX tools, those stored in the directory /bin. If you are lucky, you'll be able to mount other partitions by hand with the **mount** command to get at more sophisticated programs such as **vi**.

If the system does come up single-user, use the **fsck** command before anything else, as described in Chapter 4. This will fix many problems, and will inform you about others even if they cannot be automatically fixed. Run **fsck** first on the root partition, and if any problems are uncovered, reboot and repeat the process until the root comes up clean. Then use **fsck** to check the remaining filesystems. If at any point an unfixable error becomes evident, stop messing around and find someone that knows what they are doing to help you out.

2.1.3.4 Improperly configured kernels

Chapter 8 describes the process of building a new UNIX kernel. Every time you rebuild and replace your kernel, you run the risk that it won't work right and that you will be left in a difficult situation. Be sure to consistently make arrangements for the old kernel to be booted in case of problems. It is a good idea to keep an old kernel around even during day-to-day operation.

2.1.3.5 Errors in the /etc/rc* scripts

This is the most common impediment to successful booting, and is also the easiest to fix. What typically happens is that you make a change to one of the /etc/rc* scripts and the system then refuses to come up multi-user.

You need to identify the problem and fix it as you would when debugging any other shell script, but from single-user mode. Often the only editor available in the single-user environment is **ed**, but you can use the **mount** command to mount the /usr partition, allowing you access to **vi** and other editors. You will need to adjust your terminal type and environment by hand before screen editors will work properly. Remember to either modify your search path or reference programs in /usr by their full pathnames.

Commands that do some sort of initialization on the system may fail if run more than once, so on some systems you must reboot from scratch after each change to an rc script rather than trying to run the script from the shell.

2.2 Shutting down and rebooting

While there are many occasions when shutting down or rebooting a UNIX system is perfectly appropriate, neither operation should be performed indiscriminately. While it is generally not something to worry about, there is a degree of hardware fatigue associated with turning a computer system off and on again, and it is often better to let it run 24 hours a day than to shut it down at night. Since you won't have to wait for the system to boot and shut down every day, this will save you time and trouble as well.

Many people who move from a personal computer to a UNIX environment seem to view rebooting as a kind of magic fix for many different kinds of problems. While rebooting doesn't hurt the system, it takes time and inconveniences users – you should try to avoid it unless it is really likely to help. There are only four common situations in which rebooting the system is called for:

- If you make changes to any of the system software or configuration files that are examined or executed only when the system is bootstrapped, you must reboot for these changes to take effect. Examples of this are changes in the /etc/rc* scripts and installation of a new kernel.
- Some devices, especially printer and modem ports, can become confused enough that resetting them is not possible without reinitializing the system. In a similar vein, the BSD printing system can sometimes get so fouled up that rebooting is the only fix.
- If the system has been up constantly for more than a week, you may wish to bring the system back down to single-user mode to run **fsck** checks. If any fixes are made to the root partition, the system must be rebooted from scratch; otherwise, you can simply return to multi-user mode by exiting the single-user shell.
- If the system console becomes irrecoverably hung, you should reboot.

2.2.1 Methods of shutting down and rebooting

Unlike bootstrapping, which can be done in essentially only one way, there are a number of ways to shut down or reboot UNIX system. They are:

- Turning off the power
- Using the **shutdown** command
- Using the BSD **halt** command
- Using the BSD **reboot** command
- Sending **init** a TERM signal
- Using the BSD **fasthalt** or **fastboot** commands
- Killing **init**

2.2.1.1 Turning off the power

Even on a small-scale UNIX system, this is a poor way to shut down. Not only will you leave the system's files in an inconsistent state, but you may also damage certain kinds of disk drives which expect to have a protect switch activated or have their heads parked before being powered off.

While we mention this method primarily to steer you away from it, you should also know that it is sometimes a reasonable thing to do in the case of a dire emergency, such as when the computer is on fire or the machine room is about to be flooded. If you can get to a terminal and halt the system quickly, do so; otherwise, pull the plug.

2.2.1.2 Using the shutdown command

shutdown is the crown prince of system-halting programs; it is the safest, most considerate, and most thorough way to initiate a halt, reboot, or return to single-user mode. The following discussion refers to the BSD **shutdown** command, but most systems include a version of **shutdown** that works in a similar manner. However, many versions are not as robust as the BSD version, so consult you system documentation before using **shutdown**. The basic form of the **shutdown** command is:

> **shutdown** *time* [*message*]

Where *time* is the time at which the system is to be shut down and *message* is an explanatory message (usually enclosed in quotes) which will be shown to users as a warning and placed in /usr/adm/shutdownlog, the system shutdown log. The time may be expressed as "+*X*", where *X* is the number of minutes from the current time that the shutdown should take place, or may be expressed in standard 24-hour notation (e.g., "13:30"). The word "now" may also be used to effect an immediate shutdown.

shutdown writes warning messages to each user's terminal at progressively shorter intervals as the time for shutdown approaches. The messages tell the time of the shutdown, and include the explanatory message that was provided on the **shutdown** command line. Five minutes before the time of shutdown, the /etc/nologin file is created to prevent any more users from logging in. At the appropriate time, **shutdown** carefully brings the system down to single-user mode and removes the /etc/nologin file.

shutdown can also be used with a **-r** flag to initiate a reboot instead of a return to single-user mode, or with a **-h** flag to halt the system completely. The **-k** "kidding" flag makes **shutdown** do nothing but send out messages, so you can use it to make people think the system is going down when it actually isn't.

2.2.1.3 Using the halt command (BSD)

halt is what **shutdown -h** uses to bring the system to a complete halt after putting out all those warning messages. You can use the **halt** command directly as well. **halt** logs the shutdown, kills the system's processes, executes the **sync** system call (called by and equivalent to the **sync** command) to schedule the kernel's internally buffered information for writing out to disk, waits for the writes to complete, and then halts the processor. A **-n** flag prevents the **sync** call, and a **-q** flag instigates an almost immediate halt, without synchronization, killing of processes, or writing of logs. The use of these flags is not recommended unless **fsck** has just been used to repair the root partition.

2.2.1.4 Using the reboot command (BSD)

reboot is almost identical to **halt**, but it causes the machine to reboot from scratch rather than halting. **reboot** is the program called by **shutdown -r**. **reboot** supports the **-n** and **-q** flags.

2.2.1.5 Sending init a TERM signal

The results of killing **init** are unpredictable and often nasty. Consult your documentation before sending **init** any signals. When **init** receives a TERM signal (usually signal number fifteen, check your /usr/include/signal.h file to be sure), it usually interprets it as a command to kill all user processes, daemons, and **getty**'s and return to single-user mode. This is how **shutdown** effects this return. To send a signal to a process, you normally need to find its process id number using **ps**, but **init** is always process number one. To send this signal, the **kill** command is used, as in:

```
sync
kill -15 1
```

More information about signals is presented in Chapter 5: *Controlling Processes.*

2.2.1.6 Using the fasthalt and fastboot commands (BSD)

These commands are simple shell scripts that create the file /fastboot before executing **halt** or **reboot,** respectively. Use these commands if you don't want to perform **fsck** checks automatically when the system boots up. These are dangerous commands, and you should use them only when you're sure the filesystems are in good shape.

2.2.1.7 Killing init

init is so important to the operation of a UNIX system that if it is killed, the system will reboot automatically. This is kind of a rough way to go about rebooting, so you should use **reboot** instead.

3

Superuser Privileges

3.1 Ownership

The concept of ownership is present in almost all large operating systems to one degree or another, and in UNIX its role in regulating the operation of the machine is quite significant. In this chapter we'll explore ownership under UNIX and discuss the special access privileges available to the system administrator.

3.1.1 Ownership of files

Every UNIX file has one true owner and one group owner. The true owner of the file enjoys only *one* special privilege that is not shared with *everyone* on the system – the ability to modify the permissions of the file. However, the owner of the file may set the permissions on it so restrictively that no one but he may access it. The **chmod** command, discussed in the next chapter, is used to modify the permissions of a file.

While the true owner of a file is always a single person, the group owner of a file names a UNIX *group*, which may contain any number of people. The groups that exist on a particular system are enumerated in the file /etc/group. Here is a sample line from our /etc/group file:

```
authors:*:42:evi,garth,scott
```

This line asserts the existence of a group called "authors" which has three members: evi, garth, and scott. We'll delay a complete discussion of the group file until Chapter 6: *Adding New Users*; for now, just be aware that groups are special names for collections of people.

The true owner of a file may give special permissions to the group owners of the file. This facilitates file sharing between members of the same project. For example, we used a group similar to the preceding one to let us share access to the source files for this book. The owner and group of a file may be changed with the **chown** and **chgrp** commands, which are described in Chapter 4.

Both ownerships of a file can be determined with the command **ls -lg** *filename* under BSD and the command **ls -l** *filename* under ATT. The following example was produced with **ls -lg /staff/scott/pie.recipe** under BSD, but the ATT format is identical:

```
-rw------- 1 scott staff 1258 Jun  4 18:15 /staff/scott/pie.recipe
```

This particular file contains the secret recipe for Scott's grandmother's cherry pie; it is owned by scott and has a group ownership of "staff".

UNIX's idea of an owner or group is simply a number. Owner numbers (userids or UID's for short) are mapped to user names in /etc/passwd, and group numbers (GID's) are mapped to group names in /etc/group. The names that correspond to these numbers are purely for the convenience of the human users of the system; UNIX always maintains ownership information internally in numeric form. When a command such as **ls** wants to display the owners in a textual form, it must look up each number in the appropriate file.

3.1.2 Ownership of processes

Ownership of processes is slightly more complex than ownership of files. The kernel associates four numbers with each process: a *real* and *effective* UID and a *real* and *effective* GID. The "real" numbers are used for purposes of accounting and the "effective" numbers are used for the purposes of determining access permissions. For normal processes, the real and effective numbers are the same.

The true owner of a process enjoys two privileges with respect to the process: He may send the process *signals* and may to some extent alter the scheduling priority of the process.

A signal is a special type of notification that is delivered to a process asynchronously. What happens when a process is sent a signal depends upon the particular signal (there are about thirty different kinds) and the signal handling requests that the process has delivered to the kernel. The scheduling priority of a process helps to determine how much of the system's resources are devoted to the process in comparison with the other processes on the system. Signals and scheduling priorities are covered in Chapter 5: *Controlling Processes*.

3.1.3 Changing ownership of processes

While it is not normally possible for a process to alter its four ownership numbers, there is a special situation in which the effective user and group id's may be changed.

A process wishing to start executing a different program file calls one of the **exec** family of system calls. When this happens, the effective UID and GID may be set to the UID and GID of the *file* containing the new program image *if* the file has its *setuid* or *setgid* permission bits set. The transformation of UID and GID is automatic, and the file permissions may be set so that any combination of UID and GID is changed.

For example, let us suppose that the user jane writes and compiles a program called **calcvectors** and then uses **chmod 4755 calcvectors** to activate the setuid bit of the executable file. Suppose that the user laszlo executes jane's program, creating a new process. The process's real UID will be laszlo's UID, and the process's effective UID will be jane's UID. Both the real and effective GID's will be laszlo's.

As far as UNIX is concerned, the process is allowed the permissions normally accorded to jane on the basis of her UID and the permissions normally accorded to laszlo on the basis of his GID. If jane had also activated the setgid bit on her program, then laszlo's process would have permissions determined by both the UID and GID of the executable file. If accounting is enabled, laszlo will be charged for any resources used by the process regardless of what its effective permissions are.

3.2 The superuser

The UNIX ownership paradigm insures that users can prevent others from interfering with their files and processes without permission, but the system administrator needs to be able to override these protections in a variety of situations. To make this possible, UNIX treats one particular user differently from all others. This is the *superuser* – any user with UID 0, usually with the login name “root”.

UNIX allows the superuser to perform any operation on a file or process. In addition, some system calls may be executed only by the superuser, and a few have special options that may only be exercised if the caller is the superuser. Some examples of operations restricted to root are:

- Mounting and dismounting filesystems
- Changing the root directory of a process
- Creating device files
- Setting the system clock
- Changing ownership of files (on some systems)
- Raising resource usage limits
- Setting the system’s hostname
- Configuring network interfaces
- Setting the sticky bit on a file
- Shutting down the system

An example of the powers of the superuser is the ability of a process owned by root to change each of its ownership numbers at will. The **login** process is a case in point; the process that prompts you for your password when you log into the system initially runs as the superuser. If the password and user name typed in are appropriate, however, it changes its ownerships to that of the specified user and executes the user’s shell. Once the superuser process changes its ownerships to become a normal user process, it cannot regain its former standing.

Using the root login is like driving an expensive sports car; it gets you where you need to go quickly, but an accident will result in a big repair bill. You should use the root login with great reverence and caution, and never take it out for a spin at a time when you wouldn’t trust yourself to operate an automobile or other heavy machinery.

3.3 The root password

The superuser account is handled just like any other. Because this account is critical to the operation of the system, all UNIX systems come with this account established, and you should not have to perform any special operations to activate it.

Like other logins, access to the superuser account is controlled by a password. Someone who knows the password for the root account can do whatever they want to within the system. It is therefore critical that the root password remain a closely guarded secret. There is normally no reason for anyone but the system administrator(s) to know the root password.

3.4 Choosing the root password

It is important that the root password be selected so that it not be easily guessed or discovered by trial and error. The most secure type of password consists of a random sequence of upper and lower case letters and digits, but because this type of password is hard to remember and usually difficult to type we don't recommend that you take security to these lengths. A password consisting of two randomly selected lower case words separated by a punctuation mark is usually secure enough. Passwords of this form also comply with some systems' requirement that all passwords contain at least one number or special character.

Your primary consideration when choosing a root password should be that it be easy to type, since you may be typing it often. An easy-to-type password can also be typed faster, reducing the chance that someone looking over your shoulder will be able to determine the password by watching your fingers. There is usually a limit on the number of letters in a password that are actually encrypted, so there is no advantage to choosing a password longer than about ten letters.

You should change the root password

- At least every two months or so
- Every time someone who knows the password leaves your organization
- Whenever you think security may have been compromised

3.5 Becoming root

There are several ways that you can access the superuser account. The simplest is to just log in as root. Unfortunately, logging out of your own account and logging in as the superuser is inconvenient and time-consuming. A much better way is to use the **su** (set user identity) command. If invoked without any arguments, **su** will prompt you for the root password and start up a root shell. The superuser privileges of this shell remain in effect until the shell is terminated.

Since **su** starts up a completely new shell, if root uses the **csh** shell, the ".cshrc" file will be read and executed. It is important to set root's search path (the PATH environment variable) so that it does not include ".", the current directory. **csh** users would normally do this in the ".login" file instead of the ".cshrc" file, but because ".login" is not read during an **su** the ".cshrc" file for root must be a special case. On ATT systems where root typically uses the **sh** shell, the path is automatically reset to /bin:/etc:/usr/bin. On BSD systems **sh** neither reads root's ".profile" nor resets the path to a default value.

Under BSD, if both your shell and root's shell are the C-shell, there is no need for you to terminate the root shell to get back to your original shell; you can use the built-in command **suspend** to stop the root shell temporarily and return to it later with **fg** or by naming its job number. For example:

```
% /bin/su
Password: <root password was typed here>
1 # whoami
root
2 # suspend
% whoami
garth
```

Note that after an **su** root's prompt changes from a percent sign to a hash mark preceded by a command number. The new prompt is set in root's ".cshrc" file and serves as a reminder that superuser privileges are in effect.

If you do keep a root shell around in the background, be sure that you don't forget that it's there. Never leave a terminal with a root shell on it – even for a minute!

The **su** command is also capable of substituting identities other than root. If you know someone's password, you can substitute directly to their account by executing **su** *username*. As with an **su** to root, you will be prompted for their password. On some systems, the root password will allow an **su** or **login** to any account; on others, you must first **su** explicitly to root before **su**'ing to a user account.

3.5.1 sudo - a limited su

One problem with UNIX is that the privileges of the superuser account cannot be subdivided. This makes it hard to give someone the ability to do backups (which must be done as root) without giving them free run of the entire system.

Our solution to this problem is a program called **sudo**. The **sudo** program takes as its arguments a full command line that is to be executed as the superuser. **sudo** first checks the file /usr/local/adm/sudoers, which is a list of people authorized to use **sudo** and what programs they may run. If the command to be run is allowed, **sudo** prompts for the *user's own* password and executes the command as root. Further **sudo** commands may be executed without having to retype the password until a five-minute period has elapsed in which no **sudo**'s have been posted. This password check serves to protect the system against users with **sudo** privileges who leave their terminals unattended.

In addition to initiating the requested command, the **sudo** program also keeps a log which shows all of the command lines that were handled, the people who requested them, and the times at which the commands were executed. By default this log is kept in /usr/local/adm/logs/sudo.log.

For example, suppose that the user laura wants to look up information about her computer's telephone connection with the computer "colossus" in the /usr/lib/uucp/L.sys file, which is not world-readable. Since she knows that as herself she cannot access the file, she decides to use the **sudo** command. She types:

sudo grep colossus /usr/lib/uucp/L.sys

Unfortunately, laura's entry in /usr/local/adm/sudoers only allows her to execute **/bin/du** and **/etc/dump**, so she gets the message:

```
sudo: I know you, but I can't let you: grep
```

If laura were to try to use **sudo** to do a **/bin/du** or an **/etc/dump**, then the **sudo** program would be completely transparent except for asking for a password, and her request would be honored. Note that commands in /usr/local/adm/sudoers are specified using full pathnames to prevent people from being able to execute their own programs and scripts as root.

Using **sudo** has the following advantages:

- It is faster to use **sudo** than to **su** or log in as root.
- Operators can do chores without being given unlimited root privileges.
- The root password remains a secret shared by only one or two people.
- Accountability is higher due to command logging.
- Root privileges may be revoked without changing the root password.

- A canonical list of all users with root privileges is maintained.
- There is less chance of someone leaving a root shell around accidentally.

There are a couple of disadvantages as well. The worst of these is the fact that any breach in the security of a user's account can be equivalent to breaching the root account itself; there is little that you can do to counter this threat aside from cautioning your sudoers that they must protect their own accounts like they would the root account. Because **sudo** does allow users to execute commands as root, **sudo** privileges should only be extended to users whom you can trust not to abuse their power. **sudo**'s command logging can be easily subverted by doing things like **sudo csh** or **sudo su**. However, recent versions of the C-shell allow the shell command history to be preserved across sessions, providing a logging facility of sorts. This feature is especially useful for the root login. Including the lines

```
set history = 1000
set savehist
```

in root's ".cshrc" file will keep a 1000-command log for root whether a root shell is obtained by logging in or via **su** or **sudo**. Warning: A knowledgeable (and presumably clandestine) user of the root login can contrive to subvert or falsify this continuous log, so its use as a security trace is limited. Allowing **sudo** *xxx* where *xxx* is a command that can spawn a shell is equivalent to giving unlimited access.

The **sudo** program (for BSD) is included in Appendix A. Unlike most of the sample programs, which are shell scripts, **sudo** is written in C. Compilation instructions and a manual page are included with the source code.

3.6 Restrictions on the use of root

Two useful tools for controlling the use of the root login have recently been introduced into BSD UNIX. These restrictions are not available in most versions of ATT or earlier versions of BSD.

The first restriction is a simple change to the **su** program. Any user attempting to **su** to root is checked to be sure that he belongs to group number zero, usually named "wheel". If he does not, an apologetic message is printed and no root shell is generated. Thus, even if a user should somehow discover the root password he would not be able to **su** without specific permission from the system administrator.

Of course, this restriction is completely circumvented if the miscreant simply logs out and logs back in again as root. To prevent this, 4.3BSD has introduced the concept of a *secure* terminal. A terminal will not accept root logins unless it is designated as secure in the file /etc/ttys. A full discussion of /etc/ttys is available in Chapter 9: *Installing Terminals and Modems*. Typically, the secure terminals are the system console and the terminals housed in the personal offices of people who know the root password.

3.7 Other important users

Root is the only user that has special status in the eyes of the UNIX kernel, but there are several other special, nonhuman logins that are used for various purposes. It is customary to replace the passwords of these special users in the /etc/passwd file with an asterisk so that their accounts cannot be logged into.

3.7.1 daemon: an owner of unprivileged software

Just as root always has a userid of zero, daemon usually has a userid of one. Files that should properly belong to UNIX rather than a particular user are often given to daemon rather than root to avoid the security hazards associated with ownership by root. Programs that need access to restricted files often have those files owned by daemon and run setuid to daemon so that in case of a catastrophic error the danger of critical system files being damaged is low. daemon usually owns the printer logs and printer accounting files and the programs in /usr/games.

There is also a UNIX group called "daemon", created for similar reasons. Some of the uucp software must have access to this group (see Chapter 16: *Uucp*).

On some older systems, UID 1 (usually daemon) is allowed to **su** to root without supplying a password. This can be a security problem if you have any interactive programs that run as daemon and allow the user to generate a subshell without resetting the UID and GID. Fortunately, there are few systems that extend this privilege to daemon.

3.7.2 bin: an owner of system commands

The user bin often owns the directories that contain the bulk of the system's commands. In earlier versions of UNIX, bin owned most of the executable files as well. Newer versions of UNIX don't use bin that much, and some have even done away with it entirely.

3.7.3 sys: owner of the kernel and memory images

On some systems, the user sys is the owner of the special files /dev/kmem, /dev/mem, and /dev/drum or /dev/swap, which are respectively the kernel's address space, an image of the physical memory of the system, and an image of the system's swap space. Few programs access these files, but those that do run setuid to sys if this ownership convention is in use. On some systems, the username kmem is used rather than sys.

4

The Filesystem

Up to now, we've been concerned with the contents of files rather than the files themselves. In this chapter, we'll take a closer look at the UNIX filesystem. After making a general survey of the UNIX hierarchy and the various types of files that can be created, we will look at some tools for checking and keeping track of filesystems.

Some of the material in this chapter is directly related to system administration, and some is merely cultural background information. The latter has been included in an effort to help you understand how the filesystem works as well as how to administer it.

4.1 What the user sees

UNIX presents the filesystem to users as a single tree, starting at the directory / and continuing downwards through an essentially arbitrary number of directories. This top level directory is called the *root* directory. The complete list of directories that must be traversed to locate a given file is called the file's *pathname*. For example, /usr/local/moosefile is the pathname for a file named "moosefile". moosefile may be any type of file, since the pathname gives information only about *location* and not the uses to which a file may be put.

The kernel associates with each running process a current directory. When the kernel is asked to interpret a pathname that does not begin with the character "/", descent of the directory tree begins with the current directory rather than the root directory. It is by this mechanism that commands such as **ls adm** and **cat passwd** can be used rather than **ls /usr/local/adm** and **cat /etc/passwd** if the user's current directory is /usr/local or /etc, respectively.

Various flavors of UNIX enforce different restrictions on how files may be named. For example, ATT and early BSD filenames can be no more than 14 characters long. On BSD-based systems there is essentially no limit to how deeply in the filesystem tree a file may be created, but the kernel can only handle pathnames with individual components of 255 characters or less, and a total path length of 1023 characters.

4.1.1 Filesystems

The UNIX file tree is actually made up of smaller chunks called *filesystems*, each of which consists of one directory and its subdirectories and files. Filesystems are attached to the file tree by use of the **mount** command. **mount** tells the kernel that a given directory somewhere within the existing file tree, called a *mount point*, is to be considered equivalent to the top level directory of a filesystem when pathnames are resolved. The previous contents of the mount point become unavailable as long as a filesystem is mounted there, but are not permanently affected by the mounting process. Mount point directories are usually empty, however.

Early versions of UNIX required that filesystems be mounted inside the "/" directory, but now some Unices allow filesystems to be mounted anywhere, even under other filesystems. When we say that a filesystem consists of a single directory, we are speaking of the filesystem in its unmounted condition. For example, /usr and /usr/spool can be completely separate filesystems even though /usr/spool is mounted under /usr.

Filesystems are removed from the directory tree with the **umount** command, which uses a syntax similar to that of **mount**. Attempts to unmount a filesystem while it is still in use will result in the error message "device busy". Busyness is widely construed; even something as innocuous as an idle user having **cd**'ed onto the filesystem will keep the device active and prevent you from unmounting it. Any open file or program being executed from the filesystem will have a similar effect.

Note that the word "filesystem" actually has two separate meanings when discussing UNIX. As we have used it in the preceding paragraph, "filesystem" denotes a subsection of the UNIX file tree. As it is used in the title of this chapter, "filesystem" denotes the entire file tree and the methods and algorithms that UNIX uses to handle it. It is normally apparent from context which meaning is intended in any given situation.

There is a portion of the filesystem (second meaning) that cannot be mounted and unmounted like the rest; this is called the *root* filesystem and is composed of the directory / and a minimal set of files and subdirectories. The executable file for the kernel always lives here and is usually called /vmunix or /unix. The directories /dev for device files, /etc for critical system files and maintenance programs, /bin for important utilities, and often /tmp for the storage of temporary files are also kept as part of the root filesystem. The root filesystem is available as soon as the kernel is running.

The only other filesystem that is necessary for the correct functioning of UNIX is /usr, where many of the standard UNIX programs are kept, along with various other things such as on-line manuals, libraries, spooling directories, and accounting information. It is not strictly necessary that /usr be a separate filesystem, but for convenience in administration it almost always is.

Personal files and home directories of users are often kept on their own filesystem, usually mounted in the root directory or occasionally beneath /usr. Other filesystems may be used to house particular projects or store specific material such as source code libraries and database files.

Some systems allow entire filesystems to be shared over a network by a number of computers. In these systems, one computer called the *server* is physically attached to the disk and provides a network service for reading and writing files. The computers that wish to partake of the service, called the *clients*, hook up to the server and ask for files to be transmitted to them as needed.

The mechanisms for implementing network filesystems are of necessity quite different from those used in implementing disk filesystems on a disk, so support for network filesystems must usually be built directly into the kernel as a special case of filesystem handling. Consequently, most network file sharing systems are incompatible with each other. Some systems, such as NFS (Network File System), were designed with portability in mind and can be converted to work between different types of computers and even different operating systems. See Chapter 14: *Networking under BSD* for more information about NFS.

4.2 System organization

The organization of the UNIX filesystem was designed with flexibility in mind, and the global organization of the hierarchy is easy to change. Nevertheless, there are customary places for things to be stored, and these conventions should be honored if you want to make your life as system administrator as easy as possible. Much of the software written for UNIX can be installed with almost no reconfiguration if your system is structured in the usual way; conversely, you may have to spend considerable time hacking code and configuration files to get a particular package to work within the context of a nonstandard organization.

Don't expect the default system to be perfect, however. Under this system, files are divided up by *function* and not by how likely they are to change, making it somewhat difficult to upgrade the operating system. The /etc directory, for example, contains some files that are almost never customized for a particular system and some files which are almost entirely local.

Some of the more important standard directories are listed in Figure 4.1.

4.3 Types of files

Between BSD and ATT, there are eight types of UNIX files:

- Regular files
- Directories
- Character device files
- Block device files
- UNIX-domain sockets (BSD)
- Named pipes (FIFO's) (ATT)
- Hard links
- Symbolic links (BSD)

4.3.1 Regular files

The most common type of file is the regular file. Regular files just hold data. The data may be a program, a text file, source code, or anything else that just has to be stored somewhere. The kernel supports both sequential and random access on all regular files.

4.3.2 Directories

Directories are like regular files in that they contain a set of data bytes, but here the data is restricted to being a list of other files, the contents of the

FIGURE 4.1

Standard directories and their contents	
Pathname	**Contents**
/	The root directory, contains the UNIX binary image
/bin	Commands needed for minimal system operability
/5bin	System V compatibility commands for BSD-based systems
/dev	Device entries for terminals, disks, modems, etc.
/etc	Critical system configuration files and maintenance commands
/lib	The C compiler and preprocessor
/tmp	Temporary files – usually a small amount of space
/sys	Kernel building work area, kernel configuration files (BSD)
/stand	Standalone utilities (disk formatters, etc.)
/usr/adm	Accounting files, records of resource usage
/usr/bin	Executable files
/usr/dict	The spelling dictionary (BSD)
/usr/doc	Larger UNIX-related documents, no manual pages
/usr/games	Games and diversions
/usr/include	All UNIX-defined C header files
/usr/etc	Where Sun puts things that everyone else puts in /etc
/usr/lib	Support files for standard UNIX programs
/usr/man	Online manual pages
/usr/old	Obsolete software that will soon be unsupported (BSD)
/usr/new	New software that will soon be supported (BSD)
/usr/preserve	Backup copies of files created by the editors vi and ex
/usr/spool	Spooling directories for printers, uucp, mail, etc.
/usr/tmp	More temporary space
/usr/src	Source code for UNIX standard commands, if you have it
/usr/src/uts	Kernel building work area, kernel configuration files (ATT)
/usr/ucb	Berkeley utilities and programs (BSD)
/usr/lbin	Local binaries (ATT)
/usr/local	Local software (BSD)
/usr/local/adm	Accounting log files
/usr/local/bin	Executables
/usr/local/etc	System maintenance commands
/usr/local/lib	Support files
/usr/local/src	Source for /usr/local/bin, /usr/local/lib, and /usr/local/etc
/usr/src/local	Alternative location for /usr/local/src

directory. There are no limitations on the types of files that the directory can contain. Directory files are kept up-to-date by the operating system. BSD systems support variable-length filenames, and therefore have a more complex structure than ATT directories. BSD and newer ATT systems provide library routines to help read directories; it can be done through the regular **read** system call on older ATT systems. Directories can be created with **mkdir** and deleted with **rmdir** if empty. Non-empty directories can be deleted using **rm -rf**.

4.3.3 Character and block device files

UNIX programs communicate with hardware devices through two special types of files, called *character* and *block device files*. When a UNIX kernel is built, code modules called *device drivers* are included which know the details of how to communicate with particular devices such as disk drives, tape drives, and network interfaces. The device driver for a particular device hides all the messy details of dealing with the device from the kernel and from the end user, and presents a standard communication interface which mimics that of a regular file. When the kernel is issued a file manipulation request that references a character or block device file, it knows not to handle the request itself and passes the request on to the appropriate device driver instead.

Character device files reference device·drivers which want to do their own input and output buffering, such as the terminal and pseudo-terminal drivers. Block device files are associated with device drivers that perform I/O only in large 512- or 1024-byte chunks, and want the kernel to perform buffering for them. Some types of hardware, such as disks and tapes, can be represented by both block and character device files.

Since a single device driver may handle more than one device, device files are always identified by two numbers, called the *major* and *minor device numbers*. The major device number tells the kernel which device driver the file references, while the minor device number tells the device driver which physical unit is to be referenced. For example, the terminal driver on a Vax is device driver #12: The fifth terminal on a Vax would have major device number 12 and minor device number 4.

Some device drivers use the information provided by the minor device number in a nonstandard way. Magnetic tape drivers, for example, typically use the minor device number to select an appropriate density to use when writing tapes, and to determine whether or not the tape should be rewound when the device file is closed. On some systems the terminal driver (which handles both terminals and modems) uses minor device numbers to distinguish modems used as outgoing dialers from modems used as incoming dial-in ports.

Device files can be created with the **mknod** command and removed with the **rm** command.

4.3.4 UNIX domain sockets (BSD)

UNIX sockets are connections between processes that allow them to communicate in a fast, reliable manner. There are several different kinds of sockets under UNIX, most of which involve the use of a network. UNIX domain sockets are local to a particular host and are referenced through a filesystem object rather than a network port. Although socket files are visible to other processes as directory entries, they cannot be read or written by processes not involved in the socket connection. The only standard UNIX programs that use a UNIX domain socket are those that deal with the printing system.

UNIX domain sockets are created with the **socket** system call, and can be removed with **rm** or the **unlink** system call, when the socket no longer has any users.

4.3.5 Named pipes (ATT)

Like UNIX domain sockets, named pipes allow communication between two unrelated processes running on the same host. Named pipes may be created with the **mknod** command and removed with **rm**

4.3.6 Hard links

A link is not really a file type, but rather an additional name for another file. Each file has at least one link, usually the name under which it was originally created. When a new link is made to a file, an alias for the file is created. A link is *indistinguishable* from the file it is linked to; as far as UNIX is concerned, they are identical. UNIX maintains a count of how many links point to a particular file and does not free the data space of the file until the very last link has been deleted. Since a link is a direct connection between files, hard links cannot exist across filesystem boundaries.

Links are usually called "hard links" these days to distinguish them from symbolic links.

4.3.7 Symbolic links (BSD)

Symbolic links are files which simply contain the name of another file. When the kernel tries to open or pass through a symbolic link, its focus is directed to the file that the symbolic link points to rather than the symbolic link itself. The important distinction between hard links and symbolic links is that a hard link is a direct reference, while a symbolic link is a reference by filename. Symbolic links are files in their own right, and have their own owners and permissions.

Beware of using ".." in pathnames that involve symbolic links since ".." always references the true parent directory regardless of how the current directory was reached. Symbolic links may be created with the **ln -s** command.

4.4 File permissions

Every UNIX file has a set of nine permission bits associated with it that control who may read, write, and execute the contents of the file. Together with three other bits that affect the operation of executable program files, these permission bits constitute the *mode* of the file. The twelve mode bits are stored together with four bits of file-type information in a 16-bit word. The four file-type bits are set when the file is created and can't be changed, but the twelve mode bits can all be modified by the owner of the file or the superuser using the **chmod** (change mode) command.

The **ls** command is used to examine the values of these bits. An example is presented later.

4.4.1 The setuid and setgid bits

The bits with octal values 4000 and 2000 are the setuid and setgid bits. As we saw in the last chapter, these bits are used to let programs have access to files and processes that would otherwise be off limits to normal users. Although all files can have these bits set, most Unices ascribe meaning to them only when set on executable files. On some systems, such as SunOS 4.0, the setgid bit may be set on a directory to designate how the default group ownership of files under that directory will be computed.

4.4.2 The sticky bit

The bit with octal value 1000 is called the *sticky* bit. When set on an executable file, the sticky bit tells UNIX that the file is liable to be executed frequently and should be retained in the swap area even when not being executed. This wastes swap space but reduces the time to execute the program dramatically. Some programs are sticky by default; for example, **vi**. The sticky bit is an example of UNIX outgrowing something but not being able to keep it from tagging along anyway. Small-memory systems, like the PDP-11/45's where UNIX spent its teenage years, needed some programs to remain in memory. The sticky bit was very important then.

Some systems also allow the sticky bit to be set on a directory, which modifies the requirements for deleting and renaming files within that directory as described next.

4.4.3 The permission bits

The other nine permission bits are used in determining what operations may be performed on the file, and by whom. UNIX does not allow file permissions to be set on a per-user basis. Instead, there are sets of permissions for the owner of the file, the group owners of the file, and everyone else. Each set of permissions has three bits: a read bit, a write bit, and an execute bit.

The topmost three bits (with octal values of 400, 200, and 100) control the access allowed to the owner. The second three (with octal values of 40, 20, and 10) control the access allowed to the group. The last three (with octal values of 4, 2, and 1) control the access allowed to everyone else. In each of these triplets, the high bit is the read bit, the middle bit is the write bit, and the low bit is the execute bit.

Each user attempting to use a file is limited by the appropriate set of permission bits. By definition, each user fits into only one of the three permission sets. The permission set used is the one that is classwise most restrictive. For example, the owner of a file always has access determined by the owner permission bits and never the group permission bits, even though he usually belongs to the group as well. It is possible for the owner of the file to actually give *more* access to users in the "other" and "group" categories than he gives himself, although no one really does this.

For a regular file, the read bit allows opening and reading of the file. The write bit allows the contents of the file to be modified or truncated; however, the file cannot be completely deleted. The execute bit allows the file to be executed. There are two types of executable files: binaries, which can be directly executed by the processor, and scripts, which must be interpreted by a shell or some other program. By convention, scripts begin with a line like

```
#!/bin/csh -f
```

which specifies the program by which the script should be interpreted. Under ATT, the shell must check to determine what type of file is being executed and arrange for special treatment for scripts. Under BSD, the kernel has taken over this function. Nonbinary files which do not specify an interpreter are assumed to be **sh** scripts.

For a directory, the execute bit (often called the "search" bit in this context) enables the directory to be entered, but not to have its contents listed. This is useful when placing a public directory beneath a restricted one, since pathnames into the public directory can be allowed to pass through the restricted directory without a permission violation. The combination of read and execute bits allows the contents of the directory to be listed. The combination of write and execute bits allows files to be created, deleted, and renamed within the directory. Note that deletion of a file is controlled by the permissions of the directory it occupies, not by the write bit on the file itself.

If the sticky bit is set on a directory, some Unices require you to be either the owner of the directory, the owner of the file to be manipulated, or the superuser to delete or rename a file. Having write permission on the directory is not enough. This is an attempt to make directories like /tmp a little more private. Most Unices just ignore the sticky bit on directories.

File permissions are initially set by the program that creates the file. Most system programs create regular files with read/write permission for the owner and read permission for everyone else. Compilers also set execute permission for the owner on executable binaries.

4.4.4 Changing permissions

The **chmod** (change mode) command is used to change the permissions on a file. Only the owner of a file and the superuser may change its permissions. To use the command on early UNIX systems you had to learn a bit of binary/octal notation, but current versions accept either absolute octal arguments or a relatively mnemonic syntax. We will describe the octal syntax here.

The first argument to **chmod** is the octal number which represents the permissions to be assigned, and the second and subsequent arguments are names of files whose permissions should be changed. The first digit of the permissions is for the owner, the second digit is for the group, and the third digit is for everyone else. Each octal digit corresponds to three binary digits. The first binary digit stands for read permission, the second, for write permission, and the third, for execute permission. If the digit is 1, permission is granted; if it is 0, permission is denied.

Figure 4.2 illustrates the eight possible permission combinations in each set, where “r”, “w”, and “x” stand for read, write, and execute, respectively.

FIGURE 4.2

Permission encoding used by **chmod**

Octal	Binary	Permissions
0	000	(none)
1	001	--x
2	010	-w-
3	011	-wx
4	100	r--
5	101	r-x
6	110	rw-
7	111	rwx

Thus, **chmod 711 calcvectors** gives all permissions on the **calcvectors** program to the owner, and execute-only permission to everyone else.

4.4.5 Assigning default permissions

The built-in shell command **umask** may be used to set default values for the permissions on files created by a user. It should be executed in the ".cshrc" or ".profile" shell startup files. **umask** is given a 3 digit octal value, which represents the *binary inverse* of the permissions which may be assigned to files. When a file is created, its permissions are set to what the creating program asks for *minus* what the **umask** setting forbids. The digits give the permissions shown in Figure 4.3.

FIGURE 4.3

Permission encoding used by **umask**		
Octal	Binary	Permissions
0	000	rwx
1	001	rw-
2	010	r-x
3	011	r--
4	100	-wx
5	101	-w-
6	110	--x
7	111	(none)

Thus **umask 037** would give the owner all permissions, the group, read permission, and the world, no permission. Most systems' default umask value is 022 which gives all permission to the owner and read and execute permission to the group owner and everyone else. A more security-conscious system or user might wish to use the value 027, which gives read and execute permission only to the group, or even the value 077, allowing no permissions for anyone except the owner.

On BSD systems, the default **umask** value can be changed by compiling a different value into the kernel. Refer to Section 8.4.4.6 for more information.

There is no way you can force users to use a particular **umask** value, since they can always reset their **umask** immediately after logging in or just edit their ".cshrc" or ".profile" to reflect the value they feel most comfortable with. All you can do is edit the sample ".cshrc" and ".profile" files which you provide to new users so that, until they learn to adjust it to their own taste, they will have a suitable default value.

4.5 Inodes

The kernel maintains information about each existing file in a structure called an *inode*. Inodes tables for a filesystem are laid out when the filesystem is created and their extent and physical location on the disk never change. Each inode contains over forty separate pieces of information, but most of these are useful only to the kernel. As a system administrator you will be concerned mostly with the link count, owner, group, mode, size, last access time, last modification time, and type.

All of these can be found by using the **ls** command with various options. Under BSD, **ls -lg** gives a listing showing mode, size, last modification time, owner, group, link count, and type. Under ATT, **ls -l** shows a similar display.

Consider the following line, produced by **ls -lg /bin/sh**:

```
-rwxr-xr-x  1 root     bin         57344 Sep 15  1986 /bin/sh
```

The first field specifies the file type and its mode. Since the first character is a "-", the file is just a regular file. The one-character codes shown in Figure 4.4 are used to represent the various types of files.

FIGURE 4.4

File-type encoding used by **ls**			
File type	Symbol	Created by	Removed by
Regular file	"-"	editors, **cp**, etc.	**rm**
Directory	"d"	**mkdir**	**rmdir**, **rm -r**
Character device file	"c"	**mknod**	**rm**
Block device file	"b"	**mknod**	**rm**
UNIX domain socket (BSD)	"s"	**socket**(2)	**rm**
Named pipe (ATT)	"p"	**mknod**	**rm**
Symbolic link (BSD)	"l"	**ln -s**	**rm**

The next nine characters in this field are the three sets of permission bits. Although these bits have only binary values, **ls** shows them symbolically with the letters "r", "w", and "x" for read, write, and execute. In this case, we can see that the owner has all permissions on the file and that group and world have only read and execute permissions.

If the setuid bit had been set, the "x" representing the owner's execute permission would have been replaced with an "s", and if the setgid bit had been set the "x" for the group would also have been replaced with an "s". The last character of the permissions (execute permission for "other") is shown as "t" if the sticky bit of the file is turned on. If either the setuid bit or the sticky bit is set but the execute bit is not, then they will appear as "S" or "T".

The next field in the listing is the link count for the file. In this case it is only one, indicating that "/bin/sh" is the only name by which this file is known. Every time a hard link is made to a file this count is incremented by one. All directories will have at least two links: the link from the parent directory and the link from the special file "." inside the directory itself. Symbolic links do not affect the link count.

The next two fields are the owner and group owner of the file. We can see that the file's owner is "root" and that the file belongs to the group "bin". Of course, the inode for the file actually stores these as the user and group id numbers rather than strings.

The next field is the size of the file in bytes. This particular file is 57,344 bytes long, or slightly more than 56K.[1] Next comes the date of last modification: September 15, 1986. The last field in the listing is the name of the file itself, "/bin/sh".

If a block or character device file is the object of an **ls -lg** command, the output is slightly different. The following example was produced with **ls -lg /dev/ttya**:

```
crw-rw-rw-  1 root     daemon     12,   0 Dec 14  1986 /dev/ttya
```

Most of the fields are the same, but instead of a size in bytes, the major and minor device numbers are shown. From the preceding line we can see that /dev/ttya is the number zero unit controlled by device driver #12 (on this system, the terminal driver).

The system keeps track of the last modification time, link count, and file size information for you automatically. The permission bits, ownership, and group ownership will only change if they are specifically altered. The **chown** command is used to change the ownership of a file, and the **chgrp** command is used to change the group ownership.[2]

The syntax of **chown** and **chgrp** mirrors that of **chmod**, except that the first argument is the new owner or group owner, respectively. You must either be the owner of a file and belong to the group to which the file is to be changed, or be the superuser to use **chgrp**. On some older systems, only the superuser can use **chgrp**.

[1] One K is 2^{10} or 1024 bytes, not 1000 bytes as many people believe.

[2] On some systems, **chown** can change both the owner and group of a file at once.

Under ATT, the only restriction on the **chown** command is that you must be the owner of the file or the superuser. Be aware, however, that once you have given a file away to someone else you are no longer its owner and cannot regain ownership of the file without logging in as root. Since BSD may optionally support disk quotas, the BSD version of **chown** is always restricted to the superuser. Quota enforcement would not be very effective if people could give away their files.

The **chown** and **chgrp** commands are often used in conjunction with the **find** command to change the group or ownership of a directory and all of the files and directories underneath it. For example, to make the user jake the owner of the directory /users/jake and everything underneath it, the command

```
find /users/jake -exec chown jake {} \;
```

will do the trick. On ATT systems and some enhanced BSD systems, an even better way of doing this is available:

```
find /users/jake -print | xargs chown jake
```

The ATT version will produce exactly the same results, but will run much faster. The **chown** and **chgrp** commands on some systems will descend directory trees recursively if a **-R** option is specified. On these systems, an equivalent command is:

```
chown -R jake /users/jake
```

A public domain implementation of **xargs** is included in Appendix Q.

4.6 Keeping track of filesystems (BSD only)

The UNIX abstraction of filesystems is based on a lower-level method of segmenting disk drives into *partitions*. This low-level formatting and partitioning of disk drives is covered in Chapter 12: *Adding a Disk*. At our current level of abstraction, we'll assume that the disk is completely set up and that device files have been made for each separate partition in the /dev directory. For now, assume a one-to-one correspondence between partitions and filesystems.

4.6.1 The /etc/fstab file

Every BSD system has a file named /etc/fstab (also called /etc/filesystems in some flavors of UNIX) that lists all the disk partitions available to the system and their use. For regular partitions, /etc/fstab also specifies the customary mount point; swap partitions are never mounted and so do not have a mount point.

For example, the /etc/fstab file on "boulder" (a Vax) consists of the following lines:

```
/dev/hp0a:/:rw:0:1
/dev/hp0b::sw:0:0
/dev/ra0b::sw:0:0
/dev/ra0h:/usr:rw:0:2
/dev/ra1h:/usr/local:rw:0:2
/dev/hp0g:/usr/spool:rw:0:2
/dev/ra0a:/usr/spool/uucp:rw:0:4
/dev/ra0g:/faculty:rw:0:3
/dev/ra1g:/student:rw:0:3
/dev/ra1a:/tmp:rw:0:5
```

Each line of the file has five parameters (usually separated by colons) which describe a single partition. The first field is the name of the block device file that represents the partition. The second field contains the name of the customary mount point for partitions that hold filesystems, or is empty if the partition is used for swapping. The third field contains a two-letter code that tells how the filesystem is to be used. The codes that can appear here are listed in Figure 4.5. The fourth field is used in scheduling use of the **dump** command on the partition and the fifth is used to affect the order in which partitions are checked for consistency by the **fsck** command at boot time.

FIGURE 4.5

Two-character codes used in /etc/fstab	
Code	Meaning
"rw"	Filesystem: mount for reading and writing
"ro"	Filesystem: mount for reading only
"rq"	Filesystem: mount for reading and writing with quotas
"sw"	Swap partition, do not mount

From line 6 in the preceding example, we can see that the disk partition addressed by the file /dev/hp0g contains a filesystem that is usually mounted on /usr/spool, and that both reading and writing are allowed on this filesystem. Since we do not use /etc/fstab to schedule our dumps, the entry in the fourth field is zero. The fifth field says that the filesystem should be checked on the second pass, in tandem with /dev/ra1h; we will come back to this field in more detail in the next section. Note that /dev/ra1h is a *block* device file, not a character device file — the partition name begins with an "r" only because the name of the disk is "ra". The corresponding raw device file for this partition is /dev/rra1h.

Some systems, especially those that support network filesystems, change the format of /etc/fstab a little bit. The changes are minor, however.

The /etc/fstab file is read by the **mount**, **umount**, **swapon**, and **fsck** commands, so it is important that the data presented there be correct and complete. /etc/fstab must be maintained entirely by the system administrator, since none of the commands that read it ever attempt to adjust it.

mount and **umount** use the /etc/fstab file to figure out what you want done if you specify only a partition name or a mount point name on the command line. For example, using the fstab just shown, the command **mount /usr/local** would be completed to **mount /dev/ra1h /usr/local**. The command **mount -a** mounts all filesystems listed in /etc/fstab; it is usually executed in /etc/rc.local at boot time, so /etc/fstab must be accurate in order to avoid problems.

mount reads /etc/fstab sequentially; therefore, filesystems that are mounted beneath other filesystems must follow their parent partitions in /etc/fstab in order for their mount points to exist. For example, the line for /usr/local must follow the line for /usr. The **umount** command for unmounting filesystems accepts a similar syntax. You cannot unmount a filesystem on which files are currently open, or on which a process's current directory is located.

4.7 Swapping and paging

UNIX uses some disk partitions for temporary storage rather than for holding filesystems. These swap partitions are brought into play when the operating system finds itself with less physical memory than all of its processes need.

While the work load of the system is light, UNIX will use *paging* to manage memory. Paging is the process of moving individual memory segments that have not been recently referenced out to a swap partition to free up space. When a process tries to access a segment of memory that has been removed, an event called a *page fault* occurs and the process is suspended until the operating system is able to copy the segment back into memory.

If the work load of the system is heavy, UNIX may also begin *swapping* as well as paging. Swapping is like paging in that it involves portions of the memory being rolled out to disk, but in this case the kernel will systematically hunt through the memory to find all segments belonging to a particular process and get rid of them all at once, keeping the process from running for a comparatively lengthy time. UNIX always tries to pick a process that is not likely to run in the near future when searching for a swapping victim.

Different versions of UNIX have different capabilities with respect to swapping and paging. BSD can do both. Some ATT systems do not page.

There may be more than one swap partition available to the kernel. If so, the kernel will attempt to interleave its use of the partitions so that time spent waiting for disk operations to complete is kept to a minimum. ATT systems usually do not have separate swap partitions; instead they use the end of a partition allocated for a filesystem for swap space.

4.8 Filesystem integrity

The UNIX filesystem is complex, and it is remarkable that UNIX is able to insulate itself as well as it does from the negative effects of unexpected system crashes, flaky hardware, and all the other minor catastrophes that plague even the most reliable of computer systems. Not even UNIX can be perfect all of the time, however. There are a number of ways that filesystems can become damaged or inconsistent.

By far the most common cause of filesystem corruption is an abrupt termination of UNIX; this may happen through loss of power, turning the computer off without shutting down properly, unplugging the computer by accident, or a software error internal to the kernel. Since the kernel buffers disk blocks and summary information (in a structure called a *super-block*) in memory to enhance throughput, a sudden termination of power leaves the kernel with no opportunity to make the appropriate adjustments to the physical disk that are necessary to insure consistency of the filesystem.

The cause of a power termination is usually obvious, but kernel errors can be subtle and difficult to track down. Because the job of the kernel is so critical, no operational anomalies can be allowed to occur. To protect its image of perfection, the UNIX kernel attempts to detect even the slightest inconsistency in its internal tables and will immediately shut down the system if one is found. Because the kernel has control over this type of termination it is able to attempt to synchronize the disks with its own in-memory information, minimizing the effects of a sudden halt.

Before termination, the kernel will usually write a cryptic one-line description of the problem that caused the shutdown on the system console. These messages can provide helpful clues to the root of the problem if it recurs with any frequency, but often the best thing to do is just to log the message, shrug, and reboot the system.

Older versions of UNIX had a kernel bug that would severely injure a filesystem if it was dismounted while still in use. This bug and several others have been fixed in current releases, but it is possible, on occasion, to produce a minor filesystem quirk by playing with mounting and dismounting at strange times and by manipulating filesystems that are full to capacity. Generally, though, it is not possible for user processes that do not access the disk directly to cause filesystem problems.

It is possible to completely destroy a filesystem in seconds by writing randomly on the disk, so disk device files should have their permissions set quite restrictively. We allow read and write access for root (the owner) and read access for operator (the group owner); this allows **dump** to be run by operators without superuser privileges.

Network filesystems have their own problems with respect to filesystem damage, and because they require an additional layer of protocol and transport over the normal operation of a filesystem, they are slightly more susceptible to inconsistencies. Some networking systems attempt to minimize this effect by employing only normal filesystem operations on the part of the server and limiting the involvement of the kernel to the client's end only.

Luckily, the damage caused by all of these problems is typically innocuous. The five most common types of damage are:

- Unreferenced inodes
- Inexplicably large link counts
- Unused data blocks not recorded in the block maps
- Data blocks listed as free which are also used in storing a file
- Incorrect summary information in the super-block

These five discrepancies can all be fixed safely and automatically by using the **fsck** (file system consistency check, spelled aloud or pronounced "fisk" or "fossick") command. The **fsck** command is the most useful tool available to you for ferreting out and repairing damage to a filesystem. **fsck** subsumes the functions of the older programs **bcheck**, **dcheck**, **ncheck**, **icheck**, and **clri**, and provides much additional utility over and above all of these combined.

The following is just a quick introduction to **fsck**. There is usually a document supplied with UNIX that describes **fsck** in greater detail than the manual page. You should refer to your system's version of this document for more information about how to handle filesystem problems.

4.8.1 Filesystem checking under BSD

One of the things typically done in the /etc/rc scripts executed at boot time is to check the disks with **fsck -p**, which causes **fsck** to examine every partition listed in /etc/fstab (except swap partitions) for consistency and to correct automatically the five errors just listed. **fsck -p** may also be run on a particular filesystem, as in **fsck -p /dev/rra1h**. Either the raw and the block device names for a disk partition may be given to **fsck**, but the check is usually faster on the raw device.

When **fsck** reads the /etc/fstab file to find out what filesystems to check, it obeys the sequence indicated by the fifth field in each of the /etc/fstab entries. Filesystems are checked in increasing numeric order. If two filesystems are on different disks they may be given the same sequence number; in this case, **fsck** will attempt to check both filesystems at the same time, minimizing time spent waiting for disk accesses.

Errors that do not fall into one of the five automatic categories are potentially more dangerous and cause **fsck -p** to print a call for help and quit. In this case you must run **fsck** without the **-p** option. In nonautomatic mode, **fsck** will ask you to confirm each of the repairs that it thinks should be made to bring the filesystem back to a reasonable state. Some errors that **fsck** considers dangerous are:

- Blocks claimed by more than one file
- Blocks claimed that are outside the range of the filesystem
- Link counts that are too small
- Blocks that are not accounted for
- Directories that reference unallocated inodes
- Various format errors

Unfortunately, patching up the filesystem by hand is an operation that requires significant experience. Unless you feel sure that you know what you are doing, you should never attempt to write directly to the disk through its device files. What this means in practice is that you have little choice but to accept the fixes that **fsck** proposes. You can minimize problems by carefully writing down the messages that **fsck** produces in the system's log, since they will usually provide the name of the file that is causing problems. If **fsck** asks for permission to delete a non-empty file, you should try to copy it to a different filesystem before allowing **fsck** to go ahead with the removal. The chances that this will cause further damage to the filesystem under repair are small. If only the inode number of the file is known, **ncheck** can be used to find its filename.

If **fsck** finds a file whose parent directory cannot be determined, it will place the file into the directory "lost+found" in the top level of the filesystem on which the file is found. Since the name given to a file is recorded only in the file's home directory, names for orphan files will not be available and the files placed into the lost+found directory will be renamed with their inode numbers.

Some older systems have a program called **fsdb** that can be used to debug filesystems. Newer systems have done away with this command because it is dangerous and difficult to use correctly. It operates at a much lower level than **fsck** and is useful mostly for patching damaged super-blocks.

4.8.2 Filesystem checking under ATT

A version of **fsck** comes with every ATT system. Most ATT versions are very similar to the BSD **fsck** just described, except that few support the **-p** option. The system administrator has to pay close attention to what is going on with the filesystem check and make the decisions about what is to be fixed automatically. ATT uses the file /etc/checklist instead of /etc/fstab to identify partitions. /etc/checklist is just a list of partition names, one per line.

5

Controlling Processes

5.1 Introduction

The many programs that are running on a UNIX system at any one time are called processes. Although UNIX gives the impression that many things are happening at once, only one process is actually executing at any particular moment.[1] The abstraction of concurrently running programs is provided by a method called time-slicing, by which UNIX changes which process is executing at regular, short intervals (usually at least every 100 ms). The active process changes so quickly that it appears that all of the processes are running at once, when in actuality each process is executing only a small percentage of the time. The system administrator has the ability to monitor the status of processes, control how much of the CPU's time a process gets, and suspend or halt the execution of a process.

[1] Strictly speaking, this is true only for single-CPU computers. Some machines have more than one processor, but the concept remains the same.

5.2 What is a process?

A process consists of an address space and a set of data structures inside the kernel. The address space is a section of memory that the kernel has marked for the use of the process; it contains space for the code of the program, the variables that the process uses, the process's stack, and some other information needed by the kernel while the process is running.

The kernel's internal data structures contain information used to handle the process. Some of the more important data are:

- The process's address space map
- The current status of the process
- The execution priority of the process
- The process's resource usage summaries
- The process's current signal mask
- The owner of the process

Saying that the address space is a section of memory is actually a slight lie, because on virtual memory systems the address space may be all, partially, or not at all in physical memory at any one time. Even on systems without virtual memory the address space may be swapped out to disk rather than residing in physical memory.

5.3 Attributes of processes

Many of the parameters associated with a process directly affect the execution of the process: the amount of processor time it gets, the files it can access, and so on. Storage for these parameters is split between the kernel's internal tables and the tables kept inside the process's address space, but you need not know anything about the mechanics of this schema to understand and use the information at the system administration level.

5.3.1 PID

The PID, or Process IDentification, is the number that the kernel uses to identify the process. The PID is like a process's social security number in that it is used to uniquely determine the process. Like a social security number, the actual value of the PID has little significance. PID's are assigned in order as new process are created. If the kernel runs out of PID's it simply restarts the numbering process, skipping over PIDs that are still in use.

5.3.2 PPID

The PPID is the PID of the process's *parent*. The parent is the process that created the current process, which is its *child*. The parent process need not outlive the processes it creates.

5.3.3 UID and EUID

The UID, which stands for User IDentification, contains the user number (third field in the /etc/passwd entry) of the user who created the process.[2] That user is considered the *owner* of the process and is the only person besides the superuser who can change its operational parameters. The owner is charged by the accounting system for any resources that the process uses.

The EUID contains the Effective User IDentification of the process. It is this number that is used to determine what resources the process has permission to access. In most processes the UID and EUID are the same, the usual exception being programs that are setuid (see Section 3.1.2).

5.3.4 GID and EGID

The GID is the Group IDentification number of the process. Valid group numbers are enumerated in /etc/group, and in the GID field of /etc/passwd. When a process is started, its GID is set to the GID of its parent.

The EGID is related to the GID in the same way that the EUID is related to the UID. If the process tries to access a file on which it does not have owner permission, the kernel will automatically check to see if permission may be granted on the basis of the EGID.

On modern BSD systems a user or process can be in more than one group at a time. In this case the GID is actually a list of group numbers, and when you attempt to access a resource, the list is checked to see if you belong to the appropriate group.

[2] This is yet another micro-lie. The kernel doesn't care whether the UID or GID is one which has been assigned meaning in /etc/passwd or /etc/group; any integer will do. Only the superuser can change the UID to something undefined, however, and this is almost never done in practice.

5.3.5 Priority

A process's priority determines how much CPU time the process gets. When the kernel needs another process to run, it picks the process with the highest internal priority. A logical system would make higher priority numbers mean higher priority (meaning more CPU time), but this is not in fact how UNIX handles priorities. It uses the opposite system, with more negative numbers yielding higher execution priorities. ATT priorities run from 40 to -20, and BSD priorities run from +19 to -19.

Except for the different priority numbering schemes, BSD and ATT handle execution priorities in much the same way. Unless the user takes special action, a newly created process inherits the priority of its creator process. This will normally be the systemwide default priority if the process is created from an interactive shell. The owner of the process can decrease its priority but may not raise it, even to return the process to the default priority. (This is to prevent processes spawned with low priority from bearing high-priority children). The process can change its own priority, but only in the same way that the owner can. The superuser has complete freedom in setting priorities, and may even set the priority on a process so high that no other processes can run. On some systems, the kernel will decrease the priority of processes that have accumulated what it considers "excessive" CPU time. Processes that are run in the background usually have their priority lowered automatically.

The priority of a process is not the only thing that determines when a process will be run. To determine which process should be run next, the scheduling mechanism in the kernel uses a formula that takes into account each process's priority, how much CPU time each process has gotten recently, and how long it has been since each process has run.

5.3.6 Control terminal

Most processes have associated with them a control terminal. The control terminal determines default linkages for the standard input, output, and error channels in the absence of redirection; when you start a simple command from the shell, your terminal normally becomes the process's control terminal. The kernel's concept of the control terminal is simply a device name, so the system works equally well for "pseudo" and "real" terminals.

The concept of a control terminal is also of vital importance in handling the distribution of signals, but we must delay discussion of this mechanism until Section 5.8.

5.4 The secret life of processes

Process do not just magically appear on the system, nor are they created directly by the kernel. New processes are created by other processes, just like new humans.[3]

When a process wants to create a new process, it begins by making a copy of itself using the **fork** system call. The fork creates a copy of the original process, called the *child* process, which is identical in every way to the parent except for the following differences:

- The new process has a distinct PID
- The new process's PPID references the original process
- The new process is assumed to have used no resources
- The new process has its own copy of the parent's file descriptors

It is the last of these items that can be somewhat tricky. File descriptors are reference numbers that the kernel gives out to processes when an input/output operation is started. These numbers are actually indexes into a small table which contains pointers back to the kernel's own data structures. When a fork occurs, it is the table that is copied, **not** the underlying kernel structures. This means that anything the child does to the actual object will be reflected in the parent.

For example, suppose the child reads some data from a file descriptor. The next time the parent tries to read from this descriptor it will start reading at the place where the *child* left off, not from where it would have started reading before the fork.

fork has the unique property of returning two values. From the child's point of view, **fork** always returns zero. The parent, on the other hand, is returned the PID of the newly created child. This is how the two processes can tell who they are, and act accordingly. In C, it looks like this:

```
int     kid_pid;

kid_pid = fork();

if (kid_pid == 0)
{
        /* I'm the child, act childish. */
}
else
{
        /* I'm the parent, do whatever the parent's supposed to do. */
}
```

[3] New humans are created by other humans, of course, not by processes.

You've probably noticed that this doesn't explain how programs get executed, just how new processes are created. The **fork** system call is only half the story. The other half is the **exec** family of system calls.[4]

All calls in the **exec** family perform roughly the same function; they change the code text that the process is executing and reset the data and stack segments to a predefined initial state. When an **exec** is called, it overwrites the address space with the contents of some file, and then resumes execution at the entry point of the new code. The various forms of **exec** differ only in the ways that they specify the command-line arguments and environment to be given to the new text.

It's easiest to think of **exec** as a kind of demonic possession. The "body" of the process (file descriptor table, environment variables, priority, etc.) remains intact, but the "mind" (code text, variable space, stack) has been replaced with something completely new. There can be no return from a successful **exec**.

For a simple example of how **fork** and **exec** are used to spawn a new process, consider the following C code:

```
if (fork() == 0)
{
        /* I'm the child... */

        execl("/bin/ls", "ls", "/usr/bin", (char *)0);
}
```

In this example, the program that is running starts a new process that becomes an invocation of the **ls** command. The effect is identical to typing **ls /usr/bin** from the shell. Note that the name of the program is the first argument to the new text. The shell normally enforces this convention when you are at command level, but you must do it yourself when programming.

You are probably wondering how processes get started if they can only be created by other processes. When the system boots, the kernel does in fact create and install several processes autonomously, most notably **/etc/init**. **init** is always PID 1, and is responsible for forking a shell to execute the /etc/rc scripts and installing **getty**'s on each terminal. All processes other than the ones the kernel creates are thus descendents (either children, or children of children, etc.) of **init**.

[4] Not all of the routines in "the **exec** family of system calls" are really system calls. Under BSD, for example, all but one are really library routines.

init also plays another important role in process management. When a process wants to die, it calls a routine named **_exit** to notify the kernel that it has completed. It supplies as a parameter to **_exit** an *exit code*, an integer which tells why the process is exiting. By convention, an exit code of zero means that the process was successful.

The exit code is supplied for the benefit of the process's parent, so the kernel must keep it around until the parent requests it by using the **wait** or **wait3** system call.[5] The address space of the process that exited is released and the process is no longer executed, but it does retain its identity. A process in this state is called a *zombie*.

This system works well if the parent outlives its children and is conscientious about calling **wait** so that zombie processes don't hang around for long periods of time. If the parent dies first, however, the kernel recognizes that no **wait** is forthcoming and donates the zombie to **init**. Theoretically, **init** is prepared for this change of lineage and performs the **wait** needed to free the zombie. **init** occasionally does not do its job properly and zombies are left on the system, but they do not cause any real problems.

5.5 Monitoring processes - the ps command

ps is the system administrator's main tool for monitoring processes. While ATT **ps** and BSD **ps** are completely different in their arguments and display, they both provide essentially the same information. **ps** can be used to show the PID, UID, priority, control terminal, as well as a host of other information. **ps** also gives information about how much memory a process is using, how much CPU time it has used, its current status (running, stopped, sleeping, idle, etc.). Zombies can be readily spotted because they show up in a **ps** listing as "<exiting>" or "<defunct>". Consult the manual page to learn all of the gory details of your version of **ps**.

5.6 Signals

A signal is a way of telling a process, "Something really important has happened, so you'd better drop whatever you're doing and handle it." When a signal is delivered to a process, one of two things happens. If the process has

[5] The exit code is actually only one of several pieces of information the kernel preserves for processes that have exited. If a process was terminated externally (with a signal), the parent can find out what that signal was and whether or not a core dump was performed. A summary of the resources used by the child is also available.

specified a routine, called a *handler*, to be executed for a particular signal, it is executed. Otherwise, the kernel supplies a default handler for the signal. Default actions vary from signal to signal; many terminate the process, some causing a core dump. Specifying a handler for a signal is referred to as *catching* the signal.

To prevent delivery, programs can request that a particular signal be either ignored or blocked. A signal that is ignored is simply never delivered and goes away without a trace. A signal that is blocked can be delivered, but the kernel won't require the process to act on it until the process unblocks the signal. The handler for a newly unblocked signal is called only once, even if multiple instances of the signal were received while the signal was blocked. When the handler is finished doing whatever it is supposed to, the program continues execution where it left off.

There are two signals that can be neither caught nor blocked nor ignored: KILL and STOP. The KILL signal mandates the destruction of the receiving process, while the STOP signal merely suspends execution of the process. The CONT signal, used to continue after a STOP, may be caught or ignored but not blocked. Of these three signals, ATT systems only have the KILL signal, so it is the only one that can not be caught or blocked.

Signals are used in many ways. Signals can be sent by other processes as a means of communication, by the system in any number of situations, by the control terminal of the process, and even by the process to itself. There are 17 standard signals on ATT systems, and 31 signals on BSD systems. Each signal has its own number and meaning.[6] Signals also have symbolic names (such as KILL) for ease of reference.

As a simple example of signals in action, consider what happens when an interrupt character is typed on the keyboard. The terminal driver receives the character and sends out an INT (interrupt) signal to the active process group. Since the default handler for the INT specifies termination, most programs stop execution when they receive this signal.

Figures 5.1 and 5.2 contain lists of the standard BSD and ATT signals, respectively.

[6] The meaning of signals USR1 and USR2 is application-defined.

FIGURE 5.1

Standard BSD signals						
Number	Symbolic Name	Description	Default	Can Be Caught	Can Be Blocked	Dumps Core
1	SIGHUP	Hangup	Terminate	Yes	Yes	No
2	SIGINT	Interrupt	Terminate	Yes	Yes	No
3	SIGQUIT	Quit	Terminate	Yes	Yes	Yes
4	SIGILL	Illegal instruction	Terminate	Yes	Yes	Yes
5	SIGTRAP	Trace trap	Terminate	Yes	Yes	Yes
6	SIGIOT	IOT trap	Terminate	Yes	Yes	Yes
7	SIGEMT	EMT trap	Terminate	Yes	Yes	Yes
8	SIGFPE	Arithmetic exception	Terminate	Yes	Yes	Yes
9	SIGKILL	Kill	Terminate	No	No	No
10	SIGBUS	Bus error	Terminate	Yes	Yes	Yes
11	SIGSEGV	Segmentation violation	Terminate	Yes	Yes	Yes
12	SIGSYS	Bad argument to system call	Terminate	Yes	Yes	Yes
13	SIGPIPE	Write on a pipe with no reader	Terminate	Yes	Yes	No
14	SIGALRM	Alarm clock	Terminate	Yes	Yes	No
15	SIGTERM	Software termination signal	Terminate	Yes	Yes	No
16	SIGURG	Urgent socket condition	Ignore	Yes	Yes	No
17	SIGSTOP	Stop	Stop	No	No	No
18	SIGTSTP	Keyboard stop signal	Stop	Yes	Yes	No
19	SIGCONT	Continue after stop	Ignore	Yes	No	No
20	SIGCHLD	Child status has changed	Ignore	Yes	Yes	No
21	SIGTTIN	Bkgnd read from control terminal	Stop	Yes	Yes	No
22	SIGTTOU	Bkgnd write to control terminal	Stop	Yes	Yes	No
23	SIGIO	I/O is possible on a descriptor	Ignore	Yes	Yes	No
24	SIGXCPU	Cpu time limit exceeded	Terminate	Yes	Yes	No
25	SIGXFSZ	File size limit exceeded	Terminate	Yes	Yes	No
26	SIGVTALRM	Virtual time alarm	Terminate	Yes	Yes	No
27	SIGPROF	Profiling timer alarm	Terminate	Yes	Yes	No
28	SIGWINCH	Window changed	Ignore	Yes	Yes	No
29	SIGLOST	Resource lost	Terminate	Yes	Yes	Yes
30	SIGUSR1	First user defined signal	Terminate	Yes	Yes	No
31	SIGUSR2	Second user defined signal	Terminate	Yes	Yes	No

5.7 Process states

Just because a process exists does not mean it is eligible for CPU time. There are basically five execution states that you need to be aware of.

- Runnable - the process can be executed
- Sleeping - the process is waiting for some resource
- Swapped - the process is not in memory
- Zombie - the process is trying to die
- Stopped - the process is not allowed to execute (BSD)

FIGURE 5.2

Standard ATT signals						
Number	Symbolic Name	Description	Default	Can Be Caught	Can Be Blocked	Dumps Core
1	SIGHUP	Hangup	Terminate	Yes	Yes	No
2	SIGINT	Interrupt	Terminate	Yes	Yes	No
3	SIGQUIT	Quit	Terminate	Yes	Yes	Yes
4	SIGILL	Illegal instruction	Terminate	Yes	Yes	Yes
5	SIGTRAP	Trace trap	Terminate	Yes	Yes	Yes
6	SIGIOT	IOT trap	Terminate	Yes	Yes	Yes
7	SIGEMT	EMT trap	Terminate	Yes	Yes	Yes
8	SIGFPE	Arithmetic exception	Terminate	Yes	Yes	Yes
9	SIGKILL	Kill	Terminate	No	No	No
10	SIGBUS	Bus error	Terminate	Yes	Yes	Yes
11	SIGSEGV	Segmentation violation	Terminate	Yes	Yes	Yes
12	SIGSYS	Bad argument to system call	Terminate	Yes	Yes	Yes
13	SIGPIPE	Write on a pipe with no reader	Terminate	Yes	Yes	No
14	SIGALRM	Alarm clock	Terminate	Yes	Yes	No
15	SIGTERM	Software termination signal	Terminate	Yes	Yes	No
16	SIGUSR1	First user defined signal	Terminate	Yes	Yes	No
17	SIGUSR2	Second user defined signal	Terminate	Yes	Yes	No

A runnable process is ready to go whenever there is CPU time available. It has acquired all the resources it needs to operate and merely needs some time to chew through whatever data it is processing. As soon as the process makes a system call that cannot be instantly completed (such as reading part of a file), UNIX will put it to sleep.

A sleeping process waits for a specific event to occur. Interactive shells and system daemons spend most of their time sleeping, waiting for terminal input or network connections. Since the main execution thread of a sleeping process is effectively blocked until its request has been satisfied, it will get no CPU time unless a signal is delivered to it.

A sleep can last anywhere from microseconds to days, but the lion's share are on the order of hundredths of a second. A process that has been sleeping much longer than this is assumed to be interactive and is accorded special considerations by the kernel. When the sleep finally ends, the kernel will insure that the process gets to execute soon. This insures that you don't have to wait too long for your shell to acknowledge your existence between keystrokes.

A swapped process is one that has been completely written out to disk and removed from the computer's main memory. BSD swaps out processes only when contention for memory is so intense that paging completely bogs down and too much time is spent on processing page faults rather than useful work. Systems that do not have virtual memory must swap out processes whenever physical memory is full.

Strictly speaking, being swapped is not a true process state. A swapped process can also be sleeping, stopped, or even nominally runnable; it remains frozen in whatever state it had when it was swapped out until it is brought back into core.

You already know about zombie processes. They cannot be swapped because they are composed of nothing but a few shreds of kernel information.

A stopped process is one that has been marked by the kernel as completely unrunnable. Processes are stopped by receiving a STOP or TSTP signal, and are restarted by being sent a CONT signal. Being stopped is similar to sleeping, but there's no way to get out of the stopped state aside from having some other process wake you up.

BSD stops processes in only three distinct situations:

- When a Control-Z is typed to an interactive process from **csh**
- At the specific request of a user or program
- When a process tries to access the terminal from the background

If you're a **csh** user under BSD, you're almost certainly familiar with this first case. Here's how it works: When the terminal driver receives the Control-Z that you've typed, it figures out what the active foreground processes attached to that terminal are and sends them a TSTP signal. The default handler for TSTP simply stops the process, but because TSTP can be caught the process has the option of doing cleanup operations before stopping. For example, **vi** makes sure that the cursor goes to the bottom of the screen before it stops so that you don't get stuck with the cursor in some offbeat place.

The second case is the most general. Since the STOP signal cannot be caught, it's the signal you use when you want to definitely stop some process on the system. The STOP signal is the only sure way to halt processes that catch TSTP; the TSTP handler for an interface conforming program like **vi** must actually arrange to have a STOP delivered to itself as the last step in its pre-stop cleanup routine.

The last of these cases is used to prevent the coexistence of two or more programs that both believe themselves to be interactive foreground processes. The discipline imposed by the terminal driver is simply to prevent background processes from accessing the terminal. As soon as a background process tries to act interactive, it gets sent a TTIN or a TTOU signal, the default handler for which puts the process to sleep.

5.8 BSD process groups and job control

The BSD terminal driver supports a very elegant model for interactive job control, but you have to be a **csh** user to take advantage of it. **csh** keeps track of all the processes you start and lets you move them to and fro between the background and the foreground, stop them, and restart them.

From the system's point of view there are two basic problems in doing this kind of job control. The first is how to let the shell find out about everything that happens to its child processes. The second is how to be sure that signals generated by the terminal driver in response to keyboard input are sent to the correct processes.

The first problem is easily solved with the **wait3** system call. Recall that a **wait** is normally used to find out about dead child processes. **wait3** is kind of an extension to this paradigm; it lets the parent know about children that stop as well as those that die. **csh** periodically uses this call to find out if anything interesting has happened to the processes it starts on behalf of the user and changes its internal tables accordingly.

The second problem is a little bit trickier and is solved using the notion of a *process group*. Process groups are used exclusively for the distribution of signals, so there is little security built into the mechanism. A process may join any process group on the system, but all it will get from this is the opportunity to be sent a bunch of somebody else's signals. A process may also be conscripted into a process group by another process, normally the shell.

Terminals as well as processes have process group affiliations. When a signal-producing character is received on a terminal, the terminal driver checks to see what its dominant process group is, then sends the signal to all processes in this group. As the shell goes about its business of pushing jobs around between the foreground and background, it manipulates the process groups so that things match up correctly and signals are always distributed to the right process group.

The process group is also used in determining who may read or write to a terminal. When a read or write request is posted, the terminal driver checks to see if the calling process is in the same process group as the terminal; if not, the request may be refused.[7] This is the distinguishing characteristic of background processes under BSD: They do not belong to the process group of their control terminal.

5.9 Sending signals - the kill command

As the name implies, **kill** is most often used to stop the execution of a process. **kill** can send any signal to a process, but by default it sends the signal 15, TERM, which is the software termination signal. **kill** can be used by normal users on their own process, or by the superuser on any process. The syntax for a kill is:

kill [*-signal*] *PID*

Where *signal* is the number or symbolic name (BSD) of the signal to be sent and PID is the process identification number of the target process. By convention, a PID of zero sends the signal to all members of the shell's process group. On some systems, a PID of -1 broadcasts the signal to all processes except system processes and the current shell. A **kill** without a signal number does not guarantee that the process will stop execution, because the TERM signal can be caught, blocked, or ignored. Using the command:

kill -9 *PID*

will guarantee that the process will die because signal 9, KILL, cannot be caught by any process. Sending a KILL is often necessary when the process you are trying to kill is a system or hung process.

Another signal that is commonly used with **kill** is the hangup (HUP) signal, signal 1. Many system daemons catch the hangup signal and interpret it as a command. For example, sending most versions of **init** a HUP signal will cause it to reread its initialization file (/etc/ttys or /etc/inittab) and respawn the appropriate **getty** processes. It is *always* a good idea to send a HUP signal before sending a KILL to *any* process — many programs interpret a HUP to mean, "You might be killed, so do whatever you can to cope with this."

5.9.1 csh kill

csh implements its own version of **kill**. It is identical to the generic **kill** except for two small differences. First, the **csh kill** allows processes to be

[7] Read requests are always blocked, but the user may choose whether or not to allow write requests with **stty tostop** or **stty -tostop**.

killed to be specified by their **csh** job number rather than PID. For example, to kill job number 1, you would type:

```
kill %1
```

This is a useful feature because it allows you to kill a process without knowing its PID, eliminating the need for a **ps**. Be careful not to forget the % if you are the superuser, or you might kill **init** or some other important system process with a low PID.

The second difference is that sending a signal to all members of the login process group by specifying PID 0 is not supported. This convention is useless under **csh** anyway, since **csh** makes so many changes to the processes' process groups.

5.10 Setting priority: nice and renice

The priority of a process can be changed to increase or decrease the amount of CPU time it receives. Remember that users are limited to monotonically decreasing the priority of their own processes. The superuser can both increase and decrease priorities.

Priority can be set at the time of process creation using the **nice** command, and on BSD can be changed during execution with the **renice** command. The strange names are derived from the practice of referring to priority as "niceness," because it determines how nice you are going to be to other users of the system.

It is vital that users who run long, CPU-intensive jobs be asked to run them at low priority. Large processes not only steal CPU from the interactive users to whom it more properly belongs, but also magnify the paging or swapping overhead of the system.

Low priority is not a complete solution, however. No matter how low the priority on a large process is set, UNIX will still let it run when there is a small amount of unused processor time available. This can be a severe hit to interactive performance because although CPU is available, memory may not be. If your site is one where users will have to write and execute their own long-term jobs, you should ask that they insert code to make the processes automatically go into a long-term sleep when the system gets busy or during normal working hours.

You may have problems cajoling users into lowering the priority of their processes, as people tend to forget or not realize that it's important. A good way to deal with persistent offenders is to tell them, "Lower the priority of your own jobs, or the system administrator will do it, and he won't be very generous when he is setting the new priority." If you have a problem with a user who does not comply with your requests for self-restraint, setting a few of their jobs to the lowest possible priority will usually change their attitude.

There are very few situations in which you will need to increase priorities above the default level. The most common use of increased priorities is when the system is so overloaded that even the simplest commands can take a long time. The system administrator must find processes that can be killed, suspended, or have their priorities lowered. Because the system is so overloaded, it can be almost impossible to make any progress at finding the source of trouble. The solution is to create a high priority shell. Because a process's priority is passed on to its children, a high priority shell will allow all of the commands you execute to run at high priority.

If a process's priority is set too high, it cannot be interrupted, and therefore cannot be sent signals. The solution to this problem is to lower the priority of the process and then kill it.

As if the fact that ATT and BSD use different ranges of numbers to represent priorities were not enough, the standard version of **nice** and the **nice** implemented by **csh** interpret their arguments differently.

5.10.1 ATT nice

In ATT systems, the default priority is 20. The standard version of **nice** (not the one included in **csh**) does not accept absolute values, it interprets its arguments as adjustments to the current priority level. If **nice** is used with a numeric argument; for example:

```
nice -5 myprog
```

the current niceness will be increased by that number, in this case 5. If no numeric argument is specified, the niceness is increased by 10. The superuser may lower the niceness (increasing priority) to a minimum of -20; for example:

```
nice --10 /bin/sh
```

would create a shell with niceness 10 less then the default. If the superuser specifies an argument of -100 or less, the process becomes "real time," in which case the process gets all the CPU cycles it wants. Running a process in "real time" severely degrades the performance of all other processes on the system so it should be used sparingly, if at all. Processes running in real time still show up as niceness -20 in a **ps** listing, and this special priority is not inherited by children of the process.

On ATT systems that have implementations of **csh**, the **nice** command that is built into the shell acts differently than the actual **nice** command. In the **csh** version, the default increase in niceness is 4 rather than 10.

5.10.2 BSD nice

The BSD version of nice that is not built into the shell (/bin/nice) has the following command format:

nice [*level*] *command* [*args*]

This will execute **command** at niceness 10 if no level is given. If a level is specified, it is added to the default niceness to determine the new priority. Since the default niceness is usually 0, it in effect sets the niceness to *level.* To increase the priority, specify a negative number for the niceness. For example:

nice -10 /bin/sh

would start a shell with -10 niceness, meaning very high priority.

The **csh** version of **nice** accepts a similar command format, except that the *command* argument is also optional and that *level* is interpreted relative to the niceness of the shell rather than the default system niceness.

For example:

nice +10 longprog
nice -8 runquick

The first command would run **longprog** at a niceness incremented by 10, meaning a lower priority, and the second command would run **runquick** a niceness decreased by 8, meaning a higher priority. If no command is given, the level affects the current shell (and in effect, all of its future children). If no level is given, the niceness is incremented by 4.

5.10.3 BSD renice

The BSD command **renice** allows the niceness of individual processes, processes groups, or all processes belonging to a particular user to be changed after the processes are already running. The syntax for the command is:

/etc/renice *level* [**-p** *PID* ...] [**-g** *pgrp* ...] [**-u** *user* ...]

The niceness of all processes affected is set to *level*. If only PIDs are specified, the **-p** option is not necessary. The **-g** option allows you to specify process groups, in which case the **renice** affects all processes belonging to each specified group. The **-u** option causes all processes belonging to *user* to be reniced.

5.10.4 ATT nohup

On ATT systems, when a shell is terminated it sends a hangup (HUP) signal to all of its descendants. If a process was running in the background, it will often be terminated by this signal, which is not usually what was intended. If you want to run a program in the background which will continue to execute after you log out, it should be started with the **nohup** command. The format of this command is:

nohup *command* **&**

This command makes the specified command ignore the hangup signal. It also has the side effect of increasing the niceness by 5. Any output the process generates will be placed in the file nohup.out if stdout and stderr are not redirected. If **csh** is being run, **nohup** is not needed because the shell automatically makes all processes started in the background ignore the hangup signal.

5.11 Errant processes

Occasionally there are processes on the system that for some reason or another need to be managed by the system administrator.

The most common type of problematic process is a *hung* process. A hung process is no longer executing properly, does not respond to requests from its control terminal, and generally just hangs around doing nothing, hence the name. Hung processes often show up on a **ps** listing as "<exiting>". In general, hung processes are not much of a problem unless they are tying up a terminal, in which case they should be killed. Because they are somehow messed up, hung process are notoriously hard to kill. They usually need to be sent the KILL signal to end their execution. Sometimes they need to be sent the KILL signal more than once before they die. An easy way to do this is to use your shell's built-in loop capability. For example, in **csh** the commands

```
% while 1
? kill -9 254
? end
```

will continually try to kill process 254. The loop will terminate with the message "254: No such process" when the process is actually killed. Hung processes that are not causing any problems other than cluttering up the **ps** listings can be ignored. They will go away the next time the system is rebooted.

A much more unpleasant type of errant process is a runaway process. Runaways come in two flavors: user processes that use up excessive amounts of a system resource such as CPU or disk space, and system processes that suddenly go berserk and exhibit similar behavior. The first type of runaway is simply being a resource hog and is not necessarily malfunctioning. On BSD systems, **sendmail**, **routed**, and **lpd** seem to be the system processes most prone to becoming runaways.

Processes using excessive CPU time can be identified by looking at the CPU entry of a **ps** listing. If it is obvious that a user process is using far more CPU than can be reasonably expected, the process should be investigated. The easiest way to handle the situation is to contact the process's owner and ask what is going on, but if this can't be done you will have to do some poking around of your own. Although maintaining the privacy of users' accounts should be a prime concern of any system administrator, you are justified in tracking down and reading the source code or shell script that a runaway process is executing from.

There are two reasons for this. First, the process may be both legitimate and important to the user. It isn't too great an idea to go around randomly blowing away people's jobs just because they happen to use a lot of CPU. Second, the process may be malicious or destructive. In this case, you've got to know exactly what the process was doing so you can fix the damage.

If the reason for a runaway process's existence can't be determined, suspend the process with a STOP signal on BSD, or terminate it with a TERM signal on ATT, and send electronic mail to the owner explaining what has happened. If a process is using an excessive amount of CPU, but appears to be doing something reasonable and working correctly, the process should be reniced to a lower priority and the owner notified to nice their own programs in the future. Because ATT systems do not have **renice**, you have no choice but to unmercilessly **kill** runaway processes.

On systems that do not implement quotas (see Chapter 22), runaway processes can fill up an entire filesystem, causing numerous problems. When a filesystem fills up, lots of messages will be logged to the console, and any attempt to write on the filesystem will produce an error message. On some old versions of UNIX, filling up a filesystem can even cause the system to crash.

The first thing to do in this situation is to stop the process that was filling up the disk. Assuming you have been keeping a reasonable amount of breathing room on the disk, you can be fairly sure that something is amiss if it suddenly fills up. You'll have to use some sleuthing skills in finding a disk-eating runaway, since there's no tool analogous to **ps** which will tell you who's consuming disk space at the fastest rate. Besides, by the time you get to looking for it, it won't really be active any more.

Because a full filesystem is a semi-panic situation, you may want to suspend all processes that look suspicious until you find the culprit (but remember to go back and start the innocents back up when you are done). When you find the culprit, remove the file or files it was creating, and your filesystem should be back to normal. An old and well-known "prank" is to start an infinite loop from the shell that does:

```
while 1
        mkdir adir
        cd adir
        touch afile
done
```

This occasionally shows up originating from an unprotected login or from a terminal that was left logged in. There is nothing you can do except clean up the aftermath and warn users again about protecting their accounts. Because the directory tree that is left behind by this little prank is too large for **rm -r** to handle, you will have to write a script that descends to the bottom of the tree and then removes the directories as it backs out.

6

Adding New Users

Adding and removing users is one of a system administrator's primary chores. It is also a constant and boring chore, so most administrators build tools to do it and then let a secretary or operator do the actual work. Copies of our **adduser** and **rmuser** scripts are in Appendices B and C, respectively.

6.1 Adding users

This section describes the steps necessary to add a user by hand. Even if you intend to use an **adduser** program instead of adding each user by hand, you should still read the ensuing discussion to understand how the program works.

Adding a new user to the system consists of two required steps, an additional three to five steps to create an initial environment for the new user, and several steps that are for your own convenience as system administrator.

Required:

- Edit the password file
- Make the home directory

For the user:

- Edit the group file
- Copy in the startup files
- Set an initial password
- Set a default universe (for dual universe ATT/BSD systems)
- Authorize for the **ingres** database system (BSD)

For you:

- Set disk quotas (BSD only)
- Set a mail home
- Record accounting information
- Enter in user database
- Enter in local phone book

The **adduser** program in Appendix B performs most of these operations for you. A cookbook-style recipe for adding a new user by hand follows. The chores associated with adding a new user to the system usually require you to be logged in as root; on some ATT systems a restricted root login, "sysadmin", is provided.

6.1.1 Edit the /etc/passwd file

The passwd file is a list of users the system recognizes. To use the system, your login name must be in this file. Each line in /etc/passwd represents one user and contains seven pieces of information, separated by colons:

- Login name
- Encrypted password
- UID number
- Default GID number
- GCOS field — full name, office, extension, home phone
- Home directory
- Login shell

The following lines are all valid /etc/passwd entries:

```
root:Igl6derBr45Tc:0:0:the system,,x6096,:/:/bin/csh
bin:*:1:1:pseudo-system,,,:/:/bin/sh
evi:JJ4wg6qi6:100:10:Evi Nemeth, ECOT 8-3,,:/staff/evi:/bin/csh
dotty:ntkYbliIo:101:20:Dotty Foerst, ECOT 7-7, x6361,
    :/student/dotty:/bin/csh
```

The last of these lines has been split to fit on the page.

To add a new user to the system, you must add a line for him in the passwd file. On BSD systems, use **vipw** to edit the passwd file so that your editing session and a user's attempt to change his password cannot collide. **vipw** invokes the text editor specified by the environment variable EDITOR or **vi** if EDITOR is not defined.

The line:

```
tyler::103:10:Tyler Stevens, ECEE 3-27, x7919,:/staff/tyler:/bin/csh
```

appended to the file /etc/passwd would add "tyler" to the list of users the system recognizes.

6.1.1.1 Login name

Login names must be unique and no more than eight characters long. They may include numbers and may be upper- or lowercase; however, login names are typically all lowercase. Uppercase-only login names cause UNIX to think you have a terminal which does not support lowercase letters, so it is best to avoid these. Login names should be relatively easy to remember, so random sequences of consonants do not make good login names. It is also wise to avoid "handles" and cutesy pseudonyms.

It is useful to establish a standard way of forming login names: first names, last names, initials, or some combination of these. Any fixed scheme eventually results in duplicates or login names that are too long, so you will occasionally have to make exceptions. In the case of a long name, the /usr/lib/aliases (/etc/aliases on some systems) file can be used to equivalence the name that fits the rules with the actual login name, at least as far as mail is concerned. For example, Sun Microsystems uses an employee's first initial and last name as a paradigm. There, Brent Browning there would be "bbrowning", which is nine characters and therefore too long. His login is actually "brentb", but an entry in the aliases file lets us send mail to Brent using the address bbrowning@sun.com.

If you have more than one machine, the login names you assign should be unique in two senses. First, a user should have the same login on every machine for which he is authorized. This is mostly for convenience, both yours and his. Second, a particular login name should always refer to the same person. Potential security holes are created if the same login name refers to two different users in a networked environment. For example, if scott@boulder was Scott Seebass and scott@sigi (on the same Ethernet as boulder) was Scott Hudson, then under certain circumstances either *scott* could access the other's files.

If your system has a global mail aliases file, then each new login name must also be distinct from any alias in this file. If it is not, mail will be delivered to the alias, rather than the actual user.

In our example, the new user's login name is "tyler".

6.1.1.2 Encrypted password

The encrypted password is set using the **passwd** program.[1] When you edit the /etc/passwd file to add a new user, you should put a * in this field.

6.1.1.3 UID number

Userid numbers must be distinct integers between 0 and 32767. In a networked environment using NFS (see Chapter 14), they must be unique across the entire network. That is, a particular UID must refer to the same login and the same person throughout the network. By definition, root has UID 0. Most systems also have pseudo-users bin (UID 1) and daemon (UID 2). It is customary to put **uucp** logins and fake logins like who, tty, and ttytype in the beginning of the /etc/passwd file with low UID's. To give yourself plenty of room for non-human users, start assigning UID's to real users with 100 and continue upwards from there. Never reuse a UID, even after someone has been **rmuser**'ed and has left your organization for good. This avoids later confusion if files are restored from magnetic tape, where UID's are used to identify users rather than login names.

In our example, Tyler's userid number is 103.

6.1.1.4 Default GID number

A group id number must also be an integer between 0 and 32767. Tyler's default group id is 10. GID 0 is reserved for the group "root" or, in recent BSD distributions, the group "wheel";[2] GID 1 is usually used for the group "daemon".

Under ATT and early BSD versions of UNIX, a user can only be in one group at a time. The GID in the /etc/passwd file sets the user's initial group, and other groups he belongs to are specified in the /etc/group file. The **newgroup** command is used to change the current working group.

In recent releases of BSD a user is simultaneously in up to eight groups and the use of **newgroup** is obsolete. The meaning of the GID has changed as

[1] Or **yppasswd** under the NFS yellow pages.

[2] The name wheel comes from the TOPS-20 operating system, where the root account is called "wheel".

well: The group owner of a directory is now the default group owner of any files the user creates beneath that directory. Thus, the default group owner of a file is determined by the file's parent directory, not by the GID value in the user's /etc/passwd entry. The **chgrp** command for changing the group ownership of files is now a user command and is no longer restricted to the superuser.

6.1.1.5 GCOS field

This field has no strictly defined syntax. It was originally used to hold the login information needed to submit batch jobs to a mainframe running GCOS from UNIX systems at Bell Labs; now only the name remains. It is commonly used to record personal information for each user. An "&" in the GCOS field expands to the user's login name under BSD and saves a bit of typing, although this does seem a little penny-wise and pound-foolish. Tyler's GCOS field could have read:

```
& Stevens, ECEE 3-27, x7919,
```

Although you are free to use any encoding scheme you like, the BSD **finger** command interprets the comma-separated entries in the following order:

- Full name
- Office number and building
- Office telephone extension
- Home phone number

Since "tyler" has not provided a home phone number, there is a trailing comma after his extension to indicate that the field is null. See the bin or root entries in the /etc/passwd examples above for more comma magic. The BSD command **chfn** (change **finger** info) allows a user to change his own GCOS information.

chfn is useful for keeping things like phone numbers up-to-date, but can be misused. A user can change the information to be either obscene or incorrect. Our academic computing center, which caters to hoards of undergraduates, has disabled the **chfn** command.

6.1.1.6 Home directory

A user's home directory is his own chunk of the disk where his files will be stored. Users are placed in their home directories when they log in. If a user's home directory is missing when he tries to log in, a message such as "no home directory" is printed. Some systems allow the login to proceed and put the user into the root directory. Other systems do not allow you to log in at all without a home directory. It is customary to use the login name as the name of the home directory. Tyler's home directory is /staff/tyler.

6.1.1.7 Login shell

The login shell is the program that **login** starts up for you when you log in. Normally this is a command interpreter such as the Bourne or C shell (**/bin/sh** or **/bin/csh**). The Bourne shell is the default on most systems, and is used if the passwd entry does not specify a login shell. Other shells that are available, but not always distributed with standard UNIX, include **ksh**, the Korn shell and **tcsh**, the Tenex shell.

On BSD systems a user can change his shell with the **chsh** command. The file /etc/shells contains a list of valid shells that **chsh** will recognize for users; root may use **chsh** without restrictions.

6.1.2 Make the home directory

The name of the directory created for "tyler" must be the same as the home directory entry for him in the /etc/passwd file. Initially, any directory you make will be owned by root, so you must also change the ownership and group ownership with the **chown** and **chgrp** commands, respectively. The following command sequence creates a home directory appropriate for our example user Tyler.

```
mkdir /staff/tyler
chown tyler /staff/tyler
chgrp staff /staff/tyler
```

6.1.3 Edit the /etc/group file

/etc/group contains the names of valid UNIX groups and a list of their members' logins. For example:

```
wheel:*:0:root,evi,garth,scott
staff:*:10:lloyd,evi
student:*:20:dotty
```

Each line represents one group and contains four fields:

- Group name
- Encrypted password (never used)
- GID number
- List of group members (separated by commas)

As in /etc/passwd, fields are separated by colons. The group name must be eight or fewer characters on ATT systems. There is no limit on BSD systems. The standard UNIX distributions do not provide for group passwords, although the field is allocated in the /etc/group file. Many sites put asterisks in this field.

To continue the processing of the new user "tyler", we must add his login name to the list of users in group 10, since that was the default group to which we assigned him in the /etc/passwd file. Strictly speaking, tyler will be in group 10 whether he's listed in /etc/group or not because his password entry has already given him this membership. Always remember to update /etc/group when adding a user, however, as it should be dependable as a list of what users are in each group for security reasons.

Suppose we also wanted to put tyler in the group "wheel". We would simply make the following changes to /etc/group:

```
wheel:*:0:root,evi,garth,scott,tyler
staff::10:lloyd,evi,tyler
```

6.1.4 Copy the startup files

Some commands can be customized by placing configuration files in your home directory. Startup files traditionally begin with a dot and end with the letters *rc*, short for "runcom" (run command), a relic of the CTSS operating system. The initial dot causes **ls** not to show these files in directory listings unless the **-a** option is used, since they are considered uninteresting.

The functions of some common startup files are illustrated in Figure 6.1.

Sample startup files are listed in Appendix D. They are also called skeletal startup files, and are often kept in the directory /usr/local/skel. If you do not

FIGURE 6.1

Startup files and their uses		
Filename	Command	Typical Uses
.login	**/bin/csh**	Set terminal type Set environment variables Set cdpath for filename searches Set **biff** and **mesg** switches
.cshrc	**/bin/csh**	Set command aliases Set path for command searches Set **umask** to control modes of files created Set variables that should follow subshells prompt history and savehist
.logout	**/bin/csh**	Print "things to do" reminder list Print fortune Clear screen
.profile	**/bin/sh**	Same as preceding .login and .cshrc
.exrc	**/usr/ucb/vi**	Set **vi** editor options
.emacs_pro	**/usr/new/bin/emacs**	Set **emacs** editor options Set **emacs** key bindings
.mailrc	**/usr/ucb/mail**	Set mail aliases Set mail parameters
.dbxinit	**/usr/ucb/dbx**	Set debugger command aliases
.newsrc	**/usr/new/rn**	Specify newsgroups of interest

already have a set of good, general startup files, make a directory /usr/local/skel and create them with a text editor. For tyler, the command sequence for installing the skeletal startup files would look like this:

```
cp /usr/local/skel/.[a-z]* /staff/tyler
chmod 644 /staff/tyler/.[a-z]*
chown tyler /staff/tyler/.[a-z]*
chgrp staff /staff/tyler/.[a-z]*
```

Notice that we cannot use **chown tyler /staff/tyler/.*** because then Tyler would own not only his own files but also ".." or /staff as well. Be careful not to make this mistake; it is a very common and dangerous one.

6.1.5 Set an initial password

The **passwd** command is used to set an initial password for a user, or to change an old password. **passwd** will prompt for the password, and will ask you to repeat it. If you choose a short, all lowercase password, **passwd** will complain and ask you to use a longer password. If you insist on the same short password about three times, BSD will grudgingly accept it, but most versions of ATT UNIX will force you to use a password that contains mixed case (upper/lower/punctuation/numbers) or is longer. **passwd** will let you know what the rules are for your particular UNIX if it doesn't like your initial attempt.

Never leave a new account, or any account with access to a shell, without a password.

6.1.6 Set up ingres database access file

BSD systems include the public domain relational database system **ingres**, which is usually installed beneath the directory /usr/ingres. The /usr/ingres/files/users file contains password-like entries that control access to **ingres** database files. The following entry in this file would allow tyler to use the **ingres** system.

```
tyler:al:103:10:000001:::/staff/tyler/.ingres::
```

Fields are separated by colons. The first, third, and fourth fields are the login name, UID, and GID from the /etc/passwd file. The second field is a two-letter string that must be unique and is used by **ingres** to control access to files. These strings follow the sequence aa, ab, ..., az, a0,..., a9, ba, ..., z9 and are used in the naming of the database files. The fifth field is a permissions vector interpreted by **ingres**; the value shown is for a regular user with no special permissions. The final field shown is the path to the **ingres** startup file, usually called ".ingres". The empty fields are not usually used but are described in the **ingres** documentation. In order for users to access **ingres**, they must have /usr/ingres/bin in their search path, which is set in the .login or .profile startup files.

6.1.7 Set the mail home

It is convenient for a user to receive all of his electronic mail on one machine. This is often done by an entry in the global aliases file /usr/lib/aliases, which forwards mail addressed to that login name to a particular machine. For example, the lines:

```
tyler: tyler@tigger
tstevens: tyler
```

would route all of Tyler's mail to the machine "tigger" and set up an alias so that mail sent to "tstevens" would also be forwarded correctly. See Chapter 15 for more information about mail aliases.

6.1.8 Record accounting information

An extensive accounting system needs the user's full name, billing address, account number to charge, and rate structure to use. If your site intends to do such accounting, this information should be entered when each user is added.

6.1.9 Update the user database and phone book

An online user database and phone book can easily be created from the GCOS field of the passwd file, especially if the comma conventions of the **finger** program are followed. A simple **phone** script can be written to search for items in the database. Our local version first searches a private file .phonelist in the users home directory and then looks in the system-wide database. Under **csh** this is simply:

```
grep -i $1 ~/.phonelist /usr/local/pub/phonelist
```

6.1.10 Verify the new login

To verify that everything works for the new login "tyler", logout as root, login as tyler, and execute the following commands:

```
pwd       /* to see what Tyler's home directory is */
ls -lag   /* BSD: check the owner and group of Tyler's home and startup files */
ls -la    /* ATT: check the owner and group of Tyler's home and startup files */
```

When the new user has been added, notify him of his login name and initial password. This is also a good time to supply documentation on local customs and expected behavior as a good citizen of the user community. Remind him to change his password.

6.1.11 NFS and the yellow pages

Machines running NFS, the Network File System, use a mechanism called the yellow pages to manage the /etc/passwd and /etc/group files centrally on one machine. This master machine is called the YP server. Other machines, called client machines, access these files from the server's copies via the network.

New users are added to the /etc/passwd and /etc/group files on the YP server, which then must reread them and update its internal YP database. This is done through a Makefile in the /etc/yp (/var/yp on some systems) directory by:

```
cd /etc/yp
make
```

Client machines that access /etc/passwd through the yellow pages do not have a complete local password file. The **passwd** command is not yet smart enough to ask the server automatically for the YP version of the passwd entry. Users should use the **yppasswd** command to change their password instead.

If you use or plan to use the NFS distributed filesystem, there are other considerations you must take into account when adding users. NFS and the yellow pages are covered in Chapter 14: *Networking under BSD*.

6.1.12 Pyramid variations: ATT or BSD universe

Pyramid's dual-universe implementation of UNIX maintains a default universe file, /etc/u_universe. Entries in this file are of the form: *login:universe*; for example:

```
evi:bsd
garth:bsd
scott:att
```

Users should be added to this file when their accounts are created.

Several other vendors who have implemented both ATT and BSD UNIX, including Masscomp, Sequent, and Apollo, have a similar mechanism for selecting a default universe.

6.1.13 Setting quotas (BSD only)

If your site is configured for disk quotas (see Chapter 8: *Configuring the Kernel*), you should set a quota for each user at the time when his account is created with the **edquota** command. **edquota** can be used to interactively specify various limits, but it is more commonly used in "prototype" mode to set the quotas of the new user to be just like those of another user. For example:

edquota -p *proto-user new-user*

sets *new-user*'s quota limits to be the same as *proto-user*'s. This way of using **edquota** is especially useful in **adduser** scripts.

Refer to Chapter 22 for more information about quotas.

6.2 Removing users

When a user leaves, his login and files need to be removed from the system. This involves removing him from all the files that the **adduser** program put him, including user databases, phonelists, accounting databases, groups, etc. Before you remove a user's home directory, you should relocate any files that are needed by other users. Accounting is typically done on a monthly basis, so sites that use accounting must implement a two-stage removal process. The login must first be disabled, yet still exist for the accounting programs. After accounting has been run, all traces of the login should disappear.

The **rmuser** program presented in Appendix C complements the **adduser** program in Appendix B. It replaces the user's encrypted password with the date, thus disabling the login but leaving it in the /etc/passwd file for accounting. All the other chores of removing users are done by **rmuser** at this time. After accounting is run, any entry in the password file with the date as the encrypted password can be deleted with a text editor.

6.3 User management

This section contains a potpourri of facts about users and user management.

6.3.1 Pseudo-logins

A pseudo login is one that does not correspond to a real person. The "bin" and "daemon" pseudo-logins are distributed with the system. It is often convenient to create additional pseudo logins to execute a single command or to use for a special purpose. For example, pseudo-logins "who", "tty", "ttytype", or "hostname", which execute the corresponding command, are very handy. Pseudo-logins such as "diskhog", "nolimit", or "tiny" can be used as prototypes for disk quotas.

6.3.2 Organizing users on the disk

Disk space should be organized to make maintenance easy. Backups and operating system upgrades each need the disk organization to be cleanly divided between the stable system files and the more volatile user files. When system upgrades occur, most system directories are overwritten. Home directories in the /usr or /etc directories, for example, would be lost.

When dumps are done, they need to occur more often on user partitions, where the data changes daily, than on system partitions, where it changes more slowly. Separate partitions for home directories are preferable, although not always practical for small systems. Users should be divided by usage patterns or political status. Home directories beneath category directories, such as /staff, /student, /guest, or /systems, allow users to be grouped conveniently. If users are temporary, a separate directory tree makes it easy to delete them when their need for a login is over.

Guest logins with no password or "guest" as password are a convenience, yet present a security hole, especially if they are set up with a regular shell. If the guest login is given a real password, it is easy to lose track of the people who have it.

Limited user environments can be set up for guest logins and for logins like **uucp** or **ftp** using the **chroot** system call or a restricted shell. Chapter 14: *Networking under BSD* and Chapter 16: *Uucp* cover such environments for **uucp** and **ftp**.

6.3.3 Disabling logins

Occasionally a user's login must be temporarily disabled. Before networking invaded our campus, we would just put an asterisk in front of the encrypted password, making it impossible for the user to login. But he can still login across the network. Now, instead, we replace the user's shell with a program that prints a message explaining why the login has been disabled and how to rectify the situation.

6.3.4 Password aging

Password aging is a feature of many ATT-based implementations. It forces a user to change his password on a regular basis. We find that in our environment (a university campus) this is not necessary, and in fact a bit of a nuisance. A more complete discussion of password aging is given in Chapter 24: *Security*.

6.4 Random facts and folklore

These snippets didn't fit in anywhere else, yet they are important to know when adding users.

6.4.1 Editor autoconfiguration

In earlier versions of the **vi** editor, **vi** configuration commands could be embedded in text files so that they would autoconfigure the editor when loaded. For example, if you wanted **vi** to always use four-space tab settings, you could include a line in the file being edited to set the tabs for **vi**. **vi** interprets material following a vi: or ex: token within the first ten lines of a file as embedded commands. Thus the line:

```
evi:JJ4wg6qi6:100:10:Evi Nemeth, ECOT 8-3, x5385,:/staff/evi:/bin/csh
```

within the first ten lines of the /etc/passwd file will cause **vi** to interpret the characters following the vi: in the name "evi", as editor commands. Needless to say, this could be disastrous for the password file. The encrypted password follows the vi: and might encrypt to a string beginning with "dG", which is **vi**ese for "delete to the end of the file".

6.4.2 Password ordering

The password file should be maintained in UID order, with root first, then pseudo-users with UID's below 100, and then regular users. This allows an **adduser** program to simply increment the UID of the last entry in the file to get the next UID and works quite well for a single machine with no network. On a network, however, UID's should be unique among all machines on the network. An **adduser** program in this environment must have some other way to determine the next unused UID.

6.4.3 The nobody login

Some recent versions of UNIX have included a user called "nobody" with UID -1 or -2. UID's are short integers and thus -1 might appear as 32767, which would thwart the adduser scheme for determining the next unused UID. "nobody" is the owner of software that doesn't need or shouldn't have any special permissions. Sun workstations use it to protect the security of fileservers on a network where diskless clients can be rebooted in single-user mode by anyone with physical access to them. Some daemon programs under BSD run as nobody, such as **fingerd**, the **finger** daemon.

7

Devices and Drivers

Adding new hardware to a UNIX system requires that it be physically attached and that the operating system be told it is there. The hardware and software sides of adding a device are well separated, both in concept and in practice.

The way that a new device attaches to your system varies depending on the size of your machine and its bus architecture. An interface board is typically connected to the system's bus to act as a bridge between the protocols spoken by the computer and those spoken by the actual device.

In order for UNIX to recognize the existence of the device, a device driver for it must be included in the kernel. UNIX comes with drivers for many peripherals, including terminals, printers, disks, tapes, network interfaces, and more. Under both ATT and BSD, device drivers must be compiled directly into the kernel, so adding a new device often means building and testing a new version of the operating system. Source code for the operating system (or for the device driver) is not generally required, yet some vendors do not make including new drivers easy. Consult your manufacturer's documentation for exact details. Chapter 7: *Devices and Drivers* and Chapter 8: *Configuring the Kernel* are a bit like Siamese twins and present a serious chicken-and-egg problem. Read them in parallel!

To see exactly which drivers are on your particular system, refer to the system directory (where the object files for building a new kernel reside, see Chapter 8: *Configuring the Kernel*) and to the section of the UNIX manual dealing with devices. Figure 7.1 details these locations for some systems.

In compiling the information for Figure 7.1, we became painfully aware of the diversity of "standard" ATT distributions for which the answers in the table were totally different. We looked a vanilla ATT System V on 3B hardware,

FIGURE 7.1

Locations of device driver information		
Item	Location	Description
BSD - general info	/sys/conf/files	Common files to rebuild system
	/sys/conf/files.vax	Vax specific files
	/sys/conf/files.*kernel-name*	Files specific to a machine
	/sys/conf/devices.vax	Maps device names <-> major dev. #'s
BSD - drivers	/sys/vaxif	Communications interfaces
	/sys/vaxuba	Unibus peripherals
	/sys/vaxmba	Massbus disks and tapes
BSD - documentation	/usr/man/man4	Device driver documentation
	Usenix-/usr/group tutorial	Writing Device Drivers
ATT - general info	/etc/master	The device switch itself
	/src/sys/cf/master	The device switch itself
	/usr/lib/sys/cf/master	The device switch itself
	/etc/master.d	A directory of files for each device
ATT - drivers	/usr/src/uts/*machine*/io	Device drivers, location varies
ATT - documentation	/usr/man/man4	Format of the master file
	order from ATT	Document on writing device drivers
	/usr/group tutorial	Writing Device Drivers
SUN - general info	Same as BSD	Files named sun*X* instead of vax
SUN - drivers	/sys/sundev	Header files for devices
	/sys/sunif	Communications interfaces
	/sys/OBJ	Object files for rebuilding kernel
SUN - documentation	/usr/man/man4	Device driver documentation
	Ch. 5, Sys. Admin. Manual	Hardware installation manual
HP - general info	/etc/conf/README	Tells how to rebuild system
	/etc/conf/*.a	Libraries of system object files
Pyramid	/sys/kernel_m/*.a	Libraries of system object files
	/sys/kernel/NAME.#ports	Device configuration file
	/sys/conf/conf.c	Device jump tables
	/usr/.ucbman/man4	Device driver documentation
Xenix	/sys/conf/master	The device switch itself
	/sys/cfg/makefile	Device driver names in VASOBJS
	/sys/cfg.iparams	List of new device driver .o files
	/sys/cfg/*driver.o*	New driver modules themselves
	/sys/io/makefile	i/o device driver names in VASOBJS
	/sys/io/io.iparams	List of new i/o device driver .o files
	/sys/io/*driver.o*	New i/o driver modules

on Vaxen, on Xenix implementations, on HP bobcats, on Pyramids, on 386s, ... It was discouraging to see such lack of uniformity, even among versions that were based on the same release from ATT.

7.1 Device files and their relationship to drivers

UNIX represents devices as block- or character-special files located in the /dev directory. Each has a major device number and a minor device number. The major device number identifies which device driver should be used to communicate with the device, thus telling what type of device the file references. The minor device number identifies which particular device of a given type is to be addressed by the file, and is often called the unit number or *instance* of the device. The minor device number is also sometimes used by the driver to set a particular characteristic of the device. For example, a single tape drive has several files representing it in various configurations of recording density and rewind characteristics.

Device drivers have a standard interface to the kernel. Each driver has routines for performing some or all of the following functions: **probe**, **attach**, **open**, **close**, **read**, **write**, **reset**, **stop**, **timeout**, **select**, **strategy**, **dump**, **psize**, process a transmit interrupt, process a receive interrupt and **ioctl** (input/output control). Inside the kernel, the names of these functions (typically prefixed with the abbreviation for the device type) are stored in jump tables, *cdevsw* for character devices and *bdevsw* for block devices, indexed by the major device number. When a program references a device file, the kernel automatically traps the reference, looks up the appropriate function name in the jump table, and transfers control to it. The jump table is stored in different places depending on the flavor of UNIX. In version 7-based systems, it is in the source file "conf.c" kept in the /sys directory. In Berkeley based systems, the jump tables are usually in the file /usr/sys/*machine-type*/conf.c. Several other files contribute to the final makeup of the kernel: in 4.2BSD there is a single file called "files" in which all devices must be listed. In 4.3BSD this file has been separated into four pieces:

- files – common files for all kernels
- files.*machine-type* – architecture-specific files
- files.*kernel-name* – files specific to a particular machine
- devices.*machine-type* – device name to major device # mappings for an architecture

These files are used by the **config** program to form the ioconf.c file which describes the device drivers to the kernel. In System V based versions of

UNIX, the jump tables are built from a "master" file which lives in either /etc, /src/sys/cf, or /usr/lib/sys/cf.

Several binary distributions of UNIX include a document on writing device drivers. For example, Sun provides a document called *Writing Device Drivers for the Sun Workstation* and HP provides *Using HP-HIL Devices with HP-UX.* In addition, both the Usenix Association and the /usr/group organization present popular tutorials on writing UNIX device drivers at their semiannual meetings.

By convention, device files are kept in the /dev directory. On large systems, especially those with networking and pseudo-terminals, there may be hundreds of devices: an **ls** of the /dev directory zooms off the terminal screen. ATT systems handle this quite nicely by using a separate subdirectory of /dev for each type of device: disk, tape, terminal, etc.

Just as directory files are created with the **mkdir** command, device files are created with the **mknod** command. The **mknod** command has the form:

> **mknod** *device-name type major minor*

where *device-name* is the name of the resulting file that will represent the device, *type* is the letter "c" for a character device or "b" for a block device, *major* is the major device number associated with this type of device and *minor* is the minor device number of this particular device.

For example to make the eight terminal devices associated with the first "dz" interface on a Vax ("dz" is major device number 1), you would type:

```
cd /dev  (or /dev/terminals)
mknod tty0 c 1 0
mknod tty1 c 1 1
mknod tty2 c 1 2
 . . .
mknod tty7 c 1 7
```

A shell script called **MAKEDEV** is sometimes provided in the /dev directory to automatically supply default values to the **mknod** command. Using **MAKEDEV**, creation of the preceding eight terminal files could be performed with the single line:

```
MAKEDEV dz0
```

It is advisable to read and understand the **MAKEDEV** script before executing it.

7.2 Naming conventions for devices

Naming conventions for devices are somewhat random, and are often hold-overs from the way things were done a long time ago on DEC PDP-11 hardware. A few naming guidelines that are in common usage are mentioned next.

Some devices have both block and character device files. Disks and tapes lead dual lives; terminals and printers do not. Devices that have both block and character identities preface the character device name with the letter "r" for raw.[1]

Terminals names always begin with "tty", followed by up to two letters that identify the device interface the terminal is attached to, followed by a single digit (in hex) identifying the port on that interface. For example, ttyh3 is the fourth port on the first "dh" interface on a Vax. Terminal ports used for modems often use a "d" instead of the letter identifying the interface. Thus, if the "dh" interface was used for dialup ports, the fourth dialup would be called ttyd3.

Disk names often begin with a two-letter abbreviation for either the drive or the controller, followed by the drive number and partition name. For example, xy0a is the block device representing the "a" partition of the first disk drive on a Xylogics controller; rxy0a is the corresponding character device.

The names of tape devices often include not only a reference to the drive itself, but also an indication of whether the device rewinds after each tape operation and the density at which it reads and writes. A tape drive's name is typically formed from two parts: a two-letter device designation and a unit number. The two letters are usually either "mt" (for magnetic tape) or an abbreviation for the tape drive or its controller. The encoding of the unit numbers is as follows:

0-3	lowest density, rewind on close
3-7	lowest density, no rewind on close
8-11	next higher density, rewind
12-15	next higher density, no rewind
16-23	highest density, rewind
20-23	highest density, no rewind

[1] An "r" does not always imply a raw device file, however. On a Vax, for example, /dev/rx0 is a block device that references a floppy disk drive.

There are four numbers in each set, so four separate tape drives can be supported under this scheme.

On BSD, tape devices often have two names, one using just the unit number encoding, and one prefixed with the letter “n” for “no rewind”. Thus, the device mt12 and the device nmt8 are the same nonrewinding, medium density block device. Unfortunately, the “r” for “raw”, when placed next to the “n” for “no rewind”, looks like it forms “nr” for “no rewind”, but instead means the no rewind, raw device.

7.3 Installing new hardware

This section gives an overview of the installation of a generic device. Procedures for handling printed circuit boards and installing them in a computer are covered in Chapter 13: *Hardware Maintenance Tips*. Details for terminals, modems, and printers are given in Chapter 9, for disks in Chapter 12, and for network interfaces in Chapter 14.

7.3.1 Strapping options

Many devices have user-programmable options called strapping options. Before installing a new board, you should read the manufacturer’s installation instructions and configure the board to fit your situation. Almost all hardware has the concept of a bus address and interrupt vector. These sometimes have traditional values that should be honored in order to maintain timing relationships on the bus. On Vaxen, there are also prescribed separations between the bus address and interrupt vector of multiple instances of a particular device. Some hardware has extensive diagnostics; learn to use them.

7.3.2 Device categories

All new hardware falls into one of the two categories listed here:

- Initial or additional units of *known* UNIX devices
- *Brand-new* and nonstandard devices

An example of a known device is a second disk on an existing controller or a system’s first network interface. A brand-new device could be just about anything; for example, an automated cranberry picker. Note that under this classification system it doesn’t matter what the device actually *is*, just to what extent it or others like it are *known* to your UNIX system.

7.3.3 Installing a known device

The software chores to install a known device are quite simple. Add the device to the kernel configuration file and rebuild UNIX as described in Chapter 8. The MAKEDEV script in /dev, if it exists, can be used to make the device files, since the major and minor device numbers for the device you are adding are standard. Edit any configuration files for the device (e.g., /etc/fstab or /etc/ttys) and you're done.

The hardware tasks are summarized here:

- Read the manual to set the strapping options correctly.
- Label both ends of all cables with name and unit number; use waterproof marker.
- Shut down UNIX and power down the system.
- Install the new hardware per manufacturer's instructions.
- Power up the system, booting the new kernel.

7.3.4 Installing a brand-new device

Devices whose drivers came with the standard distribution need only be mentioned in the kernel configuration file to be correctly included in the kernel. When you write your own device driver for a new piece of hardware or obtain it from a third-party vendor, you need to configure a few more files so that the driver will be correctly linked into the kernel. The example that follows is 4.3BSD specific (SunOS, although 4.2BSD based, uses a similar system); the steps for an ATT kernel are similar. The hardware in the example is the Vax called "boulder", whose kernel configuration file is called BOULDER. SYS is not a real directory, but is used to represent the path to the system files, in this case /usr/sys.

Adding a completely new driver requires the following steps:

- Write, beg, borrow, or steal a device driver for the new device.
- Declare the device in the configuration file like any other device; see Chapter 8.
- Edit the SYS/conf/files.*kernel-name* file to declare your driver's number.
- Install the device driver code in the SYS area.
- Edit the SYS/*machine-type*/conf.c file to declare your driver's service routines.
- Make the device's device files in /dev or /dev/*device-type*.

7.3.4.1 Acquire a device driver

If you acquire the device driver from a third-party vendor, try to obtain source code and encourage them to give the sources to the computer manufacturer. It is sometimes difficult to obtain new versions of the driver that run under new releases of the operating system, which can impact your ability to upgrade as new releases come out.

7.3.4.2 Declare the device

This is the most difficult part of adding the new driver. You have to make an entry in the kernel configuration file (see Chapter 8: *Configuring the Kernel*) for the new device, but instead of being able to copy it from the generic configuration you have to create it by hand.

If the new device is supplied by a third-party manufacturer, there will probably be enough information included with it to make the correct entry in the configuration file, but if you've built the device yourself, or no longer have instructions for it, you may have to do some experimentation. You'll also need to know something about the address space of the bus to which your device is connected in order to figure out what value to declare for its command and status registers in the configuration file.

7.3.4.3 Let the config command know about the device

The file SYS/conf/files.*machine-type*, where *machine-type* is the type of CPU and is also the argument to the *machine* keyword in the kernel configuration file, contains a list of device driver object files that may be included when the kernel is built. Some of these files are always included, but others depend upon whether or not a given device has been included in the configuration. In this step, you must either create or append to a similar file called SYS/conf/files.*kernel-name*, adding information about your device. This will let the **config** program find the device driver for the device you are adding. **config** knows to look in this file automatically.

You may put as many lines in this file as there are object files in the device driver code. For example, suppose you are adding to your Vax a device driver for an electronic cranberry picker whose device name is "cb". You plan to call the first of these devices "/dev/cb0", the second "/dev/cb1", and so on. Let's also suppose that this cranberry picker driver is so complicated that you had to split the code into two separate files, "cb_thing1.o" and "cb_thing2.o". The cranberry picker will be attached to the Unibus, so you plan to put the object files for the driver in the directory SYS/vaxuba.

The correct lines to add to the SYS/conf/files.*kernel-name* file are:

```
vaxuba/cb_thing1.c          optional cb device-driver
vaxuba/cb_thing2.c          optional cb device-driver
```

The first field is the pathname of the file relative to the SYS directory. The second field can be either "standard" or "optional"; when adding a device driver the "optional" keyword will always be used, since a system that doesn't already have the driver doesn't need it to function correctly. The third field is the name of the device, and the fourth field indicates that the files contain device driver code rather than symbolic information.

7.3.4.4 Install the object files

Now that you've promised in SYS/conf/files.*kernel-name* to put the object files in a certain place, you need to really put them there. The choice of where to place extra code is completely up to you; you can even put the files somewhere outside the SYS directory by specifying a pathname that begins with one or more ".."'s in the files.*kernel-name* file. (This does not transport well to machines with symbolic links in the SYS area.) There are really only two viable options, however.

The first is to put the files in the same directory with other kernel files of the same nature. This is what we've done in the cranberry picker example, since we put the code in the same directory with all the other Unibus devices. This arrangement is nice because you always know where everything is and because it obeys an elegant and simple classification system.

The second is to put the files in a directory called something like SYS/local. This way you'll know what to save when you upgrade the operating system and need to isolate the things you've added in a hurry. This is probably the better alternative because you probably won't be adding so many new device drivers that you have trouble classifying them into Unibus devices, Massbus devices, etc.

7.3.4.5 Edit the SYS/*machine-type*/conf.c file

The *machine-type* part of this pathname should be the machine type as specified by the *machine* keyword within the kernel: in this example, "vax". This file is written in C and does the actual interfacing between the device driver and the rest of the operating system. The format is quite simple. There are two main tasks that you need to accomplish with your editing here: one is to declare the interface routines for your device, and the other is to put these routines into the switch structures so that references to the major device number that is to control the device will be routed appropriately.

A typical declaration section looks something like this:

```
#include "sd.h"
#if NSD > 0
extern int sdopen(), sdstrategy(), sdread(), sdwrite();
extern int sddump(), sdioctl(), sdsize();
#else
#define sdopen          nodev
#define sdstrategy      nodev
#define sdread          nodev
#define sdwrite         nodev
#define sddump          nodev
#define sdioctl         nodev
#define sdsize          0
#endif
```

This example is for a device called "sd", the Sun SCSI disk controller. The first line, #include "sd.h", inserts the contents of the file "sd.h" into the C code right at that point. This included file will contain only one line: An instruction to make the symbol NSD equivalent to an integer representing the number of "sd" devices connected to the system. Don't bother looking for the "sd.h" file, though, since it doesn't exist until **config** creates it. You can depend upon a file called "cb.h" being created for your new "cb" device, too.

The next line is a check to see whether there are any "sd" devices. If there are, the two lines that begin with "extern" will be looked at; otherwise, everything between the #else line and the #endif line will be. Those lines that begin with "extern" declare all the publicly accessible routines of the "sd" device driver to be supplied from somewhere else (the object files of the device driver), and declare that all the routines return integers. Every listed routine name (sdopen, sdstrategy, etc.) is an entrypoint into the device driver for "sd". If there are no instances of a device, the "extern" declarations are not looked at, and all of the routine names are equivalenced to "nodev".

There are a number of standard routines that a device driver may support, some of which are:

- **open** - prepare to start using the device
- **close** - stop using the device
- **write** - transmit data or control codes to the device
- **read** - get data from device
- **ioctl** - configure device driver

Some routines are optional and some are required. If you wrote the device driver you'll know what routines are defined for it; if it comes from somewhere else there will be a listing of routines supplied with it.

What you need to do for this part of the conf.c file is make a copy of one of these declaration blocks, replacing each routine name with the name of the routine of a similar function from the new device driver. Usually the names are formed from the name of the device concatenated with the name of the basic routine. If your device driver does not have some of the optional routines, delete references to those routines from the block.

The next thing to do is modify the appropriate device switch to include your device driver. It is at this point that the driver will become associated with a major device number.

There are two device switches: one for character devices, called *cdevsw*, and one for block devices, called *bdevsw*. If your new device will use a character device file, modify the character device switch; if it uses a block device file, modify the block device switch. Devices that may use either should have entries in both switches.

Each of these device switches is a structure that contains the name of all the appropriate control routines for a given device. Each slot in the switch holds a fixed number of names, and there are as many slots in the switch as there can be major device numbers.

The first few lines of the character device switch look something like this:

```
struct cdevsw          cdevsw[] =
{
    {
            cnopen,    cnclose,   cnread,    cnwrite,   /*0*/
            cnioctl,   nulldev,   nulldev,   &cons,
            cnselect,  0,         0,
    },
    {
            nodev,     nodev,     nodev,     nodev,     /*1*/
            nodev,     nodev,     nodev,     0,
            nodev,     0,         0,
    },

            .  .  .  .
```

The first two lines initiate the declaration of the entire switch, and each subsequent group of five lines gives information about one driver. Notice the numbers enclosed between /* and */: these are comments that tell you the major device number of the set being declared. Major device numbers are determined by offsets into the switch, so this numbering is implicit in the format.

What you need to do next is find a set that contains only null declarations. Something that looks like the preceding second set is what you are looking for, but it is much better to take one near the end rather than the beginning, because there may be obscure reasons why an early slot was left unused in the first place. It is also possible on some systems to extend the device switches by simply adding new entries. If you have to do this, that's OK; try to avoid it if possible, though.

Once you've staked out your territory, replace the "nodev"s with the names of your device driver's routines. You must put the routines into the switch in the correct order; look at other entries of the switch to determine what this is. If your driver does not support a particular routine, put the name "nulldev" into the spot where the routine name would have gone.

7.3.4.6 Make the device files in /dev

The last thing to do is make the device files themselves. The files in /dev are used during bootstrapping autoconfiguration to figure out what devices are really connected and what aren't. If you make all the other appropriate entries but neglect the device files, the driver won't be able to autoconfigure and the device will be unusable.

The MAKEDEV script usually found in /dev for making the standard devices won't work for a totally new device. You can modify it to include your new device or use the **mknod** command by hand, making sure that the major and minor device numbers and device names you use are the same as you used in the device switches and configuration files.

7.3.4.7 Install the hardware as for the known devices

The hardware installation procedure is the same as for known devices. Be sure to check the manufacturer's documentation for debugging procedures and hints.

7.4 Specifics per machine

In this section, some of the specific considerations for a particular brand of host computer are covered. These facts are organized by hardware type.

7.4.1 Vaxen

The Unibus on a Vax is not keyed, and so it is possible to put the boards in backwards. (Don't ask how we know!) There are little invisible labels that tell you the board is backwards after you have fried it. A Vax is not likely to have a totally empty Unibus cabinet, but an IBM 4381 that wants to go on the network uses a DEC Unibus on a channel adapter to house the Ethernet board. That Unibus part arrives from IBM empty and without documentation.

The Unibus, like many other busses, requires continuity through the bus slots that do not have boards installed. DEC supplies a small (2 inch square) card called a flip chip for maintaining continuity through empty slots on the bus. Unfortunately, few system administrators have hands that are the thickness of a Unibus slot, so in order to install one of these cards either adjacent boards must be pulled or the administrator's hands get all cut up from the backside of nearby boards. DEC now has tall versions of these flip chips, and installation of the new type is trivial.

The Unibus on Vax computers assumes that no installed devices will have the ability to do DMA (direct memory access) data transfers. While this was true of early DEC boards, it is the exception today rather than the rule. There is a jumper on the Unibus backplane, called the NPG jumper (nonprocessor grant), between pins CA1 and CB1, which disables DMA transfers. In order to install a DMA board, this jumper must be removed with a wire-wrap tool. Once you have found it, mark the jumper wire with a red magic marker for each of the backplane slots (usually nine), so that the job of finding the proper two pins from among the 2268 on the backplane is only done once.

If a board is removed from a slot that has had the DMA jumper removed, the jumper must be replaced. DEC used to use little jumper wires that slid onto the pins on the backplane. Now there are tall continuity cards that also reinstall the DMA jumper.

It is not uncommon for boards on the Unibus, especially boards from DEC, to fit in a single slot, yet require the two adjacent slots to be empty for proper cooling and air flow. This fact must be taken into consideration when planning the addition of Unibus peripherals. DEC boards are also notorious power hogs. A Unibus with a UDA50 disk controller and a couple of DMF32 8 port terminal interfaces has only three or four of the nine slots filled, but all the power (+5 volts) is gone.

7.4.2 Pyramids

The bus priority is determined on a Pyramid by the slot number; thus not all slots are created equal. In fact, certain boards must be in specific slots. Consult your Pyramid customer engineer for the exact specification.

Memory boards contain dip switches that specify the starting address for the first location of memory on the board. Older pyramids required the more dense boards first (lower addresses), followed by less dense boards. Early memory boards have a wire crossed that makes the addressing sequence not quite straightforward; very careful attention to the instructions is required.

Hardware is configured by the system support processor, which controls what microcode to download. The configuration is written to a floppy that is read during the boot process. Tools are provided to add new standard devices to the floppy, but adding totally new and strange devices requires that the microcode to download be provided as well.

7.4.3 Suns

The continuity on the bus of the Sun 3/160, 3/260, and 4/260 workstations is controlled by jumpers inside the front pull-down door of the chassis. The Sun hardware installation manual details which jumpers to pull for which types of board. This means you cannot in general move boards from slot to slot without also adjusting the jumpers.

The manual contains seemingly contradictory information about which bus slot each peripheral board should go into. The only slot/device mapping that is mandatory is slot 7, which must house the SCSI disk/tape interface board.

The terminal interface board can go anywhere, but unless it is placed in the last slot it doesn't fit very well. Its distribution faceplate is wider than a single slot, so the last two slots are usually used for this board.

7.4.4 HP Bobcats

HP uses "select codes," which are the equivalent of major device numbers. Dip switches on each board control the select code value, which is preset to a factory default, but can and sometimes must be changed. The HP System Administrator's Manual describes appropriate values and how to set them. It is a good idea to record the select code on the label attached to the outside of each board.

Memory boards have dip switches for setting the starting addresses. The proper settings can be looked up in the hardware manuals on memory, or can be determined using a circular memory configuration chart supplied with each system. This simple device is two circular pieces of paper resembling a star-finder chart. You enter the current memory configuration and the size of the board you want to add. It then tells you the proper dip switch settings to accomplish it.

7.4.5 IBM RT's under AIX

The IBM RT offers either a very solid and honest port of 4.3BSD, or AIX, which is based on an Interactive Systems port of ATT UNIX. AIX actually runs on top of an IBM low-level system called VRM (Virtual Resource Manager). AIX handles devices a bit differently than either ATT or BSD UNIX. They are defined with the **devices** command. The major device number is constant for a given device type, such as disks or terminals, independent of the actual interface that the device is attached to. Minor device numbers are assigned sequentially and can jump around from interface to interface at random.

7.5 Testing and debugging

The final test of any new hardware installation is to see the device working as advertised. But sometimes devices do not come up right away. Details of troubleshooting particular devices are covered in the chapters on installing those devices. The manufacturer's hardware manual often contains debugging procedures.

8

Configuring the Kernel

8.1 An overview of the kernel

Most of the operations performed by system administrators don't really have that much to do with the UNIX operating system itself — rather, they deal with what has come to be known as the "UNIX programming environment." The distinction between these two is important to make. The operating system is the traffic cop of a UNIX system, the foundation upon which the user environment is built. It is responsible for creating, scheduling, and terminating all processes, managing the system's hardware, keeping track of the filesystem, and performing many other critical functions.

The operating system is just a program like any other. This program is called the *kernel*, and is unlike normal programs in several very important respects. For one thing, the kernel runs completely outside of the UNIX environment. You can't find it in a **ps** listing and you can't run it from the shell. It doesn't have a current working directory, or a umask, or an owner, or a process id, or any of the other standard features. These abstractions are not directly meaningful to computer hardware; it is up to the kernel to define them and to implement them.

Every time a process opens a file, it is asking the kernel to go out and find the file on the disk, buffer it in memory, and be ready to modify its contents. Every time a process duplicates itself, it is asking the kernel to do the real work of creating and maintaining a new set of process records, copying the data areas, and arranging for the newly created process to get access to the CPU and hardware devices. Processes can do very little on their own.

The kernel uses device drivers in much the same way that UNIX processes use the kernel. Processes issue high-level requests ("open this file") which the kernel translates into a sequence of lower-level requests ("get block 25,348 from device 3") for the device drivers to carry out.

The kernel is written mostly in C with a little assembly language thrown in for low-level processing. The kernel is not really a large program. The compiled size of the kernel is usually well under half a megabyte. Compared with something like the **emacs** editor (which in some implementations runs upwards of 700K), the UNIX kernel is quite modest.

8.2 Your role in building the kernel

All you have to do as an administrator is tweak a few of your kernel's operational parameters and tell it about the hardware you are using. After this initial configuration your kernel should require no further maintenance until you have to upgrade your operating system or add a new device driver.

Like other C programs, the kernel is usually compiled and installed using the **make** command. When you build a new kernel, **make** will take care of most of the actual steps in the compilation process for you, using configuration information you provide in a text file. Most Unices supply a program that reads the kernel configuration file you supply and then whips up the appropriate **make** control file and instantiates all the necessary support files for your particular kernel. This program is called **config** on both BSD and ATT systems.

8.2.1 Binary versus source

Most UNIX distributions contain only compiled versions of the source files that comprise the kernel and do not include the actual kernel source code. UNIX was originally developed by Dennis Ritchie and Ken Thompson at AT&T, so all UNIX kernels are proprietary to AT&T to some extent. Most are also proprietary to the manufacturer of the individual system, since the changes to the kernel needed to make UNIX run on a new machine are not insignificant. Some manufacturers are willing to provide the kernel source for their machines (for a price), provided that you can guarantee its security and confidentiality. You must have an AT&T source license to buy source code for any version of UNIX.

The process of building a kernel is pretty much the same whether you have a source code or binary distribution, but the object-only distribution implies less flexibility. Some vendors are better than others at making binary distributions flexible and allowing you to adjust system parameters.

If you have a source code distribution, you may occasionally wish to install patches to the kernel to fix bugs. Some manufacturers periodically rerelease updated kernels, while others supply instructions for making the fixes yourself. Kernel patches may also originate from other sources such as local user groups and Usenet (see Chapter 17: *News*). If the source of a kernel patch is not the manufacturer, you should not apply it blindly without first trying to understand what it entails.

8.3 When to configure the kernel

There are only a few situations in which kernel reconfiguration is necessary. The following sections describe the three most common ones.

8.3.1 The initial kernel

You should reconfigure the kernel every time you bring up a new machine and every time you upgrade the operating system. Most versions of UNIX come with a generic kernel already configured. You will usually be supplied with both a generic configuration file and an executable kernel.

The generic kernel probably works just fine with your system, but you should reconfigure for reasons of efficiency. Generic kernels are designed to cope with any kind of hardware you might care to attach to your new system. They often include *all* of the commonly used device drivers available on your system, all the pseudo-devices, and most of the kernel options. This makes them flexible, but *big*. Initial reconfiguration is therefore a process of getting rid of extra baggage, removing drivers for devices you don't have, and eliminating options that you don't want to use. Once you strip out all the unused material, your kernel will be a lean, mean fighting machine.

8.3.2 Adding device drivers

You must reconfigure the kernel every time you add a new device driver. As you know from Chapter 7, adding a new device to your system requires that a driver for the device be included in your system's kernel. The device driver code can't just be mooshed onto the side of your kernel like a gob of Play-Doh — it has to be integrated into the kernel's device data structures. This requires that you go all the way back to the configuration files for the kernel and add in the new device, rebuilding the kernel from scratch. It does not, however, require that you have source code for the operating system.

8.3.3 Tuning table sizes

The kernel runs in constant space. When you boot the system, the kernel figures out the number of process table slots, filesystem buffers, and file table entries to allocate, then goes out and scarfs up the appropriate amount of memory to hold these.

You cannot use more process table slots or open more files than the kernel is configured for. When you operate with too few table entries free the system will behave inconsistently: The shell will sometimes be unable to execute commands, periodic daemons will never get off the ground, and attempts to open files will fail at arbitrary times. This situation can occur because there are too many simultaneous users, or even because of a few high-activity processes. Reconfiguring the kernel is only a short-term solution, as the extra memory taken up by the bloated kernel tables will reduce overall performance of the system.

Conversely, there is no point in wasting good memory space storing table slots that will never be used. While having lots of extra slots does reduce the amount of time the kernel will spend searching for free buffers and such, the law of diminishing returns soon comes into play. The solution is the same: reconfigure.

8.4 Configuring and building the BSD kernel

Both BSD and ATT kernels are fairly easy to configure. The configuration processes are completely different, but the ideas behind them are pretty much the same. The ATT construction process is covered later in this chapter.

8.4.1 A scenic tour of the kernel construction site

The files used in building a BSD kernel all lie beneath the directory /usr/sys, which is usually symbolically linked to /sys. In the following discussion we will use the uppercase name SYS to refer to this directory, just to emphasize that it doesn't really matter where it is located. If you cannot find the kernel configuration directory for your machine, consult the manuals that came with your system.

The following is the output from an **ls -F** of the 4.3BSD SYS directory of a Vax 11/785:

```
BOULDER/      conf/     machine/   netns/    vaxmba/
consolerl/    mdec/     stand/     vaxuba/   vaxif/
GENERIC/      dist/     net/       sys/
SIGI/         floppy/   netimp/    vax/
cassette/     h/        netinet/
```

Note that some directories have uppercase names. This convention identifies directories that are compilation areas for particular kernels. Each kernel configuration has a name, and the name of the kernel is the same as the name of its compilation directory. The most common naming convention is to simply name kernels after the machine they run on, but any convention will work as long as it helps you keep things straight. The GENERIC directory was provided with the operating system and contains control information for a generic kernel.

Another important directory in the SYS area is "conf". It is in this directory that the actual kernel configuration files are kept, one file to a kernel.

The rest of the directories in SYS contain various parts of the kernel. Figure 8.1 should give you a general idea of what goes where. When you build a new kernel the **config** program will handle all of these other directories for you, so you don't need to examine them unless you want to.

FIGURE 8.1

Some subdirectories of SYS	
Name of directory	Contents
SYS/cassette	Directory used when building boot cassettes (11/730 and 11/750)
SYS/consolerl	Used for making boot rl disks (Vax 8xxx)
SYS/dist	Scripts, programs, and required files for boot tapes
SYS/floppy	Used for making boot floppies
SYS/h	Copies of all kernel header files, most are also in /usr/include/sys
SYS/machine	Machine-dependent parts of the basic kernel
SYS/mdec	Boot-block program code
SYS/net	Kernel files for control of network hardware interfaces
SYS/netimp	ARPANET driver code
SYS/netinet	Protocol handlers for Internet networking
SYS/netns	Xerox NS protocol code
SYS/stand	Standalone code, diagnostics, mini-UNIX, etc.
SYS/sys	Machine-independent portions of the UNIX kernel
SYS/vax	Machine-dependent code
SYS/vaxif	Network interface device drivers
SYS/vaxmba	Massbus device drivers
SYS/vaxuba	Unibus device drivers

8.4.2 The kernel construction process

Building a new kernel is a nine-step process:

- Audit the system's hardware
- Create and edit the kernel's configuration file in SYS/conf
- Create the kernel's control directory in SYS
- Run the **config** program from the conf directory

- Run **make depend** to build the #include file dependencies
- Run **make** *kernel-name* in the kernel's control directory
- Archive the old kernel and install the new one
- Test and debug the new kernel
- Document the new kernel

8.4.3 Audit your system's hardware

Before you can configure a kernel, you need to know what devices it must handle. Take a hardware inventory of your system. Make a list of the devices connected to the computer, including:

- Terminal interfaces
- Disk drives and their controllers
- Tape drives and their controllers
- Network interfaces
- Coprocessors (encryption chips, graphics processors, etc.)
- Frame buffers
- Mice

8.4.4 Build the kernel's configuration file in SYS/conf

Once you know how you want your kernel configured, you must put this information into a form that the **config** program can understand. To do this, you will create a single configuration file in the SYS/conf directory. The file that you create should have the same name as the kernel you are configuring. This can be the name of the machine destined to run to the kernel, or the name of a class of machines if more than one machine is to run the same kernel. The name can be any valid filename, but should be descriptive enough so that a stranger to your SYS directory can tell what each kernel is for.

You can create your configuration file from scratch if you like, but it's much easier to make changes to a copy of an existing configuration file. The GENERIC configuration file will contain almost everything that can possibly be crammed into a configuration file, so adapting it is mostly a matter of gouging out the unwanted parts.

If you get stuck on something related to the configuration file and can't figure it out from the material here, you should refer to the SMM (System Manager's Manual) documentation for **config**.

The kernel configuration file is a list of control phrases, one per line. Any line beginning with a tab character is considered a continuation of the previous line. Anything between a hash mark ("#") and the end of a line is considered a comment, and blank lines are ignored. Keywords must be separated by white space, but except for this and the special meaning of tabs as continuation characters, spaces and tabs are ignored.

Any words in the configuration file that are integers may be entered in decimal, octal, or hexadecimal notation, using the standard C syntax. Octal numbers are identified by a leading zero, and hexadecimal numbers by a leading "0x". Arguments must be double quoted if they contain numbers used as part of a text string rather than for their actual numeric value.

A control phrase begins with a single keyword that indicates how the remainder of the line is to be interpreted. The rest of the fields within the phrase constitute arguments to the keyword. Some keywords can accept a list of arguments separated by spaces or commas, but it is wise to use only one keyword/argument pair per phrase. Most keywords that can accept multiple argument sets can have arbitrarily many control lines.

The order in which the types of control phrases appear is usually not important, but there is a traditional order:

- Set the machine type (the *machine* keyword)
- Set the CPU type (the *cpu* keyword)
- Identify the kernel (the *ident* keyword)
- Set the timezone (the *timezone* keyword)
- Set the kernel's internal table sizes (the *maxusers* keyword)
- Set the compilation options (the *options* keyword)
- Locate the root and swap areas (the *config* keyword)
- Declare devices with controllers (the *controller*, *disk*, and *tape* keywords)
- Declare devices without controllers (the *device* keyword)
- Declare pseudo-devices (the *pseudo-device* keyword)

8.4.4.1 The *machine* keyword

The *machine* keyword sets the type of machine that the kernel is destined to be run on. Only one machine type may be specified in the configuration file. On Vax systems the argument to the *machine* keyword is usually just "vax", and on Sun systems it is something like "sun2" or "sun3", depending on what series machines you are running. Remember that since this argument is just a name it must be enclosed in double quotes if it contains any numbers.

Note the generality of the *machine* keyword. It does not specify anything about the particular variety or configuration of the machine the kernel will be run on; rather, it is kind of a brand name identification that helps **config** to home in on the machine's general architecture and locate the correct list of kernel files to be used.

8.4.4.2 The *cpu* keyword

The *cpu* keyword enumerates the CPU types that the kernel will be run on. Unlike *machine*, *cpu* can accept many arguments. This syntax is somewhat misleading; as it implies that a kernel can be built to run on two different CPU's. This is untrue. Only CPU's that are binary-compatible can run the same kernel. We recommend specifying only a single CPU type. Other, binary-compatible machines should have their own kernels. If you absolutely must specify more than one CPU, at least put only one on each line. The phrase

```
cpu             "SUN3_160","SUN3_50"
```

is equivalent to the phrases

```
cpu             "SUN3_160"
cpu             "SUN3_50"
```

To determine the code for your particular CPU, look in the GENERIC configuration file or your system's manual page for **config**.

8.4.4.3 The *indent* keyword

The *ident* keyword sets the name of the kernel. This should be the same as the name of the configuration file.[1] The kernel identification is compiled into the kernel, so it can prove useful in identifying UFK's.[2]

Most kernels are maintained under SCCS (Source Code Control System), so a better way of identifying kernels is to use the **what** command. For example, **what /vmunix** on one of our Vaxen produces the output:

```
/vmunix
  4.3 BSD #16: Tue Jul  7 19:57:44 MDT 1989 (forys@sigi:/usr/sys/SIGI)
  Copyright (c) 1980, 1986 Regents of the University of California.
```

If your kernel is maintained using an alternative source code management system such as RCS (Revision Control System), the command to identify the kernel will be different (**ident** under RCS, for example).

Don't forget to quote kernel names that have numbers in them.

[1] **config** looks for a SYS/conf/files.*kernel-name* file that lists additional, nonstandard source files that should be compiled into the kernel. This feature is useful for various types of hackery, but you probably won't have occasion to use it.

[2] Unidentified Flying Kernels, of course.

8.4.4.4 The timezone keyword

timezone is used to set the timezone in which the computer lives. Like most time-sensitive systems, UNIX keeps track of time using Greenwich Mean Time. Login and logout times, file modification dates, and system boot records are all kept as seconds and microseconds since midnight, January 1, 1970 GMT. Users hardly ever see these raw times, however. Since the kernel knows its timezone, administrative duties never *ever* need to be carried out in GMT. Local time is always the right way to go.

The argument to **timezone** is the number of hours *west* of (i.e., earlier than) Greenwich, England that your system lives. Timezones east of Greenwich must be entered as negative numbers. There are four timezones in the continental United States, ranging from Eastern Standard Time (five hours west of Greenwich) to Pacific Standard Time (eight hours west of Greenwich).

FIGURE 8.2

Timezone computation algorithms in 4.3 BSD	
Algorithm	Appropriate for
0	No daylight saving time
1	United States
2	Australia
3	Western Europe
4	Middle Europe
5	Eastern Europe
6	Canada

timezone may also take as second and third arguments the word "dst" and an optional number which specifies an algorithm for computing daylight saving time. If the "dst" keyword alone is specified, an algorithm is selected for you based on your timezone. Figure 8.2 lists the available algorithms.

On some systems, the **zic** program is used to specify timezone data. This system is more complicated than the one just described, but it allows nonstandard kinds of daylight saving time to be used. Tasmania, for example, does not fall into any of the categories in Figure 8.2.

8.4.4.5 The maxusers keyword

The *maxusers* keyword sets the sizes of several important system tables. As its name suggests, the argument to *maxusers* is analogous to the maximum number of simultaneous users that the system is expected to support. This name is slightly misleading since UNIX doesn't actually enforce a limit on the number of users. In general, you should increment maxusers by one for each real user you expect to be simultaneously logged on and, if you are configuring the kernel for a network disk server, for each client machine. And add two for each frame buffer on which a windowing system can be run.

Figure 8.3 shows some formulas that are used to determine table sizes for a given value of maxusers.

FIGURE 8.3

Formulas used to determine system table sizes	
Item to be sized	Formula
Maximum number of processes	20 + 8 * MAXUSERS
Maximum number of active shared texts	36 + MAXUSERS
Maximum number of active files	68 + 9 * MAXUSERS
Number of system file table entries	32 + (8/5) * (36 + 9 * MAXUSERS)
Number of callout structures	36 + 8 * MAXUSERS
Number of clist structures	60 + 12 * MAXUSERS
Number of quota structures	3 + (9/7) * MAXUSERS
System page table size (in pages)	20 + MAXUSERS

All of these calculations are enumerated in the file SYS/conf/param.c, a private copy of which is made in the control directory for each kernel when **config** is run. If you want to modify these formulas, use the kernel's private copy of param.c *after* running **config** — never modify the master copy.

The formulas shown in Figure 8.3 have been boosted on some systems to accommodate the heavy loads imposed by windowing systems or large databases. This should be taken into account when determining a value of *maxusers*.

The **pstat -T** command can be used to examine the size and utilization of the current kernel tables. This use of **pstat** is discussed in Chapter 23: *Monitoring the System*.

8.4.4.6 The *options* keyword

The *options* keyword is a catch-all for any kind of special option that can be exercised when building the kernel. Clauses asserted in an *options* control phrase become variables that are defined for the C preprocessor during compilation of the kernel. Thus, *options* can be regarded as a conduit through which the compilation of the kernel can be directly influenced.

The *options* keyword can be used even at binary-only sites because the source and header files for the routines that glue the different parts of the kernel together are distributed even if the meatier kernel sources aren't. Some options are incompatible or mutually exclusive, however; the tell-tale sign of this type of error is the appearance of error messages indicating that something has been multiply defined or redefined at compile time.

Since arguments to *options* are really C preprocessor tokens, they may be of two forms. In the first form tokens are defined but given no particular value. These tokens are used to specify whether an option is on or off using the preprocessor directives #ifdef and #ifndef. If a token is supplied as an argument to *options*, then the corresponding preprocessor symbol is defined and the option is enabled. For example, the phrase to include quotas in the kernel is:

```
options  QUOTA
```

The second form of argument to *options* not only defines a symbol but also gives it a particular value. This type of symbol is not usually checked for with #ifdef. Instead, the symbol is used as if it were a constant, and the C preprocessor makes the appropriate substitution wherever it appears. When this type of symbol is declared in the configuration file, the syntax SYMBOL="VALUE" must be used. Every instance of a reference to SYMBOL will be replaced with VALUE in the kernel source code.

If a symbol is likely to be redefined inside the config file, its value will usually be assigned to a statically initialized variable inside the actual source code. This way, instead of having all references to its value hard-coded into the kernel, the value is placed in a single location where it is later referenced as the kernel runs. The values of these options can then be tuned with **adb** without having to recompile the kernel all over again. We'll talk about **adb** later in the chapter.

For example, one use of this second kind of argument is to modify the default value of MAXDSIZ, the maximum amount of virtual memory that may be allocated to the data segment of a single process. A line such as

```
options  MAXDSIZ="(64*1024*1024)"
```

sets this parameter at a value of 64 megabytes.

Because there are literally hundreds of preprocessor symbols used within the kernel we won't list them all here. Don't despair, though, only a few of the options are in common use. A complete list of options should be provided by your manufacturer.

The QUOTA option

The most common kernel option under BSD is probably QUOTA, which asks that code to limit each user's disk space be included in the kernel. QUOTA does not need to be assigned a value. Compiling quota support into the kernel is just the very beginning of a successful quota regime – the rest of the story on quotas is told in Chapter 22: *Quotas and OS Limits*.

The INET option

If you plan to operate a local area network such as Ethernet you must include the INET option, which requests kernel support for the standard Internet networking protocols. Like QUOTA, INET does not need to be assigned a value. Binary-only distributions may require that the INET option be used even if no network is to be installed. When you enable INET, you should also activate the pseudo-devices "loop" and "ether".

Note that the INET option does not request any kind of *hardware* support for your network; that comes later in the configuration file.

The NS option

In the same way that INET draws Internet protocols into the kernel, NS includes the Xerox NS (XNS) protocols.

The COMPAT option

If the kernel is built with the COMPAT option, the system will be able to run executables programmed and compiled under 4.1BSD as well as the normal 4.2 and 4.3 binaries. This option really isn't that useful unless you have a lot of old programs for which you seem to have misplaced the source code or which you are unwilling to port. New systems should have no use for it at all.

Beware! COMPAT provides only kernel-level compatibility and does not magically make your system able to run executables from incompatible, older hardware.

COMPAT does not need to be assigned a value.

The CMASK option

This is the systemwide default **umask** value. On most systems the default is 022. **umask** values are most conveniently specified in octal notation, as in:

```
options  CMASK="0027"
```

The most secure value of CMASK is 077; the most liberal is 000. Do not block any permissions for the owner of the file.

The MAXDSIZ and MAXTSIZ options

These options set the absolute maximum data and text segment sizes for all processes. MAXTSIZ usually defaults to 6 megabytes, and MAXDSIZ usually defaults to 17 megabytes. MAXTSIZ may be adjusted to any arbitrary number, but may never be larger than MAXDSIZ. MAXDSIZ can only assume values of 17 megabytes, 33 megabytes, and 64 megabytes on some systems.

Since these options require values, the second form of the syntax must be used when setting them. For example, to set a text segment size of 10 megabytes and a data segment size of 33 megabytes, the following lines could be used:

```
options  MAXDSIZ="(33 * 1024 * 1024)"
options  MAXTSIZ="(10 * 1024 * 1024)"
```

The values to be assigned to these two symbols are quoted not because the numbers inside are used as text, but because the second form of syntax requires them.

It is unlikely that you will need to change the default values of these options unless you plan to run extremely large programs (like LISP) on your system. In keeping with the permissive UNIX philosophy, you probably should not lower them. Processes that attempt to exceed the default limits are rare and should be dealt with on a case-by-case basis if they cause problems.

The GATEWAY option

The GATEWAY option should be used on machines that have more than one network interface and are intended to perform Internet routing and forwarding functions. This option currently has only minor ramifications; it increases the size of some internal networking structures so that they can cope with the expected load and provides for special network behavior if one of the network interfaces becomes nonfunctional. The GATEWAY option is now obsolete in some systems.

The NSIP option

The NSIP option can only be invoked when both INET and NS are present. This option provides a method of encapsulating XNS packets inside IP (Internet Protocol) packets for transmission through network gateways.

The TCP_COMPAT_42 option

This option is only applicable to 4.3BSD systems with INET installed. Because of a bug in 4.2BSD, there are problems with TCP connections between machines running 4.2BSD and 4.3BSD. The TCP_COMPAT_42 option will instruct the 4.3BSD TCP software to ignore the checksums on packets originating at 4.2 hosts. Since the name of this option contains numbers, it must be double quoted in the configuration file.

The IPFORWARDING and IPSENDREDIRECTS options

The IPFORWARDING option can be used to disable the packet forwarding functions of IP. By default, this option has a value of one – setting it to zero will disable it. In cases where IPFORWARDING is not disabled, the IPSENDREDIRECTS option instructs the IP software to correct other machines' notions of the network's connectivity if it discovers it is being asked to forward packets that do not require the intervention of a forwarding host. IPSENDREDIRECTS does not take any value.

Since it is almost always desirable to have IP do packet forwarding and since the network routing daemons do a pretty good job of figuring out the structure of the network, neither of these options is commonly used.

The THREEWAYSHAKE option

This option affects the operation of XNS. If it is present in the configuration file, NS connections will use a souped-up version of the standard handshake. The reliability of most network operations is quite high, so this option is usually not necessary.

8.4.4.7 The *config* keyword

config is used to specify the location of the root partition, crash dump area, and swapping/paging areas on the system's disks.

As you know from Chapter 4, the root partition is the top level of the UNIX filesystem and contains the directory / and several other important files and directories as well. There is a kind of chicken and egg problem here – the filesystem mounting information is in /etc/fstab, but UNIX can't get to it until the root partition is mounted, which it can't do unless it knows where it is, which it normally would find out from /etc/fstab, but it can't get to /etc/fstab... etc. To remedy this, information about the disk partition that holds the root filesystem must be compiled into the kernel.

The situation for swapping is not quite as dire, since it is unlikely that the kernel will have to begin paging until the /etc/rc scripts have completed their enumeration of the swapping areas with the **swapon** command. While the syntax of **swapon** suggests that swapping may be initiated on any partition, this is not the case. Only those swapping partitions actually configured into the kernel may be swapped on.

When a UNIX process encounters some kind of fault, the kernel usually dumps an image of the process's address space into a file named "core" in its current directory. This is nice because a human can come along later and examine the core file with **adb** or some other debugger and try to determine what went wrong. The kernel can't do this for itself, for several reasons.

First of all, it doesn't have a current directory to dump to. The root partition might be a sensible place to put a dump, but normally it isn't big enough to hold a complete image of the running kernel. Another reason why the kernel doesn't dump core is that it doesn't trust itself to correctly handle the filesystem after a catastrophic error – it could do an awful lot of damage if its internal data tables were scrambled.

To remedy this situation, the kernel will dump an image of itself to one of the swap partitions. It puts this core image at the very end of the partition so that it is not likely to be overwritten if the image is read and copied soon after the system is rebooted. The image saved in the swap partition can be recovered with the **savecore** command. The partition on which to place this core dump needs to be compiled into the kernel so that no hunting need be done for the information under less than ideal circumstances, and so that **savecore** always knows where to look for crash dumps.

We said earlier that each configuration file in the SYS/conf directory represents exactly one kernel. This is a slight lie, because there may be any number of *config* control phrases in the configuration file, and each one represents a kernel that can be built from within the control directory. Since these kernels will differ only in the location of their root, swap, and dump areas it is fair to say that they are "the same kernel," though.

The ability to build these variant kernels can be very handy when your root disk crashes. If you've had the foresight to establish an alternative root partition on another disk and build a duplicate kernel that uses it, you can probably bring the system right up on the other kernel with a minimum of fuss. If your alternative root partition is on the same disk drive or controller as the one that got trashed, you run the risk of destroying it in the same way as the original disk, though: It is wise to verify the stability of your hardware before rebooting.

On some systems a floppy disk or cartridge tape must be prepared to control the boot procedure. This floppy disk knows the location of the kernel and is able to control its invocation. If you maintain an alternative root partition or kernel, you may have to build a new boot floppy to make use of it.

Each *config* control phrase conveys four pieces of information:

- The name of the variant kernel
- The location of the root partition
- The location of the swap partitions
- The partition to use for crash dumps

The kernel's name

The name you give a kernel in its "config" phrase is not the name of the configuration file or the name you specified in the kernel's *ident* phrase. This is the filename that the kernel will appear under when you finish building it with the **make** command. Since the system's kernel must be called /vmunix, you should call your primary kernel "vmunix". Alternative kernels should be named "vmunix" prefixed with the name of the disk their root partition is located on (e.g., "ravmunix").

Location of the root partition

The syntax of this segment is simply "root on *partition-name*" where *partition-name* is a standard UNIX partition such as "xy0a" or "ra1a".

Location of swap partitions

The syntax for this segment is like that for the root partition. Different partitions are separated with the word "and" – to indicate that swapping should be performed on both "xy0b" and "xy1b" you can say "swap on xy0b and xy1b". There may be any number of swap partitions.

It is possible to ask that only a certain portion of a swapping partition be used for swapping activity. To do this, follow the name of the swap partition with the word "size" and the number of disk sectors to be used. If the number you specify is more than the actual size of the partition it will be ignored. There's not much point to restricting the swap area size, since you can't do anything else with the unused space.

Location of crash dumps

The location for kernel core dumps is specified in exactly the same way as the location of the root partition — just substitute "dumps" for "root", as in "dumps on xy1b". If this segment of the specification is omitted, the dump device is assumed to be the first device named in the swap partition specification.

Every time you name a disk partition in the *config* phrase it is possible to underspecify to some extent. If you give a complete disk name without a partition (e.g., "ra0"), the **config** program will fill in a default partition for you. The default is to have the root partition on "a" and swap partitions on "b". If you do not even specify a unit number (e.g., "xy"), then the default partition and disk unit zero are assumed.

The **config** program takes all of these partition names and looks up the devices they refer to in the file SYS/conf/devices.*machine-type*, where *machine-type* is the machine architecture type you gave as an argument to the *machine* keyword. This file maps the device names to the major device numbers of their drivers. Let's look at part of a a sample "devices" file, here the SYS/conf/devices.vax file from a Vax 11/785.

```
hp      0
up      2
hk      3
rk      3
ra      9
```

The left column is a list of device names and the right column is a list of their major device numbers. This file should already be set up for you, but if you do some weird device driver reorganizations, you may have to modify it.

There is also a way that you can specify major and minor device numbers in your configuration file rather than partition names. Instead of saying something like "ra0a" you can say "major 9 minor 0".

The following lines are examples of complete *config* phrases:

```
config     vmunix      root on ra swap on ra0b and ra1b dumps on ra0b
config     hpvmunix    root on major 0 minor 0 swap on major 0 minor 1
```

These lines configure two kernels: one named "vmunix" with default root and swap partitions on ra0 and an extra swap partition on ra1, and one named "hpvmunix" with its root partition on hp0a and its swap (and dump) partition on hp0b.

Before going on, we should mention the existence of an option called "swap generic," which is a method of entering a *config* phrase without having to specify the location of anything. An example control line using this is

```
config     vmunix      swap generic
```

When a "swap generic" kernel is booted you must enter the name of the disk on which the root partition resides on the machine's console. The swap partition is assumed to be the "b" partition of this disk, and dumps are done to this "b" partition as well. This is great if you want to keep a safety kernel that can boot from anywhere around, but not very elegant for a kernel you really intend to use. Some systems don't support this.

There is one other thing about the *config* keyword that we have not mentioned here. This is the ability to designate a particular swap partition as the one to hold arguments to the **execve** system call while processes are in limbo between texts. If you have one especially fast swapping disk you might wish to add something like "args on ra0b" to your *config* line, but otherwise there is no reason to worry about this.

8.4.4.8 The *controller, tape, disk* and *device* keywords

These keywords are used to tell the kernel about what devices are present. Every device must be declared if it is to be used. Declaring a nonexistent device *does* cause the appropriate driver to be included in the kernel as deadweight, however; you should pare down your configuration file until it references only devices that you actually own.

The *controller* keyword is used to designate:

- Disk and tape drive controllers
- Bus interfaces or adapters

The *device* keyword is used to designate:

- Terminal interfaces
- Network interfaces
- Frame buffers and graphics accelerators
- Other devices that do not interface through a controller

The *tape* keyword is used to designate tape drives connected through a tape controller, and the *disk* keyword is used in a similar way for disk drives. On Vaxen, the *master* keyword must be used instead of *controller* for tape controllers connected to the Massbus. This keyword is not found elsewhere, but your system may have equally bizarre vagaries. Take the following instructions with a grain of salt.

The syntax for device specifications is confusing, and the basic entries required to make the system run vary from machine to machine. We will discuss the syntax, but since we expect that you will just be paring down your system's GENERIC configuration for the most part, we won't talk that much about how to write your own device specifications from scratch.

The basic form of a control line using one of these keywords is:

```
keyword    device-name at connection-info csr address
           drive drive-number flags flags
           priority priority-level vector vector-info
```

One or more of the "csr," "drive," "flags," "priority," and "vector" clauses may not be present for a given device, and not all clauses are applicable to all devices. Furthermore, the drive numbers of disks, and sometimes parts of *connection-info*, may be replaced with a question mark, indicating that the system is to be investigated at boot time to determine what values are appropriate.

The device name

The device name is the standard name for the device (usually two or three letters), plus the logical unit number. For example, the device name for the first Unibus adapter on a Vax is "uba0". As you wade through the GENERIC configuration you can look up each device in Section 4 of the UNIX manuals to find out what it is and if it applies to you.

Note that the logical unit number has no relationship to any hardware-specified selection number of the device.

The connection information

The connection information for a device tells the kernel where to find it. For disk and tape drives, this is usually just the name of a controller. For controllers and devices, it is usually the name of a bus or bus controller, or a token to indicate that the device is located on I/O circuitry inside the machine itself. Bus interfaces are configured as controllers, and their connection information is usually the token "nexus" plus a question mark to indicate that the exact connection point of the bus is to be determined at boot time. The term "nexus" only has a literal meaning on Vaxen; on other systems it is a crossover term from the Berkeley Vax distributions.

It is almost always sufficient to state that a device is connected to a particular type of controller without specifying which one. For example, indicating that a disk controller is connected to one of the Unibus adapters on a Vax by giving its connection information as "uba?" will work fine.

The device address

This is the argument to the "csr" keyword. It represents the location of the device's command and status registers in the address space of the bus or backplane to which it is connected. All controllers and devices connected directly to a bus must have this parameter filled in. (On many systems, this address must be entered into the configuration dip switches on the board itself, too.)

Each kind of device has a certain number of address locations that it takes up in the bus address space. When new units of existing devices are added, their csr registers must be contiguous. Thus, if each unit of a particular device type takes eight bytes and the first register set is located at 0160010, the second and third units must be located at 0160020 and 0160030, respectively.

The drive number

This is the logical unit number of a disk or tape drive. If this field is filled in with a question mark, the drive number is determined at boot time. This wildcarding can be useful only if you swap disk drives around frequently; you should fill in actual drive numbers unless there is a specific reason not to.

The flags

The flags for a device are passed on to its driver at boot time without being interpreted by the kernel. This allows configuration information to be smuggled into a driver in much the same way that the *options* keyword allows preprocessor tokens to be sneaked into the kernel compilation environment.

The flags are just a simple integer. Usually this integer is interpreted bit-by-bit. For example, the terminal driver uses the flags on an interface to distinguish between serial ports that must supply soft carrier and those that can expect hard carrier, with one bit being dedicated to each port. See Chapter 9: *Installing Terminals and Modems* for more information about this.

The interrupt priority level

The priority level of a device gives an indication of how pressing interrupts from the device should be considered. Device types usually have standard priorities which should not be readjusted at whim. Some systems do not use the priority keyword.

The interrupt vector information

Some hardware systems, such as Vaxen, use a single channel to handle hardware interrupts. Since interrupts cannot be distinguished by the channel they arrive on, each device must be able to identify itself to the kernel when it signals a hardware exception. This is done using a hardware interrupt vector. Some devices have a single vector (small integer) and others use two, one for transmit and one for receive. Look in the hardware manual that came with your peripheral device to determine the value of the interrupt vector.

The most effective way to start organizing your specifications is to identify the control phrases that declare devices to which nothing else is connected. These outer-level devices include disk and tape drives (but not controllers), terminal interfaces, and networking interfaces. Once the control lines for these devices are found, you can see what other devices they depend on and follow the configurations back to the root of the device hierarchy, the "nexus".

If you do not know the short names for all of your devices, you can use **man -k** with an appropriate keyword to get a listing of all the manual pages with that keyword in their description line. If your keyword is too general you will be deluged with a list of manual pages; if it is too specific you will probably not find any entries at all. If you know the brand name of your hardware that can be a good keyword to look under. Otherwise, use keywords like "streaming" for streaming tape drives and "Ethernet" for network interfaces. You can ignore any manual pages that are not in Section 4.

For example, let's suppose you need to find the names of the nine-track tape drive and the Ethernet interface on a Sun3. The commands shown next actually turn up a few more entries not in Section 4 of the manual, but these have been removed for clarity.

```
% man -k tape
ar (4S)    - Archive 1/4 inch Streaming Tape Drive
mtio (4)   - UNIX system magnetic tape interface
st (4S)    - Driver for Sysgen SC 4000 (Archive)
tm (4S)    - tapemaster 1/2 inch tape drive
xt (4S)    - Xylogics 472 1/2 inch tape controller

% man -k Ethernet
ec (4S)    - 3Com 10 Mb/s Ethernet interface
ie (4S)    - Intel 10 Mb/s Ethernet interface
le (4S)    - Sun-3/50 10 Mb/s Ethernet interface
```

Suppose that "tm" and "ie" are the manual pages we were actually looking for; if an identification cannot be made from the output of **man -k** you may have to read the complete manual pages. If we look at the manual page for "tm" we'll find that "tm" is actually the name of the tape *controller* and not the name of the tape itself; the name of the actual tape drives is "mt".

The kernel configuration entries for these particular devices are:

```
tape      mt0 at tm0 drive 0 flags 1
tape      mt1 at tm1 drive 0 flags 1
device    ie0 at obio ? csr 0xc0000 priority 3
device    ie1 at vme24d16 ? csr 0xe88000 priority 3 vector ieintr 0x75
```

Once the control phrases for these devices have been identified, look at the connection-info field of each phrase to find out on what bus or controller the device depends. Let's look at the Ethernet interface first.

The connection info for "ie0" says that it is at "obio ?". "obio" is a Sun-specific keyword meaning "on-board I/O"; its presence here indicates that the first Ethernet interface is on the CPU board and is not located on any bus or controller. The question mark indicates that nothing more is known about its exact location and that it will have to be probed for at boot time.

The control phrase for "ie1", the second Ethernet interface, indicates that it is connected to something called "vme24d16." We'll cheat by telling you that this means the Sun VMEbus with 24 bits of address and 16 bits of data, but it's possible to do a good configuration job without knowing what the tokens represent.

The entries for the tape drives indicate that they are connected to "controllers called "tm0" and "tm1". We know that in this configuration each controller is only supporting one tape drive; otherwise, the controllers for the two drives would have been the same. Both drives are configured as drive zero for their respective controllers.

Once these relationships have been established, we now need to go back and look up every device and controller that we found something depending on. In this case, we must look up "vme24d16," "obio", "tm0," and "tm1." The control lines for these are:

```
controller    obio 1 at nexus ?
controller    vme24d16 1 at nexus ?
controller    tm0 at vme16d16 ? csr 0xa0 priority 3 vector tmintr 0x60
controller    tm1 at vme16d16 ? csr 0xa2 priority 3 vector tmintr 0x61
```

Both "obio" and "vme24d16" are connected to "nexus": we have reached the end of the dependency chain for these threads.

The tape controllers "tm0" and "tm1" are connected to the bus "vme16d16". Looking this up again in the configuration file, we find:

```
controller    vme16d16 1 at nexus ?
```

which completes our dependency search for these two devices.

Every one of the control phrases found during a dependency search must be included in the ultimate configuration file, or some necessary link will not be made and the device will not be accessible. In addition to configuration lines identified in this way, some machines require a few items to always be declared — these are usually marked in the generic configuration file for you.

The easiest error to make when configuring devices is to "forget" to declare hardware you didn't even know you had. A good example of this is the DES (Data Encryption Standard) hardware chip present on some Suns, used to speed up data encryption operations. It needs to be declared before it can be used, even though it is just a chip on the computer's main board. To forestall any possibility of this happening, glance briefly at the manual page for each device to be sure it does not apply to you.[3]

As a final check, go back to your equipment inventory and be sure that everything listed there has been mentioned in some way in the configuration file.

[3] Due to export regulations, Suns manufactured for export do not have this chip.

8.4.4.9 The *pseudo-device* keyword

Theoretically, pseudo-device drivers are programs that act like device drivers but don't have any real hardware to back them up. We say "theoretically" because some kernel options that masquerade as pseudo-devices do not act like device drivers at all, at least from the user-level point of view. The syntax for pseudo-device control phrases is:

pseudo-device *device-name number-of-instances*

where *device-name* is the name of the pseudo-device and *number-of-instances* is an optional integer telling how many of the imaginary devices the pseudo-device driver is supposed to pretend are present. The number of instances is not meaningful for some drivers. Usage of the instance count is rare.

There are very few pseudo-devices, but most of them are obligatory for correct operation of the system. Some systems have a number of nonstandard pseudo-devices that support windowing systems, extra keyboards, or auxiliary displays — consult the manuals of your system to learn how to deal with these, or simply include all the pseudo-devices from your generic configuration file for a more festive atmosphere.

The pty pseudo-device

pty's are pseudo-terminals. They mimic terminals, but instead of having an actual terminal on one end they are connected to a process. pty's are heavily used by networking programs such as **rlogin** and **rsh**, and they are also used by a few standard utilities such as **script** to do input processing.

The pty driver can accept an instance count which indicates how many pseudo-terminals may be active at any one time. The default is usually 32, more than enough in most circumstances.

The loop pseudo-device

This driver manages software loopback on Ethernet interfaces. When a host is detected attempting to send itself messages on the Ethernet, the communication is aborted and the message is delivered directly to the receiving process. If you enable the INET option, you must also enable loop.

The ether pseudo-device

This pseudo-device is used to include various Ethernet-related material in the kernel. It is required with INET.

The imp pseudo-device

Like "ether", but relating to the "intelligent message processor" hardware used to talk to the ARPANET. Imp must be enabled if you are an ARPANET site.

The ns pseudo-device

This pseudo-device is used in conjunction with the XNS option to enable the Xerox Networking System protocol suite.

8.4.4.10 A sample configuration file

Let's look at a sample configuration file for a very simple kernel. Let's call this kernel EXAMPLE, and set it up appropriately for a Vax 11/780.

```
#
# A sample kernel configuration file for a kernel called EXAMPLE.
#
machine             vax
cpu                 "VAX780"
ident               EXAMPLE
timezone            7 dst
maxusers            32
```

The first two lines of the file set the machine type to be a Vax and assure that the kernel will only be run on a Vax 11/780. The name of the kernel is EXAMPLE, and it is destined for a machine which lives in the timezone seven hours west of Greenwich, in an area that has daylight saving time. This kernel is configured for at most 32 simultaneous users, actually many more than the machine can reasonably handle.

```
options             QUOTA
options             INET
options             GATEWAY
```

Our sample kernel is configured with only two basic options: quotas and Internet networking. The GATEWAY option serves only to help the machine in handling its two separate Ethernet interfaces, between which it is expected to forward packets.

```
config              vmunix root on ra0 swap on ra0 and ra1 dumps on ra1
```

This configuration file specifies only one particular kernel configuration. The root filesystem is located on the "a" partition of the drive "ra0", and the kernel has two swapping areas available to it: the "ra0b" partition and the "ra1b" partition. Since "ra0" appears first in the specification, the "ra0b" partition will be the primary swap area; crash dumps, however, will be done to "ra1b", decreasing the likelihood of their being erased by swapping activity before they can be saved. Note that only the disk names are specified here. The partitions are assigned using the default rules.

```
controller          uba0 at nexus ?
```

This line declares the first and only Unibus adapter of the machine.

```
controller        uda0 at uba? csr 0172150 vector udintr
```

This line declares that a single DEC UDA-50 disk controller is connected somewhere on the Unibus. Note that the bus addresses are usually expressed in octal on the Vax. You should be aware that not all the bits of the address are always significant; for example, the Unibus address space is only 16 bits wide, so the top two bits of a six-digit octal address are not significant. 0172150 could just as well have been written as 0772150.

```
disk              ra0 at uda0 drive 0
disk              ra1 at uda0 drive 1
```

The system has two disk drives, both of which are connected through the UDA-50 controller.

```
device            de0 at uba? csr 0174510 vector deintr
device            de1 at uba? csr 0174520 vector deintr
```

These two lines declare two Ethernet interfaces, both on the Unibus.

```
device            dmf0 at uba? csr 0160340 flags 0xFF
                  vector dmfsrint dmfsxint dmfdaint dmfdbint
                  dmfrint dmfxint dmflint
```

These two lines declare the existence of a DMF-32 eight-line serial terminal interface connected to the Unibus adapter, on which every port has soft carrier.

```
pseudo-device     pty
pseudo-device     ether
pseudo-device     loop
```

These pseudo-devices are necessary for a system with networking.

The configuration just outlined could not actually be used in real life — connecting this much equipment to one Unibus adapter would probably cause a meltdown. Older Unibus adapters are rated for only 25 amps, and even the newer ones can only support 32 amps. The disk controller, Ethernet interfaces, and serial interface draw a combined power load of about 40 amps.

8.4.5 Create the kernel's control directory in SYS

This is easy; just **cd** to your SYS area and do a **mkdir** *kernel-name*.

8.4.6 Run config from the conf directory

When **config** is run, it expects to find the kernel configuration file specified on the command line in the current directory, along with some other information files. Therefore, for **config** to be of any use to you, you must **cd** to your SYS/conf directory before running it. **config** will read the configuration file and place a number of files in the compilation directory which you created in the last step.

Simple versions of **config** take only one argument: the name of the configuration file for your new kernel. Fancier versions have a number of options. **config** is very quiet, so don't be alarmed if nothing seems to be happening. It has a lot of work to do, so it may take up to a minute to complete.

For our example kernel, we would do

```
cd conf
config EXAMPLE
```

Some versions of **config** (for example, Sun's) will do the next step (**make depend**) for you automatically. If you see a message that says "Doing a **make depend**", it is probably safe to skip it. You won't hurt anything by doing it again, though.

If **config** produces error messages, you must go back and fix your configuration file before continuing. If you get through **config** without any errors, you can assume that your configuration was at least syntactically valid and that the kernel compilation can proceed.

8.4.7 Run make depend in the compilation directory

After **config** finishes, **cd** to the *../KERNELNAME* directory for the new kernel and do an **ls**. You should see lots and lots of files. Don't worry about their contents, **config** knows what it's doing.

Now, type **make depend** inside the compilation directory. This will initialize the file dependency information for the upcoming kernel building. This command may produce voluminous output, especially if you have a source distribution.

8.4.8 make the kernel

This is the point at which the new kernel comes into existence. While you are still in the compilation directory, type **make** *kernel*, where *kernel* is the name of one of the configurations you specified with the *config* keyword inside the configuration file. This will usually be "vmunix". If you want to make the kernel that was specified in the first *config* line, you can simply type **make**.

You must watch carefully for error messages during the kernel compilation. **make** will usually detect errors and abort the compilation, but it always helps to be alert. For extra protection, have **make** keep a record of everything that gets output to the terminal with the **tee** command; for example:

```
make vmunix |& tee ERRS.LOG
```

The **&** behind the pipe mark insures that both error messages and status messages will be directed through the pipe. Bourne shell users should precede the pipe mark with the notation **2>&1** to achieve the same effect.

If there is an error during compilation, you should first suspect your configuration file. If you get messages about missing files or undefined routines, you have probably left something out. If you get messages complaining about syntax errors, the fault may be with your configuration file or with the system, although the latter is not likely. Consult your system's manuals or contact your service representative.

8.4.9 Install the new kernel

Before you boot a new kernel, you must take steps to insure that you can back it out if it doesn't work. You must *never ever* replace your old kernel directly with a new one, as that will leave you with nothing to boot from in the event of a catastrophe. If your system supports booting an arbitrary program, you can just **mv** your old /vmunix to something like /vmunix.works, and **cp** your new kernel onto /vmunix.

It is possible to make /vmunix a link to some other filename, so you can actually put the real kernel anywhere within the root filesystem. If the kernel is not called /vmunix and you don't make this link, programs like **ps** and **w** that need to access the kernel's namelist will not work.

Even if this linking strategy doesn't work for you, your system *will* provide some way to keep an old kernel bootable while you test a new one. You must once again return to your system's manuals for specific information.

Do not be in a hurry to get a new kernel shoved into the system. Send mail to the users explaining what is going to happen and when before taking the machine down, preferably a week in advance. The /etc/motd file is a good place to put warnings like this.

8.4.10 Test and debug the new kernel

The next thing to do is boot the new kernel. Before you bring the machine down completely, however, bring it down single-user and use **fsck -p** to clean the root partition of the disk. This may save you some time later if you have problems booting the new kernel.

After this, reboot the machine. If the system comes up you are probably in good shape, but there are a few checks you can try just to make sure. First, do a **ps**. If you get a message that says "no namelist", either the kernel has the wrong name, the permissions on it are set wrong, or something didn't get compiled into the kernel correctly.[4]

Try to **ls** at least one directory in each filesystem. Success indicates that the correct partition tables are in the kernel and that the filesystem is functioning correctly.

If you are unlucky and the new kernel begins its career by erasing the system's hard disks, you should refer to the SMM document on debugging the kernel with **adb**.

Once you are confident that the new kernel will work correctly, you can move the old kernel to your alternative root partition or to somewhere else out of the way.

8.4.11 Document the new kernel

Before you can consider your job completed, you should go back to your original SYS/conf/*KERNELNAME* file and put in copious comments so that you will understand what you have done when you come back to read it six months or a year later. If you have lots of free space, you can go ahead and keep the SYS/*KERNELNAME* directory around to speed up subsequent alterations. If you don't, you can just delete it; there is nothing there that can't be reproduced automatically using **config**.

Finally, send mail to the users of your system describing the changes that have been made.

[4] Never use **strip** on the kernel, as this will remove the symolic information **ps** needs to function properly.

8.5 Modifying the kernel with adb

adb is UNIX's oldest and most traditional debugger. The user interface is horrible and the command syntax is obscure, but what **adb** lacks in charm and charisma it makes up for in competence. It can be used not only for interactively debugging software but also for modifying the permanent contents of quiescent executables. It's this kind of meddling that comes in handy when tuning the kernel.

adb's most useful function is its ability to change the values of autoinitialized variables. If a global variable is declared with a particular initial value, instead of generating code to load in the value automatically at run-time, the C compiler will write that value directly in to the data space image of the executable. When the executable is loaded, the value of that variable will then be preset appropriately.

Many kernel options are just assigned to variables for safekeeping. In these circumstances it is rare for the value of the variable to be changed, and redefining the value of the variable inside the kernel image is equivalent to modifying the options in the configuration file.

Before changing the kernel's image directly, you should consider the associated costs. To begin with, there will be no documentation of the change unless you do it yourself. This may not sound like such a problem, but maintaining documentation for **adb** kernel hacks in such a way that anyone who needs to rebuild the kernel will know to repeat them is difficult. Second, you are bypassing all the safety and consistency checks imposed by the **config** program and the C compiler. In some cases this is exactly the point, but you should be aware of the risks.

There are, however, two situations where **adb** is the tool of choice. The first is when experimenting with a variety of operational parameters to determine what is best for your system. You don't want to go back to the configuration file and go through the whole building process every time you change the value of one variable. Use **adb** to do the experimentation, but as soon as you know what you want you should install the changes permanently in the configuration file. Don't run a production kernel that you can't reproduce by typing **make** somewhere.

The second legitimate use of **adb** is to change the value of options that are not accessible from the configuration file. In some cases the reason you can't make the change properly is that you do not have source code, while in others it is that the variable happens to have been placed outside the purview of **config**.

The best way to begin an **adb** session is to make a copy of /vmunix somewhere where you can work on it. You *could* work on the actual kernel itself, but it is important to keep a backup, since mistakes can easily be made when using **adb**. Assuming that you've called your private copy of the kernel "vmunix", just type **adb -w vmunix** to get into **adb.** The **-w** flag specifies that both reading and writing are to be allowed. (You may wish to dry-run this without the **-w** flag.)

adb will not print anything back to you; this is normal. To examine the current value of a variable, you type the name of the variable, followed immediately by a question mark and one of the letter codes shown in Figure 8.4 to identify the type of the variable.

FIGURE 8.4

adb codes for identifying variable types		
Letter code	Type	Display base
o	short unsigned integer	octal
O	long unsigned integer	octal
q	short signed integer	octal
Q	long signed integer	octal
u	short unsigned integer	decimal
U	long unsigned integer	decimal
d	short signed integer	decimal
D	long signed integer	decimal
x	short unsigned integer	hex
X	long unsigned integer	hex
f	single precision float	decimal
F	double precision float	decimal

Thus, to print the decimal value of a variable called "mbuf_cnt" declared as a long, unsigned integer, the line

mbuf_cnt?U

could be used. This line will produce output something like

```
_mbuf_cnt:
_mbuf_cnt:      42
```

indicating that 42 is the preinitialized value. Changing the value of "mbuf_cnt" is somewhat harder, since **adb** has only two modes of value replacement, both of which use hexadecimal notation. The syntax is similar to that for printing: the name of the variable followed by a question mark, a control letter, and then the new value. The control letter "w" indicates that a two-byte quantity is to be written, and the control letter "W" indicates a four-byte quantity. To set the initial value of "mbuf_cnt" to 69 (45 in base 16), you could use the line:

mbuf_cnt?W45

adb's response to this would be

_mbuf_cnt: 0x2A = 0x45

The value on the left of the equals sign is the old value, and the new value appears on the right. To exit **adb** type <control-D> or "$q".

adb can also be used to modify the variables of the running kernel. The syntax is similar to that preceding, except that the question marks should be replaced with slashes to indicate that the items are to be searched for in the "core file" (here, actually the kernel's address space) rather than the executable file. To initiate an **adb** session on the currently running kernel, the command is **adb -w vmunix /dev/kmem.** Be very careful when **adb**'ing a live kernel, since the slightest mistake can cause the system to crash.

8.6 Adding a totally new device to the kernel

Devices whose drivers come with the manufacturer's distribution of UNIX just need to be included in the kernel configuration file to become part of the kernel. But totally new devices with drivers from third-party sources or homegrown drivers require additional configuration to let the kernel know they exist. The details of adding both brand-new and standard devices are covered in Section 7.3.

8.7 Configuring the ATT kernel

Unlike the BSD kernel, the ATT kernel usually comes with almost no devices configured, and you must add information about all of your system's hardware. Each version of ATT has slightly different procedures for configuring the kernel. As in the preceding section, we will use a Vax as our example machine.

There are five steps to configuring an ATT kernel:

- Edit the kernel Makefile
- Create or modify a description file
- Run **config** to create the description code
- Make the new kernel
- Install and test the new kernel

The files required to build a new kernel are usually located either in /usr/src/uts/cf or in /usr/src/uts/*machine*/cf, where *machine* is the type of machine that the kernel is destined to be run on. From now on, this directory will be referred to as the CONF directory.

8.7.1 Edit the kernel Makefile

The CONF directory contains a **make** control file (Makefile) that is used to build new kernels. This Makefile uses several internal variables that affect the naming of the kernel. You should change these variables to whatever is appropriate for your site. The values you assign cannot exceed eight characters in length.

The SYS variable

This is the hostname of the machine for which the kernel is being built. For example, "boulder", "sigi", or "tigger".

The NODE variable

This is the uucp name of the system. NODE is almost always given the same value as SYS; we have no idea why anyone would want to introduce unnecessary confusion by using two different names.

The REL variable

REL specifies the release number of the operating system; for example, "5.3". There is no need to change this parameter.

The VER variable

This is the version of the kernel being built, which is separate from the release number set with the REL variable. The kernel version is for your convenience in identifying various kernels. A common naming convention is to use the date that the kernel was configured as the version name. For example, "070489" might identify a kernel created on July 4, 1989. Descriptive names, such as "addrp06" for a kernel with an additional rp06 drive, are also common.

While the VER variable can be set inside the Makefile itself, it is more common to see it set on the **make** command line using the **-D** (define variable) flag. This is because all the kernels that you build share a single Makefile. It is easier not to modify this central file each time you build a new version of the kernel.

The MACH variable

This is the hardware name of the machine; for example, "vax-780". This parameter should not need to be changed.

The name for the new kernel is formed by concatenating the SYS and VER variables. Thus, a kernel named from the preceding examples might be called "boulder070487". The new kernel will be compiled into the CONF directory.

8.7.2 The description file

The kernel description file contains entries describing each peripheral attached to your system and setting various kernel parameters. The **config** program reads the description file and creates several (usually two) C programs that are compiled into the kernel. The description file resides in the CONF directory, and can be named anything.

Most systems come with a generic or example description file. You can either adapt one of these, or you can use the description file used to build the existing kernel, if there is one. If you cannot find a suitable description file, the **sysdef** command can be used to create a description file based on the current kernel.

The ability to name the description file in an unrestricted way has led to many abuses, so you may have to poke around in the CONF directory to find these files. To make it easy to find your description file, we suggest that you name it after your system name, as set with the Makefile SYS variable, spelled in capital letters. For the preceding example, the description file would be named BOULDER.

Any line in the configuration file that begins with an asterisk ("*") is considered a comment.

The first section of the description file describes the devices connected to the system. Each line describes one device, and has the following format:

> *devname vector address bus number nexus*

The first four parameters are mandatory.

devname is the name of the device as it appears in the /etc/master (see the description of /etc/master in your manuals) device table. *vector* is the address of the device's interrupt vector, in octal, and, *address* is the address of the device, also in octal. *bus* is the bus request level or priority of the device. Most devices have standard priorities that should not be changed arbitrarily. *number* is the number of devices associated with the given controller, in decimal. If *number* is not specified, it defaults to the maximum number of devices that the controller can handle. *nexus* is the number of the Unibus adapter to which the controller is connected. If *nexus* is not specified, it defaults to whatever is appropriate for the machine. If *nexus* is specified, *number* must also be specified. The *nexus* parameter is Vax-specific.

For example, the configuration line for an rp06 disk controller with two drives would look like this:

```
rp06   254   776700   5   2
```

The second part of the configuration file is a list of modifiable parameters. There are many parameters, and each system has a slightly different set. Only the most important ones will be discussed here. After you are confident in your ability to build new kernels, you can plow through the documentation and fiddle with the other parameters.

The *root* parameter

This parameter tells the system which device the root filesystem can be found on. The device must be both readable and writable, and must be a block device. The arguments are given as a device name and a minor device number, in octal. For example:

```
root     rp06 0
```

locates the root partition on the first partition of the first rp06 drive.

The *pipe* parameter

Pipes are interprocess communication channels. From a process's point of view, a pipe is very similar to a file, except that there is another process on the other end of the pipe and not a disk drive.

The pipe parameter tells the system which filesystem should be used for storage of pipes. When the amount of data waiting in a pipe becomes too large to be comfortably buffered in memory, it is written out to a filesystem. The pipe parameter must specify a mounted file system, so the root file system is normally used. Arguments are specified the same way as for root.

The *swap* parameter

swap tells what disk areas may be used for swapping and/or paging. Unlike BSD, ATT does not always have separate swap partitions. Instead, swapping space is usually allocated at the end of a partition that is used for a filesystem.

The syntax of the swap specification is:

swap   *devname minor swaplow numswap*

devname and *minor* are used as with the *root* parameter to identify the disk partition on which swapping is to be performed. *swaplow* is the first block number within this partition that should be used for swapping, and *numswap* is the number of blocks that are allocated (contiguously) for swapping. For example, if the root partition in the preceding example was 12000 blocks long, the root filesystem could be made 9000 blocks long, and the last 3000 blocks could be used for swapping. The configuration line for this arrangement would look like this:

```
swap   rp06  0  9000 3000
```

It would be a complete disaster if you allocated the swap space so that it overlapped a filesystem. For performance reasons, the swap space may be placed on a different disk drive than the root partition. If you do this, it is a good idea to build a backup kernel that swaps on the same drive as the root, allowing the system to run with only one drive.

The *dump* parameter

dump tells the system where to dump an image of the kernel's address space in the event of a system crash. There are usually only a few hardware devices supported for this purpose, so consult your local documentation. The devices supported are usually tape drives, which means that you must have a tape mounted when the system crashes if you want to save the core image.

The *procs* parameter

procs sets the total number of active processes that can exist on the system at any particular time. About 25 process slots should be reserved for the system, plus five slots for each simultaneous user. If the system runs out of processes under normal use, this number should be increased. Each slot takes up memory, so this number should not be set unreasonably high.

The *maxproc* parameter

maxproc sets the maximum number of concurrent processes a normal user may have. The superuser can have as many processes as are available on the system, as defined by the *procs* parameter. This should be set somewhere between four and eight; if users complain about not having enough processes, this number may be increased.

The *file* parameter

file determines how many total files may be opened at any given time. A kernel table entry is allocated for each file, so again the number should not be unreasonably large. If the system runs out of table entries, the message "no file" will be printed on the console, indicating that this parameter should be increased.

Refer to your system documentation to find out about the other parameters for your system.

8.7.3 Running config

After you have finished modifying the description file, it is time to run **config**. **config** converts the information in the description file into code files that are compiled into the kernel. Since you are already in the CONF directory, to run config simply type **/etc/config** *descf* where *descf* is the name of you description file (BOULDER in the preceding example).

config will give self-explanatory error messages if it finds problems with the description file. After config has completed with no errors, you are ready to make a kernel.

8.7.4 Making the new kernel

The Makefile in the CONF directory is used to bring together all of the various parts of the kernel into one executable version. Only a few small parts of the kernel actually need to be compiled (such as the files created by **config**), but there is a lot of code to be linked. Making the kernel can take a long time, up to half an hour in some cases. To start the **make**, type:

make VER=*ver* **>& ERRORS**

or its equivalent for your shell. Where *ver* is the value you wish to set for the VER Makefile variable, if you did not change it in the Makefile and want to set it on the command line. If you already set the VER in the Makefile, simply type

make >& ERRORS

Read the output in the ERRORS file to be sure that no errors are reported. If the make completes successfully, it will have created the file *SYSVER* in the CONF directory. This file is your new kernel.

8.7.5 Installing and testing the new kernel

Now that you have made a new kernel, you can install and test it. This involves bringing the system down, so you should give the users plenty of warning. The first thing to do is to copy the kernel into the root directory.

After copying the new kernel to the root directory, reboot the system, specifying *SYSVER* instead of /unix as the kernel. Refer to your system documentation to determine how to boot a kernel that is not named /unix. If the system boots, your kernel is at least partially viable. If the system does not boot, reboot using the old /unix kernel and carefully examine the description file for errors. If you made more than one change, back out all but one change and test the resulting kernel. Repeat this process for each change until you have isolated the problem.

After your kernel boots, test to make sure that the changes you made in the description file had the desired effect. For example, if you added an entry for a new tape drive, you would want to check that you can read and write from the tape drive.

When you are convinced that the new kernel is working properly, it is time to rename it /unix. While you can run kernels with any name, certain commands, such as **ps**, will not work properly if /unix does not contain the image of the active kernel. Do an **ls -l** on / to determine which file /unix is a link to. If /unix is not a link, **mv** it to another file, such as /oldunix, and write that name down in the system log. If it is a link, write down the name of the file it was a link to, and then **rm /unix**. These measures allow you to reboot the old kernel if you discover at that there is something wrong with your new kernel. It is important that you write the name down because if the system crashes there will be no way to figure it out. Now that the old kernel is put away in a safe place, install your new kernel as /unix by typing:

ln */SYSVER* **/unix**

It is a good idea to put a line in /etc/motd telling the users that a new kernel has been installed, and to report any problems that might be associated with a new kernel. Also, keep an eye on any console error messages for a few days to make sure everything is OK.

9

Installing Terminals and Modems

This chapter details the specific steps needed to attach new terminals and modems to your system, including more than you ever want to know about cable specifications, hard and soft carrier, flags to the device driver, configuration files, and the terminal capabilities databases. Modems are similar to terminals as far as the device interface is concerned; the section on modems will deal with the cabling and configuration differences that are specific to modem installation.

9.1 Wiring design

If your site has several machines, each with several terminal ports which must be connected to various offices and laboratories throughout the building, you need a *patch panel* or data switch. As users change offices or machines, the wiring from their office terminal to their machine must also change. Just finding the proper wire to reroute is often a challenge.

In our machine room, we have constructed a large patch panel that resembles a 1930s telephone switchboard. Wires from offices and wires to the various computer ports terminate at the patch panel in three-wire stereo jacks from Radio Shack. A short length of cable connecting two such jacks makes the final connection from a particular office to a particular terminal port on a host computer. When a user changes offices, the CPU of our data switch (a student operator) unplugs the user's connection to the old office and plugs it into the slot corresponding to the new office.

The stereo jacks were the easiest, cheapest way to construct the patch panel when we did it several years ago. They cannot handle modem lines, which require more than three wires. Today, modular phone jacks (RJ45's, for example) are cheaper, more reliable, and are able to accommodate modem connections. Software-programmable data switches are also available from companies like Rolm, Northern Telecom, and AT&T, but people-programmable patch panels are considerably less expensive. Patch panels that use telephone jacks are also commercially available from Nevada Western in Sunnyvale, CA.

Careful, complete documentation of each jack on the patch panel is essential. We maintain detailed wiring maps like those in Section 26.1.2, that show the routing of cables, location of connections, and details of pin assignments and wire colors. These are indispensable when trying to debug faulty connections.

9.2 Cables

Terminals attach to a computer using a standard RS-232.[1] interface. The RS-232 standard determines the electrical characteristics of the interface, as well as the connector types and meaning of the signals on each pin. RS-232 uses twisted pair cable, usually stranded 22-gauge wire and DB-25 25-pin connectors (DB25P, male, and DB25S, female). RS-232 voltages are ±12 volts DC (sometimes 5 or even 3 volts are used). The RS-232 pin assignments are listed in Figure 9.1; signal names are included where they exist.

A terminal can be attached either directly with a physical wire (hard-wired), or through telephone lines (dial-up) and a pair of modems at either end to

[1] RS-232-C actually.

FIGURE 9.1

RS-232 pin assignments					
Pin	Name	Function	Pin	Name	Function
1	FG	Frame ground	14	STD	Secondary transmitted data
2	TD	Transmitted data	15	TC	Transmit clock
3	RD	Received data	16	SRD	Secondary received data
4	RTS	Request to send	17	RC	Receive clock
5	CTS	Clear to send	18		Not assigned
6	DSR	Data set ready	19	SRTS	Secondary request to send
7	SG	Signal ground	20	DTR	Data terminal ready
8	DCD	Data carrier detect	21	SQ	Signal quality detector
9		Positive test voltage	22	RI	Ring indicator
10		Negative test voltage	23	DRS	Data rate selector
11		Not assigned	24	SCTE	Serial clock transmit external
12	SDCD	Secondary carrier detect	25	BUSY	Busy
13	SCTS	Secondary clear to send			

modulate and demodulate the signals. There are two cabling configurations: DTE (Data Terminal Equipment) and DCE (Data Communications Equipment) that determine which signals a device expects on which connector pins. Each device is configured as either DTE or DCE. Some support both. Most computers and terminals are configured as DTE, and most modems are configured as DCE. This means that the cables for hard-wired terminals are different from those for modem connections.

Dial-ups use a straight cable (modem cable), in which all wires go straight through to the corresponding pins. Terminals that are hard-wired must use a null-modem cable, in which send/receive and data-terminal-ready/data-set-ready pairs are crossed. The wires through the patch panel described in the previous section are all straight cables with no special connections made. If a terminal requires special cabling, changes are made between the wall jack and the terminal.

The 25 pin connectors at the ends of terminal wires are either male (with the little pins sticking out) or female (with the matching holes). There are tiny invisible numbers near the pins or holes which label them from 1 to 25. You can see them best by holding them up to the light and looking at them at an angle. Sometimes only pins 1, 13, 14, and 25 are actually numbered. There is no real standardization with regard to the sex of the connectors. Both terminals and computers may have either male or female. Modems usually have a female connector.

Many of the signals shown in Figure 9.1 are not normally used in RS-232 cables. Figures 9.2 and 9.3 show the pin assignments for both straight cables and null-modem cables.

FIGURE 9.2

Straight cable — modem connection		
Terminal pin	Computer pin	Function
1	1	Frame ground
2	2	Transmitted data
3	3	Received data
4	4	Ready to send
5	5	Clear to send
6	6	Data set ready
7	7	Signal ground
8	8	Data carrier detect
20	20	Data terminal ready

FIGURE 9.3

Null-modem cable — hard-wired connection		
Terminal pin	Computer pin	Function
1	1	Frame ground
2	3	Transmitted data - received data
3	2	Received data - transmitted data
4	4	Ready to send
5	5	Clear to send
6	20	Data set ready - data terminal ready
7	7	Signal ground
8	20	Carrier detect - data terminal ready
20	6,8	Data terminal ready - data set ready, carrier detect

9.2.1 Soft carrier and hard carrier

Not all the wires just listed are necessary for hard-wired terminals. Pins 2, 3, and 7, (send, receive, and signal ground) are always required. UNIX expects to see pin 8, carrier detect, go high (+12 volts) when a terminal is attached and turned on. The term *hard carrier* refers to the signal actually existing on pin 8 of the terminal cable; *soft carrier* refers to the software pretending that the carrier signal is there. Modem connections need to really see a signal on pin 8; if a terminal is connected through a modem and the carrier signal is lost, the modem must hang up (especially if it is a long distance call). There are many war stories of astronomical phone bills incurred when a modem hung and did not drop carrier for days.

Various versions of UNIX have dealt with soft carrier in different ways. Early versions required a patch to the terminal driver, such as:

```
if (CARRIER)  { ...
```

changed to:

```
if (TRUE)  { ...
```

ATT System V based versions of UNIX have solved this problem and can set a default carrier mode for terminal ports in the system configuration files. In addition, the CLOCAL flag to the **stty** command can be used to signal a terminal to assume soft carrier on a running system. For example:

stty -CLOCAL < /dev/tty03

would change the terminal configuration for port tty03 to soft carrier.

On BSD systems, to change a port from hard to soft carrier, or vice versa, the kernel must be recompiled, the system brought down, and the new kernel booted. This is unreasonable, but is still true in both 4.2 and 4.3. The kernel configuration file entries for terminal interfaces use a *flags* variable which is a bit mask indicating which ports of the interface expect hard carrier (the default) and which should supply soft carrier. The bit mask is expressed in hexadecimal, with the low-order bit, (the bit farthest to the right in the flags argument), corresponding to the lowest numbered terminal on the interface. If the bit is set to 0, hard carrier is required; otherwise soft carrier is asserted. For example, the entry in the configuration file for a "dh" interface on a Vax with ports ttyh0-h7 expecting hard carrier and ports ttyh8-hf expecting soft carrier is:

```
device  dh0   at uba? csr 0160420  flags 0xff00 vector dhrint dhxint
```

Most terminals ignore the CTS and RTS signals (pins 4 and 5) but some, such as those made by IBM, require a handshake across these two pins before they will talk to the computer. The hardware can be fooled by jumpering pins 4 and 5 together at the terminal end of the cable, so that when the terminal sends out a signal on pin 4 saying "I'm ready", it gets the same signal back on pin 5 saying "go ahead". The same can be done for the DTR/DSR/CD protocol exchange.

Figure 9.4 shows the pin assignments for a hard-wired cable connected to a port that supplies soft carrier.

FIGURE 9.4

Soft carrier null-modem cable — hard-wired connection		
Terminal pin	Computer pin	Function
1		sometimes jumpered to pin 7 (FG - SG)
2	3	Transmitted data - Received data
3	2	Received data - Transmitted data
4,5		sometimes jumpered (RTS - CTS)
7	7	Signal ground

The RS-232 standard specifies a maximum cable length of 75 feet. The length rating is tied to the baud rate; we are using values for 9600 baud.

Standards are usually very conservative, and RS-232 is no exception. We routinely run RS-232 cables much greater distances, up to about 1000 feet. We have hit the limit somewhere between 800 and 1000 feet, but have found that the particular brand of terminal made quite a bit of difference. DEC terminals are very robust and were no problem, while other cheaper brands failed at those distances. If you need to exceed the specification by more than a factor of 5 or 6, good quality individually shielded twisted pair cable should be used.

The proper way to connect shielded twisted pair wire is to use one pair for send (pin 2) and another pair for receive (pin 3). The second wire of each pair should go to signal ground (pin 7). The shields should be connected to frame ground (pin 1) at one end and not connected at all at the other end.

Some installations cheat (for example, ours) and use only one shielded twisted pair per terminal. If a terminal connected this way were struck by lightning, it would be fried. You pays your money and you takes your chances.

The presence of chassis ground (pin 1) that is grounded at one end and unconnected (electrically floats) at the other end is required for full safety of the installation. In addition, the use of the second wire in the twisted pair for signal ground insures that if there is a power spike, which can easily happen if terminal wires are run near high-voltage lines, spikes on the data pins (2 or 3) will be compensated for by equivalent spikes on signal ground, and the hardware will only see the difference, the true signal.

9.2.2 Cable and connector types

While terminal cables have traditionally been stranded, twisted pair wire with soldered DB25 connectors, there are now at least four choices:

- Soldered connectors, twisted pair wire
- Crimped connectors, twisted pair wire
- Press-on connectors, ribbon cable
- Modular phone jack connectors, molded flat phone wire

The crimp connections are easier to make than soldered connections and when done carefully are equally reliable. They require an expensive crimp tool and die set. The press-on connectors can be either pounded onto the ribbon cable with a hammer or pressed on with a vise. Care must be taken to align the teeth on the connector with the wires in the ribbon cable. The cost of the parts and tools are comparable for soldered, crimped, or pressed connections. Labor costs are less for crimp and press-on connectors.

The nicest system uses modular phone jacks which work with eight-conductor phone cable. The phone jacks plug into special DB25 connectors to form the completed cable. Inside the DB25's, short crimped wires connect the cable in either the DTE or DCE configuration.

9.3 The login process

The process required to allow a user to login involves several programs whose actions are controlled to some extent by the contents of the terminal configuration files described in the next section.

As UNIX boots, the **/etc/init** daemon is started up. One of **init**'s jobs is to start the **/etc/getty** program running on all terminal ports that are turned on. The files /etc/ttys or /etc/inittab determine whether a port is turned on or off. The **getty** program produces a login prompt, and sets the port's initial characteristics, such as speed and parity.

The user types his login name to the prompt on the terminal screen and waits while:

- **getty** executes the **login** program with the login name as an argument
- **login** requests a password and validates the login name and password against those stored in the /etc/passwd file
- **login** prints the message of the day file, /etc/motd
- **login** executes the shell specified in the passwd file for that user and under BSD sets the TERM environment variable to the value specified in the terminal configuration file (/etc/ttys on 4.3BSD, /etc/ttytype on 4.2BSD)
- The shell executes the appropriate startup files (.profile for **sh**, .login and .cshrc for **csh**)
- The shell prints the UNIX prompt and waits for the user's input

When the user logs out, control returns to **init**, which wakes up and spawns a new **getty** on the terminal port.

9.4 Terminal configuration files

Configuration files in the /etc directory control the terminal characteristics associated with each port. These include the presence of a login prompt and **getty** process running on the port, the baud rate UNIX expects, and on BSD systems, the terminal type and whether or not it is secure.

9.4.1 BSD files: /etc/ttys, /etc/ttytype, /etc/gettytab

Before 4.3BSD, terminal configuration data was maintained in two files: /etc/ttys and /etc/ttytype. Berkeley's 4.3 and later releases have merged this information into a single file, still called /etc/ttys.

The format of the original style /etc/ttys file is:

on/off *speed-code device*

with no spaces between fields. If the first digit is 0, the terminal port is turned off and no **getty** process is run on it; if the first digit is 1 the port is turned on and a **getty** process will be created to generate a login prompt. The *speed-code* is an index into the file /etc/gettytab which specifies the baud rate and some initial characteristics of the terminal line. The *device* is the name of the device file from the /dev directory that represents the terminal port. For example, the 4.2BSD /etc/ttys file on a Vax might contain:

```
12console
13ttyi0
13ttyi1
12ttyi2
12ttyi3
12ttyi4
12ttyi5
12ttyi6
03ttyi7
```

The format of the 4.2BSD /etc/ttytype file is:

terminal-type device

where *terminal-type* is a type of terminal that is described in /etc/termcap or /etc/termlib, and *device* is the name of the device file representing the port. If your port has an entry in /etc/ttytype, your TERM environment variable will be set at login time. A sample /etc/ttytype file follows:

```
wyse    console
dialup  ttyi0
dialup  ttyi1
vt100   ttyi2
h19     ttyi3
h19     ttyi4
h19     ttyi5
ibm-pc  ttyi6
dialout ttyi7
```

Under 4.3BSD the information in both the ttys and ttytype files has been merged. The format of the new /etc/ttys file is:

device program-to-run terminal-type on/off [secure]

The entries are separated by white space. *program-to-run* is the file that **init** should start if the port is turned on. Notice that **getty**, the usual entry in this position, takes as an argument a symbolic version of the *speed-code*. *terminal-type* is the terminal type previously kept in the /etc/ttytype file; on/off is as in the preceding discussion. If the secure keyword is present, root is allowed to login from this terminal. Many sites do not allow root to log in on machines in public terminal rooms or from dial-ins. An excerpt from the 4.3BSD style /etc/ttys file that corresponds to the preceding 4.2BSD files, follows:

```
console    "/etc/getty Console-9600"    wyse      on     secure
ttyi0      "/etc/getty isn.1200"        dialup    on
ttyi1      "/etc/getty isn.1200"        dialup    on
ttyi2      "/etc/getty std.9600"        vt100     on
ttyi3      "/etc/getty std.9600"        h19       on
ttyi4      "/etc/getty std.9600"        h19       on
ttyi5      "/etc/getty std.9600"        h19       on
ttyi6      "/etc/getty std.9600"        ibm-pc    on
ttyi7      "/etc/getty dial.1200"       dialout   off
```

A **getty** process is started by the **init** process at boot time for each terminal that is turned on in the /etc/ttys file. The speed code is determined by the **getty** program either from compiled-in tables (older versions of UNIX) or from the text files /etc/gettytab (BSD and some ATT), /etc/gettydefs (some ATT), and /etc/inittab (ATT). The codes are a single letter, and therefore not very mnemonic, but they are well commented in either getty.c, the files themselves, or Volume 1, Section 4 (ATT)/Section 5 (BSD) of the UNIX documentation. A sample /etc/gettytab file follows.

```
#
# fixed speed entries
#
c|std.300|300-baud:nd#1:cd#1:sp#300:
f|std.1200|1200-baud:fd#1:sp#1200:
6|std.2400|2400-baud:sp#2400:ht:
2|std.9600|9600-baud:sp#9600:
#
# dialup terminals, 2400/1200/300 rotary, use 'break' to cycle
#
1|D2400|Fast-Dial-2400:nx=D1200:tc=2400-baud:
3|D1200|Fast-Dial-1200:nx=D300:tc=1200-baud:
5|D300|Fast-Dial-300:nx=D2400:tc=300-baud:
```

```
D|Down|Download:\
:im=\r\n\nPyramid Technology 4.3/5.2 (%h) (dialup)\r\n\n> \
If possible, please use the ISN instead of the direct dialups.\r\n> \
These lines are needed for Emacs, and up/down-loading of software.\r\n> \
To use the ISN; dial 4921900, type "eng/annex", and "rlogin tut".\r\n\n \
:tc=D1200:
#
# X windows
#
v|Vs100|Xwindow|X window system:fd@:nd@:cd@:rw:sp#9600:
```

The line with names separated by a vertical bar ("|") lists all the names that a particular configuration is recognized by. The single character name is the one used in the /etc/ttys file to set the speed and other getty characteristics, thus the entry in an old-style ttys file of 12ttyi2 states that the terminal known as /dev/ttyi2 is turned on, should have a login prompt, and is running at 9600 baud. The other fields in the entry set the characteristics of the port and are described fully in your UNIX manuals.

Modems can often "talk" at several speeds. The preceding dial-up entries are set up to switch to another speed when the break key is hit; the break key sends a longer pulse than regular characters and therefore can be recognized by the answering modem at any speed setting. **getty** transfers to the entry specified in the ":nx" field when it detects a break. The first three dial-up entries cycle from 2400 baud to 1200 baud to 300 baud and back to 2400 baud. The final dial-up entry is included to show how to use a customized login prompt in a *:im* field to deliver a message to a specific port.

/etc/ttys is read by the **init** process when the system is booted. If a change is made to this file, **init** must be told to reread it. The **kill -1 1** command will send the HUP (hangup) signal to **init**, process number 1. In early versions of UNIX, this would actually kill the **init** process, thereby bringing the running system to single-user mode rather abruptly. If **init** does not handle the HUP signal gracefully in your version of UNIX, shut down the system before killing the **init** process.

9.4.2 ATT files: /etc/inittab, /etc/gettydefs, /etc/gettytab

On ATT systems, terminal configuration is done in the files /etc/inittab and either /etc/gettydefs or /etc/gettytab. Unfortunately, there is no single ATT standard with respect to these files. We found systems with the terminal configuration data in each of these three places. The /etc/gettytab file is similar to that just described for BSD.

The System V version of **init** supports various "run-levels." These levels determine which system resources are enabled. There are eight run-levels: 0

to 6 and "s" (single-user). When you leave single-user mode, *init* prompts you for a run-level (unless an *initdefault* field exists in /etc/inittab, as described next). **init** then scans the /etc/inittab file for all lines that match the specified run-level. Run-levels are usually set up so you have a level where only the console is enabled, and another level that enables all terminals. You can define the run-levels to mean whatever you feel is appropriate for your system. The /etc/inittab file looks something like this:

```
::sysinit:/etc/setclk </dev/console >/dev/console 2>&1
co:234:respawn:/etc/getty console console
11:234:respawn:/etc/getty tty11 9600
12:234:off:/etc/getty tty12 9600
```

The format of the inittab file is:

id:run-levels:action:process

In this format, *id* is a one- or two-character string used to identify the entry, which may be null, as in the first line. On terminal entries, it is customary to use the terminal number as the *id*, as in the preceding example. *run-levels* lists the **init** run-levels that the entry pertains to. If no levels are specified, as in the first line, the entry is considered valid for all run-levels. The *action* field tells how to handle the process field. Figure 9.5 contains a listing of the valid entries for the *action* field.

FIGURE 9.5

Possible values for the **inittab** *action* field

Value	Meaning	Wait For Termination
boot	Run when inittab is read for the first time	No
bootwait	Run when inittab is read for the first time	Yes
initdefault	Set initial run-level	N/A
off	Terminate the process if it is running	N/A
once	Start the process once	No
ondemand	Always keep the process running (same as respawn)	No
powerfail	Execute when **init** receives a power fail signal	No
powerwait	Execute when **init** receives a power fail signal	Yes
sysinit	Execute before accessing console	Yes
respawn	Always keep the process running	No
wait	Start the process once	Yes

If one of the entries in *run-levels* matchs the current run-level and the *action* field is appropriate, **init** will use **sh** to execute (or terminate) the command specified in the *process* field. In the preceding example, the first line sets the clock, the middle lines spawn **getty** processes, and the last line insures that there is no **getty** on tty12. **init** can be signaled to reread the inittab file with the command **telinit -q**.

The /etc/gettydefs file is used to tell the **getty** program how to act. The file looks like this:

```
console# B9600 HUPCL OPOST ONLCR # B9600 SANE IXANY #Console Login: #console
19200# B19200 HUPCL # B19200 SANE IXANY TAB3 HUPCL #login: #9600
9600# B9600 HUPCL # B9600 SANE IXANY TAB3 HUPCL #login: #4800
4800# B4800 HUPCL # B4800 SANE IXANY TAB3 HUPCL #login: #2400
2400# B2400 HUPCL # B2400 SANE IXANY TAB3 HUPCL #login: #1200
1200# B1200 HUPCL # B1200 SANE IXANY TAB3 HUPCL #login: #300
300# B300 HUPCL # B300 SANE IXANY TAB3 HUPCL #login: #9600
```

The format of the gettydefs file is:

label#initial flags#final flags#login prompt#next label

getty tries to match its second argument with one of the *label* entrys. If it is called without a second argument, the first entry in the file is used. The *initial flags* field sets **ioctl** flags that should be set on the device until **login** is executed. The *final flags* field sets **ioctl** flags that should be set on the device when **login** is executed. The speed entry is required for both *initial flags* and *final flags*. The fourth field contains the *login prompt*, which may include tabs and newlines in backslash notation (\t and \n, respectively). The *next label* field contains the label of the inittab entry that should be substituted for the current one if a break is received. This is useful for dial-up lines where you might want to cycle through various baud rates, as in the preceding example. If the entry is for a hard-wired terminal, *next label* should reference its own label. Each time you change the gettydefs file, you should run **getty -c gettydefs**, which checks the syntax of the file to make sure that all of the entries are valid.

The IBM RT under AIX, although based on ATT UNIX, uses a totally different system for terminal configuration. You wouldn't recognize /etc: there is no inittab file or ttys file. Utilities are provided that handle terminal configuration fairly well; consult your manuals for details.

9.5 Terminal support: the termcap/terminfo database

UNIX supports many different terminal types, as opposed to some large vendors (with three-letter acronyms) whose software only supports their own brand of terminals. UNIX does this through a database of terminal capabilities that specifies the features and programming quirks of each brand of terminal. The database (as distributed with 4.3BSD) contains entries for about 480 different terminals. Programs can look at the user's environment to determine the terminal type and then look up the characteristics of the terminal to decide how to manipulate data on the screen. Usually the user arranges for his TERM and TERMCAP environment variables to be set up in his .login or .profile file. On BSD systems, it is advisable to put the most commonly used terminals at your site at the beginning of the database to speed lookup. The format of a termcap/terminfo entry is described in detail in Section 5 of the BSD manuals or Section 4 of the ATT manuals.

9.6 Specific steps in installing a terminal

The following pseudo-code outlines the specific steps to install a terminal on an existing interface.

```
/* assume device files already exist */

1.  Make cable, plug in terminal, turn it on.
2.  Set the terminal options, duplex, speed, parity, etc.
3.  if (soft carrier is required)
    {
            if (BSD and port not configured for soft carrier)
            {
                    Read section on soft carrier.
                    Set flags in kernel configuration file.
                    Recompile kernel.
                    Shutdown system and reboot new kernel.
            }
            else if (ATT and port not configured for soft carrier)
            {
                    Use CLOCAL flag to stty command.
            }
    }
4.  Edit the terminal configuration files that apply to include the new tty
    device.
5.  Execute kill -1 1 (gently on older systems).
6.  Hit return on the terminal to get a login prompt.
```

If the installation involves the terminal interface as well as terminals, follow the manufacturers instructions for installing the terminal interface and refer to Chapter 7: *Devices and Drivers*.

9.7 Modems

Modems are used to connect devices via phone lines. The original modems transmitted data at 110 baud (110 bits/sec) or about 11 characters per second, agonizingly slow. Data rates for modems have increased through 150 baud, 300 baud, 1200 baud, 2400 baud to 9600 baud. As speeds increased, the price decreased. 9600 baud modems contain logic to packetize outgoing data and to do error correction on incoming data. The packet delays make them better for file transfer than for interactive use, although improved firmware has made interactive use over voice-grade phone lines almost as good as hardwired connections.

9.7.1 Protocols

300 baud modems use a Bell protocol in the US and a CCITT protocol in the rest of the world. 1200 baud modems use either the Vadic protocol or Bell 103. The popularity of the Hayes modem a few years ago established it and the Bell protocol as de facto standards at 1200 baud. 2400 baud modems seem to be standardizing on the CCITT protocol, but variations on it are common and it is possible for different vendors' 2400 baud modems to be unable to talk to each other reliably. Currently there are no clear standards above the 2400 baud data rate, and although the V.32 standard at 9600 baud is emerging, it is still necessary to use the same brand of modem at each end of the connection.

Most modems have configuration parameters to allow you to set up the modem as a dial-in port (answering the call) or as a dial-out (originating the call). Some allow both. Your modem's manual will detail the switch settings.

9.7.2 Line turnaround

Ports are configured differently for dial-ins and dial-outs: a dial-in requires the port to be turned on and to supply a login prompt; a dial-out requires the port turned off. Some software systems allow a single port and modem to be used in either direction by creating two devices for each port and using the minor device number to differentiate between them, or by turning the line around in the programs that use it as a dial-out port.

9.7.3 Auto-dialers

Many of the programs that use modems refer to the call-out devices cua0 and cul0 instead of the actual name of the modem's terminal port, which varies from site to site. These include **tip** (BSD only), **cu**, and uucp. These calling device names should be linked to the actual terminal ports where the auto-dial modem is attached. For example, if the dialer is on port /dev/ttyd5, then:

```
ln /dev/ttyd5 /dev/cua0
ln /dev/ttyd5 /dev/cul0
```

will equate the actual device name to the names that the dial-out programs expect. In addition, some programs require that the modem device be owned by the user uucp and the group daemon.

cu and **tip** (BSD) are programs that use a modem to dial out and establish a full duplex terminal connection to another computer. Each supports bidirectional file transfer, alas, with no error detection or correction. Uucp is the UNIX to UNIX copy system, which lets two computers exchange files and allows remote execution of commands (see Chapter 16: *Uucp*, for details).

9.7.4 BSD Configuration files: /etc/phones and /etc/remote

Two configuration files are used with **tip** to record phone numbers (/etc/phones) and remote host dial-in descriptions (/etc/remote). Samples from these two files follow.

```
#
# /etc/remote:  Dialer definitions
#
dial2400|2400 Baud hayes:dv=/dev/cul0:br#2400:cu=/dev/cul0:at=hayes:du:
dial1200|dialer|1200 Baud hayes:dv=/dev/cul0:br#1200:cu=/dev/cul0:at=hayes:du:
UNIX-1200|1200 Baud dial-out to another UNIX system:el=^U^C^R^O^D^S^Q@:\
     :ie=#%$:oe=^D:tc=dial1200:
#
# Commonly dialed hosts
#
tut:pn=3338958:di=logout:tc=UNIX-1200:
ucc:pn=3338118:tc=dial2400
cc:pn=@:tc=UNIX-1200:
dca:dv=/dev/ttyh1,/dev/ttyh2:br#9600:pa=none
#
# Hang up on close, don't allow hogging the dialups
#
HUP on close
```

The first three entries describe the dialer configurations. The next section, commonly dialed hosts, is used as a shortcut in typing **tip** or **cu** commands. Notice in the *cc* entry that the phone number is not specifically stated, but rather written as *pn=@* which means to look for the phone number(s) in the file /etc/phones. **tip**, **cu**, or uucp will then try the first number for cc in /etc/phones. If the number is busy, it will rotate on to the next, and the next, ...

```
#
#  /etc/phones:  Phone numbers, please note: this file can contain long
#       distance billing numbers and unpublished telephone numbers, so
#       is usually not readable by the world.
#
cc   4472530
cc   4928811
cc   4495054
monet    8,,415,123-4567,,,,xxx-xxxx
```

The phones file contains symbolic definitions of phone numbers. The preceding xxx-xxxx could represent a long distance billing number. Punctuation in phone numbers is used to signify delays, or to wait for a second dial tone. The punctuation characters used depend on the brand of modem: commas, hyphens, equal signs, and asterisks are all commonly used in this way.

9.8 Debugging

Debugging terminal lines is not difficult. Some typical errors are:

- Forgetting to tell the **init** process to reinitialize
- Forgetting to set soft carrier if using three-wire connections
- Using a cable with the wrong nullness
- Soldering/crimping the DB-25 connectors upside down
- Connecting the terminal to the wrong wire because of faulty wire maps
- Setting the terminal options incorrectly

9.8.1 Breakout box

A breakout box is an indispensable tool in debugging terminal cabling problems. It is placed in the terminal line and displays the signals on each pin as they pass through the cable. The better ones have both male and female connectors on each side and so are totally flexible and bisexual in their positioning. LED lights associated with each "interesting" pin (pins 2,3,4,5,6,8,20) show when a pin is active. Some breakout boxes are read-only and just allow you to monitor the signals; others allow you to rewire the connection and assert either +5V or -5V on a particular pin. For example, if you suspected that the cable needed to be nulled (crossed) you could use the breakout box to override the actual cable wiring: swapping pins 2 and 3 and also pins 6 and 20.

9.8.2 Fake logins

Adding a fake login called "tty" that has as a shell the **tty** command simplifies the task of verifying to which port a terminal is connected. If you really want to get fancy, you can write a program called **ttytype** that displays all of the terminal characteristics, and include a fake login entry for it. It is important to give these logins a limited shell that exits after the **tty** or **ttytype** command is executed, as they should have no password associated with them. /etc/passwd entries for these logins should look something like:

```
tty::69:3:tty login,,,:/usr/fake:/usr/bin/tty
ttytype::68:3:Check terminal type,,,:/usr/fake:/usr/local/bin/ttytype
```

9.8.3 Modem speaker

The speaker on a Hayes modem or compatible is quite useful in debugging a modem installation. You can hear the modem dial the phone, the phone ring, and the other modem (or person or recording) answer. Volume is usually controlled by a knob on the back and can be turned loud enough to hear even above machine room air conditioning noise.

9.9 Setting the terminal modes

We now leave the hardware world of cables and carriers and look at the terminal driver and its interface to users. While this section is all user-level stuff, it is important for a system administrator to understand. A user's most common complaint is that his terminal is not working properly, either because the characteristics set for it are inappropriate, or because he has run a program that has aborted unexpectedly, leaving the terminal in an unknown and uncooperative state.

Three user-level programs — **stty**, **reset**, and **tset** — can set the operational mode of the terminal driver from the shell. **stty** is available in both ATT and BSD systems; **tset** and **reset** are only available under BSD ("for wimps," some hardcores say). These programs allow a multitude of terminal characteristics to be set, including speed, characters used to signal interrupts, end of line delays, etc. A call to **tset** or **stty** is usually included in each user's .login or .profile file to set up the terminal characteristics at login time. **reset** is normally used only after the terminal modes have been messed up by a defective program and the terminal is in need of first aid.

9.9.1 Special characters and the terminal driver

The terminal driver maintains a list of characters that have special meaning on input and how to handle them. These special characters may be changed with either **tset** or **stty** commands. Figure 9.6 is a list of some of these special characters, along with their default values.

9.9.2 The stty command

stty allows you to change and query the various terminal options directly. There are a zillion options to the terminal driver which are documented in the man page for **stty**. Many options are the same for ATT and BSD versions of UNIX, but there are enough differences, even among the flavors of UNIX, that you should consult the manual entry on your local system. Options to **stty** can be placed on the command line in any order and in any combination; a dash before an option is used to negate it. For example, to configure a terminal for 2400 baud operation with even parity and without hardware tabs, the command line:

stty 2400 even -tabs

can be used.

A good combination of options to use for a vanilla crt terminal on a BSD system is:

stty new crt cr0 intr ^C kill ^U erase ^H -tabs

FIGURE 9.6

Special characters			
Symbolic name	ATT default value	BSD default value	Meaning
ERASE	#	^H	Erase one character of input
WERASE	N/A	^W	Erase one word of input
KILL	@	^U	Erase entire line
EOF	^D	^D	End of file
INTR	^?	^C	Interrupt current process
QUIT	^\\	^\\	Kill current process with core dump
STOP	^S	^S	Stop output to screen
START	^Q	^Q	Restart output to screen
DISCARD	N/A	^O	Throw away pending output
SUSPEND	N/A	^Z	Suspend current process
LNEXT	N/A	^V	Interpret next character literally

In this set of options, **new** specifies the new BSD-style terminal driver (which is necessary to support the C shell and job control), **crt** sets modes appropriate for a crt (includes the modes **crtbs** to echo backspaces, **crterase** to erase characters with backspace-space-backspace, **crtkill** to erase the input line on the screen when the line kill character is received, and **ctlecho** to make control characters print as ^char), **cr0** prevents putting delays in the output stream after each carriage return, **-tabs** prevents the terminal driver from taking advantage of the terminal's built-in tabulation mechanism (useful since some terminals are brain damaged about tabs), and the other options set the interrupt, kill, and erase characters to <Control-C>, <Control-U>, and <Control-H> (backspace), respectively.

For backwards compatibility, the Bourne shell perversely treats carets in a similar manner to the pipe character. Thus, to execute this command line with the **sh** you must escape each of the carets with a backslash. Under ATT, the **new** and **crt** arguments have no meaning and must be removed from the command line.

The **stty** command can also be used to examine the current modes of the terminal driver as well as set them. **stty** without any arguments produces output like:

```
new tty, speed 9600 baud; -tabs crt
decctlq
erase = ^H
```

A more verbose status report can be obtained with the **stty everything**, **stty -a**, or **stty all** depending on your system. The output here is something like:

```
new tty, speed 9600 baud, 34 rows, 80 columns
even odd -raw -nl echo -lcase -tandem -tabs -cbreak
crt: (crtbs crterase crtkill ctlecho) -tostop
-tilde -flusho -mdmbuf -litout -pass8 -nohang
-pendin decctlq -noflsh
-nopost -noisig -stopb
erase kill werase rprnt flush lnext susp  intr quit stop  eof
^H    ^U   ^W     ^R    ^O    ^V    ^Z/^Y ^C   ^\   ^S/^Q ^D
```

which is similar in format, but lists all available information. The knowledge-starved reader can look up all of these modes in the manual page for **stty**.

Since **stty** just operates on the file descriptor of its standard input or standard output (depending on your particular UNIX), it is possible to set and query the modes of a terminal other than the one currently being used through use of the shell redirection characters ">" and "<", available in both the Bourne and C shells. BSD systems use ">"; ATT systems use "<". For example, to set the speed of terminal /dev/ttyi2 to 1200 baud on a BSD system execute the command **stty 1200 > /dev/ttyi2**; on ATT **stty 1200 < /dev/ttyi2**. On some systems you will need to be the superuser to change the modes on someone else's terminal.

9.9.3 The tset command (BSD)

tset is used to initialize the terminal driver to a mode appropriate for a given terminal type. If a terminal type is specified on the command line, the terminal driver is configured appropriately for that terminal. Otherwise, **tset** looks at the environment variable TERM to find out what kind of terminal to set up for.

tset also supports a syntax for mapping given values of the TERM environment variable into other values. This is useful if you often log in through a modem or data switch and would like to have the terminal driver configured correctly for the type of terminal you are likely to be using on the other end of the connection rather than something generic and totally unhelpful such as "dialup".

For example, suppose that you have a DEC vt100 at home and that the /etc/ttytype or /etc/ttys file is configured to think that the terminal type of a modem is "dialup". If you put the line:

tset -m dialup:vt100

in your .login or .profile file, then whenever you log in through a modem **tset** will set you up correctly for a vt100 terminal.

If there are a number of terminals that you are likely to use when coming through a modem, you can have **tset** ask you what you're using every time you log in, with a suitable default provided if you just hit return. For example, the line:

tset -m dialup:?vt100

produces the question:

TERM = (vt100)?

At this prompt you may just hit return to select a vt100 configuration, or enter the type of terminal that you are using if it is not a vt100.

Unfortunately, the **tset** command is not really as simple as it pretends to be; to have it adjust your environment variables TERM and TERMCAP in addition to setting your terminal modes, you will need a line something like (this example is for the C shell only):

set noglob ; eval 'tset -s -Q -m dialup:?vt100 -m switch:z29' ; unset noglob

This invocation specifies that the "Erase is ^H, Kill is ^U" messages that tset normally outputs be suppressed (the **-Q** flag), and that shell commands to set the environment correctly be output (the **-s** flag). In addition, it says that if the user logs in on a dial-up he is to be prompted for his terminal type with a default of vt100, and if he logs in through the local data switch (configured at terminal type "switch") then the terminal is really a Zenith Z29.

The shell commands output by **tset** are captured by the backquotes and fed to the shell as input through use of the built-in command **eval**, causing them to have the same effect as if the user had typed them himself. The **set noglob** and **unset noglob** directives prevent the shell from expanding any meta-characters like "*" and "?" that might be output by **tset**.

The **set noglob** and **unset noglob** commands are not needed by Bourne shell users, since **sh** does not normally expand metacharacters within backquotes. The rest of the line remains the same, making it simply:

```
eval `tset -s -Q -m dialup:?vt100 -m switch:z29`
```

tset looks at the environment variable SHELL to determine what flavor of commands are to be returned for evaluation.

9.9.4 Resetting the terminal

Some programs, such as **vi**, make drastic changes to the terminal state while they are running. This meddling is normally invisible to the user, since the terminal state is carefully restored when the editor exits or is suspended. It is possible for the editor to crash or be killed externally without doing this cleanup. When this happens, the terminal will appear to completely freak out; it will fail to handle newlines correctly, to echo characters typed, or to execute commands properly.

To fix this situation, you need only execute the **reset** command on BSD systems or **stty sane** on ATT systems. **reset** is actually just a link to **tset** on most systems, and it can accept most of **tset**'s arguments. It is usually used just by itself, however, without any arguments at all. Either **reset** or **stty sane** restores the sanity of the terminal driver and outputs an appropriate terminal resetting code from /etc/termcap or /etc/terminfo, if one is available.

In many cases where a **reset** is appropriate, the terminal has been left in a special mode where no processing is done on input characters. Because most terminals generate carriage returns rather than newlines when the "return" or "enter" key is pressed, the return key is no longer correctly equivalenced in this situation and thus becomes nonfunctional. Instead of acting normally, the return key now generates <Control-M>'s. The workaround for this is simple: instead of using the return key to terminate lines, use the "line feed" key or <Control-J> instead. The complete sequence for resetting a terminal is therefore:

```
<line feed>             /* to clear accumulated junk chars */
reset or stty sane      /* to reset the terminal */
<line feed>             /* to send the reset */
```

Some terminals (DEC vt100s and clones) have a <no-scroll> key right where you might think the shift key should be. Once it has been typed, accidentally or not, it is as though the user has typed <Control-S> to stop all output on his terminal. This gives the appearance of a hung terminal; it won't respond to anything that is typed, except if you happen to type the <Control-Q> or <no-

scroll> key again to undo it. Another common keyboard/terminal problem, is with the text editor, **vi**, where commands have drastically different meanings if they are capital letters than if they are lowercase letters. Inadvertently hitting the caps lock key (Caps or F1, which are adjacent to Shift and Esc on a Sun workstation) throws **vi** for a loop and totally confuses the user, who still has lowercase fingers.

10

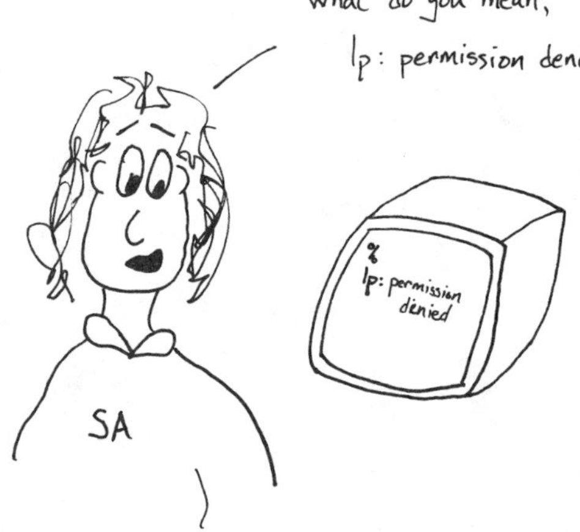

Printing under ATT

10.1 Introduction

When a user wants to print something, he must either use the program **lp** directly or a command that invokes **lp**. Only **lp** can queue data for printing. **lp** takes input and places it in a file in the spool directory appropriate for its final destination. The **lpsched** daemon determines when and where a particular file should be printed and then executes an interface program which formats the data and outputs it to the correct printer. Figure 10.1 gives a brief description of the commands that make up the printing system.

FIGURE 10.1

lp system commands	
Command	Description
accept	Begin accepting jobs to be queued
cancel	Cancel a queued or printing job
disable	Disable printing to a device
enable	Enable printing to a device
lp	Queue jobs for printing
lpadmin	Configure the printing system
lpmove	Move jobs from one device to another
lpsched	**lp** scheduling daemon
lpshut	Disable **lpsched**
lpstat	Show the status of the system
reject	Stop accepting jobs to be queued.

The AIX UNIX system for the IBM RT is based on ATT UNIX, but IBM has implemented yet another print spooling system, which bears no resemblance to either the **lp** system described here or the BSD **lpr** system described in Chapter 11. The AIX system is not covered.

10.2 Destinations and classes

A *destination* has a name, which consists of up to 14 alphanumeric characters and underscores. In addition to being named, a destination may belong to zero or more *classes*. A destination is usually a printer, but it does not have to be. For example, a destination could be an ordinary text file that needs to be appended to by many users. The printing system could be used to avoid the situation where two people attempt to add to the file at one time. A class of destinations is a group of destinations that all serve the same purpose in some way. For example, if a site had two line printers in the same room, they could be placed in a class. **lpsched** would direct output for that class to whichever printer became available first. Class names have the same restrictions as destination names. In the rest of this chapter the word "printer" is used generically to refer to destinations.

10.3 A brief description of lp

lp is a user-level command that is used to queue data for printing. **lp** makes a copy of the data to be printed (which may come either from named files or from standard input) and places it in a file or files in a spool directory. The spool directory is usually /usr/spool/*dest* where *dest* is the name by which **lp** knows the printer or class of printers. The file(s) are named *dest-N* where *N* is a job identification number assigned by **lp**. This filename is used to identify the job both to the user and internally to the printing system. We will henceforth refer to this name as the job identification (*jobid*, for short).

If the **-d** *destination* option is specified to **lp**, the input is queued for output to *destination*, where *destination* is either a printer or a class. If the **-d** option is not used, **lp** checks the LPDEST environment variable and uses its contents as the name of the output device. If LPDEST is not set, **lp** queues the data for output to the default device if one has been specified by the system administrator, or rejects the request if there is no default device.

10.3.1 Setting up lp

On some systems, you must build and configure **lp** from the source before it can be used. (A good way to check if **lp** has been built is to try to print something.) To build **lp**, create a login on the system called "lp" (this login should have a "*" in the password field), and make sure that the directory /usr/spool/lp does not exist. Then, **cd** to /usr/src/cmd/lp, and type **make -f lp.mk install**. After **lp** has been built, it must be told about your site configuration with the **lpadmin** (see Section 10.5) command. This only needs to be done when you install the system and when you make changes, because the configuration survives reboots.

10.4 The lpsched and lpshut commands

lpsched is a daemon that takes the files placed in the spool directory by **lp** and sends them to an appropriate device as soon as one is available. **lpsched** keeps a log of each file it processes and any errors that occur, usually in /usr/spool/lp/log. When **lpsched** is started, it moves /usr/spool/lp/log into /usr/spool/lp/oldlog and starts a new log file. A log file looks something like this:

```
***** LP LOG: Jul  6 12:05 *****
pr1-107        garth   pr1     Jul  6 12:10
pr-112         scott   pr1     Jul  6 12:22
pr-117         evi     pr2     Jul  6 12:22
pr1-118        garth   pr1     Jul  6 12:25
pr1-119        garth   pr1     Jul  6 13:38
pr-132         evi     pr1     Jul  6 13:42
```

The first column is the jobid of each job, the second column is the user that requested the job, the third column is the actual printer the job was sent to, and the last entry is the time that the job was queued. On the system in this example, there are two printers — "pr1" and "pr2" — both of which are in the class "pr". The user garth always specified the specific printer "pr1", so his jobs were always sent to "pr1". The users scott and evi, on the other hand, specified the class "pr", so their jobs were sent to the first available printer in that class. If jobs disappear from the system or something else unexpected occurs, the log file is the first place you should look to try to determine the problem.

To stop **lpsched** for any reason (to run **lpadmin**, for example), type **/usr/lib/lpshut**. When **lpsched** is not running, no jobs will actually be printed, though **lp** may still be used to queue jobs for printing. Any jobs in the process of being printed when the daemon is stopped will be reprinted in their entirety when the daemon is restarted. To restart the daemon, simply type **/usr/lib/lpsched**.

lpsched should be started when the system comes up multi-user, so the following lines should be placed in the /etc/rc file:

```
rm -f /usr/spool/lp/SCHEDLOCK
/usr/lib/lpsched
echo "lpsched started"
```

The file /usr/spool/lp/SCHEDLOCK is a file that is created to make sure only one copy of **lpsched** is running. If **lpsched** is stopped by any means other than **lpshut**, SCHEDLOCK must be removed by hand before **lpsched** can be restarted.

10.5 The lpadmin command

The **lpadmin** command is used to tell the printing system about your local printer configuration. It is used to give each printer a name, to create classes, and to specify the default printer. All the **lpadmin** command really does is create text files in the directory /usr/spool/lp. However, you should not try to edit these files directly because they are very format-sensitive and break easily. If you are curious, you can peruse these files after you have set everything up to see what is there. These files are a good place to practice the old adage "look but don't touch." Most **lpadmin** commands will not work when **lpsched** is running, so **lpsched** must be stopped with **lpshut** before **lpadmin** is used.

Before the printing system can output jobs to a particular printer, it must be told that the printer exists. To add a new device, execute:

/usr/lib/lpadmin -p*printer* **-v***device* { **-e***pr* | **-m***mod* | **-i***inter*} [**-c***class* ...] [{**-l** | **-h**}]

Where:

- *printer* is the name of the printer, both internally in the queuing system and to the user. Remember, the name is limited to 14 alphanumerics and underscores.
- *device* is the file that the printer is associated with. This is usually a special file in /dev (for example, /dev/pr1 or /dev/tty03), but it can be any file.
- The flag **e**, **m**, or **i** is used to tell the queuing system which printer interface program should be used. The printer interface program is responsible for actually formatting jobs before they are sent to the printer. Section 10.11 describes interface programs. The interface program may be specified in three ways:

    1. With the **-e***printer* option, where *printer* is the name of an already existing printer. This method of specifying the interface program is useful if you are adding a printer that is exactly like an existing one.

2. With the **-m***model* option, where *model* is a type of device that your system has an interface program for. Refer to your system documentation or look in the directory /usr/spool/lp/model to determine which models your system supports.

3. With the **-i***interface* option, where *interface* is the full pathname of a program that is to be used as an interface.

In addition to the required flags, **lpadmin** can be given the following options:

- **-c***class*, where *class* is the name of a class that the printer should be included in. Any number of **-c** flags may be specified for a given printer. If a class is specified that does not already exist, it will be created. Again, the name is limited to 14 characters.
- **-l** may be specified to tell **lpsched** to automatically disable the printer when it starts up. This option is intended to be used when the printer is a login terminal (hence the **-l**), but it can also be used for a device that is only attached to the system occasionally. Before any output can be sent to a printer specified with the **-l** option, the printer must be enabled (see Section 10.8). The **-h** option, the default, specifies that the printer is hardwired and can be used to disable the **-l** option.

lp will not accept requests for a new printer until it is told to do so with the **accept** command (see Section 10.7).

lpadmin can be used to modify the specification of an existing printer by specifying **-p***printer* and any options you wish to change. In general, **lpadmin** should not be used while **lpsched** is running. However, the device file may be changed with the **-v** option without stopping **lpsched**.

The **lpadmin -p***printer* **-r***class* flag may be specified, which removes *printer* from *class*. If the specified printer is the only member of *class*, this causes *class* to be removed. The **-x***printer* flag may be used to remove *printer*. If *printer* is the only member of a class, then that class is also removed. Neither a printer nor a class may be removed if it has jobs queued for output. The **lpmove** or the **cancel** commands may be used to remove jobs queued for a printer (see Sections 10.9 or 10.6 respectively).

When printing system commands take an argument with a flag, and it makes sense for the command to refer to more than one object, the argument may either be a single item or a list of items in the form "arg1,arg2,arg3,...". For example,

```
lpstat -p"pr1,pr2"
```

would show the status of pr1 and pr2.

Figure 10.2 gives a brief summary of the **lpadmin** flags that have just been explained.

FIGURE 10.2

lpadmin flags	
Flag	Result
-d*dest*	Makes *dest* the system default destination
-x*dest*	Removes *dest* from the printing system
-p*printer*	Specifies printer to which all of the following options apply:
-c*class*	Adds *printer* to *class*
-r*class*	Removes *printer* from *class*
-e*dest*	Copies the interface program from *dest* for use by *printer*
-i*interface*	Makes *interface* the interface program for *printer*
-m*model*	Specifies that *printer* should use the interface program for *model*
-h	Indicates that *printer* is hard-wired
-l	Indicates that *printer* is a login terminal
-v*file*	Indicates that output to *printer* should be appended to *file*

Here are some examples of **lpadmin** commands, with brief explanations of what they do:

/usr/lib/lpadmin -ppr1 -v/dev/tty06 -mdumb -cpr

This tells the printing system that a printer to be called "pr1" is connected to /dev/tty06, that the printer should be in the class "pr", and that the interface program for dumb printers should be used.

/usr/lib/lpadmin -ppr2 -v/dev/tty07 -epr1 -cpr

This tells the printing system that a printer to be called "pr2" is connected to /dev/tty07, that the printer should be in the class "pr", and that it should use the same interface program as "pr1".

/usr/lib/lpadmin -ppr2 -v/dev/tty08

Changes the file associated with the already existing printer "pr2" to /dev/tty08. All other parameters of "pr2" remain the same.

/usr/lib/lpadmin -dpr

Sets the system default destination to class "pr".

/usr/lib/lpadmin -ppr1 -rpr -cfast

Removes printer "pr1" from class "pr" and adds it to class "fast".

/usr/lib/lpadmin -xpr1

Removes printer "pr1" completely. This also removes the class "fast" if "pr1" was its only member.

10.6 The cancel command

cancel allows jobs that are queued or being printed to be canceled. **cancel** can either be invoked with a job number (this can be determined with **lpstat**, see Section 10.10) with a printer name. If a printer is specified, the job currently being printed is canceled. For example, **cancel 576** would cancel job 576, and **cancel pr1** would cancel the job currently on printer pr1. **cancel** is usually owned by the pseudo-user "lp" with group bin and mode 6775 so that any user can use it to cancel jobs that are obviously bogus. If someone who did not send a job cancels it, mail is sent to the user who submitted the job. If users abuse this privilege, the mode of the command may be set so it does not run setuid.

10.7 The accept and reject commands

If a printer will be unavailable for a long time (for example, due to hardware failure), jobs should not be queued for that device to avoid filling the spool directory with files. The **reject** command is used to tell **lp** to stop queuing jobs for a particular device. The command:

/usr/lib/reject -r"Printer pr1 is broken until Tuesday" pr1

would cause **lp** to reject requests for pr1 and print a message like:

```
% lp -dpr1 afile
lp: cannot accept requests for destination "pr1"
    -- Printer pr1 is broken until Tuesday
```

The **-r** flag is optional, but it is a nice way to tell users the reason that the printer is rejecting requests. The **/usr/lib/accept** *printer* command tells **lp** to begin accepting requests for *printer*. **accept** must be executed once for each new printer added with **lpadmin** because when a printer is created, it rejects requests by default.

accept and **reject** may be given a class name instead of a destination name to suspend printing for an entire class.

10.8 The enable and disable commands

The **disable** command tells **lpsched** to stop sending jobs to a particular printer. Unlike **reject**, **disable** does not stop **lp** from queuing jobs for the printer. However, queued jobs will not be output until the printer is re-enabled with the **enable** command. **disable** does not normally stop printing of the job currently being output to the printer, but if the **-c** option is specified it will cancel the current job. Like **reject**, **disable** supports a **-r** flag to allow an explanation of why a printer is disabled which will be displayed if you try to use the device. For example, to disable printing on pr1, execute:

/usr/lib/disable -r"Printer being cleaned, back up in 15 minutes" pr1

To tell pr1 to begin printing again, type:

/usr/lib/enable pr1

10.9 The lpmove command

Sometimes it is necessary to move jobs queued for one printer or class to another printer. This is accomplished with the **lpmove** command. **lpmove** is executed with a list of jobids and the name of a new printer; for example:

/usr/lib/lpmove pr1-324 pr1-325 pr2

would move the jobs numbered 324 and 325 from the queue for printer pr1 to the queue for printer pr2. **lpmove** can also be given a printer or class as a source; for example:

/usr/lib/lpmove pr1 pr2

would move all jobs queued for pr1 to the queue for pr2. When **lpmove** is used in this manner, it has the side effect of executing a **reject** on the printer. In the preceding example, **lp** would no longer accept requests for pr1. **lpmove** cannot be used when **lpsched** is running.

10.10 The lpstat command

The **lpstat** command is used to find the status of all parts of the queuing system. If executed without any arguments, it gives the status of all jobs that belong to the user who executed it. With the **-p***printer* argument, **lpstat** gives information on the status of *printer*. For example:

```
% lpstat -ppr1
printer pr1 is now printing pr-125. enabled since Jul 4 12:25
```

shows the status of printer pr1. The status of **lpsched** can be determined with the **lpstat -r** command; for example:

```
% lpstat -r
scheduler is running
```

shows you that everything is OK. Figure 10.3 lists the flags for **lpstat**.

FIGURE 10.3

lpstat flags	
Flag	Result
-r	Show the status of the **lpsched** daemon
-d	Show the default destination
-c*class*	List the members of *class*
-o*arg*	Show the status of output requests for *arg* *arg* is a printer, a class, or a jobid
-u*user*	Show the status of jobs submitted by *user*
-p*printer*	Show the status of *printer*
-v*printer*	List the output device associated with *printer*
-a*dest*	Show the acceptance status of *dest*
-s	Show a summary of status information
-t	Show all of the status information

10.11 Interface programs

An interface program must take information from a file that **lpsched** specifies, format it, and place it on the standard output. How the output is formated is completely up to the interface program. Interface programs are usually shell scripts, but they can be any executable program that performs the desired function. The interface program for a particular printer is kept in /usr/spool/lp/interface/*printer*. A user-supplied interface program specified with the **lpadmin -i** option should be owned by the pseudo-user "lp", with group owner "bin" and mode 644. The interface program is also responsible for setting the correct modes on the output device and generating headers and trailers if they are desired. When **lpsched** executes an interface program, it passes the following arguments:

/usr/spool/lp/interface/*printer jobid user title copies options file [file ...]*

Where:

- *jobid* is the job identification that is given by **lp**
- *user* is the user to whom the job belongs
- *title* is an optional title supplied by the user
- *copies* is the number of copies to print

- *options* are user-supplied options
- *file(s)* are full pathnames of files to be printed

All of the arguments will appear each time the interface program is executed, but some may be null strings. The interface program gets its standard input from /dev/null and both stdout and stderr are directed to the destination device as specified by the **lpadmin -v** command. An interface program should exit with a 0 on successful completion, and with an integer in the range 1 to 127 if an error is encountered. If a serious error occurs, the interface program should **disable** (see Section 10.8) the printer. If you need a simple interface program but none of those in the /usr/spool/lp/model directory will do, /usr/spool/lp/model/dumb is a good program to copy and modify.

11

Printing under BSD

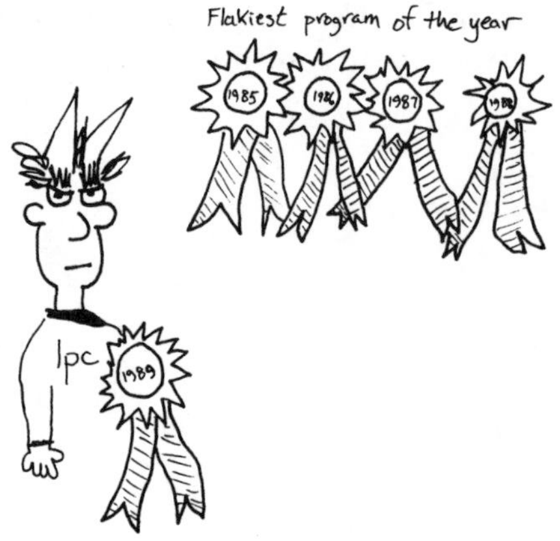

The printing facilities provided by BSD are somewhat mediocre. They allow only simple operations, are hard to maintain, and sometimes just plain don't work right. The saving grace of the BSD printing model is that it extends well to large networks, allowing many computers to share printers.

Just like any other piece of hardware, a printer must be properly connected and configured into its host's kernel before anything useful can happen. Most printers connect through a serial port like a terminal, and for these no special kernel configuration need be done. The procedure for adding other types of interfaces is described in Chapter 7: *Devices and Drivers*.

11.1 An overview of the printing process

Under BSD, all access to printers is controlled by the **lpd** daemon (located in /usr/lib) and the **lpr** program (in /usr/ucb). **lpr** takes data to be printed and puts it in a spooling queue, where **lpd** finds it prints it out. **lpr** is the only program on a UNIX system that can queue files for printing. Other programs that cause files to be printed do so by calling **lpr**.

When **lpr** is executed it gathers the data to be printed and information that specifies how the job should be handled. There are three sources for this handling information: the command-line arguments supplied to **lpr**, the environment variables of the process which executes **lpr**, and the system environment. In some cases, all three are potential sources for the same piece of information.

A case in point is the selection of the printer to which the job should be sent. If a **-P***printer* argument is passed to **lpr**, *printer* becomes the destination. Otherwise, the environment is checked to see if a variable named PRINTER is defined, and if so its value is assumed to be the name of the desired printer. If all else fails, the job is pawned off on the systemwide default printer. (Almost all printing-related commands accept a **-P** argument or a PRINTER environment variable, including **lpq** and **lprm**.)

As soon as **lpr** knows what printer the current job is headed for, it looks the printer up in the system's printer information database, /etc/printcap. This file tells **lpr** the name of a directory where print jobs headed for that printer should be placed. This is usually /usr/spool/*printername* and is called the *spool directory*.

lpr creates two files in the spool directory for each job. The first file's name consists of the letters "cf" followed by a number that identifies the job; this file contains reference and handling information for the job, such as to whom the job belongs. The second file's name begins with "df" instead of "cf". This file contains the actual data to be printed. After the file has been spooled, **lpr** notifies **lpd** of the job's existence.

When **lpd** receives this notification, it consults /etc/printcap to determine whether the print job is local or remote.[1] If the /etc/printcap file says that the destination printer is connected locally, **lpd** checks to be sure there is a printing daemon operating on the appropriate queue, and creates one (a copy of itself) if there is not.

If the requested printer is connected to a different machine, **lpd** opens a connection to the **lpd** running on the remote machine and transfers both the data and the control file. The local **lpd** then deletes the local copies of these files.

[1] Actually, the **lpd** spawned from /etc/rc doesn't do any of the real work; it just waits for network connections from other programs and makes copies of itself to handle any specific requests. When we say **lpd** does such-and-such, you can take it to mean that some *copy* of **lpd** does the work.

Scheduling for print jobs is done on a strictly first-in-first-out (FIFO) basis, but the system administrator can modify the printing agenda using the **lpc** program if desired. Unfortunately, there is no way to permanently instruct the printing system to give preferential treatment to jobs spooled by a particular user or machine.

When the job is ready to print, **lpd** creates a pathway between the spool file and the printing hardware through which the data to be printed can flow. In the middle of this pathway **lpd** places a *filter process*, a kind of electronic roadblock which gets to see and modify everything in the data stream before it hits the printer. Filter processes may perform various transformations on the data, or none at all: Their chief function is to provide formatting for special applications and any device-specific arbitration that is required when dealing with a particular printer. A printer's default filter may be overridden by specifying an alternative filter on the **lpr** command line.

11.2 The /etc/printcap file

The /etc/printcap file is the heart of the BSD printing system. Every printer accessible from a particular machine must be described in /etc/printcap.

/etc/printcap has the same format as the files /etc/termcap, /etc/gettytab, /etc/disktab, and /etc/remote files. The first object in each entry is a list of names for the printer, separated by a vertical bar ("|") character. This is followed by a number of configuration settings separated by colons, each of which is of the form "*XX=string*", "*XX*", or "*XX#number*", where *XX* is the two-character name of some parameter and *string* and *number* are values to be assigned to it. The null string may be assigned. When no value is assigned, the variable is Boolean and its presence indicates true. The null assignment is acceptable, so two colons may be placed side-by-side. It is often helpful to end each line of assignments with a colon *and* begin the following line with a colon to ease modifications. Comments in /etc/printcap are delineated by a hash mark ("#"). Entries may be continued from line to line by ending intermediate lines with a backslash.

The syntax of /etc/printcap is illustrated by the following short printcap entry. A more complete example will follow the discussion of the printcap variables.

```
#
# Apple LaserWriter remote printcap.  CS Department.
#
anchor-lw|cer|cer printer in ee1-56|:\
        :lp=:sd=/usr/spool/anchor-lw:rm=anchor:rp=anchor-lw:\
        :lf=/usr/adm/lpd-errs:
```

From the first line, we can see that "cer", "anchor-lw", and "cer printer in ee1-56" are all equivalent names for the same printer. While you are free to give your printers as many names as you like, you should include at least three forms of the primary name:

- Short name - no more than four characters, easy to type (e.g., "cer")
- Full name - specifies type of printer and owner (e.g., "anchor-lw")
- Descriptive name - other information (e.g., "cer printer in ee1-56")

All jobs submitted to the printing system without a specific destination are routed to the printer "lp", so one of your printers needs to have "lp" as an alias. You should not abandon the three-name system just described when configuring you default printer; simply tack on "lp" as an extra alias.

11.2.1 Printcap variables

The printcap variables are well documented in **printcap**(5), so we'll discuss only the most common ones. Most of the variables fall into one of five basic categories:

- File and directory specifications
- Remote access information
- Printing filters
- Communication settings
- Page information

11.2.1.1 File and directory specifications

All printcap entries should make at least two of these specifications: the spool directory (the "sd" variable) and the error log (the "lf" directory).

Each printer should have its own spool directory. All spool directories should be in the same parent directory (usually /usr/spool), and should have the same name as the full name of the printer they serve (e.g., "anchor-lw" in the preceding example). A spool directory is needed even if the printer being described lives on a different machine: Remember that spooled files will be stored locally until they can be transmitted for printing.

The spool directory is also used to contain two status files: "lock" and "status". The status file contains a one-line description of the printer's state; this information is maintained by **lpd** and referenced by the **lpq** command. The lock file is used to prevent multiple invocations of **lpd** from becoming active on a single queue and to hold information about the active job. The permission bits on the lock file are manipulated by **lpc** to enable or disable spooling and printing on the printer.

When you install a new printer, you must create the spool directory by hand. Permissions should be 775, with both owner and group-owner set to the pseudo-user "daemon".

The error log file may be shared by all printers, and may be placed anywhere you like. When a log entry is made, the name of the offending printer will be included. The log file in the example above is /usr/adm/lpd-errs.

The device name (the "lp" variable) for the printer must also be specified on the machine to which the printer is connected. This is the device file in the /dev directory which references the printer hardware. Often, this is some kind of serial port, but it can be any kind of interface. If the printer can send status information back to the host, the Boolean variable "rw" should be specified to open the device for both reading and writing rather than write-only.

If you intend to charge for printer usage or simply want to keep tabs on how much your users are printing, you should enable accounting for the printer by specifying an accounting information file (the "af" variable). The accounting file should only be specified on the machine where the printer lives, since accounting records are written when a job is printed out. Printer accounting information may be summarized with the **pac** command. See Chapter 19: *Accounting* for more information.

11.2.1.2 Remote access information

If a printer is to be used by more than one machine on a network, each printcap entry describing it must contain network configuration information. In the most tightly controlled case, two security conditions must be met before a user may spool jobs to a remote printer. First, the local machine must be in the remote machine's /etc/hosts.equiv file (or, under 4.3BSD, in the remote machine's /etc/hosts.lpd file). Second, the user must have an account on the remote machine. The second check is optional. On the machine connected to the printer, the only variable which need be set is the Boolean variable "rs". If "rs" is true, remote users are required to have local accounts before they can use a local printer; if false, anyone may use it.

On a machine which wishes to access a remote printer, the variables "rp" and "rm" must both be set. "rm" is the name of the machine to which the printer is physically connected and "rp" is the name by which the remote machine knows the printer. The "rp" variable allows you to call a printer by a different name on each host, but this is *not* recommended. An exception to this is the assignment of the default printer alias, "lp".

The preceding printcap example references a remote printer on the machine anchor. The printer is known by the name "anchor-lw" on both machines.

11.2.1.3 Printing filters

Filters perform a number of functions. The default filter **(/usr/lib/lpf)** does little but copy input to output, fixing up various nonprinting sequences and writing out an accounting record if appropriate. In the early days of UNIX, printer filters were often relied upon to perform various formatting tasks, but this practice is not as widespread as it once was. The only special filters you really need to worry about are those for handling **troff** output, TEX and LATEX[2] output, and screen dumps (on graphic workstations), and these only if you have a laser printer.

If you have a dot-matrix or other character-only printer you don't really need to be concerned with filters, and if you have a laser printer, phototypesetter, or electrostatic plotter the necessary filters will usually be provided to you with the printer's software.

11.2.1.4 Communication settings

A printer is like any other piece of hardware in that for correct operation it and its host computer must agree on a common set of communication parameters such as speed, parity, and flow control. Printers are typically connected to serial ports, so configuration of a printer is much like configuration of a terminal, except that you have to do everything by hand rather than relying on **tset**. Communication settings should only be specified on the printer's host machine.

There are three settings you control through printcap: the baud rate, the flag bits, and the local mode bits. The baud rate is the speed at which communication occurs (in bits per second), and is a simple integer. The other two parameters are more complicated; they too are simply integers, but each bit within the number modifies the behavior of the port in its own way. Setting up these parameters correctly requires that you look up the meaning of each bit in the **tty**(4) manual page and add up the values for all the bits you want to set or clear.

Baud rate

Baud rate is controlled by the "br" variable. Since it is a numeric variable, you'll use the hash mark ("#") to set it. For example, "br#9600" sets the baud rate to 9600 baud.

[2] We cannot be held responsible for the appearance of the names of "that other typesetting system."

Baud rate can only assume the standard values 50, 75, 110, 134.5, 150, 200, 300, 600, 1200, 1800, 2400, 4800, 9600, and 19,200. Some of these values (especially the slower speeds) are no longer in common use. You will probably want to run your printers at 1200, 2400, 9600, or 19,200 bits per second. The speed you select will depend on the speeds at which the printer is capable of receiving data, the speed at which the printer actually prints, and the quality of your connection cables.

As a general rule, the more expensive the printer, the greater the range of communication speeds it can handle. Desktop dot-matrix printers will usually only support one speed. Telling the printer at what speed it should communicate involves twiddling the printer hardware in some way; turning a knob on the back or setting some DIP switches (the amazing switches-on-a-chip) inside the driver circuitry. Your printer manual will tell you how.

It is not useful to run the communications to a printer much faster than the rate at which it can print. While most printers are smart enough to tell their host to stop sending data when their internal buffers are full, you increase the number of interrupts the host must handle and may reduce the reliability of the connection by running it at higher speeds.

Flag bits

The flag bits set parity, flow control, duplex, buffering, and mechanical delays. Figure 11.1 shows the meanings of the most important bits.

FIGURE 11.1

Meaning of the flag bits for a serial printer

Name	Octal value	Description
FF1	0040000	Form feed delay (2 seconds)
CR1	0010000	Carriage return delay (0.08 second)
CR2	0020000	Carriage return delay (0.16 second)
TAB1	0002000	Tab delay (dependent on amount of motion)
NL1	0000400	Newline delay (dependent on current column)
NL2	0001000	Newline delay (0.1 second)
EVENP	0000200	Even parity allowed on input and generated on output
ODDP	0000100	Odd parity allowed on input and generated on output
RAW	0000040	Pass all characters from printer to filter immediately
CRMOD	0000020	Output linefeed as "carriage-return linefeed"
ECHO	0000010	Echo (full duplex)
CBREAK	0000002	Pass characters from printer to filter immediately
TANDEM	0000001	Automatic flow control

There are two variables that can be assigned when adjusting the flag bits: “fc” and “fs”. The “fc” variable specifies those bits that should be turned off, and the "fs" variable specifies the ones that should be turned on. Bits assigned to neither variable assume default values. It is meaningless to both set a bit and clear it.

The values that should be assigned to "fc" and "fs" are computed by adding up (in octal) the values as listed in Figure 11.1. An octal number may be entered into /etc/printcap by prefacing it with a zero, so conversion to decimal is not necessary.

Suppose you want to allow both even and odd parity, enable automatic flow control, and disable full-duplex communication. You would want to set ODDP, EVENP, and TANDEM, and clear ECHO. Since ODDP + EVENP + TANDEM = 0100 + 0200 + 0001 = 0301, you would use "fs#0301" to set these bits and "fc#010" to clear ECHO.

The various delay bits are for use with old impact printers that do not have internal buffers, such as teletypes. Since it takes these printers much longer to perform carriage return, newline, and tab operations than to simply print a character, they may drop characters following these operations if the host computer does not pause to let them catch up. Be sure to clear all delay bits on printers that don't need them (99.9%).

Parity is not usually significant for printers, so EVENP and ODDP should either be both on or both off.

Setting the TANDEM bit lets the host computer issue flow control characters to the printer. This is useful only for smart peripherals like laser printers that both send status messages back to the host and also understand how to do output flow control.

The **tty**(4) manual page explains the meaning of each terminal mode bit in gory detail.

11.2.1.5 Local mode bits

The difference between the flag bits and the local mode bits is that flag bits configure the actual communication link and local mode bits configure the serial driver. The configuration method for both is the same, with the variables "xc" and "xs" being analogous to "fc" and "fs".

Most of the mode bits are intended for use on interactive video terminals and so are not relevant to printer configuration. The three bits you might want to set are listed in Figure 11.2.

FIGURE 11.2

Meaning of local mode bits for a serial printer		
Name	Octal value	Description
LLITOUT	000040	Suppress output translations
LDECCTQ	040000	Only <Control-Q> restarts output after <Control-S>
LCRTBS	000001	Backspace on erase rather than echoing erase

You will probably want to set LLITOUT to keep the serial driver from meddling with any output codes that are destined for the printer. LCRTBS is used for impact printers that need overstrike capability for printing underlined text (i.e., **nroff** output). LDECCTQ is used in handling flow control. If the printer uses the standard <Control-S>/<Control-Q> flow control characters this bit should be set to minimize any flow control interference that might be caused by line noise.

11.2.1.6 Page information

Some filters need to know the size of the output page so they can do cropping and line folding correctly. For character printers, the "pl" and "pw" variables specify the page length in lines and the page width in characters, respectively. For high-resolution printers the analogous variables are "py" and "px", both of which are specified in pixels. Some printers can act in either mode, so both sets of variables should be specified.

11.2.1.7 Miscellaneous printcap variables

Figure 11.3 is a short summary of some other printcap variables with which you should be familiar.

FIGURE 11.3

Some miscellaneous /etc/printcap variables			
Name	Type	Meaning	Default
ff	string	String that causes printer to form feed	<Control-L>
fo	bool	Output form feed when device is opened?	no
mc	num	Maximum number of copies allowed for job	0 (unlimited)
mx	num	Maximum file size of job (in blocks)	0 (unlimited)
sc	bool	Suppress multiple copies?	no
sf	bool	Suppress form feeds?	no
sh	bool	Suppress printing of burst page header?	no

11.2.2 A sample /etc/printcap entry

In this section we will look at local and remote printcap entries for an Apple LaserWriter named "gutenberg" ("gb" for short) connected to the machine sigi. Our intent is merely to give a taste of what a "real" entry is like rather than to explain every nuance fully.

The local printcap entry, on sigi, is:

```
gutenberg|gb|7-24|CS LaserWriter OT7-24:\
    :lp=/dev/gutenberg:sd=/usr/spool/gutenberg:\
    :lf=/usr/adm/gutenberg-log:af=/usr/adm/gutenberg.acct:\
    :br#9600:rw:fc#0000374:fs#0000003:xc#0:xs#0040040:mx#0:sf:sb:\
    :if=/usr/local/lib/ps/psif:\
    :of=/usr/local/lib/ps/psof:gf=/usr/local/lib/ps/psgf:\
    :nf=/usr/local/lib/ps/psnf:tf=/usr/local/lib/ps/pstf:\
    :rf=/usr/local/lib/ps/psrf:vf=/usr/local/lib/ps/psvf:\
    :cf=/usr/local/lib/ps/pscf:df=/usr/local/lib/ps/psdf:
```

Note that the machine has four separate names, one of which is the room number. This is useful if you know where you want your output to be printed, but don't remember the name of the printer there. The device file that represents the printer is identified as /dev/gutenberg; this file is actually a link to a serial port named /dev/ttyB7. The spool directory for the printer is /usr/spool/gutenberg. The error log file is /usr/adm/gutenberg-log, and accounting information is kept in the file /usr/adm/gutenberg.acct.

Gutenberg's serial line is run at 9600 baud. Since LaserWriters are intelligent printers that are capable of sending status information back to the host computer, the "rw" option is given to specify that /dev/gutenberg be opened both for reading and for writing as a job is printed.

The flag bits, set with the "fs" and "fc" variables, configure the port for no parity, no character buffering, full duplex with no echo, bidirectional flow control, no translation of newline characters, and both uppercase and lowercase text. The local mode bits prevent the serial driver from doing output translation on control characters, and specify that only a <Control-Q> may be used to restart output after a <Control-S>.

The "mx" variable is set to zero to allow files of any size to be printed, as is appropriate for a printer with graphics capabilities. "sf" suppresses form feeds, and "sb" asks for only short banners to be printed.

The rest of the variables assigned in this entry are filter programs for various types of output. The default output filter is **/usr/local/lib/psof**, and the filter which does accounting is **/usr/local/lib/psif**.

On a remote machine, the printcap entry for gutenberg is much shorter:

```
gutenberg|gb|7-24|CS LaserWriter OT7-24:\
    :lp=:sd=/usr/spool/gutenberg:\
    :rm=sigi:rp=gutenberg:\
    :lf=/usr/adm/gutenberg-log:mx#0:
```

The spool directory and error log file are named the same as on sigi. Note that no accounting file is specified since all accounting is done on the printer's local host. The "mx" variable is set here because file size checks are done when a job is spooled. Each host that uses the printer remotely must have its own copy of the spooling restrictions. The "rm" variable identifies the printer's host as sigi, and the "rp" variable explains that sigi knows the printer as "gutenberg".

11.3 Controlling the printing environment

Day-to-day maintenance of the printing system requires that you know how to use only three commands: **lpq**, **lprm**, and **lpc**. **lpq** lets you examine the queue of jobs waiting to be printed on a particular printer, and **lprm** lets you delete one or more of these jobs, erasing their stored data files and removing any reference to them within the printing system. Both of these commands are available to users, and both work transparently across the Ethernet.

lpc lets you make a number of changes to the printing environment, such as disabling printers and reordering the printing queues. Although some of its functions are available to users, **lpc** is primarily an administrative tool.

11.3.1 The lpq command - view the printing queue

lpq is normally used with only a **-P** option, although command-line arguments may be used to restrict which jobs are shown. Output from **lpq** looks like this:

```
anchor-lw is ready and printing
Rank   Owner      Job  Files                             Total Size
active garth      314  domain.2x1.ps, domain.3x2.ps      298778 bytes
1st    kingery    286  standard input                    17691 bytes
2nd    evi        12   appendices                        828 bytes
3rd    garth      13   proc                              43229 bytes
4th    scott      14   periodic                          16676 bytes
5th    garth      16   standard input                    489 bytes
```

The first column tells you what order the jobs will be printed in. This is kind of superfluous since the output lines are always in order, with the active job on top and the last job to be printed on the bottom. The second column tells you the user who spooled the job. The third column gives the job identification number for each job; this is important to know if you intend to manipulate the job later using **lprm** or **lpc**. The fourth column reiterates the files listed on the **lpr** command line used to spool the job. If the spooled data came in via a pipe (as the 5th job did), this column will say "standard input". The fifth and final column tells you the size of the job. Note that this number includes all formatting codes sent to the printer, so it doesn't necessarily represent the number of characters to be printed.

11.3.2 The lprm command - remove jobs

The most common form of **lprm** is **lprm** *jobid*, where *jobid* is the job identification number as reported by **lpq**. **lprm** *user* removes all jobs belonging to *user*. **lprm** without arguments removes the currently active job. **lprm -** removes all the jobs you submitted; if you are root, it removes every job in the queue. No ordinary user may remove another user's jobs; however, the superuser may remove any job.

The printing system maintains a notion of the origin of a job as well as the user who spooled it, and **lprm**'s matching process takes both into account. Thus garth@boulder is not considered equivalent to garth@sigi, and neither can remove the other's jobs. Some systems (like Suns) are even more cagey about removing jobs and don't allow the superuser to remove jobs over the network.

Trying to **lprm** the active job can cause problems on some printers (especially LaserWriters using Transcript software). The filter process for the job doesn't get properly notified of the termination and the whole system comes to a grinding halt with the filter process holding an exclusive lock on the printer's port, preventing other processes from using the printer.

The only way to fix this situation is to use **ps** to identify all the filter processes and kill them off by hand. **lpc** is not of use in this situation. Rebooting the system will always cure a hung printer, but this is an awfully drastic measure to take. Before you resort to a reboot, kill and restart the master copy of **lpd** just as it is done in /etc/rc.

11.3.3 The lpc command - make administrative changes

The **lpc** command can perform the following functions:

- Enable or disable queuing for a particular printer
- Enable or disable printing on a particular printer
- Remove all jobs from a printer's queue
- Move a job to the top of a printer's queue
- Manipulate the **lpd** daemon
- Get printer status information

lpc wins our award for "flakiest program of 1989". It was also awarded this honor in 1985, 1986, 1987, and 1988. When the printing system is running smoothly **lpc** works just fine, but as soon as a filter gets stuck or some other minor problem appears, it wigs out completely. And **lpc** lies: It sometimes pretends to have fixed everything while in reality having done nothing at all. You may have to fix things up by hand or even power-cycle your equipment when printing gets badly snarled.

lpc cannot be used across a network. It is normally used interactively, although it may be invoked in a one-shot mode by putting an interactive command on the **lpc** command line. Once inside **lpc**, the following commands are available:

help [*command*] or **?** [*command*]
The **help** command without arguments shows you a short list of all available **lpc** commands. With an argument, it shows a one-line description of a particular command.

enable *printer* or **disable** *printer*
Enables or disables spooling of jobs to the named printer. Users who attempt to queue files will be politely informed that spooling has been disabled. Jobs that are already in the queue are not affected. This operation is performed by simply setting or clearing group execute permission on the /usr/spool/*printer*/lock file.

start *printer* or **stop** *printer*
Enables or disables printing on the named printer. Jobs may still be spooled when a printer has been stopped, but will not be printed until printing is restarted. **start** and **stop** operate by setting or clearing owner execute permission on /usr/spool/*printer*/lock. They also kill and start the appropriate daemons for the printer. The **stop** command allows the active job to complete before disabling printing.

abort *printer*
abort is just like **stop**, but it doesn't allow the active job to complete. When printing is re-enabled, this job will be printed over again.

down *printer message* or **up** *printer*
These commands affect both spooling and printing. They are used when a printer is really broken or has to be taken off-line for an extended period. The *message* parameter supplied to **down** can be as long as you like and need not be quoted; it will be placed in the printer's /usr/spool/*printer*/status file so that it will be shown to users who execute the **lpq** command. You'll normally want to use this to register a short explanation of why the printer is unavailable and when it will be back in service. The **up** command reverses the effect of a **down**.

clean *printer*
This command removes all jobs from the printer's queue, including the active job. Since the printing daemon for the queue will still hold

references to the files of the current job, UNIX will not really delete them and the current job will complete.

topq *printer jobid* or **topq** *printer username* The first form moves the named job to the top of the printer's queue. The second form moves all jobs belonging to *username* to the top of the queue.

restart *printer*
restart is used to restart a printing daemon that has mysteriously died. You'll know that the daemon is dead when **lpq** tells you "no daemon present".

status *printer*
This shows you four things about the named printer: whether or not spooling is enabled, whether or not printing is enabled, the number of entries in the queue, and the status of the daemon for that printer. If there are no entries in the queue, you'll see something like this:

```
lpc> status cer
cer:
        queuing is enabled
        printing is enabled
        no entries
        no daemon present
```

The fact that there is no daemon present is not a cause for concern; per-printer daemons go away after the queue is empty and aren't restarted by the master copy of **lpd** until another job is spooled.

11.4 Printer philosophy

It's hard to create a truly bad printing configuration, but you may find the following rules helpful.

11.4.1 On a network, put only one printer on each machine

There are three reasons for this. First, when a printer locks up and needs to be manipulated by hand, you'll appreciate having only one set of processes to deal with. If you have more than one printer on a single machine you won't be able to tell which copies of **lpd** belong to which printer. You'll have to kill off all of them.

Second, you don't want all your printing facilities to be tied to only one machine. You might be willing to go without printing for short periods of time while the machine is being rebooted or dumped, but what if it breaks and goes down for a week?

Third, supporting a printer is somewhat of a load on the host computer. It's a modest load, but not completely negligible. Just as it wouldn't be wise to put all your users on one computer, it is best to distribute the printing load as evenly as possible.

11.4.2 Use file size limits appropriately

The "mx" printcap variable lets you set a limit on the amount of data that can be spooled at one time. If all your users are knowledgeable and directly accountable, *don't* use this feature. Some people have legitimate reasons for printing huge files.

On the other hand, naive users sometimes do incredible things like try to print binaries. This is a bad situation because binaries tend to contain a lot of form feed characters and other miscellaneous garbage that the printer is sure to misinterpret. Even a small file can use up reams of paper. Some versions of **lpr** try to protect against this by examining the input file, but such a heuristic approach is never perfect.

Fortunately, binary files tend to be fairly large. If you expect to have such problems, you can experiment with restricting maximum file size.

Another thing to consider when using file size limitations is the type of printer. For an ASCII-only line printer, you can be sure that the number of characters spooled approximates the actual number of characters to be printed, but what about laser printers and electrostatic plotters? If bitmaps are being downloaded to the printer, it may take several hundred thousand characters to describe a single page. Our advice is never to use size limitations on anything but line printers.

11.4.3 Use printer accounting

You should enable printer accounting even if you don't plan to charge for printer use. The overhead is very slight and you get to see exactly who is using the printer.

11.4.4 Use burst pages only when necessary

By default, the printing system prefaces each job with a page showing various pieces of information associated with the job. This header page is essential for heavily used printers, but it is a waste of time and paper for light-duty printers or printers used only by a one or two people. If you don't need it, suppress it by setting the Boolean printcap variable "sh" true.

11.4.5 Provide recycling bins

A large proportion of the pages printed by any printer are discarded within half an hour. Since all kinds of computer paper are recyclable, it is a shame for this paper to be thrown in the trash. You can use the boxes that paper comes in as recycling bins. Post a sign asking that no foreign material (like staples, paper clips, and newspaper) be discarded there.

12

Adding a Disk

12.1 Introduction

There is never enough disk space. The minute a new disk is added to the system, it is half full, or so it seems. Getting users to clean up their disk space is as difficult as getting a teenager to clean his room. Therefore, the system administrator will occasionally have to install new disk drives.

All disks are different; new ones come out every few months. The host machines are all different, too. All this is a giant excuse for not covering disks thoroughly, but rather covering the ideas in a broad way, and then specifically covering only one disk, the Fujitsu Eagle SMD drive (Model 2351).

First we will survey the hardware available, then the anatomy of a disk, the hardware options and formatting, and finally, the software partitioning and filesystems. The organization of the filesystem beyond the partition level is covered in Chapter 4: *The Filesystem*.

12.2 The hardware

In this section we define the terms that are used to describe a disk system.

12.2.1 Disk controllers

A disk controller interfaces the host computer to the disk drive, where data is actually stored. In the beginning, computer manufacturers all had proprietary interfaces to their peripherals. At that point, small third-party vendors started manufacturing IBM- and DEC-compatible disk systems, which were very cost effective and totally compatible. Universities and other cost-conscious consumers supported the third-party vendors, which forced the big guys to start thinking about not-invented-here products and industry standard interfaces. Today, it is not uncommon for a computer manufacturer to specify, sell, and support third-party disks that are built to an industry standard. Two disk standards that have emerged are the SMD and SCSI families. Each is described briefly.

12.2.1.1 SMD family

SMD (Storage Module Disk) controllers are separate boards that are installed on the computer bus to arbitrate between device driver commands and actions performed on the disk. Each controller can handle one to four drives. The controller has a single 60-pin command cable that attaches to the interface board and daisy chains to each drive. The last drive in the line must have a little mini-board called a terminator installed. Individual 26-pin data cables attach each drive to the controller. The command or control cable is called the A cable; the data cable is called the B cable. Both are usually ribbon cables; however, FCC regulations disallow ribbon cables in secure installations. One manufacturer has gone to great lengths to create a complicated, but secure, cabling system using RF shielded cables with DB25 and DB37 type connectors, at an additional cost of about $200 per drive.

12.2.1.2 SCSI family

The SCSI (Small Computer Systems Interface), pronounced "scuzzy", interface is often right on the CPU board or peripherals board. SCSI is a standard interface to disk and tape controllers for small peripherals. While SCSI disks tend to be small, the new ESDI interface that uses the SCSI port on workstations has improved throughput and can control larger disks. The SCSI standard specifies a 50-pin connector; vendors use several types, including DB25 terminal connectors. SCSI disk cables daisy chain to multiple drives and use an internal terminator.

12.2.2 Disk drives

Several types of disk drives are used on modern computers. Removable media drives have been obsoleted by Winchesters, which may soon be obsoleted by optical disks and solid state memory. Our focus in this chapter is on Winchester disks in the 100 Mb to 1gb range.

12.2.2.1 Removable media drives

Previously, disk storage was primarily on removable disk packs. It was thought that this convenience would be heavily used, but in fact it was almost never used. The only time disk packs were removed was for cleaning, a scary process in which your precious disk pack was submerged in a small portable washing machine device and swished around for several minutes. This process presumably prevented head crashes due to dirt and dust.

12.2.2.2 Winchester drives

Winchester disks are sealed units that are built into the drive. They cannot be removed and sometimes cannot be taken apart and repaired. They are much more reliable than the old removable media, which were susceptible to smoke particles, airborne lint, and dust. The recording methods used in most modern hard disks require such precise performance that no contamination can be tolerated.

12.2.2.3 WORM drives

WORM drives are Write Once, Read Many optical disks. They are starting to be used for backups and stable read-only databases. See Chapter 18: *Backups and Transportable Media* for a more complete discussion.

12.2.2.4 Solid state disk

Solid state disk drives are really just memory that is used as a disk. Many programs show significant performance gains when directories like /tmp are on solid state drives.

12.3 Disk geometry

The geometry of a modern Winchester disk and the terminology used to refer to its various parts are shown in Figure 12.1. A computer disk today resembles a stack of records on a record changer. The disk records information in the same way that a cassette tape recorder does, by using a magnetic field to change the spatial orientation of particles of metallic oxide. These changes in

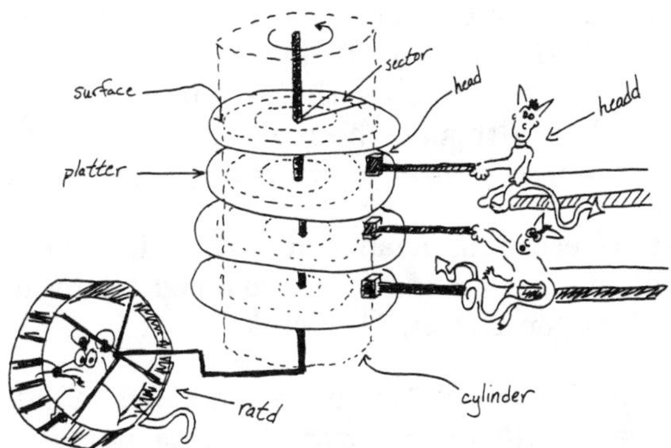

FIGURE 12.1 Disk geometry

orientation can be detected at a later time by passing the medium through a magnetic field and measuring the disturbance that the particles induce. In a cassette tape, the medium that carries the oxide particles is a long ribbon of plastic tape, while in a hard disk the medium is a circular plate called a *platter*. Each platter is usually coated with oxide on both *surfaces*, and therefore, can store data on both sides, just like a phonograph record.

In the very early days of computer hardware, disks usually had only one platter. An increase in storage capacity was provided by increasing the diameter of the platter. On the wall of our user area is an ancient platter over four feet in diameter which held approximately 280K of data. This is about one-fifth of the capacity of a 3.5-inch Macintosh floppy diskette. Today, hard disks usually have a number of smaller platters stacked one above the other, rather than one large platter.

Instead of just moving the oxide past stationary magnetic heads as a cassette player does, a hard disk moves both the medium and the recording heads. The platter is rotated at a high rate of speed, and the recording heads are mounted on arms that can be moved to various radial distances from the center of the platter. These correspond to the tonearm and needle in the record player analogy. Theoretically, the heads float very close to the surface of the platter, never actually touching it. If the head does touch the platter, this is called a *head crash* and can be very destructive. Once contact has been made, the heads tend to dig and gouge into the oxide like vicious little daggers, scratching off important data bytes, inodes, and timing marks. The recovery of data from crashed packs is a black art.

The radial movement of the head to the correct position over a particular piece of data is called *seeking*. At least one head is required for each surface of the disk. The disk heads on the early disks with a single large platter had to move huge distances to seek. Today's geometry of small stacked platters is much more efficient. The diameter of disks continues to decrease from a standard of 14 inches a few years ago, to 5$^{1}/_{4}$ inches today. In a stacked-platter system, it is possible for the arms for the various heads to be somewhat independent of one another, although the reading heads for the bottom of one platter and the top of the next platter down usually share an arm.

Each radial position that a recording head can occupy is called a *track*. Tracks are further divided into *sectors* which are mapped to the basic data block size in the software. A sector is often 512 bytes.

The set of tracks on a group of platters that have the same radial distance from the center of the platter is called a *cylinder*. All data stored in a single cylinder can be read without additional mechanical movement of the heads. Although heads move amazingly fast, they are still much slower than electrons. Therefore, any disk access that does not require the head to seek to a new position will be fast. The software driver for the disk tries to take advantage of this fact. The term *cylinder group* refers to a group of 1 to 32 contiguous cylinders and is used in the BSD fast filesystem.

12.4 Formatting the disk drive

Disk capacities are often quoted in numbers of unformatted bytes by overeager vendors. Typically, about 20% of the capacity is used in the overhead of marking the disk surfaces so the hardware/software can find the data written there. This is not optional; you must spend this space. In purchasing disks, always think in terms of formatted size and compare prices accordingly.

Formatting a disk drive writes address information and timing marks on the drive to delineate each sector, and identifies *bad blocks*. A bad block is an imperfection in the surface oxide on the disk media and results in one or more disk sectors that cannot be reliably read or written. Most formatting systems handle bad blocks as they are discovered by mapping them to alternate cylinders at the end of the disk. Sun uses a smarter system and slips bad blocks to extra sectors on the same cylinder. This allows more efficient access to the block, but costs some capacity. In addition, BSD provides utilities called **bad144** and **badsect** and ATT provides **badblk** which can be used to fix bad blocks which occur after the formatting has been done (see Section 12.10.4 for details).

The manufacturer of the disk will usually include a list of media defects that were found when quality control testing was done on the drive. A couple of additional bad spots normally develop during shipping. As you run the formatter, you should see the bad blocks reported. Check these against the media defect list provided with the drive to be sure there are not too many (hundreds) extras. It is not uncommon to have 100 bad blocks reported by the manufacturer.

Each system should provide a utility to format disks as part of a stand-alone diagnostics package rather than a UNIX command. Refer to your local documentation to see how to run the formatting command. We will describe the process when we detail the installation of a Fujitsu Eagle drive in Section 12.10.

12.5 Partitions

After the disk has been formatted and the bad sectors handled, the disk must be divided into separate[1] chunks called *partitions* for the UNIX software. A partition is a logical device that makes it easier to use a disk for many diverse purposes. Partitions make dumping easier, limit users from being total disk hogs, help performance, and confine potential damage from runaway programs. Partitions are traditionally named "a", "b", "c", ..., "h"; many systems limit each disk to a maximum of eight partitions. There are some defaults you should honor in naming your partitions: the "a" partition is the root, the "b" partition the swap and paging area and the "c" partition the whole disk. The "a" partition is always at the beginning of the disk; the "b" partition usually follows it. "d" through "h" divide up the rest of the disk into several partitions which probably overlap. This allows the system administrator to choose either several small partitions or one or two larger ones. *Do not use conflicting partitions.*

12.5.1 /etc/disktab file

The disk device driver must know about any partitions you intend for a given disk, as it treats each partition as though it were a small disk drive on its own. Early Unices had the tables defining partition locations and sizes compiled into the driver. You either had to live with the defaults delivered with the system or patch the driver with values you liked better. Fortunately the patching was not hard. More recent versions of BSD have "sort of" moved this partition definition table out of the disk device driver and into a text file, /etc/disktab. If the disk you are adding is known to your system, there will probably already be a disktab entry for that type of drive. The /etc/disktab entry for a Fujitsu Eagle from one of our BSD Vaxen is shown next.

[1] This is a lie. Partitions *do* overlap to allow the system administrator to decide between several layouts. The "c" device is by convention the whole disk drive and overlaps all partitions. It is VERY unhealthy to have active overlapping partitions.

```
eagle|Eagle|2351|2351A|Fujitsu Eagle 2351A (48 sectors):\
        :ty=winchester:ns#48:nt#20:nc#842:rm#3961:sf:\
        :pa#15884:ba#8192:fa#1024:\
        :pb#66880:bb#8192:fb#1024:\
        :pc#808128:bc#8192:fc#1024:\
        :pd#15884:bd#4096:fd#512:\
        :pe#307200:be#8192:fe#1024:\
        :pf#109248:bf#8192:ff#1024:\
        :pg#432768:bg#8192:fg#1024:\
        :ph#291346:bh#8192:fh#1024:
```

An /etc/disktab entry consists of a sequence of items separated by colons. The backslashes in the example serve to indicate that the entry continues onto the next line and do not affect its meaning. The first item is a set of names by which the disk may be called, separated by vertical bars. This drive may be called either an "eagle", an "Eagle", a "2351", a "2351A", or a "Fujitsu Eagle 2351A (48 sectors)".

Each of the other fields contains a two-letter code optionally followed by a string or numeric argument. If the argument is a number, a "#" must be inserted between it and the two-letter code – if the argument is a string, then an "=" must be inserted. Codes that do not take arguments require no extra characters. The valid codes that may appear are listed in Figure 12.2.

FIGURE 12.2

/etc/disktab codes		
Code	Meaning	Argument
ty	Type of disk	String
ns	Number of sectors per track	Numeric
nt	Number of tracks per cylinder	Numeric
nc	Number of cylinders per disk	Numeric
rm	Rotational speed, in rpm	Numeric
se	Sector size	Numeric
sf	Disk supports bad144-style bad sector forwarding	None
so	Partition offsets in sectors	None
p[a-h]	Default partition sizes in sectors	Numeric
b[a-h]	Default partition block sizes in bytes	Numeric
f[a-h]	Default partition fragment sizes in bytes	Numeric

We can see from the preceding entry that a Fujitsu Eagle is a Winchester disk, and that it has 48 sectors per track. Each cylinder is composed of 20 tracks, and there are 842 cylinders in the disk. The platters rotate at a speed of 3961 rpm, and the disk supports bad144-style bad sector forwarding. Each partition's size is specified in 512-byte blocks, and the block and fragment sizes for each partition are also given. Partitions, with the exception of the "d" partition, use 8K blocks and 1K fragments. (The BSD fast filesystem uses two sizes of data block called *blocks* and *frags*.)

We now explain the "sort of" in the earlier reference to moving the disk information out of the driver. While superficially it appears that the disk drivers could use the /etc/disktab file to determine partitioning of each disk, disktab in fact has a crucial piece of information missing: the cylinder offsets of each partition. The ":so" field is a Boolean and cannot express eight partition offsets. These offsets are hard-coded into a table in the driver on both 4.2BSD and 4.3BSD systems. The commands to build a filesystem on a partition use /etc/disktab to define the disk's geometry, but not its partitions. The manual page for disktab notes under the BUGS heading that it (the file) should not exist, but rather that the information should be stored directly on the disk drive itself.

Whenever the system has the partition information stored in the driver, it is difficult to change the default partitions. In addition, the device driver has only one table of partition information for each type of drive that it controls. Therefore, it is hard to ask that driver to handle two drives of the same type with different partition layouts. In general, even if this were simple to do, it is not advisable. It's too easy to forget a nonstandard partitioning and clobber the whole disk.

12.5.2 Disk labels

On Sun systems, a label containing the partition information is written on the first block of the disk (sector 0, track 0, cylinder 0). The /etc/disktab file does not exist. Backup copies of the label are stored at the end of the disk as well. The command **dkinfo** will display the information stored in the disk label. The Sun disk drivers reference this information from the disk.

Any naive **dd** of the root partition to another disk, say a backup root partition, needs to be to a disk of the same type and using the same partitions. If not, the label will be overwritten with an incorrect one and it will appear that you cannot read any of the other partitions. The driver will be using the wrong partition geometry and looking in the middle of data for the superblock and other special sections at the beginning of any partition. This is very scary the first time it happens. The way around it is to add arguments to the **dd** command to skip over the label.

The MIPS workstation running 4.3BSD has done disk labels really right. The label containing the disk geometry and partition information is stored on the disk in a volume header. It is not just the first block of the "a" partition, but rather a separate partition itself. It can only be accessed by utilities like **vdhtool** for reading and writing partition information. The bad sector information is also in a separate header partition of the disk.

The 4.3BSD Tahoe release also contains support for disk labels.

12.5.3 Partition layout

Disk partitions are related to the disk geometry just discussed. Partitions typically begin and end on whole cylinders and are composed of a number of radially concentric cylinders. For example, the Eagle disk has the following layout:

FIGURE 12.3

Eagle disk partition layout		
Partition	Cylinders	Typical use
a	0 - 16	Root
b	17 - 86	Swap
c	0 - 841	Whole disk
d	391 - 407	Alternate root
e	408 - 727	
f	728 - 841	
g	391 - 841	
h	87 - 390	

Graphically, but not to scale, this partitioning scheme can be depicted as:

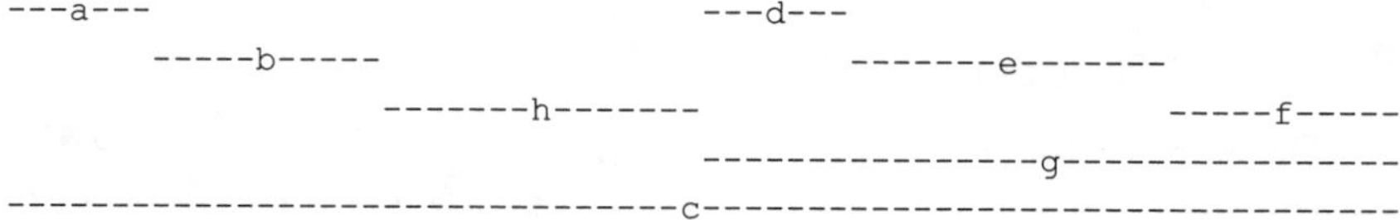

With this scheme, the system administrator can choose between using partitions a,b,h,g or using a,b,h,d,e,f or using just c.

Some systems require you to segment the disk by blocks, megabytes, or tracks, rather than cylinders — in these cases you should either be sure that the program will round to the nearest cylinder or double check your arithmetic: Partitions that do not begin on cylinder boundaries can cripple the throughput of the drive. 4.3BSD drivers force partitions to begin on cylinder boundaries.

12.5.4 Filesystems

Even after a hard disk has been conceptually divided into partitions it is still not ready to hold UNIX files. UNIX needs to add a little of its own disk overhead before the disk is ready for use.

This section describes the fast filesystem implemented by McKusick, Joy, and Leffler for 4.2BSD. The new filesystem is faster and more efficient than the old, and has improved crash-resistance mechanisms. ATT filesystems are generally similar to the 4.1BSD filesystem.

The partition is divided into one or more cylinder groups of 1 to 32 cylinders each. The discussion that follows applies to cylinder groups for the fast filesystem and to partitions for all filesystems. We use the partition terminology, rather than cylinder groups.

When a filesystem is built on a partition, the structure imposed contains five parts: a list of inode storage cells, a set of scattered *super-blocks*, a disk block map, a block usage summary, and a set of data blocks.

We've already talked about the role of inodes in storing information about files in Chapter 4. Since space for inodes must be set aside when UNIX does its initial structuring of the partition, it is necessary to decide in advance how many inodes to create. Predicting exactly how many files (inodes) will someday be needed in the filesystem is impossible; UNIX uses an empirically determined formula to estimate the number of inodes that should be allocated based on the amount of raw storage space that the partition contains. A ratio of one inode for each 2K of storage space is the default, and this usually provides more inodes than could ever conceivably be used. You can adjust the number of inodes per partition either up or down when you structure the partition — more inodes for filesystems with lots of small files, fewer for filesystems with large files. We recommend that, unless your needs are highly atypical, you just use the default.

The super-block is a block of data that describes the characteristics of the partition. Inside the super-block, information is recorded that describes the length in bytes of a disk block, the size and location of the inode table, the disk block map and usage information, the size of the cylinder groups, and a few other pieces of critical information. Because loss or damage of the super-block would remove information necessary to make the disk readable, several copies of the super-block are maintained in widely scattered locations within the partition. This was not always true; early filesystems were totally destroyed if *the* super-block became corrupted. UNIX wizards had to be adept at patching the super-block with **fsdb** on the raw device files.

For each partition, UNIX keeps both an in-memory copy of the superblock and several on-disk copies. The UNIX kernel provides the **sync** system call to flush in-memory super-blocks to their permanent storage places on disk, making the filesystem consistent for a split second. This minimizes the amount of damage that would occur if the machine were to crash when the filesystem has not updated the appropriate super-blocks. **sync** also flushes modified inodes and cached data blocks. The **update** daemon makes sure that **sync** is called at least once every thirty seconds, and additional calls may be invoked by executing the **sync** command.

The disk block map for a partition is simply a map of the free and used blocks within the partition. When new files are written this map is examined to devise a layout scheme that will minimize the rotational delays caused when the file is read. The block usage summary records basic information about the blocks that are already in use.

12.6 Device entries for disks

In order to build a filesystem on a partition, the device special files must exist in the /dev directory. General naming issues for devices and how to create the device files are described in Chapter 7: *Devices and Drivers*. Disks are both *block* and *character* devices. The block and character major device numbers are independent and are specified in either the **MAKEDEV** script (if it exists) or the text file used by the configuration program for rebuilding the kernel. See Chapter 7, Figure 7.1, and Chapter 8. The minor device numbers reflect the partition names and the drive unit number. Minor device numbers 0 to 7 correspond to partitions a to h on drive 0, 8 to 15 correspond to a to h on drive 1, etc. BSD devices are all in the /dev directory; ATT devices are often in subdirectories — /dev/dsk and /dev/rdsk for disks.

An excerpt from a **MAKEDEV** script used to create the device files for a Fujitsu Eagle drive on a Vax Massbus controller follows. It is written in **sh** and is typically cryptic. As a hint, the **expr** says do some arithmetic, and the quotes are to protect wildcard characters from the **sh** shell, like the *, which is multiply to **expr**. If invoked as **MAKEDEV hp1**, the first **mknod** line expands to:

/etc/mknod hp1a b 0 8

```
hp*)
    umask 2 ; unit=`expr $i : '..)'`
    name=hp; blk=0; chr=4
    case $unit in
    0|1|2|3|4|5|6|7|8)
        /etc/mknod ${name}${unit}a   b $blk `expr $unit '*' 8 + 0`
        /etc/mknod ${name}${unit}b   b $blk `expr $unit '*' 8 + 1`
        ...
        /etc/mknod ${name}${unit}h   b $blk `expr $unit '*' 8 + 7`
        /etc/mknod r${name}${unit}a  c $chr `expr $unit '*' 8 + 0`
        /etc/mknod r${name}${unit}b  c $chr `expr $unit '*' 8 + 1`
        ...
        /etc/mknod r${name}${unit}h  c $chr `expr $unit '*' 8 + 7`
        chgrp operator ${name}${unit}[a-h] r${name}${unit}[a-h]
        chmod 640 ${name}${unit}[a-h] r${name}${unit}[a-h]
        ;;
    *)
        echo bad unit for disk in: $i
```

```
        ;;
    esac
    umask 77
    ;;
```

If the Eagle drive were the second "hp" type drive (unit 1) then

MAKEDEV hp1

would produce the following block and character devices.

```
brw-r-----  1 root    operator   0,   8 Jan 21  1989 /dev/hp1a
brw-r-----  1 root    operator   0,   9 Jan 21  1989 /dev/hp1b
 ...
brw-r-----  1 root    operator   0,  15 Jan 21  1989 /dev/hp1h
crw-r-----  1 root    operator   4,   8 Jan 21  1989 /dev/rhp1a
crw-r-----  1 root    operator   4,   9 Jan 21  1989 /dev/rhp1b
 ...
crw-r-----  1 root    operator   4,  15 Jan 21  1989 /dev/rhp1h
```

In both the **MAKEDEV** script and the devices produced by it, devices for all eight partitions are created but not all are shown.

12.7 Partitioning decisions

The way that you choose to partition your disk will influence disk performance, dump strategy, and the overall hygiene of your disks. We will discuss a few strategies that apply to Eagle-sized disks, but not really to a 20 Mb hard disk on an IBM PC running Xenix.

12.7.1 Separation

The root filesystem, /usr filesystem and users' home directories should be on separate partitions. If root and /usr are on separate drives (and controllers) then system performance is improved. Users' files should be separate from system files for all sorts of reasons: to dump more frequently, to protect the system from runaway programs that fill the disk partition, and for general robustness. Other prime candidates for their own partition are /tmp and /usr/spool. These directories can easily overflow, and if they are on separate partitions such overflow will cause minimal damage.

12.7.2 Sizes reflect dump/backup strategy

If your dump media is nine-track tape at 1600 bpi, then about 40 Mb fits on a tape. Daily dumps write only a fraction of the files on disk to tape, but it is most convenient if these daily dumps do not exceed one tape.

12.7.3 Consistency

Using the same partitioning schemes between multiple drives of the same type avoids some nasty gotchas if partitioning is forgotten and allows more flexibility in the event of a head crash. Files can be restored from tape directly to a spare drive with the same partitioning.

12.7.4 Swap and paging areas

Swap and paging areas must be large enough to support the extended memories that are now commonplace. The days of 4 Mb Vaxen and 17 Mb swap partitions are gone. Machines today routinely have 16, 32, even 64 Mb of central memory. In order for a program to even load, there must be sufficient swap space free to completely swap the image out, even on a virtual memory system. Several swap partitions on different drives allow performance enhancements as the operating system takes advantage of separate disk arms. Early ATT systems did not include virtual memory; therefore programs were limited in size to the actual physical memory and did not require as much swap space as BSD systems.

12.8 Building filesystems

To format a crude disk partition into a fully fledged UNIX filesystem, either the **mkfs** or the **newfs** command may be used. **mkfs** takes a disk partition and divides it up into areas for data blocks, inodes, and free lists, and writes out the appropriate inode tables, super-blocks, and block maps. It places the directory lost+found into the newly created filesystem. **newfs** is a quasi-intelligent front end for **mkfs** that will execute **mkfs** with suitable values taken from /etc/disktab. You should use **newfs** if it exists on your system unless you have special requirements (e.g., need more inodes) or have reason to believe that it will not produce acceptable results for your particular drive. The **fsck** program should be run on the new drive immediately after making a new filesystem to verify that the disk is consistent and that you can access all of it. Examples for both **newfs** and **mkfs** for the "a" partition of the Eagle drive follow.

```
BSD:   newfs /dev/rhp1a eagle
       mkfs /dev/rhp1a 15884 48 20 8192 1024 16 10 66 2048 t
       fsck /dev/rhp1a

ATT:   mkfs /dev/dsk/rhp1a /stand/diskboot
       fsck /dev/dsk/rhp1a
```

The ATT **mkfs** also allows you to specify a configuration file called a prototype for the filesystem to be created. In the prototype you can set options such as the size of the filesystem to be built and the boot program to be installed in its zero block. In BSD this operation is done by the **mkproto** command.

12.9 The tunefs command (BSD only)

The **tunefs**[2] command is used to alter the kernel's layout policies on a particular disk partition. **tunefs** doesn't actually change the contents of the partition; it merely modifies the way in which future writes to the partition will be handled so that future reads will be more efficient. The following filesystem parameters may be adjusted using **tunefs**:

- The rotational delay to allow between blocks of a file
- The number of contiguous blocks that may be written in one transfer
- The number of blocks a single file may claim from a cylinder group
- The minimum amount of disk space to reserve as free

Note also that reading from a partition is completely independent of the policies set with **tunefs**. The first three items are usually set when the partition is made and are unlikely to need changing. But the minimum free space influences the point at which the operating system decides the filesystem is full. Changing the *minfree* parameter with **tunefs** is a common (cheap) way to create more disk space, at the expense of performance.

For **tunefs** to really work, the filesystems must be unmounted. **tunefs** does not complain if it is used on a mounted filesystem, but it also does not take any lasting action.

12.10 Brand-new disk in a box

We now turn to an actual new disk in a box, for this discussion the Fujitsu Eagle drive. The Eagle has an unformatted capacity of 474 Mb, which formats down to about 400 Mb. It is an SMD drive, is about 20 inches by 35 inches by 10 inches, and weighs about 150 pounds. It fits a standard 19-inch rack, but requires an especially deep one. If you order it from a Fujitsu dealer, it will include documentation and mounting rails, but will not automatically come with either a terminator or disk cables. Have two strong people handy when you try to mount it in a rack. The documentation shipped with the drive is a very complete hardware manual: M2351A/AF Mini-Disk Drive CE Manual. It is well written and contains all you need to know and more.

[2] Yes, some people pronounce this "tuna fish".

The level of detail in subsequent sections, particularly the section on strapping options, is really too much. The Eagle drive is a popular old standard, but not what you would buy today. However, the discussion is indicative of the level of detail that you need in order to understand how to format your favorite drive. If you buy the drive from the computer manufacturer, instead of from the disk manufacturer, it will already be formatted and ready to go. This section is only relevant if you are a do-it-yourselfer anxious to save money by using third-party peripherals.

12.10.1 Unpacking

Many disks have explicit unpacking instructions. Follow them. It is not uncommon to have special straps, foam chunks, wedges, etc. that are for shipping and not related to the functioning of the disk drive. These need to be removed. Early Eagle drives had a vibration prevention block (VPB), a piece of stiff foam that was placed inside the cover to stabilize the head/platter assembly during shipping. Later drives did not use the VPB as it was called, but the instructions still told you to remove it.

12.10.2 Locking heads

Disk drives should not be moved with the read/write heads bouncing around on the magnetic oxide surfaces. Some drives automatically lock them, and some have a lever or switch that must be set. For shipping or moving around, the heads should be locked; to run, the heads must be unlocked. The Eagle has a small lever held in place with a knurled Philips head screw. Remove the cover and find the lever. It has two positions, marked "lock" and "free". Loosen the screw and leave it finger tight. Then, if you have a skinny hand, you will be able to change it without removing the cover. Once the drive has been mounted in a rack, it is difficult to remove the cover.

12.10.3 Strapping options

The term *strapping options* refers to the features and functionality on a printed circuit board that can be customized with switches, jumpers, and thumb-wheels. An occasional board will require soldering or cutting jumper wires, but usually either DIP switches or jumpers are used. Disks have a variety of parameters that are set via the strapping options, including the sector size and various options to the controller interface, such as error behavior, and even obscure parameters such as whether the disk will be mounted horizontally or vertically.

The steps involved in setting these options for the Eagle are listed here:

- Remove the cover from the drive.
- Remove the logic board.

- Set the interface selection jumpers.
- Set the sector size jumpers.
- Reassemble.

The strapping options for the Eagle that are of concern in setting up a new disk are located on the logic printed circuit board (the middle board). Remove the sheet metal cover from the drive. There are six or eight small screws near the bottom of the cover that can be removed with a Philips head screw driver. There are two different types of screws, so pay attention to which kind goes where. The logic board is the middle one with two ribbon cables attached at one side. A small flat metal tool about four inches long with a kink in the middle was shipped with the drive. Find it. It is the tool to remove the printed circuit boards. One is shipped with each drive, which is both too many and not enough. You need two of these tools to remove the boards, so the first time you install such as drive you are short one, and subsequent times you have plenty.

The next step is to find out what values to use for the interface selection and the sector size. The manufacturer's documentation for the computer itself or for the controller board should tell you, and your friendly computer repairman for the particular brand of computer will also know. The values for a Vax with Systems Industries controller, Sun 3 with Xylogics controller, and Pyramid 90X with their standard multibus controller are shown in Figure 12.4 below.

FIGURE 12.4

Fujitsu Eagle disk strapping options			
Option	Sun	Pyramid	Vax
Interface selection	03-04 06-07 10-11	03-04 06-07 09-10	03-04 06-07 09-10
Sector size	Sector count = 47	Sector count = 12	Sector count = 48

Sector count = *NN* is an index into a table in the documentation that specifies the values for 16 sets of jumpers. The sector size can be fine tuned by selecting some entries from one line of the table and some from an adjacent line. For example, the Sun settings for an Eagle are optimal as: BC7: 3-4, 5-6, 10-11, 13-14; BD7: 2-3, 6-7, 9-10, 13-14; BE7: 3-4, 5-6, 10-11, 13-14; BF7: 3-4, 6-7, 10-11, 13-14 which is a combination of rows 47 and 48. The arithmetic to figure out optimal settings is explained nicely in the documentation. There are diagrams in the manual that show where the sets of jumpers are on the board. The diagram shows the jumper sets labeled from left to right, but the tables of values are labeled from right to left, so you need to carefully follow the labeling not your intuition.

12.10.4 Formatting the drive

Stand-alone formatting programs exist for our three target architectures: Sun, Pyramid, and Vax. On the Sun, **format** is an option to the **diag** program that you can boot in /stand/diag, or under SunOS 4.0 it is also available as a UNIX command **format**. On the Pyramid, there is a special diagnostics floppy that can format disks from the SSP, System Support Processor. The disk is connected directly to the SSP with the data cable and to the controller with the command cable. On the Vax the boot floppy can be used with the LSI 11 boot processor to format drives under the DEC diagnostic monitor. In addition, if you are running BSD there is a **format** command that can be run standalone from the boot floppy. There are complete instructions in the manual page for **format**(8).

Formatting is done with the system down, UNIX not running,[3] and the disk connected to its controller. (Note the cabling differences just mentioned for Pyramids.) If you are installing a second drive, disconnect the first one while you format the second, just in case. The new drive must be connected with both a command cable (60-pin) and a data cable (26-pin). A terminator must be installed since the command cable will not continue on to a second drive. The terminator fits in the output connector for the command cable. Select unit 0 for the drive number. The heads must be unlocked. If they are locked either find someone with a skinny hand to reach in and unlock them, or remove the cover and unlock them. Run the formatting software for your particular system. It takes a long time, so plan several hours of down time to format and verify the new disk. The output of the formatting process is usually a list of bad blocks and some summary information on how they were dealt with. Unfortunately, this list goes to the console terminal screen, instead of to a file. But without UNIX running, it's tough to send it to a file.

12.10.4.1 Handling bad blocks (BSD)

All blocks that are bad at the time the disk is formatted will be marked and remapped to the last cylinder on the disk which is reserved for this purpose. If subsequent bad blocks occur they can be handled by the utilities **bad144** or **badsect**. You can recognize a problem with a block when you notice an abundance of messages on the system console mentioning an ECC error on block #*XXX*. ECC stands for Error Correction Code and indicates that an error occurred and was corrected by the ECC mechanism. An occasional ECC error is nothing to worry about, but recurrent errors with the same block number do indicate a bad block.

[3] Except under SunOS 4.0 using **format**. Early versions are filled with bugs, but soon there will be updates.

bad144 marks bad disk blocks for forwarding using DEC Standard 144. New blocks are allocated on the alternate cylinders at the end of the disk. The bookkeeping is done automatically; thus a driver that supports the bad sector forwarding standard will see the disk as perfect. If your driver does not support the bad144 standard, the **badsect** command can be used to trap the bad block in a file in /BAD. **fsck** will cooperate and ask you about removing it, to which you can say no.

UNIX is picky about bad blocks in the kernel since the fancy code to look at the replacement blocks and use them instead is not yet available. Likewise, bad blocks in the swap area are not tolerated by UNIX because crash dumps are written there. It is particularly nasty if you have a bad block on the root partition in the middle of the new UNIX kernel that you are trying to install from tape. You must trap the bad block, leaving it in a copy of the kernel, and boot a different copy that is hopefully sitting on an error-free chunk of the disk. After you have UNIX up, you can use **badsect** to trap the block more gracefully.

12.10.4.2 Handling bad blocks (ATT)

Most bad blocks are identified when the disk is initially formatted, and are remapped to alternate blocks. If additional bad blocks are found, the **bdblk** command can be used to remap them. The remapping of blocks is transparent to everyone except the kernel.

12.10.5 Hook it up

Now that the hardware is happily formatted, partitioned, and perfect (no bad blocks left), we can install the disk and begin to build filesystems. The drive should be renumbered as unit 1; there is a small switch in the back that allows you to select drive numbers 0 to 3. Attach a single command cable, daisy-chaining it from the controller to drive 0 and on to drive 1. Remove the terminator from drive 0 and install it on drive 1. Attach data cables from the controller slots drive 0 and drive 1 to the respective drives.

12.10.6 Partitioning

Choose partition sizes; let's assume the standard ones already wired into the driver are OK or are chosen as the default. This means that you can choose which partitions to use, but you cannot choose their sizes or locations. Do not choose partitions that overlap; e.g., partitions "d" and "g" conflict in the partitioning detailed in Figure 12.3 and should not both be chosen. Suppose for the sake of discussion that we will use partitions "a", "b", "g", and "h" and that the drive is the second (unit 1) as in the previous examples. Sun has a snazzy program for setting partition sizes, and since it has done them correctly and put them in the label on the disk drive, you really do get choices.

12.10.7 Add the device to kernel

Refer to Chapter 4: *Configuring the Kernel* to determine the correct configuration line for the Eagle drive and your controller. If it were the second drive on the massbus controller on a Vax and you wanted to use its "b" partition as additional swap space, the lines would be:

```
BSD: config       vmunix   root on hp0 swap on hp0 and hp1 dumps on hp0
     controller   mba0     at nexus ?
     disk         hp1      at mba0 drive 1

ATT: eagle        254      776700  2
     root         eagle    0
     swap         eagle    1   0    66880
```

Rebuild the kernel as described in Chapter 8.

12.10.8 Make /dev entries

Make the entries in /dev (BSD) or /dev/dsk (ATT) corresponding to your drive. Remember that the second drive is unit 1. Although we have decided to use only partitions "a", "b", "g", and "h", it does not usually hurt to leave the other device files lying around, especially the "c" device. You can use the **MAKEDEV** script with argument **hp1**, or can execute **mknod** by hand. Remember to make both block and raw devices.

12.10.9 Reboot the new kernel

The new kernel with the additional drive must be booted in order for the system to recognize it. In addition, if we want to use the "b" partition as swap and the "h" partition with quotas (BSD), the /etc/rc file must explicitly execute either the generic versions of **swapon** and **quotaon** listed next or specific versions for the partitions involved. It is customary to use the generic versions.

```
/etc/swapon -a                          >/dev/console 2>&1
/etc/quotaon -a                         >/dev/console 2>&1
```

These lines are usually already in /etc/rc and so no modifications are needed. The -a flag means to apply the operation to all the devices in /etc/fstab for which it makes sense. Since we have not yet made filesystems or added the partitions to /etc/fstab, our new disk will be accessible from the new kernel, but is not yet fully configured.

12.10.10 Make filesystems on the partitions

We will assume that the "a" partition will be used as /tmp, the "b" partition will be additional swap space, the "g" partition for /usr/spool, and the "h" partition for guest users. Actually, the "g" partition is about 200-Mb, which is too large for the spool directory unless the machine is a major mail and news hub. Only partitions "a", "g", and "h" need filesystems; use either **newfs** or **mkfs** to build them; don't forget to run **fsck** on them.

12.10.11 Add partitions to /etc/fstab

The details of the /etc/fstab file are covered in Chapter 4: *The Filesystem.* Add the following lines to fstab; we have left the sequence for **fsck** and **dump** set to zero since sensible values will have to reflect what is already there.

```
/dev/hp1a:/tmp:rw:0:0
/dev/hp1b::sw:0:0
/dev/hp1g:/usr/spool:rw:0:0
/dev/hp1h:/boulder/guests:rq:0:0
```

12.10.12 Use it or lose it

You should now be able to mount the new filesystems and write files on them. Since disks are mounted during the boot sequence from /etc/rc (/etc/rc.local) using /etc/fstab and we modified fstab after rebooting, we must mount the new filesystems by hand just this once. Normally that would entail the commands:

/etc/mount /dev/hp1a /tmp
/etc/mount /dev/hp1g /usr/spool
/etc/mount /dev/hp1h /boulder/guests

But, both the /tmp and /usr/spool directories are actively in use and contain files in their current locations. These files would become inaccessible if the new filesystems were mounted on top. To do these mounts properly:

- Bring the machine to single user with the **shutdown** command.
- Make two temporary directories: /mnt.tmp and /mnt.spool.
- Mount the hp1a and hp1g partitions on them.
- Copy the contents of /tmp and /usr/spool to /mnt.tmp and /mnt.spool.
- Remove any files and directories from /tmp and /usr/spool.
- Unmount the new filesystems.
- Remount them on /tmp and /usr/spool.
- Remove the directories /mnt.tmp and /mnt.spool.

Subsequent reboots will automatically mount the new filesystems in the proper places.

In building a filesystem and running **fsck** you have effectively already accessed each block of the disk and are assured that the installation is reasonably correct and complete. Make a directory, edit a file, fill up the disk.

12.11 Debugging

Debugging disks, like debugging the network, is often 20-20 hindsight. As you gain experience, you will begin to recognize types of problems, and even if you have not met the same situation before, will develop a good feel for the hardware and its care and feeding.

A partial list of problems we have met with new disks follows:

- Cables installed incorrectly
- Cables made incorrectly
- Strapping options on the drive wrong
- Strapping options on the controller wrong
- Terminator not installed or installed backwards
- Boot PROMS not the right revision
- Heads locked while trying to read/write
- Write-Protect on while trying to write

One of the most common problems in installing a new disk is cabling. Improperly installed cables and bad cables seem to occur about equally frequently. The ribbon cable connectors are often different types and their orientation seems arbitrary. They still fit each other, but one is from the controller manufacturer and the other from the drive manufacturer. Sometimes they are keyed, sometimes not. If both the cable and the socket are keyed, you will not be able to make a mistake, as the cable will only fit one way. If they are not both keyed, there is often a little triangular mark that you might find on each side of the connection. And if that fails, all 60 pin connectors have little invisible marks on one side, one pin in from the end, and on the other side two pins in from the end. With sharp eyes, it should be possible to find these on both the cable and the controller or drive. Once you have determined the correct orientation of the cables, mark them with waterproof magic marker.

The terminator must be installed in the last drive opposite the daisy-chained command cable. If you don't have something to follow to decide which way to install it, look for the ground wire and a small Philips head screw that it attaches to. The ground wire and the screw go on the same side. Install the terminator so that the wire is closest to the screw.

Incorrect strapping options or strapping on the drive that is not compatible with the strapping on the controller can cause weird disk behavior. If the error is just in choosing the number of sectors per track and the sector size, the formatting program will complain and usually give you enough information to determine the problem. If you are installing an additional disk of a type you are already using successfully, then dismantling the working system will tell you the correct strapping. If the drive is a brand-new first-ever one, then you need information from the manufacturers of the disk, the controller and the host computer.

In addition, the host computer must be able to boot from the disk, so its EPROMs must be able to talk to the disk and tell it to copy block 0 directly into memory and transfer control to it. Block 0 is the boot block, and contains just enough information to load in a boot program, which then executes to load the kernel and start it running.

The heads must be locked to move the disk, but must not be locked to read or write on it. Formatting writes to the disk. The heads must be unlocked and the Write-Protect button must be off.

The Eagle drive contains a status indicator that will show a two-digit error code number indicating any problems with the drive. There are two green leds on the back that must be lit green when the disk is happy. The "I'm happy" value on the status indicator is 65.

If the hardware seems fine, but the software is not, recheck each section of software steps, and try to verify that it completed correctly. For example, after making the block and character special device files, do an **ls -l**.

13

Hardware Maintenance Tips

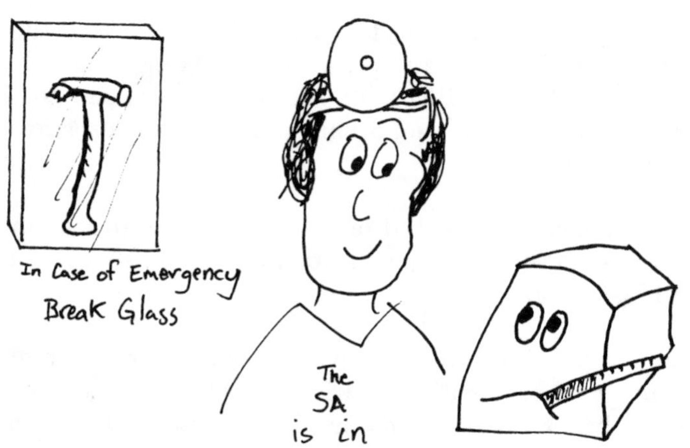

Hardware maintenance at one time was reported to account for one-third of DEC's gross revenue. With numbers like that, it is no wonder that computer hardware seems to be built like Detroit cars used to be, with planned obsolescence in mind. Maintenance rates are typically 10-12% of the list price per year. The only real anomaly from this in the industry is Hewlett-Packard, whose maintenance charges for workstations are closer to 3-4% per year. If you can afford hardware maintenance from the manufacturer or a reputable third-party vendor, by all means use it. If not, you can soon develop a pretty good sense of what might be wrong and how much you can do about it. If you keep a log book, as suggested in Chapter 26: *Bunch 'o Stuff*, a quick glance at the hardware maintenance records for the last six to twelve months will give you an idea of your failure rates. It is a good idea to keep a careful record of failures and replacement parts used, so you can evaluate different maintenance options accurately. But remember, there comes a time when all hardware should be replaced, not maintained. Know your hardware and don't mess with it beyond its useful lifetime.[1]

[1] You may even consider donating the outdated equipment to your local university or institute of learning. For them, equipment is rarely outdated.

13.1 Board handling lore

Circuit boards should be handled gently, not dropped, not have coffee spilled on them, books piled on them, etc. Most customer engineers (those friendly repair people) are ten times rougher on boards than seems reasonable.

13.1.1 Static

Electronic parts are sensitive to static electricity, and to handle boards safely you must ground yourself before and during installation. A static ground strap worn on the wrist and attached to a special mat that you kneel on (most computers require you to show proper respect!) will isolate you properly. We copied our friendly DEC repairman's setup. Remember that you need to worry about static when you open the package containing a printed circuit board, not just when you install the board. This is particularly true if the office where you receive your mail (and might be tempted to open your circuit board packages) is carpeted: Carpet generates more static electricity than hard floors.

13.1.2 Installing a board

Many busses are not keyed; i.e., each board will usually fit both the right way and backwards. If there are boards already in the machine's card cage, insert new boards using the same orientation as the old ones. If there are no boards in the card cage, find documentation, either on the card cage itself or in the manuals, before installing any boards. To insert a board into the bus, carefully slip it into the guides provided at the top and bottom of the slot, and push it into the slot until you meet resistance (about a half-inch from flush). At that point, put one hand on the top and one hand on the bottom of the board and rock it gently back and forth until it is properly seated. Some boards have thumb levers which help with this final step.

Edge connector type boards are easier to seat than pin/socket type boards. Before attempting to install a pin/socket board, visually inspect the board for bent or broken pins, and carefully straighten them if necessary. Each little pin-and-socket pair must line up exactly. This is not always easy: for example, there are 192 of them on a Sun VME board.

Most interface boards come with instructions from the manufacturer, although in some cases you must pay extra for them. It is important to follow these instructions, at least until you are experienced enough to know the safe shortcuts.

13.1.3 Reseating instructions

Many times when hardware is down, simply powering the machine down, reseating the boards and powering back up fixes it. To reseat a board, pull it out about an inch from its "seat" in the backplane, and reinstall it. If this works, but the same thing happens next week or next month, it probably means the contacts between the board and the backplane are not perfect. If the board uses edge connectors to the backplane, take the board all the way out and clean the contacts with a pencil eraser. Don't use one that is old and hard. If your eraser doesn't work well erasing pencil marks from paper, it won't work well on the board contacts either. Try to keep your fingers off the contacts, just erase them with the pencil eraser (a mild abrasive), brush off the eraser droppings, and reinstall the board in the backplane.

13.2 Preventive maintenance

Some hardware has filters that need to be cleaned or changed regularly. Clogged filters impede the flow of air to essential parts and may result in premature component failures. It is important to keep the air intakes open. It is not uncommon to find a book or newspaper lying on top of the air intakes. Keep things clean.

Anything with moving parts may need regular lubrication, cleaning, and belt maintenance. Line printers are prime candidates, also tape drives and old disk drives. Newer disks are totally sealed and maintenance free. Listen to squeaks from your older equipment and pamper it.

13.3 Third-party or manufacturer's maintenance contracts

Several major companies have begun offering hardware maintenance on computer equipment that they do not manufacture. These vendors are often very anxious to displace the manufacturer and get their foot in the door so to speak. You can sometimes negotiate very attractive maintenance contracts by playing manufacturer against new provider. Get references, if possible, on all maintenance vendors, preferably from people you know and trust.

It is rare for any maintenance provider today to diagnose beyond the board level. The old joke: "How many <generic> repairmen does it take to fix a flat tire? Four — one to replace each wheel." is somewhat true. It is not unusual for the customer engineer to swap boards until it works, without much more thought than that given to fixing a flat tire by replacing all tires to be sure you got the flat one. Given this level of understanding required, a popular maintenance alternative is board swap, where you, the user, diagnose the problem, request a spare board from the manufacturer, and install it. After the problem is resolved, broken boards are returned to the factory for diagnosis and repair. Keeping good records of failures and the symptoms and reasons will quickly train you as a qualified board swapper.

13.4 Typical maintenance call scenario

A typical maintenance call involves several steps, and its nature depends on the type of service.

13.4.1 On-site maintenance

With an on-site maintenance contract, the repairman (who is usually called a customer engineer) will come directly to your machine with his spare parts and fix it. Response time varies between guaranteed four-hour response (during working hours) to next-day response.

13.4.2 Board exchange maintenance

A board exchange maintenance program means that you and your staff will diagnose the problem, perhaps with the help of the telephone support hot line personnel at the manufacturer's site. After diagnosis, a call is placed to a maintenance number, the problem described, and the replacement board ordered. It is usually shipped Federal Express that same day and arrives the next day. You then install the board, get the hardware back up and happy, and return the old board in the box that was used to ship the new board. Often the manufacturer wants to assign a return authorization number to the transaction. It should be written on the shipping documents and included with the bad board. This number aids the manufacturer in keeping track of where the board belongs and just why the board was sent back.

13.5 Manufacturer's warranties

The length of a manufacturer's warranty should play an active role in the computation of the cost of ownership of any machine. Three months' warranty is standard, but increasingly warranties of a year or more are being offered, especially to universities.

It seems to be much easier in a university environment to get federal funding for capital equipment than for support personnel or maintenance. We have occasionally requested an "extended warranty" which could also be described as long-term prepaid maintenance, to convert equipment dollars to maintenance.

Often when ordering a computer system from several vendors, the parts do not all arrive at the same time. In this case the warranty should not start until the equipment is all there and can be installed. Most vendors are cooperative about delaying (for a month or two) the beginning of the warranty period. This is quite important, since with many pieces of hardware the real maintenance and reliability problems occur quite soon after installation. Infant mortality is the term given to hardware failures that occur within a day or two of installation. DOA (or dead on arrival) refers to hardware that arrives from the vendor broken.

13.6 Computer room environment

The environment in the area where the computer is located is quite important. Back in the old days of central machine rooms, this meant large air conditioners, false floors, halon fire control systems, power conditioners, and maybe even uninterruptible power supplies. Now many computers are in people's offices, trying to survive on building air conditioning (that is often turned off at night and on weekends), unconditioned power, and quite a healthy dose of papers and books on the cooling vents. When you place a computer in an office, keep in mind that computers steal air conditioning intended for humans. In this case, you may wish to put the offender in a room with its own air conditioner.

13.6.1 Power

Computer hardware would like to see nice stable clean power. In a machine room this means a power conditioner, an expensive box that filters out spikes and can be adjusted to provide the correct voltage levels and phases. In offices, surge protectors between the machines and the wall power help to insulate the hardware from power spikes.

Our Electrical Engineering Department has maintained a lightning generator. Originally it was used for research, but of late has become a demonstration tool for entertaining parents and prospective students. The surge in the building when the lightning machine goes off will bring down our entire machine room of computers. After the first such demo and our subsequent screams and curses, we were informed of the impending strike and took the machines down for the duration. During natural lightning storms, machines should also be taken down and left down until the storm passes. Abrupt power cycling of computer hardware is hard on it, and while it may not fail immediately, it does hurt.

13.6.2 Temperature

The ideal operating temperature for computer equipment is 64 to 68 degrees with about 45% humidity. This does not coincide with the ideal operating temperature of the computer user. Temperatures above 80 degrees in the computer room imply about 120 degrees inside the machines. Commercial grade chips have an operational range up to about 120 degrees, at which point they stop working; beyond about 160 degrees they break. As silicon heats up it has less resistance, and therefore the current a component draws increases, causing it to heat up even faster. This rate is exponential.

So, keep your machine room cool, know if your air conditioning breaks. We use a system called /dev/thermometer which is a temperature sensor with an RS-232 interface built by one of our students. Software queries it every ten minutes and if the temperature in the machine room reaches a first threshold, mail is sent to the systems folks and operators warning of increasing temperature in the machine room. If the temperature reaches a second threshold, the software dials on our dialout modem to a digital pager carried by the person on call and produces a code on the pager that means the computers are about to burn, the machine room is getting dangerously hot, drop everything, and come in to investigate.

13.6.3 Humidity

The ideal humidity for most computer hardware is in the range of 40% to 60%. If the humidity is too low, static electricity becomes a problem. If it is too high, condensation can form on the boards, which causes shorting and oxidation.

13.6.4 Vibration

A computer on a hard surface in a room next to heavy machinery will vibrate across the floor. The chips will vibrate out of their sockets, the boards out of their slots, and the bearings out of their races. Seriously, vibration can be a problem; just use common sense.

14

Networking under BSD

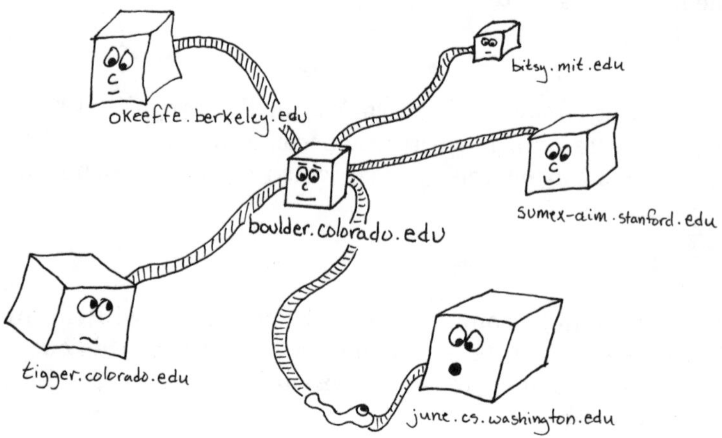

14.1 Introduction

A computer network is a collection of computers connected together by both hardware and software. Networking began in the research labs at Cal Tech, Cambridge University, Xerox PARC, and Berkeley (among others) in the late 1960s and early 1970s. The first major United States national network, the ARPANET, was funded by the Department of Defense to link universities, government labs, and key DoD industries. The initial networks used dedicated telephone circuits, Digital PDP 11 computers, and BBN (Bolt, Beranek and Newman) software to form virtual circuits between any two nodes on the network.

Ethernet, a high-speed local area networking technology, was invented in 1973, but product development and specification was not forthcoming until 1980 with the introduction of 3 Mb Ethernet hardware developed jointly by DEC, Intel, and Xerox. Three major events popularized networking in the 1980s: Ethernet support in Berkeley UNIX 4.2BSD, personal computer networks, and National Science Foundation funding to support both regional and high-speed national networks. Leased telephone lines and communication satellites are the primary transport media for wide area high-speed networks.

The main reason to connect computers via a network is to facilitate the sharing of resources. Both peripherals and CPU cycles can be shared. For example, a single networked printer can service many host computers while being physically connected to only one of them. Terminal ports can be shared via a terminal server, disks via a distributed file system, and tape drives via commands that operate both locally and remotely. Software systems exist that facilitate the use of a remote machine's CPU.

At first glance, networking seems like a system manager's dream. Disconnected machines are magically linked: All chores can be done from a single terminal via the network. Unfortunately, while system administration becomes easier for a few machines, it doesn't scale up. Techniques that worked for several separate machines don't work when applied through a network to hundreds or thousands of machines. The system administrator must not only learn to design, manage, build, and maintain the network, but must relearn and redesign old familiar tasks such as the assignment of login names and userids.

This chapter covers Berkeley networking using Ethernet hardware and the TCP/IP protocols. It focuses on local area networks (LANs), but discusses connections to wide area networks (WANs). We are excluding telephone-based, batch networks such as uucp, the UNIX-to-UNIX-copy network (see Chapter 16), CSNET, the Computer Science community's mail network, and BITNET, an IBM-based mail network. Network design, management issues, hardware and software installation, and maintenance topics are discussed. Issues facing administrators of a medium-sized network (50 to 100 hosts) are the focus; the examples chosen will necessarily be smaller, but will represent good solutions for a medium-sized organization or campus. The hardware and software systems included are:

- Ethernet hardware
- TCP/IP protocol suite
- NFS distributed file system

We have specifically chosen not to cover some networking technology either because we have no direct experience with it or because it is an emerging technology and anything said may well be incorrect by the time this book is published. The following systems are not included in this chapter:

- Token ring hardware
- XNS protocol suite
- ISO protocols
- System V.3 networking
- RFS remote file sharing

14.1.1 The ISO/OSI network model

Most networking is based on a software/hardware model called the Open Systems Interconnection (OSI) Reference Model first proposed by the International Standards Organization (ISO). The model, referred to as either the ISO or OSI model, consists of seven distinct layers of software and/or hardware, each representing a level of abstraction. At the bottom layer, the model specifies how the hardware passes bits of information across the network; at the higher layers, end user services, such as reliability, security, and data representation, are specified. Details of the ISO model are shown in Figure 14.1.

FIGURE 14.1

ISO/OSI network model		
Layer	Name	Function
1	Physical layer	The cable or physical media itself
2	Data Link layer	Transmit and receive packets, identify addresses
3	Network layer	Determine routing and keep accounting
4	Transport layer	Guarantee end-to-end correct data transfer
5	Session layer	Handle authentication and authorization
6	Presentation layer	Deal with data problems and data compression
7	Application layer	Provide end user services, mail, remote login or copy

Some think a Financial layer and a Political layer should be added to these.

At each layer of the model, a protocol is established which must be followed in order to communicate. This is sometimes called the protocol stack. The ISO model is a theoretical model and most existing protocol implementations do not follow it exactly. For example, in Berkeley networking, the IP protocol is between layers 3 and 4, the TCP protocol is part of layer 4, and there is no protocol at layer 5. But all implementations do use the layer idea for isolation and standardization. Communications between two machines at any layer travel down the protocol stack on the originating machine across the network cable, and up the other side to that same layer.

The basic unit of network data is called a *packet*. The packet has a source or origination address and a destination address. Addresses identify computers on the network and exist in three forms: a name for people to use, a software or IP address for programs to use, and a hardware or Ethernet address for the hardware to use. We will refer to the software address as the IP address and the hardware address as the Ethernet address.

The data inside a packet has several forms. At the first layer of the ISO model, it is simply bits of data. At the second layer, the bits are grouped into frames that contain Ethernet addresses. At the third layer, the frames are grouped into datagrams to which an IP address has been added, and finally, at the fourth layer, information is added to guarantee that the packets are delivered in the correct order with no errors or duplication. Each step up the protocol stack adds more overhead to the packet.

14.1.2 The Internet

The Internet is a collection of networks, both LAN's and WAN's that *interoperate* using the TCP/IP protocol suite. By interoperate, we mean that this collection of thousands of host computers at hundreds of locations, functions as if all the machines are on the same network at the same location. This is quite a feat, since the Internet spans the country and many vendors' hardware (over 150 at last count). It is made possible by the use of a standard set of protocols, called the TCP/IP protocol suite.

For data:

- IP - Internet Protocol, at layers 3 and 4 of the ISO model
- TCP - Transmission Control Protocol, at layer 4
- UDP - User Datagram Protocol, at layer 4
- FTP - File Transfer Protocol, at layer 6
- TELNET - Network Terminal Protocol, at layer 6
- SMTP - Simple Mail Transport Protocol, at layer 7

For control:

- ICMP - Internet Control Message Protocol
- ARP - Address Resolution Protocol
- RARP - Reverse Address Resolution Protocol
- RIP - Routing Information Protocol
- EGP - External Gateway Protocol

The Internet includes the ARPANET, NSFNet, MILNET, and regional networks such as NYSERNET in New York, Westnet in Colorado, Utah, New Mexico, and Arizona, BARRNET in the San Francisco Bay Area, and several others. It has grown phenomenally in recent years, expanding from a designed maximum of about 50 networks to over 300 with no expansion of the bandwidth and only minor upgrading of switching hardware at various nodes. Needless to say, it is overcrowded to the point of being close to unusable at times. Current upgrading of the lines forming the NSFNet backbone should alleviate some of the congestion for a while.

The Internet is loosely administered by the Network Information Center (NIC) at the Stanford Research Institute (SRI), where documents and standards are archived, IP addresses are allocated, and network and domain names are registered.

The specification of Internet protocols and standards is done through documents called RFC's (Request for Comments). Usually, someone gets an idea, writes it up, and submits it to SRI-NIC as an RFC. It is then assigned a number and distributed via electronic mail to the Internet community for comment. Comments are integrated into the document until the community is satisfied with the specification. In some cases it is then submitted to other organizations such as the IEEE or the National Bureau of Standards for further processing as a standard. There are five categories of RFC:

- Required - must be implemented to connect to the Internet
- Suggested - should also be implemented to truly interoperate
- Directional - ideas that have been agreed to, but not widely adopted
- Informational - factual information about the Internet
- Obsolete - ideas whose time has gone

RFC's are sometimes so precise that they are unreadable by novices who are not intimately familiar with the area being specified.

The RFC's are archived on the machine sri-nic.arpa and are available through anonymous **ftp** (see Section 14.9.2). If you wish to browse the RFC's, a good starting place is the file rfc-index.txt that lists the names and a brief description of each. The most important RFC's (through 1985) have been collected in a three-volume publication, *The DDN Protocol Handbook*, which is available from SRI International in Menlo Park, California.

14.1.3 Documentation

There are several good beginner's documents on Berkeley networking and the Internet; references follow. *Notable Computer Networks*, by John Quarterman and Josiah Hoskins, Communications of the ACM, (October, 1986) surveys networking technology in use at universities and commercial organizations both here and in Europe. *The Hitchhiker's Guide to the Internet*, by Ed Krol, University of Illinois, (August, 1987) includes descriptions of the Internet, addressing, RFC's, the Internet Engineering Board and its standardization efforts, routing protocols, and problems. It is full of useful pointers to sources of further information. *Introduction to the Internet Protocols*, by Chuck Hedrick, Rutgers University, (1987) is a good tutorial introduction to the Internet, its protocols, and packet formats for TCP and IP. *Introduction to Administration of an Internet-based Local Network*, also by Chuck Hedrick (July, 1988), summarizes addressing, routing, and Ethernet hardware.

14.2 Ethernet hardware

Ethernet supports a branching bus topology and uses a CSMA-CD (Carrier Sense, Multiple Access with Collision Detection) protocol at the hardware level. A branching bus topology means there are no loops; i.e., there is only one way for a packet to travel between any two hosts on the same network. CSMA-CD is easily described in terms of a polite dinner party where guests (computers) don't interrupt each other, but rather wait for a lull in the conversation (no traffic on the network cable) to start speaking. If two guests start to talk at the same time (collision) they both stop, listen, wait a bit, and then one of them starts talking again.

The actual delay upon collision detection is somewhat random, preventing the scenario in which two hosts simultaneously transmit to the network, detect the collision, wait the same amount of time, and retransmit, thus flooding the network with collisions. (This was not always true!) The current delay algorithm is called truncated binary exponential backoff. Each time a host tries to transmit and detects a collision, the algorithm changes a bit. For the nth try ($0 \le n \le 10$), the delay is 51.2 μsec times a uniformly distributed random number between 0 and $2^n - 1$; for attempts 11 to 15 the interval remains 0 to 1023; above 15, give up. The unit of time delay, 51.2 μsec, is the time required to transmit 512 bits.

An Ethernet installation consists of the network cable itself, terminated at each end, and a connection to that cable for each host on the network. Each connection involves a tap, a transceiver or media access unit (MAU), a transceiver drop cable, and an interface board in the host computer. Figure 14.3 depicts a typical Ethernet connection.

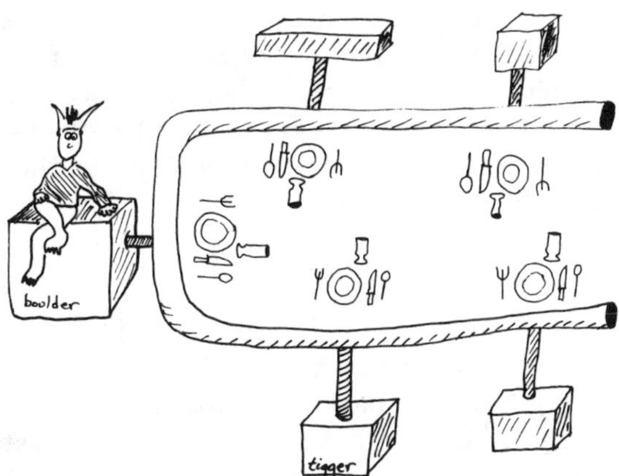

FIGURE 14.2 Ethernet dinner table

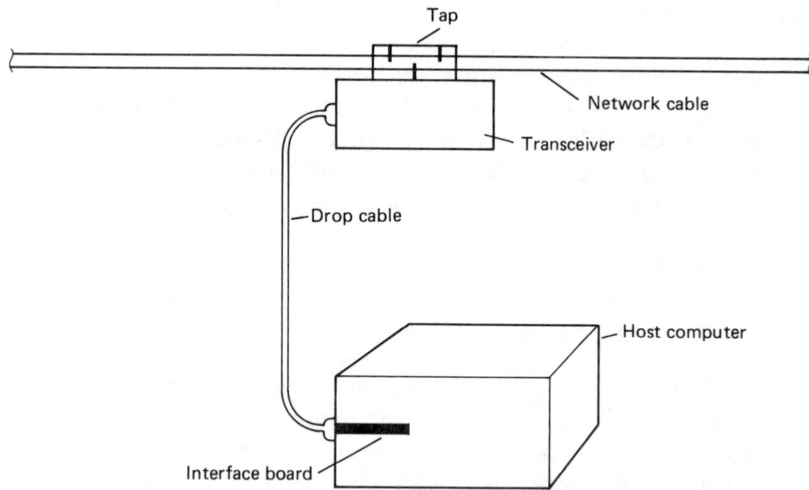

FIGURE 14.3 Diagram of Ethernet interface, transceiver, tap.

The tap makes electrical connections to the inner and outer conductors of the network coaxial cable. Attached to the tap is the transceiver which relays the signals on the network cable to the Ethernet interface board on the host computer via the drop cable. These terms are described more fully in Section 14.2.3.

14.2.1 Versions

Ethernet comes in three versions: version 1 (original DEC-Intel-Xerox 1980 specification), version 2 (revised DEC-Intel-Xerox 1982 specification), and IEEE 802.3 (official IEEE standard, 1983). The three versions can interoperate, but for any individual host computer attached to the network, its transceiver, drop cable, and interface board must all be the same version. Most new Ethernet hardware uses the IEEE standard; version mismatches are primarily a problem in older installations. The differences between the various versions have to do with the connection between the transceiver that sits on the network cable, the drop cable that connects it to the host computer, and the interface board in the host computer.

14.2.2 Limits and sizes

The distance limitations and component maximums for building an Ethernet discussed in the following section are driven by a time window specified in the Ethernet standard during which a packet of data must travel between any two hosts on the network. The Ethernet standard is conservative; many war stories exist of breaking these limits by factors of 2 or more. Many sites totally ignore some aspects of the specification. If your site is one of these and your network becomes unreliable or too slow as you add more hosts, this is a good place to look for trouble.

A bit of terminology (our own): By a *section* of cable, we mean a physical piece of continuous cable; by a *segment* of cable we mean a logical piece of cable, perhaps made up of several sections; by an *Ethernet* we mean a group of terminated segments connected by other hardware to form a logical network. These differences are emphasized in Figure 14.4.

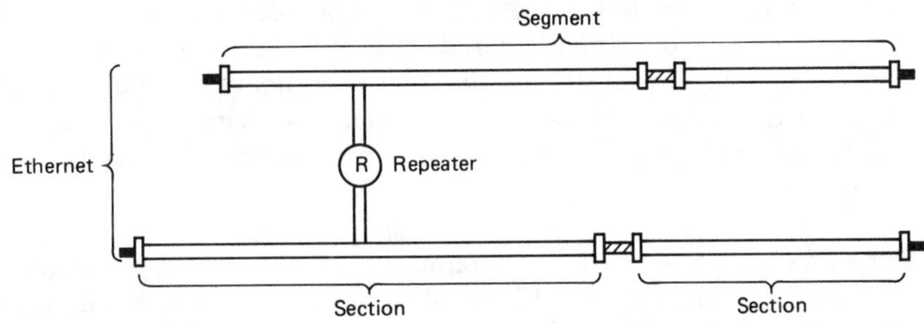

FIGURE 14.4 Cable terminology

14.2.3 Ethernet components

This section describes the hardware components that make up an Ethernet installation, the overall limits that the Ethernet standard places on these components, and the version-specific features that exist. While Ethernet was experimentally developed as a 3 Mb/sec network technology, almost all Ethernet installations use the more recent 10 Mb/sec technology. We will discuss only this newer technology.

14.2.3.1 Physical media: the network cable

The standard physical media for Ethernet is half-inch 50 Ω impedance coaxial cable (10BASE5) with N-type connectors; this cable is relatively expensive (dollars/ft). Specifications and interfaces now exist for quarter-inch coaxial cable (10BASE2) with BNC connectors, much like that used for television antennas, and also for twisted pair (10BASET) terminal or telephone wire; these media are cheaper (pennies/ft), but their networks are restricted to a fraction of the total length specified in the Ethernet standard. Broadband Ethernet cable (10BROAD36), fiber optic cable, and digital microwave and satellite transmission channels can also be used as physical media, thus substantially extending the physical size of an Ethernet. Of these, only satellite transmission does not (yet) sustain the 10 Mb/sec speed of Ethernet, but is limited to either 56kb/sec or 1.5 Mb/sec. The emerging FDDI (Fiber Distributed Data Interface) standard with 100 Mb/sec bandwidth and high-speed Metropolitan Area Networks from the phone companies promise to impact local area networks in the next few years.

Standard 10BASE5 cable

The standard Ethernet cable comes in two varieties: PVC (polyvinyl chloride) jacketed and teflon jacketed. Fire code requires that PVC cable be run through conduit when installed in air plenums (the return air areas above drop ceiling tiles), since PVC produces poisonous gasses when burned.

The national fire code adopted in July 1988 actually specifies four types of cable: plenum cable (CL2P), vertical rise cable (CL2R), general purpose cable (CL2), and restricted cable (CL2X). The plenum cable must not put toxic fumes into the heating/air conditioning system; the vertical rise cable must not burn, (thereby spreading fires between floors of a building); the restricted cable is for residential use or commercial use when run in conduit. Manufacturers are not yet manufacturing cable specifically for the vertical rise restriction.

The PVC jacketed cable is colloquially called *yellow hose* because of its bright yellow color; the teflon cable is often orange and has a translucent look from the teflon coating. The teflon cable is somewhat stiffer than the PVC cable, is slightly less than a half-inch in diameter, and has a slightly larger bend radius. The bend radius is the minimum radius the cable can be bent without adversely affecting its signal transmission properties. For the PVC cable this is seven inches, for teflon about nine or ten inches. The two types can be mixed.

Ethernet segments should be made up of sections of cable of standard lengths. The standard lengths are: 23.4 meters, 70.2 meters, and 117 meters. These values produce optimal transmission properties and it is recommended that they be mixed randomly. Note that 70.2 and 117 are multiples of 23.4; thus any cable made up of standard length sections must have a total length that is evenly divisible by 23.4 meters. Unfortunately, this implies some inefficient use of cable: for example, if you need a 100-meter segment of cable, to use standard lengths means you will have to "waste" 17 meters of cable. Ethernet segments can vary from 10 to 500 meters in length. This is in contradiction to the preceding, since neither 10 nor 500 is evenly divisible by 23.4. But that's the spec!

Most Ethernet cable has black marks (half-inch black bands) every 2.5 meters which indicate where transceivers or connectors may be placed. The half-wavelength of the signal is 2.5 meters, therefore placing devices at these points is optimal.

Thinnet 10BASE2 cable

Thinnet or "cheapernet" cable also comes with either a PVC or a teflon outer covering. A network with thinnet segments has two disadvantages: The overall maximum size of the network is reduced, and each transceiver/host pair become an active part of the network, and if broken, will disable the entire net. This makes thinnet segments of a network similar to the old-style Christmas tree lights with the bulbs in series: If one bulb was bad, the entire string of lights died. Thinnet is cheaper and easier to work with. Many small installations find it preferable. Thinnet and thicknet can be mixed using repeaters (within the spec) or connectors (violates the spec). Thinnet is usually black and therefore does not contain discernible black marks; transceivers and connectors are placed randomly.

The maximum length of a cable containing a thinnet segment is 185 meters. T connectors that place the transceivers directly in series on the network cable are used instead of drop cables. Transceivers should be at least .5 meters apart. There can be at most 30 devices per cable segment.

Twisted pair 10BASET cable

The twisted pair Ethernet cable is relatively new, and its specification, 10BASET, is not yet an IEEE standard. One of its big attractions is the possibility of installing an Ethernet over existing telephone lines and avoiding the cost of running new cable. Twisted pair telephone wire, like thinnet coaxial cable, is cheaper and easier to work with than standard Ethernet cable.

14.2.3.2 Ethernet hardware: terminators, connectors, adapters

Four basic parts are needed to build Ethernet cable segments: the cable itself, connectors to mate to the ends of sections of cable, barrel adapters to attach two sections of cable together, and terminators to put on the very ends. In Figure 14.5, two sections of Ethernet cable are joined; T indicates terminator, C connector, and B barrel adapter. Connectors are attached directly to the end of the cable to form a plug (male) end for attaching barrel adapters or terminators. Barrel adapters (socket-socket) attach to these connectors to join two sections of cable. Each logical Ethernet segment must be terminated by a 50 Ω impedance inductor called a terminator; resistors won't really work. The job of the terminator is to absorb all signals coming along the cable, allowing no reflections. Socket connectors and plug-plug adapters exist but are not standard.

Ethernet hardware comes in two basic types: solder and crimp. With the proper tool, the crimp hardware is easy to install and very reliable. Expect to spend over $100 for a good crimping tool.

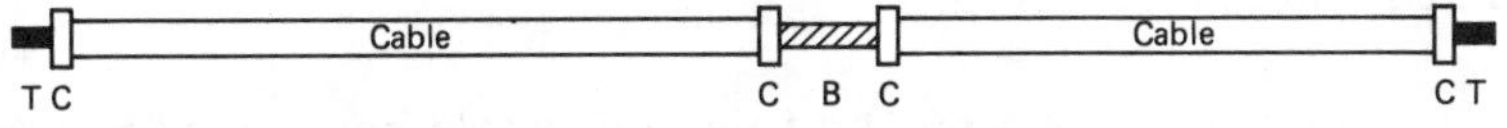

FIGURE 14.5 Ethernet cable segment

You should use the standard plug connectors with socket barrel adapters and terminators to make the end of each cable the same sex. This facilitates troubleshooting when it is necessary to logically (not physically) cut out a section of cable. While troubleshooting is a bit easier, extra parts are required for each connection using this scheme. For example, Figure 14.5 shows socket-type barrels and terminators and plug-type connectors. It would require two sections of network cable, two socket type terminators, one socket-socket barrel adapter, and four plug connectors. Each section of cable ends with a plug connector and can accept either a socket terminator or a socket-socket barrel adapter. The alternative is to mate a plug connector directly to a socket connector saving the barrel adapter, but this requires you to have both plug and socket terminators on hand for debugging. It also violates the spec.

14.2.3.3 Transceivers and taps

A transceiver is a hardware device that attaches to the network cable and connects via a drop cable to a host computer's Ethernet interface board. Transceivers do not require external power, but take their power from the host interface via the drop cable. There are slight version differences in transceivers. Version 1 uses DC coupling with the idle state high. Version 2 uses AC coupling with idle state zero and a heartbeat signal; IEEE 802.3 adds jabber control to the version 2 specification. Jabber control keeps broken hardware from flooding the network with bogus packets. The version of an interface board can be determined by checking the DC voltage across pins 3 and 10:

- Version 1 - approximately .7 volts
- Version 2 - approximately .2 volts
- IEEE 802.3 - close to 0 volts

There are three kinds of transceivers: *intrusive*, which require that the network cable be cut; *vampire*, which puncture the cable; and *internal*, which attach to the cable with T connectors. Intrusive and vampire types are used for the standard Ethernet cable, and the internal type is used for thinnet cable. Until the advent of the AMP standardized tap, arguments for intrusive versus vampire transceivers resembled religious or political wars. With the intrusives it is difficult to maintain the 2.5-meter separation between black marks, the whole network goes down during installation, and the cable ends up in lots of pieces of random length. The vampires are a bit more difficult to install, require special tools for each brand, and leave a hole in the cable if removed.

The vampires have won the thicknet battle because of the AMP tap that has quickly become a de facto standard. The tap is easy to install, does not disturb an active network, and stays on the cable when the transceiver is removed. It has been adopted by virtually all manufacturers. Thinnet installations usually use BNC T connections to internal transceivers mounted directly inside the host computer. Diagrams of each type are shown in Figures 14.6, 14.7, and 14.8.

Transceivers must be between at least 2.5 meters apart and should be placed at the black marks on standard Ethernet cable. The maximum number of transceivers per segment is 100; the maximum per Ethernet is 1024.

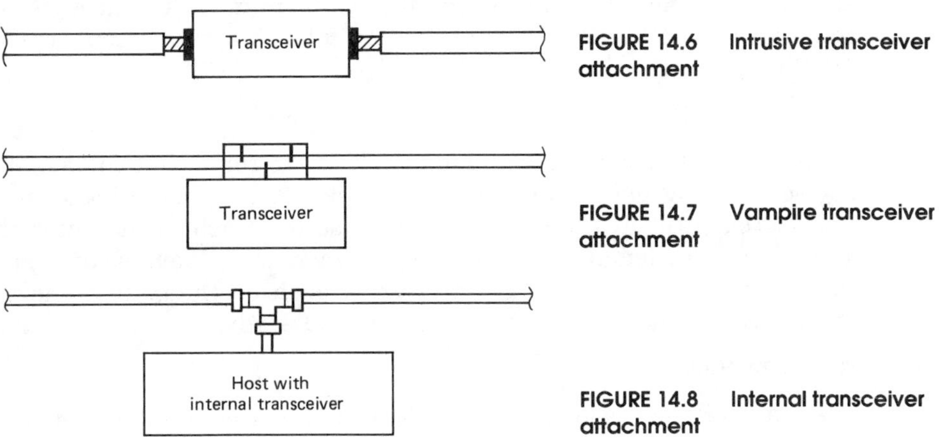

FIGURE 14.6 Intrusive transceiver attachment

FIGURE 14.7 Vampire transceiver attachment

FIGURE 14.8 Internal transceiver attachment

14.2.3.4 Multiport transceivers

For areas with a high concentration of machines, multiport transceivers, or "fanout boxes" as they are sometimes called, provide an alternative to individual taps. Typically, the network cable is tapped once and a regular transceiver installed. A drop cable then feeds from that transceiver into the multiport. Up to eight drop cables can be attached directly from the multiport's output ports to host computers. Multiports can be cascaded one level deep, providing 64 Ethernet connections for a single tap on the network cable. Each multiport level reduces the maximum length of the drop cable by about 20% since it is a passive device and does not reconstitute packets. Some multiports come with eight output ports already installed, while others come with an empty card cage and up to eight individual output port cards packaged separately; the user just plugs in the port cards as needed.

Multiports do require an external power source. They can sometimes hide or disguise problems of version mismatches. Many multiports can act as standalone networks.

Thinnet multiports are really multiport repeaters and are used to connect eight thinnet segments of cable. Since multiports can be cascaded two deep, you could build a very large thinnet installation by starting with a standard multiport feeding eight multiport thinnet repeaters each feeding eight thinnet segments, each servicing 29 hosts for a grand total of 1856 hosts. But again, that violates the spec.

14.2.3.5 Drop cables

Drop cables connect the transceiver attached to the network cable to the interface board in the host computer. They can be purchased from most network hardware vendors, or can be fabricated from shielded twisted pair cable as specified in Figure 14.9. Like coaxial cable, a drop cable's outer covering also comes in both plenum (teflon) and nonplenum (PVC) varieties. Internal transceivers for thinnet do not use a drop cable, but rather connect directly to the thinnet coax.

Connectors

Drop cables use one female and one male DB15 connector: the female for the transceiver end and the male for the computer end. Metal hoods are used to protect the wires at the connector and also to attach to the outer shield for grounding. The female connector has a bizarre slide latch locking mechanism that sometimes works; it mates to locking posts on the male connector but is often hard to slide on or off and tends to bend easily.

Pin assignments

The pin assignments for drop cables are summarized in Figure 14.9.

Drop cables are version-specific and should match the interface board and transceiver. Version 1 drop cables use one pair of 20 gauge wire and three pairs of 22 gauge wire; pin 1 is ground, and the inner and outer shields are tied together at pin 1 and the metal hood. Version 2 drop cables are the same

FIGURE 14.9

Drop cable pin assignments		
Pin	Versions 1 and 2	IEEE 802.3
1	Shield	Not connected
2	Collision presence +	Collision presence +
3	Transmit +	Transmit +
4	Reserved	Logic reference
5	Receive +	Receive +
6	Power return	Power return
7	Reserved	Not connected
8	Reserved	Not connected
9	Collision presence –	Collision presence –
10	Transmit –	Transmit –
11	Reserved	Not connected
12	Receive –	Receive –
13	Power	Power
14	Reserved	Not connected
15	Reserved	Not connected

as version 1 except that all four pairs are 20 gauge wire. IEEE 802.3 cables use pin 4 as ground, isolate the inner and outer shields, and tie the inner shield to pin 4, and the outer shield to the metal shell. (We have found that an IEEE 802.3 drop cable in which all pins that are specified as "not-connected" in Figure 14.9 are wired to ground, will serve as a universal drop cable.) Some manufacturers are marketing so-called "office drop cables" which are four pairs of 24 gauge wire, and reduce distance specifications by a factor of four. They are easier and more flexible to run than the standard 20 gauge wire, and also cheaper, but quickly exceed their length limitations.

The Ethernet specification sets limits on the lengths of drop cables: the minimum length is 5 meters; the maximum to a host from a regular transceiver is 50 meters, and from a multiport transceiver, 40 meters. Office drop cables are limited to about 12 meters total length and should not be used to feed multiports. If drop cable distance limitations are exceeded by just a bit, performance is degraded, as evidenced by the number of collisions and errors being too high. If it is exceeded by too much the device will simply not work at all. Optical fiber transceiver cables can be from 5 meters to about 5 km long and form the basis for optical repeaters, such as those manufactured by American Photonics.

14.2.3.6 Connecting and expanding Ethernets

Ethernet segments can be logically connected at several points in the seven-layer ISO network model. At layer 1, the Physical layer, one uses either hardware connectors or repeaters; the bits are transferred with only hardware. At layer 2, the Data Link layer, bridges are used; frames are transferred, again using only hardware. At layer 3, the Network layer, routers are used; whole messages are transferred, using both hardware and software.

Repeaters

A repeater is an active device used to connect Ethernet segments that are too far apart to be joined with barrel adapters. They require external power. A repeater reconstitutes and retimes packets, but does not interpret them; it has no idea where a packet is going or what protocol it is using. Local repeaters sit between network segments and attach to each cable with transceivers and drop cables. Remote repeaters come in pairs, one for each side of the connection. They are attached to the cable segments with transceivers and drop cables and to each other by up to 1000 meters of optical fiber. Both are illustrated in Figure 14.10. Local repeaters are used for two cable segments that are between 10 and 100 meters apart; remote repeaters (sometimes called half-repeaters) can be between 10 and 1100 meters apart (0 to 1000 meters of fiber and two 5 to 50 meter drop cables). Repeaters are often used to connect segments of Ethernet within a single building or adjacent buildings.

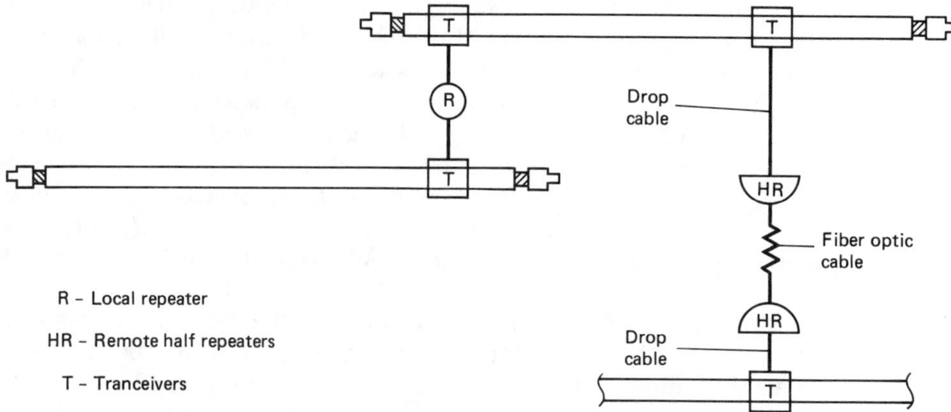

FIGURE 14.10 Local and remote repeater connections.

Ethernet versions 1 and 2 specify at most two repeaters in series per network; IEEE 802.3 has extended this to at most four repeaters.

Remote repeaters occasionally require attention from a system administrator, and so should not be in obscure and difficult-to-access locations. Usually power cycling them allows them to recover from a wedged state.

Bridges

Bridges connect Ethernets at the Data Link level (layer 2) of the ISO model. They do not require software, but receive, regenerate, and retransmit packets in hardware. Many bridges have a dynamic learning algorithm in firmware: The bridge notices which source addresses come from its left side and which come from its right side and forwards packets to the opposite side only when the destination host is actually on the other side. At first all packets are forwarded, but in a few minutes the bridge has learned the location, from its point of view, of all hosts who have sent a packet. Bridges are protocol-independent and can handle any mix of packets.

Bridges must scan every packet to determine if they should forward it. Their performance is usually measured by both the packet scanning rate and the packet forwarding rate. Many vendors do not mention the packet sizes in the performance figures they quote; therefore, actual performance may be less than advertised. Bridges, if they are fast enough, are a very good, but slightly expensive, way to connect Ethernets.

Bridges become hopelessly confused if your total network contains loops, because packets from a single host appear to be on both sides of the bridge. A single Ethernet cannot have loops, but as you connect several Ethernets together with routers or bridges, the topology can include multiple routes to a host. Some bridges can handle this situation by holding the alternate routes that actually form the loop in reserve in case the primary route goes down. They do a pruning operation on the network they see until the remaining sections present only one route to each node on the network. Some bridges can also handle duplicate links between the same two networks and route traffic in a round-robin fashion on them.

Bridges keep getting smarter as more functionality is built into their firmware. Some can be used to monitor security on the network. They record any foreign Ethernet addresses they see, thereby detecting and reporting new taps on the cable.

The TransLAN bridge can connect two Ethernets which are far apart via a digital communications system such as a satellite or leased land line. The bandwidth of current systems is either 56 Kb/sec or 1.54 Mb/sec (T1 is the telephone company's terminology for the 1.54 Mb channels). The TransLAN functions as a bridge, but due to the long round trip times on satellite links, the user feels a delay if working interactively. It uses an Ethernet interface at the local side and the V.35 standard or RS-232 standard at the satellite or leased line side. TransLAN's are programmed from the console box itself and contain nice management software to allow the user to configure the hardware to control packet filtering. They are also transparent to higher-level protocols.

The network configuration of local and TransLAN bridges is illustrated in Figure 14.11. The Ethernet time budget limits networks to a maximum of seven bridges in series.

Routers

Routers are dedicated computers that contain two or more Ethernet interfaces and function as a traffic cop at a busy intersection. They are protocol-specific; thus an IP router cannot forward DECNET packets. A general purpose computer is often used as a router if an institution's budget is tight. One just buys an extra Ethernet interface and sets up the UNIX software to know about the two interfaces and to forward packets between them. This process steals some resources from the host machine, and if the machine is a crucial link in a high traffic area, a dedicated router is a better solution. We use our fileservers as routers for networks of diskless workstations because the bulk of the traffic is on the local network, between the server and its clients; thus the extra load placed on the server by functioning as a router is not substantial.

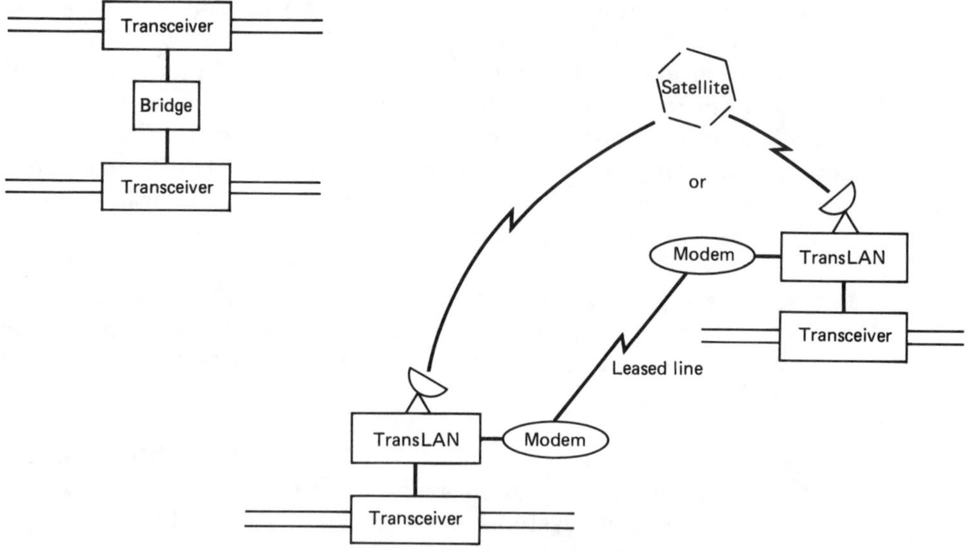

FIGURE 14.11 Local and long distance bridges

The performance of a router is measured in terms of packets per second throughput. One popular manufacturer counts the packets twice: As they arrive on one interface and again as they leave on the other! Router performance is nearly linear in packet size:

throughput = overhead + (packet-size * time-per-byte)

Gateways

Gateways are host machines that do protocol conversion as well as routing. Thus a machine that talked both Ethernet and X.25 or IBM's SNA and passed packets between them would be called a gateway. Routers are often called gateways, especially if they are overworked general computers instead of dedicated boxes. Another type of gateway is a mail gateway that might do the conversions necessary to allow messages destined for an IBM BITNET host to arrive over the TCP/IP Internet and be rerouted and repackaged into a form understood by the BITNET system.

14.2.3.7 Ethernet parts, tools, limits, and sizes

This section summarizes the various components of an Ethernet installation and the limits imposed by the Ethernet specification. Figure 14.12 shows

FIGURE 14.12

Ethernet parts and tools—parts is parts[1]			
Description	Specification	Supplier	Approx. cost
PVC cable	50 Ω RG11, Belden #9880	Belden, Geneva IL, or	$ .55/ft.
Teflon cable	50 Ω RG11, Belden #89880	Anixter	1.25/ft.
PVC thinnet cable	50 Ω RG58, Belden #8240	etc.	.15/ft.
Teflon thinnet cable	50 Ω RG58, Belden #88240		.65/ft.
PVC drop cable, Version 1	4 pair shielded, Belden #9891		
PVC drop cable, V2 or 802.3	4 pair shielded, Belden #9892		
Teflon drop cable	4 pair shielded, Belden #89892		1.00/ft.
PVC office drop cable	4 pair shielded, Belden #9504		.35/ft.
Teflon office drop cable	4 pair shielded, Belden #89504		
N-type terminators, socket	Amphenol 82-5721	Anixter or	16.00
N-type connectors, plug	Amphenol 82-313	Newark Electronics or	5.00
N-type connectors, socket	Amphenol 82-340	Glasgal Comm.	5.00
N-type barrels, socket-socket	Amphenol 82-101	etc.	5.00
N-type barrels, plug-plug	Amphenol 82-100		5.00
N-type insulating booties	Amphenol 31-5010		1.00
BNC T connectors			6.00
BNC terminators			6.50
BNC to N adapters			11.00
Transceiver	ST500	Cabletron	250.00
Multiport transceiver	8-port fanout, Model 2110	TCL	1,000.00
Local repeater	DEREP-AA	DEC	1,400.00
Remote repeater	DEREP-RA	DEC	1,300.00
Optical expander		American Photonics	2,000.00
Thinnet fanout	DEMPR	DEC	2,800.00
Bridge		Retix Corp	1,800.00
TransLAN bridge		VitaLink Corp	20,000.00
IP Router		Cisco	10,000.00
Crimp tool	HX4 and Y206P die	Daniels Mfg, Orlando FL	125.00
AMP tap coring tool			40.00

[1] Many vendors exist for most of these products. We have listed just one for each part, but have tried to include some of the big names.

detailed specifications for the various parts and tools mentioned in the preceding sections.

We are not recommending any of the products in Figure 14.12, with the exception of the Cabletron ST500 transceiver and the Cisco router which we consider the best on the market today. The Anixter catalog is a particularly good one, with diagrams and detailed instructions on many of the cables and connectors.

Figure 14.13 summarizes the limits described by the Ethernet specification.

FIGURE 14.13

Ethernet limits and sizes	
Component	Limits
Thicknet sections Thicknet segments Thinnet sections	Standard lengths: 23.4 meters, 70.2 meters, 117 meters Length from 10 to 500 meters Maximum length: 185 meters
Transceivers	At black marks on thicknet Between 2.5 and 1500 meters apart At most 100 per segment At most 1023 per Ethernet At least .5 meters apart for thinnet
Drop cables Office drop cables	5 to 50 meters long for discrete transceivers 5 to 40 meters long for multiport transceivers 5 meters to 5000 meters for optical fiber 2 to 12.5 meters long for discretes
Repeaters	Version 1: maximum of two in series Version 2 and IEEE 802.3: maximum of four in series 10 to 100 meters between Ethernet segments for local repeaters 10 to 1100 meters between Ethernet segments for remote repeaters 10 meters to 3 km between Ethernet segments for optical repeaters
Bridges	Maximum of seven in series

Further limits are imposed by the routing protocols used on the Internet, which will be discussed in Section 14.4.7.

14.3 Hardware installation

In this section we will discuss the actual installation of the network cable, attaching transceivers to that cable, building drop cables, and installing the Ethernet interface board in a computer. The latter will be a generic description since each interface board and host computer will have the manufacturer's specific instructions. Be sure to ask for manuals when you order the parts. One popular manufacturer sells the installation manuals separately.

14.3.1 The network cable

The most important issue in installing or specifying the installation of the network cable is maintainability. Before starting, refer to Section 14.2 on Ethernet parts and to Section 14.6 on network design issues to determine:

- The route the cable is to take
- The section/segment lengths
- The types of cable — teflon versus PVC, standard versus thinnet

Also assemble the following parts and tools:

Parts:

- The network cable
- Wire ties of several sizes (lots)
- Conduit and conduit tools, if necessary
- Connectors and barrel adapters
- Terminators

Tools:

- Paper and pencil to map cable
- Wire cutters
- Hammer drill (a drill that drills and pounds at the same time)
- Crimp tool for connectors
- A way to unroll the cable smoothly
- Enough people so the cable *never* kinks
- Ladders
- A tall rolling cart
- And, at a university, pizza, beer, and tall students

14.3.1.1 Handling the cable

The transmission properties of the network cable are influenced by kinks, sharp bends, squishes, etc., and so it must be handled carefully. It wants to twist and kink, of course, as it comes off the reel; unrolling it with the reel vertical helps to avoid these problems. The suggested minimum bend radius for thicknet is seven inches, so turn corners as you would if driving a bus. Avoid stepping on the cable or dropping heavy objects on it.

14.3.1.2 Routing the cable

There are conflicting goals when choosing a route: ease of maintenance versus safety from vandalism, physical security from intentional misuse, and cosmetic appearance. These must be balanced to a particular organization's needs. Ethernet is fairly sturdy and maintenance-free once the installation and initial debugging are complete.

Laying the cable in cable trays with medium voltage electrical wires does not seem to hurt the Ethernet's transmission properties, but it is against electrical code in some areas. The two types of cable can be in the same tray if they are separated by a metal divider. A better solution is to try to follow the telephone cable, because there are no restrictions on the proximity of these two types of cable.

While not always unsafe, facilities people frown on tying the cable to water pipes, electrical conduit, gas lines, and the like. In the case of electrical conduit, the cables, especially if there are several of them, will prevent the conduit from cooling the electrical wires inside it properly. In the other cases, if leaks occur, the repairs often involve soldering and could damage the Ethernet cable itself.

14.3.1.3 The actual cable installation

Now that you have designed your network, determined the route of the cable, purchased and collected all the required parts, tools, and helpers, you are ready to go. The first time you install network cable, it will take two to three times longer than you estimate. One person should be assigned the task of making the cable maps as the installation proceeds. It is often easier to first lay an entire cable section and then attach the hardware to connect it to other sections or to terminate it. As the cable is being laid out, leave extra black marks at areas where you expect to add several transceivers and even where you don't. Loops which waste a few feet of cable, but leave a couple of extra black marks, as you turn a corner, can really save time and headaches later as the network design changes. (And it will!) Use plenty of wire ties where the cable must be attached to overhead pipes or utility races.

14.3.1.4 Attaching connectors

Detailed instructions, with diagrams, for installing both N-type and BNC connectors can be found in suppliers' catalogs; for example, in the Anixter Ethernet publication available from Anixter Bros., Inc. Here are some hints.

Cut the cable so that, when assembled with connectors and barrel adapters, the 2.5 meter separation of black marks is maintained. Both N-type connectors and BNC connectors consist of a *contact* that is either crimped or soldered onto the center conductor and a body that mates to the contact, insulating it from the outer braid. Installation requires sharp tools to cut the cable squarely and cleanly, and either a crimping tool with correctly sized dies or skill in soldering. Soldered connections must be strong, yet not get too hot; excessive heat can cause the dielectric to swell and the connector body will not fit properly.

14.3.1.5 Grounding the cable

The entire Ethernet should be either ungrounded or be grounded in just one place. Little insulating booties are available for the Ethernet connectors to insure that they are not inadvertently grounding the cable. Older DC coupled Ethernets (version 1) are hum-sensitive and have ground loop problems if not grounded.

14.3.2 Attaching transceivers

Before attempting to install a transceiver, verify that the Ethernet version of the transceiver and host interface match. Some interface boards and even some transceivers have switches that allow them to change their version compliance. Refer to Sections 14.2.1 and 14.2.3.3 for more information on Ethernet versions and how they relate to transceivers.

14.3.2.1 Intrusive type

If your network is active, you should notify users and schedule 15 minutes (30 minutes if it is your first time) of downtime for the installation. Cut the network cable at a black mark and trim off enough for the connector and transceiver to maintain the 2.5 meter separation between black marks. Of course, if you change your mind and replace the transceiver with a barrel adapter, the distances are off a bit. Attach plug connectors to each side of the cut. Exact instructions for the installation of connectors depends on the particular kind you buy; refer to your vendor's catalog for details. Attach the socket-socket transceiver between the two plug connectors. If by cutting the cable you have cut off the number at the black mark (see Section 14.6.2), remark the cable near the transceiver.

14.3.2.2 Vampire type

We will only describe how to install vampire transceivers that use the standard AMP tap; if yours does not have the AMP tap, refer to the manufacturer's instructions and be sure you have that manufacturer's tools.

Have handy the AMP tap coring tool, a small screwdriver (some need slotted, some Philips), a small flashlight, and a smallish Allen wrench. The standard tap comes in six pieces:

- Tap body, which is black, a couple of inches long, and usually has a white plastic cover attached
- Clamp assembly, which is aluminum and that same two inches long
- Probe assembly, which looks almost like a miniature Volkswagen oil drain plug with a brass wire sticking through it
- Two braid picks, that look sort of like little metal flags
- Screw that holds it all together

To install it, place the wire flagpole of the braid picks in the small holes of the tap body. The braid picks can go either orientation. Lay the Ethernet cable in the slot of the tap body placing the cable's black mark at the center.

Place the clamp assembly on the cable an inch or two away from the tap body and slide it over the tap body. The open side of the clamp assembly has a flange that fits into a grove on the tap body and can go on either way, but the tap body itself will only accept the clamp assembly from one side. Insert the screw in the hole at the center of the clamp assembly and screw it all together hand tight with the Allen key hex wrench. It's easy to tighten it too much, so be gentle. Turn the whole thing over (if you are now lying precariously above the ceiling tiles or in the elevator shaft, this may well be the hardest part!), remove the plastic cap, and drill a hole in the cable using the coring tool. You can't go too deep, as the tool won't let you. Inspect and clean out the hole, using the flashlight to verify that there are no pieces of braid left in the hole. Screw in the "drain plug" with the other end of the coring tool or a socket wrench. Make sure the socket is long enough to clear the brass pin sticking out. Check your work by putting an ohmmeter between the center pin (from the drain plug) and either of the outer pins (the braid picks); you should see:

- On an active net: 20 to 30 Ω, depending on traffic
- On an inactive net: very close to 25 Ω
- On an unterminated net: infinity
- If your installation is faulty and not making contact: infinity
- If your installation is faulty and shorted: close to 0

Unscrew the screws on the transceiver that will eventually hold it in place, slide the transceiver onto the tap (doesn't matter which way it goes, idiot-proof hardware!!), and replace the screws. Renumber the black mark if the transceiver blocks the original number. If you replace an AMP tap or move it (which you shouldn't), always use new braid picks as they are very cheap and are easily scrunched together.

14.3.2.3 Internal type

Most thinnet transceivers are internal to the host computer and are daisy-chained with BNC T connectors. The BNC connectors crimp to the RG58 cable; a separate die for the same expensive crimp tool works quite nicely. Separate thinnet transceivers do exist which attach to the cable like intrusives and use a thinnet drop cable to the host computer.

14.3.3 Drop cables

Section 14.2.3.5 gives specifications for building drop cables; note that drop cables are version-specific. The version 1 and version 2 drop cables can be intermixed, but IEEE 802.3 cables are sufficiently different to require modification if version mismatches occur. Drop cables can also be purchased ready-made.

To install a drop cable, attach the male end to the host computer's Ethernet interface board and the female end to the transceiver. Slide the clip fasteners over the posts on the connector to lock the cable in place. These clips are often difficult to move, it's easiest if you look at the cable (device) first and determine which way the clip slides, then install the cable, which sometimes involves awkward positions in poor light, and finally, slide the clips into place by feel. If the drop cable is improperly wired it can blow the fuse on the interface board. The fuse is sometimes hard to find, for example on a Sun it is the size of a pea and is well concealed.

14.3.4 Installing the interface board

Follow the manufacturer's instructions to install the Ethernet interface board in the host computer. Before you start, be sure to notify users of downtime, have the transceiver installed on the cable, have the drop cable attached to the transceiver and strung back to the host computer, and have a kernel ready to boot that understands the new Ethernet interface. Also, before you start, you should have read the instructions and set any option switches on the board, such as the version. *Do not* change the hardware Ethernet address on the board, even if the instructions tell you how. This 48-bit address is guaranteed unique in all the world, and as a system administrator you will be severely punished if you allow two hardware Ethernet addresses to be the same. The network will know.

Now that you are equipped with instructions, a new kernel, the new interface board, and a transceiver drop cable to plug into it, power down the machine, install the board, connect the transceiver cable, power it up, and reboot that new kernel.

14.4 Network software

Networking, in particular the TCP/IP protocol, is built into the BSD kernel. TCP/IP was chosen because it was the only mature protocol for Ethernet available at the time; it is supported by over 150 vendors.

A kernel data structure called a *socket* and several system calls to access it form the basic interface for programs that use the network. The socket represents an endpoint of a network connection. Data transferred through the socket is guaranteed to be reliable (correct and complete) if the TCP protocol is used.

The software chores associated with maintaining the network include:

- Installation tasks to set up the network initially or add new machines
- Additional configuration if your site intends to connect to the Internet
- Additional setup if your users write their own networking programs
- Monitoring the network to see that it all runs smoothly

Of these, item two requires the most background information. We will assume that your site will have both a local area network of 50 to 100 hosts and a connection to the Internet. Much of the folklore about networking is not written down all in one place, yet it is often necessary to understand the inner workings of the network to troubleshoot a problem and solve it. We will attempt to cover the background information needed to build and maintain a healthy network.

14.4.1 Names

Each host computer must have a unique name on the network. Names for UNIX computers are not new with networking, but their uniqueness has become more important. As networking grew in popularity after the release of 4.2BSD, guaranteeing the uniqueness of the hostname became a growing problem. Mailers got smart and stopped looking at explicit routing information in the mail headers and instead looked up routes in a local database that knew the "optimal" way to get mail to its destination. As a result, when the University of Colorado named a machine "tut", and there was a machine at New York University also named "tut", mail was misrouted.

In a small organization it is relatively easy to guarantee unique names, but as networking spreads throughout the organization and the organization joins regional or national networks, machines under separate administrative control may have name collisions.

To solve this problem, a hierarchical naming scheme called the domain naming system has been introduced. It attempts to solve two problems: the uniqueness of names and the distribution of the database that contains the name-to-address mapping information. There are several top-level domains, as shown in Figure 14.14.

FIGURE 14.14

Top-level domains	
Name	Description
COM	Commercial organizations
EDU	Educational institutions
GOV	Other government agencies
ORG	Nonprofit organizations
MIL	Military government agencies
NET	Networks, to provide changeover path
XX	Two-letter country codes
ARPA	ARPANET, should go away

Each top-level domain is broken up into a set of second-level domains. Top-level domains reflect broad categories of institutions; second-level domains usually represent a whole organization. Third and lower-level domains are departments or subdivisions of that organization. The top-level domains are fixed. The second-level domain names, like hostnames, must be unique, but that is easy since they are administered centrally by SRI-NIC (Stanford Research Institute's Network Information Center). To apply for a second-level domain name, request an electronic version of form DOMAIN-TEMPLATE.TXT, shown in Appendix L, by sending computer mail to hostmaster@sri-nic.arpa. Complete the form and return it electronically. In a week or so (usually), you will receive mail confirming or changing the domain name you requested. Domain names must be 12 or fewer characters and usually reflect the name of the organization requesting them. For example, the University of Colorado has the domain name Colorado.EDU. Domain names are not case sensitive, thus we are also colorado.edu and even CoLoRaDo.eDu. Third- and lower-level names are totally managed by the institution; we have subdivided the Colorado.EDU domain by university departments and further by research projects within those departments. These naming conventions are totally local and do not have to be registered with the NIC.

The name collision just mentioned is now not a collision at all, since one machine is tut.Colorado.EDU and the other is tut.NYU.EDU.

14.4.2 Ethernet addresses

Host computers on an Ethernet are identified by two addresses, the Ethernet address (a 48-bit hardware address) and an IP or software address. Ethernet addresses are guaranteed unique because vendors building Ethernet interfaces have a set of addresses assigned to them. The IEEE Standards Board in New York City assigns the first 24 bits to a manufacturer, which then allocates the last 24 bits sequentially. The address is either built into the interface board or stored in ROM on the board.

14.4.3 IP addresses

Internet or IP addresses are used by networking software to identify machines. An IP address is four bytes or more properly octets (since they are eight bits, and bytes are not guaranteed to be eight bits); each byte is interpreted as either defining the network address or the host address on that network. The network portion is denoted by N; the host portion by H. There are three primary address classes: Class A of the form N.H.H.H, Class B of the form N.N.H.H, and Class C of the form N.N.N.H. The N portions of an address are assigned by the NIC, and the H portions are up to the local site to assign. The numbers 0, 127, and 255 have special meanings:

- 0 is reserved for machines that don't know their address
- 127 is reserved for the localhost or loopback host
- 255 is reserved for broadcast packets[1]

A 0 in any part of an address indicates that the sending host does not know that part of his own address. Each host knows himself by the name "localhost" and the address 127.0.0.1 in addition to knowing himself by his actual assigned name and address. Any packets destined for the localhost do not actually go out onto the network cable but instead are recognized and looped back through software in the kernel. This software is configured into the kernel with the pseudo-device option *loop*. 255 is a broadcast address which all hosts must listen for. The 255 may be all four bytes of the broadcast address or just the host part, with the network part remaining that of the host initiating the broadcast packet. 255 is sometimes written as -1, which is OK on a 2's-complement machine but is 254 on a 1's-complement machine (if there are any still out there). The broadcast address was not yet specified when 4.2BSD came out and so 0 was used. This creates problems on networks containing both 4.3BSD- and 4.2BSD-based machines.

Class A addresses interpret the bytes as N.H.H.H and therefore allow for many hosts on the same network. These are essentially impossible to get now unless you are a new major national or international network; for example, the ARPANET is net 10. The first bit of a Class A address must be 0, which forces the network numbers to be between 1 and 126.

Class B addresses interpret the bytes as N.N.H.H, allowing for many networks and many hosts per network. The first two bits of the first network byte must be 10, yielding network numbers between 128.1 and 191.254. Sites with Class A and Class B addresses usually use the first host byte for local subnets.

Class C addresses interpret the bytes as N.N.N.H, which only supports 254 hosts. The leading bits must be 11, yielding network numbers between 192.1.1 and 223.254.254. Medium sized sites which cannot commandeer a Class B address from the NIC can request a sequence of several Class C addresses.

The numbers at the end of the Class C range, from 224 to 254, are now reserved for Class D, Multicast addresses, and Class E, Experimental addresses.

[1] When 4.2BSD was released the broadcast address was specified as a 0 byte in the host portions of the address. 4.3BSD followed the subsequent RFC and used 255.

14.4.4 Requesting an IP address

IP addresses must be unique on the Internet, the national network that is a conglomeration of ARPANET, NSFNet, regional networks and campus/organizational networks. In the past, the only way to get a guaranteed unique set of addresses was to be on the ARPANET; however, SRI-NIC is currently allocating Internet addresses to anyone who asks. Request INTERNET-NUMBER-TEMPLATE.TXT by electonic mail from hostmaster@sri-nic.arpa to receive the proper application form (see Appendix M), and submit it electronically. IP addresses assigned by SRI-NIC are guaranteed to be unique from all others blessed by the NIC, but not necessarily from sites that assign their network numbers randomly.

The NIC not only assigns network numbers, but also approves (guarantees unique) the network names you have chosen. Network names are used in some software configuration files to symbolically name networks for routing. In choosing network names, it is a good idea to use an identifying prefix. For example, we initially requested a set of ten Class C addresses because some machines on our network could not handle subnetted Class B addresses. For each Class C address we had to supply a name for the network; the University of Colorado is often called CU and so we prefixed our network names with *cu-*, which yielded both unique names and mnemonic names as well.

14.4.5 Name-to-IP address mappings

Each machine on the network has a name, an IP address, and an Ethernet address. Each is used to refer to the machine. Mappings between names and IP addresses were originally done statically in the /etc/hosts file. Host tables, like the host name space, have not scaled up to current sizes and complexity. Just as "choose a name and hope no one else (nationwide) has used it first," failed to handle the naming gracefully, static host tables are inadequate. For a busy machine on the Internet, the hosts file would be thousands of lines long, always out of date, hard to administer in a distributed fashion, and impossible to administer centrally.

Thus was born the domain naming system and the *name server* to dynamically provide host-to-address lookups. BIND, the Berkeley Internet Name Domain server, is the tool distributed with 4.3BSD to help maintain a distributed database of hostname-to-IP address mappings. Each name server must know how to supply information about the hostname address mappings in its domain of authority and how to pass on requests for information outside its domain. Name servers accomplish this by talking to their counterparts in other domains. The user interface to the name server is called a *resolver*.

There have been several implementations of domain name servers and resolvers for various operating systems: BSD UNIX, TOPS-20, MS-DOS,

Symbolics, Harris, and VMS to name a few. Of these, BIND for BSD UNIX and JEEVES for TOPS-20 are the most mature. The MS-DOS Server and Resolver is a port of BIND by FTP Software; it runs in their PC/TCP environment. Symbolics has implemented a resolver for the 3600 series Lisp machines. Xerox PARC has a resolver running written in the Cedar language/environment. There is a domain resolver for the Harris H series that has most of the functionality of the BIND system. There is a partial resolver implementation written in Bliss which is part of the CMU/TEK TCP/IP package for VAX/VMS. Of these we will describe only BIND, since it pertains to Berkeley UNIX and is the most complete and widely used implementation.

BIND was written by Kevin Dunlap of DEC while on loan to the Computer Systems Research Group at Berkeley. The latest version is available via anonymous **ftp** from ucbarpa.Berkeley.EDU. Documentation is included with the package, both in the form of manual pages for the user-level commands and library routines, and in the form of a complete document on the BIND system, its installation, and operation: *Name Server Operations Guide for BIND*. This document is included with the 4.3BSD distribution, but is not yet integrated into the System Manager's Manual. In addition, there is a mailing list maintained by Berkeley where relevant information is distributed. To join the mailing list, send electronic mail to bind-request@ucbarpa.berkeley.edu.

BIND administration is discussed in detail in Section 14.9.1.

14.4.6 Routing

Routing is the process by which a packet is directed through the maze of machines that stand between its source and destination. Routing's simplistic design goals were that it be transparent to the user and that it work, hopefully, relatively efficiently. Chuck Hedrick of Rutgers University likens routing to the algorithm a small child uses to find his parents' table in a crowded restaurant. An adult can see the whole restaurant, including obstacles such as waiter's carts or new guests being seated that might block certain paths, and can determine quickly an efficient route back to the table. The child, on the other hand, cannot see over the tables and therefore does a random walk through the restaurant until he recognizes the correct table. If your local area network is connected to the Internet, then that restaurant spans a huge amount of territory. Routing is still considered by many to be an unsolved research problem. Algorithms seem to need foresight, hindsight, and luck. Since it is still in the research domain, the state of routing, its algorithms, and protocols is very dynamic, making any description out of date before published.

Typical routing information is of the form: "to reach network-A from machine-B, send packets to the machine-C. The cost is 1 hop." Routing information is stored in routing tables in the kernel. Entries in these tables have several parameters, including a time-to-live field and a reliability field which determines which route to use if the tables contain conflicting information.

Routing can be done either statically, dynamically, or by using a combination of the two. The **/etc/route** command installs a route in the routing tables. It is usually executed in the /etc/rc.local startup file at boot time. Static routing is adequate for small, isolated networks, but is totally impractical for a busy host on the Internet. It requires that the system administrator know the topology of the network accurately at boot time, and that the topology not change between boots. In a relatively stable local network, static routing is an efficient solution, is not difficult to administer, and is reliable.

The routing daemon, **/etc/routed** (pronounced as two words, "route dee") performs dynamic routing by communicating with **routed** programs on other machines to learn what the actual network topology really is and how to reach any host on the network. Although a bit of a resource hog, **routed** does a good job when a network is changing often or when connected to external networks whose topology is not known.

A good routing strategy for a medium-sized installation with a relatively stable local structure and a connection to the Internet is to use a combination of static and dynamic routing. Machines within the local structure that do not gateway to external networks can use static routing, forwarding all unknown packets to a default machine that understands the outside world and does dynamic routing.

14.4.7 Routing protocols

Where separate networks meet, either at the local level where a campus network interfaces to the outside world, or nationally where ARPANET and NSFNet meet, an external, mutually understood routing protocol must be used to help packets cross the boundary. There are several such routing protocols in use:

- EGP - External Gateway Protocol
- RIP - Routing Information Protocol
- IGRP - Internal Gateway Routing Protocol
- Hello - Original gateway protocol for NSFNet

Routing protocols use a cost metric to assign weights to each route that reflects how long it takes a packet to traverse the route. The protocols try to distinguish between good and bad routes with this cost metric. Most will only use "the best" route from their point of view. Each protocol uses a different metric for measuring cost.

EGP is the gateway protocol spoken by the ARPANET gateways. It uses a cost metric with only three values and infinity (there are actually eight values, but only four are distinguishable) and therefore is more accurately described as a reachability protocol.

RIP is an XNS protocol adapted for IP networks. It is the protocol used by the **/etc/routed** command. The cost metric is the hop count, where each machine that a packet flows through is counted as one hop; 16 is equal to infinity, signifying that the destination host is down. Thus large local networks with more than 16 gateway machines along a single path cannot use RIP. **/etc/gated**, a replacement for **routed**, allows a machine to cheat and alter the hop counts to support larger networks.

IGRP is a new proprietary interior routing protocol used by Cisco Systems. It broadcasts its routing information every 90 seconds and has metrics which depend on the delay experienced and the bandwidth of the link.

Hello was the original gateway protocol for the NSFNet backbone which used "fuzzball" routers. Fuzzballs are PDP-11s with software from Dave Mills of the University of Maryland. The Hello protocol uses milliseconds of delay as a cost metric and contains very sophisticated algorithms for determining values of the metric. Time on the NSFNet under Hello routing was synchronized to within milliseconds — quite a feat.

The **/etc/gated** program understands the RIP, Hello, and EGP protocols, and thus can be used when two networks speaking different gateway protocols meet and must transfer packets. It translates between the various metrics and includes important flexibility under control of a configuration file, /etc/gated.conf. It can control broadcasts, filter the routes advertised, include static routing, and recognize trusted gateways. **gated** is not part of distributed 4.3BSD, but will probably be included in later releases. It was written by Mark Fedor from Cornell University and can be obtained via anonymous **ftp** from devvax.tn.cornell.edu. **gated** has replaced **routed** at many sites, including ours.

14.4.8 Subnets

Many organizations with Class B addresses find it convenient to use the third byte of the address to designate particular Ethernets within the organization. For example, Colorado's machine "boulder" with address 128.138.240.1 and "boulder-gw" with address 128.138.238.18 are the same machine, with interfaces on two local networks: the 240 net, cu-engineer, and the 238 net, cu-boulder. Routing from the outside world remains the same, but within the University, different routes are used to reach the 238 net than to reach the 240 net. The use of such high numbers for the third byte is arbitrary. We converted from a group of Class C addresses to a single Class B address by just changing the first two bytes of the network number, thus inheriting the last network byte of our old Class C addresses. The use of a Class B address with subnetting hides the structure within the University from the outside world. It is only necessary to advertise the single net, 128.138, to the Internet. If each institution needed to advertise all its local structure, routing tables would quickly overflow.

Subnetting is implemented using the NETMASK field of the **ifconfig** command, which defines the network part and the host part of an IP address. For example, a machine with a class B address used as a gateway to the Internet might define a NETMASK of 0xffff0000 on the Internet interface and a NETMASK of either 0xffffff00 if the campus net is subnetted, or 0xffff0000 if the campus net is not subnetted, on the campus interface.

The subnet code was not implemented in 4.2BSD and therefore systems that are 4.2 based do not understand subnets. This means they must use static routing in a subnetted environment.

14.4.9 ARP - the Address Resolution Protocol

ARP, the address resolution protocol, is used when a host's name or IP address is known, but the 48-bit hardware Ethernet address is not. An ARP request is broadcast asking for the hardware address in question. When a reply comes back, the host needing the information will add the address mapping to its ARP tables. ARP uses an Ethernet broadcast address of all 1's (48 of 'em) as its broadcast address; it does not use IP packets.

14.4.10 Trailers

Trailers are header information that is tacked onto the end of a packet to avoid having to recopy the packet. Packets arriving with trailers are aligned on a page boundary, the trailer information is checked and removed, and a pointer to the page is turned over to the receiving program with no data moves necessary. Unfortunately, trailers have never been formally adopted in an RFC (although RFC 893 describes trailers as implemented in 4.2BSD pretty well) and not all implementations of TCP/IP understand them. 4.3BSD machines negotiate trailers with ARP, but for 4.2BSD machines it is all or nothing; that is, either all machines on the net understand and use trailers, or none can. Trailers can be used on local nets but should not be used on the Internet. Trailers are set with an option to **ifconfig**.

14.4.11 TCP/IP differences

Several differences between 4.2BSD and 4.3BSD networking code exist; the important ones are described next:

- Congestion algorithm
- ICMP redirects
- Broadcast address
- Subnetting
- Checksum bug

TCP is the layer above IP and guarantees the transmission of a flow controlled, correctly ordered, unduplicated, message between two points. This means that if a packet does not arrive in time at the receiving end of the conversation, no acknowledgment is returned to the sender and after an appropriate period the sender times out and retransmits the same packet again. If the timeout occurs because the network is congested, this just aggravates the situation by flooding the network with unnecessary retransmissions. The TCP code under 4.2BSD retransmitted packets quickly and often, thus reacting too quickly to a congested network. It is slow to adapt to current congestion conditions. The algorithm used in 4.3BSD is better.

ICMP redirects are routing control messages that a gateway can use to avoid congestion by telling the sender of a particular message that a different route is more direct or preferable. 4.2BSD ignores ICMP redirects; 4.3BSD uses them to upgrade its routing tables, entering the new routes learned through ICMP redirects for a fixed period of time, after which they expire and the old default route is resumed.

4.2BSD was released before RFC 972, which specified the IP broadcast address as 255. It used a 0 in the host bytes of the IP address to specify a broadcast packet. 4.3BSD uses 255 or all 1's in the host bytes for an IP broadcast address and all 1's for the Ethernet broadcast address.

4.2BSD does not support subnetting; 4.3BSD and later releases do.

The checksum code shipped with 4.2BSD contained a bug that was ported to many vendors' products. This was not discovered until 4.3BSD was released with the checksum error corrected and could not interoperate with 4.2 based systems. The workaround is to define the option TCP_COMPAT_42 in the kernel configuration file (see Chapter 8: *Configuring the Kernel*), causing the checksums to be ignored in packets that originate on 4.2BSD machines.

Recently TCP has been improved further by Van Jacobson of Lawrence Berkeley Labs. The new code is part of the 4.3BSD Tahoe release, or can be obtained by anonymous **ftp** from ucbarpa.berkeley.edu (in ~ftp/pub/4.3 the five files: tcp.tar, inet.tar, netns.tar, socket.tar, and imp.tar). Performance, especially under heavy loads, is greatly enhanced.

14.5 Required software

The discussion that follows assumes that the network is being built from scratch, and therefore refers to creating the various configuration files rather than just updating them as you would if adding a new host to an existing network. The example chosen for this section is very simple: two machines: "boulder", a Vax 11/780 with two network interfaces, and "tigger", a MIPS 1000 with one.

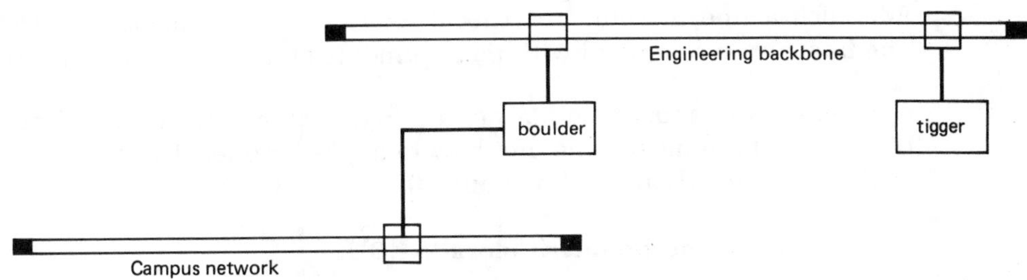

FIGURE 14.15 tigger-boulder network configuration

There are several software management decisions that must be made for a new network; i.e., static versus dynamic routing, running BIND, global versus local name spaces, etc. Both sides of these issues are presented here, but you should read Section 14.7 on management issues to decide which scheme is best for your site. This discussion is limited to the actual steps necessary to configure the software to use the network:

- Set hostname and domain name
- Modify the /etc/hosts file
- Modify the /etc/networks file
- Build a new kernel
- Set up the /etc/rc.local file
- Set up routing
- Create pseudo-terminals and update terminal configuration files
- Set up /etc/hosts.equiv, /etc/hosts.lpd, and /.rhosts
- Boot the new kernel
- Make links in /usr/hosts
- Set up /etc/inetd.conf, /etc/services, and /etc/protocols

- Set up /etc/gated.conf
- Set up BIND configuration files

The order of these steps is not critical, however all steps before "Boot the new kernel", must be done prior to the reboot.

14.5.1 Choose and assign names

Each host computer must have a unique name on the network. Under BSD hostnames can be up to 32 characters. But it is convenient to have shorter names because programs such as **uucp**, only look at the first six or seven characters. The hostname is set in the file /etc/rc.local with the **hostname** command; for example:

/bin/hostname boulder

Add such a line to your /etc/rc.local (or /etc/rc, /etc/rc.boot, /etc/brc, ...) file. The **hostname** command with no arguments shows the current hostname.

A domain name must also be chosen. See Section 14.4.1 for a description of the domain naming scheme and how to apply for one. The domain name can be included directly in the hostname; for example:

/bin/hostname boulder.Colorado.EDU

The full hostname can also be specified by an alias in the /etc/hosts file (see Section 14.5.2) and in the /usr/lib/sendmail.cf file by a definition in the localization part (see Section 15.3.2.1). If you intend to run the name server the true hostname must include the domain name.

14.5.2 Set up the /etc/hosts file

The /etc/hosts file is used by any command or program that must do a hostname-to-IP address mapping, that is, by any command using the network.[2] The hosts file contains a list of IP addresses, hostnames, hostname aliases, and optional comments. The format is illustrated by the following example for our tiny network.

```
#  Tiny Ethernet Example: /etc/hosts file
#
128.138.240.1    boulder boulder.colorado.edu          # vax780, ECEE 00-71A
128.138.238.18   boulder-gw boulder-gw.colorado.edu  # vax780, ECEE 00-71A
128.138.240.26   tigger tigger.colorado.edu            # mips M1000, ECCR 0-20A
```

[2] This is not quite true, since this mapping is dynamically determined if you run BIND, the Berkeley Internet Name Domain server, which can bypass the static /etc/hosts file, but we will ignore this for now.

In 4.3BSD, host tables are hashed by the **mkhosts** command to create .pag and .dir files that are used by the **ndbm** (3) routines for fast lookups. Any time the file /etc/hosts is changed you must run **/etc/mkhosts**.

14.5.3 Set up the /etc/networks file

The file /etc/networks allows hosts on the same network or subnet to be referred to as a group. This is quite convenient for things like static routing, which take as an argument either an individual hostname or a net name to refer to all hosts on that network. The format of the file is illustrated by the following example:

```
#
#  Tiny Ethernet Example: /etc/networks file
#
loopback-net     127.0.0          Software loopback net
cu-netmask       255.255.255      Netmask on campus
#
colorado         128.138          University of Colorado, Class B address
cu-engineer      128.138.240      Engineering Center Backbone
cu-boulder       128.138.238      Campus Backbone
```

Notice that only the network portion, including the subnet byte, of the Internet address is used. The cu-netmask entry defines symbolically the string 255.255.255 or 0xffffff00 which identifies the network portion of addresses.

14.5.4 Building a new kernel

To build a new kernel that will understand the network, you must include the network interface device driver and the networking code in the kernel.

14.5.4.1 Device drivers supported

Figure 14.16 lists the networking devices supported under Berkeley 4.3.

To verify exactly which networking devices are supported for your system, refer to the documentation or look in the directory where device drivers are kept (/usr/src/sys/vaxif on 4.3BSD for a Vax). If the device driver for the device you have purchased (or are purchasing) is not supported by your software, you may be able to obtain a driver from the manufacturer of the interface board, but be aware that the computer manufacturer and the interface board manufacturer will probably not cooperate to get you the latest driver for the latest version of the operating system at exactly the time you would like to do your upgrade. If you have the clout, consider asking the interface board manufacturer to give the driver to either the public domain or the computer manufacturer.

FIGURE 14.16

Network device drivers supported in 4.3BSD	
Device name	Manufacturer and model number
acc	ACC LH/DH interface to IMP
css	DEC IMP-11A interface to IMP
ddn	4.2 DDN X.25 network driver
de	DEC DEUNA 10Mb/s Ethernet
dmc	DEC DMC-11 (also works with DMR-11)
ec	3Com 10Mb/s Ethernet
en	Xerox 3Mb/s prototype Ethernet (not a product)
ex	Excelan EXOS 204 interface
hdh	ACC IF-11/HDH interface
hy	NSC Hyperchannel, w/ DR-11B and PI-13 interfaces
il	Interlan 10Mb/s Ethernet
pcl	DEC PCL-11
qe	Digital Q-BUS to NI adapter
uba	UNIBUS network interfaces
un	Ungermann-Bass network w/ DR-11W interface
vv	Proteon ring network (V2LNI)

14.5.4.2 Configure a networking kernel

In addition to including a line for the network interface in the devices section of the configuration file, you must also turn on several networking options to include all the code needed to operate the network. The following lines are indicative of what must be included in the configuration file to build a networking kernel. The interfaces in this example are the Interlan Unibus interface, il0, and the DEC DEUNA interface, de0, for the Vax "boulder".

```
options         INET
options         GATEWAY
options         TCP_COMPAT_42
device          il0      at uba? csr 0164000 vector ilrint ilcint
device          de0      at uba? csr 0174510 vector deintr
pseudo-device   pty
pseudo-device   loop
pseudo-device   ether
```

The GATEWAY option increases the sizes of some data structures and tables in the kernel and is appropriate for machines with multiple network interfaces. These lines do not just get tacked onto the end of the configuration file. See Chapter 8: *Configuring the Kernel*, for details on where these lines should be placed and how to rebuild the kernel from the configuration file.

14.5.5 Set up the /etc/rc.local file

The /etc/rc.local file contains machine-specific initialization commands. In addition to setting the hostname as described in Section 14.5.1, two chores regarding the network are done here: initializing the network interface and setting up the routing tables.

14.5.5.1 The ifconfig command

ifconfig is used to turn an Ethernet interface on and off from a software point of view, and to set the options and parameters that the interface is to use. An example for the machine boulder, which has two network interfaces, follows:

```
/etc/ifconfig il0 boulder up subarp netmask cu-netmask arp\
        broadcast 128.138.240.255 > /dev/console
/etc/ifconfig  de0  boulder-gw up subarp netmask cu-netmask arp\
        broadcast 128.138.238.255 >/dev/console
/etc/ifconfig  lo0  localhost  up  arp > /dev/console
```

The first line configures il0, an Interlan board. It is turned on (up), told to use certain options (subarp and arp), to use a particular netmask (netmask cu-netmask), and to use a particular broadcast address (broadcast 128.138.240.255). The netmask cu-netmask is defined in the file /etc/networks and refers to the two network bytes and the subnet byte of our Class B address. Notice that the broadcast address has the form net.subnet.255 and therefore will not be recognized as a broadcast address except on the 240 subnet. The second line configures the de0 interface, a DEC DEUNA board, to the campus backbone network. The final line configures the localhost pseudo-device lo0 for software loopback.

Actually, it is better to use the IP address rather than the symbolic name for machines in **ifconfig** commands because the nameserver (BIND) can have initialization problems with the symbolic names. The same is true for the netmask. Symbolic names are used just for readability.

ifconfig has many options that are used to tell the software driver exactly how smart the hardware and host computer are. The basic form of the command is to name the interface as configured into the kernel, the hostname, and the keyword "up" to turn on the interface or "down" to turn it off. It is common to use a distinct hostname for each interface on machines with multiple interfaces; for example: "boulder" and "boulder-gw". Further options have to do with the routing, including subnet routing, ARP, the address resolution protocol, broadcast addressing, and packet format. These are described in detail in the manual page for **ifconfig**(8); we will describe only the gotchas that are not mentioned in the manual page.

4.2BSD based systems must either see each packet with trailers or no packets with trailers. Thus if any machines on a network cannot support trailers, no machines can use them. 4.3BSD, on the other hand, negotiates trailers (with ARP) on a host-by-host basis.

Hosts that do not use ARP cannot respond when queried for their hardware address. Another machine can answer for them, using a system called proxy ARP, in which a machine that speaks ARP keeps tables of ARP data for hosts that do not. The option to **ifconfig** is "subarp." Code for proxy ARP is not part of 4.3BSD, but is in the public domain; **diff**s were posted to Usenet for sites which have sources. In order to set up the ARP tables in the first place, the hardware Ethernet addresses in question must be determined from the interface board or by listening on the network as machines boot.

The **ifconfig** command with just the interface as an argument prints the current values of the options that are set on the interface.

14.5.5.2 Routing

Refer to Section 14.4.6 on general routing issues to determine a routing policy: static, dynamic, or a combination of the two. This section discusses how to implement static or dynamic routing, not which scheme you should choose.

Static routing, /etc/route

The **/etc/route** command establishes static routes — that is, entries in the routing tables that do not change. For example, the lines:

```
/etc/route add `/bin/hostname` localhost 0  # for loopback
/etc/route add cu-boulder boulder-gw 1      # everyone thru gateway
/etc/route add default boulder 1            # boulder knows all
```

executed from the /etc/rc.local file would allow tigger to know that local packets should use the pseudo-host localhost (zero hops), that packets for machines on the cu-boulder network should be sent to the machine boulder-gw for forwarding (one hop), and that all other packets should go through the host boulder (also one hop).

The exact format of the **route** command is:

> **/etc/route** [-f] {add,delete} *destination gateway hop-count*

The *destination* can be a hostname, a network name, or the keyword "default", which will handle any route not explicitly mentioned. The *gateway* is the machine name to send packets to for forwarding; the *hop-count* is the number of such forwardings to finally reach the destination. The -f argument flushes the routing tables. The **route** command is in the /usr/etc directory on Sun workstations.

If your site has many networks and uses static routing, it is more convenient to bundle the **/etc/route** invocations into one file and execute that command file from rc.local such as the **setuproute** command illustrated next.

In rc.local:

```
/usr/local/etc/setuproute
```

In setuproute itself:

```
PATH=/usr/etc:/etc:$PATH
route add cu-srl                goober-gateway 1
route add cu-cer                anchor-gateway 1
route add cu-ot                 piper-gateway 1
route add cu-enterprise         kirk-gateway 1
route add cu-balcony            sigi 2
route add cu-optics             fred-gateway 1
route add cu-esuper             boulder 2
route add cu-psuper             boulder 2
route add wasser-gw             boulder 1
route add cu-cadswes            boulder 2
route add default               boulder 1
```

If you run the nameserver on a gateway machine and that gateway happens to be down, then the local machine executing the **route add** command will hang as it boots trying to resolve the address for boulder. This can be alleviated by using the IP address instead of the name for the gateways. No packets can get through the gateway if it is down, of course, but at least the boot can proceed.

Dynamic routing, /etc/routed

Dynamic routing uses **/etc/routed** to build the routing tables on the fly as they are needed by the packet traffic. To implement dynamic routing, add the following lines to rc.local:

```
if [ -f /etc/routed ]; then
       /etc/routed & (echo -n ' router')     >/dev/console
```

routed is a resource hog and early versions occasionally locked up, bringing the machine to its knees and forcing a reboot.

Better dynamic routing, /etc/gated

/etc/gated is a replacement for **/etc/routed** that understands multiple routing protocols and translates routing metrics between them. It is driven by the configuration file /etc/gated.conf, which allows the administrator to have much more control over the routes advertised, the broadcast addresses, trust, metrics, etc. **gated** can be run with debugging turned on, causing its actions to be archived to a log file. This is very useful when first setting up the gated.conf configuration file, and in fact provides a good history of routing information. It grows quite quickly and so should be restarted or truncated weekly. If **gated** is sent a HUP signal, it turns off debugging, allowing you to rename or truncate the log file. A second HUP signal turns the debugging back on. **gated** does not have to be restarted if the parameters to a network interface change; simply **ifconfig** the interface down, wait a minute, and **ifconfig** it up with the new parameters. **gated** will notice shortly.

gated is started in /etc/rc.local as follows:

```
if [ -f /etc/gated ]; then
   rm -rf /usr/adm/gatedlog
   /etc/gated -t /usr/adm/gatedlog & echo -n ' gated' >/dev/console
fi
```

The manual page for **gated**(8) contains complete guidelines for setting up the configuration file.

14.5.6 Set up terminal interactions

The remote login program **rlogin** uses pseudo-terminals (software masquerading as hardware) which must be present in the terminal configuration files.

14.5.6.1 Pseudo-terminal devices

Pseudo-terminals, *pty*'s, must be created in the /dev directory. These are character devices that use software to emulate a terminal; the kernel support for pty's is included with the "`pseudo-device pty`" line in the configuration file. Pty's are named p0-pf for the first 16, q0-qf for the second 16, and so on. The following commands create 32 ptys with names beginning with ptyp0 (master) and ttyp0 (slave).

cd /dev
MAKEDEV pty0
MAKEDEV pty1

On a workstation, which is essentially a single-user machine, 16 ptys are probably enough. However, on a time-sharing machine supporting many users, more may be required. In addition to the network, window systems, the **emacs** editor, and some commands use ptys.

14.5.6.2 Terminal configuration files

The pseudo-terminals must be listed in the configuration files /etc/ttys and /etc/ttytype (the latter only under 4.2BSD). Typical entries follow:

4.3BSD /etc/ttys:

```
ttyp0   none                    network
ttyp1   none                    network
 ...
ttyqf   none                    network
```

4.2BSD /etc/ttys:

```
02ttyp0
02ttyp1
  ...
02ttyqf
```

4.2BSD /etc/ttytype:

```
network ttyp0
network ttyp1
  ...
network ttyqf
```

14.5.7 Set up the /etc/hosts.equiv and /.rhosts files

Security on the network is feebly controlled with two files: /etc/hosts.equiv for machine-level control and ~/.rhosts for user-level control. The /etc/hosts.equiv file specifies which machines are globally equivalent and trusted. Trusted means that all users, including root, with logins on the remote machine may access the machine via **rlogin**, **rsh**, or **rcp** without supplying a password. This is very convenient for system administrators who need to bounce around the network fixing or monitoring things, but leads to some security issues which are discussed in Section 14.7.4. We recommend very limited and controlled use of hosts.equiv. Sun ships their software with a "+" in the hosts.equiv file; for systems using the Yellow Pages distributed database, this means that all machines on the whole network are equivalent. If you have Suns, change this.

The /etc/hosts.equiv file contains the names of the equivalent machines, one per line. For example, if tigger wished to trust boulder:

```
boulder
boulder-gw
```

If you are running the nameserver, then it is not necessary to list both boulder and boulder-gw; if you do host lookups statically in the /etc/hosts file, then both are necessary.

The file ~/.rhosts allows an individual user to specify which machines are equivalent for him and even which login names on those machines are equivalent. In particular, the file /.rhosts controls root access, and is a better and safer way to equivalence machines for system administration. It is, in fact, the only way to equivalence machines for root access under 4.3BSD. In the following sample /.rhosts file for the machine tigger, the entry "boulder sysadmin" allows the user "sysadmin" on the boulder machine to log in to tigger as root without supplying a password.

```
boulder
boulder-gw
boulder sysadmin
```

Note that if two machines are equivalenced through hosts.equiv, then user login names MUST be unique. If "bob" on boulder is not the same person as "bob" on tigger, then the security and privacy of each bob can be violated by the other, as no password will be requested if either tries to remotely log in or copy files across the network. Generally this is not a problem for machines in the same administrative group, but can cause headaches in large organizations. It is best not to globally equivalence machines.

The file /etc/hosts.lpd on 4.3BSD systems allows a limited form of equivalence. It lists the names of machines whose users are allowed to print on local printers, but gives no further access rights. /etc/hosts.lpd is described in Chapter 11.

14.5.8 Boot the new kernel

At this point the kernel, configuration files, and initialization files have been told about the network. It's time to reboot the new kernel and test drive the network. Just in case, keep the old kernel around and know how to boot it, even if it isn't called /vmunix. For example:

```
mv /vmunix /vmunix.nonet                       /* save the working kernel */
cp /usr/sys/.../vmunix /vmunix.network         /* copy in the new one */
ln /vmunix.network /vmunix                     /* and name it */
shutdown +5 "rebooting to test network"        /* notify users */
reboot (or fastboot)                           /* reboot the new kernel */
```

As the kernel boots you should see the network interface mentioned as the devices are scanned (assuming your particular hardware does this) and should see **routed** started if you elected dynamic routing.

14.5.9 Test drive the network, gently

Not all of the networking commands will work yet, since there are still more software setup chores to do. But try some simple ones:

- **ping** - to verify the connection
- **telnet** - to login to a remote machine
- **ftp** - to copy files to/from a remote machine
- **rlogin** - also to login to a remote machine

- **rcp** - also to copy files to/from a remote machine
- **rsh** - to execute a command on a remote machine

If **ping**, **telnet**, **ftp**, and **rlogin** fail, the network is probably not configured correctly. Refer to Section 14.10 on debugging. If **rcp** or **rsh** fail because of permissions, the hosts.equiv or .rhosts files are not set up correctly on the remote machine. Both **rcp** and **rsh** require that the user be equivalenced on the remote machine through either ~/.rhosts or /etc/hosts.equiv.

14.5.10 Make links in /usr/hosts

Making links between **rsh** (the remote shell) and the hostnames of all machines on the network allows some typing shortcuts; for example:

> **cd /usr/hosts**
> **ln /usr/ucb/rsh tigger**

allows users to type:

> **tigger** instead of **rlogin tigger** and
> **tigger** *command* instead of **rsh tigger** *command*

The directory /usr/hosts contains a script called MAKEHOSTS which makes these links automatically from the /etc/hosts file. The "#" symbol in the /etc/hosts file denotes a comment, either an entire line of comments or the beginning of a comment on a non-comment line. Some versions of MAKEHOSTS don't understand comments within a line and thus break on a well-commented hosts file. Fortunately this presents an inconvenience and not a real error, but you might want to read MAKEHOSTS before executing it. You should remind users to put /usr/hosts in their directory search path (near the end) to take advantage of these shortcuts.

14.5.11 Start the rwhod daemon

The remote **who** daemon **rwhod** broadcasts packets periodically announcing who is logged in on the machine. **rwhod** also receives such packets from other **rwhod**s on the network and builds a database in /usr/spool/rwho of all users and machines on the network. The **rwho** and **ruptime** commands use this database to provide a snapshot of the status of the network. **rwhod** is started in the file /etc/rc by the lines:

```
if [ -f /etc/rwhod ]; then
        /etc/rwhod;      echo -n ' rwhod'     >/dev/console
```

BSD systems usually already have this line in /etc/rc. **rwhod** can be a resource hog on a busy network because every machine must listen to all broadcast packets. The default granularity of **rwhod** broadcasts is three minutes, therefore the data reported by **ruptime** and **rwho** are slightly out of date.

14.5.12 The inetd daemon

Network daemons were quite a resource hog in 4.2BSD; 4.3BSD has introduced a super daemon which manages the other network daemons to improve performance. This overseer of the network daemons is **/etc/inetd**, which manages the network service daemons according to instructions contained in the /etc/inetd.conf configuration file. **inetd** listens for connections on well-known sockets and starts the proper daemon if a connection is requested. The performance win over the alternative of having every possible daemon running all the time is substantial, and daemon startup procedures are simplified.

The **inetd** configuration file comes properly set up for the standard network programs distributed with Berkeley UNIX. However, if your users are writing code that uses the network, they may want to semi-officially install their own programs as **inetd** clients. To change the daemons managed by **inetd**, simply adjust the configuration file as appropriate and send **inetd** a HUP signal:

```
ps ax | grep inetd          /* to get the PID */
kill -HUP PID               /* to signal inetd */
```

14.5.12.1 The /etc/inetd.conf file

Each line of the **inetd** configuration file, /etc/inetd.conf, contains the information to manage a particular server process:

- Service name - from the /etc/services file
- Socket type - from {stream, dgram, raw, rdm, seqpacket}
- Protocol - from /etc/protocols file
- wait/nowait - for datagram sockets to specify if **inetd** must wait until the current instance of the server must finish and exit before processing another request on that socket
- User - the user name that the server should run as (not necessarily root)
- Server program - pathname to the program **inetd** should start
- Server arguments - arguments to the server program including the program name itself

Fields are separated by either spaces or tabs; comments begin with the "#" symbol. **inetd** performs a few services itself, in which case the server program is indicated by "internal".

The format of the configuration file is illustrated by the following excerpt.

```
#
# Internet server configuration database
#
ftp     stream  tcp     nowait  root    /etc/ftpd       ftpd -l
telnet  stream  tcp     nowait  root    /etc/telnetd    telnetd
time    stream  tcp     nowait  root    internal
time    dgram   udp     wait    root    internal
```

14.5.12.2 The /etc/services file

The /etc/services file is a registry of programs and so-called *well-known* port numbers. If two programs on different machines want to talk to each other, they agree on a well-known port number to rendezvous through. For example, the **sendmail** program, **/usr/lib/sendmail**, uses port 25 on every machine it runs on. When the **sendmail** on one machine contacts the **sendmail** on another machine, it uses the SMTP high-level protocol and connects to port 25 using the lower-level TCP protocol.

Any program wanting to reserve a port number should be in the /etc/services file. This allows the use of the **getservbyname** library routine instead of bypassing the /etc/services file and binding directly to the port. All of the servers to be managed by **inetd** must be in the /etc/services file. Each line in the file describes one program and its well-known port. The format of the file is:

- Official name of the service
- Port-number/protocol-name
- Aliases

Fields are separated by blanks or tabs; comments begin with the "#" symbol. An excerpt corresponding to the preceding /etc/inetd.conf example follows:

```
#       @(#)services    1.16 (Berkeley) 86/04/20
#
# Network services, Internet style
#
ftp       21/tcp
telnet    23/tcp
smtp      25/tcp      mail
time      37/tcp      timserver
time      37/udp      timserver
 ...
#
# local stuff goes below
```

```
uniquid   700/tcp    uniquidd      # Unique UID daemon (forys)
cardd     4201/tcp                 # Card access daemon (coggs)
#
# X windows
X0        5800/tcp                 # Needs well-known socket but
X1        5801/tcp                 #   no daemon for inetd to manage
 ...
```

It is a good idea to use the comments field to identify local daemons with both a descriptive phrase and the name of the user for whom they are installed.

14.5.12.3 The /etc/protocols file

If a user writes his own protocol using the raw socket interface provided for such purposes, it will have to be listed in the /etc/protocols file in order for **inetd** to manage daemons using it. Each line of the file describes a protocol used on the network:

- Official protocol name
- Protocol number
- Aliases

Fields are separated by blanks or tabs; the # symbol indicates the beginning of a comment. The following excerpt illustrates its format:

```
#
# Internet (IP) protocols
#
ip      0      IP      # internet protocol, pseudo protocol number
icmp    1      ICMP    # internet control message protocol
tcp     6      TCP     # transmission control protocol
egp     8      EGP     # exterior gateway protocol
udp     17     UDP     # user datagram protocol
```

14.5.13 Network commands

This section will introduce you to the user-level commands, as well as those handy for a systems administrator, that use the network. If you are an old hand, skip this section.

14.5.13.1 telnet(1) and rlogin(1)

telnet is a user interface to the ARPANET remote login TELNET protocol; **rlogin** is the BSD remote login command. Each allows you to login across the network to another machine. **rlogin** expects to find another UNIX machine at the other end. **telnet** is less picky; it just expects something that also talks the TELNET protocol.

14.5.13.2 ftp(1) and rcp(1)

ftp is the user interface to the ARPANET File Transfer Protocol; **rcp** is the BSD remote copy program. Each is used to copy files between machines on the network. **ftp** allows you to log in on the remote host; **rcp** requires that the two hosts be equivalent, either through /etc/hosts.equiv or ~/.rhosts.

14.5.13.3 rtar(l), rmt(l), and rdd(l)

rtar, **rmt**, and **rdd** are remote versions of **tar**(1), **mt**(1), and **dd**(1), respectively. They allow the use of remote tape drives by any host on the network. The argument specifying the tape drive is written in the form host:device, which causes the command to be passed to **/etc/rmt**(8), the remote mag tape protocol module for execution on the remote machine. These three programs were not distributed with 4.2BSD or 4.3BSD, but were posted to the net (Usenet, see Chapter 17: *News*). They are so widely used that they are sure to be on future Berkeley releases. They were written by Donn Seeley while he was at UC, San Diego.

14.5.13.4 rdump(8) and rrestore(8)

rdump and **rrestore** are the remote cousins of **dump** and **restore**. They support filesystem backups to devices across the network (see Chapter 18: *Backups and Transportable Media*, for details). The tape device is specified with the **-f** flag as host:device.

14.5.13.5 rdist(1)

rdist is like **make**, but understands the network. A system administrator can use **rdist** quite effectively in the installation of bug fixes or new software on all machines on the network (see Section 14.7.5.2).

14.5.14 Loose ends

Several loose ends remain and are covered in detail in other chapters or in later sections of this chapter. Network printers are covered in Chapter 11, mail using the network in Chapter 15, and dumps via the network in Chapter 18. The administration of BIND, the name server and resolver is covered in Section 14.9.1. NFS, the Network File System, is covered in Section 14.8. **ftp** is covered in Section 14.9.2.

14.6 Designing the network

This section addresses the logical and physical design of the network; software design issues are covered in Section 14.4. Remember that we are targeting for medium sized network installations. The ideas presented will scale up to a few hundred hosts, but are overkill for three machines and inadequate for thousands. We are also assuming that you have an adequate budget and are starting from scratch, which is probably only partially true. You will have to adapt your inherited environment to the set of guidelines presented. A good reference for network design, independent of which vendor's hardware you use, is the DEC Networks and Communications Buyer's Guide. It is updated every six months; older versions are more useful as a general Ethernet reference, as the new ones are very product oriented.

14.6.1 Issues

The issues presented here are typical of those that must be folded into any network design.

14.6.1.1 Network architecture versus building architecture

The network architecture is usually more flexible than the building architecture, yet the two must co-exist. If you are lucky enough to be able to specify the network before the building is constructed, be lavish. For most of us, both the building and a facilities management department already exist and are somewhat rigid.

In existing buildings, the network must use the building architecture, not fight it. Modern buildings often contain utility raceways for data and telephone cable in addition to high-voltage electrical wiring and water/gas piping. They also often contain drop ceilings, a boon to network installers. Many campuses and organizations have underground utility tunnels that facilitate network installation as well. Use them. The integrity of fire walls must be maintained; if you route a cable through a fire wall the hole must be snug and filled in with a non-combustible substance. Respect air plenums in your choice of cable.

The logical design you choose must fit into the physical constraint of the buildings it services. Keep this in mind as you specify the network; it's too easy to draw a logically good solution and then find that it is physically difficult or impossible to implement.

14.6.1.2 Existing networks

Computer networks are the focus of this discussion, yet many organizations already have CATV networks and telephone networks capable of transmitting data. Often these include fiber links. If your organization is ready to install a new telephone system, buy lots of extra fiber and have it installed at the same time. We had that opportunity a couple of years ago and asked the contractors if they would string some fiber for us. They said sure, no charge, and were a bit miffed when we showed up with $35,000 worth of fiber for them to install.

14.6.1.3 Expansion

It is very difficult to predict needs ten years from now, especially in the computer/networking field. Therefore it is important to design the network with expansion and increased bandwidth in mind. As the cable is being installed, especially in out-of-the-way, hard-to-reach places, leave extra black marks so additional transceivers can be installed. Plan in advance to handle the growing terminal load and growing numbers of diskless workstations.

14.6.1.4 Congestion

A network is like a chain — only as good as its weakest or slowest link. Several things put a serious load on the network, and Ethernet does not perform well as it gets loaded. Because of the nature of the Ethernet algorithm, it is not possible to use the entire bandwidth of the network. Diskless nodes, terminal concentrators, low-speed links, and mismatched interfaces all lead to congestion. Creating subnets to localize traffic and using interconnection devices such as the learning bridges described earlier are helpful in controlling congestion. Subnets can also be used to isolate machines needed for dedicated experiments; it is very difficult to run an experiment that involves several machines if there is no easy way to isolate those machines both physically and logically from the rest of the network.

14.6.1.5 Maintenance

Ease of maintenance is an important design goal. Probably the single most crucial ingredient in an easy-to-maintain network is accurate, complete, up-to-date documentation. Such a documentation scheme is discussed in detail in Section 14.6.2. Joints between major population centers in the form of bridges, routers, or even connectors facilitate debugging by allowing parts of the network to be isolated and debugged separately. Use a consistent sex for connectors so that a barrel adapter that connects two cable sections can be easily replaced with a terminator to verify part of the segment. Place the transceivers where they are easy to reach, yet not likely to be disturbed or vandalized. Know where they are. Avoid sharp bends in the cable and avoid running it too near high-voltage cables and other sources of electrical noise.

14.6.2 Documentation

Maps of the cable's route, location of walls, transceivers, connectors, and terminators are essential to maintain the network. Problems with the cable itself are diagnosed with a device called a time domain reflectometer (TDR) which indicates disturbances in the signal in units of distance from the end of the cable. If the TDR says there is a problem 483 feet from the end of the cable, you must be able to find that spot.

Our recommended procedures, although tedious, facilitate cable maintenance. First, identify different Ethernets with colors, segments of a single Ethernet with letters, and within that scheme, number *each* black mark. Permanent magic marker works fairly well, but tends to smear or wipe off if the cable is handled too much. There are also cable markers which resemble adhesive tape with preprinted numbers that can be used. It is best to place the numbers a few inches away from the black mark, so that if a transceiver is attached at the black mark the number is still visible. Colored tape can be used to identify the Ethernet, especially in places where several cables are placed in the same bundle.

Cable maps should not only identify the Ethernet and the segment, but should include the endpoints, location of transceivers, manufacturer, model, and version of the transceiver, length, color, and version of the drop cable, and the location of physical landmarks like walls, partitions, etc. Figure 14.17 illustrates a typical cable map; the room numbers within the engineering building are indicated in parentheses.

FIGURE 14.17

Red cable - Engineering backbone, segment A	
Black mark	Description
A0	Terminator, beneath machine room (EE-0071) floor, SE corner under "boulder" machine.
A2	"boulder" transceiver, Interlan NT10, Version 1, no AMP tap, 15 ft flat blue drop cable.
...	
A5	Cable punctured, bad transceiver installation, repaired (??) with electrical tape.
A11	Thru the wall of the machine room to the storage area (EE-0072), middle of west wall.
...	
A23	Into CER lab (EE1-54).
A25	"anchor" net TCL discrete to TCL multiport in CER machine room (EE1-55).
A26	"piper-gateway" Cabletron discrete in CER machine room (EE1-55).
A32-B0	Barrel connector to segment B in hallway outside CER lab (EE1-54).

In addition to the detailed cable map in Figure 14.17, it is useful to have an actual physical map and a logical map. For the physical map, a reduced size blueprint of the building with the various cables indicated in color coded felt tip marker suffices quite nicely. The logical map should show gateway/router machines, repeaters, bridges, and other devices, but not necessarily general hosts. For example, that same engineering backbone network is logically depicted in Figure 14.18.

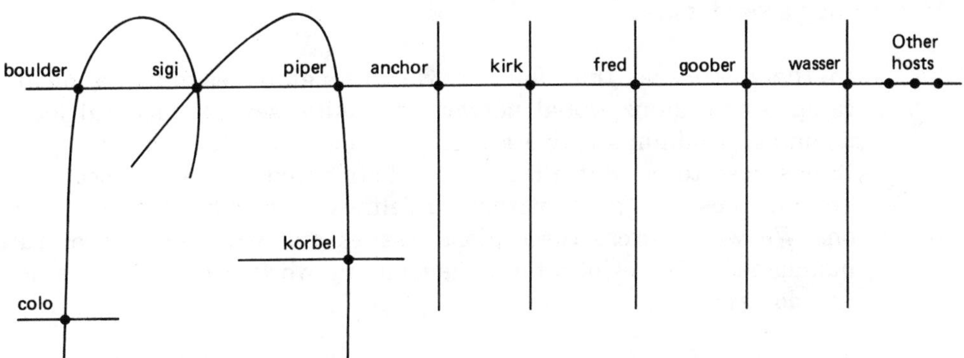

FIGURE 14.18 Logical map of the engineering backbone cable

A more correct representation of the intersection of two networks, for example the engineering backbone-campus backbone connection is:

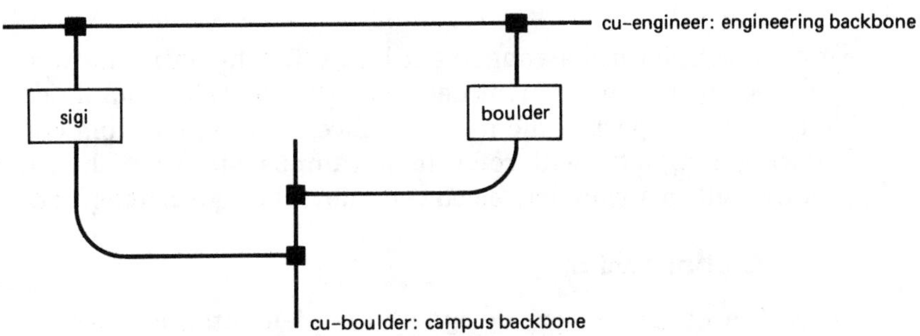

FIGURE 14.19 Detailed diagram of network connections

Documentation must be done while the cable is being installed; it is too late when you are all finished. If the cable is above a drop ceiling, it is also useful to mark its route by placing small colored paper stickers (we use three-quarter-inch diameter circles) on the aluminum ceiling framing where the cable enters and exits a room. These markers are essentially invisible to all but cable maintainers who walk around looking up. We color code the stickers to the color that identifies the particular Ethernet and write the segment label on them. Both stickers and colored tape are available at office supply places. For example, as the cable mapped in the previous figure enters the room EE 1-54, a small red sticker marked A23 is attached to the under side of the ceiling near its entry and one marked A30 near its exit.

14.7 Management issues

In the discussion that follows, we are again assuming a medium sized campus or organizational network spanning several physical locations and domains of administrative control. If the network is to interoperate, some things need to be centralized, some distributed, and some local. Reasonable ground rules and "good citizen" guidelines need to be formulated and agreed on. We will address these global issues and will then concentrate on the management issues of a heterogeneous network within a single administrative domain.

The typical environment we assume includes:

- A backbone network between buildings
- Departmental subnets connected to the backbone
- Group subnets within a department
- Connections to the outside world: the Internet, BITNET/CSNET, and uucp

First we will discuss management issues for the entire network, and then the more technical management decisions that a system administrator, responsible for only his part of the network, faces in the preceding environment. The following language will refer to a campus situation, but the ideas apply equally well to a similarly sized commercial or government organization.

14.7.1 Global control

Several facets of network design and implementation must have campuswide control, responsibility, maintenance, and financing. Networks with chargeback algorithms for each connection grow in very bizarre and predictable ways as departments try to minimize their own local costs. Prime targets for central control are:

- The network design, including the use of subnets, routers, bridges, etc.
- The backbone cable itself, including connections to it
- Host IP addresses, hostnames, subdomain names
- Protocols, mostly to insure that they interoperate
- Routing policy to the Internet

Domain names, IP network addresses, and network names are already controlled centrally by SRI-NIC. Central control and support of each of these target areas is justified next.

14.7.1.1 Network design

A central authority has an overall view of the network, its design, capacity, and expected growth. It can afford to own monitoring equipment (and staff to run it) to keep the backbone network healthy. It can insist on correct network design, even when that means telling one department to buy a router and build a subnet to connect to the campus backbone cable. Such a decision might be necessary so that a new connection would not adversely impact existing machines on the network.

Included in network design is:

- The topology and routing of the cable
- Type of cable
- Type of transceivers
- Use of repeaters, bridges, and routers

The overall size of the network may preclude using thinnet or twisted pair segments on the backbone. Maintainability, uptime, and religion may preclude the use of intrusive transceivers. The network must remain usable by all.

Another key issue of network design is congestion control. Distributed file systems tax the network quite heavily, and so file serving on a backbone cable is undesirable. Diskless workstations tend to multiply like rabbits and promises of "only a server and one client" may be genuine this year but will have grown to six to eight clients by next year. Terminal servers also put heavy loads on the network cable. When connecting two segments of Ethernet cable, bridges and routers help with congestion control better than repeaters or barrel adapters that pass every packet. They are correspondingly more expensive.

If a network runs heterogeneous machines, operating systems, and protocols, it is almost essential to have either a very smart router (e.g., Cisco) or a 4.3BSD machine with source code on the network in a gateway/router role to fix the little incompatibilities between protocols, to handle machines that do not understand ARP, and to clean up things before they go onto the Internet. Such as:

- Proxy ARP
- DEC tty server LAT broadcast storms
- 4.2BSD - 4.3BSD incompatibilities
- Broadcast munging

14.7.1.2 The backbone cable

The central authority must have control of the physical cable. It must know where and what the taps on the cable are and in many cases may want to either install all the taps itself or perhaps delegate that responsibility in a dictatorial fashion; i.e., yes to one department, no to another. A shorted transceiver installation could take down the entire network. A clandestine tap (for example, by a PC in a student's dorm room that happens to be next to the utility closet containing the campus cable) threatens the security and privacy of all machines on the network.

14.7.1.3 Host IP addresses, hostnames, and subdomain names

The host portion of the IP address is assigned by the institution, but must be unique across that institution. Unless the entire campus is subnetted, with each administrative domain receiving a subnet and handling routing to that subnet, this host number assignment must be centrally administered. Likewise, hostnames and subdomain names must also be unique. At Colorado, individual machine owners suggest names to the Computing Center, which approves them if they are unique and assigns them an IP address or a subnet number. Administration within a subnet is local, but since routing needs to work properly from a global point of view, local decisions must be communicated to all concerned. The management of host tables and network tables is a good candidate for distributed control, with different administrators having authority over different sections of the host tables. (The scheme illustrated in Appendix O works well in this instance.)

14.7.1.4 Protocols

Protocols on the Ethernet must interoperate. If one user wants to add a machine whose software is incompatible with other machines on the network, a central authority must arbitrate. Most protocols just break the Internet rules a little bit, and so a machine running BSD (with source code) can fix most of these things. For example, machines that do not speak ARP can be handled with another machine running proxy ARP and answering for them. Subnetting can be handled by using static routes, and some of the protocol issues between DECNET, TCP/IP, and Chaosnet can also be handled with source code.

14.7.1.5 Routing

An overall routing scheme for the site needs to be chosen and implemented on the key gateway machines. The connection to the Internet will become so important to an institution that it should be under the central authority's control and financing. Electronic mail must flow, and to stay off the net for weeks when the department with the Internet connection takes their machine down is unthinkable. Local routing is important too, since passing broadcast packets around a network can put quite a load on all machines. Some mixes of hardware and software lead to broadcast storms on the cable that will bring the net to its knees. These need to be analyzed quickly, diagnosed with the expensive hardware the central authority can afford, and the problem solved or worked around.

14.7.2 Maintenance and financing

If an institutional network is to function properly, items like the backbone cable, key routers or gateways, and leased lines must be centrally maintained and centrally financed. Chargeback schemes cause cancerous growth patterns. For example, if the cost to attach a PC to the network is $100/year, but to attach a Vax is $1000/year, you will find many Vaxen and other larger machines hiding behind the PC to optimize overall cost to a department.

14.7.3 Software licensing

As PC's and workstations invaded the computing environment, software licensing became a problem. Pirated software abounds. Vendors were slow to address the problems of site licenses and to accommodate the idea of a license not being tied directly to a particular CPU. For example, in a student lab containing 50 machines, the University might hold 30 licenses to the Pascal compiler and 30 licenses to the FORTRAN compiler. A student needing Pascal checks out the software as he would a library book and sits at any free machine to use it. This requires the software vendor to trust the institution to really buy as many copies as they typically use. Diskless workstations also present licensing questions. If a server and ten clients all use one copy of the software, is that one license or eleven? Some vendors have addressed this problem by selling server licenses and some have not, still requiring individual CPU licenses.

Centralizing the purchase of popular software packages has advantages. Better prices can often be obtained, and the central computing center can handle the details of licensing and distribution.

14.7.4 Network security

Security has often been accused of being inversely proportional to convenience, and alas it's true. Networking presents many more opportunities for security violations than a single machine in a locked machine room with hard-wired terminals in terminal rooms. A PC connected to the Ethernet and running the public domain software Netwatch from MIT can see and monitor the content of every packet. Workstations can be easily rebooted in single-user mode, the root password modified or deleted, and rebooted again in multi-user mode. Without physical security of the network cable the network is vulnerable, yet physical security in most organizations is impractical. A

TDR (time domain reflectometer, see Section 14.10.1) can be used to discover and locate clandestine taps on the cable, and a protocol analyzer can look for addresses that are not in its database of valid hosts. Some bridges can also report unknown addresses. Software can control root access across the network. Administratively, cooperation is necessary to track an intruder once a security violation has been discovered. Most security violations cross administrative boundaries; i.e., one of my users breaks into your system or vice versa.

While building a totally secure installation also makes it very inconvenient to use, there are some things that can be done to track an intrusion once it is noticed, especially if the intruder is a novice (as is often the case.) The root shell, if it is **csh**, can have a long history stack kept and can survive login sessions. It is often possible to trace back the history stack and see exactly what the user "root" was doing. Accounting files also provide information about logins, ports, where across the network the login originated, etc.

14.7.5 Local technical issues

We now turn to management issues within one administrative domain. The scale is say 20 to 50 or 100 machines. Usually the number of machines grows faster than the number of system administrators, as it should. But to keep up, system administrators must build tools to make the administration of *n* copies of the same machine substantially less work than *n* times the work for one copy of that machine.

14.7.5.1 Global versus local copies

In this section we discuss some of the growing pains of an expanding network, more from a technical side of system administration than from the management side. A network makes sharing easier, but as the network grows, it becomes impractical to make a change somewhere and then propagate that change by hand to 100 other machines throughout the network. If several machines are under one administrative unit the following items are good candidates for one global copy rather than *n* local copies:

- The source code, maintain one "source" machine for each CPU type
- The network files, /etc/hosts and /etc/networks
- The /etc/passwd file with unique UID's, GID's, and login names
- The group file, /etc/group
- The mail aliases file, /usr/lib/aliases
- Part of the message of the day file, /etc/motd
- The user database, /usr/local/adm/users
- The news database, /usr/spool/news

- The manuals, /usr/man
- Help libraries; for example, /usr/local/doc/naghelp

Some of these are dynamic and therefore easier to keep current if there are only a few machines where changes must be made and those changes are then propagated to the rest of the machines. Others are static but very large, and thus multiple copies, while not difficult to maintain, use disk resources.

14.7.5.2 Tools

Tools are needed to maintain these files in a consistent and up-to-date state. We will describe several, some from the standard BSD releases, some that have been posted to the net, and some that were developed locally. Sources are listed for each.

The rdist(1) command

The following piece of code is regularly executed at sites across the country.

```
while (1)
{
    rlogin host;
    fix bug;
    forget to fix it everywhere;
}
```

FIGURE 14.20 Difference between a bug and a feature

rdist, a remote file distribution program, can be used to automate this loop. **rdist** maintains identical copies of files across multiple hosts on a network. Not all hosts need to be of the same type; for example, the files could be source code which gets distributed and then compiled on each target host. **rdist** uses a data file called Distfile that is similar to a Makefile for the **make** program, but that understands the basics of the network. The following example distributes software from the Vax boulder to sigi, tigger, and anchor (Vax, MIPS, and Sun, respectively).

```
#
#  Distfile for remote program
#
MACHINES = (boulder sigi tigger anchor)

FILES = (Makefile remote.c)

${FILES} -> ${MACHINES}
        install;
        special remote.c "make";
        notify evi@rupertsberg;
```

The output as this program is run on the host boulder follows; it has been truncated slightly:

```
% rdist
updating host boulder
installing: Makefile
installing: remote.c
special "make"
cc -c remote.c
cc -o remote remote.o
notify @boulder ( evi@rupertsberg )
 ...
updating host anchor
installing: Makefile
installing: remote.c
special "make"
cc -c remote.c
cc -o remote remote.o
notify @anchor ( evi@rupertsberg )
```

The updatehosts(l) command

The /etc/hosts and /etc/networks files must be global for the institution, yet often span administrative domains. Parts of the files fall under different system administrators authority and distributed control is needed. The **updatehosts** system, written by Bob Coggeshall at the University of Colorado, allows distributed control of a hosts or networks file through specially formated comments embedded in it. The source code for the **updatehosts** command is listed in Appendix O. An excerpt from a hosts file maintained by **updatehosts** follows:

```
##
# CU/Boulder TCP/IP hosts
# Mail changes to 'updatehosts@boulder.colorado.edu'
```

```
# LastRevised: Thu Jul 14 20:05:27 MDT 1988
##
##
# Begin: Host-dependent
#
127.0.0.1       localhost loghost
#
# End: Host-dependent
##
##
# Begin: UNIXOps
# AdminMail: netadmin@boulder.colorado.edu
#
128.138.240.1   boulder boulder.colorado.edu    # Vax780, ecee0071A
128.138.243.14  encore encore.colorado.edu      # Encore, ecee0071A
128.138.240.20  tut tut.colorado.edu            # Pyr90x, ecee0071A
128.138.240.26  tigger tigger.colorado.edu      # Mips M1000, ecee0071A
#
# End: UNIXOps
##
##
# Begin: cs-suns
# AdminMail: brentb@boulder.colorado.edu
# NextNumbers: 12, 13, 14
# LastRevised: Sun Sep 25 14:49:56 MDT 1988
#
#       CER Lab Sub-Net         (ec-cer)
#
# GATEWAY:      anchor-gateway
#
128.138.240.119 anchor-gateway anchor-gateway.colorado.edu
128.138.242.1   anchor anchor.colorado.edu      # 4/260, ecee1-54
#
# anchor clients
#
128.138.242.4   heineken heineken.colorado.edu  # 3/60, ecee1-56
128.138.242.7   guiness guiness.colorado.edu    # 3/60, ecee1-56
128.138.242.8   molson molson.colorado.edu      # 3/60, ecee1-56
128.138.242.9   pilsner pilsner.colorado.edu    # 3/60, ecee1-56
#
# CS GatorBox Gateway and subnet
#
128.138.243.30  csgator-gw csgator-gw.colorado.edu
128.138.237.1   csgator csgator.colorado.edu
128.138.237.2   fatmac fatmac.colorado.edu      #  MACII, ecee0-69
#
##
# End: cs-suns
```

Keywords are used to delineate sections and identify the primary person responsible for a given part of the hosts file. To change a section of the hosts file, a system administrator at Colorado mails a copy of the correct entries for his portion of the host file to updatehosts@boulder, which passes it to the **updatehosts** program listed in Appendix O. The following line in the /usr/lib/aliases file routes the mail to the updatehosts program:

```
updatehosts: "|/usr/local/adm/hosts/updatehosts"
```

The /etc/networks file also can be administered using updatehosts.

The mkrevhosts(l) script

mkrevhosts is a script to produce the name server startup files, /etc/named.{hosts,rev}, which require the IP address in reverse address order, from the /etc/hosts file. By using **mkrevhosts**, the name server files will always be current, yet the system administrator can use the hosts file format (which is easier and more intuitive) for administration. A copy of **mkrevhosts** is in Appendix P.

The adduser(l) program

An **adduser** program that maintains unique UID's, GID's, and login names is required for an NFS distributed filesystem environment and is highly recommended for simplicity and security in any single administrative domain. The **adduser** program in Appendix B is not suitable for a networked environment, but one that is suitable was written by Jeff Forys at Colorado. While that program is too long to list in an appendix, it is available via anonymous **ftp** from boulder.colorado.edu.

The remote(l) utility

remote is a program to allow any machine to act as a terminal server for the network. A listing of a preliminary version of **remote** is included in Appendix N.

The vialiases(l) script

vialiases is a script used to edit the /usr/lib/aliases file, run the **dbm** routines on it, and distribute the resulting .pag and .dir files. This script is too site dependent to be of general interest. If you are a system administrator of a large networked installation with a global aliases file you should create such a script since the maintenance of the aliases file is expensive and tedious. Our version of **vialiases** collects changes during the daytime through an interface to mail and a special user "aliases" and then rebuilds the file and distributes it in the wee hours.

The vimotd(l) command

The message of the day file, /etc/motd, needs at least three parts: global (for messages that pertain to all machines in an administrative domain), semilocal (for messages that are for a subgroup of that domain, perhaps a particular network), and local (for messages that apply only to a particular machine). For example, a planned power outage in the entire building impacts everyone, a gateway machine going down for dumps impacts machines downstream from it, and an individual machine going down to install a new board impacts only its users.

There are several possible solutions for this problem. The **login** program could be modified to display not only the /etc/motd file but also additional files for semilocal and global information. Unfortunately, this solution requires UNIX source code.

Our solution uses Sun's netgroup idea, which is a natural for this kind of thing. We identify each line of the single /etc/motd file on each machine with a special character keyed to the line's globalness. For example, the /etc/motd file on tigger contains:

```
] Hardware problems    -  mail wiring
] Software problems    -  mail trouble
] Dump scheduling      -  mail operations

> boulder down noon-midnight, Saturday, Sept 25, for level 0 dumps.

< tigger has a new disk drive, fill 'er up !!
```

Items with the "]" at the left margin are global and on every machine in our administrative group. Items with ">" are local to the netgroups that this machine belongs to, in this case, machines dependent on boulder for connection to the rest of the campus network. Items with "<" at the left margin are totally local to this machine. Scripts manipulate each section.

14.7.5.3 Communication and documentation

In a university, the system administration staff often includes students who work odd hours and have poor documentation skills. It is difficult with lots of administrators and lots of machines to remember exactly what you have done to each machine. We keep a diary file on each machine to record changes, fixes, problems, and the like. It is quite useful for training new system administrators or for remembering just how you fixed it six months ago at 3:00 a.m. the last time the network was wedged.

In addition, a paper logbook is next to each machine and is used to record hardware configuration, disk partitions, maintenance information, and hardware problems. An accurate maintenance log can help you understand your maintenance needs and costs and is especially important if you are considering doing self-maintenance.

14.8 NFS - the Network File System

NFS was introduced by Sun Microsystems in 1985. It is an unfortunate mnemonic for university folk who also have to keep their tongue around NSF, the National Science Foundation. It seems difficult to have both of these acronyms correctly stored in one's working vocabulary. The specification for NFS is in the public domain; it has become a de facto standard and has been implemented by most UNIX vendors that support BSD networking.

NFS provides a distributed file system. The file system is almost transparent to users, is stateless, and uses a generalization of the inode called the vnode or virtual inode. Stateless means that there is no client state information lost if the server crashes. The client can just wait until the server comes back up and then can continue as if nothing had happened. NFS includes remote mount semantics; RPC, a remote procedure call interface; XDR, an external data representation scheme; and YP, the Yellow Pages, a distributed database for managing system administration files. Each of these topics and how they affect the system administrator will be described in more detail in the sections that follow.

The RFS system available under ATT System V.3 and later releases provides similar functionality.

14.8.1 The mount command

The mount command has been modified under NFS to understand the extended path notation

hostname:directory

as meaning the pathname *directory* interpreted according to the host *hostname*. Note that any remote directory may be mounted via NFS; the local host need not be concerned with the details of where one disk partition ends and another begins on the remote system. For example, from the machine tigger the command

/etc/mount boulder:/boulder/users /boulder/users

would make the /boulder/users directory tree from a disk on the machine boulder appear as the local directory tree /boulder/users on tigger. When executed on tigger, the **df** command shows both local and remotely mounted filesystems:

```
Filesystem              kbytes    used    avail capacity  Mounted on
/dev/ip0a                20783   11170     7534    60%    /
/dev/ip0g                62063   53017     2839    95%    /usr
boulder:/boulder/users
                        354207   28136   290650     9%    /boulder/users
```

Prefacing the directory names with the remote hostname is a convention used to avoid naming conflicts and note where the files really live. There are several options to **mount** that should be considered when remotely mounting a filesystem. The manual page for mount describes them in detail. Important options include:

- soft–return an error if the server doesn't answer
- hard–keep trying (maybe forever)
- bg–background, don't wait for the server to come up
- rw–read-write filesystem
- ro–read-only filesystem

To automatically mount that same remote filesystem on tigger at boot time, changes must be made to /etc/fstab on tigger and to /etc/exports on boulder. On tigger, set up /etc/fstab to include an entry for the remote partition:

```
boulder:/boulder/users  /boulder/users  nfs  rw,soft,bg  0  0
```

On boulder, set up /etc/exports to include the line:

```
/boulder/users  tigger
```

Be sure the following daemons are running:

- **portmap**–the RPC port lookup daemon
- **mountd**–the remote mount daemon
- **nfsd**–the NFS daemon
- **biod**–the block i/o daemon

mountd and **nfsd** need to be running on only the server machine, in this case boulder; **portmap** and **biod** must be running on both the server and the client. **mountd** is usually managed by **inetd** (see Section 14.5.12). **portmap**, **nfsd**, and **biod** are started in the /etc/rc.local file at boot time. Multiple copies, usually four to eight, of **nfsd** and **biod** are started to handle the file serving load.

Excerpts from /etc/rc.local illustrate typical entries; notice that **nfsd** is only started if /etc/exports exists (machine is server):

```
(echo -n 'starting rpc and net services:')        >/dev/console
if [ -f /etc/portmap ]; then
        /etc/portmap; (echo -n ' portmap')         >/dev/console
fi
#
```

```
if [ -f /etc/biod ]; then
        /etc/biod 4; (echo -n ' biod')          >/dev/console
fi
#
# if nfs daemon exists and /etc/exports file exists become nfs server
#
if [ -f /etc/nfsd -a -f /etc/exports ]; then
        /etc/nfsd 4 & (echo -n ' nfsd')         >/dev/console
fi
```

The "if" around each invocation allows the same /etc/rc.local file to be used on both servers and clients.

14.8.2 RPC, the remote procedure call interface

RPC, the remote procedure call interface, is the workhorse of the NFS system. It is implemented through a library of procedures and a daemon process on the remote host which acts as an agent to execute the procedure call on behalf of the calling process. The programmer's interface is at a higher level than the Berkeley socket abstraction and the networking system calls provided by the kernel.

14.8.3 XDR, external data representation

XDR, the external data representation component of NFS, supports data exchange between heterogeneous machines with perhaps different byte order, word length, alignment, and floating point representation. It also supports the exchange of structured data between heterogeneous compilers where the representation of bit fields and padding of structs or records may be different. XDR routines allow programmers to write network applications between heterogeneous systems more easily.

14.8.4 YP, the Yellow Pages

The Yellow Pages is a distributed database for managing certain system data files. Under YP, a single copy of a file is maintained for the whole network rather than keeping individual copies on each host. From a system administrator's point of view, this is a real boon. One copy is much easier to maintain than many. The database can be replicated on several server machines for safety. YP servers cannot serve machines that are not on the same Ethernet; that is, YP does not work through routers or gateways. It does work through bridges. This is because broadcast packets are not passed by routers and gateways, and if the YP system gets stuck, clients broadcast for help from any server who is listening.

Yellow Pages *domains* are used to group client machines; each domain can be served by a master YP server and zero or more (optional) YP slave servers.

YP domains map nicely to administrative domains. The basic data object in the YP database is called a *map* and corresponds loosely to a UNIX file. The maps are managed by the **ndbm** extendible hashing routines to improve the efficiency of lookups. Maintenance of YP files is relatively easy: Change the file on the master server, propagate it to slave servers, and you're done.

YP also supports groups of machines called netgroups. Netgroups, which are defined in the file /etc/netgroup, are independent of domains and are used primarily for naming.

14.8.4.1 YP files

YP manages three classes of files:

- Local files–local machines' copy overrides YP copy
- Global files–YP copy overrides local copy
- Optional files–YP copy used if local copy contains net-group notation

Local files

The passwd file /etc/passwd and the group file /etc/group are considered by YP to be local. They are consulted first in lookups, and then, if the files contain the "go check the Yellow Pages magic token", the character "+", the YP database is also consulted.

Global files

The system totally ignores local copies of the global files and goes directly to the YP server for their contents, with the exception of the file /etc/hosts, which is consulted at boot time. A diskless client needs to boot across the network and consults /etc/hosts to see which host to try to boot from. The global files are: /etc/hosts, /etc/networks, /etc/protocols, /etc/services, and /etc/netgroup.

Optional files

Optional files are managed by YP if they contain entries of the form ± netgroup-name. The optional files are: /etc/hosts.equiv and /.rhosts. A gaping security hole exists if the file /etc/hosts.equiv contains the YP magic cookie "+" — all hosts on your local Ethernet and the Internet are equivalenced. Until recently Sun workstations were shipped with the /etc/host.equiv file set up this way.

14.8.4.2 YP programs

Several programs are used to manipulate the YP database files. Most are in the /etc or /usr/etc directory. These are listed in Figure 14.21 with a brief description of their function; the number in parentheses after the command name is the section of the UNIX manual containing documentation on the command.

FIGURE 14.21

YP programs	
Command name	Description
ypserv(8)	YP server daemon started in /etc/rc
ypbind(8)	Remembers binding, which server, where, etc.
ypinit(8)	Builds the database from files
ypmake(8)	Rebuilds YP database, after a change, for example
makedbm(8)	Build a YP database file directly
ypxfr(8)	Transfer a YP file or map to another domain
yppush(8)	Forces an update on a YP map
ypset(8)	Tells **ypbind** to use a particular server
yppoll(8)	Asks for info about a particular map and its server
ypcat(1)	Print values in a YP database
ypmatch(8)	Prints database values for a particular key
ypwhich(8)	Tells your YP server's hostname
yppasswd(1)	Change your YP passwd (**rpc.yppasswdd** must be running)
ypupdated(8)	Updates data in YP maps (managed by **inetd**)
ypclnt(3)	C library interface to YP database

14.8.4.3 YP setup

Setting up the Yellow Pages involves several steps, each of which is detailed next.

Determine the YP domain design

It is convenient to have all the machines in an administrative domain also in the same YP domain. Domains can be wider than just a server and its clients and can span an entire Ethernet.

The names of the YP domains and machines in each domain must be decided. Also the master and slave servers must be chosen. Domain names are set with the **/bin/domainname** command, usually in the file /etc/rc.local.

Set up YP files, server and client versions

In general, files distributed via Yellow Pages need only exist on the Yellow Pages server. However, this is not true for the files /etc/passwd, /etc/group, and /etc/hosts, of which each client must have a minimal private version. /etc/passwd and /etc/group are necessary to allow root to log in should no YP server be available. The /etc/hosts file must be present to allow the client to locate the Yellow Pages server itself.

The server's versions of YP-managed files are identical to the complete files which exist independently of the Yellow Pages (with the exception of the /etc/netgroup file, which exists only under the Yellow Pages). Selected sample YP files are shown next.

Client version, /etc/hosts:

```
#
# If the Yellow Pages is running, this file is only consulted when booting
#
# These lines added by the Sun Setup Program from server anchor
#
128.138.242.1    anchor anchor.colorado.edu loghost
128.138.242.2    becks becks.colorado.edu
128.138.242.3    xx xx.colorado.edu
 ...
128.138.242.5    bass bass.colorado.edu
128.138.242.6    watneys watneys.colorado.edu
127.0.0.1        localhost
#
# End of lines added by the Sun Setup Program
#
```

Client version, /etc/passwd:

```
+root::0:1:Operator:/:/bin/csh
nobody:*:-2:-2::/:
daemon:*:1:1::/:
sys:*:2:2::/:/bin/csh
bin:*:3:3::/bin:
uucp:*:4:4::/usr/spool/uucppublic:
news:*:6:6::/usr/spool/news:/bin/csh
ingres:*:7:7::/usr/ingres:/bin/csh
sync::1:1::/:/bin/sync
+sysdiag::0:1:System Diagnostic:/usr/diag/sysdiag:/usr/diag/sysdiag/sysdiag
+::0:0:::
```

The "+" is the YP magic token that signals programs needing information from a file to go to the YP server for further information. Although it appears from this example that the root login has no password, the entry is in fact "+root," which forces the passwd lookup to happen on the YP server, not on the client. The "+" at the end of the /etc/passwd file routes all lookups for logins not found in the local passwd file to the server. However, on machines not running YP, that same line would allow a root login with no password and with login name "+"!

Client version, /etc/group:

```
wheel:*:0:
daemon:*:1:
kmem:*:2:
bin:*:3:
news:*:6:
+:
```

The client defers all group lookups to the server, except those of system logins.

Server version, /etc/netgroup:

```
vaxen           (boulder,,) (sigi,,)
pyramids        (beagle,,) (euclid,,) (icarus,,) (jove,,) (tut,,)
symbolics       (monet,,) (cassatt,,) (matisse,,) (renoir,,) (degas,,)
multis          (cubie,,) (encore,,)
bobcats         (snake,,) (headrest,,)
servers         (anchor,,) (moet,,) (piper,,) (kirk,,) (titan,,) (sol,,)
anchorclients   (bass,,) (becks,,) (guiness,,) (heineken,,) (molson,,) \
                (pilsner,,) (watneys,,) (xx,,)
beers           (anchor,,) (anchor-gateway,,) anchorclients
cstrusts        vaxen beers
allhosts        pyramids vaxen multis beers bobcats
```

The /etc/netgroup file only exists on the server and is used by YP to verify permissions for remote mounts (in /etc/exports), remote logins, and remote shells. The form of an entry is: *groupname list-of-members.* A member is either another groupname or a triplet (hostname, username, domainname). An empty field is a wild card, thus the entry (boulder,,) refers to all users in all domains on the host boulder. A "-" in a field is negation, so the entry (boulder,-,) refers to just the machine boulder and no users. Notice that groupnames can be nested multiple levels.

Network groups are a nice idea. A system administrator often needs to do something for a group of machines, such as post a message on the message-of-the-day file, or notify all users of an event.

Initialize the Yellow Pages

The YP system must be initialized on the master server, on the slave servers, and on the clients. This is typically done in two steps: **ypinit** must be run on all servers once to define the master and slave roles. The Yellow Pages are started with the **ypserv** command for servers and the **ypbind** command for clients. Servers also run **ypbind**, usually bound to themselves. This is typically done at boot time in the file /etc/rc.local. Both direct command sequences and rc.local entries are shown next.

On the master server:

```
cd /usr/etc                    /* /etc/yp on some systems */
ypinit -m                      /* initialize as master server */
ypserv
```

On the slave servers:

> **cd /usr/etc**
> **ypinit -s** *master-hostname* /* initialize as slave to master */
> **ypserv**

On the clients, after updating the YP files:

> **cd /usr/etc**
> **ypbind**

From /etc/rc.local on either a server or client:

```
#
/bin/domainname cssuns
#
if [ -f /usr/etc/ypserv -a -d /usr/etc/yp/`domainname` ]; then
        /usr/etc/ypserv; (echo -n ' ypserv')          >/dev/console
#       /usr/etc/ypserv -i; (echo -n ' ypserv')       >/dev/console
fi
#
if [ -f /etc/ypbind ]; then
        /etc/ypbind; (echo -n ' ypbind')              >/dev/console
fi
```

Changing YP domains

If you find you need to make a change to a YP domain, for example to add a new server or client or to change the master server, the changes can be made while the NFS system is running. Here is an outline of what to do in each situation.

Adding a server:

- Add the server to the servers map and propagate it
  Use **makedbm** to dump servers map
  Edit it to add the new server
  Use **makedbm** to build new servers map
  Use **yppush** to force folks to use the new map
- Initialize the new server, as already indicated.

Changing the master server:

- Build the servers map on the new master server, as detailed
- Propagate it with **ypxfr**

Adding a new client:

- Set the domain with **domainname**
- Run **ypbind** to hitch up with a server

Updating YP files:

- Make any changes on the YP master server
- Run **make** in the /etc/yp (/var/yp) directory to propagate the changes

Administrative hints

Running NFS forces some system administrative decisions and suggests others. Any user who wants to access a file on the distributed file system must have a login on the machine where the file actually lives. He does not necessarily have to have a real shell associated with that login, but the login must be in the password file. Furthermore, both UID's and GID's must be unique across all machines that participate in the distributed file system, and should be unique across all machines.

Having a standard naming and partitioning scheme makes it easier to manage NFS partitions. Names that include the server are a good scheme. Standard partitions also give some added flexibility when you must recover from disaster by reassigning disks. Raw copies of partitions only work if the partition sizes are comparable; dumps and total restores cannot always be used if partition sizes change.

If you are running NFS with diskless clients, try to balance the number of clients between the various servers and the disks attached to them. Use at least two YP servers (if you have a least two file servers!), because the whole system grinds to a halt if you lose the Yellow Pages. Add each user to all servers, even if they are in different YP domains. Use a fake shell if the user is not authorized to use all of the machines.

NFS has some security problems, so consider mounting partitions with the "nosuid" option enabled and enabling privileged port checking in both **rpc.mountd** and the kernel by setting the variable _nfs_portmon to 1 with **adb**. Don't equivalence machines. If your environment is very insecure (for example, a student environment), get the Kerberos system from MIT that runs on top of NFS and implements a security/privacy system. It seems quite robust, having withstood all those clever engineering students for a year or two.

14.9 Optional software

This section describes the BIND nameserver and anonymous **ftp**. We concentrate on installation and maintenance.

14.9.1 BIND: the Berkeley Internet Name Domain server

The domain system and BIND, its nameserver, are introduced in Section 14.4.5. Here, we describe the components of BIND and its administration. BIND consists of a name daemon, **named**, and a resolver, /usr/lib/resolv.a. **named** satisfies resolver queries, queries other name servers, and caches information from previous queries. With **named** running, all programs that execute the system call **gethostent( )** and its variations get routed to **named** for resolution. If **named** is not running, calls to the **gethostent( )** family of functions are looked up in the /etc/hosts file. BIND includes user-level commands and library functions to query name server databases: **nslookup**(1) and **resolver**(3).

Each copy of **named** running on the network is responsible for a group of machines called a *zone of authority*. **named** can run in several modes:

- Primary master–startup data stored locally in files
- Secondary master–startup data downloaded from primary server at boot time
- Caching only–no local data, queries other servers, caches answers
- Remote–server resides on another machine

Each site should have a primary master server and at least one secondary master server.

The resolver in BIND replaces **gethostbyname**( ), **gethostbyaddr**( ), and **sethostent**( ) in either libc.a or libresolv.a. If you switch from host lookup via the /etc/hosts file to **named** you must recompile EVERYTHING that uses these calls[3] unless your system supports dynamic libraries (e.g., SunOS 4.0). The C library should be recompiled before recompiling the rest of the system. Set the variable HOSTLOOKUP to **named** in the Makefile for the library (/usr/src/lib/libc/Makefile) and run **make**.

14.9.1.1 BIND configuration files

Each **named** answers queries about hostname-to-address mappings for machines in its zone of authority. It must know where to look for information outside this zone of authority, where to get initial data files, who the

[3] Have fun!

alternate servers are, and a host of other things about the network configuration. The answers to these questions are contained in configuration files that are read as **named** starts up. Annotated examples, for both primary and secondary servers, of the configuration files that control such things are illustrated next. The BIND configuration files are:

- named.boot - server startup file
- named.local - client startup file
- named.ca - initial cache of names and addresses

In all of the BIND configuration files, the ";" character in column 1 denotes a comment line. The master server's startup file named.boot is different from a slave server's startup file; therefore, examples of both are shown.

14.9.1.2 named.boot - master server startup

The named.boot configuration file used by **named** at startup is usually invoked from /etc/rc.local; for example:

```
if [ -f /etc/named ]; then
        /etc/named /etc/named.boot; echo -n ' named'  >/dev/console
```

The boot file tells **named** what things are and where to find them. An example is listed next; it is for the machine boulder, the primary master server at the University of Colorado.

```
;
;  bind4.8 boot file  (primary server for Colorado.EDU)
;
sortlist  128.89.0.0 128.0.0.0 192.0.0.0
directory /etc
;
; type          domain                      source file or host
;
cache                                       named.ca
;
primary         Colorado.EDU                named.hosts
primary         138.128.IN-ADDR.ARPA        named.rev
primary         0.0.127.IN-ADDR.ARPA        named.local
```

The file is a bit cryptic; we will dissect it line by line. The first noncomment line, the *sortlist* line, states the order you want addresses returned by the name server if there is more than one answer to a given query. For example, the mail machine for CSNET has both an ARPANET address, 10.x.x.x and its own Class B address, 128.89.x.x. In the boot file just illustrated, the sortlist would cause the 128.89.x.x address to be returned before the ARPANET address. The second line states that all file names are relative to the directory /etc.

The third line initializes caching servers from the file named.ca. The fourth line states that the primary source of authoritative data on name-to-address mappings for the Colorado.EDU domain is the file named.hosts. An IP address can also be specified as the source of data for a server, in which case **named** tries to connect to that address and transfer the host information from the **named** socket of the specified host. It is common for the primary server record to contain a filename and the secondary server record to contain the IP address of the primary server. You may have noticed a proliferation of capitalization styles in hostnames and domain names; the software using these names is not case sensitive.

The fifth line states that the mapping data for the 128.138 network is in the file named.rev. The IP addresses are reversed (byte swapped) in both the configuration line and the data file. The file contains pointer records from the host bytes of our Class B address (in reverse order) to the hostname. A script to transform host tables into reverse address mappings is included in Appendix P.

The final line specifies the location of localhost information. Notice that the localhost address is reversed also.

14.9.1.3 named.boot - secondary server startup

The machine boulder is the primary server in these examples, but there are two secondary servers on our network as well: spot and sigi, whose named.boot file is illustrated next.

```
;
; bind4.8 boot file (secondary for Colorado.EDU)
;
sortlist  128.89.0.0 128.0.0.0 192.0.0.0
directory /etc
;
; type      domain                   source file or host
;
cache                                named.ca
;
secondary   Colorado.EDU             128.138.240.1 128.138.238.18 named.hosts
secondary   138.128.IN-ADDR.ARPA     128.138.240.1 128.138.238.18 named.rev
primary     0.0.127.IN-ADDR.ARPA     named.local
;
forwarders  128.138.240.1
```

The secondary servers point back to the IP addresses of the primary server, boulder (and boulder-gw). boulder is also the *forwarder*. All querys will be forwarded to boulder for resolution, rather than going directly to a root server. Thus, boulder will build a big cache and be able to resolve most queries locally.

14.9.1.4 named.local - client startup

The file *named.local* is used to specify the local loopback interface for the primary domain server. The location of this file is specified in the named.boot file. It should contain one SOA or Start of Authority record and the localhost resource record. boulder's named.local file follows:

```
@   IN   SOA   boulder.Colorado.EDU. netadmin.boulder.Colorado.EDU. (
                     10.2      ; Serial
                     3600      ; Refresh
                     300       ; Retry
                     3600000 ; Expire
                     3600 )    ; Minimum
    IN  NS     sigi.Colorado.EDU.
1   IN  PTR    localhost.
```

The SOA record defines the start of a zone. The @ in the first field is the name of the zone; @ denotes the current *origin* or Colorado.EDU in this case. The fourth field contains the name of the primary server for this domain (boulder.Colorado.EDU). The fifth field is the person in charge: in this case it is an alias for the folks who administer our network. This field must be an electronic mail address; a person's name won't do. The next parts of the SOA record set the parameters for the domain. *Serial* is a serial number and should be incremented every time the file is changed. *Refresh* is the frequency in seconds that secondary servers should query the primary server to see if updated tables are available. *Retry* is the time in seconds that the secondary should wait for the primary to reply when requesting a refresh. *Expire* is the total time, again in seconds, for a secondary server to carry on without a refresh before throwing away the whole database. *Minimum* is the default value for the TTL (time to live) parameter on resource records with none specified.

The second record in the file states that sigi.Colorado.EDU is the name server; the third record specifies a reverse pointer to localhost. The 1 in the first column of the last entry is short for 1.0.0.127, the reverse version of the localhost address 127.0.0.1.

14.9.1.5 named.ca - initial cache

The named.ca file is used to prime the cache with data for looking up names outside the Colorado.EDU domain. A sample follows:

```
;
;       Initial cache data for root domain servers
;
.               99999999        IN      NS      C.NYSER.NET.
                99999999        IN      NS      NS.NASA.GOV.
                99999999        IN      NS      SRI-NIC.ARPA.
                99999999        IN      NS      A.ISI.EDU.
;
;       Prep the cache (hotwire the addresses), order doesn't matter
;
A.ISI.EDU.      99999999        IN      A       26.2.0.103
C.NYSER.NET.    99999999        IN      A       128.213.5.17
NS.NASA.GOV.    99999999        IN      A       128.102.16.10
SRI-NIC.ARPA.   99999999        IN      A       10.0.0.51
SRI-NIC.ARPA.   99999999        IN      A       26.0.0.73
```

Each of the sites just listed can serve one of the top-level domains. The first field is the domain; the second, the TTL (set to infinity here); the third, the class (INternet, CSnet, etc.); the fourth, the type of record (NameServer, Address); and finally the hostname or address. Fields are separated by tabs. The dot in the beginning of the first noncomment line is important: it means the root domain. A blank entry in a field uses the last entry defined for that field. Thus those first four lines are for the root servers. The final dot in the hostnames in the first and last fields is also significant: It terminates the name and does not allow anything else to be tacked on.

BIND is a developing system and new releases are frequent (more than once a year). The latest code can be obtained by anonymous **ftp** from the machine ucbarpa.Berkeley.EDU.

14.9.2 Anonymous ftp

Anonymous **ftp** is the primary way software and documents are distributed on the Internet. **ftp** connects to a remote machine and allows users to login as "anonymous" with any password accepted. Some sites expect the password given to be the word *guest* or *ident*; others expect the user's name or his email address. Once logged in, the user can execute **ls**, some built-in shell commands, and several **ftp** commands.

ftpd, the server daemon process that makes it all work, is managed by **inetd** and therefore must have an entry in the /etc/inetd.conf and /etc/services files. When an anonymous login is made, **ftpd** does a **chroot**(2) system call to make files outside of the ~ftp directory invisible and inaccessible. This adds security, since **ftpd** must run setuid to root to manipulate privileged socket ports.

14.9.2.1 Taking via anonymous ftp

Throughout this book, we have occasionally said that software package *xxx* is available via anonymous **ftp** from *yyy*. Now we will finally tell you how to get all these goodies. There are a few prerequisites: You must have a connection to the Internet, you must have **ftp** set up in your environment, and you must know the name of the machine that has the software you need. The following example illustrates an **ftp** session from the machine boulder to the machine ucbarpa.Berkeley.EDU to pick up the latest copy of BIND. If you do not have the nameserver running, you must either have ucbarpa.Berkeley.EDU in your host tables or know its IP address and use that in place of the machine name in the following **ftp** command. Transfers of large files can take a while. Most files are in compressed **tar** format and require the **uncompress** utility to unpack.

```
% ftp ucbarpa.berkeley.edu
Connected to ucbarpa.berkeley.edu.
220 ucbarpa.Berkeley.EDU FTP server (Version 4.3 Thu Jun 9 22:32:59 PDT 1988) ready.
Name (ucbarpa.berkeley.edu:evi): anonymous
331 Guest login ok, send ident as password.
Password:   (typed evi@boulder.colorado.edu here but it did not echo)
230 Guest login ok, access restrictions apply.
ftp> cd pub/4.3
250 CWD command successful.
ftp> ls
200 PORT command successful.
150 Opening data connection for /bin/ls (128.138.238.18,1696) (0 bytes).
README
bench.tar.Z
bind.4.8.tar
bind.4.8.tar.Z
disklabel.h
 ...
ucb-fixes
226 Transfer complete.
251 bytes received in 0.14 seconds (1.7 Kbytes/s)
ftp> binary
200 Type set to I.
ftp> get bind.4.8.tar.Z
200 PORT command successful.
150 Opening data connection for bind.4.8.tar.Z (128.138.238.18,1697) (376483 bytes).
226 Transfer complete.
local: bind.4.8.tar.Z remote: bind.4.8.tar.Z
376483 bytes received in 2.7e+02 seconds (1.4 Kbytes/s)
ftp> bye
221 Goodbye.
```

The file transfer took about 4.5 minutes for the one-third Mb file. Your mileage will definitely vary; this transfer was Saturday afternoon, but at 10:00 a.m. Monday morning allow a half-hour or more! The BIND software is in compressed tar format; to unpack it:

```
uncompress bind.4.8.tar.Z
tar xf bind.4.8.tar
```

14.9.2.2 Giving via anonymous ftp

In order to let others share your software via anonymous **ftp**, you must set up a fake user ftp, configure its home directory, and verify that the ftp daemon process, **ftpd**, is included in **inetd**'s configuration file.

To allow anonymous **ftp** from your site:

- Add the pseudo-user "ftp" to your regular password file.
- Create subdirectories bin, etc, and pub beneath ~ftp.
- Copy the **ls** program to the ~ftp/bin directory.
- Copy the /etc/passwd and /etc/group files to the ~ftp/etc directory.
- Edit both the passwd file and the group file, truncating them drastically.
- Set the permissions on the files and directories as below.
- Make sure **ftpd** is in /etc/inetd.conf.
- Fill ~ftp/pub with goodies.

Beneath the ~ftp directory are subdirectories bin, etc, and pub. bin contains the shell commands that ftp is allowed to execute, etc contains a passwd file and a group file, and pub is where the data files to share are stored. bin must contain the **ls** command; usually that is all it contains. The passwd file should only contain users root, daemon, uucp and ftp. The contents of the group file must include ftp's group, in our case the group misc. Permissions on the various files and directories are quite important. It is recommended that the permissions be set as shown in Figure 14.22.

FIGURE 14.22

Recommended anonymous **ftp** permissions

File	Owner	Group	Permissions
~ftp	ftp	misc	555
~ftp/bin	root	wheel	555
~ftp/bin/ls	root	wheel	111
~ftp/etc	root	wheel	555
~ftp/etc/passwd	root	wheel	444
~ftp/etc/group	root	wheel	444
~ftp/pub	ftp	misc	777

14.10 Debugging and monitoring the network

This section will cover debugging the network, both the hardware components and the software components. Hardware tools are used to monitor the hardware of the network and the low-level packet structure. Software tools typically allow a much higher level of abstraction.

14.10.1 Hardware

Two of the most effective network monitoring tools are the TDR and the network analyzer.

14.10.1.1 Time domain reflectometer

A TDR or time domain reflectometer can be attached to the network cable in place of a terminator to view impedance variations along the cable. In operation, the TDR simply bounces a signal down the cable and listens to the echoes produced as the signal bounces around. Each quiver in the signal indicates a disturbance in the cable. Transceiver taps can be seen quite clearly and resemble a small pip up. The location of the pip is calibrated to the distance from the TDR (the end of the cable).

The Cabletron TDR can operate on an active network; early versions of the Tektronix could not. A TDR costs several thousand dollars ($5,000 to $10,000 list).

Problems with the cable can be seen quite clearly, both potential problems like a sloppy transceiver installation or too-tight bend, and immediate problems like a short or open in the cable. The standard items to look for are summarized next:

- Open cable, no terminator – signal goes up off the screen
- Shorted cable, bad transceiver tap – signal goes down off the screen
- Healthy transceiver tap – small pip up
- Healthy connector and barrel adapter – very small pip up
- Sharp bend, crunch, kink – itty bitty small pip up

If you have or can borrow a TDR, it is a good idea to map your cable and keep a permanent record either on Polaroid film (Cabletron) or a strip chart record (Tektronix) of the cable. If clandestine taps are suspected, a second picture of the cable can be compared to the original and the taps located.

The poor man's TDR is a simple volt/ohmmeter. It cannot tell as much as the TDR, but can help to identify poor transceiver installations. Each transceiver tap can be verified by attaching the meter to the center conductor of the network cable and the outer braid to measure the resistance. After drilling the hole for the tap, and before installing it, attach one lead to the shield and the other lead via the stinger to the center core. The meter should read about 25 Ω. If it reads less than 23 Ω there is a short somewhere; if more than 27 Ω the cable is open somewhere.

Drop cables contain eight wires. The continuity of these wires can be tested with an ohmmeter. If you have lots of them to test, a simple cable tester can be purchased or built.

The Cabletron transceivers can also be debugging tools. They contain little LED lights that show power, heartbeat, transmitted data, received data, and collision presence. High collision rates can be the result of a version mismatch.

14.10.1.2 Network analyzer

A network analyzer attaches to the network cable like any host, but runs software for analyzing the packets and data that are coming across the network cable. All packets are seen, but many analyzers cannot keep up with the packet rate on the network. Hewlett-Packard makes one that can keep up to the network; many other companies make analyzers based on the IBM PC and software done at MIT called Netwatch. These PC-based systems cannot keep up with the network.

The analyzer can be programmed to filter packets in just about any way you can imagine. It can also generate traffic and measure network load. So if a transceiver is faulty and generating collisions all the time, the analyzer can see it and identify the Ethernet address of the host with the bad transceiver.

Network analyzers can see the data in packets on the cable. This is certainly a violation of privacy if not also security. Some devices can be set (voluntarily) to show only the IP addresses and header information, and not display the actual data sent. It is relatively easy to set up a PC that grabs packets and looks for the string "ssword", for example, and saves the data in the next few packets when that string is seen. Logging in as root across the network might be unwise in some environments.

14.10.2 Software

Several standard BSD software tools help debug the network. Many vendors of graphics workstations have taken these tools and built nice front-ends to them to improve their user-friendliness and utility. We will briefly describe the standard tools and the value-added tools distributed by Sun Microsystems.

14.10.2.1 ping

ping *machinename* uses the ICMP protocol's mandatory ECHO_REQUEST datagram to force a response from *machinename*. **ping** (without a count argument) runs in an infinite loop and so must be terminated with an interrupt signal (usually <Control-C>). **ping** as distributed with BSD is pretty drab, but a new public domain version written by Mike Muuss from BRL is quite snazzy. Here are examples of both:

```
% oldping tigger
tigger is alive

% newping tigger
PING tigger.Colorado.EDU (128.138.240.26): 56 data bytes
64 bytes from 128.138.240.26: icmp_seq=0 time=12 ms
64 bytes from 128.138.240.26: icmp_seq=1 time=11 ms
64 bytes from 128.138.240.26: icmp_seq=2 time=11 ms
64 bytes from 128.138.240.26: icmp_seq=3 time=11 ms
64 bytes from 128.138.240.26: icmp_seq=4 time=10 ms
^C

----tigger.Colorado.EDU PING Statistics----
6 packets transmitted, 6 packets received, 0% packet loss
round-trip (ms)  min/avg/max = 10/11/12

% newping gingko
PING gingko.Colorado.EDU (128.138.241.3): 56 data bytes
^C

----gingko.Colorado.EDU PING Statistics----
7 packets transmitted, 0 packets received, 100% packet loss
```

The output for tigger shows the IP address of the host pinged, the ICMP sequence number of the packet and the round trip travel time. The host gingko in the second example is down. **ping** is the first program to try in a new network installation. If ping can't get through, nothing can.

14.10.2.2 netstat

netstat displays the network status as seen from the point of view of the host where it is executed. There are several flags to **netstat** that can be used to filter data. Some of the more useful ones for monitoring an active network will be described.

FIGURE 14.23

Selected **netstat** options	
Option	Description
-a	Show active Internet connections and their status
-i	Show summary information on each network interface
-m	Show mbuf (memory buffer) usage
-s	Show packet summaries by protocol
-r	Show routing tables, their status, and usage summary

netstat takes an optional interval argument which is interpreted as the interval to sleep between invocations of **netstat** in an infinite loop. For example, here is output from the command **netstat -i** on our boulder machine at a relatively quiet time (2:30 a.m.). The first form shows each interface; the second form shows the default interface and its continuing traffic at three-second intervals.

```
% netstat -i
Name  Mtu   Network      Address       Ipkts Ierrs    Opkts Oerrs   Coll
il0   1500  cu-engineer  boulder      733444     0   556187     0    175
il1   1500  cu-boulder   boulder      429618     0   330798     0    826
sl0   1006  cu-engineer  boulder       36139     0    35672   102      0
lo0   1536  127          localhost     39034     0    39034     0      0
```

Notice that the collision rate is quite low relative to the number of packets handled. There were no errors on the regular interfaces, but on the interface sl0, a serial line IP (SLIP) connection over voice grade phone lines, the error rate is quite high.

```
% netstat -i 3
    input    (il0)      output               input   (Total)      output
packets errs  packets errs colls  packets   errs  packets   errs colls
 733486    0   556216    0   175  1238313     0   961744    102  1001
      5    0        3    0     0       30     0        4      0     0
      2    0        2    0     0        8     0        6      0     0
      3    0        3    0     0       11     0        9      0     0
      2    0        2    0     0       13     0        9      0     0
      3    0        1    0     0       13     0       12      0     0
```

The first line of the display shows totals since the last reboot (16 hours ago), subsequent lines show the number of packets handled in each three-second time interval. The left columns are displaying data for the il0 interface, the right columns show totals for all interfaces.

netstat -r can be used to find out exactly what routing a host is using. A sample from our boulder machine with two network interfaces follows:

```
% netstat -r
Routing tables
Destination      Gateway            Flags    Refs     Use  Interface
pprince          colo               UGH         0     2054  il1
eprince          colo               UGH         0     5189  il1
localhost        localhost          UH          4   251844  lo0
piper            piper              UH          0    34331  il0
boulder          localhost          UH          1    95467  lo0
wasser           boulder            UH          0   401411  sl0
cu-boulder       boulder            U           5  2845294  il1
cu-engineer      boulder            U           1   168589  il0
cu-cer           anchor             UG          0    41279  il0
midnet           128.138.238.36     UG          0        0  il1
130.118          128.138.238.36     UG          0        0  il1
```

The destination and the gateway can be either hostnames or IP addresses. The flags quantify the route: U is up, G is a gateway, H is a host, D (not shown) is a route resulting from an ICMP redirect. ICMP redirects allow gateways to exchange information about their idea of the best routes. The remaining fields give statistics on the route: the current number of active uses, the number of packets sent, and the interface used.

14.10.2.3 ruptime and rwho

ruptime and **rwho** use the broadcast packets produced by **rwhod** to supply snapshots of the networks hosts status and who is logged on where. If **rwhod** is not broadcasting correctly then the **ruptime** and **rwho** commands will not work. Broadcast packets are not normally propagated through gateways.

14.10.2.4 routed and gated

If you use dynamic routing, **routed** or **gated** are very important to the health of your network. They each can be invoked with a log file for debugging and verifying initial configurations. Check these log files to be sure they are behaving as expected. You can flush the routing tables and then watch them build up again as RIP requests fly around your network.

14.10.2.5 telnet and ftp

telnet and **ftp** often work when their counterparts, **rlogin** and **rcp**, fail. If this happens it is usually because **rcp** and **rlogin** do some authentication before blindly allowing you to connect or copy files. Check the hosts.equiv or ~/.rhosts files again to be sure they are set up correctly, and try again. If a machine is a gateway and has two names, such as boulder and boulder-gw, it is necessary to include both of these names in the host.equiv and ~/.rhosts files if you are not using the nameserver.

14.10.2.6 Sun's traffic program

The **traffic** program graphically displays network load, packet sizes, protocol traffic, or packet origins and destinations. If you have a spare Sun lying around, install it as a network watcher. To run **traffic**, several daemons must also be running; consult your manual for details. Sun also supports a tool called **etherfind** that can be used to track packets with specified features on the network, much like the network analyzers do.

15

Mail and Berkeley Sendmail

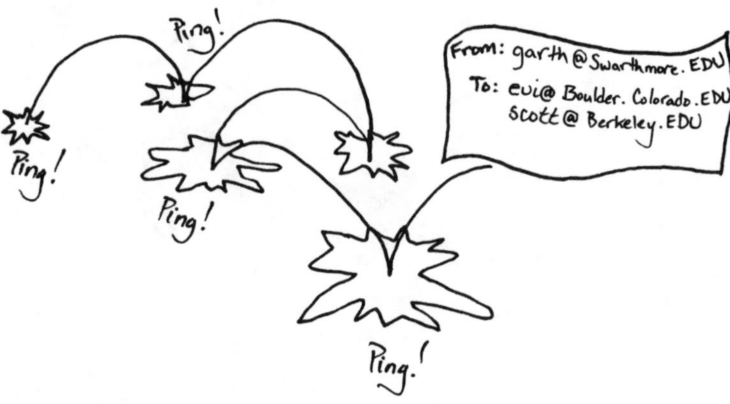

15.1 The electronic mail explosion

A few years ago, electronic mail (email) was a new thing that was mostly used by computer nerds. Today, if mail is broken on our machines, the secretaries are the first to complain; almost all departmental communication is done by electronic mail rather than by telephone, memos, or discussions. This has introduced some interesting social behavior. Electronic mail seems to be less formal than a paper letter, and therefore people tend to say more directly what they mean and feel. It is also somehow less personal and more removed than direct voice contact, and so rage and frustration tend to emerge. The result is that computer mail "flames" occur in which two people exchange messages they would never say or write on paper to each other. One of our users is easily upset and used to abuse the systems administrators regularly. The only defense seemed to be to save his messages and then send them back to him a few weeks later when all had cooled down. He was appalled at the things he had committed to print.

Unfortunately, electronic mail does not always work properly, mostly due to its haphazard development over the years. Different networks have different standards. For example, uucp uses one (initially unwritten) standard, while the Internet uses another standard described by various RFC's (Request for Comment) — and even these have changed. You only need to lift the RFC's that specify what a mail system connected to the Internet should understand and what it should do to realize that mail, while simple in concept, is not a simple program to implement.

15.1.1 Mail systems

When user A mails a message to local user B with a carbon copy to local user C, the mail system accepts A's message, verifies that users B and C exist on the machine, and then appends the message to the mailbox files of B and C. If for any reason the BSD mail system cannot deliver a message as addressed, it is returned to the sender along with an error message reporting the apparent reason. This error service is not available under ATT mail.

A mail system may consist of a single program or several programs functioning as a user agent and a transport agent.

15.1.1.1 User agent

The user agent interfaces to the user for sending and receiving mail. ATT's **/bin/mail** is the original user agent. Several others now exist:

- **/bin/mail**
- **/usr/ucb/mail**
- **/usr/new/mh**
- **/usr/local/bin/dmail**
- Sun's **mailtool**

We will not really cover the user agent in detail, but will briefly mention the **/usr/ucb/mail** user agent and its administration.

15.1.1.2 The transport agent

The transport agent is responsible for actually receiving and delivering messages. It should:

- Accept messages from the user agent
- Understand destination addresses
- Deliver mail originating on the local machine to the proper mailbox[es] if local, or to a delivery agent if not local
- Receive incoming mail from other delivery agents and deliver it to local users

Several transport agents exist, two of which are quite comprehensive: Berkeley's **sendmail** and CSNET's **mmdf** (**pmdf**). We will discuss only **sendmail**.

15.1.2 Mail addressing

When mail is local, addressing it is quite simple, because the user's login name uniquely identifies him. But if the addressee is not on the local machine, then the delivery gets more complicated.

There are two basic forms of mail addresses: *route-based* addresses and *location-independent* addresses. Route-based addressing is rather like requiring anyone who wishes to send a letter to know not only the recipient's address but also the exact route one must take to get from the sender's place to the recipient's place, or requiring you to know all the switching nodes in the telephone company's circuits in order to place a telephone call. To include this routing information in the statement of the address is clumsy and not necessary. The post office and telephone company have long ago relegated both the storage, lookup, and use of this routing information to the transport agent. All the user of these systems needs to know is the location-independent final destination address of the recipient. Computer mail is coming of age and we see a move toward location independent addressing being accelerated by the switch to the domain hierarchical naming scheme for computers across the country.

There are two common forms of mail addresses on UNIX systems, one route-based and one location-independent. Examples of each follow:

host!path!user
user@host.domain

The former normally represents an address on the uucp network (see Chapter 16: *Uucp*), while the latter commonly indicates use of a high-speed network such as ARPANET (see Chapter 14: *Networking under BSD*). UNIX mail software, in particular the transport and delivery agents, is getting smarter and routinely translates from route-based to location-independent addressing.

Let's assume that user C is local (Colorado), and that B is a user on the machine ucbvax in Berkeley, California, and explore some possible addresses for B.

hao!hplabs!ucbvax!B

This address says that B is a user on ucbvax which can be reached using uucp via the machines hplabs and hao. The order of the machine names is significant: The current machine talks to hao, which in turn forwards the mail to hplabs, which forwards it on to ucbvax. This address could also be:

utah-cs!ucbvax!B

which would again use uucp as a delivery agent, but would send the mail to the machine utah-cs for forwarding. If the address

B@ucbvax.Berkeley.EDU

was used, the message would go to Berkeley via the Internet (ARPANET/NSFNet/CSNET). Another valid address would be

ucbvax!B@bbn.COM

which would send the message to bbn.COM via the Internet and then on to ucbvax via uucp.

As you can see, when mail leaves the realm of the local machine the complexity of the delivery mechanism increases greatly. Also, as the last address illustrates, the distinction between route-based and location-independent addressing is blurred.

15.1.3 Reading mail headers

Following is a typical mail message (generated by the mail system **sendmail**) that has been routed through both the Internet and the uucp system. The line numbers at the left are for reference in the following discussion and not part of the message. They will be used as we dissect this message and identify which mailer on which machine created the various lines of the header.

```
1:  From @UCBVAX.BERKELEY.EDU:mcvax!ukc!dat@seismo.css.gov Tue Jun 16 14:48:20 1987
2:  Received: from boulder.Colorado.EDU by rupertsberg.Colorado.EDU (3.2/4.7)
3:       id AA14111; Tue, 16 Jun 87 14:48:15 MDT
4:  Received: by boulder.Colorado.EDU (cu.csnet-uucp.052787)
5:  Received: from ucbvax.berkeley.edu by RELAY.CS.NET id aa16172;
6:       16 Jun 87 14:08 EDT
7:  Received: by ucbvax.Berkeley.EDU (5.57/1.25)
8:       id AA03037; Tue, 16 Jun 87 11:05:48 PDT
9:  Received: from mcvax.UUCP by seismo.CSS.GOV (5.54/1.14) with UUCP
10:      id AA05869; Tue, 16 Jun 87 14:05:07 EDT
```

```
11: Received: by mcvax.cwi.nl; Tue, 16 Jun 87 19:57:13 +0200 (MET)
12: Message-Id: <8706161757.AA04040@mcvax.cwi.nl>
13: Received: from hawk by kestrel.Ukc.AC.UK   Over Ring with SMTP  id aa21053;
14:      16 Jun 87 13:17 BST
15: Date: Tue, 16 Jun 87 13:13:06 BST
16: From: mcvax!ukc.ac.uk!dat@seismo.css.gov
17: To: phoenix@UCBVAX.BERKELEY.EDU
18: Subject: Miranda paper
19: Status: RO

20: Message was here.
```

This message was from user "dat" in England to "phoenix" at Berkeley. "phoenix" is a mail alias that expands (on the Berkeley machine ucbvax) to eric (a local user) and evi@boulder.Colorado.EDU. This particular message took the following path:

- From the machine *hawk* in England where it originated
- To *kestrel.ukc.ac.uk* in England via Cambridge Ring network (lines 13,14)
- To *mcvax.cwi.nl* in Holland (lines 11,12)
- To *seismo.css.gov* in Washington D.C. via uucp (lines 9,10)
- To *ucbvax.berkeley.edu* in Berkeley, California via ARPANET (lines 7,8)
- To *relay.cs.net* in Boston via CSNET (lines 5,6)
- To *boulder.colorado.edu* in Colorado via CSNET (line 4)
- To *rupertsberg.colorado.edu* in Boulder via local Ethernet (lines 2,3).

Each of the "Received:" header lines documents the message's passage through the mail system of a given machine. The message undoubtedly also passed through several machines on the Internet at the IP level — for example, in its trek from Berkeley to Colorado — but this is not recorded in the message header. Line 1 is the UNIX (non-RFC822) version of the sender's address and the date the message was received in evi's mailbox on the machine rupertsberg. The other lines, or pairs of lines, are written by the mail system on each receiving machine and record the date and time the message arrived at that machine and also, in most cases, where it came from.

For example, let's take lines 9 and 10 apart. These lines were inserted into the message by the mailer on the seismo machine. They state that seismo received the message from the machine mcvax at 2:05 p.m., June 16, 1987. The message was sent using the uucp network. While stored on seismo, the message had the identifier AA05869; this can be used to search system logs on seismo if necessary to get more information about the message.

Line 15 is the date the message was sent, where BST means British Summer Time. Line 16 is the return address of the sender; this is the address that would be used if the **mail** command "r" were used to respond to the message. In this particular message, the full name of the user who sent the message is not recorded in the header, but his login name is "dat". Line 17 is the recipient, in this case the alias "phoenix". Note that this message was not in fact delivered to evi on boulder: When it arrived on boulder it was forwarded to the machine rupertsberg where evi reads mail. This last hop was caused by an alias on the machine boulder. The status line, Line 19, states that the message has been read and is old.

As you can see, the route to Boulder, Colorado, was not the most direct one distance-wise, but may well have been the most direct based on the connectivity of the mail systems involved. Also note that due to the time difference of eight hours, this particular message from England to Colorado via Holland and Berkeley took nine hours and 35 minutes to make the seven hops in its trip across the Atlantic. Mailers must do quite a bit of work to properly deliver a message halfway around the world.

15.1.4 Spool directory

Users' system mailboxes are usually in the directory /usr/spool/mail (BSD) or /usr/mail (ATT) in files named for users' login names. This directory is created during the installation of the operating system and should have permissions set to mode 777 (BSD) or mode 775 (ATT).

15.1.5 Startup files

The standard Berkeley mail interface to the user, **/usr/ucb/mail**, uses a global startup file called /usr/lib/Mail.rc, and local startup files for each user, ~/.mailrc. A sample Mail.rc file is listed here:

```
set append dot save crt ask
ignore Received Message-Id Resent-Message-Id Status Mail-From
ignore Return-Path Via received from status message-id
```

The *set* line sets options:

append — add saved messages to the end of ~mbox instead of to the beginning
dot — recognize the dot on a line by itself as signaling the end of a message
save — save the message in progress if interrupted by <Control-C> or <Control-D>
crt — show messages only a screenful at a time via a pager like **more**
ask — asks for a subject for outgoing messages

The dot option comes from the dot in the **ed** editor which signaled the end of input and switched the user back to command mode. It has become a bit of UNIX folklore, and is used not only by **ed** and **mail**, but by other programs as well. The crt option is usually turned off, even though it's nicer to see messages a screenful at a time, because it is so slow. It is foolishly implemented by a **system**(3) call, not a pipe.

The *ignore* directives make the mail message friendlier to users, preserving only the default headers From, Date, To, and Subject. Other headers are still part of each message, but are not displayed unless requested with the P command to **/usr/ucb/mail**. Any option to **mail** may be put in the Mail.rc file; they are all described in the **mail**(1) manual page.

Users can override the Mail.rc file with the -n flag. The .mailrc file in a user's home directory is typically used to define additional options or to override those in Mail.rc and to define personal aliases (see Section 15.2.3); a sample follows:

```
unset crt
set autoprint metoo askcc ask hold
alternates evi@rupertsberg evi@tut evi@boulder evi@tigger evi@tramp \
        evi@spot evi@sigi evi@dwim
alias wayne trzyna@spot
alias deb deborah
alias ron hao!hplabs!ucbvax!allegra!watmath!water!rcmullin
alias brent brent@ucbernie.berkeley.edu
alias warren sunpeaks!sun!wteitelman
alias cs225 evi tyler carmen
```

The first line undoes the systemwide default set in the Mail.rc file. Additional options are set:

autoprint — prints the next message when the current message is deleted
metoo — includes the sender in carbon copy lists, usually the sender is ignored
askcc — asks for carbon copy recipients for outgoing messages
ask — is redundant, since it is the global default
hold — keeps undeleted messages in the system mail spool file instead of ~/mbox

The alternates list enumerates other addresses that the user is known by. This list is used to prevent multiple copies of mail you respond to from flying back in your face because the software doesn't realize that evi, evi@boulder, and evi@rupertsberg are all the same person. Personal aliases can be set in the .mailrc file to allow either shorter names for a single recipient or the creation of a personal mailing list. The format of an alias line[1] is:

alias new-name old-name1 old-name2 ...

Note that a user's .mailrc file is not portable if it contains route-based addresses. The move to location-independent addressing and the use of fully qualified addresses (addresses that include not only the machine name, but also its domain) improves the portability of this file substantially. In this example, only the entry for brent is portable, and would work from any machine with access to the Internet.

15.2 sendmail

The most complex and complete mail delivery system in common use is the **sendmail** program written by Eric Allman while a student at Berkeley. At the time of **sendmail**'s inception, Eric had recently taken a computer science course in which he used production systems, so he decided to tackle the mail delivery problem with a similar approach. At the time, he thought he was attacking a fly with a sledge hammer, intending to move to a simpler technique when he better understood the problem, but **sendmail**'s generality allowed him to keep up with the changing electronic mail world — several important email standards were just taking form, often changing every week. He came to realize that the fly was in fact an elephant and that the sledge hammer was not a sufficiently powerful tool.

sendmail is a transport agent, interfacing between mail programs like **/bin/mail**, **/usr/ucb/mail**, and **/usr/new/mh** and mail delivery agents like **/usr/lib/uucp/uux** (uucp), and **/usr/local/bin/{mmdf,pmdf}** (CSNET). **sendmail** is itself a delivery agent for the Internet. **sendmail** controls the mail messages as they leave the user's keyboard, understands the recipients' addresses, chooses an appropriate delivery agent, rewrites the addresses to a form understood by the delivery agent, reformats the headers as required, and, finally, passes the transformed message off to the agent for delivery. **sendmail** also generates error messages and returns the message to the sender if it is undeliverable.

If you expect incoming mail over a network connection, **sendmail** should be run in daemon mode (see Chapter 20: *Daemons*). In this mode, **sendmail** listens on network port 25 and waits for work. It is started at boot time from the file /etc/rc* as follows:

[1] In this file. We will see that there are three places aliases can be expressed, each with a different format!

```
if [ -f /usr/lib/sendmail ]; then
    (cd /usr/spool/mqueue; rm -f lf*)
    /usr/lib/sendmail -bd -q1h; echo -n ' sendmail'  >/dev/console
fi
```

The **-bd** flag tells **sendmail** to run in daemon mode; the **-q1h** flag sets the frequency to process the queue, in this case one hour. Each time **sendmail** processes the queue it forks off a child process; therefore, this time should be set carefully. For example, processing the queue every minute could be very expensive on a busy machine.

sendmail's actions are controlled by a configuration file, /usr/lib/sendmail.cf, called the *config file* for short. The config file determines **sendmail**'s

- Choice of delivery agents
- Address rewriting rules
- Mail header format

The config file format was designed to be easy to parse since **sendmail** must read and understand it every time it starts up. This has made it a bit lacking in warm, user-friendly features. The biggest system administration chore in using **sendmail** is maintaining the config file. But before we jump into the syntax and semantics of rewriting rules, which make up the real meat of the config file, we will first reference the documentation available and then discuss some issues in the design of your site's mail system.

15.2.1 Documentation

The invocation of **sendmail** is described in Section 8 of the BSD manuals, **sendmail**(8). An overview can be found in *Sendmail — An Internetwork Mail Router*. Installation and a good description of the configuration file are covered in *Sendmail Installation and Operation Guide*, which is in Section 7 of the 4.3BSD System Manager's Manual. Each of these documents is written by Eric Allman. In addition, RFC 819 on domain addressing and RFC 822 on network mail systems, which are in a sense the functional specifications to which **sendmail** was built, were included with the 4.2BSD release in the directory /usr/src/usr.lib/sendmail/doc. RFC 821 defines SMTP (Simple Mail Transport Protocol), the protocol that **sendmail** speaks. It was included with the 4.3BSD release in that same directory. RFC's are also available from the machine sri-nic via anonymous **ftp** (see Chapter 14: *Networking under BSD*).

15.2.2 Mail philosophy

We are going to propose a mail philosophy that is appropriate for medium and large sites, but may be overkill for smaller sites or individual home UNIX machines. On the small machines you won't have **sendmail** anyway, so you should skip this chapter. If you have a small system, you can usually just send your mail to a nearby uucp site which is running **sendmail**, and let them forward it for you.

In setting up mail for a large site, there are two principles that lead to easy administration: a master mail machine and a mail home for each user. Another important philosophy: Don't reinvent the wheel — find a **sendmail** configuration file that is close to what you need, steal it, and modify it to fit your situation.

15.2.2.1 Master mail machine

A single machine at your site should be designated the master mail machine, to which other machines at the site forward mail they cannot deliver. The configuration file on the master machine can deal with all the bizarre addresses, and the rest of the machines can have a simple, relatively stupid config file that forwards the hard stuff to the master. Tables of hosts and routing information only need be maintained on the one "smart" machine. Out-of-date config files on the other machines may result in some inefficiency but will not result in any lost or misdelivered mail. **sendmail** with an out-of-date config file might forward a message to the master machine when it could have delivered it more directly had its config file been up-to-date.

Another use of a master mail machine is to hide the local structure of your organization and present one face to the outside world. Thus, any user at our site is user@boulder, even if he does not even have a login on the boulder machine and gets his mail somewhere else. This is implemented through *aliases* which are discussed in the next section. This reason for a master mail machine has been largely rendered invalid by the domain system discussed later in this chapter and in Chapter 14.

Only the config file on the master mail machine needs to be maintained on a regular basis. The slave config files can be all identical and seldom require attention. The master machine should handle the connections to external networks such as uucp, CSNET, and ARPANET, but if this is not convenient it is not required, as long as the master machine knows how to reach these networks. The master mail machine should be one that is stable and reliable.

15.2.2.2 Mail home

It is convenient for users to be able to read mail on a single machine even if they have logins on several different systems. This can be accomplished with the aliasing mechanism described in the next section. The aliasing scheme we use allows the alias files to be the same on all machines in the same administrative domain at a site. (We are assuming here that login names are unique across all machines at the same site.)

15.2.3 Aliases

Aliases can be used for either assigning additional names to a user, routing a user's mail to a particular machine, or defining mailing lists. Examples of each type follow:

```
nemeth: evi
evi: evi@boulder
authors: evi,garth,scott
```

The first line says that mail sent to "nemeth" should be delivered to evi, the second line says that mail to evi should be delivered on the machine boulder, and the third line says that mail addressed to "authors" should be delivered to evi, garth, and scott.

The systemwide aliases are contained in the file /usr/lib/aliases. The format of an entry in this file is

alias-name: *recipient1*, *recipient2*,...

where *alias-name* is how mail can be addressed and the recipient list contains either actual recipient addresses or further aliases. **sendmail** does detect alias loops which would cause mail to be forwarded back and forth forever. We have already seen that an individual user can set personal aliases in their ".mailrc" file, but unfortunately the format is different (see Section 15.1.5).

The user can also reroute his mail through the ".forward" file in his home directory, which uses yet another format to express a mail address. It is typically used when someone leaves your site to forward his mail to the new location. The .forward file consists of a single line of comma-separated addresses such as:

```
evi@okeeffe.berkeley.edu
```

and

```
\mcbryan, mcbr@ducru, unido!supgmbh!mcbryan@uunet.UU.NET
```

The \mcbryan entry indicates that mail should not only be forwarded to the rest of the list, but that it should also be kept on the current machine. For temporary changes in mail routing, use of the .forward file is preferable to use of the global aliases file because the overhead (computer time and people time) required to change large systemwide alias files is quite high. Permanent changes should go in the systemwide aliases file, since the user's login and files will eventually be removed.

Note that if a user on a network has a mail home (and therefore an entry in the global aliases file), he cannot use the .forward file to reroute his mail to another machine at his own site. For example, the alias

```
evi: evi@boulder
```

and the .forward file on the machine boulder containing

```
evi@tigger
```

would create a loop. Mail addressed to evi would be forwarded to boulder, where the .forward file would cause it to be sent to tigger, where the aliases file would cause it to be forwarded back to boulder, ... After 17 hops (the default, you can configure this when you compile sendmail), the mail would be returned to the sender as undeliverable.

Some typical entries a system administrator might use in /usr/lib/aliases are:

```
postmaster: coggs,evi,forys
root: coggs,forys,trent,trouble
# include for local trouble
trouble: troubletrap@boulder,tmr,:include:/usr/local/adm/trouble.alias
troubletrap: "/usr/local/adm/logs/troublemail"
tmr: stevenr,trent,brownj
```

The postmaster alias *must* be in the /usr/lib/aliases file and should refer to whoever maintains the mail system.

If the aliases file is global to all machines on your network (or in your administrative domain), you must be clever to have the file be global, yet produce locally appropriate actions. The preceding trouble alias is an example of one way to do that. "trouble" is the mail address where problems are reported, but those reports should not necessarily go to the same people across all machines. The alias consists of an archive file (troubletrap), a global part (tmr, for "trouble mail readers"), and a local part (trouble.alias) taken from a file on the particular machine.

For example, on the machine boulder the trouble.alias file contains "coggs,micah" but on the machine tigger it contains "haleden,tag,kooros." Using this scheme, trouble mail is seen by stevenr, trent, brownj, and whoever is in the trouble.alias file for the particular machine with the problem. A special rule is added to the sendmail configuration file to handle the ":include:" directive (see Line #336, Appendix J).

The aliases file supersedes the password file from mail's point of view, so the entry

```
david: david@somewhere-else
```

in the /usr/lib/aliases file would prevent the local user david from ever getting any mail.

Global aliases are stored in a hashed database which is built with the program **newaliases**. **newaliases** is really just **sendmail** with appropriate flags for regenerating the special files of the database. Running **newaliases** on a large aliases file can take a long time; it is best to run it at night when fewer users are impacted.

15.3 The sendmail configuration file

The **sendmail** configuration file controls the behavior of the **sendmail** program. It rewrites addresses from the form supplied by the user to the form expected by the mail delivery agent, sets parameters and arguments to mail delivery programs, and performs many other chores.

The only way to understand the **sendmail** configuration file is to liken it to a frog in high school biology and dissect it piece by piece. That is what the following sections will attempt to do, and like that poor frog, there will be a few unidentified parts that just *are*. The lines used as examples in the sections that follow are taken from the config file in Appendix J for boulder, our master mail machine. The line numbers in Appendix J are not part of the config file, but are there for reference.

The config file is organized into three broad sections:

- Definitions of symbols, classes, options and parameters
- Address rewriting rules
- Definitions of mailers and delivery programs, and how to invoke them

15.3.1 General syntax

sendmail commands begin in column 1; the first character determines the type of command and the format of the rest of the line. Each line is a complete command, except for lines beginning with spaces or tabs, which are continuations of preceding lines. Lines beginning with a "#" are comments; blank lines are also treated as comments. The characters

```
< > ( ) " \
```

have special meanings for **sendmail**. Any attempt to change their meaning with the config file is doomed to failure. DECNET has a bad habit of using the " character when forming UNIX mail addresses such as:

```
spot::"evi@boulder"
```

where spot is a machine running Ultrix, DEC's brand of UNIX. We tried quite unsuccessfully to use the config file to eradicate the " from our DECNET-generated addresses.

15.3.2 Defining variables

sendmail allows the system administrator to define symbols, classes, options, priorities, and many other configuration parameters for mail delivery. The commands to do this usually precede the meat of the config file, the address rewriting rules. This is nice, since they are relatively easy to understand and give someone new to the config file a healthy case of overconfidence. The details of these ground rules are discussed in the following sections.

15.3.2.1 D : define symbol

Variables or *macros* as they are called in the sendmail documentation, may be defined using the D keyword with the syntax: D*name value* (in the actual definition, there is no space between the name and value). Macros are named with a single character, and since **sendmail** itself uses most of the lowercase letters, additional macro definitions should have uppercase names. The value of a macro is referenced as $*name*.

sendmail's predefined macros (variables) are listed in Figure 15.1.[2]

[2] We define the phrase "Snatched from Eric" to mean "taken from the *Sendmail Installation and Operation Guide* by Eric Allman, modified a bit, and included here with permission." This table was Snatched from Eric.

FIGURE 15.1

sendmail's built-in variables	
Name	Meaning
a	The origination date in ARPANET format
b	The current date in ARPANET format
c	The hop count
d	The date in UNIX (ctime) format
e	The SMTP entry message
f	The sender (from) address
g	The sender address relative to the recipient
h	The recipient host
i	The queue id
j	The "official" domain name for this site
l	The format of the UNIX from line
n	The name of the daemon (for error messages)
o	The set of "operators" in addresses
p	**sendmail**'s process id
q	Default format of sender address
r	Protocol used
s	Sender's host name
t	A numeric representation of the current time
u	The recipient user
v	The version number of **sendmail**
w	The hostname of this site
x	The full name of the sender
z	The home directory of the recipient

Some examples of the use of the D command taken from our sample config file follow:

```
# this host's official domain
DDColorado.EDU                                              (Line #44)
# official name for site (taken from $w which is from /bin/hostname)
#     usually this is $w.$D, but to run the name server the domain
#     must be part of the hostname reported by /bin/hostname
Dj$w                                                        (Line #48)
# delimiter (operator) characters
Do.!:@^%/[]                                                 (Line #83)
# format of a total name
Dq $?x $x <$g> $| $g $.                                     (Line #85)
```

The first defines the symbol D, the domain of the boulder machine as Colorado.EDU; the second defines the **sendmail** variable or macro j, the official name of the boulder machine, as boulder.Colorado.EDU. The third defines the special symbols that **sendmail** will recognize in addresses as separator characters rather than part of the address. The fourth uses the conditional form of a macro with syntax:

$?*x* *true* $| *false* $.

where if the variable *x* is defined, then *true* is processed, otherwise *false* is processed. The "$| else" clause is optional; the "$." (note that the "." must be there) terminates the conditional macro expansion. Armed with this, let's attack that third line of gibberish, which defines **sendmail's** macro q, the default format of the sender's address, as $x, the full name of the sender (if it is defined), followed by <$g>, the sender's electronic address relative to the recipient. Thus, this might expand to

Evi Nemeth <evi@boulder.Colorado.EDU>

If the variable *x* were not defined, it would expand to just:

<evi@boulder.Colorado.EDU>

15.3.2.2 C : define a class from a list

A class of symbols (for example, all VMS machines on the network) can be defined using the C command. The syntax is: C*name list-of-members*, where name is a single character. Again, use uppercase letters for class names since the system reserves several of the lowercase letters. The members of the class are separated by spaces and may span lines. Examples of the C command follow:

```
CFvaxa vaxb vaxc
CGtigger
CGanchor
```

The first line defines a Class F with three members: vaxa, vaxb, and vaxc; and the second and third lines define a Class G with two members: tigger and anchor. Either syntax is acceptable. Later in the rewriting rules, we will be able to identify a symbol (machine, in this case) in a particular class with the notation $=*classname*, such as $=F or $=G. Classes are often used to define groups of machines that need to be treated in the same way, such as the DECNET hosts whose mail should go to a particular gateway machine for forwarding. Lines 59 to 76 in Appendix J define classes; lines 61, 68, and 75 consisting of ellipses ("...") indicate that several lines have been omitted from the example.

15.3.2.3 F : define a class from a file

F is identical to C in function, except that the list of members is read from a file. The format to use while reading the file is specified using **scanf**(3) notation. For example:

```
FV/usr/local/lib/sendmail/vms.hosts %s
FU/usr/lib/uucp/L.sys %[abcdefghijklmnopqrstuvwxyzABCDEFGHIJKLMNOPQ
      RSTUVWXYZ1234567890_-]
```

The first defines V as the class of machines whose names are contained in the file /usr/local/lib/sendmail/vms.hosts to be read with **scanf** format string "%s". This method of defining a long list of hosts is preferable; if there are only a few hosts then use the C command. The second example defines the Class U, the uucp hosts that the machine boulder talks to, as the contents of the L.sys file read with a **scanf** format that eliminates comment lines and everything after the first blank. The format string has been broken here to fit on the page; it should be a single line in the config file. This will pick off just the host names (refer to Chapter 16: *Uucp*, to see the format of the L.sys file). Notice that this method of determining uucp hosts does not require changing the config file when new uucp hosts are added; they will automatically be included in the next invocation of **sendmail**. However, since **sendmail** is usually run in daemon mode, always running and listening to socket 25 for connections from other mail agents, it must be restarted to force it to reread the config file.

15.3.2.4 O : set options, a google of 'em

The O command can be used to set options in much the same way as D defines macros, the syntax is O*name value* (again there is no space between *name* and *value*). Option names are represented by a single character, which may be set to a string, integer, Boolean, or time interval. There are many, many options; a partial list is shown in Figure 15.2. Examples of the use of the O command follow:

```
# default delivery mode (deliver in background)
Odbackground                                          (Line #94)
# temporary file mode
OF0600                                                (Line #96)
# default timeout interval
OT2d                                                  (Line #114)
```

The first sets the default delivery mode to background; the second sets the temporary file mode to 600 (note the leading 0 to specify an octal integer). The third sets the timeout value to two days, that is messages can remain in the queue for two days, after which they will be returned to the sender as undeliverable. If your master mail machine goes down for any length of time, the value of this variable should be increased and **sendmail** should be restarted.

FIGURE 15.2[3]

sendmail's O options	
Option	Meaning
A	Location of the aliases file
a	Rebuild alias database if "@:@" does not appear in time
B	Default blank substitution character to *c* in addresses
c	Don't connect to an expensive outgoing mailer
d	Default delivery mode ("interactive," "background," or "queue" only)
D	Rebuild the alias database if necessary and possible
e	Default error mode (print, exit status, return mail, etc.)
F	The temporary file mode, in octal
f	Save UNIX-style "From" lines at the front of headers
g	Default group id for mailers
H	Location of the help file for SMTP
i	Ignore dots in incoming messages
L	Default log level
m	Send to me too
N	Name of the home network; "ARPA" by default.
o	Assume headers may be in old format
Q	Location of the queue directory
q	Multiplier for load average determination of delivery mode
r	Default timeout for reads
S	Location of statistics file for logging
s	Be safe, always instantiate the queue file, even for immediate delivery
T	Default queue timeout, return expired messages
t	Set the local time zone daylight savings under version 6 UNIX
u	Default userid for mailers
v	Run in verbose mode
x	Load average limit, if above just queue messages
X	Load average limit, if above refuse incoming SMTP connections
y	Lower priority of jobs with large numbers of recipients
Y	Run each job as a separate process, good if you are short of memory
z	Modify priority from precedence class
Z	Also modifies priority

[3]Snatched from Eric.

15.3.2.5 P : message precedence

Each mail message is assigned a priority as it enters **sendmail**'s queue based on the time it was submitted, its size, the number of recipients, and its precedence value. The precedence value determines the class of service and can be set by a user by including a "Precedence:" field in his message. The config file defines the meanings of the various precedence classes using the P command: P*name=number*. Negative numbers imply that no error message will be sent if the message is undeliverable. Typical P entries are:

```
Pfirst-class=0
Pspecial-delivery=100
Pjunk=-100
```

15.3.2.6 T : trusted users

A trusted user, set by T*user1 user2* ..., has additional permissions within **sendmail**. Trusted users can override the sender address using the **–f** flag, which is necessary, for example, if a mailer wants to return an error message to the sender. In the distributed sendmail.cf file, the trusted users are usually root, daemon, network, uucp, and eric (Eric Allman). At our site, eric is our department chairman's ten-year-old son, so we changed this entry. As well as allowing respectable users like daemon to impersonate someone else in mail messages, the trusted user concept allows the system administrator the opportunity to show they have read the manual and to send mail as anyone they like. One of our Pyramid machines regularly sends me mail begging to have his hardware upgraded to include a data cache board. This was accomplished by logging in as root and executing:

sendmail –f *anyname recipient*

followed by a message, yielding, for example:

```
From biff Sat Aug 27 22:04:45 1988
Date: Sat, 27 Aug 88 22:04:33 MDT
Apparently-To: evi

hiya, evi, please fill my water dish!!!

biff
```

15.3.2.7 H : header format

Mail headers produced by **sendmail** can be very verbose and use more space than the message itself. Verbose headers are useful for debugging, but a bit redundant for ordinary use, not to mention painful to print on slow dial-up lines. The headers are set with the H command, with the syntax: H*name: format*, and are applied to each outgoing message. The syntax is actually a bit more general: H*?list-of-mailer-flags?name: format*, where if the mailer that the message will use has one of the mailer flags specified, then the header line will be included. A complete list of mailer flags and their meanings is given in Section 15.3.4. For example:

```
H?P?Return-Path: <$g>                                    (Line #143)
```

says that if the P flag is passed to the mailer, include the header line:

Return-Path: *<sender address relative to the recipient>*

For instance:

Return-Path: <evi@boulder.Colorado.EDU>

Notice that in the sample config file, the definitions of the Internet and CSNET mailers include the P flag, while the definitions of the other mailers do not. The header line:

```
HReceived: by $W.$D ($X); $b; id $i; from $s        (Line #144)
```

does not contain the conditional clause and so will always be included as:

Received: by *official-name* (*mailer id*); *date*; id *message id*; from *sender's host*

For instance:

Received: by boulder.Colorado.EDU (cu.grandpoohbah.082888);
Fri Sep 30 11:46:04 MDT 1988; id AA16656; from tigger.Colorado.EDU

15.3.3 Rewriting rules

We have now gotten the skin off the frog and are ready to proceed with the real meat of the config file, the rewriting rules. Rewriting rules are used to transform addresses from one form to another. First we will describe the general idea and specific syntax, then proceed to dissect a couple of rulesets from our sample config file. Finally, we will track an entire mail message as it winds its way through the fun house called the config file.

sendmail accepts addresses in many forms and tries to rewrite them in a generic form where the meanings "user", "host", and "domain" can be attached to various parts of the address. From the host and domain portion of the address the correct mailer program is determined. This seems a simple task if the address is:

evi@boulder.Colorado.EDU

but what if it is:

@boulder:haidozo!evi%wasteheat%dogfood%goodkarma%snake@sigi

Some mail addresses have no obvious operator precedence, and thus are difficult to parse correctly. Much of the "magic" in the **sendmail** configuration file is used to take care of hard problems like operator precedence and scoping.

Rewriting rules have three parts, separated by tabs: the left-hand side (denoted by LHS), the right-hand side (by RHS), and an optional comment field. When an address matches the LHS, it is rewritten as specified by the RHS.

15.3.3.1 Rulesets

The rewriting rules are grouped into rulesets, designated by a ruleset number, Sn where n is an integer < 30 (this can be changed, see Section 15.3.5) naming the ruleset. In general, each rule in a ruleset is applied to a particular address; thus, an address might be rewritten several times within a ruleset. The rulesets are applied in the order outlined in Figure 15.3. Ruleset 3, denoted S3, is the first ruleset applied to all addresses and tries to put them into the canonical form:

local-part@host-domain-specification

It also adds the magic tokens < and > to help set precedence. Ruleset 3 is probably the hardest to understand; if you are trying to figure out the config file you might want to start elsewhere.

Ruleset 0 decides what the destination really is and which mailer program should get the message there. It resolves the destination address into a triple (mailer, host, user).

Ruleset D adds sender domain information to addresses that have no domain; for example, given: "From: evi@boulder.Colorado.EDU" and "To: garth", it would modify the latter to "To: garth@boulder.Colorado.EDU."

Rulesets 1 and 2 rewrite sender and recipient addresses, respectively. Don't forget that by the time an address has reached ruleset 1 or 2, the resolution of where and to whom the message is going has already been made. Any recipient rewriting is purely cosmetic and will not influence where the message is delivered. In addition, each mailer can specify additional rulesets for both the sender and recipient addresses to do final mailer-specific cleanup. These rulesets have different names for each mailer and are denoted S and R in the diagram.

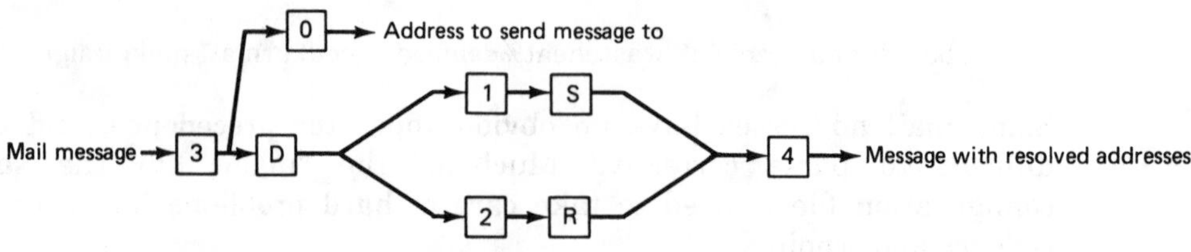

FIGURE 15.3 Application of rulesets[4]

[4]Snatched from Eric.

Ruleset 4 rewrites all addresses, usually from internal to external form. It is the final rewriting.

15.3.3.2 Tokens

Parsing is a computer jargon word that means reading an input string, understanding it by dividing it into parts, called tokens, and determining the type and meaning of each token. In these terms, mail addresses are parsed into tokens. The tokens are recognized as the strings between the separators defined in the "o" macro, namely:

```
! . : @ % / [ ]
```

in our sample config file. Thus the address evi@boulder.Colorado.EDU contains seven tokens: "evi", "@", "boulder", ".", "Colorado", ".", and "EDU". These seven tokens are referred to as $1, $2, ..., $7, respectively, in the rewriting rules. You will see more than enough of this notation in the sections that follow.

15.3.3.3 Rules

Each rewriting rule is on a line by itself and has syntax:

R*LHS* <tab> *RHS* <tab> *optional-comment*

The **R** indicates that it is a rule. If an address matches the LHS of the rule, then the RHS replaces the address. When there is a match, the rule is reapplied until it fails. The syntax for the pattern matching tokens for the LHS is summarized in Figure 15.4.

FIGURE 15.4[5]

LHS pattern matching tokens		
Token	Debug Symbol	Meaning
$*	^P	Match 0 or more tokens
$+	^Q	Match 1 or more tokens
$–	^R	Match exactly 1 token
$=*X*	^S*X*	Match any token in class *X*
$~*X*	^T*X*	Match any token NOT in class *X*

[5]Snatched from Eric.

The debug symbol above shows what is printed to represent each pattern matching token in a rule when **sendmail** is run in debug mode.

The pattern matching for the left-hand side uses a greedy algorithm, digesting as many of the nonliteral (indefinite) tokens as it possibly can, until it hits a literal token that matches. Figure 15.5 gives sample LHS rules each applied to the same address: evi%rupertsberg@boulder.colorado.edu, and the values of the indefinite tokens, $1, $2, etc., relative to that rule. Each rule is applied only once, since the RHS is unspecified.

FIGURE 15.5

Tokens and the LHS		
LHS rule	Indefinite tokens	Comments
$*	$1=evi%rupertsberg@boulder.colorado.edu	Matches
$+	$1=evi%rupertsberg@boulder.colorado.edu	Matches
$-		Does not match
$+@$+	$1=evi%rupertsberg, $2=boulder.colorado.edu	Matches
$+%$+	$1=evi, $2=rupertsberg@boulder.colorado.edu	Matches
$-%$+	$1=evi, $2=rupertsberg@boulder.colorado.edu	Matches
$+%$-		Does not match, >1 token after %
$+@$W.$D	$1=evi%rupertsberg	Matches, $W.$D are literal tokens
$-!$+		Does not match, no !
$+.$+	$1=evi%rupertsberg@boulder, $2=colorado.edu	Matches, $1 stops at first .
$+.$+.$=T	$1=evi%rupertsberg@boulder, $2=colorado, $3=edu	Matches, class T counts

The RHS of a rule can contain any of the tokens matched from the LHS, arbitrary text, and some special symbols as well. These are summarized in Figure 15.6.

FIGURE 15.6[6]

RHS special symbols		
Token	Debug Symbol	Meaning
$*n*	^U*n*	Use token *n* from the LHS
$>*n*	^Y *n*	Call ruleset *n* (like a subroutine call)
$#*mailer*	^V *mailer*	Resolve to *mailer*
$@*host*	^W *host*	Specify *host* to *mailer*
$:*user*	^X *user*	Specify *user* to *mailer*
$[*hostname*$]	^] *hostname*	Canonicalize *hostname* as in **gethostent**(3)
$@	^W	As a prefix, terminates ruleset (like *return;* in C)
$:	^X	As a prefix, terminates current rule (like *break;* in C)

[6] Snatched from Eric.

The $@ and $: prefixes are used to control evaluation and to avoid infinite loops when an address needs to be massaged and then sent back through the same ruleset again. The $@ terminates the current ruleset and returns with the rest of the RHS. The $: terminates the current rule, but the ruleset continues; it is stripped before continuing to avoid further application of the rule. Recall that rules are reapplied when there is a successful match, unless overridden by the $: on the RHS. The $[token asks the name server (see Chapter 14: *Networking under BSD*) to resolve the hostname following it and look for an MX (mail exchanger) record for the best routing. MX records allow mail to use the dynamic routing supported by the BIND system so that mail can be delivered through an alternate route (if one exists) when the preferred route is down. As the old post office slogan says, "The mail must go through."

Armed with this friendly notation, let's look at some examples. In Figure 15.7, we have shown the rule and then its effect on several addresses, both those that match and those that don't match. The first example for any rule is a typical successful application of the rule. The LHS of the first rule matches any number of tokens ($*), followed by an "@", followed by the variable $w, which is predefined by **sendmail** to mean this host. The address evi@boulder[7] matches this rule with the "evi" corresponding to the $*, the "@" matching itself, and "boulder" being $w. It is rewritten, according to the rule, as $1 (the token matching $*, here "evi"), an @, the $w (boulder), a ".", and finally $D, which has been defined as the domain of this machine (Colorado.EDU). The next application of this same rule also matches, with $* matching the multiple tokens "evi%dwim." The next two applications do not match, the first because $w is not ucbvax, and the second because there is no"@" in the address.

The second rule in Figure 15.7 uses the $- notation, which matches a single token. Thus the first address succeeds, but the second does not, because while "spot" matches $- and :: is OK, "evi@boulder" does not match $-. It would match either $+ or $*, however.

FIGURE 15.7

Examples of rewriting rules and their application				
LHS	RHS	Address In	Address Out	Comments
R$*@$w	$1@$w.$D	evi@boulder	evi@boulder.Colorado.EDU	$w is this host
		evi%dwim@boulder	evi%dwim@boulder.Colorado.EDU	$D is this domain
		eric@ucbvax	eric@ucbvax	Does not match
		vaxa::kjk	vaxa::kjk	Does not match
R$-::$-	$2@$1	vaxa::kjk	kjk@vaxa	DECNET syntax
		spot::evi@boulder	spot::evi@boulder	Does not match
		evi@boulder	evi@boulder	Does not match
R$+<@$=A>	$@$1<@$w.$D>	evi<@anchor>	evi<@boulder.Colorado.EDU>	hide localness
		evi<@vaxf>	evi<@vaxf>	Does not match
		blia!eric	blia!eric	Does not match

[7] This is a slight white lie, since the config file we are referencing runs the nameserver and therefore has the domain as part of $w.

The third rule illustrates the use of a class. The Class A (defined in the sample config file in Appendix J) contains the machine "anchor" but not the machine "vaxf", thus @$=A matches @anchor but does not match @vaxf. This rule is used to hide the local structure and make addresses from local machines behind boulder go out to the rest of the world as user@boulder.Colorado.EDU independent of the local machine of origin.

One of the major pitfalls in dealing with the config file is that the address you build a special rule for is often rewritten several times before it even reaches your rule. As a result, when it finally gets there it doesn't match. The rulesets are applied in a specific order, and rules are applied sequentially within the ruleset. But rulesets can be called recursively, directly or indirectly; the $>*n* (*n* = ruleset number) does a subroutine call, the $@ prefix does a return, and the $: prefix does a break. The path an address takes through the config file is often not clear.

Ruleset 3 is always applied first and adds the < > around the relevant host domain to help parse the address. It often calls other rulesets; for example, in our configuration file in Appendix J, ruleset 3 calls ruleset 8. Ruleset 0, which decides where a message is going, is invoked after ruleset 3. It calls ruleset 3 once and then calls rulesets 7 and 6 before finally resolving the destination to a {mailer, host, user} triple. With this bouncing between rulesets, it's no wonder your poor little address is unrecognizable by the time it reaches the new rule you wrote for it. Figure 15.10 provides a roadmap to the rules and the order in which they are applied, corresponding to the sample config file in Appendix J.

sendmail contains very powerful debugging and trace code to help track addresses through the config file (see Section 15.4).

15.3.4 Mailers

Many standard mailer descriptions are included in the generic sendmail.cf file that comes with BSD UNIX. Figure 15.8 shows the more common ones and a couple of local ones.

The first column is the name of the mailer. In the config file a mailer is specified by the string M*mailername* beginning a line (Lines #408, 426, 478, etc. in our example file). The second column is the program to be called as delivery agent. [IPC] refers to the interprocess communication in BSD networking, for which **sendmail** itself is the delivery agent. The third column is the set of flags to be passed to the mailer. These are the same flags that are in the conditional definitions of header lines for messages (Line #143). There are too many flag options, although many are quite simple and are used just to format the headers for a particular mail system. The list of mailer options

FIGURE 15.8

Mailer specifications				
Name	Program	Flags	Arguments	Used for
local	**/bin/mail**	DFlmnrs	mail -d $u	Mail on this machine
prog	**/bin/sh**	DFMels	sh -c $u	Mail to a program (stdin)
uucp	**/usr/bin/uux**	CDRMUhmsu	uux - -gC -a$f $h!rmail ($u)	**uucp** neighbor
palias	**/usr/local/etc/uumail**	CDFMSUhsu	uumail -f $g $h!$u	Pathalias **uucp**
uusndmail	[IPC]	CDFMRhmsu	uux - -gC -z -a$f $h!\ sendmail (-f $g $u)	SMTP via **uucp**
csnet	[IPC]	DFLMPRXemsu	IPC $h	CSNET via Internet
lclsmtp	[IPC]	CDFMXmsu	IPC $h	Local SMTP
nonlclsmtp	[IPC]	DFLMPRXemsu	IPC $h	The Internet

is detailed in the **sendmail** installation document. The fourth column shows the arguments used in calling the delivery program.

15.3.5 Parameters

sendmail has several parameters that are compiled into the code which you may wish to tune. The ones most commonly bumped into are listed in Figure 15.9 with their default values.

A more complete list of the **sendmail** parameters is in the *Sendmail Installation and Operation Guide*; the complete list is in the file conf.h in the **sendmail** source directory. If you need to change a parameter, edit the file conf.h in the **sendmail** source directory and recompile; a simple **make** should do it.

15.4 Testing and debugging

sendmail provides extensive debugging facilities, using a two-dimensional debug flag and debug level scheme to specify both a topic and the amount of information to display. If **sendmail** is invoked with the **-d***ff.nn* flag debugging output is directed to the screen (stderr). The debug level *ff.nn* (21.00-21.99 for rulesets) determines how much output you see. Special testing procedures exist for the rewriting rules as well.

FIGURE 15.9

sendmail's parameters		
Parameter	Default value	Description
MAXPV	40	Maximum number of parameters to a mailer. This limits the number of simultaneous recipients.
MAXLINE	1024	Max line length, for example, an alias line.
MAXRWSETS	30	Maximum number of rewriting rulesets, ruleset names cannot exceed MAXRWSETS-1.

15.4.1 Testing rewriting rules

sendmail can be run in test mode, in which only address rewriting is shown:

sendmail -bt -C*config-file-name*

In this mode, you enter the rulesets you want to test followed by an address; for example:

2,13,4 blia!eric

Ruleset 3 is always applied first, even if you don't request it, followed by those specified, in this case, rulesets 2, 13, and 4, in that order. To see where the message is really going, use ruleset 0. To see the exact effect of a single rule, you can make a ruleset containing just that rule or turn on debugging (see Section 15.4.2). The output of **sendmail -bt** with the config file in Appendix J and input **2,13,4 blia!eric** and **0 blia!eric** follows.

```
% /usr/lib/sendmail -bt
ADDRESS TEST MODE
Enter <ruleset> <address>
> 2,13,4 blia!eric
rewrite: ruleset  3   input: "blia" "!" "eric"
rewrite: ruleset  3 returns: "eric" "<" "@" "blia" "." "UUCP" ">"
rewrite: ruleset  2   input: "eric" "<" "@" "blia" "." "UUCP" ">"
rewrite: ruleset  2 returns: "eric" "<" "@" "blia" "." "UUCP" ">"
rewrite: ruleset 13   input: "eric" "<" "@" "blia" "." "UUCP" ">"
rewrite: ruleset 13 returns: "blia" "!" "eric"
rewrite: ruleset  4   input: "blia" "!" "eric"
rewrite: ruleset  4 returns: "blia" "!" "eric"
> 0 blia!eric
rewrite: ruleset  3   input: "blia" "!" "eric"
rewrite: ruleset  3 returns: "eric" "<" "@" "blia" "." "UUCP" ">"
rewrite: ruleset  0   input: "eric" "<" "@" "blia" "." "UUCP" ">"
rewrite: ruleset  3   input: "eric" "@" "blia" "." "UUCP"
rewrite: ruleset  3 returns: "eric" "<" "@" "blia" "." "UUCP" ">"
rewrite: ruleset  7   input: "eric" "<" "@" "blia" "." "UUCP" ">"
rewrite: ruleset  7 returns: "eric" "<" "@" "blia" "." "UUCP" ">"
rewrite: ruleset  6   input: "eric" "<" "@" "blia" "." "UUCP" ">"
rewrite: ruleset  6 returns: "eric" "<" "@" "blia" "." "UUCP" ">"
rewrite: ruleset  0 returns: "^V" "uucp" "^W" "blia" "^X" "eric"
```

The recipient address starts as blia!eric and ends up that way in this case. Ruleset 0 resolves the address to the mailer (^V) uucp, the host (^W) blia, and the user (^X) eric.

The sender's address would traverse rulesets 1, 12, and 4 for the **uucp** mailer and would be rewritten as follows:

```
> 1,12,4 tigger!evi
rewrite: ruleset  3   input: "tigger" "!" "evi"
rewrite: ruleset  3 returns: "evi" "<" "@" "tigger" "." "UUCP" ">"
rewrite: ruleset  1   input: "evi" "<" "@" "tigger" "." "UUCP" ">"
rewrite: ruleset  1 returns: "evi" "<" "@" "tigger" "." "UUCP" ">"
rewrite: ruleset 12   input: "evi" "<" "@" "tigger" "." "UUCP" ">"
rewrite: ruleset 12 returns: "boulder" "!" "evi"
rewrite: ruleset  4   input: "boulder" "!" "evi"
rewrite: ruleset  4 returns: "boulder" "!" "evi"
```

In this case the local machine tigger is hidden behind the machine boulder by ruleset 12 (Line #439).

15.4.2 Debug levels in sendmail

sendmail has very good tracing support. There are umpteen levels of debugging output you can choose. To see more information regarding the rewriting rules just tested, try:

sendmail -bt -C*config-file-name* **-d21.99**

Pages and pages of output go zooming off your screen, 686 lines to be exact, explaining in detail what the ten preceding lines summarize. The output contains the debugging symbols shown in Figures 15.4 and 15.6 to express each part of a rewriting rule. A sample for a rule that fails and for one that matches is shown next.

```
Version 5.58
ADDRESS TEST MODE
Enter <ruleset> <address>
> 0 blia!eric
 ...
rewrite: ruleset  3   input: "blia" "!" "eric"
-----trying rule: "^P" "<" "^Q" ">" "^P"                    (Line #178)
ap="blia", rp="^P"
ap="blia", rp="<"
ap="!", rp="<"
ap="eric", rp="<"
ap=<null>, rp="<"
----- rule fails
 ...
-----trying rule: "^R" "!" "^Q"                              (Line #194)
```

```
ap="blia", rp="^R"
ap="!", rp="!"
ap="eric", rp="^Q"
-----rule matches: "^W" "^U2" "<" "@" "^U1" "." "UUCP" ">"
$2: 7fffe49f="eric"
$1: 7fffe498="blia"
rewritten as: "eric" "<" "@" "blia" "." "UUCP" ">"
rewrite: ruleset  3 returns: "eric" "<" "@" "blia" "." "UUCP" ">"
rewrite: ruleset  0   input: "eric" "<" "@" "blia" "." "UUCP" ">"
 ...
```

To make this easier to understand, we repeat the meanings of the common debug symbols ^P, ^Q, etc., and their corresponding rewriting tokens.

From the left-hand side:

$*	^P	0 or more tokens
$+	^Q	1 or more tokens
$-	^R	exactly 1 token
$=*X*	^S*X*	token from class *X*

From the right-hand side:

$*n*	^U*n*	the *n*th token
$>*n*	^Y*n*	go to ruleset *n*
$@	^W	break out of ruleset
$:	^X	break out of rule, continue ruleset

"ap" is the address pointer and follows the address being matched; "rp" is the rewrite pointer and follows the rule itself, sliding along as it must if the rule specifies $* or $+, which are variable length. Notice that the right-hand side of the rule on Line #194 specifies the $@, which is indicated as ^W, and which causes ruleset 3 to terminate, resulting in ruleset 0 being called next.

With debugging set to level 21.99, you can see each rule applied and each token matched in infinite detail. Level 21.15 is also a useful level; it shows each rule being applied and its fail/match status without each token being identified. The output produced by the same command with debug level set to -d21.15 is only 210 lines; an excerpt follows:

```
Version 5.58
ADDRESS TEST MODE
Enter <ruleset> <address>
> 0 blia!eric
rewrite: ruleset  3   input: "blia" "!" "eric"
 ...
```

```
-----trying rule: "^P" "<" "^P" "<" "^Q" ">" "^P" ">" "^P" (Line #177)
----- rule fails
-----trying rule: "^P" "<" "^Q" ">" "^P"                     (Line #178)
----- rule fails
-----trying rule: "^Q" "at" "^Q"                            (Line #179)
----- rule fails
 ...
-----trying rule: "^R" "!" "^Q"                             (Line #194)
-----rule matches: "^W" "^U2" "<" "@" "^U1" "." "UUCP" ">"
$2: 7fffe49f="eric"
$1: 7fffe498="blia"
rewritten as: "eric" "<" "@" "blia" "." "UUCP" ">"
rewrite: ruleset  3 returns: "eric" "<" "@" "blia" "." "UUCP" ">"
rewrite: ruleset  0   input: "eric" "<" "@" "blia" "." "UUCP" ">"
```

A prerequisite to understanding the rewriting rules, and therefore the config file, is understanding which rules are applied to which addresses and when. For example, mail messages using the config file in Appendix J will apply rulesets as shown in Figure 15.10. Another config file may have different mailer-specific rulesets, but you should be able to construct such a table to use as a roadmap to debugging. Note that the rulesets are in the order applied and do not contain any references to rulesets called as subroutines or called recursively. The exact rulesets called from other rulesets are context sensitive and depend on the address being parsed.

FIGURE 15.10

Roadmap to the rulesets			
Mailer	Decide destination	Sender address	Recipient address
lclsmtp	3,0	3,1,20,4	3,2,21,4
nonlclsmtp	3,0	3,1,14,4	3,2,4
local	3,0	3,1,10,4	3,2,11,4
uucp	3,0	3,1,12,4	3,2,13,4
csnet	3,0	3,1,18,4	3,2,4
uusndmail	3,0	3,1,24,4	3,2,25,4

15.4.3 The –v flag to mail

mail can be run with the **–v** flag which shows the steps that **sendmail** takes as it delivers the message. An example of the output produced by **mail –v** executed on the machine boulder, using the config file in Appendix J, follows:

mail –v evi@okeeffe.berkeley.edu
Subject: hi
<Control-D>
Cc:
Null message body; hope that's ok

```
evi@okeeffe.berkeley.edu... Connecting to okeeffe.berkeley.edu.nonlclsmtp...
220 okeeffe.Berkeley.EDU Sendmail 5.60/1.29 ready at Tue, 30 Aug 88 17:37:02 PDT
>>> HELO boulder.Colorado.EDU
250 okeeffe.Berkeley.EDU Hello boulder.Colorado.EDU, pleased to meet you
>>> MAIL From:<evi@boulder.Colorado.EDU>
250 <evi@boulder.Colorado.EDU>... Sender ok
>>> RCPT To:<evi@okeeffe.berkeley.edu>
250 <evi@okeeffe.berkeley.edu>... Recipient ok
>>> DATA
354 Enter mail, end with "." on a line by itself
>>> .
250 Ok
>>> QUIT
221 okeeffe.Berkeley.EDU closing connection
evi@okeeffe.berkeley.edu... Sent
```

As you can see, the **sendmail** on boulder.Colorado.EDU connected to the **sendmail** on the machine okeeffe.Berkeley.EDU and talked the SMTP protocol to negotiate the exchange of the message. All **sendmail** processes listen for connection requests from other **sendmail** processes across the Internet on port 25.

15.4.4 Talk to SMTP directly

The SMTP (simple mail transport protocol) is easy enough to use directly in debugging the mail system. It is used with the **telnet** command on port 25. Some SMTP commands are:

HELO – to start a conversation
MAIL From: <reverse-path> – initiate a mail transaction, identify sender
RCPT To: <forward-path> – identify recipient
DATA – begin the message, terminate with a "."
QUIT – to end the conversation
HELP – get help

There are only 14 commands in the whole language so it is quite easy to learn and use. It is not case sensitive. Complete specification of SMTP is contained in RFC 821 by Jon Postel of ISI at the University of Southern California.

15.5 Security

sendmail has long had a reputation for creating security loopholes. The UNIX virus[8] which stormed the U.S. in November, 1988 attempted

[8] We use the term "virus" here loosely, as it was used by the press during the program's rampage. Strictly speaking, the program was a “worm” and not a virus. System-cracking software can only be called a virus if it operates by recoding other programs and using them for its own purposes.

(successfully in many cases) to exploit weaknesses in **sendmail**, although it used other break-in methods as well. Security problems in **sendmail** have been fixed in some current releases, but many vendors' UNIX products still use older, uncorrected versions.

Because of the existence of these unprotected systems, we cannot ethically describe the security problems associated with **sendmail** (or any of UNIX, for that matter) in detail. Just be aware that mail is not secure.

It is possible to impersonate any user in mail messages. Thus, be careful if mail messages are the authorization vehicle in your organization for things like keys, access card authorizations, and money. You should warn administrative users of this fact and suggest that if they see mail, apparently from a person in authority, asking that unreasonable privileges be given to an unusual person that they verify the validity of the mail message. Requests authorizing a grand-master key for an undergraduate student might be suspect!

16

Uucp

16.1 An overview of uucp

Uucp (UNIX-to-UNIX copy) is a simple intermachine communication system that can be run over direct serial lines, network connections, or ordinary telephone lines. It supports two operations: file copying and remote command execution. Thus, uucp can be thought of as a kind of asynchronous Ethernet that only supports the **rcp** and **rsh** commands.

Remote command execution requests are handled by the **uux** program, and file copying is handled by the **uusend** and **uucp** programs. Don't be confused by the fact that "uucp" is the name of both the entire system and one of its component utilities: We will always boldface the command.

The primary use of uucp is to act as a transport mechanism for electronic mail and Usenet news. It is rare for users to take direct advantage of uucp's facilities, both because it is finicky and hard to use, and because better methods of transferring files exist.

Uucp does not support third-party forwarding of files or of command sequences; you may only communicate with machines to which you have established direct connections. Transactions may involve more than one directly connected host, however. For example, you can copy a file directly from one neighbor to another.

Since third-party forwarding is essential for both mail and news, these systems provide their own forwarding facilities. Each time a mail message or news article makes a "hop" from one machine to another, it must reenter the appropriate software system for further routing. Both mail and news make use of remote command execution rather than file copying — mail messages and news articles are sent as standard input to special mail- or news-reception programs which determine their ultimate destination. The reception programs may either grab them for local use or feed them back to uucp for retransmission.

Direct uucp connections are fast, but may involve a long distance phone call if the destination is far away. It is possible to economize by making calls only in the middle of the night and using only low-price long distance carriers. Indirect uucp "connections" are usually free, but are of course slower and less reliable. When your jobs are routed indirectly, you are depending upon the system administrator of each intervening host to have properly configured that host's software. This may sound somewhat risky, but the system works well in general.

The price you must pay for all of this free forwarding is to return to other systems the same favors and services that they extend to you, even at the expense of an occasional long distance phone call. This means maintaining good uucp connectivity with other sites, publishing information about your connections in the uucp maps, keeping your system in working condition, and keeping your system secure so that uucp traffic is not intercepted or interfered with.

If you are not prepared to devote enough time and money to hold up your end of things, you should consider leaving uucp uninstalled. However, unless you already have access to a high-speed network such as ARPANET, or don't have a reasonably fast modem, there's probably no reason for you to miss out on this great opportunity; setting up and maintaining uucp is quite easy, and its benefits are enormous.

16.2 Flavors of uucp

There are two main flavors of uucp: standard and HoneyDanBer. Some systems are supplied with HoneyDanBer rather than standard uucp. We don't explicitly cover HoneyDanBer uucp in this chapter, but it is similar to the standard uucp, and much of the material here is applicable to both. As a rule, uucp shows little variation from UNIX to UNIX. The uucp protocols are standardized, so any version of uucp can communicate with any other.

16.3 Uucp addresses

A uucp address generally consists of a list of names separated by exclamation points. The last name is a user name, filename, or command name, depending upon whether the address is a mail address, file copy address, or remote command execution request. The other names are hostnames. The hostname list specifies a sequence of uucp hops which can be followed to get to the appropriate machine. If the address is to be used with a native **uucp** command, there can usually only be one host specified.

For example, suppose you're at the site "hao" and want to send mail to Eric Allman at Berkeley.[1] "hao" doesn't have a direct connection with "ucbvax", Berkeley's master mail machine, but it does have a connection with "hplabs", which talks to "ucbvax" over a leased line. To get mail to "ucbvax", you need to specify that it go first to "hplabs", and that "hplabs" then pass along the job to "ucbvax". The complete mail path to Eric is thus

```
hplabs!ucbvax!eric
```

Extremely long uucp paths are uncommon. Most computers can be reached from just about anywhere with under ten hops. The reason for this is the existence of a number of important uucp relay sites that act as a central connectivity ring. Though these sites are usually called the uucp backbone, a more appropriate biological analogy is to the major veins and arteries of the circulatory system. The connections between the backbone sites are like the blood vessels between the heart and the legs: reliable, long distance, high volume.

There are under a hundred backbone sites, but it is rare to be more than three hops away from one. Unfortunately, the backbone sites are not distributed evenly around the world, or even around the United States. Most of them are concentrated in the northeast and western areas of the US, with a few in between these extremes. There are few foreign backbone sites outside of Europe.

[1] Eric Allman is the author of the **-me** macros for **troff**, with which this book was typeset.

16.4 Uucp data transport - the uucico program

All intermachine uucp communication is managed by the **uucico** (UNIX-to-UNIX copy-in copy-out) program. There are a variety of programs in the uucp system for queuing requests and querying the state of connections, but only **uucico** can make actual transactions.

uucico can operate in two modes: master and slave. At any given time in a uucp conversation, one of the cooperating **uucico** processes plays each role; however, the two processes can and do freely change roles at various points in the transaction so that large outgoing or incoming jobs do not block data flowing in the other direction for long periods of time.

In master mode, **uucico** attempts to deal with requests that have been queued on the local system. Satisfying these requests may involve sending a file to the slave site, requesting a file from the slave site, or requesting execution of a program at the slave site. Note that the designation of master and slave is independent of the current sender or receiver of information: If the master has requested a file from the slave, it can and will be both the master and the receiver at the same time. In slave mode, **uucico** listens to the orders issued by the master and attempts to carry them out.

To initiate a conversation, a **uucico** process on one machine must call up another machine and start up a remote **uucico** process. The calling **uucico** starts out in master mode, and starts up the remote **uucico** in slave mode. To gain access to the remote system, the calling **uucico** follows a script set by the system administrator that guides it through whatever protocols are needed to enter its login name and password on the remote machine.

We suggest that you make the login names on your system consist of the name of the remote system prefixed with a capital "U". If the remote name is too long, you must clip it to eight characters or fewer. For example, if you were setting up your system to allow calls from the system "cranberry", you'd make the login name "Ucranber". Uucp logins must have their shell specified as **/usr/lib/uucp/uucico** in the /etc/passwd file so that a complete **uucico** connection is formed immediately upon login.

As soon as the two **uucico**'s are connected, they will negotiate a protocol to use during the ensuing conversation. Only one protocol is currently supported for each transport medium, so this negotiation is unlikely to produce any violent dissension between the two participants. The current uucp modem protocol is fully error-correcting, so transferred data are guaranteed to arrive at their destination intact.[2]

[2] Ha ha.

16.5 User-level uucp

There are only three programs which can queue uucp requests:

- **uucp** - copy files between hosts
- **uux** - execute commands on a remote host
- **uusend** - send a file to an indirectly connected host

The following sections describe each of these commands in detail.

16.5.1 The uucp command

The syntax of the **uucp** command is identical to that of the **cp** command, except that the locations of files are specified using uucp paths rather than local filenames. Each path begins with a system name, followed by an exclamation point and a remote pathname. If the system name in the path is null, the filename is assumed to refer to a file on the local system and the exclamation point is optional. The remote pathname must be specified in one of the following formats:

- A full pathname (e.g., /usr/dict/words)
- A pathname beginning with ~*user*/ (e.g., ~evi/proposal)
- A pathname beginning with ~/ (e.g., ~/explain)
- A relative pathname (e.g., bin/bust-bladder)

Using tildes ("~") to specify pathnames should be familiar to C-shell users, as **csh** supports a similar syntax. "~/" denotes the user's home directory, and "~*user*/" denotes the home directory of *user*. All tildes are interpreted on the remote system, so these expressions may mean something slightly different from what you expect. Pathnames beginning with "~/" are interpreted to start at the home directory of the current user, but since the current user will be not you but something like "Ucranber", this will expand to the directory /usr/spool/uucppublic, the uucp public access directory. We'll talk more about this in a few paragraphs.

The full pathname syntax is quite straightforward: The name is looked up in its entirety on the given system. Watch out for the relative pathname syntax, though; **uucp** always inserts the absolute pathname of the *local* directory from which it is run in front of the relative pathname. Thus, if you **cd** to the directory /staff/garth and execute the command

```
uucp akelei!files/exabyte exabyte
```

your request will cause **uucp** to try and copy the file /staff/garth/files/exabyte from the system "akelei" into /staff/garth/exabyte on the local machine, probably not what you want. (C-shell note: **csh** uses both "!" and "~" as metacharacters, so they must be backslashed on the command line if they are to reach **uucp** unmolested. This detail has been omitted for clarity in the command line examples for this chapter.)

The **uucp** command accepts a number of flags that modify its behavior in minor ways. You can have it send you mail when the copy is complete, force it to make a copy of local files for its own use rather than use the actual files themselves (in case you want to delete the file immediately), allow it to create directories as needed for storage of the transferred files, etc. It does not accept the **-r** flag to copy directory hierarchies recursively.

One thing that you must keep in mind when using any **uucp** command is that all the operations you request will be performed by processes with UID's and GID's different from your own. This essentially means that the files you want to manipulate must be world-readable and/or world-writable.

For example, if you want to copy a file from a remote system into your home directory, you must give write permission on your home directory to everyone. To copy files from the local system to a remote system, you must give read permission on them to the world. Files that **uucp** creates are owned by "uucp," not by you, no matter where they are located. If you have **uucp** copy a file into your home directory, you will probably be able to read it but not modify it. You will have to copy the file to a different filename and then delete the original (which you will be able to do because you have write permission on your home directory, even if not on the file).

It is exactly for this reason that the /usr/spool/uucppublic directory exists. It is analogous to the systemwide /tmp directory in that its permissions are set to allow all access to everybody, but it is intended for use primarily when performing **uucp** operations. You can do all the permission fudging that you need right in this directory without worrying about having to change the permissions on your home directory back and forth all the time. In addition, you'll always be able to have **uucp** deposit transferred files here for you to pick up.

16.5.2 The uusend command

uusend is like **uucp** with three important differences. First, **uusend** may only be used to send files from the local site to a remote site, not to request a file from somewhere else. Second, **uusend** can only handle one file at a time. If you want to transport a number of files you must issue a separate **uusend** command for each one. Third, and most important, **uusend** accepts a mail-type network pathname for the remote address, which may specify an arbitrary *chain* of hosts through which the file is to be routed.

The **uusend** command cannot be counted as one of the basic **uucp** commands, since it runs on top of **uux** (see the next section). It is, however, a standard **uucp** utility. The reason for **uusend**'s inability to request files as well as send them is more a matter of security than laxity on the part of the implementor. Sites to which you are directly connected allow requests because they know who you are and have some confidence in your site. Sites with which you have no real relationship cannot be expected to extend this same courtesy.

Let's look at an example. The command

```
uusend /users/scott/.cshrc pyramid!ucbvax!/usr/spool/uucppublic/new.cshrc
```

asks that the local file /users/scott/.cshrc be sent to the system "ucbvax" and stored in the file /usr/spool/uucppublic/new.cshrc. The site "pyramid" acts only as a relay.

16.5.3 The uux command

The **uux** program is used to initiate remote command execution. **uux** accepts shell-style command strings in which each file or command name is a network path, specified using the same syntax used by the **uucp** command. **uux** understands the shell metacharacters ">", "<", "|", and ";". Since the command string must appear to **uux** as a single argument, it should be properly quoted on the command line.

For example, the command

```
uux '!diff hao!/usr/jack/rabbit nbires!/research/hare > !differences'
```

invokes the local command **diff** on the files /usr/jack/rabbit from "hao" and /research/hare from "nbires", sending the standard output of the command to the file "differences" on the local machine.

16.6 Setting up uucp

There are two kinds of tasks you must do for **uucp**: those that are done only once when the system is set up, and those that you must do every time you acquire a new **uucp** neighbor.

The once-only tasks are:

- Locate the uucp software.
- Create the uucp login, give correct modes to files.
- Connect your modems.

- Describe your modems to uucp.
- Establish low-cost telephone service.
- Enter telephone access codes in the L-dialcodes file.
- Prepare your USERFILE and L.cmds files.
- Establish an initial connection.
- Reconfigure your mail system to use uucp.
- Test uucp mail.
- Publish your uucp data.

The tasks that need to be repeated are:

- Make a login for the connection.
- Make an L.sys entry for the connection.
- Edit /usr/lib/crontab to reflect the desired calling schedule.
- Debug the connection.
- Publish the connection in the uucp maps.

16.6.1 Initial uucp configuration

Setting up uucp is not difficult, but some of the steps can be time-consuming. We've presented the steps in the order that they should be completed, rather than the order they should be started. Read through all steps before beginning.

16.6.1.1 Locate the uucp software

There are three directories of importance to uucp: /usr/spool/uucp (for storage of jobs and temporary files), /usr/lib/uucp (for storage of executables and configuration files), and /usr/spool/uucppublic (for use by users). Most of the user-level commands associated with uucp are kept in /usr/bin. If you are lucky, you will find most of these already in place. Your /usr/lib/uucp directory should contain at least the following files:

```
L-devices   L-dialcodes   L.aliases   L.cmds   L.sys
USERFILE    uucico        uuclean     uuxqt
```

The uucp naming conventions are strange. Programs are handled quite reasonably, but chaos reigns in the area of configuration file naming. Why is it that some configuration files start with "L-" while others start with "L.", and what does the "L" stand for anyway? And why "USERFILE"? We don't know the answers.

If the directory does exist but contains only the commands **uucico**, **uuclean**, and **uuxqt**, then your system is probably set up, but you will not have any

FIGURE 16.1

Files in the /usr/lib/uucp directory			
Filename	Type	Purpose	HoneyDanBer
L-devices	Config	Specifies types of available modems	Dialers,Devices
L-dialcodes	Config	Phone number and access code database	Dialcodes
L.aliases	Config	Deals with hosts that change their names	
L.cmds	Config	Commands available via **uuxqt**	
L.sys	Config	List of uucp neighbors, login scripts	Systems
USERFILE	Config	Lists access available to remote sites	Permissions
uucico	Program	Manages intermachine communication	**uucico**
uuclean	Program	Cleans up spool directory	**uuclean**
uuxqt	Program	Remote command execution server	**uuxqt**

example configuration files to look at. A brief summary of the purpose of each of these files is presented in Figure 16.1. The last column of the table contains the names of the files in the HoneyDanBer (HDB) system that perform roughly the same function. There is not really a one-to-one mapping, but this should give you some idea of how the systems are related. HoneyDanBer also provides many commands which do not have equivalents in standard uucp.

If your uucp software is not already in place, it is probably not loaded onto the system at all. On some systems, it is considered optional and must be specifically loaded from the distribution tapes when you install the system. Your manuals will explain.

16.6.1.2 Create the uucp login

Everything in /usr/lib/uucp should be owned by the user "uucp", and the programs stored there should be setuid to this account. In addition, /usr/spool/uucp and /usr/spool/uucppublic should also both be owned by uucp. Do an **ls** (with appropriate flags) on the uucp directories — if the ownerships and permissions match those shown in the following example, you are in good shape and can skip on to the next section. Otherwise you will have to patch things up by hand. Don't be disturbed if you are unable to find some of the files listed here; some of them will not exist until the uucp system is in use.

For /usr/lib/uucp, the permissions should be:

```
-rw-r-----  1 uucp     daemon       151 Jan  3  1987 L-devices
-rw-r-----  1 uucp     daemon        20 Jan 12  1987 L-dialcodes
-rw-r-----  1 uucp     daemon       218 Apr  1 00:34 L.aliases
-rw-r-----  1 uucp     daemon       116 Jul 13 23:41 L.cmds
-rw-r-----  1 uucp     daemon      4315 Jul 14 02:05 L.sys
-rw-r-----  1 uucp     daemon         4 Jul 16 18:57 SEQF
-rw-r-----  1 uucp     daemon        42 Jan  4  1987 USERFILE
```

```
---s--x---  1 root     daemon      22528 Jun  7  1986 acucntrl
---s--s--x  1 uucp     daemon     106496 Apr  4 20:05 uucico
---s--x--x  1 uucp     daemon      25600 Jun  7  1986 uuclean
---s--x---  1 uucp     daemon      43008 Jun  7  1986 uuxqt
```

The /usr/spool/uucp directory should have the permissions:

```
drwxr-xr-x 13 uucp     daemon        512 Jul 15 02:32 /usr/spool/uucp
```

Inside /usr/spool/uucp directory, all subdirectories should have permission 775. The log files should have the permissions:

```
-rw-r--r--  1 uucp     daemon         71 Jul 15 23:20 ERRLOG
-rw-rw-r--  1 uucp     daemon     662326 Jul 16 19:25 LOGFILE
-rw-rw-r--  1 uucp     daemon     301847 Jul 16 19:25 SYSLOG
```

/usr/spool/uucppublic should exist, should be owned by the user "uucp" and the group "daemon", and should have the mode 777. There should not necessarily be anything inside it.

If your system does not have the correct permissions or ownerships, you may even need to add the "uucp" login to /etc/passwd before you can continue. Put an asterisk in this login's password field, since no one will be using it to actually log in.[3] The home directory of the "uucp" login should be the /usr/spool/uucppublic directory, and its shell should be /usr/lib/uucico. The UID of "uucp" should be within the UID range that you reserve for pseudo-users.

16.6.1.3 Connect your modems

If you don't already have your system's modem or modems connected and tested, now is the time to do it. Uucp uses modems in the same way that other modem-using programs do, so things should be set up as described in Chapter 9: *Installing Terminals and Modems.*

The device file for modems that are to be used with uucp should be owned by the user "uucp" and the group "daemon", and should have permissions 664; these ownerships and permissions are also those correct for use with the **tip** and **cu** programs. Either one can be used to verify that the modem is connected correctly and that you can dial into other sites.

[3] Some sites use the "uucp" login as the generic login for all clients. This works, and there is nothing wrong with it, but we advocate giving each remote system its own login. This helps to control access to your system and lets you disable one site's login without disabling everyone else's.

If you plan to use the same modem as both a dial-in port and a dial-out line for uucp, there are some additional tasks that need to be performed. Refer to Chapter 9.

16.6.1.4 Describe your modems to uucp

You know exactly what kind of modems you have and at what speeds they can communicate, but there is no way for uucp to find out this information without your help. To tell uucp about your equipment, you need to edit the file /usr/lib/uucp/L-devices.

The implementors of uucp have already done most of the detail work for you; uucp has programmed into it the knowledge of how to use a variety of modems. All you need to do is give it a shove in the right direction and it will be off and running.

All of the uucp configuration files (L-devices included) accept a standard format for comments and continuation lines. Any line beginning with a "#" character is ignored, and any line ending with a backslash is joined with the following line before interpretation.

Aside from comment lines, each line in the L-devices file represents one piece of equipment that can be used to connect with other computers. Up to now we've been assuming that this is a modem, but uucp can also make use of a number of some other communication modes, such as dedicated serial lines, Ethernets, and various data switches.

The format of a line in the L-devices file is:

Caller Device Call_Unit Class Dialer Chat

Each of the fields has the following meaning:

Caller

The caller field indicates only what type of connection the line references. For autodialing modems, this field always contains the word "ACU", which stands for "Auto Call Unit." The other codes that may appear here are shown in Figure 16.2.

Device

The device field specifies the name of the device file through which the connection is to be made. For a modem this is often something like /dev/cua0, a link to the appropriate terminal port.

Call unit

The call unit is optional, and contains the pathname of a device file to be used for performing operations on the actual modem, as opposed to the device to which data is to be sent. Theoretically, a true auto call unit

FIGURE 16.2

L-devices connection-type codes	
Code	Meaning
ACU	Autodialing modem (Hayes, etc.)
DIR	Direct connection, usually RS-232
DK	AT&T Datakit
MICOM	Micom terminal switch
PAD	X.25 PAD connection
PCP	GTE Telenet PC Pursuit
SYTEK	Sytek dedicated modem port
TCP	BSD TCP/IP or 3Com UNET

uses separate device files for data communication and modem control; in real life this paradigm is seldom implemented. If you are using one of the standard modems which does not have a separate modem control file, put the word "unused" in this field.

Class

The class field specifies the communication speed of a modem, the line speed of a direct connection, or the port number of a network connection. Modems that are capable of communicating at more than one speed should have multiple entries in the L-devices file, each entry differing only in the class field.

The class field of an entry may be proceeded by a nonnumeric prefix to distinguish modem properties that are not otherwise addressed. When **uucico** wants to initiate a call to another system, it will look through the L-devices file and attempt to find a match on both the "caller" and "class" fields as specified in other information files. This field is therefore somewhat free-format.

For example, if a particular remote host requires the Vadic modem protocol to be used, the prefix "V" might be used to distinguish modems that can handle this protocol from those that cannot — suppose that you have a modem that can speak both Vadic and Bell protocols, both at either 300 or 1200 baud. You would probably want to make four entries in L-devices, one with a class of "300", one with a class of "1200", one with a class of "V300", and one with a class of "V1200. "

Uucp does not place any particular interpretation on these prefixes; they are used only when attempting to match a device description with a device request from the L.sys file. Feel free to create your own prefixes if you have special needs.

Dialer

This field is applicable only to modems, and identifies their particular brand and model. About 20 different types are supported, and there are separate codes for tone and pulse dialing on modems that support both. Look at your manual page for "L-devices" for a list of these.

Chat

The chat field is a script used to gain access to the communications device if it is necessary to negotiate a data switch or some other such obstacle. Its format is identical to the login script used inside the L.sys file, but since the L-devices scripting mechanism is rarely used, we will delay discussing scripts until Section 16.6.2.

For example, suppose your site has both a Hayes Smartmodem referenced by /dev/cua0 that runs at both 300 and 1200 baud, and a Vadic modem referenced by /dev/cua1 that runs only at 1200 baud. Your L-devices file would look like this:

```
ACU    /dev/cua0    unused    1200     hayestone
ACU    /dev/cua0    unused    300      hayestone
ACU    /dev/cua1    unused    V1200    vadic
```

16.6.1.5 Edit your USERFILE and L.cmds files

The files /usr/lib/uucp/USERFILE and /usr/lib/uucp/L.cmds control what actions other systems may take when in contact with your site. It is *extremely* important that their contents correctly reflect the level of security you wish to impose. It is possible to restrict access so tightly that uucp cannot be used for anything but sending mail (or even tighter!); it is also possible to give your uucp neighbors access equivalent to that of a normal user.

This latter permissiveness is *not recommended* since it essentially gives everyone in the entire world a login on your machine. The danger is not that someone will be able to cause uucp to do destructive things, but rather that they will be able to obtain copies of all your world-readable system files and examine them for weaknesses that might be exploited. Almost all sites place severe limitations on the use of uucp. It is indeed rare to see a site that allows much more than the transmission of mail and news, and the use of simple system statistics programs such as **ps** and **who**.

The format of the USERFILE and L.cmds files is such that permissions can be set on a per-site and per-user basis if it is necessary to allow special access to particular people. This can be quite risky, however, and should be avoided. Our master uucp machine, which maintains about 50 regular uucp contacts, has only one across-the-board set of access permissions for all of its neighbors.

The USERFILE is used to restrict what *files* are available for access, while the L.cmds file is used to restrict what *programs* may be run via **uux**. In addition to restricting the access allowed to remote systems, these files also restrict the access that local users have to the local system when using uucp commands. For example, let's say that your system name is "saturn" and that someone on one of your uucp neighbors executes the command:

uux '!cat saturn!/etc/passwd !myfile | saturn!mail evi'

Permission to execute the **cat** command on the remote system (meaning the system that originated the command) must be granted by the /usr/lib/uucp/L.cmds file on the remote system. Likewise, permission to access the file "myfile" on the remote system must be granted by the remote system's USERFILE. Assuming that this command gets through the remote system OK, its success on saturn depends upon whether or not saturn's USERFILE permits access to the /etc/passwd file and whether or not saturn's L.cmds file allows access to the **mail** command. The argument "evi" in this example is neither a file nor a command, so it can pass through **uux** unmolested.

Format of the USERFILE

Noncomment lines are of the form:

loginname,systemname [c *] pathname ...*

loginname and *systemname* must be separated by only a comma. The other fields may have an arbitrary number of spaces or tabs between them.

When file access permissions are to be determined, this file is read sequentially until a line that fits the appropriate criterion is found. For local **uucp** or **uux** processes, or when **uucico** is run in master mode, the file is searched for a line that has a *loginname* field identical to the login name of the current user in the /etc/passwd file. When **uucico** runs in slave mode, it is the *systemname* field that is examined instead; a line is selected when this field matches the actual name of the remote site, *not* the site's login name (e.g., "cranberry" rather than "Ucranber").

If no matching lines are found, the first line with an empty field in the appropriate spot is used. If there is more than one matching line, the first matching line is used. Either or both of the two first fields may be empty on any line.

The character "c" that follows the *loginname* and *systemname* fields is to be either entered literally or left out. It has meaning only in the case where the program perusing the USERFILE is a slave-mode **uucico** process. If the "c" is present in this case, the connection between the local and remote **uucico**s is broken and the local **uucico** attempts to call the remote system back immediately, using its own concept of the remote system's telephone number. This provides a degree of security against impostors, yet insures that either side of the connection may initiate a conversation at any time.

The *pathname* list consists of a number of pathname prefixes or directory names that complete filenames must begin with to be considered accessible by the remote system. For example, the directory name /usr/spool/uucppublic would allow access to any file within that directory or one of its subdirectories.

To illustrate this point, imagine that there are two other sites that saturn talks to: one called "goodsite" and one called "badsite". You'd like to allow goodsite to access files anywhere in the /usr partition or in /etc, but you want badsite's access to be restricted to /usr/spool/uucppublic. Since goodsite will have access to sensitive information, you want to be sure that it is not impersonated. You resolve to put goodsite on call-back status. Furthermore, imagine that there is a user "iamaspy" on your system whom you suspect of being an industrial spy. You'd like to prevent him from shipping out your system's files, but you want everyone else to have free run of the system. Your USERFILE should look like this:

```
Ugoodsit,goodsite    c  /etc  /usr
Ubadsite,badsite        /usr/spool/uucppublic
iamaspy,unused          /dev/null
,unused                 /
unused,                 /usr/spool/uucppublic
```

The line that gives permissions for badsite is not strictly necessary, since those permissions match the defaults specified for other systems by line five. It is wise to include such a line in case you decide to liberalize the default access permissions. You might forget to rescind badsite's default permissions at that time.

Login and system names specified as "unused" are given to prevent matching of null fields. You would not, of course, use this notation if you talk to a site or have a local user called "unused". Note that it is important to provide the login names of the remote sites as well as their system names, since some remotely executed programs may attempt to forward files or execution requests by executing the **uucp**, **usend**, or **uux** commands.

This example setup is dangerous in several ways. To begin with, you should never, but never, give permissions on /etc or /usr to *anybody* — and certainly not permissions on the root directory! Second, new contacts will by default have access to all files on the system when remote command executions they request cause **uucp**, **uusend**, or **uux** to be executed, because of line four.

It is a shame to let uucp's functionality go to waste, but our advice is to make your USERFILE look like this:

```
                /usr/spool/uucppublic
```

Format of the L.cmds file

The format of the L.cmds file is much simpler and more intuitive than that of the USERFILE. It contains a list of commands whose execution is to be allowed via remote command execution, and, optionally, a list of directories in which to search for these commands. The default directories are /usr/bin, /bin, and /usr/ucb. If you run, or intend to run, news, you should add the directory /usr/new to this list by including a line of the form:

```
PATH=/bin:/usr/bin:/usr/ucb:/usr/new
```

somewhere within the L.cmds file.

Command names in L.cmds are listed one per line, and may have the optional suffixes ",Error" and ",No", indicating that acknowledgment messages are to be sent to the initiator of the command request only in the case of an error, or never, respectively.

Typically, the L.cmds file allows allows execution of the commands **rmail**, **ruusend**, and **rnews**. **rmail** is the mail receiving program used in conjunction with uucp, **ruusend** is the program responsible for taking **uusend** requests and forwarding them on towards their proper destinations, and **rnews** is the standard news receiving program. **rnews** should be specified as "rnews,Error". If there are other commands that you want to include in your L.cmds file, you should be sure that they do not have any kind of built-in shell escape facility, and the shells themselves should be strictly off limits. Commands that print information about the state of the system are usually OK, but watch out for commands that take filename arguments.

The L.cmds file on boulder, our master uucp machine, looks like this:

```
PATH=/bin:/usr/bin:/usr/new:/usr/ucb:/usr/new/lib/news
rmail
rnews
cunbatch
uusndmail
sendmail
```

16.6.1.6 Establish low-cost telephone service

Some people have very strong opinions on long distance telephone service. For home or office telephones there are admittedly a number of good reasons to choose a full-service telephone carrier like AT&T over low-cost alternatives such as SPRINT or MCI. Some of the bargain services are infamous for persistent billing errors.

Computers aren't like people, however. They don't need operator assistance or directory information, and can usually deal competently with noisy telephone connections. As a rule of thumb, it is best to get the cheapest long distance telephone service you can find, unless your modems can run at speeds of more than 1200 baud without error correction. The higher the speed of data transmission, the more susceptible the connection is to line noise.

When transmitting over telephone lines, uucp uses an error-correcting protocol. This doesn't mean that everything just turns out well by magic, though: Data packets that arrive at their destination damaged must be completely retransmitted. Smaller data packet sizes make this job easier, but introduce a sizable overhead cost of their own. The best solution is to insure that connection lines are good enough to keep retransmissions under ten percent. You can estimate your retransmission rate by running **uucico** in debug mode.

Many alternative long distance telephone companies allow you to subscribe without paying a monthly service charge and let you pay only for the telephone time you actually use. This is good since it allows you to test-drive them without undue expense. If you fear that the service in your area is bad enough to warrant caution in choosing a carrier, you should start with the cheapest services and climb gradually up the ladder until you find one that meets your needs.

Once you've identified the company you want to use, ask them if they will sell you telephone time in large blocks. Most carriers have a program under which you can realize substantial savings by agreeing to use at least five hours of time per month. Even AT&T does this. Details vary.

16.6.1.7 Enter telephone access codes in the L-dialcodes file

Most cities let you specify a default carrier for your outgoing lines, but in some circumstances the older dial-a-local-number-and-enter-your-access-code protocol must be observed.

It is painful to keep track of these numbers and type them in again and again as you add each new uucp connection. Luckily, uucp lets you keep this information in a centrally located place and reference it symbolically when you need to. This place is the /usr/lib/uucp/L-dialcodes file.

L-dialcodes simply specifies a mapping between names and telephone numbers, so it can be used to not only to keep track of long distance access codes but also the access phone number of each of your uucp connections, if you wish. Each noncomment line lists the symbolic name of a phone number and the phone number itself, separated by spaces and/or tabs. For example, the lines:

```
#
# Phone number for Uucpi (United Cranberry Pickers International)
#
ucpi_phone              666-8743
```

declare the symbolic name "ucpi_phone" for the phone number 666-8743.

The phone numbers in L-dialcodes are passed directly to the modem for interpretation, so if your modem supports special characters (for pauses or dialing method selection) you can enter them here without any problem. For example, a prefix used to access an alternative telephone company might be (this is for a Hayes modem):

```
#
# Access string for long distance service.
#
ldist                   492-2534,,,873253,,
```

492-2534 is the local access number, and the commas indicate pregnant pauses in the dialing sequence (to allow time for the service to answer). This example points out an important feature of the L-dialcodes file. The phone numbers it contains need not be complete; they may also be dialing sequence prefixes. To place a call to Fort Lauderdale using this long distance prefix, the appropriate entry in the connection information file (L.sys) would be something like "ldist305-763-8263".

16.6.1.8 Establish an initial connection

Before you can go any further with your uucp configuration, you should start trying to obtain a uucp connection with some local site. It may take some time for the other site to get you set up properly, so it's good to plan this part ahead.

How easy it is to get a connection depends upon where you are located, what kind of organization you represent, and whether or not you attempt to wangle a news feed. (News is discussed in the next chapter. If somebody feeds you news they will have to ship several megabytes of data to you every day via uucp.) The best sites to ask first are the local colleges and universities; call their computer science departments and ask them for the name and phone number of their computer administrator. Uucp clones exist for several operating systems, so you need not locate a site that is running UNIX.

Most system administrators are happy to give out uucp connections, provided that the expected flow is small and that you do not force them to make long distance calls. Be sure to explain to any prospective first connection that you are a new uucp site, so that the system administrator will not be surprised if problems with the connection occur. There is no call for obsequious groveling, but remember that the administrator on the other end is doing you a favor. As a general rule, you should be willing to offer uucp connections to at least two other sites for every connection you request from someone else.

If you cannot obtain a connection from an educational institution, you will need to find out what businesses in your area are on uucp and phone them individually. A good way to start this search is by asking the person who sold you your system to send you the uucp map for your area. Complete uucp maps for the entire world are posted to the news group comp.mail.maps; each map file typically represents either a country or a U.S. state. The format of the maps is appropriate for machine parsing, but it is fairly easy for a human to read them even without a description. Each map entry gives the postal address of the site and the telephone number of the administrator, so you will be able to identify good potential contacts with no problem. See Chapter 17: *News* for more information about news.

If you just can't get your hands on a bona fide uucp map, you should contact your local university for help.

Once you've convinced someone to connect with you, each of you needs to give the other the following five pieces of information:

- The machine name of the local system
- The login name for the remote system to use when logging in
- The password for the remote login
- The phone number of the local system
- The name and phone number of the local system administrator

In addition, you must reach agreement on the following items:

- The speed and modem protocol to be used
- The calling schedule for the connection

As we've mentioned before, the login name for the remote system should be the name of the system prefaced with a capital "U" and truncated to eight characters if necessary. It is best to assign a password consisting of random letters and digits to this login, since no human will need to remember or type it. For convenience, all uucp logins may share a single UID. This UID should *not* be the same as the UID of the generic "uucp" login.

If the remote system is only a local phone call away, you should attempt to establish a bi-directional, on-demand schedule until you are confident that your system is functioning properly. This means that both your site and the other site should agree to place a call as soon as there is work to be done. With things set up like this, your testing time will be quite modest. After the initial break-in period, you may wish to limit calls to certain hours of the day or to allow one of the sites to completely control the link.

To debug the new connection, turn to the steps listed under Section 16.6.2.

16.6.1.9 Reconfigure your mail system to use uucp

Now that you have uucp, you need to tell your mail system how to use it. The process of configuring your mail system for correct uucp operation depends upon your flavor of UNIX. Chapter 15: *Mail and Berkeley Sendmail* describes this process for BSD; under ATT the configuration is practically automatic.

Most mailing systems do not handle uucp mail directly. Instead, they give uucp-addressed mail to a special uucp mailer (often called **rmail**) for forwarding. The division of labor is very clear: The mail system does the address parsing and rewriting, and the uucp mailer is responsible for examining the final result and forwarding it to the appropriate machine. On most systems, the uucp mailer also receives incoming uucp mail from other machines and submits it to the local mail system.

16.6.1.10 Smart mailers

One of the problems with uucp mail is that every piece of mail usually gets routed exactly as its address specifies, host by host. This is fine when people know what they are doing and choose good uucp paths, but it can be a disaster when inefficient routes are taken. Bad uucp routing is detrimental to everybody involved: The person who sends the mail has to wait longer for it to be delivered, and the sites involved have to deal with unnecessary traffic.

There is a global uucp database that describes the location and connectivity of all uucp hosts. The global uucp map is truly gigantic, however. It would be practically impossible for a human to browse through it to find a single path between two arbitrary hosts, let alone the most efficient one. Luckily, humans don't have to do this; a program called **pathalias** will do it for them. **pathalias** chomps up all available uucp maps and spits out a list of all the known hosts on the network, along with the best paths to each from your local site.

pathalias by itself just produces a text file that can be **grep**'ed through to find uucp paths. This is very useful for looking up addresses, but the real payoff comes when **pathalias** is used to generate a database of paths for use by the mail system.

Instead of using the system's standard uucp mailer, sites having the **pathalias** database can use a **pathalias**-based mailer such as **uumail** instead. **uumail** is only one of a number of popular smart mailing systems, but it is the simplest of its kind and runs under several flavors of UNIX. **uumail** performs the same job as the standard mailer, but instead of just blindly forwarding mail, it does rerouting using its idea of the fastest, most efficient path.

It may seem slightly Machiavellian to interfere with the natural flow of mail in this way, and it is. There are a number of reasons why a user might wish to specify a nonoptimal uucp address, and smart mailers ignore all of these. For this reason, most sites that use a smart mailer rewrite addresses only when it is unclear how to proceed with a given address.

On BSD systems running **sendmail** it is easy to determine whether or not the next site in a given uucp address is one of your neighbors by defining a class based on your L.sys file that contains the names of all your neighbors. Valid addresses can be forwarded through the normal mailer and defective addresses through a smart mailer.

In any case, you should avoid installing a smart mailer until you are sure that your system's treatment of mail is stable and reliable.

Neither **pathalias** nor any of the smart mailers are standard UNIX programs. You should be able to get both from a uucp neighbor.

16.6.1.11 Test uucp mail

Testing uucp mail is generally fairly easy. You can send mail to yourself that must travel through a remote host and back again to get to you, proving that you can both send and receive mail correctly. In the following examples, we'll assume once again that "cranberry" is the name of your neighbor and that your local system's name is "saturn".

The first thing you should try is:

mail -v cranberry!saturn!_yourname_

This will let you watch **sendmail** chew on the address. A successful session looks something like this:

```
% mail -v cranberry!saturn!garth
Subject: Hi garth
<Control-D>
Cc:
Null message body; hope that's ok
```

```
cranberry!saturn!garth... Connecting to cranberry.uucp...
cranberry!saturn!garth... Sent
```

If instead of this, **sendmail** tells you that it's "totally stumped", the problem lies in your /usr/lib/sendmail.cf file. You need to go back there and review your uucp mailing rules. If you get messages saying that the host cranberry is unknown, that probably comes from the uucp system itself and requires that you go back to the files in /usr/lib/uucp to try to figure out what is wrong.

If everything goes smoothly, you should attempt to force a call to the remote system with:

/usr/lib/uucp/uucico -r1 -scranberry -x5

It may take a minute or two for the message to get turned around, so you may have to force another call after about five minutes to pick up the incoming message. Once the second session has completed, wait another minute and then check your mailbox.

If there's no mail, you should check the uucp logs in /usr/spool/uucp (they are described soon). If the mail went out but didn't come back, the problem most probably lies with your sendmail.cf file's address rewriting. Refer to Chapter 15: *Mail and Berkeley Sendmail* for help with debugging **sendmail** rulesets.

16.6.1.12 Publish your uucp data

You are now a fully fledged member of the uucp community, and it's time for you to start paying your community taxes by making your location and connectivity public. What you need to do is fill out an electronic form and mail it to rutgers!uucpmap; the Uucp Mapping Project will take care of the rest. You will need to update this map entry periodically, so it is a good idea to maintain a permanent copy of it in the /usr/lib/uucp directory.

The format of a uucp map entry is rather particular and takes several pages to describe. Rather than cover that here, we've included the standard instructions in Appendix K. This form will also be sent to you automatically if you neglect to send it in and the mapping project's network-sniffers discover your existence. The information you submit will be redistributed in the newsgroup comp.mail.maps to every site that receives news.

While the primary reason for publishing your information is to allow other sites to route mail through you, there are many benefits to your site as well. For one thing, everybody that runs **pathalias** will automatically know how to reach your site. Don't drag your feet on this. It is easy and quick to do, and you might as well get it over with while you are still working on uucp.

16.6.2 Adding a new neighbor

The following steps must be performed every time you add a new uucp connection. When you remove a connection, you must back out the installation by reversing each individual step.

16.6.2.1 Make a login for the new connection

Since the facilities available to uucp logins need not be complete, you do not need to perform all the steps outlined in Chapter 6. It is usually sufficient to simply add a line to the /etc/passwd file, like this:

```
Unbires::63:9:NBI research:/usr/spool/uucppublic:/usr/lib/uucp/uucico
```

A single UID (*not* the "uucp" UID) may be used for all uucp logins. The advantages to this are that you do not pollute the UID range you have reserved for pseudo-users with lots of uucp logins, and that files created by one login in /usr/spool/uucppublic can be read and rewritten by another. Once you've made this entry in /etc/passwd, use **passwd** (or **yppasswd**) to set the password of the remote system.

16.6.2.2 Make an entry in L.sys for the new connection

The L.sys file is the heart of the uucp system. It is this file that contains the names, phone numbers, and passwords of all systems with which you communicate. Although it is possible to compile the uucp programs so that you can communicate with systems that are not listed in L.sys, this is not recommended.

Because the L.sys file contains instructions for logging into all of your uucp neighbors, it must be considered highly confidential. If the information were to fall into the wrong hands it could lead to a breach in security of the remote sites and of the uucp and mail networks. Never give any permissions on this file to the world, and never make backup copies outside of the /usr/lib/uucp directory.

The format of an L.sys entry is:

Site Times Caller Class Device/Phone# Login-script

Where the fields have the following meanings:

Site

This is the name of the remote system. This is *not* the login name; it is the true host name.

Times

This field specifies the times when a call may be initiated to the host specified in the first field. The syntax allows restrictions to be placed on the *grade* of job that may be transferred at any given time. The grade of a uucp job is signified by one character from 0 to 9, A to Z, or a to z. Grade 0 is the very highest priority, and grade z is the lowest. Mail is usually sent at grade C, news at grade d, and uucp file copying operations at grade n. The grade of a job may be given as a command line argument to **uucp** and **uux**.

This field consists of one or more *time records* separated by commas, where a time record is of the form

timehhmm-hhmm/grade;timeout

All of the segments are optional except for *time*.

The *time* field must be instantiated with one of the time codes listed in Figure 16.3. The *time* field limits the applicability of the following hour range to certain times of the week, except in the case of the keywords "Night", "NonPeak", and "Evening", which are comprehensive specifications and do not accept the additional time range.

The range of hours *hhmm-hhmm* further qualifies the *time* keyword. The range may span midnight.

If a grade is specified, no jobs of lower priority than that specified may be transferred during the given time. The grade limitation applies to both sending and receiving.

If a retry timeout is given, it tells the number of minutes to wait between successive (unsuccessful) attempts to contact the host. The default is to start at ten minutes and increase the waiting time between each attempt until 26 tries have been made, at which point no more attempts are made. The number of retries is constant, so a too-small

FIGURE 16.3

Time slot keywords and their meanings

Keyword	Meaning
Any	Any day, any time
Wk	Weekdays
Mo	Monday
Tu	Tuesday
. . .	. . .
Su	Sunday
Evening	5 p.m.-8 a.m. M-F, All day Sat. and Sun.
Night	11 p.m.-8 a.m. M-F, All day Sat. Sun. from mid-5 p.m.
NonPeak	6 p.m.-7 a.m. M-F, All day Sat. and Sun.
Never	Never call this site (can still receive calls, though)

value for the timeout will cause the connection to be abandoned earlier than is reasonable. Retries of the call will be made subject to the original time slot restrictions.

For example, the time specification:

```
Wk0900-1330/C;5,Th0000-2200/d,Sa,Su
```

says that on any weekday, mail and higher grade jobs may be sent between the hours of 9:00 a.m. and 1:30 p.m., and that if a connection attempt fails, to wait only five minutes before trying again. In addition, anything of news grade or higher may be sent any time on Thursday, except for the hours of 10pm to midnight. On Saturday and Sunday, jobs of any grade may be transferred at any time.

Few sites really use all the extra features of the time specification field, though. A more realistic example is:

```
Any/C,Evening
```

which says that calls may be initiated at any time, but that jobs of lower priority than mail must wait until after 5pm to actually be transferred.

Caller

This field specifies a type of connection to be used, and is identical to the "Caller" field of the L-devices file. If a modem is to be used for the connection, the keyword "ACU" should go in this field.

Class

The class field's interpretation depends on the value of the caller field. If the caller is an ACU or DIR (direct connection), then the class is the line speed to be used. If the caller is TCP, then the class is the number or name (from /etc/services) of the network port to connect to over the Ethernet, usually the service "uucp" at port 540.

If an ACU is to be used, the speed may be prefaced with an arbitrary nonnumeric code that will be matched inside the L-devices file. For example, if you make L-devices entries for your Vadic protocol-speaking modems that have the line speed specified as, say, V1200 rather than just 1200, you can then specify that calls to a given system are to be made with a Vadic-type modem by putting V1200 into L.sys as the class field.

Device/phone number

If the caller field of the entry is ACU, this field gives the phone number to call when making the connection. If the phone number includes a nonnumeric prefix, this is looked up in the L-dialcodes file and substituted before dialing occurs. It is possible to specify the entire phone number in the L-dialcodes file and simply reference it here without any additional numbers. Within the final telephone number, dashes are interpreted as pauses of from two to four seconds, while equal signs are interpreted as instructions to wait for a secondary dial tone (implemented as a pause on most modems). In addition, "#" and "*" characters may be used like numbers for tone dialing systems.

If the caller field is DIR, this field contains the name of the device in the /dev directory to be used when establishing the connection. If the caller is TCP, this field contains the network name of the host to be sought over the network (usually the same as the first field, system name).

Login-script

The login script consists of a number of expect/send pairs, where an "expect" is some string of characters to be expected from the remote host, and a "send" is a string of characters to be sent once the previously expected string appears, followed by a return. There are also a number of special cases and features which are not covered here; see your manual page for L.sys for a more thorough description.

A string consisting of two double quotes indicates the null string; a null send string is still followed by a return character. Several backslash escapes are also available; see Figure 16.4.

FIGURE 16.4

L.sys escape sequences		
Backslash	Alternate	Meaning
\b	BREAK	Line break of 3/10 sec.
\b*n*	BREAK*n*	Line break of *n*/10 sec.
\c	<none>	Suppress the \r at the end of send
\d	PAUSE	Delay 1 sec for \d, 3 for PAUSE (send only)
<none>	PAUSE*n*	Delay *n* seconds
\r	CR	Carriage return
\n	NL	Newline
XXX	<none>	The character with octal value *XXX*
<none>	EOT	End-of-transmission

The expect/send strings are normally separated from each other with spaces. There is a special case in which "-" is used as the separator; statements of this type are in the form:

expect-send-expect-...

where the send field is sent only if the first expect does not materialize within 45 seconds, and after which it is the second expect field that is waited for. There may be an arbitrary number of expect and send strings taped together with dashes.

For most Unices, the login script need not be complex. The following script will suffice in 99% of all cases:

```
"" "" ogin:--ogin: Ucranber ssword: s3jHd2
```

Here, "Ucranber" is the login name and "s3jHd2" is the password. The first exchange has a null expect field, so the send is output immediately. There are no characters in the send field, but remember that send fields are always followed by carriage returns; thus this exchange has the effect of always sending a carriage return to the remote system. The next exchange waits for the string "ogin:" presumably a substring of the system's login prompt. The first character has been left off for two reasons: because the case of the first letter may vary, and because noisy telephone lines tend to affect the first characters of a line more often than characters in the middle.

If the login prompt is not received in 45 seconds, another carriage return is sent. This is indicated by the fact that there is nothing between the two dashes. After the second carriage return is sent, the script will expect the same login prompt; if this expect times out, the login script will be aborted since there are no more dash-separated clauses. Once the login prompt has been secured, the username is output, the password prompt is waited for, and the login password is sent.

When you acquire additional uucp connections, you need only add the remote system to /etc/passwd and add a line for it in L.sys. (Maybe also USERFILE if you do permissions on a case-by-case basis.) That's it!

16.6.2.3 Debug the uucp connection

Remember that the **uucico** program handles all actual uucp communication. The best way to debug your first connection is to get on the telephone with the other site's administrator and shoot a few jobs back and forth with **uucico** debugging turned on. The way to initiate such a call is to type something like

/usr/lib/uucp/uucico -r1 -s*system* -x9

where *system* is the name of the system to call. Since you are running this from the shell, the debugging output will appear right on your screen. It is the **-x9** flag that asks for the debugging output; the number following the "x" indicates the verbosity. A debugging level of 9 is fairly verbose, 5 is good for an initial audit, and numbers higher than 9 will give you more information than is useful.

If **uucico** is ever run in slave mode or in a situation where standard error output is not available, the diagnostic output will be placed in the file /usr/spool/uucp/AUDIT/*systemname*.

It is more difficult to monitor an incoming call; you will probably have to content yourself with looking at output from **ps** and **w** to trace the general flow of the uucp conversation and to be sure that the remote system was able to log in without problems.

16.6.2.4 Edit /usr/lib/crontab to control the calling schedule

Now that you know that your uucp system is functional, you need to make it completely automatic.

The /usr/lib/crontab file controls the behavior of the **cron** daemon, which executes programs at preset times. This daemon can and should be used to initiate calling sequences for uucp. **cron** is a whole topic in and of itself, and the details of its usage are covered in Chapter 21: *Periodic Processes* rather than here. In this section we will just present some boilerplate configurations that can be used directly or with only a little modification.

You cannot control the times when other systems may call you with their uucp traffic. The only thing you can do to refuse uucp connections at inopportune times is to place all your neighbors on call-back status inside the USERFILE. This is a rather drastic and wasteful measure to take. It is much better to simply call the administrator of the offending site and ask him to modify his L.sys or /usr/lib/crontab file.

You do have complete control over the times when you initiate calls to other systems, however. In the L.sys file you specified at what times it was *permissible* to call; now you have to set things up so that these calls actually get made.

The usual way to initiate calls is to run the **uucico** program in master mode (the **-r1** flag does this). With no other arguments, **uucico** simply scans its spool directories to discover for which systems work has been queued, and then makes calls to each of those systems, provided that the current time is within the range specified for each system in the L.sys file. If there is no work for a site, no call is placed.

The **uucp** and **uux** commands will, by default, attempt to initiate a **uucico** whenever a job is queued for a remote system, unless the **-r** flag is included on the command line. Mail and news always use this option, so you have much more control over their schedules than you do over the transfer times of **uucp**'s and **uux**'s initiated by real users.

The simplest way for you to set up uucp is to have **cron** run **uucico** in master mode every half hour or so. The longest amount of time any job will spend sitting in your system's uucp queue (assuming it is eligible to be transmitted) is the amount of time between executions of **uucico**.

On a 4.3BSD system, the crontab line to add for an hourly check will look something like the following (ATT syntax is different).

```
43 * * * *     uucp  /usr/lib/uucp/uucico -r1
```

This is fine as long as your neighbors are set up to call you when there are jobs for you on their end. If you call a site that doesn't call you, you have to be sure that a connection is made every once in a while *regardless* of whether or not you have work waiting to give to it. There is no way for you to know whether or not there are jobs waiting on the other end without forcing the call.

This situation is not as far-fetched as you may think; for example, we provide uucp service to a number of UNIX-running personal computers stationed in the homes of faculty members. The voice phones of the homes double as data phones for the PC's, so it would be rather annoying for the owner to be called up by a computer every hour or so. Consequently, our L.sys file has been set up to say that at no time is it permissible to call them. Instead, the owners of the systems must initiate all transactions themselves. It doesn't matter how much stuff is waiting for them at the university: They will not get it unless they call and ask for it.

It is only slightly harder to do a poll than it is to do a queue scan; the problem is that a separate command line is required for each system to be polled. The **-s***system* flag to **uucico** will cause the named system to be called regardless of whether or not there is work. This flag should be supplemented with the **-r1** flag to insure that the **uucico** is started in master mode.

The easiest way to handle your polling is to write yourself a shell script and install it in /usr/local/etc. If you do not poll many systems, you can hard-wire their names right into the script; otherwise, you should have a script that accepts as arguments the names of systems to call. You should then run this script out of crontab just as you run **uucico** directly for non-polled sites.

As a trivial example, the following C-shell script simply polls all of its arguments:

```
#!/bin/csh -f
#
# uucp.poll sitename1 sitename2 ... sitenameN
#
# call the requested sites
#
foreach site ($argv)
      /usr/lib/uucp/uucico -r1 -s${site}
end
```

If you were to use this script as part of a polling regime, you would have a line in crontab for each set of sites to be polled at the same time; for example:

```
00 7 * * *uucp  /usr/local/etc/uucp.poll bog pika hottub
23 7,16 * * *uucp  /usr/local/etc/uucp.poll tiger lunacy
```

16.6.2.5 Publish the new connection in the uucp maps

If the connection you are adding is your first, you should skip this section and read Section 16.6.1.12 on publishing your uucp data. Otherwise, you already have a registered uucp map entry that needs to be updated to reflect your new connectivity. Resend the entire map entry rather than just the changes; preface your mail with an explanation that you are sending in a change to an existing map and not a new map for a previously unregistered site.

16.7 The uucp log files

Most of the stuff in /usr/spool/uucp is internal to the uucp system and won't need to be configured or looked at. There are a couple of files and directories that may interest you, however. The information in these files tends to be extremely verbose, so you may wish to run some cleanup scripts out of **cron** to delete them every week or move them somewhere else.

16.7.1 The /usr/spool/uucp/LOGFILE file

This file contains general information about uucp activity on the local site and actions performed when connected with remote sites, whether or not the calls were initiated locally. Every time a uucp remote command execution request is queued locally, a line of the following form is entered in the LOGFILE

```
evi cranberry (7/19-21:52-5938) XQT QUE'D (rmail hao!bpa!swatsun!schwartz)
```

which shows the requester (evi) the remote site (cranberry), the date, and the command to be executed.

In addition, information about the various calls that were attempted or received, whether or not they succeeded, and what went on during the conversations are also recorded here.

16.7.2 The /usr/spool/uucp/SYSLOG file

This file shows the size in bytes of each uucp transaction, the name of the requester, the site with which the transaction occurred, the time of the transaction, and the time needed to perform the transaction.

For example, the line:

```
tyler hao (7/19-21:52) (553751571.80) sent data 694 bytes 0.01 secs
```

indicates that 694 bytes were transferred to the site "hao" on behalf of the user "tyler". The transmission time for this was only one-hundredth of a second, since the connection between the University of Colorado and hao is a TCP link. A more realistic example is:

```
news akelei (7/19-20:55) (553748130.51) sent data 8347 bytes 38.85 secs
```

in which 8347 bytes of news were transferred in just under 40 seconds.

16.7.3 The /usr/spool/uucp/ERRLOG file

This file is used to record various errors that occur during the operation of the uucp system. A line from this file looks something like this:

```
ASSERT ERROR (uux) pid: 16140 (10/4-19:15) CAN'T OPEN D.sigiX00W0 (0)
```

Here, **uux** was unable to open a file that it expected to have access to. This may have been caused by someone removing the file by hand from the /usr/spool/uucp/D. directory.

16.8 Miscellaneous uucp support programs and files

There are quite a few utilities supplied with uucp for doing things like examining the job queue, finding the status of all connections, and reading the logs in an organized way. These programs aren't really essential to the operation of uucp, but they can be helpful in tracking down problems and monitoring traffic.

16.8.1 The uuclean command

uuclean is used to remove outdated cruft from the spooling area and do general housekeeping for the whole system. It can be used to remove all files over a certain age, and can select the files to be deleted on the basis of their names, which is useful if only files of a certain type (e.g., lock files) are to be removed.

uuclean is generally run out of **cron**, just like **uucico**. Normally, **uuclean** is run every 24 hours, and only the **-m** flag is supplied; this causes **uuclean** to just do general cleanup and to send mail to any victims whose stale files are deleted.

16.8.2 The uuq command

uuq is used to monitor the uucp work queue. It supports a number of options to select only jobs having certain qualities (such as being destined for a particular system), and gives information in short, medium, or long form.

uuq can also be used by the administrator to delete jobs from the **uucp** queue; to do this, **uuq** must first be run in normal or verbose mode to provide the job names for each job, and then run again with the **-d** flag to indicate which job is to be deleted.

16.8.3 The uuname command

Without any arguments, **uuname** shows the names of all known uucp connections. With the **-l** flag, it shows the **uucp** name of the local host.

To obtain this list, **uuname** merely looks at the first field of each line in the L.sys file — hardly an amazing feat. Were it not for comments and continuation lines, the functionality of the **uuname** command could be duplicated with the shell command

```
awk '{print $1}' /usr/lib/uucp/L.sys | sort -u
```

uuname is necessary because ordinary users do not have read permission on the L.sys file, so they need an intermediary, setuid program to search this file for them.

16.8.4 The uuencode and uudecode commands

These commands are used to translate binary data into ASCII format for transmission via the uucp system. Uucp cannot handle files with binary data in them because it uses some of the nonprinting characters for its transmission protocols. Unfortunately, **uuencode** and **uudecode** run setuid to "uucp," so they have the same weird permission restrictions as the **uucp** command.

For this reason, it is best to run **uuencode** and **uudecode** from the /usr/spool/uucppublic or /tmp directories.

16.8.5 The uupoll command

This command is used to force a telephone call to a remote system. Rather than using **uucico** with polling flags, as we've advocated in this chapter, it queues a job for the system and then attempts to start **uucico** normally. **uucico** will see that there is work and initiate the call.

We don't recommend the use of the **uupoll** command, not because it doesn't work, but just because its method of operation requires cluttering up the spool directories with fake jobs. If you find that it suits your taste better than using a **uucico** shell script, by all means use it.

16.8.6 The **uusnap** command

This rather violent-sounding command displays the status of all uucp connections that currently have work waiting for them on the local system. It shows the number of files and commands waiting to be handled, and the current status of the connection. If the status is blank, it means that the system has not yet been called; otherwise, it will say that the remote system is currently being talked to, or will show any problems or comments relevant to previous connection attempts.

16.8.7 The **uulog** command

This command does different things on different versions of **uucp**.

Some versions of the uucp system actually keep log information lying around in separate files in the spool directory; this information is not compiled into the /usr/spool/uucp/LOGFILE file until **uulog** is run. On these systems, **uulog** should be run at least once per day.

On other systems the logs are kept directly in the log files and the **uulog** command is used to search through these logs for information about particular systems. Consult the manuals for your system to find out what your **uulog** does.

16.8.8 The /usr/lib/uucp/L.aliases file

This file is used to create uucp aliases for a given host, most commonly used when a remote system decides it wants to change its name. In this case, the old name and the new name can be equivalenced in the L.aliases file, and jobs queued for the old name will be handled correctly even though they are being picked up by a "strange" computer. The L.aliases file does not provide a complete fix, however, as a **uucico -s** command must still be given the name exactly as it appears in the L.sys file. The L.sys entry for the site should be changed as soon as possible to reflect the new name.

The format of the L.aliases file is

real-name alias-name

where *real name* is the current real name of the system. Alias names are any other names by which the system should be known (including the old name of the system).

17

News

The UNIX news system (Usenet) is a system for distributing messages simultaneously to many sites. It is like electronic mail, except that all articles are publicly readable. News is available to almost any site that has a uucp or network connection, and boasts a user community of tens of thousands of people at more than 4000 sites.

17.1 Distribution

Usenet is distributed through a nonhierarchical network. Most news is transmitted via uucp, so the structure of Usenet is effectively constrained to the uucp model. Each news site has one or more *feeds* from which news is obtained, and zero or more *clients*, to which news is sent. The distribution of news is not centralized. News postings may originate at any site, and are automatically propagated both "upstream" and "downstream" throughout the Usenet by the news software. Each site that receives news is responsible for correctly preparing it to be resent to all the sites that it feeds.

Over two megabytes of news are posted each day. This is a staggering figure when you consider that most news feeds are run over 1200 baud modems. Transmitting two megabytes of data at this speed takes over three hours.

The use of data compression and high-speed modems has reduced this problem significantly: two megabytes of news compressed by 60% and transmitted at 9600 baud takes under 15 minutes.

Transmission time is not the only problem with news volume, however. Stockpiling news articles for a long time also becomes very expensive in terms of disk space. Each news-receiving site typically allows individual news articles to survive for only a week or two before deleting them.

The Usenet software itself is not interactive: It simply manages the flow of news articles to and from your site, storing them in the appropriate directories. To read and post news, you must use a separate program such as **readnews**, **rn**, **vnews**, or **postnews**.

17.2 Newsgroups

Messages on Usenet are divided into *newsgroups*. Each newsgroup is dedicated to the discussion of one particular topic, which may be as broad the UNIX operating system (comp.unix) or as narrow as Celtic culture (soc.culture.celtic).

It is not necessary or even possible for all users to read everything posted to the Usenet. There are over 450 newsgroups, and some of these get over one hundred messages per day. The programs used to read news allow users to subscribe only to the groups they are interested in, and some even provide ways of hiding particular threads of discussion inside newsgroups. Even with all this help, it can take an hour or so to read 20 active newsgroups.

Much of the information posted on Usenet is computer-related: operating systems, software, human interfaces, programming languages, hardware, etc. This is not due to any restriction on subject matter but is a natural consequence of the fact that most Usenet users are computer professionals. There is no dearth of other material, however. There are newsgroups for skydivers, scuba divers, glider pilots, cooks, Buddhists, woodworkers, nudists, and almost any other category you can think of.

Most newsgroups are unmoderated, which means that anyone can post an article if they want to. Because of the lack of restrictions, some unmoderated groups feature high doses of irrelevant material and personal argumentation. Groups with a technical bent usually maintain a high signal-to-noise ratio, but more socially oriented newsgroups frequently degenerate into inane free-for-alls in which little useful information is exchanged.

On the other side of the coin are the moderated newsgroups. Instead of being able to post articles directly to a moderated newsgroup, users must send their messages to a moderator for review. Every article that appears in a moderated group has been personally approved by the moderator. Some moderators forward individual articles, and others condense submissions into digests which are posted as a single article. Most news-reading programs provide the same interface for posting to an unmoderated group and submitting an article to a moderator.

It is rare for the moderator of a group to actually reject an article, since the mere knowledge that a posting will be reviewed and judged usually freezes frivolous users dead in their tracks.

Like the UNIX file tree, Usenet newsgroups are organized into a hierarchy. The name of a newsgroup is analogous to the full pathname of a UNIX file, except that the separator character is a period instead of a slash. The similarity between these two is intentional; the news storage area is a tree of directories whose names are formed by a simple transliteration from newsgroup names to pathnames.

At the top level of the news hierarchy are the core news classes. These are listed in Figure 17.1. There are other top-level news classes (gnu, bionet, etc.) distributed on a by-request-only basis, but these may not be available from all locations. Underneath each of these classes is an arbitrary number of subdivisions. Each subdivision may be a newsgroup in its own right, have other subdivisions inside it, or both. For example, the newsgroup misc.consumers covers material of interest to consumers in general; the typical fare of this group ranges from product reviews to questions on locating a particular product to horror stories about dealing with unscrupulous meat-product salesmen. This group also has a subgroup misc.consumers.house in which the discussion is limited to the buying and selling of real estate. The more subtopics in the name of a group, the more restricted it is.

FIGURE 17.1

Top-level newsgroup classifications	
Name	Content
comp	Computer-related and source code distribution newgroups
news	Groups that discuss Usenet itself, its content and transport
rec	Discussions of recreational activities (skiing, hiking)
sci	Newsgroups of interest to the scientific community, new research, etc.
talk	Serious discussions (abortion, religion, philosophy)
soc	Socially oriented newsgroups (singles, college)
misc	Everything that doesn't fit in anywhere else (for sale, jobs offered)
alt	Alternative groups; e.g., alt.drugs, alt.sex (distributed by request only)

Usenet hasn't always had this top-level organization. The current division scheme was begun in 1986 at the request of the news and uucp backbone sites, who felt that the old system was disorganized, ad hoc, and inefficient. Newsgroups used to be classified primarily by whether or not they were moderated – moderated newsgroups were placed under the top-level designation "mod," and unmoderated newsgroups were lumped under the designation "net."

Sites that did not want to pay for transmission of "social" newsgroups didn't like the old system because it was hard to discriminate between the chaff and the grain. Before, such diverse groups as net.sources and net.garden were all bunched up together in "net"; now, the classification is by topic and separation is much more straightforward.

17.3 The news software

The news software is not a standard UNIX package, but it is "freely available"; the software is not in the public domain, but distribution is unlimited. You will have to get someone to send it to you via mail or uucp, or **ftp** it from somewhere. The most recent version can always be **ftp**'ed from the machine uunet.uu.net. Sites that don't have an ARPANET connection can obtain news from a uucp neighbor. Try to find someone with a recent distribution that has not been meddled with to accommodate their local conditions.

Most versions of the news software are primarily maintenance releases; they contain many little pokings and tweakings, but have not modified the essential format and transport of news. Older versions of the software expect an article format called Version A. This format is no longer supported and has been replaced with a Version B format. The transformation was quite some time ago, and Version B is now the global standard.

While you are looking for the basic news software, try to also find source code for the **rn** news-reading program. The news software comes with a rather minimal program called **vnews** that is adequate for light or occasional readers of news, but your site's dedicated Usenetters will not survive the heavy flow of Usenet traffic without the more powerful **rn** at their disposal.

Compilation and installation of the software is well documented in the source distribution, so the low-level details aren't covered here. News has many compile-time options that you will need to carefully review and set as appropriate for your system, but once the initial installation is completed, the operation of news is largely automatic and rarely needs attention. Be sure to test your installation with a cooperating site as described in the documentation.

Included with the news distribution are a few of the documents posted to news.announce.newusers on a rotating basis; these documents describe the essential paradigms of user-level Usenet, and will (hopefully) instill in you a permanent awareness some of very important concepts and warnings. One of the most important of these documents is Chuq Von Rospach's *A Primer on How to Work with the USENET Community*, which presents some guidelines for posting to Usenet. Be sure to read this before *posting anything* anywhere on the net.

17.4 Maintenance strategies

Because of its chronically high disk activity, the news system makes disk backups be twice as long as they should be. This is especially problematic if your news directory is on the same disk partition as users' home directories, since such partitions must be dumped often.

The solution is to make a separate filesystem (usually called /spool) on which to keep news, uucp spool files, and anything else that never needs to be dumped. See Chapter 18: *Backups and Transportable Media* for more information about setting up an appropriate dumping regime.

Always remain aware of the fact that your news neighbors are depending on you to keep your system running correctly. If you take your system down without telling your feeds, they will continue to queue news for transmission to your site. It does not usually take long before the backed-up news traffic starts to cause problems. Likewise, machines that you feed will wonder what is going on. Always notify your news connections of potential downtime and problems.

17.5 News-reading chores for system administrators

Some newsgroups are so useful to a system administrator that we consider it practically a mandatory part of any administration job to subscribe to and read them. It's hard to prioritize them, so they are not listed here in any particular order. The following newsgroups are unmoderated unless marked.

17.5.1 news.announce.important (moderated)

This group carries information of vital importance to all news-reading users. Postings to this newsgroup are required to be really important, so it is rare to see anything here more often than every month or so.

17.5.2 news.software.b

This group is used for discussion about the Usenet software. Debate about the future directions of the news software is prevalent, but other relevant topics are also covered.

17.5.3 news.sysadmin

This is a forum for administrators of news software. Important information about the news software and Usenet in general usually comes in through this group.

17.5.4 comp.unix.questions

This newsgroup is a forum for questions and answers about UNIX. In theory, the material posted to this group should be as hardware-independent as possible, but in real life many questions posted here are related to problems with specific flavors of UNIX and particular kinds of hardware. Some of the material is obscure, but you will find that much of it relates, if only indirectly, to you and your system.

If you have a system-independent question that your manuals do not answer, this is a good place to try and find an answer. If your question is better suited for a more focused newsgroup, don't post it here. As a general rule, you should learn to recognize the types of questions that are appropriate for a given newsgroup through a week or two of observation before posting anything.

17.5.5 comp.unix.wizards

This newsgroup is kind of an older sibling to comp.unix.questions, but the material discussed is more kernel-oriented. It isn't directly related to system administration, but it can give you a good feel for what is going on inside your machine.

One of the nice things about this newsgroup is that operating system bugs are often reported here as they are found (hopefully not often). A patch that you can apply to your kernel if you have source code is often supplied along with the bug report, allowing you to increase the reliability of your system in a relatively painless way. (But remember to beware of *any* patch!)

17.5.6 comp.sources.unix (moderated)

This group contains source code for use on UNIX systems. Almost any kind of program can appear here, from spelling correctors to text formatters to programming languages to utilities for use with other packages such as uucp and news itself. The code here is free and is in the public domain.

Most of the things posted to comp.sources.unix (as well as the other source newsgroups) are packed in a format called a *shell archive* or *shar* for short — this packing scheme enables multiple files to be placed inside a single file for transmission and then unpacked at their destination by running the file through **sh**. Before invoking **sh** on a file, be sure that all the header information of the article has been trimmed off, as **sh** won't understand it and will gag on the file. Programs for putting files into shar format are common, and can be obtained from a uucp neighbor or the comp.sources.unix archives.

Most packages posted to this group are reasonably well formed and complete, and most include a Makefile (see Chapter 26) for easy installation. When you install software from the net on your system, be sure to put the entire original distribution in a consistent place (/usr/new/src or /usr/local/src) so you can find it later, and be sure to install the manual pages! *Always* read the Makefile to determine what it is going to do before running **make** as root — it is rare for intentionally destructive programs to be posted, but your system configuration can differ enough from that of the poster for strange things to happen.

Be especially aware of the installation directories specified in the Makefile. For some unfathomable reason, many people write Makefiles that try to install things in the standard system directories; e.g., they put man pages for new user commands in Section 1 of the manual just like standard UNIX does. This is a horrible practice. When you upgrade your system, all of the standard directories will be wiped out, and software installed in this way will be detonated. Make sure that everything goes into the *local* versions of the system directories (i.e., /usr/man/manl for manual pages, /usr/local/bin or /usr/new/bin for programs, and /usr/local/lib or /usr/new/lib for support files.)

17.5.7 comp.sources.games (moderated)

If you don't mind users playing games on your system, there are occasionally some nice ones posted here.

17.5.8 comp.sources.*machine* and comp.binaries.*machine* (moderated)

There are hosts of source and object code newsgroups for machines whose source code is not compatible with other kinds of machines. Most of these are personal computers that don't run UNIX, since as a rule UNIX source is reasonably transportable. There's no reason for you to subscribe to any of these groups unless you also support or use computers of the appropriate type.

17.5.9 comp.sources.misc (moderated)

This is a group for posting of software that doesn't fit into other source groups. Either it is not of interest to the general public (numerical analysis routines), it isn't written in C (non-C programs are welcome in most newsgroups, but tend to be scoffed at), or it is for a specific computer that doesn't have its own source code newsgroup.

For example, past postings to comp.sources.misc have included routines for performing fast Fourier transforms, programs for printing the time in a variety of formats, a **finger** program for VAX/VMS under Eunice (gag), and a program for handling function keys on HP 2392a's and clones.

17.5.10 comp.sources.bugs

Bug reports and fixes for source code distributed through Usenet are posted here.

17.5.11 comp.sources.wanted

In this newsgroup are heard the desperate pleas of people who are trying to find out if code exists to do a particular job or who are trying to locate a copy of a particular package that they know exists. Consider this group as a kind of bank — every time you help someone else to get what they need, you are morally entitled to make a similar public request. If the other person's question is not likely to be of interest to the general Usenet community, send mail to them directly rather than posting your reply.

In many cases, it is painfully obvious that the person trying to locate source code has not done their homework very well and is trying to get someone else to do the legwork for them by posting on Usenet. This is bad because numerous people are liable to reply to easy questions, some to give the answer, and others to yell and scream about how the poster should have been able to figure it out himself. Don't get involved in this, not as an asker or answerer, and especially not as a whiner.

17.5.12 comp.sys.*machine* and comp.sys.*machine*.digest (moderated)

These are the moderated and unmoderated forums for general discussion of a particular machine or architecture. Most commercial systems are represented in the unmoderated groups, but only the more popular ones also have moderated versions. There are a few anomalously named groups of this type (e.g., comp.sys.sun is moderated).

17.5.13 comp.mail.maps (moderated)

The uucp maps for all known uucp sites in the universe are posted here every month. This is where you get the data files to feed to **pathalias**. See Section 16.6.1.10 for more information about **pathalias**.

18

Backups and Transportable Media

18.1 Why backups are essential

No matter how carefully system hardware is maintained and no matter how brilliant the users are, every system manager will eventually be confronted with lost files. Lost files range from a single file inadvertently deleted by a user to an entire filesystem destroyed by a hardware failure. No system, no matter how small or inactive, can be operated without backups. Without backups, all data that has changed since the operating system was brought up can (and probably eventually will) be lost due to a system failure.

18.2 Which filesystems to backup, and when

The more often backups are done, the safer system data is from loss; however, backups use system resources and an operator's time. The system manager must determine a balance point where adequate data backup is achieved without using too many of the system's resources. On large systems, performing backups of the user filesystems every workday is generally considered the balance point. Daily backups insure that at most one day's worth of work can be lost, but they do not overburden a large system's resources. On systems that are used less, or on which the data is less volatile, the system manager may decide that performing backups every Monday, Wednesday, and Friday or every Tuesday and Thursday is sufficient. On a small personal system that usually has only one user, performing backups once a week is probably adequate.

Filesystems that are infrequently changed, such as / or a filesystem that contains reference material, do not need to be backed up as frequently as user filesystems. If there are a few files that change on an otherwise static filesystem (such as /etc/passwd on /), those files may be copied daily to another filesystem that is regularly backed up (see Chapter 21: *Periodic Processes*).

If /tmp is a separate filesystem, it should *never* be backed up. /tmp should not contain anything that should need to be saved, so there is no reason to back it up. (In case this seems obvious, we know of one large system that does daily backups on /tmp!).

18.3 Backup devices and media

In order for backups to be effective, they must be put on some sort of removable media. The reason that the media must be removable is that system failures can destroy many pieces of hardware at the same time. For instance, backing up one disk onto another disk would provide very little protection against a controller failure, which might cause the contents of all of the disks to be destroyed. The removable media can range from floppy disks on a small, single-user system, to magnetic tapes on a larger system, to removable pack disks on a system with more spare peripherals and money than CPU and operator time. The following are brief descriptions of some of the types of media that can be used for backups.

18.3.1 Floppy diskettes

Floppy diskettes are the most inconvenient media for backups because they are slow and they do not hold very much data (up to 1.2 megabytes per disk). Floppy diskettes are not cost-effective. Per megabyte, they are much more expensive than other storage media. But, floppy drives are inexpensive and are often included on small systems.

18.3.2 Videotape

There are controllers available for many PC's that allow a VCR to be used as a backup device. This is an inexpensive way to get a lot of backup capability on a PC. However, in order to utilize such a system, a device driver will have to be written (see Chapter 7: *Devices and Drivers*).

18.3.3 Cartridge tapes

Cartridge tapes are often found on workstations and medium sized systems. They are faster and hold more information than floppies. However, cartridge tape drives are much more expensive than floppy drives. Some types of cartridge tape controllers do not have adequate buffering, causing the system to slow to a snail's pace while the tape drive is being used.

18.3.4 Nine-track magnetic tapes

Nine-track magnetic tape is probably the most commonly used backup medium on large systems. Some advantages of magnetic tape are that most large systems have a nine-track tape drive, the tapes are relatively cheap, the tapes hold a lot of information, and they are relatively reliable. There are three common densities of nine-track tapes: 800 bpi, (bpi stands for bits per inch) which is found only on very old systems, 1600 bpi, which is the most common density, and 6250 bpi, which is a more recent high-density format. The 1600 bpi format is usually used to transfer data from one system to another. Most 6250 bpi drives can also read and write at 1600 bpi. Prolonged exposure to background radiation affects the data on magnetic tapes, limiting the expected lifespan of data on a magnetic tape to approximately two years. This is not a hard limit — that is, the tape does not self-destruct — you just can't count on the tape being readable after more than two years. Magnetic tapes also have the disadvantage that UNIX cannot sense EOT (end of tape) until the tape has reached it. Therefore, programs must either use less than one whole tape, or make pessimistic size estimations to avoid running off the end of the tape. On some tape drives, UNIX can actually cause tapes to run off their spools, causing tape to spill out onto the floor in a giant spaghetti-like pile. If this happens, the tape may be recovered by rethreading the end of the tape on the spool and then manually rewinding it.

18.3.5 Exabyte cartridge tapes

Exabyte brand cartridge tape systems use standard 8mm (small-format) videotapes as the recording medium. A 90-minute tape holds about two gigabytes of data. Exabyte systems are relatively fast and allow a complete dump to be performed without operator intervention because of their large capacity. The drive itself can handle data at up to 15 megabytes/minute, but dumping over an Ethernet reduces the overall transfer rate to about two megabytes/minute. The driver software for these tape drives allows them to mimic a standard nine-track tape, so they can be accessed using standard software such as **dump**, **tar**, and **cpio**. These systems also have the advantage that the tapes are compact, reducing the need for storage space.

18.3.6 WORM disks

WORM disks are write once read many laser disks. They may be written only once, but that is all that is necessary for backups. They are a little faster than nine-track tapes, and several gigabytes can be stored on a single disk. The disks themselves are relatively expensive, but they have the advantage that they do not suffer from the deterioration that magnetic media do.

Often there is no choice of what media to use because the system has only one possible backup device. However, in some cases there may be a choice of several, or, in the case of a system on a large network, many, suitable devices on which to do backups. The system manager must evaluate the advantages and disadvantages of each available device and make a decision as to which one to use. In the following discussions, "tape" will be used as a generic term that refers to the media chosen for backups, and specific examples will use tape devices.

18.4 Setting up an incremental dumping regime

The programs **dump** and **restore** are the most commonly used method of keeping backups. However, some ATT versions of UNIX do not have these commands. If you have such a system, skim the sections on **dump** and **restore** for the philosophy of incremental backups, and then refer to Section 18.6, which describes several other archiving programs. If done correctly, dumps allow the system manager to restore a filesystem, or any part of a filesystem, to the condition it was in at the time of the last dump. The choice of the word *regime* in the heading of this section may seem militaristic and rigid, but that is intentional: dumps must be done carefully, rigorously, and on a strict schedule. While dumps are the most tedious and repetitive of a system managers duties, they are also one of the most important.

18.4.1 The **dump** command

The **dump** command builds a list similar to a directory tree of files that have been modified since a previous dump, and then packs those files into a single large file to archive to an external device.

18.4.1.1 Dump level

While it is possible to back up all of the information on the system each day, it is certainly not practical. Incremental dumps make it possible to backup only those files that have changed. **dump** uses a level number, which is an integer in the range 0 to 9, to determine which files should be backed up. A level 0 dump dumps the entire filesystem. A level *n* (*n* from 1 to 9) dump includes any file that has been modified since the last dump with level less than or equal to *n*. The times of previous dumps are determined from the file /etc/dumpdates.

18.4.1.2 The u flag

Most versions of **dump** will not update /etc/dumpdates (or the equivalent file) unless they are instructed to. No incremental dumping system will function correctly unless this file is updated, because there is no other way for **dump** to determine when the last level *n* dump occurred. On most versions of **dump**, the **u** flag causes /etc/dumpdates to be updated. The file /etc/dumpdates is a text file, and may be edited. If a filesystem's name has been changed, /etc/dumpdates must be edited to reflect that change or **dump** will become confused.

18.4.1.3 The dump device

dump will send its output to some default device, which is usually the primary tape drive on a large system, and the first floppy drive on a small system. **dump** must be instructed to send its output somewhere else if another device is to be used. This is accomplished with the **f** flag.

18.4.1.4 Other options to dump

dump makes some assumptions that may or may not be correct for your situation. These assumptions include the type of tape being used for dumps, the length of the tape, and the density of the tape. The manual for your version of **dump** should be consulted to determine if these assumptions are reasonable for your system, and, if not, to determine how to set these parameters. For example, to do a level 5 dump of the filesystem mounted on /work to a 1000 bpi, 1700 foot cartridge tape drive whose device file is called /dev/rst0, you would execute the command:

```
dump 5usdf 1700 1000 /dev/rst0 /work
```

Obviously, **dump** can take quite a few arguments, which is one of the motivations for automating the dump sequence.

18.4.2 The Towers of Hanoi sequence

There are many different sequences by which dumps may be done, one of which is based on the Towers of Hanoi mathematical problem. The connection between the sequence and the mathematical problem is limited and unimportant. This sequence has been devised as a balance between the desire to save as much information as possible for as long as possible, and practical limitations such as the amount of time, both the system administrator's and CPU, that can be devoted to performing dumps, or the number of tapes to archive. The Towers of Hanoi dump sequence is illustrated in Figure 18.1.

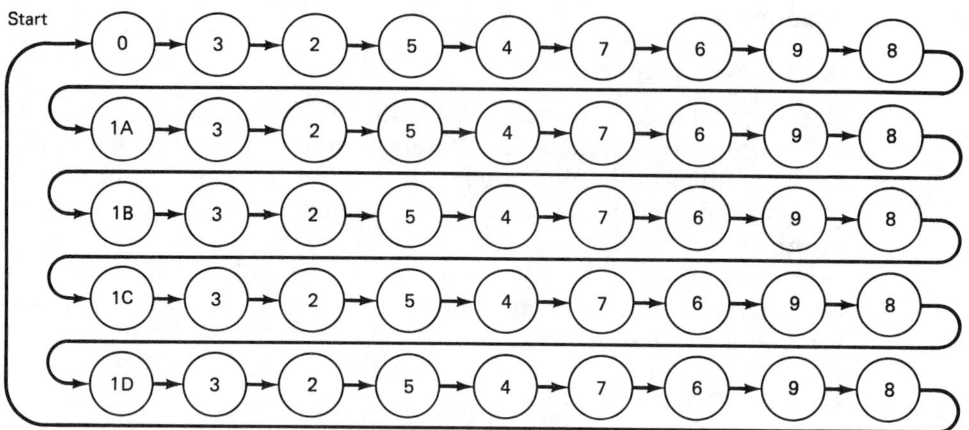

FIGURE 18.1 The Towers of Hanoi dump sequence

When this sequence is finished, it is repeated— however, new tapes are used for each level 0 dump. The level 2 to 9 tapes are reused every nine dumps, while the level 1[ABCD] tapes are re-used every 45 dumps. There are four sets of level 1 tapes for each filesystem, labeled 1A, 1B, 1C, and 1D. Level 1 dumps are done to each of these set of tapes, the [ABCD] indexing is just to distinguish between the four sets of tapes. Each filesystem will have a set of tapes for each level 1 through 9 which are to be reused. Dumps should be performed often enough, or the filesystems should be made small enough, so that the level 2 through 9 dumps fit on a single tape.

18.4.3 Different dump schedules

The Tower of Hanoi sequence is by no means the only sequence by which to do dumps. One alternative schedule entails doing a level 0 dump, and then repeated level 9 dumps to distinct tapes (that is, a new tape for each dump) until it is time to do another level 0 dump. Another variation involves putting the dumps from several filesystems on one tape. This is possible when the level 2 to 9 dumps take up only a small portion of a tape, which happens when the filesystems are small or relatively static, or the tape drive is a high density (i.e, 6250 bpi). Putting more than one filesystem on a tape saves tapes and operator time, but it makes restoring individual files a little tricky. With this method, a tape can be mounted before the operator leaves at night, and **cron** (see Chapter 21: *Periodic Processes*) can be used to run **dump** at night, because no changing of tapes is required. If a dump schedule seems particularly well suited for your system, by all means use it. If in doubt, use the Towers of Hanoi sequence. The following sections are written with specific examples and references to the Towers of Hanoi sequence, but they contain basic information that is valid regardless of the dump sequence that is used.

18.4.4 Cleaning tape drives

Tapes leave a brown residue on the parts that they come in contact with which should be cleaned off. Before a dump is done, the heads and rollers of the tape drive should be cleaned. Tape drives are cleaned with sterile alcohol cleaning pads and/or with sterile swabs that have been dipped in special tape drive cleaning solution. Never use rubbing alcohol because it contains water. The heads should be cleaned last with a new sterile pad. If you are unsure of how to clean your tape drive, refer to its documentation. While cleaning the drives before each dump may seem like overkill, it really does reduce the frequency of tape read and write errors.

18.4.5 Preparing to do dumps

The first step in preparing to do dumps is to acquire a set of tapes for the level 2 to 9 dumps and label them. The level 1 tapes cannot be labeled in advance because level 1 dumps are typically multivolume; these tapes should be relabeled every time they are used. The label on each tape should clearly show the level, the filesystem, and the machine name. These tapes will be reused, so they should be of good quality. Cheap tapes tend to become less reliable after several reuses.

The next step is to generate a dump schedule to keep track of when dumps should be done, when (and whether) the dumps were done, and by whom they were done. Schedules can be handwritten, or a simple shell script can be written to generate them automatically.

While it is possible to do the dumps by manually executing **dump** with all of its arguments, it is much easier to invoke a program that keeps track of which dumps should be done, prompts the operator to load the correct tapes, and executes **dump** with the correct arguments. This type of program also has the advantage that it does the tedious bookkeeping, making an operator error less likely. Appendix F contains a C-shell script called **dumdum** that can be modified to handle almost any combination filesystems and dump media.

It is still important to maintain careful hardcopy dump records, because there is always the chance that **dumdum** will become misaligned with the actual dump schedule. A method of performing dumps that may be used on BSD systems is to use the dump frequency field in /etc/fstab and **dump -w** to remind you when to do dumps.

After **dumdum** or a **dumdum**-like program is installed, a dump schedule has been made up, and enough tapes have been acquired, it is time to start actually doing dumps. The way to start any kind of dump regime is by doing a level 0 dump.

18.4.6 Level 0 and 1 dumps

Before you perform a level 0 dump, you should run **fsck** (see Section 4.8). To begin doing a dump, simply execute **dumdum**, preferably from the system console. The **dumdum** program will determine which dump should be done (level 0 if this is the first dump done), and then ask the operator for verification. After the operator confirms the level of the dump, **dumdum** will tell the operator to mount the first tape. After the tape is mounted, **dump** itself will be executed and begin outputting various messages. **dump** gives very verbose messages, including periodic status reports and some grossly optimistic estimations as to how many tapes and how much time will be required to complete the dump.

When a tape is removed, it should be immediately labeled (if not prelabeled) with the level of the dump, the filesystem being dumped, the date of the dump, the density of the tape, and the sequence number of the tape (i.e., number 1 of *n*, where *n* will be filled in after the entire filesystem has been dumped). If the tape is not the first of a sequence, it should also be labeled with the starting inode number as reported by **dump**. Since files are dumped in order of inode, the inode number allows an operator to identify on which tape of a long dump a particular file is stored during a later **restore**.

After a filesystem has been completely dumped, **dumdum** will prompt the operator to mount volume 1 of the dump, and it will then perform a **restore -t** to produce a table of contents for the dump. The output from this command will be placed in a disk file named /usr/local/adm/dumpdir/lev*X.filesys*, where *X* is the level of the dump and *filesys* is the filesystem being dumped. Besides providing a quick check that the first tape of the dump is readable, this **restore -t** makes it much easier to determine on which dump tape(s) a particular file resides.

If **restore** prints out an error message that the tape is unreadable, the entire dump must be repeated. There is no easy way to tell if the problem lies with the tape or the drive, so you might want to experiment with **tar**'ing some small files onto another tape to determine where the problem lies. Bad tapes should be immediately damaged (to prevent someone from coming along and "salvaging" them) and discarded.

Level 0 and 1 dump tapes should, if possible, be stored somewhere other than the machine room to guard against a catastrophe such as a fire that destroys both the machine and the dump tapes. Level 0 dumps are often saved for two years or more to provide the ability to restore files that were on the system for a long time, even if they were removed quite some time ago.

Dumps should be done with as little filesystem activity as possible because filesystem activity can cause the **dump** program to make mistakes. Filesystem activity during dumps may be limited either by doing the dumps at times when there are few or no users on the system, such as at night or on the weekends, or by making the filesystem inaccessible to anyone but the dump program. If dumps are done at night, they should be scheduled so they are not done at the same time as any programs invoked by **cron** that modify the filesystem, such as the system accounting programs. An inconsistency in a level 0 dump can make it impossible to restore the filesystem; therefore the filesystem must be absolutely stationary while a level 0 dump is being done. It is not as important to limit filesystem activity on level 2 to 9 dumps, because mistakes on these tapes will usually only cause files that were modified during the dump to be unreadable.

18.4.7 Level 2 to 9 dumps

Level 2 to 9 dumps are much easier than level 0 and 1 dumps because the tapes are already labeled, filesystem activity does not have to be restricted, and they take much less time. When a level 2 to 9 dump is being done, the operator simply has to mount each tape that **dumdum** requests and fill out the appropriate dump schedule. Although these dumps can be done while there are users on the system, **dump** is a resource hog and the loss of system performance may require that the dumps be done at a time when the system is not heavily loaded.

18.4.8 Dumping over a network

Machines that are on a high-speed network and have the **rdump** command may be dumped over the network. **rdump** allows a machine to be dumped to a remote device; that is, a device that is connected to another machine on the network. Using **rdump** over a network allows the dumping of machines that do not have adequate removable media on which to do dumps, and it also allows an operator to use a single tape drive to dump all of the machines on a network, which allows an entire network to share one fast (but probably expensive) backup device. When dumping with **rdump**, **rrestore** should be run on the machine that was dumped to restore to that machine. Dumps done with **rdump** may be restored only on machines with the same byte order. Thus a dump of a Sun filesystem with **rdump** to a Vax tape drive can be restored using **rrestore** on the Sun from the Vax's tape drive, but it cannot be restored using **restore** on the Vax.

18.4.9 Dumping to disk

On some systems, it is not possible to have an operator present to switch tapes when the level 2 to 9 dumps are being done. If the system has adequate surplus disk space, dumps may be done to disk files and then transferred to tape when an operator is available. Programs such as **tar** or **cpio** can be used to transfer the dump files to tape. Here is an example of the commands that would be executed to do a daily dump (level 3 in this example) of the filesystems /usr and /project to disk and then transfer them to tape.

```
< executed by cron or at in the middle of the night >
dump 3unf /dumps/lev3.usr /usr |& mail operator
dump 3unf /dumps/lev3.project /project |& mail operator
< done by the operator in the morning >
[ check mail and make sure the dumps executed without errors ]
[ mount a tape for level 3 /usr ]
% tar -c /dumps/lev3.usr
[ mount a tape for level 3 /project ]
% tar -c /dumps/lev3.project
```

In the preceding example, /dumps is a filesystem or a directory that has been set aside for storing incremental dumps. Dumping to disk also has the advantage that recent incremental dumps may be kept online, simplifying the task of restoring lost files. Most users realize that they have incorrectly deleted a file within microseconds of hitting the return key, and having the most recent dump on the disk can be a real time saver. For example, to restore the file /project/franklin/lostfile from the level 3 dump done in the previous example, type:

```
restore -xf /dumps/lev3.project franklin/lostfile
```

If a dump regime involving dumps to disk is used, it should be thoroughly tested by restoring various files from the dumps before it is relied upon. Note also that if the amount of data to be backed up on any given day exceeds the space available for storage, the dumps will not be completed and the system will get clogged.

18.5 Restoring from dumps

There are as many variations of the **restore** program as there are of the **dump** program. Some versions are called **restor**, and others are called **restore**. Before reading this section, consult the manual page for your particular version of **restore**.

18.5.1 Restoring individual files

A system manager or operator will probably be called on often to restore individual files that users have somehow destroyed. Appendix G contains a listing of a csh script for a command called **lostfile**, which provides a convenient way for users to notify the system administrator when they have lost a file. The first step to take when notified of a lost file is to determine which dump tapes contain versions of the file. **dumdum** automatically does a **restore -t** after it finishes each dump, and stores the output in a file. We will refer to this type of file as a *dumptoc* (for dump table of contents). **dumdum** puts the dumptocs in /usr/local/adm/dumpdir, and names them lev*N*.*filesys*, where *N* is the level of the dump and *filesys* is the name of the filesystem. If you decide to write your own dump script, it should probably create dumptocs, because dumptocs allow you to easily determine which dump tape a lost file is on. For example, to find on which tape a file /users/janet/iamlost is located, execute the command:

grep janet/iamlost /usr/local/adm/dumpdir/*users

This command might create output like this:

```
/usr/local/adm/dumpdir/lev1.users: 18576        ./janet/iamlost
/usr/local/adm/dumpdir/lev3.users: 18576        ./janet/iamlost
/usr/local/adm/dumpdir/lev3.users: 18620        ./janet/iamlost.index
/usr/local/adm/dumpdir/lev2.users: 18576        ./janet/iamlost
/usr/local/adm/dumpdir/lev5.users: 18576        ./janet/iamlost
```

This tells you that the file /users/janet/iamlost can be found on the level 1, 3, 2, and 5 tapes. The file /etc/dumpdates (or your hardcopy schedule) can be consulted to determine which of those dumps was done most recently. This **grep** also tells you that the inode of the file is 18576. The inode number is important if you are using an older version of **restore** that is only able to restore by inode number. It also allows you to determine which tape of a multi-volume dump a file is on (you did write the starting inode number on the labels, didn't you?). Usually the user will want the most current version of a file, but that is not always the case. For example, if a user lost his file by inadvertently copying another file on top of it, he would want the version of the file that existed before he copied over it, not the most current version. If the dumptocs are not kept online, the system administrator must mount dump tapes and do **restore**'s on them until the correct version of the file is found. After determining which tape the desired file is on, **cd** to a place such as /tmp or /usr/tmp where a large directory hierarchy can be created without colliding with anything; most versions of **restore** must create all of the directories leading to a particular file before that file may be restored. Then use the **restore -x** command to restore the file. For example, to restore the file /users/janet/iamlost for the user janet on a BSD system, the following sequence of commands would be used:

```
[ mount the correct tape ]
% cd /tmp
% restore x /users/janet/iamlost
< restore command prints out various messages >
% ls /tmp/users/janet
iamlost
% ls /users/janet
afile  bfile  cfile
% cp /tmp/users/janet/iamlost /users/janet/iamlost
% chown janet /users/janet/iamlost
% chgrp student /users/janet/iamlost
% mail janet
    Your file iamlost has been restored as requested
and has been placed in /users/janet/iamlost.

            Your Name, Humble System Administrator
```

If there was a file /users/janet/iamlost still in existence on the system, the restored version would have to be renamed (for example: iamlost.restored) and the mail message altered to reflect this change.

18.5.2 Interactive restore

More recent versions of **restore** support the **-i** flag which allows **restore** to seem more interactive. This option represents the files on the tape in a filesystem format, and lets you step through them just like you would a normal directory tree using **ls**, **cd**, and **pwd**. Files that you wish to restore are added to a list with the **add** command, and when you have selected all of the desired files, the **extract** command will extract them from the tape. If your version of **restore** supports the **-i** option, use it, because it makes restoring much easier. Note that **restore -i** makes dumptocs obsolete to some extent because it allows the inode number of each file on a dump tape to be determined before the file is restored.

18.5.3 Restoring entire filesystems

With luck, a system administrator will never have to restore an entire filesystem due to system failure, but the situation does occasionally arise. Before attempting to restore the filesystem, it is imperative to make sure that whatever problem caused the filesystem to be destroyed has been remedied. It would be pointless to spend numerous hours spinning tapes only to have the filesystem destroyed again. Before beginning the restore, a filesystem must be created and mounted (see Chapter 12: *Adding a Disk*). **cd** to the mount point at the root of the new filesystem, mount the first tape of the most recent level 0 dump, and type **restore -r**. **restore** will prompt for each tape in the dump. After the level 0 dump has been restored, mount and restore each dump up to the last dump done in the same order they were done. For example, if the last dump done was a level 5 using the Towers of Hanoi sequence, the sequence of commands to restore the filesystem /usr, residing on physical device /dev/rhp0g , would look like this:

% **/etc/newfs /dev/rhp0g eagle** (**newfs** is a friendly version of **mkfs**)
% **/etc/mount /dev/hp0g /usr**
% **cd /usr**
[mount first tape of most recent level 0 dump of /usr]
% **restore -r**
[mount the tapes requested by restore]
[mount first tape of last level 1 dump of /usr, if more recent than the level 0]
% **restore -r**
[mount the tapes requested by restore]
[mount the level 3 tape for /usr]
% **restore -r**
[mount the level 2 tape for /usr]
% **restore -r**
[mount the level 5 tape for /usr]
% **restore -r**

This sequence would restore the filesystem to the state it was in when the level 5 dump was done.

18.5.4 Dumping and restoring to change system software

If you want to change the version of UNIX you are running on your system, all of the user filesystems will have to be backed up and possibly restored. The filesystems must be restored only if the filesystem format has changed between the old and new versions of UNIX, or if you wish to change the partitioning or layout of your disk, but they *must* be backed up as insurance against any problems that might occur while changing software. To do this, perform a level 0 dump on each user filesystem, change the operating system, then, if necessary, restore from the level 0 dumps. Also, backup and restore any system-specific files that are on / and /usr (such as /etc/passwd, /usr/local, etc.). UNIX's slightly brain-damaged organization mixes locally tailored files with distributed files, making this quite a difficult task. Appendix H contains a listing of a Makefile called Makefile.localsys that represents our attempts to automate this process.

18.6 Other archiving programs

dump is by no means the only program you can use to archive files to tapes; however, it is usually the most efficient way to do backups of an entire system. The programs **tar**, **cpio**, and **dd** also provide ways to move files from one medium to another. The following descriptions explain how each of these commands can be used to do some sort of backup, and give brief descriptions of some of the other uses of the commands.

18.6.1 The tar command

tar is an archive program which takes multiple files or directories and stores them as one file, usually a tape file. **tar** is a useful way to back up files that you anticipate will need to be recovered. For instance, if a user is leaving for six months and the system is short of disk space, the system administrator can use **tar** to put the user's files onto a tape and then remove them from the disk. When the user returns, the system administrator can use **tar** to reload the files from the tape back onto the (not totally full) disk. **tar** is also useful as a way of moving directory trees from place to place on versions of UNIX where **cp** is not capable of copying directory trees. For example, the command:

tar -cf - *adir* **| (cd /tmp ; tar xf -)**

would create a copy of the directory tree *adir* in /tmp. A note of caution: Do not put ".."'s in the arguments for **cd** in this command, or things may get screwed up on some systems. By default, **tar** does not follow symbolic links, but it can be instructed to do so with the **-h** flag. The biggest drawback of **tar** is that most versions do not allow multiple tape volumes; that is, if the data you wish to archive will not fit on one tape, **tar** cannot be used. **tar** is also very intolerant of tape errors.

18.6.2 The cpio command

cpio is another file archiving program that it is similar to **tar** in functionality. All ATT versions of UNIX contain **cpio**, but some of them do not contain **tar**. **cpio** is therefore a good method for archiving files for transfer between systems using ATT UNIX. **cpio** can also be used to move directory trees; for example, the command:

find *adir* **-depth -print | cpio -pd /tmp**

would make a copy of the directory tree *adir* in /tmp. Like **tar**, most versions of **cpio** do not allow multiple tape volumes. Some versions of **cpio** do not handle pipes gracefully, and only the superuser can copy special files.

18.6.3 The dd command

dd is a file copying and conversion program. Unless it is told to do some sort of conversion, **dd** just copies from its input file to its output file. **dd** is often used to read tapes that are written in non-UNIX format. If a user brings a tape that was written on some non-UNIX system, **dd** may be the only way to read the tape. Another use of **dd** is to create a copy of an entire filesystem easily. On a system with multiple disks, it is a good idea to keep such a copy of / on a separate disk. This backup filesystem can be booted and used to bring up the system if the disk that contains / fails. **dd** can also be used as a quick way to make a copy of a magnetic tape, as in this example:

Two tape drives (/dev/rmt8 and /dev/rmt9):
% **dd if=/dev/rmt8 of=/dev/rmt9 cbs=16b**

One tape drive (/dev/rmt8):
% **dd if=/dev/rmt8 of=tfile cbs=16b**
[change tapes]
% **dd if=tfile of=/dev/rmt8 cbs=16b**
% **rm tfile**

Of course, if you only have one tape drive, you must have enough disk space available to store an image of the tape.

18.6.4 The volcopy command

volcopy makes an exact copy of a filesystem to another device, changing the blocksize as appropriate. It is available on most ATT versions of UNIX. **volcopy** can be used to make backups of a filesystem to to a removable pack disk. **volcopy** can also be used to make a complete copy of a filesystem to tape.

18.7 Incremental backups without dump

Some systems do not have the **dump** and restore commands, but that does not mean that incremental backups cannot be done. Some systems have other programs that perform incremental backups which may be used in a manner similar to **dump** and restore. If your system has does not have such programs, **find** and **cpio** may be used to perform incremental backups. A simple script like **dumdum** can be created to assist.

19

Accounting

19.1 Introduction

The UNIX kernel and various system programs keep accounting records for CPU time, memory usage, input/output requests, login sessions, printer usage, and much more. A system administrator must summarize these records to understand and monitor usage, and to keep the data files from growing without bound and overflowing the disks. The CPU accounting files, for example, can grow by megabytes per day and will quickly swamp the disks if not regularly truncated.

The accounting systems are quite different on ATT and BSD systems, but both systems measure essentially the same data. The BSD system has a few C programs that summarize single quantities of interest, while the ATT system is built on shell scripts which collect and summarize the data into reports. System administrators tend to write scripts that take the output of the available tools and convert it into a format that suits their needs.

19.2 Why bother with accounting?

Universities that purchase computers with federal research dollars are often required by their funding agencies to keep detailed accounting records if they charge research grants for computer usage. Government contractors may also be required to keep detailed accounting information. The most obvious reason for accounting is to bill the users for the resources they used. Aside from these mandated reasons, system administrators need to keep an eye on resources and their allocation among users, monitor usage, and determine charging algorithms for users.

19.3 What to measure and archive

It is possible to measure many quantities associated with a running UNIX system: the kernel records CPU usage data, the **init** and **login** processes record connect time, the line printer daemon records printer usage, the programs that use a dial-out modem record the phone number called, and the file system is in some sense a constant record of disk usage. Accounting is usually run automatically by **cron**.

Many of the accounting data files and system log files must be truncated periodically or they will fill the disk. Before truncating them you may want to archive accounting summaries to disk or tape for permanent records. Per-device log files are useful for debugging, but not for much else. Accounting data files, summaries of their contents, and some log files may all need to be archived if complete records are required for possible audit.

Four broad philosophies exist for archiving these files:

- Conservative - archive all accounting files and most log files to tape
- Sensible - archive summary accounting files to tape or disk, keep other accounting data and log files for a month and overwrite them next time
- Carefree - restart all accounting and log files monthly, throw away the old ones
- No accounting - turn off accounting as much as possible, truncate files nightly out of **cron**

Choose a philosophy that fits the requirements of your particular site.

19.4 Outline of a complete accounting system

The charging algorithm for a complete accounting system usually includes not only the amount of a resource used, but also when it was used. Computations for CPU usage, for example, can be based on the time of day, on the priority at which commands are run, or both. Connect time charges can depend on the type of connection, with higher rates charged for graphics terminals and dial-up ports. Figure 19.1 illustrates a complete charging algorithm.

FIGURE 19.1

A complete charging algorithm	
Quantity measured	Rates
CPU time	High rate: 9 a.m.-5 p.m. Low rate: 5 p.m.-9 a.m.
Connect time	High rate: graphics terminals Medium rate: dial-ups Low rate: cheap terminals
Disk space	High rate: file system backed up daily Medium rate: file system backed up weekly Low rate: file system never backed up
Printer	High rate: laser printer Low rate: line printer
Phone - dial-out	Local rate Long distance rate

19.5 Simple accounting systems

The charging algorithm can also be very simple — for example, a fixed rate per user per month. You may not want to charge for all services, only certain ones such as disk space, pages printed, or long distance dial-out usage. The summary data produced by the accounting commands can be used to determine equitable rates and to understand usage patterns.

19.6 Accounting in a networked environment

In an environment with lots of workstations on a local area network, separate accounting on each workstation becomes difficult to manage. Tools should be designed to allow the system administrator or operator to run accounting for all workstations from a single host. This implies local scripts that summarize data on each host and a central script that collects this data and performs further processing.

19.7 Accounting under BSD

The accounting data archived, location of data files, and a summary of commands standard with BSD systems are detailed next.

19.7.1 CPU accounting

CPU accounting can be turned on by the **/etc/accton** command. **accton** is usually executed at boot time in the /etc/rc file:

```
/etc/accton  /usr/adm/acct
```

Data is kept in the file /usr/adm/acct (or whatever file is specified as the argument to the **accton** command) and grows by megabytes per day on a busy system. The UID, CPU time, memory usage, and input/output requests for each command executed are archived as the command finishes. Note that a program which never terminates does not produce any accounting record. The **sa** command can be used to summarize this data either by user, typically to the file /usr/adm/usracct, or by command, to /usr/adm/savacct. **sa** has a zillion options, most having to do with the sorted order of the final data and which uninteresting processes to ignore. Two useful ones are the **-m** option to summarize by user and the **-s** option to summarize by command and restart the data file /usr/adm/acct. This summary by command gives the system administrator a snapshot of system utilization. **sa -s** should be run at least daily to control the size of the /usr/adm/acct file. Sample output from **sa -m** follows:

```
user    # commands  CPU-minutes  io-operations    memory used
-------------------------------------------------------------
root          646      7.10cpu       7940tio       65583k*sec
daemon          5      0.03cpu         84tio          72k*sec
evi            28      2.41cpu        669tio       12094k*sec
uucp          240      4.60cpu       7922tio       20073k*sec
news         2162     10.61cpu      16829tio       63205k*sec
marga          51      0.66cpu        504tio        2980k*sec
roger          49      0.28cpu        397tio        1694k*sec
brett          35      0.53cpu        483tio        2013k*sec
johnd          61      1.34cpu       1797tio        9875k*sec
tyler          31      0.34cpu        201tio        1543k*sec
remote         23      3.16cpu        335tio        8021k*sec
```

Column 1 is the login name of the user; column 2 is the number of commands he executed; column 3 is the CPU time (user and system) used in minutes; column 4 is the total number of input/output operations performed; and column 5 is the average memory used by the programs executed, measured in core-kilobytes per second.

sa -s summarizes CPU usage by command, producing the following output, and also truncates /usr/adm/acct to zero length:

```
#commands          CPU time             input/output    memory  command
-----------------------------------------------------------------------
    3785   8936.16re     49.11cp         12avio     91k  TOTALS
       2    139.47re     10.13cp          3avio     20k  rmt
     141   3937.77re      6.37cp         31avio    109k  csh
      96   1561.48re      3.94cp         58avio     66k  uucico
     147      6.54re      2.55cp         41avio    105k  inews
      20   1552.44re      2.34cp         17avio     41k  rlogin
     191     37.44re      2.30cp         21avio    352k  sendmail
       4      3.44re      2.21cp        159avio    140k  sa
      26    143.05re      2.18cp         29avio    169k  ***other
     232     96.08re      1.90cp          3avio     29k  sh
      16    616.28re      1.71cp          0avio     44k  rlogin
      51      3.05re      1.65cp          4avio    322k  compress
       4    574.60re      1.65cp         10avio     27k  rlogind
      63     27.41re      1.09cp         12avio     58k  nntpxmit
      15     37.97re      0.94cp         30avio    122k  vi
     ...
```

Column 1 is the number of times the command has been executed; columns 2 and 3 are the real time (elapsed time) and CPU time (user and system), both in minutes; column 4 is the average number of input/output operations per command execution; column 5 is the core usage in kilobytes averaged over the CPU time execution period; and column 6 is the command name. the "***other" entry represents all commands with unprintable characters in their name and all commands that have been executed only once.

The system automatically suspends accounting if the filesystem that contains the accounting data becomes 95% full. When space becomes available on the filesystem, accounting is restarted automatically.

If the machine crashes or is rebooted, processes that were running are not recorded in the CPU accounting file. A sneaky user could avoid CPU accounting by having his program sleep indefinitely upon completion so it is always still running when the machine is rebooted.

19.7.2 Connect time accounting

Connect time accounting is turned on by the existence of the data collection file /usr/adm/wtmp. Login name, port, login time and logout time are recorded. The **ac** command summarizes the data by person or by day and should be done at least monthly; the wtmp file should be truncated at this time. Sample output from **ac -p** follows:

```
login   connect-hrs
------------------
Uhao        0.13
Uutah-cs    0.02
remote     43.95
mcbryan    13.32
trent       3.46
forys       0.03
johnd       0.85
evi        24.26
 ...
total     117.76
```

The output of **ac -d**, shown next, which summarizes by date, illustrates that the weekends are periods of lighter usage.

```
date           connect-hrs
-------------------------
Jan  1 total     65.47
Jan  2 total     93.96
Jan  3 total    129.61
Jan  4 total    318.19
Jan  5 total    327.31
Jan  6 total    236.02
Jan  7 total    285.24
Jan  8 total    262.03
Jan  9 total     93.91
Jan 10 total     86.26
```

The **last** command can be used to display the data by port; this is useful in determining overworked or broken terminals, or dial-up usage. For example, the command **/usr/ucb/last ttyd0,** which will show the usage on the dial-up port /dev/ttyd0, produces:

```
remote    ttyd0         Sun Jan 10 08:00   still logged in
remote    ttyd0         Sun Jan 10 07:44 - 08:00  (00:15)
remote    ttyd0         Sat Jan  9 23:46 - 00:40  (00:54)
lee       ttyd0         Sat Jan  9 14:48 - 14:55  (00:07)
remote    ttyd0         Sat Jan  9 13:25 - 13:28  (00:02)
bob       ttyd0         Fri Jan  8 17:34 - 17:51  (00:16)
mercure   ttyd0         Fri Jan  8 07:40 - 07:44  (00:03)
johnd     ttyd0         Fri Jan  8 05:26 - 05:39  (00:13)
 ...
Uakelei   ttyd0         Fri Jan  1 05:52 - 05:55  (00:02)

wtmp begins Fri Jan  1 00:15
```

19.7.3 Disk usage

Snapshot data of disk usage can be obtained by the **quot** command, showing each user's total number of files and disk blocks on each partition of the filesystem. For example, **quot -f /dev/ra0h** produces:

```
blocks   files   user
----------------------

/dev/ra0h (/usr):
86138    7792    root
14469     555    news
 7926     877    ingres
 1418      21    daemon
  571      74    uucp
  336       2    laszlo
  292       3    nobody
  235       8    coggs
   ...
```

The **du** command summarizes the disk usage in a directory hierarchy. This can be quite effective in identifying disk hogs; for example: **du -s /faculty/*** produces:

```
404      andrzej
5101     bobby
1083     clayton
3949     dennis
746      driscoll
3771     evi
4598     lee
27756    roger
  ...
```

If accuracy is required, disk usage summaries should be run daily at random times and then the results averaged. Accounting records can provide the raw data for requesting users to control their disk usage; see Section 26.8 for details.

19.7.4 Printer usage

The line printer daemon **lpd** records printer usage if the /etc/printcap file entry has the *af* variable defined and if the file designated by *af* exists. See Chapter 11: *Printing under BSD* for more information about the /etc/printcap file. The accounting file is typically called /usr/adm/*printer-name*-acct (for example, lp-acct) and contains the number of pages printed, hostname, and username for each use of the printer. Data is summarized by the **pac** command; use it at least monthly. For example, the command **/etc/pac -Pgutenberg** produces the following output:

```
  Login                   pages/feet   runs    price
------------------------------------------------------
anchor:baeza                   68.00    13   $  1.36
anchor:cactisl                 11.00     2   $  0.22
anchor:heuring                 69.00    12   $  1.38
anchor:moce                     3.00     1   $  0.06
anchor:waite                   19.00     2   $  0.38
ausone:terwilli              1259.00   186   $ 25.18
bass:herbert                    8.00     2   $  0.16
bass:morfeq                     2.00     1   $  0.04
boulder.Colorado.EDU:amy       30.00     6   $  0.60
boulder.Colorado.EDU:ann       14.00     3   $  0.28
boulder.Colorado.EDU:evi      908.00   299   $ 18.16
 ...

total                       20004.00 4397    $400.08
```

The **pac** command takes a flag **-p***price* which sets the price per page (in dollars) to be used. The default is .02 or 2 cents per page; **pac** does not charge per run, so any header pages are not charged for. There are several other options to **pac**; as always consult your manual for local wisdom.

19.7.5 Dial-out usage

The **cu**, **tip**, and uucp family of commands record the login name, date and time, phone number, and status of all calls made through a dial-out modem. The data is recorded in /usr/adm/aculog, which is a text file. If you allow users to talk directly to the modem via a *dialer* entry in the file /etc/remote, then the command **tip dialer** will circumvent the accounting process since the **tip** program does not cause the phone number to be dialed directly and therefore cannot write an appropriate log entry. No standard tools exist to summarize this file; however, **grep** can be used to identify long distance calls.

19.7.6 Summaries

The following two tables detail the files that store accounting data and the commands to summarize them. Note that the owner, group, and mode (octal) of the accounting data files is important and that any program used to reinitialize these files should be sure to **chown**, **chgrp**, and **chmod** appropriately.

FIGURE 19.2

Summary of BSD accounting data files						
Data kept	Filename	Type	Owner	Group	Mode	Man entry
CPU,memory,i/o	/usr/adm/acct	Binary	root	system	644	acct(5)
Connect time	/usr/adm/wtmp	Binary	root	system	644	wtmp(5)
Disk usage	the filesystem	N/A	root	operator	640	
Printer usage	/usr/adm/lpacct	Text	daemon	daemon	644	
Dialout usage	/usr/adm/aculog	Text	uucp	daemon	664	

FIGURE 19.3

Summary of BSD accounting commands			
Data	Command	Man entry	Frequency to run
CPU	**/etc/accton**	**accton**(8)	During boot
	/etc/sa	**sa**(8)	At least daily
Connect	**/etc/ac**	**ac**(8)	Monthly
Disk	**/etc/quot**	**quot**(8)	Daily and average data
	/bin/du	**du**(1)	As needed
Printer	**/etc/pac**	**pac**(8)	Monthly for each printer

19.7.7 Archiving log files

Many UNIX programs write status information to a log file. These files are very useful in debugging and accounting, but they grow steadily and often very quickly, and so must be truncated on a regular basis. This is typically done by scripts run by **cron** at regular intervals. Figure 19.4 lists the files to archive, summarize, or truncate, the minimal frequency to do so given average disk resources, the required owner, and the mode of the new file.

FIGURE 19.4

BSD files to archive regularly					
File	Frequency	Owner	Group	Mode	Contents
/usr/adm/acct	daily	root	system	644	CPU accounting
/usr/adm/wtmp	monthly	root	system	644	Connect accounting
/usr/adm/*lpacct	monthly	daemon	daemon	644	Printer accounting
/usr/adm/aculog	monthly	uucp	daemon	664	Dial-out accounting
/usr/adm/messages	monthly	root	system	664	Console messages
/usr/adm/shutdownlog	monthly	root	system	664	Shutdown reasons
/usr/adm/timed.log	monthly	root	system	644	Time daemon log
/usr/spool/uucp/LOGFILE	monthly	uucp	daemon	664	Uucp transaction log
/usr/spool/uucp/SYSLOG	monthly	uucp	daemon	664	Uucp file transfer log
/usr/adm/gatedlog	daily	root	system	644	Network routing log
.../news/nntp/logfile	weekly	news	news	644	News connection log

19.8 Accounting under ATT

Most versions of ATT contain a fairly complete accounting system implemented with C programs and **sh** scripts. These scripts are typically run daily and monthly by **cron**. All accounting is done under the login adm with home directory /usr/adm, which is also where accounting data is kept. The accounting programs and scripts are usually in /usr/lib/acct.

19.8.1 Setting up accounting

On most systems accounting does not run by default, so you must set it up. The first thing to do is to make sure that the adm login exists. If it does not, you can create it by adding the following line to /etc/passwd:

```
adm:*:4:4:Administrative Login:/usr/adm:/bin/sh
```

adm traditionally has UID 4 but that is completely arbitrary. After creating the login, make sure that the directory /usr/adm/acct exists and is owned by adm. The /usr/adm directory should contain a .profile with the following contents:

```
PATH=/usr/lib/acct:/bin:/usr/bin
```

You should also create the subdirectories "nite", "sum", and "fiscal" in /usr/adm/acct.

Accounting information is not gathered until the **startup** command is executed. To start accounting automatically, add the following line to /etc/rc:

```
/bin/su - adm -c /usr/lib/acct/startup
```

And to turn off accounting gracefully before a reboot, add the following line to /etc/shutdown:

```
/usr/lib/acct/shutacct
```

In order for the system to charge properly for system usage, you must tell it which hours you consider *prime* time and which days are holidays. This is done in the file /usr/lib/acct/holidays. A sample holiday file looks like this:

```
* Prime/Nonprime Table for Accounting System
*
* Curr      Prime      Non-Prime
* Year      Start      Start
*
  1989      0830       1700
```

```
*
* Day of     Calendar     Company
* Year       Date         Holiday
*
    1        Jan 1        New Year's Day
   33        Feb 2        Ground Hog Day
   35        Feb 4        Ken Thompson's Birthday
  120        May 1        Biff's Birthday
  252        Sep 9        Dennis Ritchie's Birthday
  323        Oct 31       Halloween
  338        Nov 15       A-Basin Opens
  329        Nov 26       Thanksgiving Day
  330        Nov 27       Day after Thanksgiving
  358        Dec 24       Christmas Eve
  359        Dec 25       Christmas Day
```

All lines starting with an "*" are comments. The first noncomment line specifies the current year (in this case 1989), and the start and end of the prime hours. In this example prime hours are from 8:30 a.m. to 5:00 p.m. There is no easy way to increase the granularity of the prime time specification, it must be a contiguous block of hours. All other hours are considered non-prime. The rest of the lines in the file contain the days that you consider holidays, which are treated in the same way as weekends. The fields are:

Day of Year   Month   Day   Description

of these, only the Day of Year is actually used by the accounting programs. Obviously the holidays file must be updated each year. A mail message will be sent to users adm and root if the accounting is run with an out-of-date holidays file.

Running **startup** just tells the system to start archiving accounting data; it does not cause it to be processed. The following **cron** entries, usually placed in /usr/spool/cron/crontab/adm, support both daily and monthly accounting processing. They take the raw accounting data and gather it into a format that can be easily understood. The entries *min* and *hr* refer to minutes and hours in the wee hours of the night when performance degradation will not impact regular users.

```
#
#  daily and weekly accounting chores
#
min  hr  *  *  1-6   /usr/lib/acct/runacct 2> /usr/adm/acct/nite/fd2log
min  hr  *  *  4     /usr/lib/acct/dodisk
0  *   *  *  *       /usr/lib/acct/ckpacct
```

```
#
#  monthly accounting
#
min  hr  1  *  *      /usr/lib/acct/monacct
```

19.8.2 What accounting does

The **runacct** program generates several files that contain daily accounting information, and stores them in the directory /usr/adm/acct/sum. The only files in this directory that are of any real interest are the report files. There are report files for each day since **monacct** was last run called rprt*mmdd* where *mm* is the month and *dd* is the day. These reports can be printed out if you want daily accounting. The reports contain summaries of terminal utilization, command usage, disk usage, and time of last login. The format of the report files is self-explanatory. If **runacct** does not run to completion because the system crashes, it will have to be restarted by hand. The manual page gives a complete description of how to restart **runacct** so it picks up where it left off.

The **dodisk** program collects disk usage information. **dodisk** is only run once a week because it uses a lot of CPU time, and disk usage does not generally change that much. The data that **dodisk** gathers is summarized by **runacct**.

The **ckpacct** command monitors the process accounting data file /usr/adm/pacct and splits it up when it exceeds a certain size, usually 1000 blocks. **ckpacct** also monitors free space on /usr, and disables accounting if there are fewer than 500 free blocks.

The **monacct** program summarizes all of the daily reports for the previous month, stores the summaries in /usr/adm/acct/fiscal/fiscrpt*mm*, where *mm* is the month, and restarts the summary files in the sum directory. If you want to charge users for their usage, you can write a simple shell script that examines the monthly summaries and generates invoices for each user.

In addition to the information that is collected automatically when accounting is turned on, the **chargefee** program allows you to assess additional fees on specific users. This is useful if you want to charge for something that you did for them, such as loading a tape. You could use the command:

/usr/lib/acct/chargefee joe 10

to charge the user joe for ten accounting units. What the units mean is completely arbitrary. All fees that are charged with **chargefee** will appear in the report files, so you can include them in any invoices you generate.

Ideally, you should not have to worry about the nitty-gritty of how data files are processed. However, if you want to modify how accounting works, or if something is not working correctly, you may have to investigate the inner workings. The accounting system keeps a lot of internal files in the directories /usr/adm/acct/nite and /usr/adm/acct/sum. Brief descriptions of the various commands and data files can be found in the documentation. Figure 19.5 describes the files usually found in the directory /usr/lib/acct.

FIGURE 19.5

Summary of ATT accounting commands in /usr/lib/acct		
Command	Type	Description
acctdusg	Program	Computes disk usage by login
accton	Program	Turns on process accounting
acctwtmp	Program	Adds boot record to wtmp file
chargefee	**sh** script	Charges specific users
ckpacct	**sh** script	Checks size of pacct file and restarts it if too big
diskusg	Program	Generate disk accounting data by user
dodisk	**sh** script	Takes a snapshot of disk usage
fwtmp	Program	Fixes dates in wtmp when **date** command has changed them
holidays	Text	List of holidays
monacct	**sh** script	Produces monthly reports
nulladm	**sh** script	Reinitializes files and insures correct ownership
prctmp	**sh** script	Print session record file
prdaily	**sh** script	Prints previous day's accounting summaries
prtacct	**sh** script	Prints the accounting records from tacct files
remove	**sh** script	Cleans up the /usr/adm/acct/sum directory
runacct	**sh** script	Summarizes daily data
shutacct	Program	Adds shutdown record to wtmp file and turns off accounting
startup	**sh** script	Executed at boot time to enable accounting
turnacct	**sh** script	Turns on accounting to the file /usr/adm/pacct
wtmpfix	Program	Recognizes and repairs a bad wtmp file
acctcms	Program	Make command usage records - called by **runacct**
acctcon1	Program	Make connect time records - called by **runacct**
acctcon2	Program	Make connect time records - called by **runacct**
acctprc1	Program	Make process records - called by **runacct**
acctprc2	Program	Make process records - called by **runacct**
acctmerg	Program	Merge processed records - called by **runacct**
acctdisk	Program	Make disk usage records - called by **dodisk**
acctdusg	Program	Make disk usage records - called by **dodisk**

20

Daemons

20.1 Introduction

The UNIX daemons are a collection of processes that each perform a particular system task. In keeping with the UNIX philosophy of modularity, daemons are programs rather than parts of the kernel. Most of the daemons are started in the /etc/rc files and continue to run as long as the system is up.[1]

Many people equate the word “daemon” with the word “demon,” implying some kind of Satanic connection between UNIX and the underworld. This is an egregious misunderstanding. “Daemon” is actually a much older form of “demon”; daemons have no particular bias towards good or evil, but rather serve to help define a person’s character or personality. The ancient Greeks’ concept of a “personal daemon” was similar to the modern concept of a “guardian angel” — “eudaemonia” is the state of being helped or protected by a kindly spirit. As a rule, UNIX systems seem to be infested with both daemons and demons.

[1] This is no longer true on systems that use **inetd**. See Section 14.5.12 for more information.

The word daemon was first used as a computer term by Mick Bailey, a British gentleman who was working on the CTSS programming staff at MIT during the early 1960s.[2] Mick quoted the Oxford English Dictionary in support of both the meaning and spelling of the word. Daemons made their way from CTSS to Multics to UNIX, where they are so popular they need a superdaemon to manage them. Daemons are featured on the cover of the BSD UNIX manuals.

This chapter presents a brief overview of the most common daemons. Not all of the daemons listed here are supplied with UNIX, and not all daemons supplied with UNIX are listed here. Besides making you more aware of how UNIX works, knowing what all of the various daemons do will make you look really smart when one of your users asks, "What does **comsat** do?"

20.2 Daemons common to ATT and BSD

Only the **init** and **cron** daemons are common to ATT and BSD, and the implementations of both are substantially different.

20.2.1 init

init is the most important daemon, for it is the parent of all user processes. **init** is started as the last step of the boot procedure and *always* has a PID of 1. **init** either places the system in single-user mode or begins reading the /etc/rc startup files. If the system is placed in single-user mode, **init** will read the /etc/rc files upon termination of the single-user shell.

After processing the /etc/rc files, **init** consults the /etc/ttys (BSD) or /etc/inittab (ATT) file to determine on which terminal ports to expect logins, and attempts to open them. If a port cannot be opened, **init** periodically issues complaints on the system console until either the port can be opened or it is removed from the list of active ports. **init** spawns a **getty** process on each port that is successfully opened. While the system remains in multi-user mode, **init** maintains these **getty** processes on the appropriate ports. **init** is partially responsible for maintaining the /etc/utmp file, which contains information about each logged-on user, and the /usr/adm/wtmp file, which contains a diary of login and logoff times.

init also plays an important role in controlling the undead zombie processes that would otherwise accumulate on the system. This function of **init** is described in Chapter 5: *Controlling Processes*.

[2] This bit of history comes from Jerry Saltzer at MIT, via Dennis Ritchie, via Kirk McKusick.

On some systems, **init** can be told to reread the /etc/ttys file by sending it a hangup signal (SIGHUP). For example, to turn on an additional terminal port the following commands could be used:

> **vi /etc/ttys**
> (change entry for desired port)
> **kill -1 1**

On older systems, the hangup signal told **init** to bring the system down to single-user mode. This function has been subsumed by the software termination signal (TERM) on later systems. Asking **init** to return to single-user mode is the last step in most **shutdown** scripts. **init** is so essential to the operation of the system that an automatic reboot is initiated if **init** ever dies.

The **init** daemon supplied with ATT's System V is more complex than the traditional **init**. This **init** supports various "run levels" at which it can be started. These levels determine which system resources are enabled. There are eight run levels: 0 to 6 and "s" (single-user). The characteristics of each run level are determined by the /etc/inittab file. When **init** is started up, it prompts the user to enter a run level. If "s" is given, it enters single-user mode. Otherwise, it scans /etc/inittab for entries that specify the requested run level and executes the corresponding commands. The format of /etc/inittab is discussed in Section 9.4.2. The command **telinit** is used to change the run level of **init**; for example, **telinit 4** changes to **init** run level 4. **telinit**'s most useful argument is **-q**, which causes **init** to re-read /etc/inittab.

20.2.2 cron

The **cron** daemon is the system's alarm clock. It wakes up periodically and reads either the file /usr/lib/crontab or all of the files in the directory /usr/lib/cron or /usr/lib/crontab, depending on the system. The crontab files enumerate commands that need to be run periodically, ranging from running monthly accounting to polling uucp neighbors for mail.

The more intelligent versions of **cron** read ahead in their command files to find which command is to be executed next, and then sleep until the appropriate time. The format of the command files and the uses of **cron** are described in Chapter 21: *Periodic Processes*.

20.3 The BSD daemons

Of the five daemons described next, only two can really be considered daemons in the true sense of the word. The first three, **pagedaemon**, **swapper**, and **update**, perform tasks that are more on the kernel level than the user-service level.

20.3.1 pagedaemon

The **pagedaemon** is an integral part of the BSD virtual memory system. When a page of virtual memory is accessed, a *page table* is consulted to determine if that page is currently in physical memory. If the page is not in memory, a page fault occurs, and the **pagedaemon** is called upon to bring it into memory from the paging disk.

The **pagedaemon** determines the location of the page in the swap space, then reads it into an available page of physical memory. If there are no available pages of physical memory, the **pagedaemon** selects a page of physical memory and writes it to the swap device, updating the appropriate page table entries, to make room for the needed page.

20.3.2 swapper

When there are many processes running simultaneously, the system will begin to spend much of its time processing page faults, because each process has a certain number of pages that it accesses regularly. This condition is called *thrashing*, and it can cause severe performance degradation. The **swapper** daemon is the solution to thrashing.

The **swapper** monitors the number of page faults that occur in proportion to the number of memory references. If too many page faults are occurring, the **swapper** will begin selecting processes to be moved out to the swap space. The processes fingered by the **swapper** are moved entirely out of memory, and are prevented from running for a comparatively long time (seconds). The **swapper** continues to move processes out to the swap space until the page fault level is acceptable. Swapped processes do eventually get swapped back in and allowed to resume execution.

20.3.3 update

update executes the **sync** system call every 30 seconds. **sync** writes the current version of all super-blocks to disk and schedules other disk blocks buffered in memory for writing to disk. Keeping the super-blocks up to date minimizes damage to the filesystem in the event of a crash. On some early versions of UNIX, this function was performed by **cron**.

We know of one novice system administrator who, while cleaning up the crontab files on a UNIX system, removed the **update** functionality completely. The filesystem mess that resulted was monumental.

20.3.4 lpd

The **lpd** daemon is responsible for the printer queuing system. It accepts requests to be printed and forks processes to actually perform the printing. It is not uncommon for **lpd** to hang and have to be restarted manually. A detailed description of **lpd** is given in Chapter 11: *Printing under BSD*.

20.3.5 sendmail

The **sendmail** daemon processes the mail queued by various mail interface programs, translates their addresses, and sends them on to the appropriate mailers. See Chapter 15: *Mail and Berkeley Sendmail* for a complete description of mail processing, including the **sendmail** daemon.

20.4 ATT daemons

There are only two standard ATT daemons: **errdaemon** and **lpsched**.

20.4.1 errdaemon

errdaemon collects and logs system errors by reading the special file /dev/error. By default, **errdaemon** places the errors in the file /usr/adm/errfile, but another file can be specified when the daemon is started. **errdaemon** does not analyze the error data; the **errpt** command is used for this.

errdaemon should be started in /etc/rc, and can be terminated with the **kill** command or by using the command **/etc/errstop**. Only one copy of **errdaemon** should be active at any time.

20.4.2 lpsched

lpsched is ATT's version of the line printer daemon. **lpsched** receives print jobs from the **lp** program and queues them for printing. When an appropriate device becomes available, **lpsched** spawns a slave process to do the actual printing. There is a detailed description of **lpsched** in Chapter 11: *Printing under ATT*.

20.5 Internet daemons

We define "Internet daemons" very loosely to mean daemons that use Internet protocols to handle requests for service from machines on the network. Most Internet daemons spend the majority of their time servicing local requests.

The file /etc/services gives a list of all of the "well-known" services, and the port numbers at which they wait for work requests. The following are brief descriptions of some of the networking daemons. The respective manual pages should be consulted for details.

20.5.1 inetd

inetd is the Internet superdaemon. It is alway running. When **inetd** starts up, it reads /etc/inetd.conf (or /etc/servers on some Sun systems) to determine to which ports it should listen, and then waits for messages on those ports. When a message is received, **inetd** creates a copy of the appropriate daemon to actually handle the request. A more detailed description of this process is given in Section 14.5.12.

20.5.2 comsat

comsat is responsible for notifying users when new mail has arrived. When **comsat** receives an indication that there is new mail for a user, it looks in /etc/utmp to see if the user is logged on. If so, it checks to see whether the user has set biff ("bark if from found", as if that explains anything)[3] with the command **biff y**. If both of the conditions are true, **comsat** prints the beginning of the mail message to the user's terminal.

20.5.3 talkd

Requests for connection from the **talk** program are accepted by **talkd**. When it receives a request, it negotiates with the other machine to set up a network connection between the two users executing **talk**.

20.5.4 rwhod

rwhod maintains general information about who is logged on and what the load average is for all machines on the network. It collects this information for the local machine and broadcasts it; when **rwhod** receives information from other hosts, it verifies that the information is reasonable and then places it in the file /usr/spool/rwho/whod.*hostname*, where *hostname* is the name of the host that sent the information. The programs **rwho** and **ruptime** reference this information.

By default, **rwhod** broadcasts only every three minutes, so the data reported by **rwho** and **ruptime** are only approximately correct.

[3] Biff was actually the name of Heidi Stettner's dog, who always barked when the mailman came. The "bark if from found" explanation was invented after the fact.

20.5.5 ftpd

ftpd is the daemon that handles **ftp**, the ARPANET file transfer protocol. **ftpd** first verifies that the user has a passwd file entry, and verifies the password. If the user name is "anonymous" or "ftp" and an ftp login exists, any password is acceptable but access is limited to the user ftp's home directory and its subtrees. **ftpd** understands the commands placed in the ~ftp/bin directory (usually only **ls**.) It expands shell wildcards locally to make file specification easier. See Section 14.9.2 for more information about **ftpd**.

20.5.6 rexecd

rexecd stands for "remote execution daemon." Requests for command execution from a remote machine are received by **rexecd** over the Internet. After verifying the login name and password supplied by the remote user, **rexecd** will optionally set up an additional communication channel for standard error output, and attempt to set up the user's default environment. If this is successful, **rexecd** forks the user's shell, which inherits the communications channels.

20.5.7 rlogind

rlogind is responsible for handling remote logins. When invoked by **inetd**, it tries to automatically authenticate the remote user by examining the contents of the /etc/hosts.equiv file and the user's "~/.rhosts" file. If automatic authentication is successful, the user is logged in directly. Otherwise, **rlogind** executes a **login** process to prompt the user for a password.

20.5.8 rshd

Remote shell requests from the **rsh** and **rcmd** commands are handled by **rshd**. The authentication process enforced by **rshd** is similar to that of **rlogind**, except that if permissions are insufficient, the shell request is denied without allowing the user to prove his identity by typing in a password. **rshd** is also the server for **rcp** remote file copy requests.

20.5.9 timed

A number of different network time servers exist, and more than one is named **timed**. Most time servers support essentially the same paradigm. One or more machines are designated as masters and continuously maintain a notion of the correct time. The other participating machines are slaves; they periodically converse with the master to learn the time and adjust their internal clocks appropriately.

The time between settings of a slave's clock is short enough that only very slight adjustments need usually be made. If available, the slave will use the

adjtime system call[4] to smooth the adjustment of the system's clock and prevent large time leaps backwards or forwards. Setting the clock back suddenly is especially harmful; time should be a monotonically increasing function.

The notion of "correct" time is rather nebulously defined since the motivation for using time services is usually just to insure that all computers stay synchronized. Some time servers poll the network to get an average time value, while others simply declare the master correct by fiat. Time values calibrated to atomic standards are available by modem or over the ARPANET.

20.5.10 routed

The **routed** daemon maintains routing information used in sending and forwarding packets over the Ethernet. **routed** deals only with dynamic routing; routes that are statically defined (i.e., wired-in with the **route** command) are not modified. In operation, **routed** is both a sender and a receiver of routing information. See Chapter 14: *Networking under BSD* for more information about **routed**.

20.5.11 gated

gated understands several routing protocols, including that used by **routed**. **gated** translates routing information between the RIP, EGP, and Hello routing protocol systems. **gated** was written by Mark Fedor and is not yet a part of standard BSD. Chapter 14 gives more information on **gated**.

20.5.12 syslogd

syslogd acts as a clearing house for status information and error messages produced by many system programs and daemons. Before **syslogd** was written, daemons and programs either wrote their error messages directly to the system console or maintained their own private log files. Now they simply use the **syslog**(3) library routine to register a message and severity code with **syslogd**.

syslogd takes the messages it receives and routes them according to instructions contained in the /etc/syslog.conf file. Messages may be appended to a file, forwarded to a different machine, written to all or a subset of the logged-in users. There may be more than one destination for a particular message. The configuration syntax for syslog allows for fine control over message routing, as both the importance of a message and its source may be taken into account when disposing of it.

[4] **adjtime** biases the speed of the system's clock so that it very gradually falls back into correct alignment. When the system time matches the current objective time, the bias is canceled and the clock runs normally.

20.5.13 named

named is the name server for the domain-style Internet naming scheme. **named** maps host names into network addresses using a distributed database maintained by **named**'s everywhere. Section 14.9.1 describes domains and the operation of **named**.

20.5.14 nntpd

Nntp (network news transfer protocol) is a protocol used to transfer Usenet news articles across an Internet. The protocol is sufficiently general to allow it to serve both as a front-end for single users who want to read news interactively and as a mechanism for bulk propagation of news from machine to machine.

nntpd is the daemon which implements the nntp protocol. As an interactive news server it is driven by programs such as **rrn** (really just a link to **rn**) which maintain the illusion that news articles are stored on every machine, when actually only one copy of each article is stored on a master machine. As a bulk news transfer agent, it is driven by the news distribution software in much the same way that uucp is driven for transfers via telephone.

21

Periodic Processes

All UNIX systems provide a facility for automatically scheduling the execution of programs and scripts on a periodic basis. This chapter describes the operation of that mechanism and outlines a number of typical applications for system administration.

21.1 cron - the UNIX timekeeper

In the previous chapter, we introduced the UNIX daemons, programs that execute continuously behind the scenes. One of the most important of these daemons is **cron**, a program that runs other programs at specified times. **cron** reads one or more configuration files containing lists of command lines, times at which they are to be invoked, and (on some systems) UID's under which they are to run. Standard shell syntax is used to describe the command lines, so almost anything that you can do by hand from the shell you can have **cron** do for you automatically.

Older **cron**s scan their command files every so often and simply execute all commands that should have been run since the last scan. The newer ones parse the complete command file, figure out which of the listed commands needs to be run soonest, and go to sleep until the command's execution time has arrived. All implementations of **cron** read the configuration files when they start up. On some systems, sending **cron** a hangup signal forces it to reread the files.

cron normally does its work silently, but some versions provide for the maintenance of a log file (usually /usr/adm/cronlog) that tells what commands were executed, and when. For systems that have this feature, creating the log file enables logging and removing the file turns logging off. On systems with high **cron** activity, this file can grow quickly; we recommend that logging be disabled unless you are debugging a new configuration.

cron has no concept of history. Commands originally scheduled to run during a time when the system is down will not be executed, even when the system is rebooted and **cron** is restarted. It is debatable whether or not this behavior is optimal, but it does avoid jamming the system with hundreds of superfluous commands following a protracted down time.

21.2 cron's configuration files

Different Unices have different numbers of configuration files, but all the configuration files on a system typically share a common format. As far as **cron** is concerned, there might as well be just one giant file containing lines from all configuration files. There are various reasons for using more than one configuration file: Under ATT, each user may have his own configuration file, and under newer versions of BSD, there are separate files for local and global operations.

21.2.1 BSD configuration files

Under versions of BSD previous to 4.3, there is only one configuration file, /usr/lib/crontab. Under 4.3, the file /usr/lib/crontab.local is also used. Separating the standard and local parts of the crontab file helps you keep things organized during a system upgrade, but you may use only one file or the other, as you wish.

To change the information in one of these files, you simply edit it using your favorite text editor. Permissions on the BSD crontab files are usually set so that only root may edit them.

21.2.2 ATT configuration files

The ATT system is considerably more flexible. Instead of having a few designated files where configuration information is stored, ATT has a configuration *directory*. Any file in the configuration directory is considered a configuration file. Unlike BSD crontabs, ATT crontabs should never be edited directly. Instead, the **crontab** program is used to submit and recover configurations. When a user submits a configuration file, **crontab** copies the file into the configuration directory and gives it the name of the person who submitted it.

The ATT version of **cron** uses the name of a configuration file to determine under what username the commands it contains should be run. In this way, any user can enjoy the benefits of **cron** without enlisting the aid of a system administrator to make the crontab entries. On some systems, the /usr/lib/cron/cron.allow file contains a list of users who are allowed to submit configuration files. ATT-style configuration files are also used in some BSD-based systems such as SunOS 4.0.

21.2.3 Format of the configuration files

The format of **cron** configuration files is fairly constant from one flavor of UNIX to another. Comments are introduced with a hash mark ("#") in the first column of a line. Each non-comment line in a configuration file contains either six or seven fields, and represents one command. The seven-field format is:

minute hour day month weekday username command

All fields are separated by white space. The six-field format omits the *username* field.

minute, *hour*, *day*, *month*, and *weekday* give information about the times at which the command should be run. Their interpretations are:

- *minute* - the minute of the hour (00 to 59)
- *hour* - the hour of the day, in 24 hour format (00 to 23)
- *day* - the day of the month (1 to 31)
- *month* - the month of the year (1 to 12)
- *weekday* - the day of the week (1 to 7, Monday = 1, Sunday = 7)

Each of these fields may contain:

- An asterisk ("*"), which matches anything
- A single integer, which matches exactly
- A list of integers separated by commas, which matches any listed value
- Two integers separated by a dash, matching any value in the indicated range

For example, the time specification

```
0,30  9-17  13  *  5
```

selects all half-hours between 9:00 a.m. and 5:00 p.m. on any Friday the 13th in any month.

username tells under what UID the command should be run. On ATT systems, which use the six-field format, the name of the configuration file is taken to be the username. In any case, you can still have **cron** run commands as an arbitrary user. Simply preface a command run by the root crontab with **/bin/su** *username* **-c**.

command is the **sh** command line to be executed. It can be any valid shell command, and should not be quoted. *command* is considered to continue to the end of the line, and so may contain blanks or tabs.

Some **cron**s allow the use of percentage marks to indicate newlines within the *command* field. When these are used, only the text up to the first percentage mark is included in the command proper; the remaining "lines" are placed upon the command's standard input.

The following are examples of legal crontab commands:

```
echo The time is now 'date' > /dev/console
write garth % Hi garth. % Nice to meet you.
cd /etc ; cat passwd | mail -s "System File of the Month" evi
```

Let's look at some complete examples. The following example lines are in seven-field format and were taken from a Vax running 4.3BSD.

```
30  2  4  6  *  joe  ( cd /users/joe/project ; make independ )
```

This line will be activated at 2:30 a.m. on July 4th. It will change the shell's current working directory to /users/joe/project and then run the **make** command. This might be used to start a long compilation at a time when other users would not be impacted.

```
20  1  *  *  * root  find /tmp -atime +1 -exec rm -f {} ;
```

This command will be run at 1:20 a.m. each morning, and will remove from the /tmp directory all files that have not been accessed in 24 hours.

```
55  23  *  *  1,2,3,4,7  lisa  /student/evi/lisa/bin/acct-script
```

At 11:55 p.m. on Monday, Tuesday, Wednesday, Thursday, and Sunday, a script stored under the home directory of the user "lisa" will be executed. Since this example is from a BSD machine, the script can be executed directly; on an ATT machine, this would have to be changed to a more explicit `csh /student/evi/lisa/bin/acct-script`. Note that the notation "1,2,3,4,7" is really necessary, as "1-4,7" is not acceptable.

21.3 Some common uses for cron

There are a number of very standard, mundane tasks that are especially suited for performance by **cron**, and these typically make up the bulk of the material in a site's crontab files. In this section we'll look at a variety of such tasks and the crontab lines used to implement them. As always, be aware of the differences between systems when adapting these for your own use.

UNIX systems often come with some crontab entries preinstalled for you. These make for valuable reference material even if you don't like the way they do things. If you want to deactivate them, comment them out by inserting a hash mark at the beginning of each line — don't delete them completely. The preinstalled and standard crontab entries should precede any specialized or machine-dependent entries you add.

21.3.1 Running user-scheduled scripts

Both BSD and ATT support a command called **at** that can be used to request the execution of a shell script at some later time. All **at** really does is make a copy of the script and the current environment variables in the directory /usr/spool/at. The actual execution of the script is left up to **at**'s companion program **atrun**. When **atrun** is invoked, it simply runs any jobs whose requested times of execution have arrived.

It is the responsibility of **cron** to insure that **atrun** is run every once in a while. The line

```
0,15,30,45 * * * * root /usr/lib/atrun
```

runs the program once every 15 minutes, a typical frequency. If you feel that your users make special use of the **at** program you can adjust this up or down as necessary. Don't set the execution interval to lower than five minutes or higher than one hour, however.

On some ATT systems, use of the **at** command is limited to those users listed in the /usr/lib/cron/at.allow file.

21.3.2 Processing user appointment calendars (BSD)

BSD has a facility which allows each user to be automatically reminded of important dates. To partake of this service, the user must create a file called "calendar" in his home directory containing a list of all the events of which he wishes to be reminded. The user can run the **calendar** program at any time to obtain a list of all reminders entered for the current and following day.

When the superuser runs **calendar** with a dash as the only argument, **calendar** peeks into the calendar file of each user on the system and excerpts the relevant reminders, mailing the results directly to the user rather than sending them to the standard output. This operation is initiated out of **cron** and should be performed early in the morning (*not* late at night) because **calendar** processes entries for the current day.

A crontab line to implement this might be:

```
30  1  *  *  *  root  /usr/bin/calendar -
```

21.3.3 Cleaning the filesystem

A certain percentage of the files on any UNIX system are junk. For example, consider the core files created by the kernel to hold the memory image of a process that has just crashed. The core file can sometimes be of great value to someone who is debugging a program, but more often its creation is just a nuisance. Since core files tend to be rather large, it doesn't take too many of them to significantly impact the amount of free disk space.

In addition to being of time-limited utility, core files are highly reproducible. If you want to regenerate the image, you can just run the offending program again. There is thus no reason not to delete core files which no one has looked at in a few days. It is a virtual certainty that they are not wanted.

There are many other sources of junk files. Many programs create temporary files in the /tmp directory that don't get erased for one reason or another, and some programs (especially editors) like to make backup copies of each file they work with.

A partial solution to this problem is to institute some sort of nightly junk file reclamation regimen out of **cron**. The following examples all use the **find** command to delete worthless files:

```
find / -name core -atime +7 -exec rm -f {} ;
```

This command removes all core image files that have not been accessed in a week, regardless of their location within the filesystem.

```
find / '(' -name '#*' -o -name '.#*' -o -name '*.CKP' ')' /
    -atime +3 -exec rm -f {} ';'
```

This command deletes files throughout the filesystem whose names begin with "#" or ".#", or end with ".CKP", and have not been accessed in three days. These are often backup files created by GNU Emacs, but some other programs use a similar naming convention for temporary files.

```
find /usr/preserve -mtime +7 -a -exec rm -f {} ;
```

This command removes any file in the /usr/preserve directory a week after its last modification. This directory is used by **vi** to store copies of files that users were editing as the system crashed or **vi** itself was terminated. The files are just plopped in once and never modified again unless claimed by their owners.

```
cd /tmp; find . ! -name . ! -name lost+found -type d /
    -mtime +1 -exec /bin/rm -r {} ;
```

This command recursively removes all subdirectories of /tmp not modified in 24 hours. Plain files in /tmp are typically removed at boot time by commands in one of the /etc/rc scripts, but most systems do not remove directories by default. If a directory named lost+found exists, it is treated as a special case and is not removed. This handles the special case of /tmp being placed on its own filesystem.

A common practice is to place a variety of these **find** commands into a shell script called a **skulker** which is then run out of **cron**. Many **skulker**s perform additional functions such as checking for security breaches. See Section 26.8.4 for more information.

If you do use some sort of automatic cleanup regimen, you must be sure that your users are aware of it to avoid having files accidentally deleted.

21.3.4 Uucp polling

cron is an integral part of any complex uucp schedule. In the uucp context, **cron** is primarily used to initiate calls to other sites at specific times of day; however, it may also be used for other uucp-related tasks such as summarizing phone traffic information and cleaning of the uucp spool area.

The use of uucp with **cron** is covered in Chapter 16: *Uucp*.

21.3.5 Accounting

System usage accounting is a fertile field for **cron** because of the intrinsically periodic nature of the accounting tasks. CPU accounting information has to be summarized and archived several times a day, and summaries have to be reviewed every month to compute usage totals for each user. Chapter 19: *Accounting* explains specific **cron** techniques for use with accounting.

21.3.6 Setting the system time

Most Unices provide no standard facility for automatically keeping the internal clocks of a group of computers synchronized. This really didn't matter so much when computers worked alone, but now that networking and remote file sharing are becoming commonplace it can cause a variety of minor problems.

A number of solutions for this problem exist. Some vendors supply programs that allow setting the clock of one machine from the clock of another, and there are a few public domain programs that accomplish similar goals.

If you do get your hands on a time-setting mechanism, you will probably want to set things up using **cron** so that each slave machine contacts the master time machine at least once every few hours. A typical crontab entry at our site is

```
0  *  *  *  *  root  /usr/new/settime  sigi
```

which sets the time at the beginning of each hour.

21.3.7 Marking time

It is convenient to have the system write the current time on the console every half hour or 15 minutes so that you can determine how long the system was up if it crashes at night. This is easily accomplished with the crontab entry

```
0,15,30,45  *  *  *  *  root  echo Time: `date`
```

On some systems this facility is built directly into the kernel and does not need to be simulated using **cron**. If the system console is sometimes used as a terminal, having the date printed every 15 minutes is often more annoying than helpful.

21.3.8 Network distribution of mail aliases (BSD)

If you are running a network of machines, it's very convenient to maintain a single, distributed version of the mail aliases database, /usr/lib/aliases. To maintain the consistency of this master alias file across the network, it is a good idea to copy it around to all the mail slaves every night.

Once the mail alias file has been distributed using **rcp**, the **newaliases** program must be run on each machine to hash the file and convert it to the form used by **sendmail**. To increase efficiency, you may wish to copy the hashed version of the file (/usr/lib/aliases.dir and /usr/lib/aliases.pag) among machines of the same type instead of running **newaliases** on each machine.

Other machine-specific processing may have to be done as well. For example, on Suns the aliases file is often maintained using the yellow pages network information service. Installing a new aliases map on these machines involves running the **make** command inside the master yellow pages server's "yp" directory.

22

Quotas and OS Limits

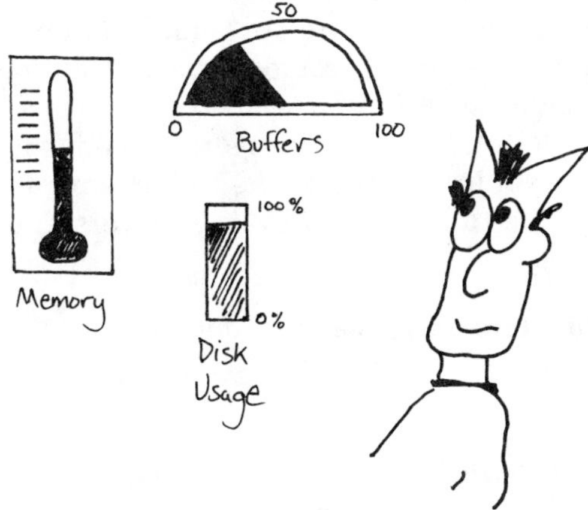

22.1 Introduction

In order for a user to get anything useful accomplished with a computer, he must appropriate some of the system's resources for his project. If he is a courteous and elegant user, he will keep his home directory clean and design his programs to be fast, efficient, and mindful of the other users of the system. If he is a horrible user, he will accumulate huge numbers of outdated files and write enormous programs that run at full speed for days on end.

Most users fall somewhere between these two extremes, but because writing bad programs is so much easier than writing good programs, and because disk space housecleaning is painful and time-consuming, most people tend to resemble the horrible users more than the ideal ones. UNIX provides a variety of unpleasant tortures that you can use to curb this kind of resource abuse, and these are the subject of this chapter.

Before we begin in earnest, we should say that we don't really advocate the use of *any* of these draconian tactics unless absolutely necessary. While a few of our machines use disk quotas, none of the other techniques described in this chapter are used anywhere on our network (with the exception of

tout, the use of which is voluntary). Our feeling is that it is better to allow users as much freedom as possible in the daily course of events, as long as they do not make unreasonable use of the system. If a transgression does occur, we typically initiate a hostile confrontation in which the specifics of the user's crimes are spelled out to him in humiliating detail.

There are several reasons for this. To begin with, peer pressure can be as effective in halting system abuse as most other methods. If other users are inconvenienced by someone's waste of disk space or enormous processes, they will certainly attempt to negotiate some kind of settlement with the miscreant. (The **spacegripe** script presented in Appendix I aids this process.) Second, disk quotas and their ilk impose an added burden on the system administrator. Getting things set up correctly is not difficult, but maintaining the mess is unpleasant (especially if users' needs are subject to frequent changes), and the extra details increase the overall complexity of the system. Some of the limitations require sneaky tricks to implement. Third, it is fairly rare for serious problems to be caused by users overstepping the bounds of good taste anyway.

The resources whose usage parameters may be adjusted are:

Resources controlled with quotas:

- Maximum disk usage on a given partition
- Maximum number of files on a given partition

Resources controlled with system calls (**setrlimit** or **ulimit**):

- Maximum per-process CPU usage
- Maximum size of any single file
- Maximum size of a process's data segment
- Maximum size of a process's stack segment
- Maximum number of process pages in core
- Maximum core dump size

Resources controlled with the (local) **tout** program:

- Maximum idle time allowed before auto-logout

All of these values may be set on a per-user basis. Unfortunately, ATT UNIX does not support most of these limitations. The only direct resource control afforded by ATT is that of maximum file size.

In the following sections, we will pursue each of these limitations separately.

22.2 The quota system (BSD)

The BSD quota system allows you to specify limits on two aspects of disk storage: the number of inodes that may be allocated to a user (roughly the number of files the user may possess) and the number of disk blocks that may be allocated to the user. Each limit is specified as two numbers: a *soft limit* after which the user is issued warnings about his impending quota violation and a *hard limit* which specifies the absolute limit on the resource, to which the system will steadfastedly limit the user.

The intention behind this dual-limit paradigm is that users be forced to stay under their soft limit most of the time (specifically, when not logged in), but that the strictures be relaxed while the user is actually active so that he may create large temporary files as he goes about his business. To this end, the BSD quota system has a time limit that specifies how long someone may remain over their soft limit but under their hard limit; after this time (usually three logins) has elapsed, the soft limit is enforced with the same strictures as the hard limit, and nothing useful can be done until the user pares his hoard down to below the soft limits. At this point, the time limit is reset and the user may once again exceed his soft limits with impunity for another three login sessions.

BSD quotas are handled on a per-user per-filesystem basis. If there is more than one filesystem on which a user is expected to create files, quotas must be set for each one separately. If no quotas have been set for a particular user on a given filesystem, that user's ability to absorb disk space is not limited. By convention, limit values of zero are also interpreted to mean "unlimited."

22.2.1 Installing quotas

Before you begin to set quotas, you have to do some configuration work. The first time you add quotas to one of your system's partitions, there are six chores you must perform. Subsequent partitions require only four of these six:

First time:

- Reconfigure the kernel with `options QUOTA`
- Modify the /etc/rc script to turn on quotas at boot time

Every time:

- Modify the partition's /etc/fstab entry
- Create the quota record file
- Run **quotacheck** to give quota records correct initial values
- Turn quotas on by hand

22.2.1.1 Reconfigure the kernel

Because disk quotas affect filesystem operations at a very basic level, they require some additional code to be compiled into your kernel. To make the kernel smaller and faster, this code is not included by default; you must specifically request it inside the configuration file with the following line:

```
options    QUOTA
```

After you have made this change, simply rebuild the kernel as described in Chapter 8, and then reboot the system.

22.2.1.2 Modify the /etc/rc script

The kernel allows quotas to be turned off and on at any time. This is convenient in certain circumstances, but also requires that quotas be turned on "by hand" when the system is booted. This is usually done in the /etc/rc script right after the filesystems are mounted. Just as the **mount -a** command mounts all the filesystems listed in /etc/fstab, the **quotaon -a** command enables quotas on all filesystems that use them. Modify the part of your /etc/rc script that controls mounting to look something like this:

```
/etc/mount -a > /dev/console 2>&1
    echo -n 'checking quotas:' >/dev/console
/etc/quotacheck -a -p >/dev/console 2>&1
    echo ' done.' >/dev/console
/etc/quotaon -a
```

In addition to **quotaon**, we've stuck in another very important quota control command: **quotacheck**. We'll delay talking about this command for a few paragraphs, since you'll need to use it when you add quotas to a new partition, too. Before you add the **quotacheck** line to your /etc/rc file, be sure that your system's version supports the **-p** (parallel check) flag. If it doesn't, just leave it out.

22.2.1.3 Modify the partition's /etc/fstab entry

As you probably recall from Chapter 4: *The Filesystem*, the /etc/fstab file contains information about how disk partitions are set up and the uses to which they are to be put. Just as **mount** reads /etc/fstab to find information about the filesystems themselves, **quotaon** (and its analog **quotaoff**) read /etc/fstab to find information about the quotas on these filesystems.

Partitions on which you have not yet instituted quotas will normally have a line in /etc/fstab that looks something like:

```
/dev/ra0g:/users:rw:1:2
```

Note that the third field contains the code "rw", meaning that the partition is to be mounted for both reading and writing. To add quotas to the filesystem, replace the "rw" code with the code "rq", meaning that the partition is to be mounted for reading and writing with quotas. Naturally, read-only filesystems with quotas are not supported.

22.2.1.4 Create the quota control file

Quota information for each partition (including the current usage summary) is contained in a file somewhere within the partition itself. The kernel allows this file to be located anywhere, but most of the quota utility programs are hard-coded to look for a file named */partitionname/*quotas, so there really is no alternative to calling it by this name.

This file should be owned by root, and should have read and write permissions for root and none for anyone else. For the preceding example /etc/fstab line, the correct sequence of commands for creating the quota control file is:

```
touch /users/quotas
chmod 600 /users/quotas
```

You must be logged in as root to do this.

22.2.1.5 Run the quotacheck program

quotacheck is used to check the actual disk usage on a particular filesystem. In normal operation, the quota system has hooks into the filesystem code that allow it to keep a running total of the number of disk blocks and inodes owned by each user, which it squirrels away in the quota control file. However, just as generic filesystem information can become inaccurate over long periods of time and need to be repaired with **fsck -p**, abrupt system halts and crashes can degrade the quota information.

Running **quotacheck** forces an entire partition to be critically examined block by block to recalculate the current disk usage, and updates the quota control file to reflect the partition's true state. It is normally run from the /etc/rc file in the form **quotacheck -a,** which performs the check on every partition declared to have quotas in the /etc/fstab file. Individual partitions may be checked with **quotacheck** *filesystem*. In this form of the command, the device name (e.g., /dev/ra0g) should be given rather than the pathname (e.g., /users) — **quotacheck** is not as smart as **mount** and **umount**. The **-v** flag can be used to obtain a list of all users and their disk usages (this can be done with the **quot** command, too).

Some systems (4.3BSD, for one) also provide an optional **-p** flag, which causes **quotacheck** to check filesystems in parallel, in a manner similar to that used by **fsck**. The **fsck** sequence numbers from /etc/fstab are used to determine the order and parallelism of the checks.

22.2.1.6 Turn quotas on by hand

Even though quotas are turned on in /etc/rc, there is no need to reboot the machine to start them up on a newly quota-ized filesystem. Use the command **quotaon** *filesystem*.

22.2.2 Miscellaneous quota commands

Now that quotas are installed on your filesystems, you still need to go through and assign everyone's quotas, an operation that is performed with the **edquota** command. If you say **edquota** *user*, you'll be put into **vi** (or whatever editor is specified in your environment variable EDITOR) to edit the quotas for that user on each partition that currently supports quotas. You can specify multiple users, but since you will not be given any indication of which user's quotas you are editing at any given time, this is not very useful. If you say

> **edquota -p** *proto-user user*

the quotas for the user *user* will be set to be the same as those of the user *proto-user*. Multiple targets may be specified, but only one prototype user.

To quickly set the quotas for every user on the system to the same value, you should first edit your own quota information by hand, then execute:

> **edquota -p** *yourlogin* 'awk -F: '$3 > 99 {print $1}' /etc/passwd'

This command assumes that you are using the C-shell, and that you assign your human UID's starting with 100. Note that the outside single quotes are backquotes, while the inside single quotes are not.

We maintain logins for a number of pseudo-users that are used only as disk quota prototypes. We used to have pseudo-users with several different quota allocations for each of about four different kinds of user. This soon became too complex, however, so we simplified it to a three-level system: "small," "medium," and "huge."

If all you want to do is see the quotas of a particular user, you can use the **quota** command. **quota** *user* gives information about *user*'s quota status on filesystems where he is over quota; complete information can be obtained with the **-v** flag. Individual users can find out their own quota information in a similar way, but only the superuser can see the quotas of other people.

The **repquota** command produces similar information to **quot** and **quotacheck -v** but reports each user's quotas as well as current disk usage.

22.3 Per-process limits

Unlike quotas, which deal only with the total disk usage of a particular user, the other limits imposed by the kernel are all dealt with on a per-process basis. The kernel maintains a list of the limits imposed on a process inside its own address space, and controls access to this data through system calls.

The limits that are implemented, their mechanism of operation, and the system calls used to change them are completely different in ATT and BSD, so we will address them separately.

22.3.1 BSD process limits

As in the case of quotas, Berkeley process limits are specified as a hard limit and a soft limit; when the soft limit is violated, the process is sent a signal. Violation of a hard limit is grounds for immediate termination of the process.

Limits are propagated by inheritance from parent process to child process; after being spawned, no one but the process itself can modify its limits, not even the superuser. Using the **setrlimit** system call, limits can be adjusted downward (made more restrictive). Unless the process is owned by the superuser, however, limits cannot be relaxed.

There is a command called **limit** that is built into the C-shell which allows easy access to the **setrlimit** system call. Just typing **limit** prints a list of all the limits and their current values. For example:

```
cputime         unlimited
filesize        unlimited
datasize        245504 kbytes
stacksize       512 kbytes
coredumpsize    0 kbytes
memoryuse       unlimited
```

The data and stack segment limits are imposed by the kernel automatically, based on the values for MAXDSIZ and MAXSSIZ specified at kernel configuration time. All other limits are initially disabled until the user gives them a value. In the preceding listing, the user has set the maximum core dump size to be zero kilobytes to prevent core dumps from ever being made. This can sometimes save time when debugging large programs on slow machines.

To prevent himself from accidentally creating a file larger than five megabytes, the user might execute **limit filesize 5 m**. Likewise, to limit the CPU usage of each program invoked by the shell to thirty seconds, the command **limit cputime 30** could be used.

This is all well and good, but unfortunately BSD does not provide any way of foisting limits off on users without their consent. If you have the source code for your system utilities, you can add calls to **setrlimit** in the code for **init**, **login**, or **getty**; otherwise, you will have to content yourself with placing **limit** commands in the default .login or .cshrc files that you give to users when they are first added to the system.

The only limitation that can really increase the interactive performance of the system as a whole (at some expense to the individual user) is that on memory usage. This limitation will prevent large processes which belong to the user from snatching up everyone else's memory pages as soon as they are idle for a few seconds. A limit of 300 kilobytes is probably reasonable and will affect the user only in extreme cases. Some programs (Lisp, **emacs**, etc.) are memory hogs which cannot function properly with less than several megabytes of memory, however.

22.3.2 ATT process limits

The only resource limited by ATT UNIX is maximum file size. As in BSD, adjustment of the limit is controlled by a system call (**ulimit**), and the limit cannot be raised unless the caller is the superuser. The ATT **ulimit** call also allows the caller to find out the maximum permissible data segment size; however, this is a constant value and may not be modified.

Unlike BSD, which does not impose a default limit on anything other than segment sizes, the ATT kernel uses a default maximum file size that is set at kernel configuration time. Most systems come with this parameter set to two megabytes, which can cause havoc with large databases and such; we suggest a much higher value.

If a single systemwide default file size does not suit your needs, you can make patches to /etc/inittab that cause the normal processes spawned by **init** to be executed by way of another program that sets file size limits before turning control over to the original executable. This does require you to do some programming in C and to be familiar with the **exec** family of system calls and library routines. Some distributions allow the limit to be specified in the GCOS field of /etc/passwd, but this is not a standard feature, so consult your specific documentation.

22.4 The tout program

We have a program written by Andrew Rudoff called **tout** that allows users to specify how long the system is to allow them to remain idle before logging them out. It is called with an argument which represents the number of minutes of idle time to be allowed. When the user has been idle for almost this long, a warning message will be printed on his terminal. If he does not press some key or other within the next minute or two, deadly signals will be sent to his shell and foreground processes, causing them to die and terminating his login session.

Idle users are not really a drain on the computer itself, but they sometimes tie up resources such as terminals and modems that others may wish to use. Under BSD, you can define all dial-in lines as having terminal type "dialup" in the /etc/ttys or /etc/ttytype file. This allows the terminal type to be checked in the ".cshrc" or ".profile" files and **tout** to be automatically started up when you are logged in through a modem.

Another common reason for using **tout** is to prevent users from leaving terminals logged in by accident, thus exposing themselves to all kinds of pranks.

A listing of the **tout** program is included in Appendix E.

23

Monitoring the System

23.1 Introduction

This chapter will point you towards some utilities that are used to monitor system statistics and overall load. Using this information is something of an art, as *you* must determine what the normal conditions are for your machines. Some of the commands described in this chapter are used only infrequently by administrators because interpreting their output requires some understanding of the data structures and algorithms built into the UNIX kernel. It would be dishonest of us to claim that the material in this chapter is anything but superficial.

We would have liked to pair this introduction to system monitoring with some material on performance enhancement. Unfortunately, there's very little to write about in that area. For all their complexity, UNIX systems are basically plug-and-chug environments; as a system administrator you have almost no say in the way the kernel manages the system's resources and few ways to tune the system to your particular environment. Instead of talking about global system performance, we've chosen a few user-level operations that are especially expensive in terms of system resources and listed some ways to make them cheaper.

23.2 Monitoring system activity

This section applies mostly to BSD systems, as ATT systems are not generally rich in system monitoring commands. Some have versions of the commands we will describe, but this is rare. Practically all systems support higher-level commands such as **ps** and **uptime**, however, and these suffice for 99% of applications. Check your manuals to find out what your system supports.

The best way to view a UNIX system for the purpose of analyzing performance is to think of it as a collection of disconnected, atomic resources. Usually, the only resources that need be considered in such analyses are memory, CPU, hard disks, and Ethernet; most other factors can be neglected due to their comparatively small influence on the system. For example, the throughput of even the fastest printers is insignificant compared to, say, the disk traffic on a lightly loaded system.

Getting information about the system is easy, but useful interpretation of this information is not. To develop a feeling for what the system statistics mean, you'll have to examine them over a long period of time and under a variety of load conditions. Once you know what is normal for your system you'll be able to spot anomalies with some accuracy; however, don't be too quick to assume that something has gone terribly wrong whenever you get strange readings.

You should read the following command descriptions with this experimental process in mind. We present the commands only to insure that you are aware of their existence and functionality, not to prescribe any particular usage regimen.

23.2.1 System statistics

In the following discussion, we use the word *statistic* somewhat loosely to mean either an average behavior over time or some type of current *state*. For subjects like disk access, trying to piece together an image of the system's activity by examining what it's doing at several discrete instants is futile. The only way to get a coherent picture of activity is to represent activity as time ratios, such as interrupts per second or pageouts per minute. State-type statistics are used to represent things that can be more immediately quantified, like the current number of network connections or number of disk writes queued.

BSD has a number of standard tools for condensing system statistics into human-readable (but cryptic!) form. The most important are:

- **iostat** - get disk and terminal throughput statistics
- **vmstat** - get virtual memory statistics
- **pstat** - get statistics on a whole bunch of system functions
- **netstat** - get information and statistics about the Ethernet

Your system may support programs that produce similar information but have a different interface. For example, 4.3BSD has the **systat** program which is similar to **pstat** with an interactive interface, and SunOS includes a program called **traffic** which graphically portrays Ethernet usage statistics. If you have access to one of these, great! — if not, it doesn't really matter. Everything you need can be obtained from the four commands just listed and a few others you already know: **w** (or **whodo**), **ps**, and your system's accounting programs.

23.2.2 The iostat command

iostat tells you how much I/O (input/output) is being done to terminals and hard disks. It also tells you what percentage of the CPU's time is spent in various states, but why the author of **iostat** felt these two statistics to be complementary is a bizarre mystery. **iostat** is most useful as a measure of disk activity.

iostat's output looks something like this:

```
      tty          ra0          ra1         cpu
 tin tout bps tps msps bps tps msps us ni sy id
  46  128   9   2  0.0  31   6  0.0 11  6 15 67
```

These lines should be interpreted as columns, with only the third row containing actual data. The columns are divided into a number of "topics" (four in this case: tty, ra0, ra1, and cpu), with the data for each topic being presented in the fields beneath it.

The "tty" topic presents data concerning terminals and pseudo-terminals. "tin" and "tout" denote the average total number of characters input and output per second by *all* of the system's terminals, respectively. In the example output, we can see that an average of 46 characters per second were input and 128 characters per second were output. If these numbers sound inordinately high, remember that pseudo-terminals may become involved in multilayer protocols which necessitate internal communication and which may disguise output characters as input. For example, when you use **rlogin** to log into another machine over Ethernet, everything the remote machine sends to you as output is interpreted locally as input to the pseudo-terminal with which you communicate. Remember also that every time someone does a screen refresh operation inside an editor, the system may output several thousand characters.

The topics "ra0" and "ra1" give information about two separate disk drives. Each of the disks has fields "bps", "tps", and "msps", indicating disk blocks transferred per second, total transfers per second, and milliseconds per seek, respectively. Each transfer operation involves at least one disk block, so the number of transfers per second can never exceed the number of blocks per second. The "bps" field tells you how busy your disks are; the "tps" field tells you whether there are many small disk requests or a few large ones. Calculation of seek times seems to work only on specific drives and sometimes gives bizarre values.

The "cpu" topic tells you how much of the system's time is spent in various states. "us" is user time, time spent executing user program code. "ni" is time spent executing jobs whose priority has been lowered with the **nice** command or an equivalent system call. "sy" is time that has been spent executing parts of the kernel. "id" is idle time.

When invoked without arguments, **iostat** displays these numbers as averages over the time since the system was booted. If a numeric argument *N* is provided, **iostat** presents a new summary each *N* seconds consisting of activity since the previous summary. An optional second argument specifies the number of summaries to print before exiting. Some systems also allow a particular disk to be specified on the command line.

23.2.3 The vmstat command

vmsat is ostensibly a program for monitoring virtual memory usage, but like **iostat** it's very chatty and gives you all kinds of extraneous information. **vmstat** can also be used to examine the kernel's summary table, which records the number of interrupts, system calls, etc. that have occurred since boot.

The command-line syntax of **vmstat** mirrors that of **iostat**, and so, unfortunately, does the output. The following material was produced by **vmstat 5 5**:

```
procs     memory          page                  disk          faults        cpu
r b w    avm   fre   re at  pi po fr   de   sr r0 r1 d2 d3   in  sy  cs us sy id
2 0 0   3128   656    1  2   1  0  0   72    0  2  5  0  0    4  75   9 11  2 88
1 0 0   3128   608    0  0   0  0  0   72    0  0  0  0  0   13 405 107  0  1 99
1 0 0   3128   600    0  0   0  0  0   72    0  1  6  0  0    3 258 104  0  0100
1 0 0   2528   600    0  0   0  0  0   72    0  1  1  0  0    0 209 104  0  0100
1 0 0   1944   600    0  0   0  0  0   72    0  0  0  0  0    0 193 104  0  0100
```

Under the "procs" heading are shown the number of processes that are, respectively, immediately runnable, blocked on I/O or short-term resources, and runnable but swapped.

The next two columns, "avm" and "fre", give some information about the status of the computer's virtual memory system. "avm" is the number of virtual memory pages[1] owned by processes that have run within the last 20 seconds, regardless of whether they are actually in memory or not. Processes like **getty** that are usually asleep don't affect this number. The "avm" number includes both data and text (program code) pages, so it can be relied upon to give you an accurate indication of how busy the virtual memory of the system is. If the number of active pages approaches the size of the physical memory minus the size of the kernel, paging will result and system throughput will be reduced.

If you habitually get sluggish performance from your system, memory usage is one of the first things to look at. A little money spent on memory can make a dramatic difference in throughput.

The "fre" column tells the number of pages on the system's free list, the list of physical memory pages that have been marked as not currently in use. In order to understand the significance of this figure, you must first understand how UNIX does page-level memory management. UNIX uses what is known as a "clock" algorithm for determining which pages of memory are the best ones to page out in the event that a running process requests more memory than the system can physically provide. Inside the kernel is code which marks each physical page of memory in turn as being inactive. This code begins to execute whenever memory gets tight, and simply goes round and round from page to page like the hand of a clock; hence the name. As each page is marked, it is placed on the free list.

Whenever a page of memory is actually referenced by a process, the "inactive" status of the page is cleared, and the page is safe until the next sweep of the clock's hand. If a page is referenced often, the chance that it will happen to be marked as inactive when the kernel comes prowling for some memory to reclaim is low. Conversely, pages that really are inactive will spend all their time marked as such and will have a high probability of being paged out. This is not a perfect algorithm for choosing which memory pages to page out, but it works fairly well.

The "fre" column thus lists the number of pages that have not been referenced by their owner process since they were marked inactive.

[1] A BSD page is usually 8K. For reasons of efficiency, it is common practice for Unices to pretend that the hardware page size is larger than it really is and group several hardware pages into a "virtual hardware page" called a *page cluster*. UNIX maintains the illusion of large hardware page sizes consistently enough that you can ignore this subtlety.

The next seven columns give information about paging activity on the system. All columns are in units of pages per second. Their meanings are:

- re - page reclaims, pages on free list which were later referenced and salvaged
- at - attaches, pages used up to form address spaces
- pi - pageins, pages read from disk on page fault
- po - pageouts, pages written to disk to free core memory
- fr - pages freed, the conceptual opposite of attaches
- de - predicted short-term memory shortfall
- sr - clock algorithm scan rate

If **vmstat** is invoked with a **-S** flag, the **re** and **at** columns will be replaced with swap-ins and swap-outs per second, respectively.

Note that in the preceding example output, all of the numbers in these columns except for the since-boot summary are zero. This is quite reasonable because the clock algorithm and paging system are not even activated until UNIX perceives the need for them. The clock algorithm actually runs at several different speeds, depending on how dire the memory shortage appears.

The next four columns give the number of disk operations per second for each of two separate drives. The two-letter code used to identify the drives varies with the hardware. Exactly four drives (columns) will be displayed, even if your system has more or less than this number. The "d2" and "d3" columns in this example are dummies inserted by **vmstat**.

The next three columns are:

- **in** - nonclock (i.e. hardware) interrupts per second
- **sy** - system calls per second
- **cs** - context switches per second

For a real thrill, try the **vmstat -s** command. This shows a summary of such information since boot time, in absolute units rather than per-time units. For example, on our master mail machine, which has been up for about a week, some of the more impressive figures are:

```
0               swap outs
24350684        cpu context switches
157316049       total interrupts (device, software, pseudo-dma)
102958811       system calls
```

Note that less than 25% of all system calls result in a context switch, and that not one process has been swapped since the system was booted.

The remaining three columns are CPU usage percentages for user, system, and idle time. This is the same information that **iostat** gives, but user time is not broken down into normal and low priority processing.

23.2.4 The pstat command

pstat is used to dump the contents of various kernel tables in an almost human-readable form. There is no unifying theme to the information **pstat** can display; it is just a clearing house for various tidbits that don't need to be time averaged or that the kernel automatically maintains time averages for.

pstat is notified of the information you'd like to see by the command-line flags. The various displays are mutually exclusive; however, **pstat** won't complain if you use more than one major flag and will just pick one of the information pages you requested. The following displays are available:

- A dump of the inode table (**-i**)
- A dump of the text table (**-x**)
- A dump of the process table, gorier than **ps** (**-P**)
- A dump of the open file table (**-f**)
- Status information for all terminals (**-t**)
- Information about a particular process (**-u**)
- Information about swap space usage (**-s**)
- Information about how full the kernel's tables are (**-T**)

The most useful of these displays to the system administrator is the kernel table usage summary produced by the **-T** option. The information you get looks like this:

```
121/364        files
85/158         inodes
34/74          processes
21/38          texts
70/169         00k swap
```

The numbers separated by slashes represent current usage versus actual size of the indicated table. From this sample output we can see that the system is currently running only 34 processes, but that it could support an additional 40 processes if necessary. Note that the limit on texts is distinct from the limit on processes; you could have 74 processes but only 38 separate program texts active at any one time.

pstat -T is useful for determining the optimal value of "maxusers" when configuring the kernel. See Chapter 8: *Configuring the Kernel* for more information.

23.2.5 The netstat command

netstat is very much like a **pstat** command for the network-related parts of the kernel. When invoked without flags, it gives a display of the network sockets the machine is currently maintaining, and their state. With the **-a** flag, **netstat** shows the status of all sockets; server sockets are normally deemed uninteresting and are not shown.

The other displays **netstat** can produce are:

- Memory management statistics for the network drivers (**-m**)
- Network interface statistics (**-i**)
- A summary of the IMP host tables, for machines on ARPANET (**-h**)
- The current routing tables (**-r**)

netstat is described in more detail in Chapter 14: *Networking under BSD*.

23.3 Maximizing system throughput

Keeping a UNIX system running smoothly is largely a matter of avoiding certain CPU and memory consumptive operations rather than of performing secret tuning operations. In this section we will list some common practices that are wasteful of system resources and ways to reduce their impact.

23.3.1 ps

No system administrator should miss the experience of waiting several minutes for output from **ps**. If you use the **time** command to find out what the holdup is, you'll find that **ps** spends most of its time executing system calls. When **ps** goes to look up the information for a process, it has to locate the process's address space, grope around in it for command-line arguments and data structures, and grope around inside the kernel for the rest of the information it needs. If a process is swapped, the relevant parts of the address space may even need to be brought in off of the swap disk.

The only way a user-level process like **ps** can do these magical manipulations of other process' address spaces is to route them through the pseudo-devices /dev/mem, /dev/kmem, and /dev/drum, which are mapped into the physical memory of the computer, the kernel's address space, and an image of the swap device, respectively. This is a slow and laborious process involving lots of seeks and microscopic reads. Even after the process information is obtained, **ps** still has to do things like look the UID's up in /etc/passwd to find their human-readable equivalents. It should not be surprising that **ps** is so slow.

Here's what you can do to speed things up:

- Don't ask to see command-line arguments.
- Don't ask to see usernames.
- Don't ask to see environments.
- Don't ask to see processes without control terminals.

For example, the show-me-everything option set on a Sun 3 is **augxe**. This takes almost 20 seconds of real time to run, although only about 5 seconds of that is actual CPU time. The low-budget alternative would be something like **agv** which runs in a little over 2.5 seconds. The difference is an order of magnitude.

For blindingly fast response, you can either limit the processes **ps** shows you to those attached to a particular terminal (using the **-t** option) or use one of the public domain **ps** substitutes such as **sps**.

23.3.2 Reading .cshrc in csh scripts

When a copy of **csh** is spawned, it tries to configure itself by reading and executing the contents of the file .cshrc in the home directory of the invoker. This is great for interactive shells, but it is a pain when a **csh** created merely to interpret a script spends a long time chewing on the .cshrc file. A **-f** flag on the **csh** command line tells **csh** not to read the .cshrc file; you can write your scripts so that this flag is automatically supplied when the script is executed. The following explains how.

The standard UNIX convention for identifying interpreted code files is to put the special marker "#!" at the very beginning of the file, followed (on the same line) by the command to which the text should be fed as input. Under BSD, this convention is supported explicitly by the kernel and interpreted files may be **exec**'ed just like binary code files. Under ATT the shell has to arrange the execution by hand.

The processor command for an interpreted file can contain flags and options just as if it were typed from the shell, although shell metacharacters like ">" and "|" are not supported. Thus to disable .cshrc processing, you can start your **csh** scripts with:

```
#!/bin/csh -f
```

23.3.3 grep, egrep, fgrep, and other pattern matching programs

Commands in the **grep** family are used to scan files for lines that match a particular pattern. **egrep** is the most feature-laden of the three and can use arbitrary regular expressions as search patterns. **grep** accepts a limited class of regular expressions and **fgrep** accepts fixed strings only.

According to the manual pages on most machines, **fgrep** is the fastest of the three programs. This is a lie. **egrep** is almost twice as fast as **fgrep**, even when searching only for fixed strings. **grep** is comparable in speed to **egrep**, but **egrep** is a much more flexible program. **egrep** does not support **grep**'s **-i** (case insensitive) option, however.

There are a number of public domain **grep** replacements that run much faster than the standard **grep**. The best of these (so far) is the **fastgrep** package written by James A. Woods. **fastgrep** can be used as a drop-in replacement for all of the standard **grep** variants. It runs about five times faster than **egrep** on a Vax and can be obtained from your nearest comp.sources.unix archive.

Another **grep**-like command that can speed up searching operations is **look**, which is supplied as standard equipment on many systems. **look** differs from **grep** in that it assumes its input to be *sorted*; this limits its useful domain to word lists and such but makes it very fast. For example, finding the word "hello" in our unabridged dictionary file is 100 times faster with **look** than with **egrep**.

24

Security

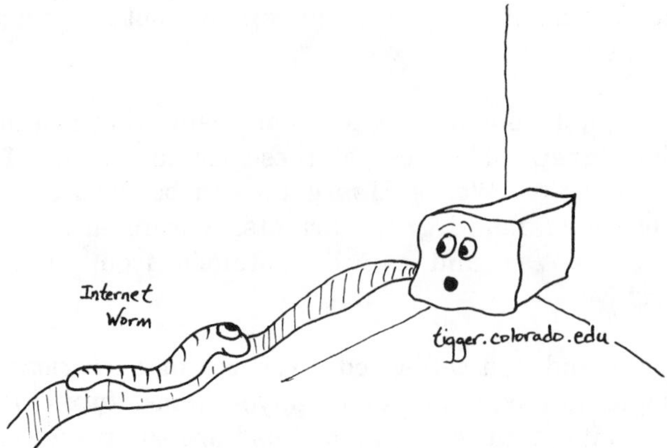

24.1 Introduction

UNIX was not designed with security in mind, and for that reason no UNIX system can be made truly secure.[1] A skilled and patient person with a thorough knowledge of UNIX's shortcomings can violate the security of even the most carefully protected system. The best the system administrator can hope to do is to make the task a difficult one by removing any gaping security holes that a relative novice could find. UNIX can be modified to correct security problems to the point that it is difficult to use and administer, but it will still not be secure. If you have a system where all of the terminals are physically secure and there are no dial-ups or network connections, you do not really need to concern yourself with security (provided you trust all of your users).

We have had great difficulty deciding on a philosophy for this chapter. There are many known security holes in UNIX which will never be fixed and others that have been fixed by some vendors but not by all vendors. In addition,

[1] Versions of UNIX that comply with governmental security standards do exist; however, the permission and security models of these operating systems have been extensively modified.

sites often do not run a vendor's latest software release, either because localization is too expensive or because they do not subscribe to the vendor's software maintenance plan. Even if the vendor has fixed a security hole, it is probably still present in currently used software. To describe these bugs and tell how to exploit them would compromise the security of many sites. Therefore, we will sometimes tell how to fix a security problem without explaining exactly what the problem is. It would be irresponsible to publish ways of violating UNIX security. Berkeley has made a similar decision regarding security problems in the BSD releases. Fixes are posted to Usenet with the annotation "Fixes security hole," but without a description of the actual problem and how to exploit it. This forces the system administrator implementing the fix to trust its correctness, but one tends to trust their primary software supplier.

The security holes that are common knowledge among the small community of UNIX experts usually do not cause problems because those people do not exploit them. If you find out about a security problem, do not tell anyone about it except trusted system administrators. System administrators need to know about security holes so they can close them, but no one else has any legitimate use for such information.

The best sources of information about specific security problems are your fellow system administrators. Information passed from administrator to administrator will almost never fall into the wrong hands. When a site suffers a security breach, all neighboring sites should be informed of the breach and how to foil it, because they will probably be attacked soon (if they have not already been).

The Internet worm[2] that took the country by storm in the fall of 1988 exploited a couple of bugs, one in the mail system and one in a C library routine, that had been known to "insiders" for several years. The worm invaded thousands of machines across the United States in a matter of hours; no data was destroyed, but it totally consumed the resources of each machine it took over. The worm guessed user's passwords by trying variations of their name or login name and a list of about 400 favorite passwords. With password in hand, the worm then propagated to other machines listed in the user's .rhosts file. The worm ran on only two architectures, yet was able to invade nearly every site on the Internet, including most major universities, some government installations, and a few commercial organizations. One of the reasons that the worm was so successful in its rampage is that, for convenience, users equivalence machines they use often. This convenience served the worm quite handily; convenience is always inversely proportional to security.

[2] The worm was called a virus by the popular press, but since it did not invade and alter any programs, it is more properly called a worm.

Security is much tighter now at many sites, so we have to ask: Did the Internet worm do us all a favor?

Some guidelines for assessing and tightening security on your system follow.

24.2 Security problems in the /etc/passwd file

The /etc/passwd file is a gateway through which every user must pass in order to use a UNIX account.[3] Its contents determine who can log in and what they can do once they get inside, so it must be scrupulously maintained and free of garbage. There are just a few cardinal rules to use when maintaining the /etc/passwd file, so there is no excuse for sloppiness.

24.2.1 Password checking, aging, and selection

The first line of defense for systems is the user passwords. It is extremely important to verify on a continuous (at least weekly) basis that every login has a password. The only exceptions to this rule are logins that have severely restricted shells, such as a "who" login that runs **/bin/who** as its shell. Entries in the /etc/passwd file that describe pseudo-users like "daemon" which are used but never log in should have a "*" in the password field.

Several specialized software packages exist to check the /etc/passwd file for security problems, but the command:

```
awk -F: '{ if ($2 == "") print $1 }' /etc/passwd
```

suffices just as well for finding null passwords. A script that performs this check and mails you the results can be easily run by **cron** every week. An added measure of security can be implemented by writing a script that checks /etc/passwd daily against a version from the previous day and mails any differences to you. You can then verify that the additions are legitimate. /etc/passwd and /etc/group must be readable by the world, but writable only by root.

UNIX allows users to choose their own passwords, and while this is a great convenience it leads to many security problems. When users are given their logins, they should also be provided with instructions for choosing a good password. They should be told not to use their name, their initials, or the name of their child, pet, or SO (significant other). Passwords derived from personal data such as telephone number, address, or social security number

[3] Some network services do not operate in a secure fashion, and can thus be considered a way of bypassing the /etc/passwd file. However, these services are willing to perform only a few basic functions (in theory).

can be easily broken by anyone who bothers to look into a user's background. Passwords like "sex", "love", and "money" are cliché; they appear on every pirate's list of commonly used passwords. All of this may seem obvious, yet the majority of inexperienced users pick passwords from one of these three categories.

Passwords should be longer than five characters, should have changes in case, include numerals, or include punctuation, and should not be in the dictionary, *especially* not in the file /usr/dict/words. Nonsense words and combinations of two or more simple words make the best passwords. Unfortunately, there is no easy way to check that your users are following your guidelines for selecting passwords.

There are public domain utilities available to implement what is called *password aging*. These systems force users to change their passwords periodically. While this may seem like a good idea at first glance, it has several problems. Users become resentful at having to change their passwords, and since they don't want to forget their new password they choose simple passwords that are easy to type and remember. Many users will switch back and forth between two passwords each time they are forced to change, so making them change their password does not really add any additional security.

The root password, on the other hand, should be changed regularly. Since you get to choose the new password yourself, you can always pick a good replacement. A root password should roll easily off the fingers so that it can be typed quickly and cannot be guessed by watching the movement of fingers on the keyboard. We find that two unrelated words separated by punctuation makes an excellent root password.

24.2.2 /etc/passwd entries with zero UID

The only distinguishing feature of the root login is its UID of zero. Since there can be more than one entry in the /etc/passwd file which assigns this UID, there can be more than one way to log in as root.

A common way for pirates to install a back door into the system once a root shell has been obtained through other means is to edit new root logins into the /etc/passwd file. Since programs like **who** and **w** (or **whodo**) reference the /etc/utmp file to find out who is logged in rather than the UID which owns the login shell, they cannot expose interlopers who are really logged in as root.

The defense against this kind of thing is an **awk** script similar to the one used for finding logins without passwords:

```
awk -F: '{if ($3 == 0) print $1}' /etc/passwd
```

You may wish to adapt this to find passwd entries with suspicious groups and/or UID's that are the same as those of key people within your organization.

You should also check for password entries that have no user name or punctuation as a user name. These entries may seem nonsensical, but they often will allow you to log in.

24.2.3 User shells

The most important rule here is to avoid using a script as the shell for an unrestricted (passwordless) login. Passwordless logins should be used only as a facility for running small, completely noninteractive utilities such as **who**, **date**, and **lpq**. Using a script as the shell for a real user is uncommon, although not dangerous.

24.3 Setuid programs

Programs that run setuid, especially ones that run setuid root, are prone to security problems. The setuid commands distributed with UNIX are theoretically secure; however, security holes have been discovered in the past and will undoubtedly be discovered in the future.

24.3.1 Writing setuid programs

The surest way to minimize setuid problems is to minimize the number of local setuid programs. If you must write something that's setuid, keep the following rules in mind as you code.

24.3.1.1 Don't write setuid shell scripts (for any shell)

The whole purpose of a shell is to let users configure their environment to their taste. This is exactly what you don't want when running setuid. You need to have complete control over execution of your code and not be affected by any monkey wrenches a user tries to throw into the works. Although a shell spawned to execute a script doesn't necessarily read the user's shell configuration files, there are other ways that it can be influenced: by the user's environment variables, by the contents of the current directory, and by the way the script is invoked.

24.3.1.2 Don't use library routines which invoke a shell

Just because you code in C or some other "real" language doesn't mean that you've escaped the dangers of the shell. Library routines which start up slave shells are almost as dangerous as setuid shell scripts. Fortunately, there are only a few of these; the two most commonly used routines are **popen**(3S) and **system**(3).

24.3.1.3 Don't use execlp or execvp

The **execlp**(3) and **execvp**(3) routines are interfaces to **execve**(2) that duplicate the path-searching functionality of a shell. The idea is that you can specify just a simple command name instead of a complete pathname and the routine will look through your search path to find the command. This is dangerous because users have complete control over their paths; if you use these routines your code can be forced to execute whatever command a user wants.

24.3.1.4 Use full pathnames to identify files

In a similar vein, don't rely on *any* kind of searching mechanism to find you the right file or program. Each time you reference a file from within a setuid program, you have to be sure that you are getting exactly what you intended to get. This means using hard-wired, absolute paths or setting the path at the beginning of the script. Also, root's path should never contain "." or any directories that are world-writable.

24.3.1.5 Don't setuid to root unless you need to

If all you need to do is restrict access to a file or database, there is no reason to make your code setuid root. Instead, make an entry in the /etc/passwd file for a pseudo-user who's only reason for existence is to own the restricted resources, and let your program setuid to that user. Such a fake login should follow the normal fake login conventions; that is, the password should be "*", and the home directory should be /dev/null.

Writing software to be setgid instead of setuid is not generally useful; being in a particular group can often be more beneficial to a pirate than being setuid to a particular UID.

24.3.1.6 Use seteuid(2) to control setuid powers

Just because a program has the setuid bit set doesn't mean that it is condemned to run setuid throughout its execution. All it means is that the program has the *option* of running setuid. While it is true that the EUID of the process is initialized to the setuid value, you can freely switch between the setuid UID and the invoker's UID.

Consider the following simple program. The executable is setuid to "jenny" and "stevenr" is executing it.

```
main(argc, argv)

int argc;
char **argv;

{
        int old_setuid_userid;

        /* Real userid is stevenr and effective userid is jenny */

        /* Save setuid # and make effective userid = real userid */

        old_setuid_userid = geteuid();
        seteuid(getruid());

        /* Now BOTH real userid and effective userid are stevenr */
        /* The process has NONE of jenny's permissions! */

        seteuid(old_setuid_userid);

        /* Now we're back running in setuid mode. */
}
```

The moral is to spend only the very smallest amount of time in actual setuid mode. Bracket all setuid-dependent operations with calls to **seteuid**(3). Remember also that permissions are checked only at specific points in the operation of a program. Once you've successfully **open**(2)'ed a file, for example, you can freely use the file descriptor you obtain even after switching back to non-setuid mode.

24.3.1.7 Don't make setuid programs world-readable

There is a difference between having permission to execute a file and having permission to read it. Use this to your advantage by setting the permissions on your setuid programs so that they can be executed but not read. This is to keep prying eyes from finding out how your code works and exploiting its weaknesses.

Suppose there is a line in your code which reads

```
date_stream = popen("date","r");
```

(which of course there shouldn't be). Anyone who has read permission on the executable can use the **strings** utility to find the printable sequences in the file, including the string "date". A possible line of attack on the program has now been made very clear.

24.3.1.8 Don't put secret back-door escapes in your code

Some people like to put secret, undocumented features in their setuid programs for debugging, performing administrative chores, or spawning setuid shells. This works great until someone else finds out about them. One early UNIX utility allowed savvy users to get a root shell at will; this is still considered somewhat of a scandal.

24.3.2 Finding setuid programs

Once someone has breached the security of your system, he or she will sometimes create private setuid shells and utilities that allow easy access to other accounts. For example, having a setuid version of a shell is equivalent to knowing the root password. Watching for these clandestine setuid programs helps to catch such intrusions early.

The command:

```
/usr/bin/find / -user root -perm -4000 -print | \
        /usr/ucb/mail -s "Setuid root files" operator
```

will generate a list of all setuid root files and mail them to the user "operator". This can be included in a weekly **skulker** script, as described in Section 26.8.2.

24.4 Trojan horses

Trojan horses, as the name implies, are programs that are not what they seem. Be wary of any software that you do not get from a reputable distributer, especially software found in the public domain or supplied by users. If you want to install any such software on your system, read the code and make sure that the program does only what it is supposed to, and that it does not do any devious things. It is easy to hide things in obscure code, so if you do not understand a piece of code, and the comments do not adequately explain it, do not run the software. Never install public domain programs that you only have binary for, because you have no idea what they actually do. Be especially wary of programs that claim they need to run setuid, and never run any user programs when you are superuser. A good example of a Trojan horse was a program called turkey that was distributed on the Usenet. The program said it would draw a picture of a turkey on your terminal, but it actually removed all of the files in your home directory. With a little care you, unlike the residents of Troy, should be able to avoid a bloody slaughter.

24.5 at and cron

The **at** program lets you schedule the execution of a shell script for some later time. When **at** is executed, it copies the specified script and records the current environment within the /usr/spool/at directory. The **cron** daemon periodically executes the **atrun** program, which scans the /usr/spool/at directory to see if the time to execute any of the jobs has arrived. If so, **atrun** setuid's to the appropriate account and runs the script.

The problem is that older versions of **atrun** determine who to setuid to by simply looking at the owner of the command file created in the /usr/spool/at directory. This works because when a user invokes **at** to schedule a job, **at** runs under his UID and he owns the command files that are ultimately created. This is poison on ATT systems which allow users to give away their files to other users, however, since a user can create a command file and then have its contents executed under another UID by manually **chown**'ing away the file after its installation in the /usr/spool/at directory. Since **at** is not usually standard equipment on such systems, the problem arises only on hybrid systems or on ATT systems which have had **at** or an **at**-clone installed externally.

24.6 Important file permissions

There are many files on a UNIX system that must have particular permissions to avoid security problems. Some vendors ship software with permissions set for their own "friendly" development environment. These permissions may not be appropriate in your environment. We will not discuss all of these files, but only those files which are often found to have incorrect permissions.

The uucp file /usr/lib/L.sys contains login names and passwords for all of your uucp neighbors. If this file has incorrect permissions, it violates the security of all of those sites. The L.sys file should have read and write permission for the owner (uucp), read permission for the group (daemon), and no permissions for anyone else. You should also check the contents of this file to make sure that it only includes sites with which you really want to communicate.

The special file /dev/kmem allows access to the kernel's address space. It is used by programs such as **ps** that need to look at kernel data structures. This file should only be readable by the owner and group members, not by the world. All programs that need to access /dev/kmem should be setgid to the group that owns the file, usually the group "kmem".

Some versions of UNIX come with /dev/kmem publicly readable. This is a major security problem because any reasonably competent programmer can then look for things like unencrypted passwords in the kernel data structures and buffers. If your system has /dev/kmem publicly readable, *change this immediately*. If this change causes any programs to stop working, make those programs setgid to the group that owns kmem.

Although it should go without saying, the /etc/passwd and /etc/group files should not be world-writable. They should have owner root and mode 644. The group should be set to some system group, such as daemon. The **passwd** program runs setuid to root so that users can change their passwords without having write permission on the file.

Another potential source of problems are device files for hard disk partitions. Having read or write permission on a disk device file is essentially the same as having read or write permission on every file in the filesystem it represents. Only root should have both read and write permission. The group sometimes gets read permission, but the world is never allowed any permissions.

24.7 Smart terminal problems

Many terminals have built-in intelligence that allows them to operate somewhat independently of a host computer. Although UNIX does not take advantage of these features directly, some of them can cause security problems. In particular, many of these terminals can be sent control sequences that cause them to echo back what is sent to them as though it was typed at the keyboard. If this feature is used to echo UNIX commands, the commands will be executed by whoever is logged in on the terminal. If root is logged in on such a terminal, the security of the entire system is compromised.

This bug is often referred to as the "25th line bug" because on many of the intelligent terminals the characters that are echoed back appear on the status line, line 25. One defense against this line of attack is to use the **mesg n** command to prevent anything, including the dreaded control sequences, from being sent directly to the terminal. Unfortunately, **mesg n** also prevents **write** and **talk** from working, and doesn't keep the control sequences from being delivered to you through other routes, such as electronic mail. This problem can be avoided by having smart terminals emulate older, dumber terminals that do not support a 25th line.

24.8 Data encryption with crypt

The **crypt** utility can be used to encrypt any files you don't want prying eyes to see. If you want to encrypt a whole directory hierarchy, first use **tar** or **cpio** to pack it into a single file. **crypt** alone does not change the size of a file; however, if you wish to use a data compression program such as **compress** in conjunction with **crypt** be sure to apply the compression program first, as the nature of encrypted files makes them quite resistant to the common compression algorithms.

crypt requires a key that becomes essentially a password for the encrypted file. The key cannot be recovered, so the use of **crypt** should not be taken lightly. **crypt** allows the key to be specified on the command line, but this option should not be used because it allows a timely **ps** to display the key.

The editors **ex** and **vi** support a **-x** option that causes a file to be stored in the same encrypted form that **crypt** uses, but decodes the file for editing. The encryption method that **crypt** uses is well known and not particularly hard to break, so **crypt** provides minimal protection at best. Many systems provide alternatives to **crypt** that use better encryption algorithms such as the NBS DES (Data Encryption Standard).[4] A **man -k crypt** should show what encryption programs are available on your machine.

24.9 Vigilance

Probably the most useful thing you can do to increase security is to randomly monitor the system. Whenever you are bored with your system administration duties, you can randomly poke around and look for security problems. Occasionally do a **ps** and look at all of the processes running on the system. This is an easy way of spotting fake login programs, programs being run by root or daemon that should not be, and a variety of other violations. Fake login programs impersonate a login prompt and then gather password data. A simple fake login can be written by even the most novice user, but they are easily discovered by doing a **ps**. As a general rule of thumb, if it looks weird, investigate. Doing **ls -l** on system directories will sometimes turn up security holes. Another thing to occasionally look for is clandestine copies of device files outside of /dev. You can do this with the command:

```
/usr/bin/find / -type b -o -type c -print
```

This can easily be included in a **skulker** script, described in Section 26.8.4.

[4] Evi broke the Diffie-Hellman key exchange often used with the DES encryption method using a HEP supercomputer in 1984. Although the DES algorithm is quite complicated, nothing encrypted with DES can be considered 100% secure. The U.S. government has been (rightly?) accused of blocking adoption of encryption standards that cannot be broken by the NSA.

25

Small UNIX Systems

In the last few years, personal computers have advanced to the point where they are fast enough to make running UNIX feasible. Numerous companies have ported versions of UNIX for small machines, especially machines in the IBM PC/XT/AT class. The cost of these systems is low enough to make them affordable even for home use. This chapter is designed to give some general information about peculiarities that are specific to these systems.

25.1 A few caveats on choosing a system

Because of disk space and processor limitations, small UNIX systems often are not as complete as their full-sized counterparts. Before you buy a small UNIX system, be very wary of what you are getting. First of all, avoid like the plague systems that are not true Unices, but "UNIX-like implementations." Anyone who has ever used a real UNIX system will be disappointed by such a system. Most of the small systems are ports of ATT System III with various enhancements, depending on the vendor. If you want the Berkeley enhancements (**vi**, **more**, etc.) make sure the system you purchase includes these. Many of the vendors make the additional compliers (F77, Pascal, Lisp) separate items, which you purchase only if you want them. Beware of any system that makes the C complier an option, because anyone who would consider that a separate package would probably not think twice about making things like **cd** and **ed** separate packages. The text formatting software (**nroff**, **tbl**, **eqn**, etc.) is usually considered a separate product.

Many systems have a limitation built into the kernel that specifies the maximum number of simultaneous **getty**'s the system will support. This is the vendor's method of limiting the number of users on the system and finding a way to charge you more money. These systems are marketed as "single-user," "two-user," or "multi-user" systems, the only difference being the number of **getty**'s that can coexist. It would not be to hard to use **adb** to modify the **init** code of a "single-user system" to make it a "multi-user system," but we could never condone that. This limitation on **getty**'s can become very annoying when you want to use one port as a dial-in for uucp and another port for a terminal.

Some systems have additional enhancements that allow various communications with other operating systems on the machine, primarily DOS. These facilities range from simple file transfer to complete emulation of the other system's environment. If you intend to buy such a system, give it a thorough test to make sure it does what you want it to, because such systems are notoriously flaky.

If you are running any sort of nonstandard hardware on your system, chances are there will not be device drivers to support it. The most common and irritating example of this problem is in the area of disk drives. Although a nonstandard disk may function without problems with DOS, the UNIX drivers tend to be much more picky. Before purchasing a system, make sure that it supports both your disk controller and the actual disk that you have. If you have any peripheral that you intend to write a device driver for, make sure that you buy a system that allows the kernel to be recomplied with additional drivers.

In the world of small UNIX systems, it is often true that you don't get what you think you paid for. Before buying any system, insist on a demonstration and look to make sure that all of the commands that you want exist on the system. A simple checklist might include: **cc**, **vi**, **uucp**, **make**, **nroff**, **sccs**, and **f77**. Although few systems will actually come with all of these packages, it will at least give you a good idea of exactly what you are getting.

25.2 Performance

If you expect a small UNIX system to give performance similar to a large system, you will be disappointed. Limited processor speed and slow peripherals (especially hard disks) severely limit the responsiveness of the system. The most severe limitation is in the ability to handle multiple users. Although many systems can support multiple users, the performance gets so bad that it makes using the system a frustrating task at best. The multi-user feature is convenient, but you should not plan on using it all of the time. Although the performance of small systems is inherently limited, you can do some tuning to get the most out of your system.

The easiest way to improve the performance of your system is to increase the size of the memory. Memory is relatively inexpensive, so put as much in your machine as you can afford. The more memory you have, the less likely you are to have to swap to disk. If programs are accessing the filesystem and have to swap, the disk head will have to move back and forth between the swap area and the filesystem, which severely degrades performance. Remember, these versions of UNIX are based on System III, so they don't have any of the nifty memory management found in current releases.

If you plan to run programs that do a lot of floating-point calculations, you should consider buying a floating-point coprocessor. Most versions of UNIX require that you build a new kernel in order to utilize the coprocessor. Refer to your specific documentation to determine how to do this (Chapter 8: *Configuring the Kernel* will help you understand what you are doing). If you are not running programs that do a lot of floating-point number crunching, a coprocessor will do you little or no good. Don't forget that **troff** is a floating-point hog.

While most of the versions of UNIX claim to support multiple hard disk drives, many of them do not work correctly if both drives are not of the same type and size. If you do happen to have two hard drives, and they work properly with your system, significant performance improvements can be gained if you place the swap area on the drive that does not contain the root filesystem. This is especially true on machines with limited memory that tend to do a lot of swapping. Moving the swap space requires building a new kernel (refer to your system documentation and Chapter 8 to do this). The performance improvements do not justify purchasing an second drive, but if you have two drives, it is worth the trouble of building a new kernel.

26

Bunch o' Stuff

This chapter contains a number of minor topics that we wanted to include but couldn't fit into other chapters.

26.1 Local documentation

It is difficult to run a large computer system smoothly without a workable system of local documentation. There are two reasons for documenting what you do:

- So that *other people* can understand what you've done
- So that *you* can understand what you've done six months later

The system's records can be concise, but they should be complete enough to be understood by someone who is not intimately familiar with your local setup. Overdocumenting is as much a problem as underdocumenting; you will quickly become frustrated with the process if you feel bogged down by details and trivialities.

Good documentation includes a description of:

- What was done and why - a one or two sentence summary
- When it was done, if germane - the date
- Who did it - your name
- How it was done - list of files modified, wires run, etc.
- Pitfalls - anything that confused you about the operation
- Parameters - any "magic numbers" you used

For example, the documentation for moving a printer from one machine to another might look like this:

```
Garth - July 23, 1988:  Moved cs-imagen from boulder to sigi because
boulder is being sold.  Modified /etc/printcap on sigi and boulder to
reflect swap - printcaps on all other machines were modified to point
at sigi as remote machine rather than boulder.  Deinstalled
/usr/lib/imagen directory with printer drivers and reinstalled on
sigi from source tape.  Freed port ttyi12 on boulder, took port
tty03 on sigi.  No new cables were made, connection was just changed.
```

The pitfalls and parameters are the most important things for you to include. Recording pitfalls is important because the first time you do something it is normal to spend 20% of your time actually getting it done and 80% of your time being confused and debugging. If you write down what your stumbling blocks were and how to get around them, you will streamline subsequent modifications. Parameters are important because they can't always be recovered by just examining the setup. For example, after formatting a disk it is painful to find out what the starting and ending block numbers for each partition are unless they are written down.

26.1.1 Methods of documentation

There are four basic ways to keep documentation:

- In a file which you edit directly
- In an electronic mail drop
- In a notebook or log
- In paper documents

Each method has its advantages, and you'll probably want to use them in combination. In the following specific applications, we've suggested a method that's most appropriate for each.

The most convenient of these four is the electronic mail drop. The idea is to set up a mail alias that routes mail to a file. When you want to make a log entry, you just send mail to the alias. This system has the following advantages:

- Your log entries are signed and dated for you automatically.
- There are no hassles with file permissions.
- The log is easy to review (just use **mail**).
- Simultaneous submissions are handled correctly.
- You can easily carbon copy relevant personal mail to the log.
- You can modify the log alias to include people who want to receive copies.
- You're unlikely to lose the log.

BSD **sendmail** supports sending mail to a file directly, but you can fake it on other systems by adding an imaginary user to the /etc/passwd file. At our site we use the alias "diary", and each machine is set up with its own diary file so that mail with addresses like "diary@boulder" and "diary@sigi" is always sent to the right log file.

It is also useful to create a mail drop called "trouble" that users can send gripes and questions to about things that are not working properly. Trouble mail should actually be forwarded to two different files: one for archival purposes that is never modified and one to be read and modified by everyone involved in system administration using **mail -f**. Messages from this second file can be deleted as they are resolved so that everyone on the maintenance team knows what problems are waiting for attention at any given time.

26.1.2 Wire maps

Whenever a new cable or terminal wire is run, its location and purpose should be clearly recorded in a wiring log. If the cable contains more than one set of conductors you must also identify where each set goes. You'll need to record what signal is carried on each conductor within a set; since the insulation colors in multiconductor cables are not standardized it is unwise to depend on a particular color coding scheme. Wiring maps can become quite complex when lengths of several different cables are spliced together to form a longer piece, but most entries will be fairly simple.

Wiring maps should be kept on-line in a file (not a mail drop) to make their modification easier when things are rewired. This makes it hard to take the log on-site to record the wiring as you do it, but we feel that overall the benefits outweight the costs. You'll have to make the initial notes on paper or in a notebook and transcribe them later.

The following example shows the connections for a cable containing ten sets of twisted-pair terminal wires. The cable runs from the machine room through a junction box, where four of the sets branch off. The other six sets continue through to a second box before reaching their final destination.

```
Wire map for cable that runs from the machine room to the
dean's office, providing service for rooms DO-0 to DO-90.
There are extra wires running to both Box #1 and
Box #2 for future use.

Label   Machine Room    Box #1              Box #2          Location
----------------------------------------------------------------
dean0   black/yellow    black/yellow        black/yellow    DO-87
dean1   black/red       black/red           black/red       DO-81
dean2   black/green     black/green         black/green     DO-67
dean3   black/white     black/white         brown/white     DO-60
dean4   black/blue      black/blue          brown/blue      DO-40
dean5   black/orange    black/orange        brown/orange    DO-15
dean6   white/blue      DO-17(red/black)
dean7   brown/green     black/brown              -
dean8   blue/yellow     DO-6  (red/black)
dean9   red/green             -


Label        - the label on the connector in the machine room.
Machine Room - the color of the wires in the machine room.
Box #1       - the color of the wires leaving Box #1, which is
               located in the ceiling outside DO-12.  If a room number
               is specified, a wire  runs from this box to that room.
Box #2       - the color of the wires leaving Box #2, which
               is located in the ceiling outside DO-16.
Location     - the room number where the cable goes after
               leaving box #2.

The first color specified refers to pin #2, and the second color
specified is connected to pin #3.  The ground from each twisted
pair is used for pin #7 on the corresponding cable.
```

This example is taken more or less directly from our wiring maps, but has been somewhat simplified; it is more complicated than most wire maps will be. Notice that most of the map is an explanation of how things were done, which is at least as important as the description of the actual wire colors.

26.1.3 Cable specifications

There are many different kinds of cables, and they are all made in different ways. Specifications on how to make nonstandard cables should be kept in a mail drop. Section 9.2 tells how to construct some of the common cables to start you on your way; you need not reproduce this information on-line.

26.1.4 Maintenance logs

A log of all hardware maintenance performed on each machine is very useful to have. Since machines are usually down when maintenance is performed, it does not make sense to keep this information on-line. A bound composition book makes a good hardware log.

Basic information should be listed on the first few pages of the log. Some important items are:

- The local hardware configuration
- The serial numbers and revision levels of all components
- Backplane and bus interface maps identifying boards and their slots
- How to call for hardware maintenance

The log should be used to document the following events:

- Service calls
- Hardware swaps and changes
- Preventive maintenance calls
- Machine crashes and their causes
- System errors (if you aren't running **syslogd** or **errdaemon**)

All entries should include all the relevant information and be dated and signed.

26.1.5 Boot instructions

While most newer systems boot automatically, older systems often have complex or cryptic boot procedures. The fewer people there are who know the boot procedure, the more likely you are to be called at odd hours and asked to reboot the machine, so it is to your advantage to make detailed booting instructions available to operators. The instructions should be good enough that someone with very little experience can use them correctly.

A good place to put the boot instructions is in the front of the maintenance log for the machine. If they are sufficiently brief, a copy of the boot instructions can also be taped to the console.

Caveat: Complex boot procedures often give plenty of opportunity for creating a root shell on the console. Boot instructions should be targeted at operators whom you trust and who are authorized to use the root account.

26.1.6 Backup schedules

A schedule of which backups need to be done and when they should be performed should always be maintained a month or more in advance. The easiest way to do this is to buy a calendar and simply write on it, but you can do it automatically with software if you're ambitious. For more information, refer to Chapter 18: *Backups and Transportable Media*.

When someone does a backup, they should record their name and the date on the backup schedule. If the backups are delegated to someone else, the system administrator should regularly consult the backup schedules to make sure that the backups are being done on time. If more than one person does backups, you can use to the schedule as an assignment sheet, too.

26.1.7 Vendor information

Every piece of hardware your site buys will come with documentation. We have found through experience that the *only* way to deal with this documentation effectively is to put it in a filing cabinet. Keeping the vendor documentation with the hardware does not work; it increases clutter dramatically and things tend to walk away. Stacking documentation in random piles or distributing it among several people's bookshelves is an unmitigated disaster.

26.1.8 Local customs

If your site is large enough that you don't know all your users personally, you should write and distribute a document that describes your local computer customs and procedures. This document should explain how to get an account, how to get started with using the system, how to communicate with the system administrators and wiring crew, how to get files archived or restored from dump tapes, and anything else you think might be useful for them to know.

26.2 /etc/motd

The motd (message of the day) is kept in the file /etc/motd. The contents of this file are shown to all users as they log in[1] and so should be used to disseminate information of general interest. It has been said that the only thing that all UNIX systems have in common is the motd message asking users to clean up their files and use less disk space.

[1] BSD users can suppress printing of the motd by creating a file called .hushlogin in their home directory.

Whether or not users read the motd depends on how long it is and whether or not you customarily abuse it. If you constantly fill it with drivel or leave time-dependent motd messages up after they are useful, you are increasing the chance that it will be habitually ignored. Since the system administrator sees the motd when logging in, there is no excuse for outdated information to remain in the motd. As a rule of thumb, the motd should not be longer than five lines.

The motd is the proper place to give information on scheduled downtime, brief descriptions of new hardware or software, and impending system changes. Do not *under any circumstances* put a sappy welcome message with a little border of asterisks around it in the motd; such messages are not user-friendly, just saccharine and dumb.[2]

26.3 make

The **make** command is used to specify the necessary steps to process a set of files. It is usually used to compile a set of source code into a command or commands, but may be used to process any set of files where hierarchical dependencies exist, such as documentation sets.

make ranks with the shell (as a programming language) as one of the most powerful system administration tools. If you are unfamiliar with the **make** command, consult the documentation. If a software package is properly maintained, you should only have to type **make** to insure that the executable is up-to-date, and **make install** to install the software and manual pages in the proper places.

When a software package is obtained from Usenet or other such source, the Makefile (the **make** control file) may have to be modified to reflect your local naming and storage conventions. You should insist that any user contributed software conform to this standard. On systems that have source code, you can see that UNIX itself is generated with **make**.

26.4 File revision handling

Any file that is frequently modified, either because it is under development or just because it needs incremental changes, should be kept under a revision control system. Two such systems are **SCCS** (Source Code Control System),

[2] This paragraph elicited strong commentary from our technical reviewers. One wrote "Hear hear!", another "Wrong"!

and **RCS** (Revision Control System). Both allow different versions of a file to be kept along with a log describing the changes it has undergone. Neither system actually keeps copies of old versions around; only the *differences* between versions are stored. This allows any version to be recreated with a minimum of storage overhead. **SCCS** is standard equipment on all Unices. **RCS**, written by Walter F. Tichy at Purdue University (tichy@purdue.edu), is available from several sources; however, the distribution status of the most recent revision is unclear.

26.5 Data compression

Most UNIX systems have at least one set of utilities for data compression and expansion. These utilities usually include a compression program, an expansion program, and a program that dynamically expands for viewing. Some common program sets are the **compress** family, the **compact** family, and the **pack** family. The best percentage compression is achieved with **compress**. **pack** is slightly faster than **compress**, but is significantly worse in overall compression. **compact** uses the same compression algorithm as **pack**, but implements it in a horrible way that takes an order of magnitude longer to run. **compress** is not a standard UNIX utility, but almost every site has a copy of it. Figure 26.1 is an informal performance comparison of **compress**, **pack**, and **compact**.

FIGURE 26.1

Input file	**compress**		**pack**		**compact**	
	Compression	Time (secs.)	Compression	Time (secs.)	Compression	Time (secs.)
1 Megabyte English text	58.3%	30.8	39.8%	28.4	39.8%	279.7
1.6 Megabytes C source code	62.5%	45.4	31.2%	43.6	31.2%	466.9
1.5 Megabytes executable binary	45.8%	53.2	23.8%	42.0	23.8%	510.2
DNA genetic code data	none		none		none	

Any large files that are only accessed occasionally are good targets for compression. Log files created by shell scripts that are run at night are often suitable for compression because it is easy to have the script automatically compress the file before it exits. When deciding whether to compress a file, you must decide whether savings in disk space warrant the CPU time and the hassle that it takes to compress and expand the file.

A **man -k compress** should give a listing of all the compression programs available on your system, and by reading the manual pages you can determine which one is most appropriate for your applications.

26.6 Local software

When a new version of UNIX is installed, there are many local files such as /etc/passwd, /usr/lib/aliases, /usr/lib/uucp/L.sys, as well as locally installed software packages, that need to be saved from the old system and restored on the new system. One way to make this job easier is to keep as many things as possible in local directories. The traditional place for local software is in /usr/local/bin, with the sources in /usr/local/src. Keeping all local software together in one place makes conversion to a new system much easier.

Even with careful segregation of local and nonlocal files, there are many system files that must be changed to reflect local conditions. Our attempt to simplify the process of upgrading to a new release of UNIX is the Makefile.localsys. An example of such a Makefile with comments is located in Appendix H. This Makefile is used in conjunction with the **make** command to create a **tar**-format tape that contains most of the local files that are scattered around the system. This Makefile may not be able to automate the entire process, but it at least provides a standard place for information about which files contain site-specific information. When any change is made to a system file that makes it locally specific, that file should be added to the Makefile.localsys. If this is done, the problems associated with installing a new version are kept to a minimum.

26.7 Bugs

All large software systems have bugs, and UNIX is no exception. UNIX is especially susceptible to bugs because new and better versions are constantly being developed and released. Most bugs will be discovered by someone else, reported, and fixed long before you ever realize that they exist, but once a solution has been determined it is the system administrator's job to implement it locally.

26.7.1 Bug fixes

There are two main sources for bug reports and fixes: the software distributor and Usenet. Chapter 17: *News* gives a list of the groups that the system administrator should monitor to get bug fixes. When a bug fix comes from the software vendor, it is usually in the form of a tape containing a new version of the program, or a detailed description of the steps to take to fix the bug.

When a bug fix comes from Usenet, it is usually less precise. Some Usenet bug reports refer to nonexistent bugs, and a few of the fixes supplied cause more serious bugs. Before implementing a bug fix from the net, collect all of the articles relating to that particular bug for several days and only then decide on a course of action. In many cases, the best fix is to not fix anything.

There is a program called **patch** that is available over the network that makes fixing bugs in source code easier. **patch** takes as input a file containing a **diff** (see **diff**(1)) of the buggy and fixed source code and reverse-engineers the needed changes onto your copy of the source code automatically. Whenever you implement a bug fix, you should thoroughly test it before installing it, and always use source code control so that you can back out the patched version easily.

Fixing bugs in the kernel or other binary-only programs requires the use of a binary editor such as **adb** or recompiling the program from object files after replacing an entire object file. Fixes that require this type of manipulation should be avoided if possible.

26.7.2 Reporting bugs

If you find something that appears to be a bug, you should be very careful before reporting it as a bug. First of all, make sure that it is actually a bug and not a feature. If you are confident that something is definitely not performing as it is documented, try to create a short test program to demonstrate the bug. If you cannot isolate the bug, there is little chance that anyone will be able to fix it.

If you are confident that there is a bug and you have a short test program that illustrates it, fill out a bug report form which can be obtained from your software vendor. Most vendors have electronic mail forms and electronic addresses where you can send bug reports as well.

26.8 Disk cleanup

A common feature of all UNIX systems is useless files that grow and multiply until all disks are full to capacity. No matter how much disk space you have, it isn't enough. In addition to user-generated garbage, the system software is responsible for creating a large amount of useless information. It is the system administrator's job to control both of these sources of trash.

UNIX provides some ways of controlling disk usage; for example, partition sizes and quotas. System administrators can also use peer pressure, threats, or rewards. We will describe both the UNIX tools and psychological tools we have used successfully.

26.8.1 Partition sizes

The placement of users' home directories can be used to manage disk space. For example, separate partitions for students and for faculty will stop faculty from taking so much space students have none left. This provides rather gross control, since partitions are often a few hundred megabytes and house many individual users.

26.8.2 BSD disk quotas

BSD systems support disk quotas on a per user, per filesystem basis. Quotas are useful not only to control true disk hogs, but also to stop runaway user programs that might try to fill the disk by mistake. Quotas provide a fine level of control, but require more maintenance than other means of controlling disk usage. Frantic users who cannot save their edit sessions become a constant administrative chore when disk space is tight. Maintaining quotas also takes a lot of system resources.

26.8.3 Peer pressure with easy archiving

Most Unices do not support quotas, so the system administrator must spend a lot of time nagging users to control their disk usage. It is often hard to convince users that they should remove any of their precious files until the disk is actually full or overflowing.

Asking users to clean up their files in /etc/motd and sending mail to all users are both useless as ways to get people to clean up because they do not assign responsibility to specific users. To get action you have to find out who the disk hogs are and let them know that you know they are the source of the problem. You can do this automatically with the **spacegripe** script presented in Appendix I. **spacegripe** identifies all users whose disk holdings are above a certain threshold and sends them polite mail requesting that they clean up their act. It is quite polite and precise, yet unfortunately it is generally ignored by our user community.

No user likes to face a message-of-the-day that labels him in the top ten disk hogs, especially if disk space is tight enough that his peers are having trouble getting their work done. We have found that publishing such a list is by far the most effective way of coercing users to clean up the disk. When the list of disk hogs is posted in the /etc/motd file, the disk space situation miraculously improves.

If some users do not reduce their disk usage even after public humiliation, you will have to deal with them on a person-by-person basis. Do not go poking around in their home directories looking for files to erase, as this is a rather egregious violation of privacy. It is, however, appropriate to run a

find on their home directory to find big files. You may see something (such as a multimegabyte core dump) that a user is not even aware of owning.

If you ask users to clean up, you must give them an alternative way to store their files. We have found that a tape drive in a public area allows users to archive files that are used infrequently with minimal fuss on our part.

26.8.4 Skulker scripts

skulker is the name usually given to a script that goes around the disk, controlling the size of system log files, removing junk files left around, and checking for security breaches. Skulker scripts are usually run by **cron** either daily or weekly. The following is an example of a simple weekly **skulker**:

```
#!/bin/csh
# Skulker - program to run weekly to clean up the disk.
#
# remove old core, a.out and .o files
/usr/bin/find / \( -name a.out -name core -name '*.o' \) -atime +7 \
    -exec /bin/rm -f {} \;

# clean up /tmp and /usr/tmp
/usr/bin/find /tmp -type f -atime +7 -exec /bin/rm -f {} \;
/usr/bin/find /usr/tmp -type f -atime +7 -exec /bin/rm -f {} \;

# remove printer logs
/bin/rm -f /usr/adm/lp-log
/bin/rm -f /usr/adm/lw-log

# find all files owned by root with setuid
/usr/bin/find / -user root -perm -4000 -print | \
    /usr/ucb/mail -s "Setuid root files" operator
```

The last line, which checks for files setuid to root, is a reasonable way to check if anyone has illegal copies of setuid programs. Notice that all command paths are hard-wired. This is an attempt at improving the security of the script; you do not want the first command named **find** in the invoker's path being executed.

The junk files that a skulker should remove vary from system to system. The ones removed in the preceding script are generally fairly safe, but there is always a chance someone will unknowingly name an important file to match one of the specifications and have it deleted. Because an acrimonious flame-fest can follow such an event, we recommend that you auto-delete files *only* after a complete, level zero dump.

26.8.5 Disk overflows

A filesystem that is completely full constitutes an emergency situation. The first step to take is to find out what caused it to overflow. If you have been keeping an eye on the filesystems and keeping them under 90% full, it is most likely some sort of runaway program that is overflowing the filesystem. Do a **ps** and look for suspicious processes. If you find the culprit, suspend its execution, remove the files it has been making, and notify the owner of the process.

If the overflow was not caused by a runaway program, you will need to remove some files to give breathing room for the filesystem until you can get people to clean up. If the overflowing filesystem is /usr, remove printer log files, uucp log files, and whatever looks like junk in /usr/tmp, and truncate /usr/adm/wtmp if you don't need it for accounting. If it is a strictly user filesystem, it may be harder to find things to delete, but core files are a good place to start.

26.9 UNIX user groups

There are many support organizations for users of UNIX. Of these, /usr/group (about 5000 members) and the Usenix Association (about 3500 members) are the largest.

The /usr/group organization is a trade organization dedicated to the promotion of products and services based on UNIX. It is much more commercially oriented than Usenix, and is geared towards training users how to use UNIX. /usr/group sponsors the annual UniForum Conference and Trade show (about 20,000 people attend this conference). These conferences have a huge trade show, tutorials, and symposia. /usr/group provides its members with a biweekly newsletter, a bimonthly magazine, and a "UNIX Products Directory."

Usenix is "The Professional and Technical UNIX Association." Usenix is oriented more toward developers and administrators of UNIX than common users. Usenix sponsors semi-annual conferences (2500 attendees) which include tutorials, a technical program, vendor exhibits, BOF's (Birds of a Feather sessions), WIP's (work in progress sessions), and contests (go, obfuscated C programming). The winter meetings are often held concurrently with /usr/group meetings. Usenix also holds focused workshops several times a year; recent topics have included TCP/IP, C++ and UNIX security. Usenix offers its members a bimonthly newsletter, a quarterly journal, printed versions of the BSD manuals, and software distribution tapes.

Many countries have UNIX organizations, and many manufacturers sponsor groups dedicated to their hardware. There are also many local user groups, most of which are affiliated with /usr/group or Usenix. The address of /usr/group is:

/usr/group
4655 Old Ironsides Drive, Suite 200
Santa Clara, California 95054
(408) 986-8840

The address for Usenix is:

USENIX Association
P.O. Box 2299
Berkeley, CA 94710
(415) 528-8649
{uunet,ucbvax,decvax}!usenix!office
office@usenix.org

A

The **sudo** *Command*

A.1 Introduction

sudo (originally written by Cliff Spencer of SUNY-Buffalo) is a program which allows authorized users to run commands as root. The operation of **sudo** is controlled by a configuration file which lists the permissible commands for each user. As a special case, a user may be given unlimited privileges. All commands executed via **sudo** are entered into a human-readable log file.

As a security precaution, **sudo** users are asked to enter their own passwords to prove who they are. For convenience, **sudo** allows a number of commands to be executed sequentially after typing the password once; when five minutes have passed without an invocation of **sudo**, the password must be reentered.

sudo is written in C and runs under BSD. No special BSD tricks were used in writing it, so it should work under ATT with little modification. The complete **sudo** package consists of four files:

- sudo.c - the main program file
- clrusr.c - user validation routines
- sudo.8 - the manual page
- Makefile - the **make** control file for compilation and installation

To install **sudo** at your site, type in these four files and edit them to reflect where you want things to go. In particular, make LOGFILE and userfile in sudo.c point to the place where you want the command log and permissions file to go, and change TIMEDIR in clrusr.c to point at the directory where **sudo's** time-keeping files should be put. The Makefile will need to be altered to reflect any changes to these three paths.

Next, read the Makefile and be sure you agree with what it is going to do. Then simply type **make install** to perform a complete installation or **make sudo** to simply compile the program. After installation, read the manual page and then edit the configuration file to give out permissions as appropriate. If you choose not to use the Makefile for installation, remember that **sudo** must be setuid to root in order to work properly.

When someone here at the University of Colorado is given unlimited access, they get sent a copy of the following message. You may wish to do something like this as well.

```
You have been given "sudo all" permissions, which means you have
unlimited superuser access.  You may have already been given a
lecture at some point as to the moral and social etiquette that you
should observe as a superuser.  Please bear with me.

With superuser permissions, It is possible to do great damage by
accident.  Use extra premeditation before doing anything. Some famous
sudo boo-boo's include removing /etc or killing init. Lots of fun.

With superuser permissions you may look at any file you wish. Resist
all temptation to look in other people's personal files, even if they
haven't locked them up properly.

By far the most prevalent use of superuser permissions are for very
routine things like killing processes, changing ownerships, removing
print jobs, etc.

However, if you use sudo to make permanent changes or fixes to
commands or files in that are used by the system or the community at
large, it is very important to check with systems people and to
document any changes made.
```

To document a change simply 'mail diary@host systems trouble'. Systems people will be much happier if you run something by them before you go ahead and do it, of course. But under emergencies and after hours, use your own discretion.

A.2 The sudo.c file

```
/*
**  sudo - run a command as root
*/

#include <stdio.h>
#include <strings.h>
#include <ctype.h>
#include <sys/time.h>
#include <sys/types.h>
#include <sys/stat.h>
#include <sys/param.h>
#include <pwd.h>

#ifndef MAXHOSTNAMELEN
#define MAXHOSTNAMELEN 64
#endif MAXHOSTNAMELEN

#define ALERTMAIL    "root"
#define LOGFILE      "/usr/local/adm/logs/sudo.log"

extern char          *ctime();
extern long          time();

char                 *userfile = "/usr/local/adm/sudoers";
char                 *progname;
long                 now;

void                 log(), errexit(), firsthostname();
int                  checkdoer();
char                 *isadoer();

main(argc, argv)

int                  argc;
char                 *argv[];

{
    char             doerline[512];
    char             cmd[512];
```

```
char            *dp;
struct passwd   *pw;
int             uid, pid;

progname = argv[0];
if(argc < 2)
{
    fprintf(stderr, "usage: %s cmd\n", progname);
    exit(1);
}

/* remember who this user really is */

uid = getuid();

/* Set userid to be root and group id to be daemon */

if((setuid(0)) < 0)
{
    eperror("setuid");
}

if((setgid(3)) < 0)
{
    eperror("setgid");
}

dp = &doerline[0];
pw = getpwuid(uid);
now = time((long*) 0);

if ((dp = isadoer(pw->pw_name,pw->pw_passwd)) == NULL)
{
    log(pw->pw_name,"FAIL",argc,argv);

    fprintf(stderr,"%s:I don't know you, and I'm telling!\n",*argv);

    if ((pid = fork()) == 0)
        mailmsg(pw->pw_name,argv,argc);
    if (pid == -1)
        eperror("fork");

    exit(1);
}

argv++, argc--;
```

```
    checkdoer(dp,*argv,cmd);

    if (strcmp(cmd,"all") == 0)
    {
        log(pw->pw_name,"",argc, argv);
        execvp(*argv, argv);     /* then do it  */
        eperror(*argv);
    }

    if (cmd[0] == '\0')
    {
        log(pw->pw_name,"FAIL",argc,argv);
        fprintf(stderr,
        "%s: I know you, but I can't let you: %s\n",progname,*argv);
        exit(1);
    }

    /* do a specific command with hard-coded path from doer file */

    log(pw->pw_name,"",argc,argv);
    execv(cmd, argv);    /* then do it  */
    eperror(*argv);
}

/*
**  isadoer(name, encrypted password) - look for a user in USERFILE
**      return doer entry on success, else NULL.
*/

char *isadoer(name,password)

char            *name;
char            *password;

{
    register FILE *fp;
    char buf[BUFSIZ];
    struct stat statb;

    if (stat(userfile, &statb))
        eperror(userfile);

    if (statb.st_uid != 0)
        errexit("%s must be owned by root\n", userfile);

    if (statb.st_mode & 022)     /* should be og-w */
        errexit("bad modes on %s\n", userfile);
```

```
    if ((fp = fopen(userfile,"r")) == 0 )
        errexit("Couldn't open %s\n",userfile);

    while ((fgets(buf,BUFSIZ,fp)) != NULL)
    {
        if(buf[0] == '#')    /* munch comments */
        {
            continue;
        }

        if((strncmp(buf,name,strlen(name))) == 0)
        {
            if (not_timed_out(name,password))
            {
                return(buf);
            }
            return(NULL);
        }
    }

    return(NULL);
}

/*
**  log this command in the log file
*/

void
log(username, info, argc, argv)

char            *username;
char            *info;
int             argc;
char            **argv;

{
    register FILE *fp;
    fp = fopen(LOGFILE,"a");

    if (fp == NULL)
    {
        errexit("can't open %s.\n", LOGFILE);
    }

    fprintf (fp, "%20.20s :", ctime(&now));
    fprintf (fp,"%s",info);
    fprintf (fp,"%7.7s :",username);
```

```
    while (argc--)
    {
        fprintf (fp,"%s ",*argv++);
    }
    fprintf (fp,"\n");
    (void) fclose (fp);
    return;
}

/*
**  eperror - print system error message and exit
**     string s is printed too.
*/

eperror(s)

register char       *s;

{
    fprintf(stderr,"%s: ",progname);
    perror(s);
    exit(1);
}

/*
**  errexit(format, message) - print formatted error and exit
**     also send mail
*/

void
errexit(fmt, arg)

register char       *fmt, *arg;

{
    FILE            *popen();
    FILE            *fd;
    char            hostname[MAXHOSTNAMELEN];
    char            cmd[80];

    fprintf(stderr,"%s: ", progname);
    fprintf(stderr, fmt, arg);

    if ((fd = popen(cmd, "w")) == NULL)
    {
        return;
    }
```

```
    firsthostname(hostname, MAXHOSTNAMELEN);

    (void) sprintf(cmd,
        "/usr/ucb/mail -s \"HELP! %s@%s has problems.\" %s ",
        progname,hostname,ALERTMAIL);

    if ((fd = popen(cmd, "w")) == NULL)
    {
        return;
    }

    fprintf(fd,"%s: ", progname);
    fprintf(fd, fmt, arg);
    (void) pclose(fd);
    exit(1);
}

/*
**  checkdoer - check to see if user is permitted to do command requested.
**     dp points to a sudoer file entry of the form:
**     'user ['all,','/dir/dir/cmd1,/dir/dir/cmd2,/dir/dir/cmdN'] ie)
**     coggs     /bin/wall,/etc/vipassw,/etc/adduser
**     operator shutdown
**     If 'all' is found, then string "all" is returned in res.
**     If command passed in ap is found, then that command, along
**     with its full path are passed back in res. If nothing is
**     found, then NULL is returned in res.
*/

checkdoer(dp,ap,res)

char            *dp;        /* doer file entry: 'user cmd1,cmd2,cmdN' */
char            *ap;
char            *res;
{
    char         *cp0, *cp1, *cp2;

    cp0 = dp;

    while(isalnum(*cp0))     /* skip past user field */
    {
        cp0++;
    }

    while(*cp0)       /* search until end of line */
    {
```

```
while(isspace(*cp0))     /* skip to beg of cmd field */
{
    cp0++;
}
if (strncmp(cp0,"all",3) == 0)  /* if cmd field is "all" */
{
    (void) strcpy(res,"all");    /* then pass it back */
    return;
}

cp1 = cp0;

/* find end of this entry */

while (*cp1 != '\n' && !isspace(*cp1))
{
    cp1++;
}

cp1--;  /* point to last character of cmd */
cp2 = cp1;

while (*cp2 != '/')      /* backup to head of command */
{
    cp2--;
}

cp2++;

cp1++; /* point cp1 to last character + 1 */

/* if command issued is found then pass whole path back */

if (strncmp(cp2,ap,strlen(ap)) == 0)
{
    (void) strncpy(res,cp0,cp1-cp0); /* copy command back */
    return;
}

/*
 * if it got to here, then command not found *yet*
 * move pointer past next comma and keep looking
 */
```

```
        while (!isspace(*cp0) && *cp0 != '\n')
        {
            cp0++;
        }

        if (*cp0 == '\n')  /* if at endo of line then fail */
        {
            break;
        }
        else
        {
            continue;
        }
    }

    *res = NULL;
    return;
}

/*
**  mailmsg - Snitch on person
*/

mailmsg (user,argv,argc)

char            *user, **argv;
int             argc;

{
    FILE        *popen();
    FILE        *fd;
    char        cmd[80];
    char        hostname[MAXHOSTNAMELEN];

    firsthostname(hostname, MAXHOSTNAMELEN);

    (void) sprintf(cmd,
        "/usr/ucb/mail -s \"*SECURITY* %s@%s tried to execute %s\" %s ",
        user,hostname,*argv,ALERTMAIL);

    if ((fd = popen(cmd, "w")) == NULL)
    {
        return;
    }

    fprintf(fd,"%s\@%s tried to do a\n\n",user,hostname);
```

```
    while(argc--)
    {
        (void) fputs(*argv++, fd);
        (void) fputc(' ', fd);
    }

    (void) fputs("\n\nThought you might want to know.",fd);

    (void) pclose(fd);
}

/*
**  firsthostname() - return hostname without domain stuff.
**     Parameters - pointer to char array for name, and length of array.
*/

void
firsthostname(n, l)

char            *n;
int             l;

{
    (void) gethostname(n, l);       /*  get full hostname  */
    n[l-1] = 0;                     /*  make sure null terminated  */
    if (n = index(n, '.')) *n = 0;  /*  blat null on top of '.' if any
}
```

A.2.1 The clrusr.c file

```
/*
** clrusr.c
*/

#include <stdio.h>
#include <sys/file.h>
#include <sys/types.h>
#include <sys/stat.h>
#include <signal.h>
#include <ctype.h>

char    *getpass();
char    *crypt();

#define TIMEDIR    "/usr/local/adm/sudocheck/"  /* Dir for time stamps *
#define INFO_FILE  "/usr/local/adm/sudocheck/sudo.doc"
```

```
#define INVALID    -1            /* Returned by system routines */
#define SUDO_OK    1             /* Flag: good validation */
#define TIME       5             /* Validation time, in mins */

/*
**  The not_timed_out() routine checks to be
**  sure a user is not prevalidated.  If he
**  (or she) is already valid, they need not
**  retype the password.
*/

not_timed_out(name,password)

char    *name;          /* Username of person */
char    *password;      /* And their encrypted passwd */

{
    char      fname[200];
    struct    stat stab;

    sprintf (fname, "%s%s",TIMEDIR,name);

    if (access(fname, F_OK))
    {
        /* Validation file doesn't exist, create it */
        get_password(password);
        create_file(fname);
        return(SUDO_OK);
    }

    if(stat(fname, &stab))
    {
        fprintf (stderr,"Gag, can't stat validation file.\n");
        exit(1);
    }

    if ((time(NULL) - stab.st_mtime) > (TIME * 60))
    {
        get_password(password);
    }
    create_file(fname);
    return (SUDO_OK);
}

/*
**  get_password() solicits a password and
**  compares it against the users own
**  password.
*/
```

```
get_password(password)

char    *password;          /* User's encrypted password */

{
    char    *paswd;
    char    *encrypted;

    paswd = getpass("Password:");
    encrypted = crypt(paswd,password);

    if (strcmp(password,encrypted))
    {
        fprintf (stderr,"Password incorrect\n");
        exit(3);
    }

    fflush(stderr);
    fflush(stdout);
}

/*
**  create_file() sets the modtime of the
**  validation file.
*/

create_file(file)

char    *file;          /* Filename to be created */

{
    int   descrip;
    long  timep[2];

    descrip = open(file, O_TRUNC | O_CREAT | O_WRONLY, 0700);

    if(descrip == INVALID)
    {
        printf("Gag, couldn't open validation file.\n");
        exit(4);
    }
    close(descrip);

    timep[0] = timep[1] = time(0);
    utime(file, timep);
}
```

A.3 The Makefile file

```
#
# sudo makefile
#
CFLAGS=-O
DESTDIR=/usr/local/bin
ADMDIR=/usr/local/adm
LOGDIR=/usr/local/adm/logs
TIMEDIR=/usr/local/adm/sudocheck

all: sudo

sudo: sudo.o clrusr.o
	cc ${CFLAGS} clrusr.o sudo.o -o sudo

install: sudo
	install -m 4755 -o root sudo ${DESTDIR}
	cp sudo.8 /usr/man/man1/sudo.1
	chmod a+r /usr/man/man1/sudo.1

	if [ \! -d ${ADMDIR} ]; then \
	mkdir ${ADMDIR};\
	chmod go-rwx ${ADMDIR};\
	fi

	echo "You will have to edit the contents of ${ADMDIR}/sudoers."

	touch ${ADMDIR}/sudoers
	chmod go-rwx ${ADMDIR}/sudoers

	if [ ! -d ${LOGDIR} ]; then \
	mkdir ${LOGDIR};\
	chmod go-rwx ${LOGDIR};\
	fi

	touch ${LOGDIR}/sudo.log
	chmod go-rwx    ${LOGDIR}/sudo.log

	if [ ! -d ${TIMEDIR} ]; then \
	mkdir ${TIMEDIR};\
	chmod go-rwx ${TIMEDIR};\
	fi

clean:
	rm -f clrusr.o sudo.o make.out sudo
```

A.4 The sudo.8 file

```
.TH SUDO 8
.SH NAME
sudo - execute a command as root
.SH SYNOPSIS
.B sudo
command
.SH DESCRIPTION
.I Sudo
allows a permitted user to execute a command as root.
.I Sudo
determines who is an authorized user by consulting the file
.I /usr/local/adm/sudoers.
If a match is found
.I command
is executed with root id.
Sudo also prompts for a user's password to initiate a validation period
of five minutes.
Lines in
.I sudoers
beginning with a
.I '#'
or ' ' are considered comments and are ignored. The lines in the sudoers
must have the format:
.nf
.b

    # comment
    #
    user1   /path/path/cmd1 /path/path/cmd2
    user2   all

.r
.fi
In this example, Lines beginning with '#' are considered comments. User1
may invoke 'cmd1' or 'cmd2' only. User2 on the other hand is permitted
to execute any command.

.I Sudo
will send mail to root
if a user that does not appear in
.I sudoers
executes
.I sudo
, or if the file
.I sudoers
is not owned and exclusively writable by root.
```

```
All
.I sudo
invocations cause a log file
.I /usr/local/adm/logs/sudo.log
to be appended with date, time and command attempted.

.SH DIAGNOSTICS
.nf

sudo: I know you, but I can't let you: cmd
sudo: I don't know you and I'm telling !
sudo: bad modes on sudoers

.fi
.SH BUGS
Shell builtins such as
.I 'cd'
will fail.

It would be nice if entire groups could be enabled.
.SH FILES
.nf
/usr/local/adm/sudoers - list of authorized users
.br
/usr/local/adm/logs/sudo.log - record of all invocations of sudo
.br
/usr/local/adm/sudocheck - five-minute validation files
.fi
.SH SEE ALSO
su(1)
```

B

An **adduser** *Script*

B.1 Introduction

This is a **csh** script which can be used to add new users to the system. This script does not take distributed system files and such into account, and so is not suitable for use on a networked environment. It will probably have to be slightly modified to suit your local environment. This script adds the user to the /etc/passwd and /etc/group files, creates a phonelist entry, and creates a home directory with the necessary startup files. It makes the user's shell be **/bin/csh** by default, and allows an initial password to be set.

B.2 An **adduser** script

```
#!/bin/csh -f
#
# adduser - simple script to add a new user.  To execute
#          simply type adduser.  Only root can run this script
#          successfully.
#
#
onintr quit:
```

```
#
set freedisk=100
# directory containing sample . files
set skeldir=/usr/local/adm/skel
#
set passwdfile=/etc/passwd
set groupfile=/etc/group
set phonelist=/usr/local/pub/phonelist
#
#
set local_host=`hostname`
#
#       get login, look for conflicts in /etc/passwd
#       and /usr/lib/aliases
#
set msg="enter login name, must be <= 8 characters"
echo "junk" > /tmp/AD1$$
echo "junk" > /tmp/AD2$$
set aliasdone = no
set good = no
while ( ${good} == no )
        echo ${msg}
        set dollar=$
        set login=$<
# look for it in the passwd file
        awk -F: '{print $1}' /etc/passwd | grep "^${login}${dollar}" \
                > /tmp/AD1$$
        if (! (-z /tmp/AD1$$)) then
                set msg="already used in passwd file, try again"
        else
# look for it in the /usr/lib/aliases file
                fgrep ':' /usr/lib/aliases | awk -F: '{print $1}' | \
                        grep "^${login}${dollar}" > /tmp/AD2$$
                if (! (-z /tmp/AD2$$)) then
                        echo -n "already used in aliases file, entry is:    "
                        grep "^${login}:" /usr/lib/aliases
                        echo -n "is that ok ???  "
                        set answer = $<
                        if (${answer} == n) then
                                set msg="then try again, enter login id"
                        else
                                set good = yes
                                set aliasdone = yes
                        endif
                else
                        set good = yes
                endif
        endif
end
```

```
rm /tmp/AD1*
rm /tmp/AD2*
#
#       get uid (biggest uid+1)
#
set uid=`sort -t: -nr +2 /etc/passwd | sed '1q' | awk -F: '{print $3}'`
@ uid++
#
#       get gid (group)
#
set gid
set null
set msg="enter unix group"
while ( ${gid} == ${null})
        echo ${msg}
        set group=$<
        set gid=`grep "^${group}:" /etc/group | awk -F: '{print $3}'`
        set msg="group not in group file, try again"
end
#
#       get parent directory
#       set up home
#
set good=no
set msg="enter location of home dir "
echo ${msg}
set top=$<
set home = /${top}/${login}
#
#       get finger info
#
echo "enter users full name, campus address, campus phone, home phone"
set finger = $<
#
set entry="${login}::${uid}:${gid}:${finger}:${home}:/bin/csh"
#
echo " "
echo login"                    "${login}
echo group"                    "${group}
echo uid"                      "${uid}
echo gid"                      "${gid}
#
echo home"                     "${home}
echo " "
#
#
echo passwd entry is:
echo ${entry}
```

```
echo " "
#
set a=n
echo "continue?(y/n) (last chance before scribbling on files)"
        set a=$<
if ( $a == n ) exit
#
#       add entry to passwd file
#
echo making passwd entry
echo ${entry} >> $passwdfile
#
#       add name to group file
#
echo making group entry
set scpt=/^${group}/s/\$/,${login}/
echo ${scpt} > /tmp/ADD$$
sed -f /tmp/ADD$$ /etc/group > /tmp/newgroup$$
rm /tmp/ADD$$
mv /tmp/newgroup$$ $groupfile
#
#
#       add to the phonelist
#
echo making phonelist entry
echo ${login}"          "${finger} >> ${phonelist}
#
#       make users home, copy in skeleton files
#
echo making home directory
mkdir ${home}
cp ${skeldir}/.login ${skeldir}/.logout ${skeldir}/.cshrc \
        ${skeldir}/.exrc ${skeldir}/.mailrc ${home}
find ${home} -exec chown ${login} {} \;  -exec chgrp ${group} \;
#
#
#       set passwd
#
passwd ${login}

quit:
        rm -f /tmp/*$$
```

C

An **rmuser** Script

C.1 Introduction

This is a **csh** script to remove users from the system; it parallels the adduser script in Appendix B. Modify it to suit your needs, but do not use it in a networked environment. **rmuser** removes the user's home directory if desired, and removes the user's entries in /usr/spool/mail, /etc/passwd, and /etc/group.

C.2 An **rmuser** script

```
#!/bin/csh -f
#
#  rmuser  - remove users, in the same vein as adduser.
#            leaves phonelist entry for future reference.
#
#          -a flag makes it actually remove from the passwd file
#          default is to replace password with the date, and leave
#          /etc/passwd.   This allows accounting to correctly
#          identify the user at the end of the month.
#
```

```
# get user if not on cmd line.
#
onintr quit:

set absolute=0
if (${#argv} < 1)  then
        echo "enter user to be removed."
        set argv=$<
endif
#
if ( $1 == "-a" ) then
        set absolute=1
        set argv[1]=
        echo "removing absolutely\!"
endif
#
#
#  initialize files to be altered.
#
set group="/etc/group"
set passwd="/etc/passwd"
set maildir="/usr/spool/mail"
#
umask 220
set datenow = `date`
set month = $datenow[2]
set year = $datenow[6]
@ yearsuffix = $year - 1900
set date = $month$yearsuffix
set null
#
#  run login loop, rm'ing each.
#
foreach login ($argv)
        set good=`grep "^${login}:" ${passwd} | awk -F: '{print $5}'`
        if ("${good}" == "${null}") then
                set msg=" not in password file."
                echo ${login} ${msg}
                continue
        endif
#
#  verify removal of this user.
#
        if (${login} == "root") then
                echo "no removing root allowed\!"
                echo "you will have to do it the hard way."
                continue
        endif
```

```
#
	echo "ok to remove ${good}? (y/n)"
		set ans=$<
	if (${ans} != y) continue
#
#  find home directory in passwd file
#
	set home=`grep "^${login}:" ${passwd} | awk -F: '{print $6}'`

	echo ${home}
	echo "ok to remove home?(${home}) (y/n)"
	set ans=$<
	if (${ans} != y) then
		echo "continue with removing this user? (y/n)"
		set ans=$<
		if (${ans} != y) continue
	else
		echo "removing home"
		rm -r ${home}
	endif
#
#  remove mail
#
	echo "removing mail"
	set mail="${maildir}/${login}"
	if (-e ${mail}) rm -f ${mail}
#
#  remove passwd entry.
#
	while (-e /etc/ptmp)
		echo "Waiting for password file to become available."
		sleep 5
	end
	touch /etc/ptmp
	echo "removing passwd entry"
	if ($absolute) then
		echo "/"^$login":[^:]*:/d" > /tmp/rmu$$
	else
		echo "s/^"$login":[^:]*:/"$login":"$date":/" > /tmp/rmu$$
	endif
	sed -f /tmp/rmu$$ ${passwd} > /etc/ptmp
	mv /etc/ptmp ${passwd}
#
#  remove login name from group file - type <tab> where you see \t
#
	echo "removing group entry"
	set scrpt="g/[^a-zA-Z0-9_]${login}[ \t]*,*/s/${login}[ \t]*,*//"
	echo ${scrpt} > /tmp/rmu$$
```

```
    set scrpt="g/,[ \t]*$/s///"
        echo ${scrpt} >> /tmp/rmu$$
        set scrpt="w"
        echo ${scrpt} >> /tmp/rmu$$
        set scrpt="q"
        echo ${scrpt} >> /tmp/rmu$$
        ed ${group} </tmp/rmu$$
#
#  wrap up and continue.
#
        rm /tmp/rmu$$
end  #foreach

quit:
        rm -f /tmp/rmu$$
```

D

Sample Startup Files

D.1 Introduction

This appendix contains the various configuation files that we give to new users. Some parts of them may need to be modified to suit you local conditions. Your mileage may vary.

D.2 A sample .login file

The .login file is executed after .cshrc, but only once. It should contain definitions of variables such as your terminal type that will not change with each invocation of the shell.

```
set path=(. /usr/local/bin /usr/ucb /bin /usr/bin /usr/new \
 /usr/games /usr/hosts )
if (($term == dialup) || ($term == switch)) then
tryagain:
   set noglob;eval 'tset -s -Q -m dialup:?vt100 -m switch:h19';unset noglob
   if ($TERM == unknown) goto tryagain
   if (-e /usr/local/bin/tout) tout 30
```

```
endif
set history=30
setenv EXINIT 'set shell=/bin/csh redraw sm'
stty new crt cr0 intr ^C kill ^U erase ^H
setenv ROGUEOPTS "jump,noterse,flush,passgo,overwrite"
rn -s6 -c
echo " "
mesg y
biff y
```

D.3 A sample .cshrc file

```
alias dir 'ls -l \!* | more '
alias where 'rwho | grep \!*'
alias mroe more
umask 027
```

D.4 A sample .profile

```
echo 'erase ^H, kill ^U, intr ^C'
stty erase ^H kill ^U intr ^C
PATH=.:/usr/local/bin:/usr/ucb:/bin:/usr/bin:/usr/new:/usr/games
export PATH
HOME=/usr/theuser
export HOME
export TERM
```

D.5 A sample .mailrc

```
set ask
set askcc
set autoprint
```

E

tout: *A Voluntary Timeout Program*

E.1 Introduction

UNIX has no built-in method for logging out users after a certain amount of idle time. This is convenient for office terminals that are logged in all the time, but it also leads to terminals being left logged in for extended periods in public user areas.

Our solution to this problem is the **tout** program written by Andrew Rudoff. **tout** is a *voluntary* timeout program; users can set the amount of time that the system will allow them to remain idle before logging them out. **tout** is usually executed at login time from the .login or .profile script.

tout should run unmodified on BSD-based systems, and with only a little modification on ATT systems. To compile **tout**, type the Makefile, tout.c, and the tout.1 manual page into the same directory and use **make tout** or **make install**.

E.2 The Makefile file

```
#
# Makefile for tout
#

tout:   tout.o
    cc -O tout.o -o tout

clean:;     rm -f tout tout.o

install:    tout
    csh -c "install -s tout /usr/local/bin"
    cp tout.1 /usr/man/manl/tout.l
    chmod 644 /usr/man/manl/tout.l
    make clean
```

E.3 The tout.c file

```
/*
**  tout - a personal timeout program
**
**  Andrew Rudoff, University of Colorado, Boulder
**
**  usage: tout minutes
**
**  This is a voluntary timeout program.  A timeout occurs when the user
**  is idle for a time larger than "minutes."  The inaccuracy can be as
**  much as 1 minute (1 minute granularity).  The user is warned 1 minute
**  before the timeout; the timeout can be prevented by typing any key to
**  clear the idle status of the terminal.
*/

#include <stdio.h>
#include <signal.h>
#include <sys/types.h>
#include <sgtty.h>
#include <sys/stat.h>

#define BEEP '\007'

main(argc, argv)

int             argc;
char            **argv;
```

```
{

char            user[50];           /* name of current user */
char            invoker[50];        /* name of invoker */
struct          stat statbuf;       /* buffer for stats on tty */
long            current, timeout;   /* times in seconds */
int             pgrp, tmp = 0;

    if (argc != 2)
    {
        fprintf(stderr, "usage: %s minutes\n", argv[0]);
        exit(1);
    }

    nice(4);    /* run gracefully in the background */

    if ((timeout = 60 * atoi(argv[1])) == 0)
    {
       fprintf(stderr, "%s: incomprehensible or zero timeout\n", argv[0]);
        exit(1);
    }

    if (!isatty(0))
    {
        fprintf(stderr, "%s: stdin not a terminal\n", argv[0]);
        exit(1);
    }

    strcpy(invoker, getlogin());

    printf("Timeout set for %s (%s minutes)\n", invoker, argv[1]);
    fflush(stdout);

    if (fork())
    {
        exit(0);
    }

    while(1)
    {
        sleep(60);  /* spend most of my spare time sleeping */
        strcpy(user, getlogin());

        /* Be sure same person is logged in */

        if (strcmp(user, invoker))
        {
            exit(0);
        }
```

```
        if ((fstat(0, &statbuf)) != 0)
        {
            fprintf(stderr, "%s: couldn't stat tty\n", argv[0]);
            exit(1);
        }

        time(&current);

        if (current - statbuf.st_atime >= timeout)
        {
            fprintf(stderr, "\n\n%s: Timeout - you're outta here!\n\n",
                argv[0]);

            while(ioctl(0, TIOCGPGRP, &pgrp), pgrp != tmp)
            {
                tmp = pgrp;
                killpg(pgrp, SIGHUP);   /* Let editors save, etc */
                sleep(5);
            }

            vhangup();
            exit(0);
        }

        if (current + 60 - statbuf.st_atime >= timeout)
        {
            fprintf(stderr, "\n%s: WARNING - timeout in 1 minute.%c\n",
                argv[0], BEEP);
        }
    }
}
```

E.4 The tout.1 file

```
.TH TOUT local
.SH NAME
tout
.SH SYNOPSIS
tout minutes
.SH DESCRIPTION
Calling
.I tout
specifies an idle-time limit for the particular
login session.  The user is warned one minute before
timeout (at which point he could hit RETURN at the keyboard
and reset his idle time).  When the timeout time is reached, all
```

```
of the foreground processes are sent HANGUP signals, and he is logged
out.  If the user logged out normally,
.I tout
will disappear within one minute.
.SH EXAMPLE
tout 20
.SP
This means that the current login session will end automatically
if the keyboard is inactive for 20 minutes.
.SH FILES
/dev/tty
.SH SEE ALSO
alarm(2)
.br
killpg(2)
.SH AUTHOR
Andrew M. Rudoff
.SH BUGS
.I tout
can only kill processes owned by the user who invoked it.  If the
user invokes a new shell with a different user id,
.I tout
can't kill it.
```

F

The **dumdum** *Script*

F.1 Introduction

The **dumdum** Script was developed to provide a easy way for operators to do dumps and to reduce the possibility of operator error. Although this script may not do dumps in exactly the manner you wish, it can be easily modified to suit local conditions. **dumdum** keeps track of which dump level should be done, allows the operator to verify that this is correct, then performs the dump and creates a dumptoc (dump table of contents) for each filesystem that should be dumped. **dumdum** keeps track of whether a dump was completed and will restart an aborted dump if necessary.

The first step in installing dumdum is to determine where the dump information should be kept. We use the directory /usr/local/adm/dumpdir, but it can be placed anywhere. The variable DUMPDIR in the script determines the location of the dump files. This directory will contain **dumdum** itself, a log file, and the dumptocs.

After creating the DUMPDIR directory, and typing the **dumdum** script in, you need to create the file WHICHDUMP. WHICHDUMP contains the sequence of dump levels to be performed and the current dump level. A WHICHDUMP for a standard Towers of Hanoi sequence looks like this:

0 3 2 5 4 7 6 9 8 1a 3 2 5 4 7 6 9 8 1b 3 2 5 4 7 6 9 8 1c 3 2 5 4 7 6 9 8 1d 3 2 5 4 7 6 9 8 0

As you can see, it just contains the dump levels in the order that they should be done. The final 0 means that the last dump that was done was the 0th in the sequence, so the next level that will be done will be the initial level 0. When **dumdum** comes to the end of the sequence, it starts at the beginning again. If you wish to perform dumps in a sequence other than the Towers of Hanoi, you can just change the numbers in the WHICHDUMP file.

After creating the WHICHDUMP file, you need to make sure that some of the variables in **dumdum** are set correctly for your system. The important variables are:

DUMPDIR - the directory containing all of the dump information
LOLEV - list of filesystems to be dumped at levels 0 and 1
ALWAYS - list of filesystems that should be dumped at levels 2 to 9
DUMP - the path of the dump program
RESTORE - the path of the restore program
DEN - the density of the tape drive
DUMPDEV - the special file name of the tape drive

After setting these variables to values appropriate for your system, you should be ready to go. Just type **dumdum** and it should prompt you as needed and perform the dumps.

F.2 The dumdum script

```
#!/bin/csh -f
#
# dumdum: script to do incremental dumps
#

onintr quit
umask 7

# filesystems to be dumped on level 0 and 1
set LOLEV =  "root usr net"

# filesystems to be dumped at every level
set ALWAYS = "usr net"
```

```
# dump program to use
set DUMP = "/etc/dump"

# restore program to use
set RESTORE = "/etc/restore"

# density of the tape
set DEN = "1600"

# device to dump to
set DUMPDEV = "/dev/mt0"

#directory where all dump information is stored
set DUMPDIR = "/usr/local/adm/dumpdir"
cd ${DUMPDIR}

#set up temporary file names
set FLAGDIR = "${DUMPDIR}/flagdir"
if (!(-d $FLAGDIR )) mkdir $FLAGDIR
set FLAGFILE = "${FLAGDIR}/dumpit"
set FNAME = "tmp"
set TEMPFILE = "${FLAGDIR}/${FNAME}$$"

# get the sequence information from the WHICHDUMP file
set which = `cat ${DUMPDIR}/WHICHDUMP`
set DATEFILE = "${DUMPDIR}/DUMPDATES"
@ lessone = ${#which} - 1
set nonomatch

start:

#if the last dump did not finish, restart it
set junk = (`ls ${FLAGDIR}`)
set isnotdone = (${junk})
if (${#isnotdone} >= 1) then
        echo "THIS IS THE CONTINUATION OF AN ABORTED DUMP"
        echo "Continuing with a level ${which[${which[${#which}]}]} dump."
        echo " "
        echo -n "Is this correct? "
        set junk = $<
        while ((${junk} != "yes") && (${junk} != "no") &&
            (${junk} != "y") && (${junk} != "n"))
                echo -n "Please answer yes or no: "
                set junk = $<
        end
        if ((${junk} == "n") || (${junk} == "no")) then
                rm -f ${FLAGDIR}/*
        goto start
        endif
```

```
        set restart
        goto getlevel
else

# increment the position counter (last element of array)
        @ which[$#which]++

# if the position counter points to its own position in the array, recycle
# back to the beginning of the array
        if (${which[${#which}]} == ${#which}) set which[${#which}] = 1
recover:
        echo ""
        echo -n "My records"
        if (${?limit}) echo -n " now"
        echo -n " indicate that this should be a "
        echo " level ${which[${which[${#which}]}]} dump."
        echo -n "Is this correct? "
        set junk = $<
        while ((${junk} != "yes") && (${junk} != "no") &&
             (${junk} != "y") && (${junk} != "n"))
                echo -n "Please answer yes or no: "
                set junk = $<
        end
        if ((${junk} == "yes") || (${junk} == "y")) then
                echo $which > ${DUMPDIR}/WHICHDUMP

# set the level - lolevel contains the number without sublevel information
getlevel:
                set level = ${which[${which[${#which}]}]}
                set lolevel = `echo $level | tr -d "a-z"`
        else
#
# list the dump sequence and corresponding numbers
#
                echo ""

                @ limit = $#which /  5
                set counter = 1
                while ($counter <= $limit)
                        set temp = $counter;
                        set i = 1
                                while ($i <= 5)
                                        echo -n "${temp}==$which[$temp]"
                                        if ($temp == $which[$#which]) then
                                                echo -n "*"
                                        endif
                                        echo -n "       "
                                        @ temp += 9;
                                        @ i++
                                end
```

```
                        echo ""
                                @ counter++;
                end

                echo "* marks the dumps I thought we were supposed to do."
                echo ""
                echo -n "What is the number of the correct dump? "


# get the correct dump number
                set junk = $<
                while ((${junk} < "1") || (${junk} >= "${#which}"))
                        echo "Please choose a number between 1 and ${lessone}\!"
                        echo -n "What is the number of the correct dump? "
                        set junk = $<
                end
                set which[${#which}] = ${junk}
                goto recover
        endif
endif

echo ""

if ((${lolevel} == "0") || (${lolevel} == "1")) then
        set fs = "${LOLEV}"
else
        set fs = "${ALWAYS}"
endif

echo "Doing these file systems: $fs"

echo " "

# cycle for each filesystem that needs to be done
foreach filesystem ( ${fs} )
        if (!(-e ${FLAGFILE}.${filesystem})) then
                unset restart

#look up raw device name in /etc/fstab
                if ($filesystem == "root") then
                        set DEV = `awk -F: '$2 ~ /\/$/ { print $1}'\
                                /etc/fstab`
                else
                        set DEV = `awk -F: '$2 ~ /'${filesystem}'$/\
                                { print $1}' /etc/fstab`
                endif

#do the dump
                echo -n "Type 'yes' when the /${filesystem} tape is online: "
```

```
        set junk=$<
                while (("${junk}" != "yes") && ("${junk}" != "y"))
                        echo -n "Type 'yes' when the /$filesystem tape is online:"
                        set junk=$<
                end

                echo "Doing the dump...."
                ${DUMP} ${lolevel}udf ${DEN} ${DUMPDEV} ${DEV} |& tee $TEMPFILE

                touch ${FLAGFILE}.${filesystem}

        else
                echo "Apparently the ${filesystem} dump has been done."
        endif

# do the dumptoc
        if (!(-e ${FLAGFILE}.r${filesystem})) then

                echo -n "Doing the dumptoc..."
                ${RESTORE} tf ${DUMPDEV} > ${DUMPDIR}/lev${level}.${filesystem}
                touch ${FLAGFILE}.r${filesystem}
                echo "Done"
                if (-z ${DUMPDIR}/lev${level}.${filesystem}) then
                        echo "PANIC\!"
                        echo "${DUMPDIR}/lev${level}.${filesystem} is empty\!"
                endif
                echo -n "Level ${level} /${filesystem}          " >> ${DATEFILE}
                echo -n `date` >> ${DATEFILE}
                echo " by ${USER}" >> ${DATEFILE}
        else
                echo "And the dumptoc for ${filesystem} has been done also."
        endif
end

rm -f ${FLAGFILE}.*

goto clean

quit:
echo ""
echo "The dump has been killed.... I hope you know what you are doing\!"
echo ""

clean:
rm -f ${FLAGDIR}/${FNAME}*
cd
```

G

The **lostfile** *Script*

G.1 Introduction

The **lostfile** script allows users to request that a file be restored from backups. This script prompts the user for all needed information and mails it to the person who is responsible for restores (operator, by default). This script is written in **csh**, but a **sh** equivalent would not be hard to write.

G.2 The lostfile script

```
#!/bin/csh
#
# lostfile - script to allow users to request file restoration from backups
#           in a consistent manner.  The user simply types 'lostfile' and
#           they are prompted for all of the necessary information.
#

onintr quit
set noglob
# login name or mail alias of whoever is responsible for
# retrieving lost files
```

```
set mailto = operator

set filename = not_null
set count = 1
echo ""
echo -n "Enter the login name of the owner of the lost files: "
set login = $<
echo "Lost files owned by ${login}"  >>  /tmp/lostxfer$$
echo ""  >>  /tmp/lostxfer$$
echo ""
echo -n "Were all of the files in the same directory? "
set dirsame = $<
echo ""
echo "Enter the names of lost files, one at a time;"
echo "A <CR> with no name ends the querys."
echo ""

while ( ${filename} != "" )
   echo -n "Enter the name of lost file ${count}: "
   set filename = $<
   if  ( ${filename} != "" )  then
      echo "Filename: ${filename}"  >>  /tmp/lostxfer$$
      echo -n "Enter the last modification date of ${filename}: "
      set modtime = $<
      echo "Modtime: ${modtime}"  >>  /tmp/lostxfer$$
      if  ( ( ${dirsame} == "no" )  ||  ( ${dirsame} == "n" ) )  then
         echo -n "Give the full pathname of the"
         echo -n " directory containing ${filename}: "
         set dirname = $<
         echo "Directory: ${dirname}"  >>  /tmp/lostxfer$$
      endif
      echo -n "Was ${filename} a directory? "
      set dir = $<
      if  ( ( ${dir} == "yes" )  ||  ( ${dir} == "y" ) )  then
         echo -n "File was a directory; "  >>  /tmp/lostxfer$$
         echo -n "Do you want subdirectories of ${filename}? "
         set subdirs = $<
         if  ( ( ${subdirs} == "yes" )  ||  ( ${subdirs} == "y" ) )  then
            echo "entire contents wanted."  >>  /tmp/lostxfer$$
         else
            echo "only the regular files wanted."  >>  /tmp/lostxfer$$
         endif
      endif
      echo ""
      echo ""  >>  /tmp/lostxfer$$
   endif
   @ count++
end
```

```
if  ( ( ${dirsame} == "yes" )  ||  ( ${dirsame} == "y" ) )  then
   echo ""
   echo -n "Give the full pathname of the directory that the files were in: "
   set dirname = $<
   echo "All files were in the directory: ${dirname}"  >>  /tmp/lostxfer$$
endif
echo ""
echo "You will be contacted by mail if further information is needed,"
echo "and you will be notified when the files have been retrieved."
echo "Your files should be recovered to the best of our ability within"
echo "a day or two.  Please 'mail ${mailto}' if you have questions or"
echo "problems concerning lost files.  Thank You."
echo ""

unalias mail
mail -s "Lost file report for $login" ${mailto}  <  /tmp/lostxfer$$

unalias rm
rm -f /tmp/lostxfer$$
exit

quit:
   echo "Interrupt received, lost aborted"
   unalias rm
   unset noglob
   rm -f /tmp/lostxfer$$
```

H

Makefile.localsys

H.1 Introduction

This file is an example of a makefile used to partially automate the job of saving and restoring system files when a new operating system is installed. Because some system files, such as etc/passwd, are embedded in directories which also contain binaries, the files must be restored individually. To use a makefile like this one to copy the system files to tape, simply type **make tape**. To restore the files onto the new operating system, simply type **make passwd** then **make restore**. Restoring the passwd file first insures that the rest of the files have correct ownership. This sample Makefile.localsys is from a SunOS 3.3 file server. Each different system will have a slightly different list of files that need to be backed up and restored.

H.2 A Makefile.localsys file

```
#
#       Makefile for saving and restoring local files embedded in the system.  Makes
#       upgrading the operating system less painful, with fewer forgotten files.
#
```

```
#       It is not intended that the restore be fully automated, but rather that the
#       names of the files remind the installer of what to do.
#
#       Note - you should run "make password" and then reinstall the old passwd file
#       before running "make restore" so that things are owned by the right uid.
#
#       This particular Makefile.localsys is from a Sun 3.3 file server.
#

TAPE = /dev/rst0
TAR = tar
TAROPTIONS = cvf
RESTOREDIR = /usr/localsys

# These lists of files need to be modified to suit local conditions
ROOT = {.profile,.emacs_pro,.login,.logout,.cshrc,.rhosts,.rootmenu,.defaults,Makefile.localsys}

PRIVATEUSR = {adm/acct,adm/aculog,adm/lastlog,adm/newsyslog,adm/savacct,adm/usracct,\
             adm/wtmp,lib/crontab,preserve,spool}

ETC = {hosts.equiv,remote,motd,servers,services,dumpdates,nd.local,syslog.conf,hosts,ethers, \
      netgroup,syslog.pid,exports,networks,ttys,ttytype,passwd,fstab,fstab.clients,printcap, \
      protocols,gettytab,group,rc,rc.boot,rc.local,rc.local.clients,rc.clients}

USRETC = {cohorts,termcap}

USRLIB = {Mail.rc,Mailrc,aliases,aliases.dir,aliases.pag,bmac,font/dev240,font/dev300,\
         font/devpsc,font/ft[RIBS],sendmail.cf,tmac/tmac.an,tmac/tmac.m}

SRCS = {new,sun,ucb}

USRSYS = {conf/ANCHOR,conf/BEERS,conf/ANCHOR.2swap}

USR = {local,new}

USRMAN = {man1}

# Type "make tape" to make a tape of all the local system files
tape: fake
        csh -c 'cd /; $(TAR) $(TAROPTIONS) - ./$(ROOT)  ./private/usr/$(PRIVATEUSR)\
         ./etc/$(ETC) ./usr/etc/$(USRETC) ./usr/lib/$(USRLIB) ./usr/src/$(SRCS)  \
         ./usr/man/$(USRMAN) ./usr/sys/$(USRSYS) | rsh anchor dd of=$(TAPE)'

# Type "make localtape" to make a tape of all /usr/local and /usr/new
localtape: fake
        csh -c 'cd /; $(TAR) $(TAROPTIONS) - ./usr/$(USR) | rsh anchor dd of=$(TAPE)'
password: fake
        cd /$(RESTOREDIR); $(TAR) xf $(TAPE) ./etc/passwd
        csh -c 'echo "You need to install /$(RESTOREDIR)/etc/passwd"'
```

```
# Type "make restore" to restore from the tape.  Should make passwd first
restore: fake
	cd /$(RESTOREDIR); $(TAR) xfp $(TAPE);


fake:
#	This makefile needs to be smart and needs to remind
#	humans, rather than automate everything, so changes
#	in new releases will not be ignored or done wrong.
#
```

I

The **spacegripe** *Script*

I.1 Introduction

spacegripe is a **csh** script that you can use to terrorize users who take up more than their fair share of disk space. Simply tell **spacegripe** the name of the partition you are concerned about on the command line and it will identify all users who have home directories on that partition and use **du** to find out what their disk usages are. **spacegripe** will then send a polite message to all of the users who occupy more than 750K of disk space asking them to clean up their act.

Since **spacegripe** has to poke around in people's home directories, it has to be run as root. You can set a different usage threshold by replacing the number 749 with the maximum number of disk blocks someone can have without being sent mail.

This script should run unmodified on any BSD system. It can probably be converted to **sh** without too much hassle.

I.2 The spacegripe script

```
#!/bin/csh -f
#
# spacegripe - identify and send mail to disk hogs
#
# usage: spacegripe partition-name
# partition-name should be a path name (/users, etc.), not a device name
#
if ($#argv != 1) then
        echo "usage: spacegripe partition-name"
        echo "partition-name should be a path name, not a device name"
        exit 0
endif

set partition = `echo $argv[1] | sed 's/\///g'`
#
# Extract users from passwd file.
#
cat /etc/passwd | \
awk -F: '{ print $6 }'   |\
grep ${argv[1]}/ > /tmp/$partition.homedirs
#
# Determine who the hogs are - people with 750 or more disk blocks
#
du -s `cat /tmp/$partition.homedirs` | sort -nr |\
awk '{if ($1 > 749) print $0}' > /tmp/$partition.du.users
#
# Extract usernames.
#
sed 's/^.*.\///' < /tmp/$partition.du.users > /tmp/$partition.users
#
# compose a letter...
#
cat << MUCK > /tmp/$partition.message
The Disk partition on which your home directory resides is almost full.

The following is a list of home directories and
their sizes measured in Kilobytes:

MUCK
cat /tmp/$partition.du.users >> /tmp/$partition.message
cat << MUCK >> /tmp/$partition.message

As a large consumer of space on this partition, you should consider
deleting unwanted files.  This disk partition is backed up at regular
intervals. Anything that you delete may be retrieved from these
backup tapes in an emergency.

For large files that you need regularly, you might consider the 'compress'
program. Do a 'man compress' for more info.
```

```
This situation is critical. It requires immediate action on your part.

If you have any technical problems, please send mail to the system
administrator.

Sincerely,

spacegripe@`hostname`.
MUCK
#
/usr/ucb/mail -s "`hostname`:/$partition is very full" \
    `cat /tmp/$partition.users` systems < /tmp/$partition.message
#
cd /tmp
rm $partition.*
```

J

A **sendmail** Configuration File

J.1 Introduction

The **sendmail** configuration file controls **sendmail**'s behavior and the delivery of mail to and from your site. **sendmail** is described in Chapter 15: *Mail and Berkeley Sendmail* in detail. The sendmail.cf file that follows is for the master mail machine at the University of Colorado and as such is expected to be able to resolve most mail. All other sendmail.cf files at the University forward their undeliverables to boulder for resolution. boulder in turn sends anything it doesn't understand up the line to the CSNET Relay machine.

The line numbers are not part of the configuration file itself, but have been added to make explicit references within the config file in Chapter 15 easier to describe.

J.2 A master sendmail.cf file

```
##############################################################################
###
### Sendmail configuration file for the University of Colorado, Boulder
###    Flavor: GrandPoohbah for use on boulder.Colorado.EDU
###    Last update: Sun Aug 28 17:32:48 MDT 1988
###
##############################################################################

#    necessary evil. would rather initialize on cmd line w/ -oMw`hostname` or something.
DWboulder
##
#    Q need only be be defined if you are using the uusndmail mailer
DQboulder
##
#    my name. comes out on error messages
Dnpostmaster@$w
##
#    revision date mmddyy
DZ082888
##
#    flavor/revision date. appears on 'Received' header and smtp sign-on
DXcu.grandpoobah.$Z
##
#    uucp hosts this machine talks to directly
FU/usr/lib/uucp/L.sys %[abcdefghijklmnopqrstuvwxyzABCDEFGHIJKLMNOPQRSTUVWXYZ1234567890_-]
##
#    local DECNET gateway
DVcolo.colorado.edu
##
#    BITNET gateway
DBvaxf.colorado.edu
##
#    CSNET gateway host
DPrelay.cs.net
#
#    ultimate authority host (if they can't get rid of it, no one can)
DSrelay.cs.net
##
#    top-level domains that csnet likes to deal with... note that these are ones that
#    get sent directly.  ones not falling in this category (and no other special ones like
#    BITNET or uucp) will get sent to $S for resolution
CTARPA EDU GOV MIL COM ORG NET
##
#    this host's official domain
DDColorado.EDU
##
```

```
#    define official host name (taken from $w which is from /bin/hostname)
#         $w must include the domain if running the name server.
Dj$w
##
#    sometimes they forget .edu so we have to answer to this too.
DMcolorado
##
#    Class of machines in $D domain that are connected via uucp links, but do not
#         want addresses in !bhangist format
CYuswat uswest mcbryan
##
#    Hosts in Colorado.EDU  (deliver direct smtp) -- should be from file
#         Last update: Wed Jan  6 09:29:19 MST 1988
CCagua          ajsh        aleft        alta         clipr    bakmes
CCanchor        annex-isn   annex03      annex04
 ...
CCyaba          yquem       zippy        quill           gw-optics    zeppo
##
#    Hosts hidden behind boulder, From line reads boulder.Colorado.EDU
#         Last update: Thu Dec  3 12:10:35 MST 1987
CAanchor        ausone      barney       bass         beagle       becks
CAbones         boulder     brion        chekov       columbine    dennis
 ...
CAnewton        gauss       picard       laguerre     raphson      mcbryan
##
#    DECNET nodes
#         Last update: Wed Jan  6 09:27:33 MST 1988
CVacspc1  acstst  albedo  algol   altair  amino1  amino2  aquila  arctic
CVaries   athena  auk     bali    booby   boris   canary  ccncsm  ccndu
 ...
CVvesta   virgo   vlsimv  wizard  wren    zeppo   zeus    zodiac  rover

######################################
###   Boilerplate: special macros   ###
######################################
#    UNIX header format
DlFrom $g  $d
#    delimiter (operator) characters
Do.!:@^%/[]
#    format of a total name
Dq$?x$x <$g>$|$g$.
#    SMTP login message
De$j Sendmail $v/$X ready at $b

###############################
###   Boilerplate: options   ###
###############################
#    location of alias file
```

```
OA/usr/lib/aliases
#     default delivery mode (deliver in background)
Odbackground
#     temporary file mode
OF0600
#     default GID
Og1
#     location of help file
OH/usr/lib/sendmail.hf
#     log level
OL0
#     default messages to old style
Oo
#     queue directory
OQ/usr/spool/mqueue
#     read timeout -- violates protocols
Or2h
#     status file
OS/usr/lib/sendmail.st
#     queue up everything before starting transmission
Os
#     default timeout interval
OT2d
#     time zone names (V6 only)
OtMST,MDT
#     default UID
Ou1
#     wizard's password
Ow************
#     maximum load average before queueing mail
Ox25
#     maximum load average before rejecting connections
OX30

############################################
###    Boilerplate: message precedences    ###
############################################
Pfirst-class=0
Pspecial-delivery=100
Pbulk=-60
Pjunk=-100

#####################################
###    Boilerplate: trusted users    ###
#####################################
Troot
Tdaemon
Tuucp
```

```
#Teric          eric is Lee's 10 year old kid on our system
Tcoggs

##########################################
###   Boilerplate: format of headers   ###
##########################################
H?P?Return-Path: <$g>
HReceived: by $W.$D ($X); $b; id $i; from $s
H?D?Resent-Date: $a
H?D?Date: $a
H?F?Resent-From: $q
H?F?From: $q
H?x?Full-Name: $x
HSubject:
H?M?Message-Id: <$t.$i@$W.$D>
H?M?Resent-Message-Id: <$t.$i@$j>

S1
################################################################################
#  Ruleset 1: Sender field pre-rewriting
################################################################################
# DECNET syntax
#R$-::$- $2@$1.decnet
R$-::$-         $2@$1
R$-::$+         $2

S2
################################################################################
#  Ruleset 2: Recipient field pre-rewriting
################################################################################
# DECNET syntax
#R$-::$- $2@$1.decnet
R$-::$-         $2@$1
R$-::$+         $2

S3
################################################################################
###  Ruleset 3: Name canonicalization
################################################################################
# handle "from:<>" special case
R<>                     $@@                          turn into magic token
# basic textual canonicalization
R$*<$*<$*<$+>$*>$*>$*   $4                           3-level <> nesting
R$*<$*<$+>$*>$*         $3                           2-level <> nesting
R$*<$+>$*               $2                           basic RFC821/822 parsi
R$+ at $+               $1@$2                        "at" -> "@" for RFC 82
R$*<$*>$*               $1$2$3                       in case recursive
# make sure <@a,@b,@c:user@d> syntax is easy to parse -- undone later
```

```
R@$+,$+                 @$1:$2                          change all "," to ":"
# handle source route address
R@$+:$+                 $@<@$1>:$2                      handle <route-addr>
# more miscellaneous cleanup
R$+:$*;@$+              $@$1:$2;@$3                     list syntax
R$+@$+                  $:$1<@$2>                       focus on domain
R$+<$+@$+>              $1$2<@$3>                       move gaze right
R$+%$+                  $:$>8$1%$2                      user%host%host
R$+<@$+>        $@$1<@$2>                       since already canonical, exit
# bhangist to domainist
R$+@$+.UUCP             $@$1<@$2.UUCP>                  already done
R$+^$+                  $1!$2                           convert ^ to !
R$-!$+                  $@$2<@$1.UUCP>                  resolve uucp names
R$-.$-.$-!$+            $@$4<@$1.$2.$3.UUCP>

S4
###########################################################################
#  Ruleset 4: Final output post-rewriting
###########################################################################
R@                      $@                              handle <> error addr
# externalize local domain info
R$*<$+>$*               $1$2$3                          defocus
R@$+:$+:$+              @$1,$2:$3                       <route-addr> canonical

S6
###########################################################################
#  Ruleset 6: Localhost deletion
###########################################################################
R$*<$*@$=w>$*           $1<$2@>$4       this host
R$*<$*@$=W>$*           $1<$2@>$4       this host
R$*<$*@$W>$*            $1<$2@>$3       this host
R$*<$*@$=w.$D>$*  $1<$2@>$4       this host
R$*<$*@$W.$D>$*         $1<$2@>$3       this host
R$*<$*@$W.$M>$*         $1<$2@>$3
R$*<$*@$D>$*            $1<$2@>$3

S7
###########################################################################
#  Ruleset 7: Explicit names of us as source route addresses
###########################################################################
R<@$=w>:$*              <@>:$1          this host
R<@$=W>:$*              <@>:$1          this host
R<@$=W.$D>:$*           <@>:$1          this host
R<@$=W.$M>:$*           <@>:$1          this host
R<@$=D>:$*              <@>:$1          this host

S8
###########################################################################
```

```
#  Ruleset 8: THE percent hack; Given multiple %'s change rightmost % to @.
################################################################################
R$*<$*>$*                $1$2$3           defocus
R$*%$*                   $1@$2            First make them all @'s.
R$*@$*@$*                $1%$2@$3 Undo all but the last.
R$*@$*                   $@$1<@$2>        Put back the brackets.

S0
################################################################################
#####
#####              RULESET ZERO PREAMBLE
#####
#####     The beginning of ruleset zero is constant through all configurations.
#####
################################################################################
# perhaps an aesthetic crime to put it here, but have to catch DECNET early...
R$w::$-                  <@>:$1
R$-::$-                  $2<@$1.decnet>
# first make canonical
R$*<$*>$*                $1$2$3                     defocus
R$+                      $:$>3$1                    make canonical
# handle special cases.....
R@                       $#local$:$n                handle <> form
# handle [a.b.c.d] host addresses
R$*<@[$+]>$*             $#nonlclsmtp$@[$2]$:$1@[$2]$3       numeric internet spec
# now delete the local info
R$+<@$W.UUCP>            $1<@>                      us as uucp address
R$*<$*$W.UUCP>$*  $1<$2>$3         thishost
R<@$w:>$*                <@>:$1                     we were head of the route
R<@$W:>$*                <@>:$1                     we were head of the route
R$+                      $:$>7$1                    more of us at head of route
R$+                      $:$>6$1                    other names for this host
R$*<$*.>$*               $1<$2>$3         drop trailing dot
# and retry
R<@>:$*                  $@$>0$1                    retry after route strip
R$*<@>                   $@$>0$1                    strip null trash & retry

################################################################################
###  Machine-dependent part of ruleset zero
###  Distinctive characteristics: serves as uucp hub, utilizes the name server
################################################################################
R<@$+>$*:$+:$+           <@$1>$2,$3:$4              <route-addr> canonical
##
# (doesn't work either)
R$+<@[128.138.240.1]>$*    $#local$:$1
# numeric internet spec (broken 'cause of name server at the moment)
R$*<@[$+]>$*             $#nonlclsmtp$@[$2]$:$1@[$2]$3
##
```

```
# first try local smtp-able neighbor, then try uucp neighbor
R$+<@$=C>               $#lclsmtp$@$2$:$1<@$2>
R$+<@$=C.$D>            $#lclsmtp$@$2$:$1<@$2>
R$+<@$=C.UUCP>          $#lclsmtp$@$2$:$1<@$2>
R$+<@$=C.$D.UUCP> $#lclsmtp$@$2$:$1<@$2>
R<@$=C>:$+              $#lclsmtp$@$1$:<@$1>:$2
R<@$=C.$D>:$+           $#lclsmtp$@$1$:<@$1>:$2
R<@$=C.$D.UUCP>:$+      $#lclsmtp$@$1$:<@$1>:$2
##
# special class of uucp neighbors (in Colorado.EDU domain) that like Internet addresses
R$+<@$=Y>               $#uusndmail$@$2$:$1<@$2>
R$+<@$=Y.$D>            $#uusndmail$@$2$:$1<@$2>
R$+<@$=Y.UUCP>          $#uusndmail$@$2$:$1<@$2>
R<@$=Y>:$+              $#uusndmail$@$1$:<@$1>:$2
R<@$=Y.$D>:$+           $#uusndmail$@$1$:<@$1>:$2
##
# next see if it is a local decmailable neighbor
R$+<@$=V.UUCP>          $#lclsmtp$@$V$:$1<@$2>          user@dnethost.UUCP
R$+<@$=V>               $#lclsmtp$@$V$:$1<@$2>          user@dnethost
R$+<@$=V.$D>            $#lclsmtp$@$V$:$1<@$2>          user@dnethost.domain
R$+<@$-.DECNET>         $#lclsmtp$@$V$:$1<@$2.DECNET>   user@dnethost.DECNET
R$+<@$-.DNET>           $#lclsmtp$@$V$:$1<@$2.DECNET>   user@dnethost.DNET
R$+<@$-.DNET.$D>  $#lclsmtp$@$V$:$1<@$2.DECNET>     user@dnethost.DNET.domain
R$+<@$-.DECNET.$D>      $#lclsmtp$@$V$:$1<@$2.DECNET>   user@dnethost.decnet.domain
R<@$=V>:$+              $#lclsmtp$@$V$:<@$1:$2>         @dnethost:whatever
R<@$-.DECNET>:$+  $#lclsmtp$@$V$:<@$1.DECNET:$2>    @dnethost.DECNET:whatever
R<@$-.DECNET.$D>:$+     $#lclsmtp$@$V$:<@$1.DECNET:$3>  @dnethost.decnet.domain:whtevr
##
#  next, see if it is a local UUCP neighbor
R$+<@$w.UUCP>           $#local$:$1             thishost.UUCP
R$+<@$w.$D.UUCP>  $#local$:$1           thishost.UUCP
R$+<@$=U.UUCP>          $#uucp$@$2$:$1          uucpneighbor.UUCP
R$+<@$=U>               $#uucp$@$2$:$1          uucpneighbor
R$+<@$=U.$D>            $#uucp$@$2$:$1          uucpneighbor.colorado.edu
##
# if it is in uucp format and still isn't resolved, foist it off on pathalias
R$+<@$+.UUCP>           $#palias$@$2$:$1  call uucp via mystical pathalias
##
# by this time we have tried everything imaginable to resolve user@host.colorado.edu,
# don't try higher authority, since they will just spit it back at us.
R$+<@$-.$D>             $#error$:Host: $2 Non-existent in the $D domain
R<@$-.$D>:$+            $#error$:Host: $1 Non-existent in the $D domain
##
# resolve 'phony' domains...
R$*<@$+.BITNET>$* $#nonlclsmtp$@$B$:$1@$2.BITNET$3
R<@$+.BITNET>:$*  $#nonlclsmtp$@$B$:@$1.BITNET:$2
##
# anything in the T class is considered nameservable..
```

```
R$+<@$+.$=T>            $#nonlclsmtp$@$2.$3$:$1<@$2.$3>
R$+<@$+.$+.$=T>         $#nonlclsmtp$@$2.$3.$4$:$1<@$2.$3.$4>
R$+<@$+.$+.$+.$=T>      $#nonlclsmtp$@$2.$3.$4.$5$:$1<@$2.$3.$4.$5>
R<@$+.$=T>:$+           $#nonlclsmtp$@$1.$2$:<@$1.$2>:$3
R<@$+.$+.$=T>:$+  $#nonlclsmtp$@$1.$2.$3$:<@$1.$2.$3>:$4
R<@$+.$+.$+.$=T>:$+     $#nonlclsmtp$@$1.$2.$3.$4$:<@$1.$2.$3.$4>:$5
##
# Let CSNET deal w/anything else...
R$+<@$+.CSNET>          $#csnet$@relay.cs.net$:$1<@$2>      user@anything.CSNET
R$+<@$+>        $#csnet$@$S$:$1<@$2>
R<@$+>:$+               $#csnet$@$S$:<@$1>:$2
##
# everything else must be a local name
R$-                     $#local$:$1                         local names
##
# let the ":include:" aliases hack get to local too.
R:include:$+            $#local$::include:$1
R/$+                    $#local$:/$1
##
# if it got to here, we are stumped.
R$+                     $#error$: $1: Unparseable address
##
# end of the fabulous ruleset 0. Go read some other short fiction.

#####################################################################################
###  Mailer lclsmtp: local smtp Internet mailer specification
#####################################################################################
Mlclsmtp,     P=[IPC], F=msCDFMuX, S=20, R=21, E=\r\n, A=IPC $h

S20
#####################################################################################
###  Ruleset 20: sender rewriting for local smtp mailer
#####################################################################################
R$+<@$=Y>               $@$1%$2<@$W>      Unfortunate, but necessary
# pass <route-addr>'s through
R<@$+>$*        $@<@$1>$2                           resolve <route-addr>
# handle other external cases
R$+<@$->        $@$1<@$2>                           user@host
R$+<@[$+]>              $@$1<@[$2]>                         [a.b.c.d]
# convert remaining addresses to old format and externalize appropriately
R$-                     $@$1@$?H$H$|$W$.
# respect bhangist
R$+<@$+.UUCP>           $:$2!$1
R$W!$W!$+               $@$W!$1

S21
```

```
###############################################################################
###  Ruleset 21: recipient rewriting for local smtp mailer
###############################################################################
# respect bhangist
R$+<@$+.UUCP>               $:$2!$1

###############################################################################
###  Mailer nonlclsmtp: non-local Internet mailer specification
###############################################################################
Mnonlclsmtp,      P=[IPC], F=msRDFPMueXL, S=14, R=15, A=IPC $h, E=\r\n

S14
###############################################################################
###  Ruleset 14: sender rewriting for non-local smtp mailer
###############################################################################
# pass <route-addr>'s through
R<@$+>$*            $@<@$1>$2          resolve <route-addr>
# machines in $A are hidden
R$+<@$=A>                   $@$1<@$W.$D>       user@clubhost -> user@thishost.domain
R$+<@$=A.$D>                $@$1<@$W.$D>       same thing w/domains
# machines in $C but not $A get fully qualified and percentified..
R$+<@$=C>                   $@$1%$2<@$W.$D>
R$+<@$=C.$D>                $@$1%$2<@$W.$D>
# machines in SV but not $A get fully qualified and percentified..
R$+<@$=V>                   $@$1%$2<@$W.$D>
R$+<@$=V.$D>                $@$1%$2<@$W.$D>
# get rid of uucp-like things..
R$+<@$+.UUCP>               $@$2!$1<@$W.$D>
# machines not in either $C or $V (with one token) get percentified..
R$-<@$+>            $@$1%$2<@$W.$D>
# machines not in either $C or $V get source routed (ugly)
R$+<@$+>            $@@$W.$D:$1<@$2>
# internet numeric literal
R$+<@[$+]>                  $@$1<@[$2]>        [a.b.c.d]
# convert remaining addresses to old format and externalize appropriately
R$-                         $@$1<@$W.$D>       tack on our hostname
# respect bhangist, but reconcile
R$+<@$+.UUCP>               $:$2!$1<@$W.$D>
R$W!$+<@$+>                 $@$1<@$2>          remove duplicate

S15
###############################################################################
###  Ruleset 15: recipient rewriting for non-local smtp mailer
###############################################################################
# null ruleset
```

```
###########################################################################
###  Mailers local and prog: local and program mailer specifications
###########################################################################
Mlocal,  P=/bin/mail, F=rlsDFmn, S=10, R=11, A=mail -d $u
Mprog,   P=/bin/sh,   F=lsDFMe,  S=10, R=11, A=sh -c $u

S10
###########################################################################
###  Ruleset 10: sender rewriting for local and prog mailers
###########################################################################
R@                          sendmail@$W?g.$D  errors to mailer-daemon
# respect bhangist
R$+<@$+.UUCP>               $:$2!$1

S11
###########################################################################
###  Ruleset 11: recipient rewriting for local and prog mailers
###########################################################################
# respect bhangist
R$+<@$+.UUCP>               $:$2!$1

###########################################################################
###  Mailers uucp and palias: UUCP and path alias mailer specification
###########################################################################
Muucp,   P=/usr/bin/uux,    F=sCDRMhumU,  S=12, R=13, M=100000,
         A=uux - -gC -a$f $h!rmail ($u)
Mpalias, P=/usr/local/etc/uumail, F=hsuCDFMSU, S=12, R=13, M=100000,
         A=uumail -f $g $h!$u

S12
###########################################################################
###  Ruleset 12: sender rewriting for uucp, palias mailers
###########################################################################
R$W!$1                      $@$W!$1
R$+%$=C<@$W>                $@$W!$2!$1
R$+<@$W.UUCP>               $@$W!$1
R$+<@$W>            $@$W!$1
R$+<@$=A.UUCP>              $@$W!$1           alias clubbers are invisible
R$+<@$=A>                   $@$W!$1
R$-                         $@$W!$1
R$+<@$->            $@$W!$2!$1
R$+<@$-.$D>                 $@$W!$2!$1
R$+<@$-.decnet>             $@$W!$2!$1
R$+<@$-.decnet.$D>          $@$W!$2!$1
R$+<@$+.UUCP>               $@$W!$2!$1
R$+<@$+>            $@$W!$2!$1
R$+                         $@$W!$1
```

```
S13
################################################################################
###  Ruleset 13: recipient rewriting for uucp, palias mailers
################################################################################
R$+<@$->		$@$2!$1
R$+<@$-.$D>		$@$2!$1
R$+<@$+.UUCP>		$@$2!$1
R$+<@$+>		$@$2!$1
#
################################################################################
###  Mailer ns: Internet name server mailer specification
################################################################################
Mns,	P=[IPC], F=msRDFPMueXL, S=22, R=23, A=IPC $h, E=\r\n

S22
################################################################################
###  Ruleset 22: sender rewriting for ns mailer
################################################################################
# pass <route-addr>'s through
R<@$+>$*		$@<@$1>$2		resolve <route-addr>
R$+<@$->		$@$1@$2.$D		user@host->user@host.ourdomain
R$-			$@$1@$W.$D		user->user@host.ourdomain
R$+<@$+.UUCP>		$:$2!$1@$W		user@host.uucp->host!user@host.ourdomain

S23
################################################################################
###  Ruleset 23: recipient rewriting for ns mailer
################################################################################
# null ruleset

################################################################################
###  Mailer csnet: CSNET mailer specification
################################################################################
Mcsnet,  P=[IPC], F=msRDFPMueXL, S=18, R=19, A=IPC $h, E=\r\n
#
#	Notice that the PMDF mailer DOES NOT USE the host field. We set this
#	field to "CSNET-RELAY" in all instances where we call the PMDF mailer
#	so as to be able to send one copy of a letter with many recipients.

S18
################################################################################
###  Ruleset 18: sender rewriting for csnet mailer
################################################################################
R$-<@$=A>		$@$1<@$W.$D>
R$-<@$=A.$D>		$@$1<@$W.$D>
R$-<@$=C>		$@$1<@$2.$D>
R$-<@$-.decnet>		$@$1<@$2.$D>
```

```
R$-                          $@$1<@$W.$D>
# respect bhangist, but reconcile slightly
R$+<@$+.UUCP>                $:$1<@$W.$D>
R$W!$+<@$+>                  $@$1<@$2>

S19
################################################################################
###  Ruleset 19: recipient rewriting for csnet mailer
################################################################################
# null ruleset

################################################################################
###  Mailer uusndmail: non-local smtp via uucp
################################################################################
Muusndmail,         P=/usr/bin/uux,    F=sCDRMFhum,  S=24, R=25, M=100000,
                    A=uux - -gC -z -a$f $h!sendmail \(-f $g     $u \)
#  basic philosophy is that a fictitious address "$Q.Colorado.EDU"
#  will be supported until it can be legitimately converted to uswest.com

S24
################################################################################
### Ruleset 24:  sender rewriting for uusndmail mailer
################################################################################
R<@$+>$*            $@<@$1>$2           resolve <route-addr>
# machines in $C are hidden
R$+<@$=C>                    $@$1<@$Q.Colorado.EDU>
R$+<@$=C.UUCP>               $@$1<@$Q.Colorado.EDU>
R$+<@$=C.COM>                $@$1<@$Q.Colorado.EDU>
R$+<@$=C.$D>                 $@$1<@$Q.Colorado.EDU>
# all others in user@host format get percentified
R$+<@$->            $@$1%$2<@$Q.Colorado.EDU>
# preserve alien bang-like junk
R$+<@$+.UUCP>                $@$2!$1<@$Q.Colorado.EDU>
# internet numeric literal
R$+<@[$+]>                   $@$1<@[$2]>        [a.b.c.d]
# convert remaining addresses to old format and externalize appropriately
R$-                          $@$1<@$Q.Colorado.EDU>     tack on our hostname
R$w!$+<@$+>                  $@$1<@$2>                  remove duplicate

S25
################################################################################
### Ruleset 25:  recipient rewriting for uusndmail mailer
################################################################################
R$-<@$=C>                    $@$1<@$Q.Colorado.EDU>     tack on our hostname
```

K

Uucp Site Registration Instructions

The following instructions for writing a uucp map entry are distributed by the Uucp Mapping Project. We've added headings and done some minor reformatting, but the text is verbatim.

K.1 Introduction

This article describes the format of the uucp map data. It was written July 9, 1985 by Erik E. Fair (ucbvax!fair), and last updated July 12, 1985 by Mark Horton (stargate!mark).

The entire map is intended to be processed by **pathalias**, a program that generates uucp routes from this data. All lines beginning in "#" are comment lines to **pathalias**, however, the Uucp Project has defined a set of these comment lines to have a specific format so that a complete database could be built.

The generic form of these lines is:

```
#<field id letter><tab><field data>
```

Each host has an entry in the following format. The entry should begin with the #N line, end with a blank line after the **pathalias** data, and not contain any other blank lines, since there are **ed**, **sed**, and **awk** scripts that use expressions like /^#N $1/,/^$/ for the purpose of separating the map out into files, each containing one site entry.

#N	uucp name of site
#S	manufacturer machine model; operating system & version
#O	organization name
#C	contact person's name
#E	contact person's electronic mail address
#T	contact person's telephone number
#P	organization's address
#L	latitude / longitude
#R	remarks
#U	netnews neighbors
#W	who last edited the entry ; date edited

#
sitename .domain
sitename remote1(FREQUENCY), remote2(FREQUENCY),
remote3(FREQUENCY)

An example of a completed entry is:

```
#N      ucbvax
#S      DEC VAX-11/750; 4.3 BSD UNIX
#O      University of California at Berkeley
#C      Robert W. Henry
#E      ucbvax!postmaster
#T      +1 415 642 1024
#P      573 Evans Hall, Berkeley, CA 94720
#L      37 52 29 N / 122 13 44 W
#R      This is also UCB-VAX.BERKELEY.EDU [10.2.0.78] on the internet
#U      decvax ibmpa ucsfcgl ucbtopaz ucbcad
#W      ucbvax!fair (Erik E. Fair); Sat Jun 22 03:35:16 PDT 1985
#
ucbvax      .ucbvax.Berkeley.EDU
ucbvax      decvax(DAILY/4), ihnp4(DAILY/2),
            sun(POLLED)
```

K.2 Specific field descriptions

All of the fields should be filled out, if possible.

K.2.1 System name (#N)

Your system's uucp name should go here. Either the **uname**(1) command from System III or System V UNIX; or the **uuname**(1) command from version 7 UNIX will tell you what uucp is using for the local uucp name.

One of the goals of the Uucp Project is to keep duplicate uucp host names from appearing, because there are mailers in the world which assume that the uucp name space contains no duplicates (and attempt uucp path optimization on that basis), and it's just plain confusing to have two different sites with the same name.

At present, the most severe restriction on uucp names is that the name must be unique somewhere in the first six characters, because of a poor software design decision made by AT&T for the System V release of UNIX.

This does not mean that your site name has to be six characters or less in length—just unique within that length.

With regard to choosing system names, remember Harris's lament: "All the good ones are taken."

K.2.2 Machine type and operating system (#S)

This is a quick description of your equipment. Machine type should be manufacturer and model, and after a semicolon (";"), the operating system name and version number (if you have it). Some examples:

SUN 3/260; 3.0 SunOS
DEC VAX-11/780; VMS 4.0
Pyramid 90x; OSx 2.1
IBM PC/XT; Coherent
CRDS Universe 68; UNOS

K.2.3 Organization name (#O)

This should be the full name of your organization, squeezed to fit inside 80 columns as necessary. Don't be afraid to abbreviate where the abbreviation would be clear to the entire world (say a famous institution like MIT or CERN), but beware of duplication (In USC the C could be either California or Carolina).

K.2.4 Contact person (#C)

This should be the full name (or names, separated by commas) of the person(s) responsible for handling queries from the outside world about your machine.

K.2.5 Email address of contact person (#E)

This should be just a machine name and a user name, like "ucbvax!fair". It should not be a full path, since we will be able to generate a path to the given address from the data you're giving us. There is no problem with the machine name not being the same as the #N field (i.e., the contact "lives" on another machine at your site).

Also, it's a good idea to give a generic address or alias (if your mail system is capable of providing aliases) like "usenet" or "postmaster", so that if the contact person leaves the institution or is reassigned to other duties, he doesn't keep getting mail about the system. In a perfect world, people would send notice to the Uucp Project, but in practice, they don't, so the data does get out-of-date. If you give a generic address you can easily change it to point at the appropriate person.

Multiple electronic addresses should be separated by commas, and all of them should be specified in the manner just described.

K.2.6 Contact person's telephone number (#T)

The format of this entry should be:

+<*country code*><space><*area code*><space><*prefix*><space><*number*>

For example:

```
#T  +1 415 642 1024
```

This is the international format for the representation of phone numbers. The country code for the United States of America (and Canada) is 1. Other country codes should be listed in your telephone book.

If you must list an extension (i.e., what to ask the receptionist for, if not the name of the contact person), list it after the main phone number with an "x" in front of it to distinguish it from the rest of the phone number. For example:

```
#T  +1 415 549 3854 x37
```

Multiple phone numbers should be separated by commas, and all of them should be completely specified as just described to prevent confusion.

K.2.7 Organization's address (#P)

This field should be one line filled with whatever else anyone would need after the contact person's name, and your organization's name (given in other fields in the preceding), to mail you something via paper mail.

K.2.8 Latitude and longitude (#L)

This should be in the following format:

#L *DD M* [*SS*] "N" | "S" / *DDD MM* [*SS*] "E" | "W" ["city"]

Two fields separated by a slash, with optional third.

First number is latitude in degrees (*DD*), minutes (*MM*), and seconds (*SS*), and a N or S to indicate north or south of the equator.

Second number is longitude in degrees (*DDD*), minutes (*MM*), and seconds (*SS*), and an E or W to indicate east or west of the prime meridian in Greenwich, England.

Seconds are optional, but it is worth noting that the more accurate you are, the more accurate the maps we can make of the network will be (including blow-ups of various high-density areas, like New Jersey or the San Francisco Bay Area).

If you give the coordinates for your city (i.e., without fudging for where you are relative to that), add the word "city" at the end of the end of the specification, to indicate that. If you know where you are relative to a given coordinate for which you have longitude and latitude data, then the following fudge factors can be useful:

1 degree	=	69.2 miles	=	111 kilometers
1 minute	=	1.15 miles	=	1.86 kilometers
1 second	=	102 feet	=	30.9 meters

For LONGITUDE, multiply the preceding numbers by the cosine of your latitude. For instance, at latitude 35 degrees, a degree of longitude is 69.2*0.819 = 56.7 miles; at latitude 40 degrees, it is 69.2*0.766 = 53.0 miles. If you don't see why the measure of longitude depends on your latitude, just think of a globe, with all those north-south meridians of longitude converging on the poles. You don't do this cosine multiplication for LATITUDE.

Here is a short cosine table in case you don't have a trig calculator handy. (But you can always write a short program in C. The cosine function in **bc**(1) doesn't seem to work as documented.)

deg	cos	deg	cos	deg	cos	deg	cos	deg	cos	deg	cos
0	1.000	5	0.996	10	0.985	15	0.966	20	0.940	25	0.906
30	0.866	35	0.819	40	0.766	45	0.707	50	0.643	55	0.574
60	0.500	65	0.423	70	0.342	75	0.259	80	0.174	85	0.087

The prime meridian is through Greenwich, England, and longitudes run from 180 degrees west of Greenwich to 180 east. Latitudes run from 90 degrees north of the equator to 90 degrees south.

K.2.9 Remarks (#R)

This is for one line of comment. As noted before, all lines beginning with a "#" character are comment lines, so if you need more than one line to tell us something about your site, do so between the end of the map data (the #? fields) and the **pathalias** data.

K.2.10 Netnews neighbors (#U)

The Usenet is the network that moves netnews around—specifically, news.announce.important. If you send news.announce.important to any of your uucp neighbors, list their names here, delimited by spaces. Example:

```
#U  ihnp4 decvax mcvax seismo
```

Since some places have lots of Usenet neighbors, continuation lines should be just another #U and more site names.

K.2.11 Last edit of entry and when (#W)

This field should contain an email address, a name in parentheses, followed by a semicolon, and the output of the **date** program. Example:

```
#W  ucbvax!fair (Erik E. Fair); Sat Jun 22 03:35:16 PDT 1985
```

The same rules for email address that apply in the contact's email address apply here also. (i.e., only one system name, and user name). It is intended that this field be used for automatic aging of the map entries so that we can do more automated checking and updating of the entire map. See **getdate**(3) from the netnews source for other acceptable date formats.

K.2.12 pathalias data

The DEMAND, DAILY, etc., entries represent imaginary connect costs (see the following) used by **pathalias** to calculate lowest cost paths. The cost breakdown is shown in Figure K.1.

FIGURE K.1

Interpretation of **pathalias** cost keywords		
Name	Points	Typical meaning
LOCAL	25	Local area network (Ethernet)
DEDICATED	95	High-speed dedicated line
DIRECT	200	Local telephone call
DEMAND	300	Long distance call, anytime
HOURLY	500	Hourly poll
EVENING	1800	Time-restricted call
DAILY	5000	Daily poll
WEEKLY	30000	Irregular poll
DEAD	huge number	Not a usable path

Additionally, HIGH and LOW (used like DAILY+HIGH) are -5 and +5 respectively, for baud-rate or quality bonuses/penalties. Arithmetic expressions can be used, however, you should be aware that the results are often counterintuitive (e.g., (DAILY*4) means every four days, not four times a day). This is because the numbers represent "cost of connection" rather than "frequency of connection."

The numbers are intended to represent cost of transferring mail over the link, measured very roughly in elapsed time, which seems to be far more important than baud rates for this type of traffic. There is an assumed high overhead for each hop; thus, HOURLY is far more than DAILY/24.

There are a few other cost names that sometimes appear in the map. Some are synonyms for the preceding preferred names (e.g., POLLED is assumed to mean overnight and is taken to be the same as DAILY), some are obsolete (e.g., the letters A through F, which are letter grades for connections). It is not acceptable to make up new names or spellings (**pathalias** gets very upset when people do that...).

K.2.12.1 Local area networks

We do not want local area network information in the published map. If you want to put your LAN in your local Path.* files, read about the LAN syntax in the **pathalias** manual page.

K.3 What to do with your entry

Once you have finished constructing your **pathalias** entry, mail it off to {uunet | gatech | ucsd | ames}!rutgers!uucpmap, from where it will be sent to the appropriate regional map coordinator. They maintain assigned geographic sections of the map, and the entire map is posted on a rolling basis in the Usenet newsgroups comp.mail.maps over the course of a month (at the end of the month they start over).

Questions or comments about this specification should also be directed to rutgers!uucpmap.

L

Domain Name Registration Form

L.1 Introduction

Domain names must be unique and therefore are centrally administered. Top-level domains identify the type of organization; the second-level domain that this form pertains to identifies the organization itself. To request an electronic copy of this form, send electronic mail to hostmaster@sri-nic.arpa (Network Information Center at Stanford Research Institute).

L.2 The domain registration form

```
[ NETINFO:DOMAIN-TEMPLATE.TXT ]                          [ 2/88 ]

   To establish a domain, the following information must be sent to
   the NIC Domain Registrar (HOSTMASTER@SRI-NIC.ARPA).  Questions
   may be addressed to the NIC Hostmaster by electronic mail at the
   above address, or by phone at (415) 859-5539 or (800) 235-3155.

   NOTE: The key people must have electronic mailboxes and NIC
   "handles," unique NIC database identifiers.  If you have access to
   "WHOIS", please check to see if you are registered and if so, make
```

sure the information is current. Include only your handle and any changes (if any) that need to be made in your entry. If you do not have access to "WHOIS", please provide all the information indicated and a NIC handle will be assigned.

(1) The name of the top-level domain to join.

For example: COM

(2) The NIC handle of the administrative head of the organization. Alternately, the person's name, title, mailing address, phone number, organization, and network mailbox. This is the contact point for administrative and policy questions about the domain. In the case of a research project, this should be the principal investigator.

For example:

```
Administrator

   Organization  The NetWorthy Corporation
   Name          Penelope Q. Sassafrass
   Title         President
   Mail Address  The NetWorthy Corporation
                 4676 Andrews Way, Suite 100
                 Santa Clara, CA 94302-1212
   Phone Number  (415) 123-4567
   Net Mailbox   Sassafrass@ECHO.TNC.COM
   NIC Handle    PQS
```

(3) The NIC handle of the technical contact for the domain. Alternately, the person's name, title, mailing address, phone number, organization, and network mailbox. This is the contact point for problems concerning the domain or zone, as well as for updating information about the domain or zone.

For example:

```
Technical and Zone Contact

   Organization  The NetWorthy Corporation
   Name          Ansel A. Aardvark
   Title         Executive Director
   Mail Address  The NetWorthy Corporation
                 4676 Andrews Way, Suite 100
                 Santa Clara, CA. 94302-1212
   Phone Number  (415) 123-6789
   Net Mailbox   Aardvark@ECHO.TNC.COM
   NIC Handle    AAA2
```

(4) The name of the domain (up to 12 characters). This is the name that will be used in tables and lists associating the domain with the domain server addresses. [While, from a technical standpoint, domain names can be quite long (programmers beware), shorter names are easier for people to cope with.]

For example: TNC

(5) A description of the servers that provide the domain service for translating names to addresses for hosts in this domain, and the date they will be operational.

A good way to answer this question is to say "Our server is supplied by person or company X and does whatever their standard issue server does."

For example: Our server is a copy of the one operated by the NIC; it will be installed and made operational on 1 November 1987.

(6) Domains must provide at least two independent servers for the domain. Establishing the servers in physically separate locations and on different PSN's is strongly recommended. A description of the server machine and its backup, including

(a) Hardware and software (using keywords from the Assigned Numbers RFC).

(b) Host domain name and network addresses (which host on which network for each connected network).

(c) Any domain-style nicknames (please limit your domain-style nickname request to one)

For example:

- Hardware and software

```
VAX-11/750   and  UNIX,     or
IBM-PC       and  MS-DOS,   or
DEC-1090     and  TOPS-20
```

- Host domain names and network addresses

BAR.FOO.COM 10.9.0.193 on ARPANET

- Domain-style nickname

BR.FOO.COM (same as BAR.FOO.COM 10.9.0.13 on ARPANET)

(7) Planned mapping of names of any other network hosts, other than the server machines, into the new domain's naming space.

For example:

```
BAR-FOO2.ARPA (10.8.0.193) -> FOO2.BAR.COM
BAR-FOO3.ARPA (10.7.0.193) -> FOO3.BAR.COM
BAR-FOO4.ARPA (10.6.0.193) -> FOO4.BAR.COM
```

(8) An estimate of the number of hosts that will be in the domain.

(a) Initially
(b) Within one year
(c) Two years
(d) Five years.

For example:

```
(a) Initially  =  50
(b) One year   = 100
(c) Two years  = 200
(d) Five years = 500
```

(9) The date you expect the fully qualified domain name to become the official host name in HOSTS.TXT.

Please note: Registration of this domain does not imply an automatic name change to previously registered ARPANET or MILNET hosts that will be included in this domain. If changing to a fully qualified domain name (e.g., FOO.BAR.COM) causes a change in the official host name of an ARPANET or MILNET host, DCA approval must be obtained. This should be done after your domain name is approved by Hostmaster. Allow 10 working days for your requested changes to be processed. ARPANET (network 10) sites should contact ARPANETMGR@DDN1.ARPA. MILNET (network 26) sites should contact MILNETMGR@DDN1.ARPA.

(10) Please describe your organization briefly.

For example: The NetWorthy Corporation is a consulting organization of people working with UNIX and the C language in an electronic networking environment. It sponsors two technical conferences annually and distributes a bimonthly newsletter.

M

Internet IP Address Request Form

M.1 Introduction

Internet IP addresses, like second-level domain names, must be unique and therefore are centrally administered. SRI-NIC doles them out for both Internet sites and non-Internet sites.

M.2 IP address request form

```
[ NETINFO:INTERNET-NUMBER-TEMPLATE.TXT ]                [ 7/87, DBDOC ]

This questionnaire must be used when applying for an Internet Protocol
(IP) Network Number.  To obtain an Internet number, please
provide the following information online to HOSTMASTER@SRI-NIC.ARPA.
Or, if electronic mail is not available to you, please mail to:

        DDN Network Information Center
        SRI International
        Room EJ217
        333 Ravenswood Avenue
        Menlo Park, CA 94025
```

```
1) If the network will be connected to the DARPA Internet or the DDN
Internet, you must provide the name of the sponsoring organization,
and the name, title, mailing address, phone number, net mailbox, and
NIC Handle (if any) of the contact person at that organization.  This
is the contact point for administrative and policy questions about the
authorization for this network to join the DARPA Internet or the DDN
Internet.

NOTE: If the network will NOT be connected to either the DARPA
Internet or the DDN Internet, then you do not need to provide this
information.

      For example:

         Sponsor

            Organization  DARPA
            Name          Dr. Robert E. Kahn
            Title         Director, IPTO
            Mail Address  DARPA
                          1400 Wilson Bl.
                          Arlington, VA. 22209
            Phone Number  (202) 694-5922
            Net Mailbox   Kahn@ISI.EDU
            NIC Handle    REK2

2) The name, title, mailing address, phone number, and organization of
the administrative head of the organization.  This is the contact
point for administrative and policy questions about the network.  In
the case of a research project this should be the Principal
Investigator.  The online mailbox and NIC Handle (if any) of this
person should also be included.

      For example:

         Administrator

            Organization      USC/Information Sciences Institute
            Name              Keith Uncapher
            Title             Executive Director
            Mail Address      USC/ISI
                              4676 Admiralty Way, Suite 1001
                              Marina del Rey, CA. 90292-6695
            Phone Number      (213) 822-1511
            Net Mailbox       Uncapher@ISI.EDU
            NIC Handle        KU
```

3) The name, title, mailing address, phone number, and organization of the technical contact. The online mailbox and NIC Handle (if any) of the technical contact should also be included. This is the contact point for problems with the network and for updating information about the network. Also, the technical contact may be responsible for hosts attached to this network.

For example:

Technical Contact

```
Organization  USC/Information Sciences Institute
Name          Craig Milo Rogers
Title         Researcher
Mail Address  USC/ISI
              4676 Admiralty Way, Suite 1001
              Marina del Rey, CA. 90292-6695
Phone Number  (213) 822-1511
Net Mailbox   Rogers@ISI.EDU
NIC Handle    CMR
```

4) The short name of the network (up to 12 characters). This is the name that will be used in tables and lists associating networks and addresses.

For example: ALPHA-BETA

5) The long name of the network (up to 20 characters). This name should be descriptive of the network. It might be used to clarify the ownership, location, or purpose of the network.

For example: Greek Alphabet Net

6) Geographically, where is this network located?

For example: USC/ISI
4676 Admiralty Way
Marina del Rey, CA. 90292-6695

7) A citation to a document that describes the network. This should identify a document that describes the network in a technical sense.

For example: "The Ethernet, a Local Area Network: Data Link Layer and Physical Layer Specification", X3T51/80-50 Xerox, Stamford Connecticut, October 1980.

```
8) Gateway information:
If the network is to be connected to the DARPA Internet or the DDN
Internet, answer questions 8a and 8b.

If the network will not be connected to the DARPA Internet or the DDN
Internet, answer question 8c.

   8a) A description of the Gateway that connects the new network to
   the DARPA Internet or the DDN Internet, and the date it will be
   operational.  The gateway must be either a core gateway supplied
   and operated by BBN, or a gateway of another Autonomous System.  If
   this gateway is not a core gateway, then some gateway in this
   gateway's Autonomous System must exchange routing information with
   some core gateway via EGP.

      A good way to answer this question is to say "Our gateway is
      supplied by person or company X and does whatever their standard
      issue gateway does".

         For example: Our gateway is the standard issue supplied and
         operated by BBN, and will be installed and made operational
         on 1-April-83.


   8b) A description of the gateway machine, including

      (a) hardware (LSI-11/23, VAX-11/750, etc. interfaces)

      (b) addresses (what host on what net for each connected net)

      (c) software (operating system and programming language)

      For example:

         (a) hardware

            PDP-11/40, ARPANET Interface by ACC, Ethernet Interfaces
            by 3COM.

         (b) address

            10.9.0.193 on ARPANET

         (c) software

            Berkeley UNIX 4.2 BSD and C
```

8c) A description of the Gateway used in the system. For example, does the Gateway:

(a) forward IP datagrams,
(b) send ICMP redirects,
(c) implement GGP, or
(d) implement EGP?

A good way to answer this question is to say "Our gateway is supplied by person or company X and does whatever their standard issue gateway does".

For example: Our gateway is the standard issue supplied and operated by BBN, and will be installed and made operational on 1-April-83.

Note that for networks connected to the DARPA Internet or the DDN Internet the gateway must be either a core gateway supplied and operated by BBN, or a gateway of another Autonomous System. If this gateway is not a core gateway, then some gateway in this gateway's Autonomous System must exchange routing information with some core gateway via EGP.

9) An estimate of the number of hosts that will be on the network

(a) initially,
(b) within one year,
(c) two years, and
(d) five years.

For example:

```
(a) initially   =   5
(b) one year    =  25
(c) two years   =  50
(d) five years = 200
```

10) Unless a strong and convincing reason is presented, the network (if it qualifies at all) will be assigned a class C network number. Is a class C network number acceptable for your purposes, and if not why not? (Note: If there are plans for more than a few local networks, and more than 100 or so hosts, we strongly urge you to consider subnetting. [See RFC 950])

For example: Class C is fine.

11) Networks are characterized as being either Research, Defense, Government - Non Defense, or Commercial, and the network address space is shared between these three areas. Which type is this network?

For example: Research

12) What is the purpose of the network?

For example: To economically connect computers used in DARPA sponsored research project FROB-BRAF to the DARPA Internet or the DDN Internet to provide communication capability with other similar projects at UNIV-X and CORP-Y.

N

The **remote** Utility

N.1 Introduction

remote allows any time sharing machine to act as a terminal server. The user logs in as the pseudo-user "remote" on any terminal connected to a machine that supports the system, and then is forwarded across the network to his destination machine. **gremote** supports eight-bit ASCII. You must add password entries for remote and gremote.

N.2 The file remote.c

```
/*
 * remote, gremote - do an 'rlogin' through a machine.
 *
 *      If invoked as gremote, it will invoke 'rlogin -8' to support
 *      graphics terminals.
 *
 *      Right now, it is hard-wired to disallow dialups on boulder only;
 *      if this becomes a popular feature, it should be generalized.
 *
 *
 */
```

```
#include <stdio.h>
#include <sys/file.h>
#include <sys/syslog.h>

#define HOSTNAME_SIZE 32
#define NAME_SIZE 8
#define LOGSTAT LOG_LOCAL0

FILE *fd,*fopen();
char *index(),*rindex(),*getenv();

main (ac,av)
        int ac;
        char **av;
{
        char host[HOSTNAME_SIZE];
        char thishost[HOSTNAME_SIZE];
        char username[NAME_SIZE];
        char *cmdname;
        char *ttytype;
        char *ttyn, *ttyname();
        int i;
        short int  eightbit = 0;        /* flag true if rlogin -8 wanted */


        cmdname = *av;
        if (*cmdname == '-')
                cmdname++;

        openlog(cmdname,0,LOGSTAT);

        /* Look at the environment and get the type of the tty */
        ttytype = getenv("TERM");

        /* if this is a machine from which you do not want dialups
                to get access to remote login capabilities -- then nuke 'em */

        gethostname(thishost,sizeof(thishost));

        if ( (strncmp("Your_machine_name",thishost,sizeof(thishost)) == 0) &&
             (strncmp("dialup",ttytype, sizeof(ttytype))  == 0)      )
        {
                printf ("%s:Sorry, %ss not permitted on dialups on %s.\n",
                        cmdname,cmdname,thishost);

                syslog(LOG_INFO,"on %s failed",thishost);
                sleep(1);
                exit(0);
        }
```

```
        if (*cmdname == 'g')
                        eightbit++;

        /* prompt for hostname */
        printf ("hostname: ");
        alarm(120);
        gets(host);

        /* prompt the remote login */
        printf ("%s login: ",host);
        scanf ("%s",username);
        alarm(0);

        /* if they invoked us as 'gremote' give them the 8 bit interface */
        if (eightbit) {
                syslog(LOG_INFO,"gremote host: %s, user: %s",host,username);
                execl
                ("/usr/ucb/rlogin",host, "-8" ,"-l",username,"-e 177",0);
        }
        else {
                syslog(LOG_INFO,"remote host: %s, user: %s",host,username);
                execl
                ("/usr/ucb/rlogin",host,"-l",username,"-e 177",0);
        }
}/* main */
```

O

Distributed Host Management System

O.1 Introduction

This appendix contains a set of utilities that allow distributed control of the /etc/hosts and /etc/networks files. The program **updatehosts** receives mail from administrators on various machines. The administrator's name is verified, and then the request for a change in the tables is processed. The script **updatedhosts.daily** is run once a day to modify the master files and distribute them to the clients. Minor modifications will have to be made to suit your environment. Your /etc/hosts and /etc/networks files should contain embedded comments similiar to the ones in the sample files in Section 14.7.5.2.

O.2 The updatehosts.c file

```
/*
** updatehosts - accept /etc/host file section updates via mail.
**
**  Accepts mail on stdin, then looks at body of message for:
**       # begin: foo
**
```

```
**   whereupon it writes this and all lines up to and including:
**       # end: foo
**
**   to the file HOSTDIR/foo... If a line of the format:
**       # adminmail: goober
**   is encountered an acknowledgment is sent to goober.
**
**   If it sees:
**       send
**   it will send the sender a copy of the current hosts file. If it
**   sees:
**       help
**   it will send the sender a copy of the help file
**
**
**   to make the program receive mail addressed to updatehosts,
**   add the following line to your /usr/lib/aliases file
**      updatehosts: "|/usr/local/adm/hosts/updatehosts"
**
**   Written by Bob Coggeshall (coggs@boulder.Colorado.EDU)
**
*/

#define JTY "Just thought you'd like to know.\n"

#include <stdio.h>
#include <ctype.h>
#include <sys/param.h>

#define HOSTDIR         "/usr/local/adm/hosts/hostsrc/"
#define HOSTS           "/usr/local/adm/hosts/hostsrc/hosts"
#define HELPFILE        "/usr/local/adm/hosts/doc/updatehosts.catme"
/** NEDITOR should be the name of the person allowed to edit **/
#define NEDITOR         "coggs"
#define TEMPFILEPREF    "/tmp/updatehosts."
#define STDERR           "/tmp/updatehosts.stderr"
#define UMASK            002

/** domainname contains your domain name **/
char *domainname = "colorado.edu";
char hostname[MAXHOSTNAMELEN];


/* values used by upexit() */

#define FAIL 1
#define FAKEFAIL 0            /* avoid generating mail bounces */
#define SUCCESS 0
```

```
/* values returned by parsline() */

#define BEGIN        1
#define END          2
#define ADMINMAIL    3
#define MAILHEAD     4
#define DATA         5
#define SEND         6
#define HELP         7
#define SUBJECT      8

/* values used by mail() */

#define INDENT   1
#define NOINDENT 0

char *gets();
char *rindex();
char *index();
char *getcuradmin();
FILE *fopen();
FILE *freopen();

char *progname;

char wrkline[256];            /* yet another */
char wrkline1[256];           /* yet another 1 */

char realsender[256];         /* sender from the 'From ' line */
char curadminmail[256];       /* current value of 'Adminmail:' arg from file */

FILE *fd = NULL;              /* file descriptor for writing section file */
FILE *tfd = NULL;             /* file descriptor for temp file */
FILE *efd = NULL;             /* file descriptor for stderr */
char *cp;                     /* general purpose character pointer */
char tempfile[256];           /* name of temporary file */

main(ac,av)
int ac;
char **av;
{

    char arg[256];                /* rhs of arguments from input file */
    char line[256];               /* general purpose line buffer */
    char secfile[256];            /* name of section file */
    char secname[256];            /* name of section */
    char adminmail[256];          /* administrator mail arg */
    int pid;                      /* process id */
```

```
int freadcount;              /* count returned from fread() */
int systatus;                /* returned by system() */

    umask(UMASK);

/*
** get the hostname and the program name.
*/
gethostname(hostname,sizeof(hostname));

if ((progname = rindex(*av,'/')) == 0)
    progname = *av;
else
    progname++;

/*
** redirect stderr to a file
*/
if ( (efd = freopen(STDERR,"w+",stderr)) == NULL) {
    sprintf(wrkline, "%s: couldn't freopen() %s", progname,STDERR);
    mail(NEDITOR,wrkline, JTY,0,0);
}


/*
** process input, parseline figures out what kind of line it is
** and this case statement decides what to do.
*/
while (gets(line) != NULL)
{
    switch (parseline(line,arg)) {

            case ADMINMAIL:          /* snarf adminmail arg */
                if (tfd) {
                    fputs(line,tfd);
                    fputc('\n',tfd);
                }
                strcpy(adminmail,arg);
                /*
                ** check that old adminmail and new adminmail args match
                */
                strcpy(wrkline,adminmail);
                if ((cp = index(wrkline,'@')) != 0)
                        *cp = '\0';

                strcpy(wrkline1,curadminmail);
                if ((cp = index(wrkline1,'@')) != 0)
                        *cp = '\0';
```

```
        if ( (strncmp(wrkline,wrkline1,sizeof(wrkline)) != 0) ) {
            sprintf(wrkline,
          "%s: new adminmail:%s and current adminmail: %s don't match",
            progname,adminmail,curadminmail);
            mail(NEDITOR,wrkline, JTY,0,0);
            upexit(FAKEFAIL);
        }
        break;

    case MAILHEAD:              /* its the mail header, skip it */
        strcpy(realsender,arg); /* snarf sender */
                          fprintf(stderr,"realsender: %s\n",realsender);
        break;

    case SUBJECT:
        break;

    case SEND:              /* they want a copy of the whole thing */
      sprintf(wrkline,"%s: copy of current hosts file:",progname);
        mail(realsender,wrkline,"",HOSTS,NOINDENT);

        sprintf(wrkline,"%s: sent %s copy of current hosts file",
                progname,realsender);
        mail(NEDITOR,wrkline,JTY,0,0);

        upexit(SUCCESS);

        break;

    case HELP:              /* send them the help file */
        sprintf(wrkline,"%s: help file",progname);
        mail(realsender,wrkline,"",HELPFILE,NOINDENT);

        sprintf(wrkline,"%s: sent %s the help file",
                progname,realsender);
        mail(NEDITOR,wrkline,JTY,0,0);

        upexit(SUCCESS);
        break;

    case DATA:                  /* its data, snarf it. */
        if (tfd) {
            fputs(line,tfd);
            fputc('\n',tfd);
        }
        break;
```

```
case BEGIN:
    /*
    ** if begin, then see if section file exists
    ** if it doesn't send mail and die. if it does
    ** open it tempfile for write.
    */
    strcpy(secfile,HOSTDIR);
    strcpy(secname,arg);
    strcat(secfile,secname);

    if (access(secfile,0) != 0) {
        sprintf(wrkline,"%s: Can't access() %s",
        progname,secfile);
        mail(NEDITOR,wrkline,
        "File needs to exist before i'll overwrite it",0,0);
        upexit(FAKEFAIL);
    }

    /*
    ** read secfile and get the current adminmail: arg
    ** and authenticate by comparing it with sender
    */
    strcpy(curadminmail,getcuradmin(secfile));

    strcpy(wrkline,curadminmail);
    if ((cp = index(wrkline,'@')) != 0)
            *cp = '\0';

    strcpy(wrkline1,realsender);
    if ((cp = index(wrkline1,'@')) != 0)
            *cp = '\0';

    if ( (strncmp(wrkline,wrkline1,sizeof(wrkline)) != 0) ) {
    /*
    ** some exceptions....
    */
    strcpy(wrkline,NEDITOR);
    if ((cp  = index(wrkline,'@')) != 0)
        *cp = '\0';
    if ( (strncmp(wrkline,wrkline1,sizeof(wrkline)) == 0)||
        strncmp(wrkline,"root",sizeof("root")) == 0)
        goto except;

    sprintf(wrkline,
    "%s: sender: %s and current adminmail: %s don't match",
    progname,realsender,curadminmail);
```

```
                mail(NEDITOR,wrkline, JTY,0,0);
                upexit(FAKEFAIL);
            }
        except:

                /*
                ** open temporary file.
                */
                pid = getpid();
                sprintf(tempfile,"%s%d",TEMPFILEPREF,pid);
                if ( (tfd = fopen(tempfile,"w+")) == 0) {
                    sprintf(wrkline,"%s: Can't fopen() %s",
                    progname,tempfile);
                    mail(NEDITOR,wrkline,JTY,0,0);
                    upexit(FAKEFAIL);
                }

                if ( (fputs("##\n",tfd)) == EOF) {
                    sprintf(wrkline,"%s: %s: Write failed",
                    progname, tempfile);
                    mail(NEDITOR,wrkline,JTY,0,0);
                    upexit(FAKEFAIL);
                }
                fputs(line,tfd);
                fputc('\n',tfd);
                break;

            case END:
                /*
                **   if end then close file, make sure begin and
                **  end agree. complain and die if not. otherwise
                **  send mail that things are ok
                */
                strcpy(wrkline,HOSTDIR);
                strcat(wrkline,arg);

                if (strncmp(wrkline,secfile,strlen(tempfile)) != 0) {
                    sprintf(wrkline,"%s %s",NEDITOR,adminmail);
                    sprintf(wrkline1,
                  "%s: 'End:' arg disagreed with 'Begin:' arg",progname);
                    mail(wrkline,wrkline1,JTY,0,0);
                    upexit(FAKEFAIL);
                }

                fputs(line,tfd);
                fputc('\n',tfd);
                fputs("##\n",tfd);
                (void)fseek(tfd,0L,0);
```

```
if ( (fd = fopen(secfile,"w")) == 0) {
    sprintf(wrkline,"%s: Can't fopen() %s",
    progname,secfile);
    mail(NEDITOR,wrkline,JTY,0,0);
    upexit(FAKEFAIL);
}

while( (freadcount = fread(wrkline,
                    sizeof(*wrkline),
                    sizeof(wrkline),tfd))  > 0)

    if ((fwrite(wrkline,
        sizeof(*wrkline),freadcount,fd))  < 0) {
        sprintf(wrkline,"%s: Can't fwrite() %s",
        progname,secfile);
        mail(NEDITOR,wrkline,JTY,0,0);
        upexit(FAKEFAIL);
    }

if ( (fclose(fd) == EOF) ) {
        sprintf(wrkline,"%s: Can't fclose() %s",
        progname,secfile);
        mail(NEDITOR,wrkline,JTY,0,0);
        upexit(FAKEFAIL);
}

fclose(tfd);
unlink(tempfile);

sprintf(wrkline,"%s, %s",NEDITOR,adminmail);
sprintf(wrkline1,
"%s: \"%s\" submitted by \"%s\" successfully",
progname,secname,adminmail);
mail(wrkline,wrkline1,"Revised file: \n",secfile,NOINDENT);

/*
** do a 'make hosts'
*/
sprintf(wrkline,"cd %s;make hosts > /dev/null\n",HOSTDIR);
if ( (systatus = system(wrkline)) != SUCCESS) {
    fclose(efd);
    sprintf(wrkline1,"%s: make returns %d",
          progname,systatus);
    mail(NEDITOR,wrkline1,wrkline,STDERR,INDENT);
    upexit(FAKEFAIL);
}

break;
```

```
                default:
                    break;
            }
        }
    upexit(SUCCESS);
}



/*
** tolowers(string) - convert string to lowercase
**
*/

tolowers(string)
char *string;
{
    char *s;

    s = string;

        while (*s++)
            *s = (isupper(*s) ? tolower(*s) : *s ) ;
}


/*
** parseline(line,arg) - determine what kinda line it is
**
**  line - input string
**  arg  - string parsed out of Begin: End: or adminmail: line
**
** returns BEGIN        - if it was a '# Begin:'
**         END          - if it was a '# End:'
**         ADMINMAIL    - if it was a '# AdminMail:'
**         MAILHEAD     - if it was a 'From '
**         DATA         - if it was anything else
**         SEND         - if it was a 'Subject: Send '
**         HELP         - if it was a 'Subject: Help '
**         SUBJECT      - if it was a 'Subject: anything'
*/
parseline(s,arg)
char *s,*arg;
{
    char wrkline[256];
    char *cp;
    int result;
```

```
strcpy(wrkline,s);

cp = wrkline;

result = DATA;

if (strncmp(cp,"From ",strlen("From ")) == 0) {
        sscanf(cp,"%*s %s",arg);
        result = MAILHEAD;
        return(result);
}

tolowers(wrkline);

/*
** check out subject line for 'help' or 'send'
*/
if (strncmp(cp,"Subject:",strlen("Subject:")) == 0) {
        sscanf(cp,"%*s %s",arg);
        if (strncmp(arg,"send",strlen("send")) == 0) {
                arg = "";
                result = SEND;
                return(result);
        }
        if (strncmp(arg,"help",strlen("help")) == 0) {
                arg = "";
                result = HELP;
                return(result);
        }
        result = SUBJECT;
        return(result);
}

if (*cp++ == '#')
{

    while (*cp == ' ' || *cp == '\t')
     cp++;

    if (strncmp(cp,"begin:",strlen("begin:")) == 0)
            result = BEGIN;

    if (strncmp(cp,"end:",strlen("end:")) == 0)
             result = END;

    if (strncmp(cp,"adminmail:",strlen("adminmail:")) == 0)
            result = ADMINMAIL;
```

```
        sscanf(cp,"%*s %s",arg);

        return(result);
        }
    return(result);
}


/*
** mail(recipient,subject,message,file,indent) - send somebuddy mail.
**
**
*/
static
mail(recip,subj,mesg,file,indent)
char *recip, *subj, *mesg, *file;
int indent;
{
    FILE *pfd;
    FILE *ifd;
    char *aav[11];
    int fildes[2];
    int stdin_fd;
    int pid;
    char retaddr[128];
    char line[128];

    /*
    ** put together arglist for sendmail
    */
    sprintf(retaddr,"%s@%s",progname,hostname);
    aav[0] = "/usr/lib/sendmail";
    aav[1] = "-t";
    aav[2] = "-oi";
    aav[3] = "-f";
    aav[4] = retaddr;
    aav[5] = "-F";
    aav[6] = "/etc/host updating facility";
    aav[7] = NULL;       /* grimble snort */

    /* prep pipe to write to child */

    pipe (fildes);

    /* save stdin  */

    stdin_fd = dup(0);
```

```
/* cauterize stdin temporarily */

dup2(fildes[0], 0);

/* fork; child execs sendmail, parent writes to child (sendmail). */

if ( (pid = vfork()) < 0) {
    fputs("vfork botch",stderr);
    perror(progname);
}
if (pid == 0) {
        execv (aav[0],aav);
}

/* make standard in normal again in parent  */

dup2 (stdin_fd, 0);

/* associate file descriptor with a stream so we can fputs, etc */
if ( (pfd = fdopen(fildes[1],"w")) ==  NULL)
    perror(progname);

fprintf(pfd,"To: %s\n",recip);
fprintf(pfd,"Subject: %s\n",subj);
fputs("\n",pfd);

fprintf(pfd,"%s", mesg);

/*
** read send file along
*/
if (file != 0) {
    if ( (ifd = fopen(file,"r")) == NULL)
        fprintf(pfd,">> Couldn't fopen() %s\n",file);

    if (indent)
            fputs("> \n",pfd);

    while(fgets(line,sizeof(line),ifd) != NULL) {
            if (indent)
                    fputs("> ",pfd);
            fputs(line,pfd);
    }
    fclose(ifd);
}

fprintf(pfd,"\nyours truly,\n\n");
fprintf(pfd,"%s",retaddr);
```

```
    fclose(pfd);
    close (fildes[1]);
    return(SUCCESS);
}

/*
** skipheader(fd) - skip over mail header
**
**  actually just read until you get a blank line...
**
*/

skipheader(fd)
FILE *fd;
{
    char line[256];
    while(fgets(line,sizeof(line),fd) != NULL) {
        if (line[0] == '\n')
                break;
    }
}
/*
** getcuradmin(secfile) - read an existing section file and
**                          return the adminmail: arg
*/

char *getcuradmin(secfile)
char *secfile;
{
    FILE *fd;
    char line[256];
    char arg[256];
    char s[256];

    if ( (fd = fopen(secfile,"r")) == 0) {
            sprintf(wrkline,"%s: Can't fopen() %s",
                    progname,secfile);
            mail(NEDITOR,wrkline,JTY,0,0);
            upexit(FAKEFAIL);
    }

    while ( (fgets(line,256,fd) != NULL ))   {

        switch (parseline(line,arg)) {

        case ADMINMAIL:
            strcpy(s,arg);
            break;
```

```
        default:
            break;
        }
    }

fclose(fd);
return(s);
}

/*
** upexit(code) - clean up and pass 'code' to system exit()
*/
upexit(code)
int code;
{
    if (tfd != NULL) fclose(tfd);
    if (efd != NULL) fclose(efd);
    if (fd  != NULL) fclose(fd);
    unlink(tempfile);
    unlink(STDERR);
    exit(code);
}
```

O.3 The Makefile file

```
LIB=/usr/local/adm/hosts/

default: updatehosts.c makefile
        cc -g updatehosts.c -o ${LIB}updatehosts
        chown daemon.daemon ${LIB}updatehosts
        chmod 4770 ${LIB}updatehosts
```

O.4 The updatehosts.l manual page

```
.TH UPDATEHOSTS LOCAL "1 February 1987"
.UC
.SH NAME
updatehosts \- maintain hosts file via mail.
.SH SYNOPSIS
mail updatehosts@boulder
.SH DESCRIPTION
.PP
.B Updatehosts\^
is a program that accepts input via mail from specific senders to that is
```

```
used to update a source for the organization's hosts file.
.B Updatehosts\^
also accepts queries for help and to have an up-to-date copy of the hosts
file be sent to the requester. Updatehosts is useful for medium to large
organizations where changes to the hosts file occurs rapidly, and where
there are more than one individuals responsible for the administration
of hosts on the local network.
.SH INSTRUCTIONS
.PP
To use
.B updatehosts,
the hosts file is divided into sections delimited with special
comments of the form:
.nf

\fB
.ti 1.0i
##
.ti 1.0i
# Begin: ACS
.ti 1.0i
# adminmail: dcmwood@spot
.ti 1.0i
# nextnumbers: 27,28,29,31,32
.ti 1.0i
#
.ti 1.0i
192.12.238.36  ncar-cu-gw          # Cisco IP gateway to NCAR
.ti 1.0i
#
.ti 1.0i
192.12.238.1    spot.colorado.edu spot
.ti 1.0i
# End: ACS
.ti 1.0i
##
\fR
.fi

.PP
The arguments to
.B Begin:
and
.B End:
must match. These are taken as the name of a file in the  host source directory.
The
.B AdminMail:
argument is taken as the mail address of the administrator responsible for
```

```
this section. To update a section file of the host source directory, The
administrator simply sends mail to the address
.B updatehosts@boulder
with their section in the form that it appears above as the body of the message.
.B Updatehosts
will send an acknowledgement back to the sender. Note that the value of the
.B AdminMail: in the update and the previous version must match or else the
update will not be accepted.

.SH OTHER CAPABILITIES
.PP
Anyone may receive updates of the most recent up to date version of the hosts
file. By mailing
.B updatehosts
with a message with the a
.B Subject:
field:
.B Send.
In this case, it will mail to the sender, the latest full version of
the hosts file.

.PP
To get a copy of this manual page, mail a message to
.B updatehosts@boulder
with the
.B Subject:
field:
.B Help

.SH ADMINISTRATION/MAINTENANCE
.PP
.B updatehosts
sends mail is to a single hosts file administrator  who verifies
that sections are being added correctly.
There is a makefile in the host source directory that is called by
.B updatehosts
to assemble the hosts  file. To create a new section, The hosts
administrator needs to create a new section file with the
\fBBegin:, End: and AdminMail:\fR fields set appropriately, and modify the
makefile to include it.

.PP
There is a companion script invoked out of cron,
.B updatehosts.daily
which rcs's the hosts file, and sends out diff's of the hosts file
to a list of recipients as changes are made. This script also
sends a full copy of the hosts file  bi-weekly. The mailing
list is kept in  the file
```

```
.B admins.mailist
in the host source directory.

.SH DIAGNOSTICS
.PP
.B Updatehosts
will transmit mail back to the  sender and the hosts administrator
as appropriate explaining various unhappinesses.

.SH BUGS
.PP
It is possible to breach the security of this system by forging mail,
however, since this mechanism only updates a passive source directory,
and the hosts administrator is notified of any update, and old versions
are kept, it is generally felt to be safe.

.SH FILES
.nf
boulder:/usr/local/adm/hosts/*
.fi

.SH SEE ALSO
.nf
hosts(5)
.fi
```

O.5 The updatehosts.daily script

```
#!/bin/csh
###
# updatehosts - remake and distribute hosts file as necessary.
###

# determines how old a file can be before it is considered unmodified..
set maxthours = 1

# ug+rwx modes for writing files
umask 002

# get the date for figuring out whether to send diffs or the whole thing
set date = `date`

# munged version of date w/o colons on time...
set now     = `date | sed 's/:/ /g'`
```

```
# make sure we can execute fun things
set path=(. ~ ~/bin /usr/ucb /usr/bin /usr/new /etc /bin /usr/local/bin \
        /usr/local/etc /usr/hosts /usr/games /usr/local/adm/hosts/tools )

# get list of machines to distribute to
set MACHINEINFO = /usr/local/etc/MACHINES

# where the real hosts file lives..
set HOSTFILE    = /etc/hosts

# which mailer to run when bothering people
set mail        = "/usr/ucb/mail"

# list of people who like to know when host list changes
set names = `cat /usr/local/adm/hosts/mailist`

# someone who wants to be bothered w/errs
set netadmin = coggs

# list of machines to distribute to...
set allhosts = \
( boulder sigi tut orbit extaci euclid sol anchor piper kirk eprince \
        pprince encore tigger )

# find out who trusts us..
#set trusted =  ( `grep -w TRUSTED ${MACHINEINFO} | awk '{print $1}' ` )

# where the action is...
set SRCDIR  = /usr/local/adm/hosts/hostsrc
cd $SRCDIR

##
# check each section, determine if it has been changed since last time.
set sections = \
(`grep "DATASECTIONS =" makefile | sed 's/[A-Z]*[    ]*=[            ]*//'`)

##
# max tolerable # of hours a file may be unmodified...
@ maxtseconds = $maxthours * 60 * 60
@ modified = 0
echo ""                                         > /tmp/updatehosts

foreach section ( $sections )
        echo $section
        set fileage = `cvdate -f $section`
        if ($fileage < $maxtseconds) then
                echo $section                   > touched-sections
                @ modified++
```

```
    endif
end
if ( $modified != 0 ) then
        set sections = `cat touched-sections`
        rm /tmp/updatehosts
        cat << EOF                                   > /tmp/updatehosts.mesg
The following section(s) of the cu/boulder hosts file have been updated.

$sections

A complete copy of the file is available via anonymous ftp from
boulder.colorado.edu

You may receive the complete updated hosts file by sending mail to
'updatehosts@boulder' with a Subject: line consisting of the string
'send'.

You may receive further information on updatehosts by replacing the
above 'send' with 'help'.

For a complete rationalization, mail 'netadmin@boulder.colorado.edu'
EOF
  $mail -s "updatehosts@boulder: hosts file update: $sections" $names $netadmin \
                                            < /tmp/updatehosts.mesg

        rm /tmp/updatehosts.mesg
endif
##
# make the hosts file...
#
if ( $modified != 0 ) then

        ##
        # make new hosts file
        make hosts                          >& /tmp/updatehosts.terr
        if ($status != 0) then
                goto reporterr
        endif
        cat /tmp/updatehosts.terr           >> /tmp/updatehosts.err
        ##
        # rcs it.
        ci -l hosts < /dev/null             >& /tmp/updatehosts.terr
        if ($status != 0) then
                goto reporterr
        endif
        cat /tmp/updatehosts.terr           >> /tmp/updatehosts.err
```

```
    ##
        # deposit copy in ~ftp/pub
        cp hosts ~ftp/pub                       >& /tmp/updatehosts.err
        if ($status != 0) then
                goto reporterr
        endif
        cat /tmp/updatehosts.terr               >> /tmp/updatehosts.err

        ##
        # stick new copy in host:/etc/hosts
        cp hosts /etc/                          >& /tmp/updatehosts.err
        if ($status != 0) then
                goto reporterr
        endif
        cat /tmp/updatehosts.terr               >> /tmp/updatehosts.err
        #
        mkhosts /etc/hosts                      >& /tmp/updatehosts.err
        if ($status != 0) then
                goto reporterr
        endif
        cat /tmp/updatehosts.terr               >> /tmp/updatehosts.err

        rm touched-sections

        ##
        # distribute hosts file
        #
        distribhosts


endif
exit(1)
##
#
reporterr:
        cat /tmp/updatehosts.terr       >> /tmp/updatehosts.err
        (echo "Errors:"; \
        cat    /tmp/updatehosts.err ) | \
        /usr/ucb/mail -s "updatehosts.daily: problems..." $netadmin
        rm /tmp/updatehosts.err
        exit(0)
```

P

Hosts to **named** *Configuration Files*

P.1 Introduction

This script can be used to map from the /etc/hosts format of hostnames and IP addresses, to the form required for the BIND nameserver files /etc/named.hosts and /etc/named.rev. The primary format difference is the reversal of the bytes of the IP address. A system administrator can maintain only one file, the /etc/hosts file, and from it generate the other files for the nameserver. The script is localized to the Colorado.EDU domain, and therefore changes will be required to use it at your site.

P.2 The **mkrevhosts** script

```
#!/bin/csh -f
#
# mkrevhost - get hostnames out of /etc/hosts file, and produce
# RR format entries suitable for insertion in /etc/named.hosts file
#
```

```
set HOSTSRC     = "/usr/local/adm/hosts/hostsrc/hosts"

set NETADMIN    = "netadmin@boulder"
set TERR        = /tmp/mkrevhosts.terr
set ERR         = /tmp/mkrevhosts.err
set AWKFILE     = /tmp/mkrevhosts.awk
set REVFILE     = /tmp/mkrevhosts.rev
set HOSTFILE    = /tmp/mkrevhosts.hosts
set PRIMEHOSTS = "boulder"
set NSDIR       = /usr/local/adm/hosts/ns/
cd $NSDIR
# zero errfile
cat /dev/null > $ERR

##
# convert 'Colorado.EDU' into 'colorado.edu'
set OUTDOMAIN = Colorado.EDU
set INDOMAIN  = `echo $OUTDOMAIN | tr A-Z a-z`

##
# put majik awk script in /tmp/.
#
# extracts lines looking like:
#
#  128.138.238.1    spot spot.colorado.edu
#
#  and spits things out that looks like:
#
# HOSTNAME       IN      A       nnn.nnn.nnn.nnn
#
cat << EOF > $AWKFILE
/$INDOMAIN/  &&    ~ /[0-9]/      &&       !~ /#/ {

        i = 2
        while( i <=  NF)
        {
                if (  == "#") { break }

                j = split(,host,".")

                 = host[1]
                if ( length(host[1]) > 7 )
                        tab = ""
                else
                        tab = ""
```

```
                printf("%s%sINA%s0,host[1],tab,)

                ++i
        }
}
EOF

##
# execute awk script.  run /etc/hosts thru it.
# should spit out all names and nicknames of hosts for a given domain.
# filter it thru tr to get hostname in upper case, sort alphabetically
# and uniq to drop duplicates
#
awk -f $AWKFILE < $HOSTSRC |  sort | uniq > $HOSTFILE

rm $AWKFILE

###
#
# take things like:
#
# hostname      IN      A       aaa.bbb.ccc.ddd
#
# and turn them into things like:
#
#  ddd.ccc      IN      PTR     hostname.Colorado.EDU
#
cat << EOF > $AWKFILE
{
 j = split(,addr,".")
 printf("%s.%sINPTR%s.%s.0,addr[4],addr[3],,"$OUTDOMAIN")
}
EOF

##
# execute awk script.  run /etc/hosts thru it.
# should spit out all names and nicknames of hosts for a given domain.
# strip -gateway and -gw, sort alphabetically and uniq to drop duplicates.
#
cat $HOSTFILE | \
awk -f $AWKFILE | \
sed -e 's/-gateway./../' -e 's/-gw./../' | sort | uniq > $REVFILE
rm $AWKFILE

# forys' hack #1
#
```

```
# make sure we don't have a dup entry for primary servers.
set JEFHOSTS = ${HOSTFILE}.jef
foreach Host ($PRIMEHOSTS)
        /bin/cp $HOSTFILE $JEFHOSTS
        /usr/bin/egrep -v "${Host}[     ]" $JEFHOSTS >$HOSTFILE
end
/bin/rm -f $JEFHOSTS

# forys' hack #2
#
# Add MX, HINFO & WKS records to HOSTFILE (if available)
/usr/local/adm/hosts/tools/addhinfo $HOSTFILE

###
#
cat ./header.rev $REVFILE > ./named.rev
cat ./header.hosts $HOSTFILE > ./named.hosts

##
# distribute to hosts running /etc/named
#
cat /dev/null > $ERR
foreach host ( $PRIMEHOSTS )
        $host "cp /etc/named.hosts /etc/named.hosts.previous; \
               cp /etc/named.rev /etc/named.rev.previous"       >& $TERR
        cat $TERR >> $ERR
        rcp ./named.hosts ./named.rev ${host}:/etc/             >& $TERR
        cat $TERR >> $ERR
        $host kill -HUP `cat /etc/named.pid`                  >& $TERR
        cat $TERR >> $ERR
        if ( !(-z $ERR)) then
                echo "Errors:"
                cat $ERR
                (echo "Errors:"; \
                cat   $ERR ) | \
                /usr/ucb/mail -s "mkrevhosts: problems..." $NETADMIN
                rm $ERR
                rm $TERR
        endif
end
exit(0)


##
# mail errors to NETADMIN and exit
#
```

```
mailexit:
        cat $TERR >> $ERR
        echo "Errors:"
        cat $ERR
        (echo "Errors:"; \
        cat   $ERR ) | \
        /usr/ucb/mail -s "mkrevhosts: problems..." $NETADMIN
        rm $ERR
        rm $TERR
        exit(0)
```

Q

xargs: *A Public Domain Implementation*

Q.1 Introduction

xargs is way to create large command lines without the use of the shell's backquote mechanism. It reads its standard input and supplies each line it finds as a separate argument to the command (and command arguments) on the command line. The command is found using the same PATH conventions as the shell and may be a script. Because of the limitations of the local UNIX system or the great volume of input lines, it may run the command several times.

xargs is found on many versions of UNIX, but the command is missing from some implementations (notably BSD). This public domain version, written by Andrew Gollan, is short enough to type in, so you need never be without **xargs** again. **xargs** is generally significantly faster than the shell backquote mechanism.

Q.2 The Makefile file

```
#
#          Makefile for xargs
#
CSRCS =  xargs.c
COBJS =  xargs.o
DEFNS =  -DBSD
CFLAGS = -O $(DEFNS)

xargs:  $(COBJS)
        cc $(COBJS) $(LIBS) -o xargs

xargs.o: xargs.c /usr/include/sys/wait.h /usr/include/stdio.h \
        /usr/include/sys/param.h

lint:
        lint -abch $(DEFNS) $(CSRCS)

clean:
        rm -f a.out core $(COBJS)
```

Q.3 The xargs.c file

```
/*
 *      Public Domain simplified version of the System V xargs program.
 *
 *      Author: Andrew Gollan
 */
#include        <sys/param.h>
#include        <stdio.h>

/*
 *      Handle the ATT/BSD ideas of wait(2).
 */
#ifdef  BSD
#include        <sys/wait.h>
typedef union wait      WAIT_T;
#else
typedef int             WAIT_T;
#endif  /* BSD */

/*
 *      Set the maximum argument list that xargs will generate.
 *      The reason this is not just NCARGS is that NCARGS can include
```

```
 *      the environment space as well, a really serious program would
 *      size the environment on the fly (but you know what you can do
 *      with that idea). This is pretty big and pretty safe.
 *
 *      Also set the maximum number of arguments that we are going to cope with.
 *      This needed so that we can allocate an array of char * for execv(). Note
 *      that on (at least some) BSD systems NCARGS is 1MB and MAXNARGS will be
 *      32K. Thank the powers for virtual memory.
 */
#define MAXCARGS        (NCARGS / 2)
#define MAXNARGS        (MAXCARGS / 32)

/*
 *      We need to set a limit on an input line for fgets, so use the
 *      longest pathname the system can cope with if available, otherwise
 *      a suitably large number.
 */
#ifdef  MAXPATHLEN
#define MAXARGLEN       MAXPATHLEN
#else
#define MAXARGLEN       1024
#endif  /* MAXPATHLEN */

/*
 *      System error handling.
 */
#define SYSERROR        (-1)

extern int      errno;
extern int      sys_nerr;
extern char     *sys_errlist[];


#define sysmess()       (\
                                (errno < 0 || errno > sys_nerr) \
                                ? \
                                "Unknown Error" \
                                :  sys_errlist[errno] \
                        )
/*
 *      Statically allocate (in the bss segment) an argument vector
 *      and a pool for collecting the arguments in.
 */
static char     *argvector[MAXNARGS];
static char     arglist[MAXCARGS];
static int      argbase;
```

```
/*
 *      Program name for error messages.
 */
static char     *myname;

/*
 *      Read lines from the standard input and pass them on as arguments
 *      to the provided command, making sure that the system limit on
 *      the number of characters in an argument is not exceeded.
 */
int     xargs()
{
        /*
         *      Keep reading while the standard input is valid.
         */
        while (!(feof(stdin) || ferror(stdin)))
        {
                register int    i;
                register int    pid;
                register char   *argptr = arglist;

                /*
                 *      Limit the number of discrete arguments to MAXNARGS -
                 *      We need the last slot for a NULL pointer to keep
                 *      execvp(2) happy.
                 */
                for (i = argbase; i < MAXNARGS - 1; ++i)
                {
                        register int    len;

                        /*
                         *      If we run out of space or we get
                         *      EOF or an error on input, stop collecting
                         *      arguments.
                         */
                        if
                        (
                                argptr + MAXARGLEN >= &arglist[MAXCARGS]
                                ||
                                fgets(argptr, MAXARGLEN, stdin) == NULL
                        )
                                break;

                        /*
                         *      Ignore empty arguments. Note that fgets leave
                         *      the newline at the end of the string.
                         */
```

```
if ((len = strlen(argptr)) <= 1)
                continue;

        /*
         *      Kill the trailing newline, add this argument to
         *      the vector and advance the buffer pointer.
         */
        argptr[len - 1] = ' ';
        argvector[i] = argptr;
        argptr += len;
}

/*
 *      Only run the command if we have some arguments.
 */
if (i <= argbase)
        break;

/*
 *      Cap the vector with the NULL pointer needed for
 *      execvp(2).
 */
argvector[i] = NULL;

/*
 *      Fork and exec the command with all the collected
 *      arguments. Watch out for failed forks.
 */
switch (pid = fork())
{
case SYSERROR:
        (void)fprintf
        (
                stderr,
                "%s: Couldn't fork: %s\n",
                myname,
                sysmess()
        );
        exit(1);
        /* NOTREACHED */

case 0:
        /*
         *      The child just execs the command.
         */
        (void)execvp(argvector[0], argvector);
        perror(argvector[0]);
        exit(1);
```

```
        default:
                        /*
                         *      Wait for the child to return. Due
                         *      to shell handling of pipelines, it
                         *      is possible to get the pid back from wait().
                         */
                        while (wait((WAIT_T *)0) != pid)
                                ;
                }
        }
        return 0;
}

/*
 *      Process the arguments and call xargs().
 */
int     main(argc, argv)
int     argc;
char    *argv[];
{
        register int    i;

        /*
         *      Get the program invocation name for error messages.
         */
        myname = argv[0];

        /*
         *      Check the arguments for consistency.
         */
        if (argc < 2)
        {
                (void)fprintf(stderr, "usage: %s command [arg] ...\n", myna
                exit(1);
        }

        /*
         *      Fill in the command.
         */
        for (i = 1; i < argc; ++i)
                argvector[argbase++] = argv[i];

        /*
         *      Call xargs() to do the real work.
         */
        return xargs();
}
```

Q.4 The xargs.1 file

```
.TH XARGS 1 "22 February 1989"
.SH NAME
xargs \- supply input lines as additional arguments to a command
.SH SYNOPSIS
.B xargs
.B command
[
.I argument
.B .\|.\|.
]
.SH DESCRIPTION
.B xargs
is way to create large command lines without the use of the shell's
backquote mechanism.
It reads its standard input and supplies each line it finds as a
separate argument to the command (and command arguments) on the command
line.
The command is found using the same PATH conventions as the shell
and may be a script.
Because of the limitations of the local UNIX system or the great volume of
input lines,
it may run the command several times.
.SH EXAMPLES
find ~evi -print | xargs chown evi
.br
find ~evi/recipes -print | xargs grep -i turkey
.SH SEE ALSO
sh(1), csh(1)
```

Bibliography

ALLMAN, ERIC. *Sendmail - An Internetwork Mail Router. UNIX Programmers Manual.* 4.3 Berkeley Software Distribution. University of California, Berkeley. April 1986. The paper describing the **sendmail** mail routing system.

BACH, M. J., *The Design of the UNIX Operating System.* Englewood Cliffs, N.J.: Prentice-Hall Inc., 1986. This book describes the internals of ATT System V.

BOURNE, S. R. *The UNIX System.* Reading, Mass.: Addison-Wesley Publishing Company, Inc. 1982. An intermediate UNIX introduction.

COMER, DOUGLAS. *Internetworking with TCP/IP: principles, protocols, and architecture.* Englewood Cliffs, N.J.: Prentice-Hall, Inc., 1988. A complete overview of the Internet, its protocol suite and auxiliary services, including subnetting, naming via domains, and routing.

CSRG. *UNIX Programmer's Manual, 4.3 Berkeley Software Distribution.* University of California Computer Systems Research Group: Berkeley, CA., 1986.

DUNLAP, K. J., *Name Server Operations Guide for BIND, UNIX System Manager's Manual.* 4.3 Berkeley Software Distribution. University of California, Berkeley. April 1986. Document that describes the BIND name server.

GRAMPP, F. T. and R. H. MORRIS. *UNIX Operating System Security AT&T Bell Laboratories Technical Journal* October 1984, Vol. 63 No. 8 Part 2. 1649-1672. A description of some UNIX security holes and how to correct them.

HEDRICK, CHUCK. *Introduction to the Internet Protocols*, Rutgers University: 1987. Anonymous **ftp** from uxc.cso.uiuc.edu. A good tutorial introduction to the Internet, its protocols, and packet formats for TCP and IP.

HEDRICK, CHUCK. *Introduction to Administration of an Internet-based Local Network*, Rutgers University: 1987. Anonymous **ftp** from uxc.cso.uiuc.edu. Summary of addressing, routing, and Ethernet hardware.

HONEYMAN, PETER. *PATHALIAS, Usenix Conference Proceedings* Summer 1986. 126-141 The paper describing the pathalias mail routing system.

KERNIGHAN, BRIAN W., and ROB PIKE. *The UNIX Programming Environment*. Englewood Cliffs, N.J.: Prentice-Hall, Inc., 1984. An introduction to using the various UNIX tools, including **sh** programming.

KERNIGHAN, BRIAN W., and DENNIS M. RITCHIE. *The C Programming Language: Second Edition*. Englewood Cliffs, N.J.: Prentice-Hall, Inc., 1988. The bible of C programming, second edition includes ANSI standard C.

KROLL, ED. *The Hitchhikers Guide to the Internet*. University of Illinois: 1987. Anonymous **ftp** from uxc.cso.uiuc.edu. 1987. A short, concise overview of the Internet.

LEFFLER, SAMUEL J., MARSHALL KIRK MCKUSICK, MICHAEL J. KARELS, and JOHN S. QUARTERMAN. *The Design and Implementation of the 4.3 BSD UNIX Operating System*. Reading, Mass: Addison-Wesley Publishing Company, Inc. This book describes the concepts, data structures, and algorithms used to implement the 4.3BSD operating system.

LOMUTO, ANN NICOLS, and NICO LOMUTO. *A UNIX Primer*. Englewood Cliffs N.J.: Prentice-Hall Inc., 1983. A basic introductory book for beginners.

REEDS, J. A and P. J. WEINBERGER. *File Security and the UNIX System Crypt Command. AT&T Bell Laboratories Technical Journal* October 1984, Vol. 63 No. 8 Part 2. 1673-1684. A discussion of the encryption method used by the **crypt** program and how to break it.

QUARTERMAN, JOHN and JOSIAH HOSHINS. *Notable Computer Networks*, Communications of the ACM, October 1986. A survey of networking technology in use at universities and commercial organizations both here and in Europe.

SUN MICROSYSTEMS, *System Administration for the Sun Workstation*. Sun specific system administration documentation.

UNIX System V/386 System Administrator's Guide, Englewood Cliffs, N.J.: Prentice Hall, Inc., 1988. System administration of System V on the Intel 386 chip.

XEROX, *Internet Transport Protocols*. Xerox System Integration Standard 028112. Stamford, CT: Xerox Co., 1981. The document which specifies the internet protocols.

Index